Reading 1 Corinthians with Philosophically Educated Women

Reading 1 Corinthians with Philosophically Educated Women

NATHAN J. BARNES

☙PICKWICK *Publications* • Eugene, Oregon

READING 1 CORINTHIANS WITH PHILOSOPHICALLY EDUCATED WOMEN

Copyright © 2014 Nathan J. Barnes. All rights reserved. Except for brief quotations in critical publications or reviews, no part of this book may be reproduced in any manner without prior written permission from the publisher. Write: Permissions, Wipf and Stock Publishers, 199 W. 8th Ave., Suite 3, Eugene, OR 97401.

Pickwick Publications
An Imprint of Wipf and Stock Publishers
199 W. 8th Ave., Suite 3
Eugene, OR 97401

www.wipfandstock.com

ISBN 13: 978-1-62032-572-8

Cataloguing-in-Publication data:

Barnes, Nathan J.

Reading 1 Corinthians with philosophically educated women / Nathan J. Barnes.

xviii + 340 pp. ; 23 cm. Includes bibliographical references.

ISBN 13: 978-1-62032-572-8

1. Bible. N.T. Corinthians, 1st—Criticism, interpretation, etc. 2. Women—Religious aspects—Christianity. I. Title.

BS2675.52 B27 2014

Manufactured in the U.S.A.

For Leslee Jean Barnes
With gratitude to the faculty of Brite Divinity School

Contents

Abbreviations | viii

1 A History of Research | 1
2 Educated Women in the Ancient World | 37
3 Women in Philosophy | 65
4 Corinth and Its Philosophers | 122
5 Patronage and Philosophically Educated Women | 167
6 Marriage, Family, and Worship in 1 Corinthians | 223
7 Self-Sufficiency in Paul and the Popular Philosophers | 251
8 Summary of Conclusions | 274

Works Cited | 279

Abbreviations

ABD	*Anchor Bible Dictionary*. Edited by D. N. Freedman. 6 vols. New York, 1992.
Ach.	*Acharnenses*
Lys.	*Lysistrata*
Ael.	Aelian
Ep.	*Epistulae*
NA	*De natura animalium*
Var. hist.	*Varia Historia*
Alciphr.	Alciphron
Ep.	*Epistulae*
ANF	Ante-Nicene Fathers
ANRW	*Aufstieg und Niedergang der römischen Welt: Geschichte und Kultur Roms im Spiegel der neueren Forschung.* Edited by H. Temporini and W. Haase. Berlin, 1972–.
Anth. Pal.	*Anthologia Palatina*
App.	Appian
Hisp.	*Wars in Spain*
Ar.	Aristophanes
Arist.	Aristotle
Eth. Eud.	*Ethica Eudemia*
Eth. Nic.	*Ethica Nicomachea*
Ath.	Athenaeus
Aul. Gell.	Aulus Gellius
NA	*Noctes Atticae*

Abbreviations

BGAD	Bauer, Walter, Frederick W. Danker, William F. Arndt, and F. Wilbur Gingrich. *A Greek-English Lexicon of the New Testament and Other Early Christian Literature*, 3rd ed. Chicago: University of Chicago Press, 2000.
BGU	Ben-Gurion University Papyri
BL	British Library Papyri
Callicratidas	Callicratidas
De. dom. felic.	*De domestica felicitate*
Cass. Dio	Cassius Dio
CH XIII	Grese, William. *Corpus Hermeticum XIII and Early Christian Literature*. Studia ad corpus Hellenisticum Novi Testamenti 5. Leiden: Brill, 1979.
Char.	Chariton
Cic.	Cicero
Acad. Post.	*Academia posteria*
Amic.	*De amicitia*
Arch.	*Pro Archia*
Att.	*Epistulae ad Atticum*
Brut.	*Brutus*
Fam.	*Epistulae ad familiares*
Fin.	*De finibus*
Leg.	*De legibus*
Nat. D.	*De natura deorum*
Off.	*De officiis*
Orat.	*Orator ad M. Brutum*
Tusc.	*Tusculanae disputationes*
Verr.	*In Verrem*
CIG	*Corpus inscriptionum graecarum*. Edited by A. Boeckh. 4 vols. Berlin: Ex Offiicina Academica, 1828–1877.
CIJ	*Corpus Inscriptionum Judaicarum*. Edited by J. B. Frey. 2 vols. Rome: Pontificio Istituto di Archeologia Cristiana, 1936–52.
CIL	*Corpus inscriptionum latinarum*. Berlin: Reimar, 1862–.

Abbreviations

Clem. Al.	Clement of Alexandria
Paed.	*Paedagogus*
Strom.	*Stromateis*
Dig. Just.	*Corpus Juris Civilis*
Dio Chrys.	Dio Chrysostom
Or.	*Orationes*
Diod. Sic.	Diodorus Siculus
Diog. Laert.	Diogenes Laertius
Dion. Hal.	Dionysius Halicarnassensis
Ant. Rom.	*Antiquitates Romanae*
Epict.	Epictetus
Disc.	*Discourses*
Epicurus	Epicurus
Ep. Hdt.	*Epistulae ad Herodotum*
Sent. Vat.	*Vatican Sayings*
Eunap.	Eunapius
VS	*Vitae sophistarum*
Eus.	Eusebius
PE	*Praeparatio evangelica*
Chron.	*Chronica*
Eust.	Eustathius
Il.	*Ad Iliadem*
FGrHist	Die Fragmente der griechischen Historiker
Gal.	Galen
Comp. med. loc.	*Compositione Medicamentorum Secundum Locus*
Hippol.	Hippollytus
Haer.	*Refutatio omnium haeresium*
Hom.	Homer
Od.	*Odyssey*
Il.	*Iliad*
Hor.	Horace
Epod.	*Epodi*
Od.	*Odes*
Serm.	*Sermones*

Abbreviations

Iambl.	Iamblichus
VP	*De vita Pythagorica liber*
I.Erythrai	Engelmann, Helmut, and Reinhold Merkelbach. *Die Inschriften von Erythrai und Klazomenai.* 2 vols. Bonn: Habelt, 1972–1973.
IAG	Moretti, L. *Iscrizioni agonistiche greche* (Rome: Angelo Signorelli, Ed.,1953)
IG	*Inscriptiones graecae.* 1873–
IGRR	*Inscriptiones graecae ad res romanas pertinentes.* Edited by René Cagnat et al. 3 vols. Paris, 1911–1927. Vol. 1, 1911. Reprint, Chicago: Ares, 1975.
IGUR	Moretti, Luigi. *Inscriptiones graecae urbis Romae.* 4 vols. in 5 parts. Rome, 1968–1990.
ILS	Dessau, Hermann. *Inscriptiones latinae selectae.* 3 vols. in 5 parts. Berlin, 1892–1916.
ILydiaKP	Keil, Josef, and Anton von Premerstein. *Berichte über eine Reise in Lydien.* Vienna: Hölder, 1908–14.
Inscr. Eph.	Engelmann, H., D. Knibbe and R. Merkelbach, eds., *Die Inschriften von Ephesos.* Habelt: Bonn, 1980.
Isoc.	Isocrates
Joseph.	Josephus
AJ	*Antiquitates Judaicae*
JSJSupp	Supplements to the Journal for the Study of Judaism in the Persian, Hellenistic, and Roman Periods
JSNTSupp	*Journal for the Study of the New Testament Supplements*
Juv.	Juvenal
Kock	*Comicorum atticorum fragmenta.* Edited by Theodorus Kock. Lipsig: Teubner, 1888.
Lactant.	Lactanius
Div. inst.	*Divinae institutiones*
LCL	Loeb Classical Library
Lucr.	Lucretius
Mart.	Martial
Mieneke	Mieneke, A. *Fragmenta comicorum Graecorum.* Berlin: Reimer, 1839–57.

Abbreviations

Milet	Milet, H. A. *Études et fragments d'économie politique.* Paris: Blot, 1891.
Min. Fel.	Minucius Felix
Oct.	*Octavius*
MSG	Jan, K. *Musici Scriptores Graeci.* Leipzig: Tuebner, 1895.
Muson.	Musonius Rufus
New Docs	*New Documents Illustrating Early Christianity.* Edited by G. H. R. Horsley and S. Llewelyn. North Ryde, N.S.W., Australia: Macquarie University, 1981–.
NovTSupp	Supplements to Novum Testamentum
NPNF	Nicene and Post-Nicene Fathers
Ov.	Ovid
Parth.	Parthenius
Amat. narr.	*Narrationes amatoriarum*
PASSupp	Proceedings of the Aristotelian Society Supplementary Volume
Paus.	Pausanius
Perictione	
De mul. harm.	*On the Harmony of Women*
PG	*Patrologiae cursus completus. Series graeca.* Compiled by Jacques-Paul Migne. 161 vols. Paris: Petit-Montrouge, 1800–1875.
P.Herc.	Herculaneum papyrus
Philo	Philo
Leg.	*Legatio ad Gaium*
Praem.	*De Praemiis et Poenis*
Quod omn. prob.	*Quod Omnis Probus*
Phot.	Photius
Bibl.	Bibliotheca Philostr.
Philostratus	
V A	*Vita Apollonii*
Pind.	Pindar
Isthm.	*Isthmian Odes*
Nem.	*Nemean Odes*

Abbreviations

Ol.	*Olympian Odes*
Pyth.	*Pythian Odes*
Pl.	Plato
Gorg.	*Gorgias*
Hip. mai.	*Hippias maior*
Menex.	*Menexenus*
Phaedr.	*Phaedrus*
Prot.	*Protagoras*
Rep.	*Republic*
Symp.	*Symposium*
Tht.	*Theatetus*
Plb.	Polybius
Plin.	Pliny the Elder
HN	*Naturalis historia*
Plin.	Pliny the Younger
Ep.	*Epistulae*
Plut.	Plutarch
Cic.	*Cicero*
Cleom.	*Cleomenes*
Lyc.	*Lycurgus*
Mor.	*Moralia*
Per.	*Pericles*
Phoc.	*Phocion*
Tib. Gracch.	*Tiberius Gracchus*
P.Med.Bar.	Papyri Mediolanenses Barelli. Published in C. Balconi, *Papyri della collezione dell'Università Cattolica di Milano provenienti da cartonnage*, Akten des 23. Intern. Papyrologenkongresses, Vienna, 2007, p. 15–18; C. Balconi, *Proceed. 24th Intern. Congress Papyrology Helsinki* (2007) 75–81.
P. Mil. Vogl.	*Papiri della R. Università di Milano*. Edited by A. Vogliano. Milan: Hoepli, 1937.
Porph.	Porphyry
VP	*Vita Plotini*

Abbreviations

P. Oxy.	*Oxyrhynchus Papyri*. Edited by B. P. Grenfell et al. 70 vols. London: Egypt Exploration Fund, 1898–2006.
Prop.	Propertius
Ptol. Alex.	Fraser, P. M. *Ptolemaic Alexandria*. 3 vols. Oxford, 1972.
RAC	*Reallexikon für Antike und Christentum*. Edited by T. Kluser et al. Stuttgart, 1950.
RE	*Real-Enzyklopädie Für Die Gebildeten Stände*. 15 vols. Edited by F. A. Brockhaus. Leipzig: Brockhaus, 1843–1848.
Samama	Samama, Évelyne. *Les médecins dans le monde grec: Sources épigraphiques sur la naissance d'un corps médical*. École pratique des Hautes Études, Sciences historiques et philologiques 3. Hautes études du monde gréco-romain 31. Geneva: Librairie Droz, 2003.
SB	*Sammelbuch griechischer Urkunden aus Aegypten*. Edited by F. Preisigke et al. Vols. 1–, 1915–.
SBLSP	Society of Biblical Literature Seminar Papers
Scrib. Larg.	Scribonius Largus
Comp.	*Compositiones*
SEG	Supplementum epigraphicum Graecum
Sen.	Seneca the Younger
Ben.	*De beneficiis*
Constan.	*De constantia sapientis*
Ep.	*Epistulae*
Helv.	*ad Helviam*
Marc.	*ad Marciam*
Prov.	*De providentia*
Tran.	*De tranquillitate animi*
Sext. Emp.	Sextus Empiricus
Pyr.	*Outlines of Pyrrhonism*
SIG	*Sylloge inscriptionum Graecarum*. Edited by W. Dittenberger. 4 vols. Leipzig, 1915–1924.
Stat.	Statius
Silv.	*Silvae*

Abbreviations

Stob.	Stobaeus
Strab.	Strabo
Suet.	Suetonius
Dom.	*Domitianus*
Gram.	*De grammaticus*
Ner.	*Nero*
Tib.	*Tiberius*
Vesp.	*Divus Vespasianus*
Tac.	Tacitus
Ann.	*Annales*
Dial.	*Dialogus de oratoribus*
Hist.	*Historiae*
Suid.	Suidas
Tat.	Tatian
Or.	*Oratio ad Graecos*
TDNT	*Theological Dictionary of the New Testament.* Edited by G. Kittel and G. Friedrich. Translated by J. T. Willis, G. W. Bromiley, and D. E. Green. 8 vols. Grand Rapids, 1974–.
Them.	Themistius
Or.	*Orationes*
Thuc.	Thucydides
TLG	*Thesaurus Linguae Graecae*
Val. Max.	Valerius Maximus
Fact. dict. mem.	*Memorable Deeds and Sayings*
Vell. Pat.	Velleius Paterculus
Xen.	Xenophon
Ages.	*Agesilaus*
Mem.	*Memorabilia*
Oec.	*Oeconomics*

1

A History of Research

PAUL EXISTS IN AT least three worlds and interacts with three rich, overlapping heritages: Judaisms,[1] Hellenisms,[2] and Roman Empire.[3] The "new perspective(s) on Paul" redefined the relationship of Paul's theology within first-century Judaism(s) and therefore questioned the former understandings of justification by faith as the center of Pauline theology.[4] E. P. Sanders initiated a "Copernican turn" in Pauline scholarship by reviewing a wide variety of Palestinian Jewish literature and arguing for a pattern of Jewish religion comprising "covenantal nomism."[5] The sharpest criticism of Sanders came from Jacob Neusner, who demonstrated that Sanders's use of rabbinic material is fundamentally flawed due to his neglect of rabbinic exegesis and the late date of these materials. Neusner also points out that Sanders's definitions of the Pharisees are incorrect, and one cannot speak of a singular "Judaism" of the first century, given that there is no single unifying tradition.[6]

1. Boccaccini, "Multiple Judaisms," 46; Nuesner, "Four Approaches," 1–34.
2. See the essays in part one of Boys-Stones, *Hellenic Studies*, 3–182.
3. Horsley, *Paul and Empire*; Horsley, *Paul and Politics*; Horsely, *Paul and the Roman Imperial Order*; Horsley, *Hidden Transcripts*; Lopez, *Apostle to the Conquered*; Marchal, *Politics of Heaven*; Elliott, *Liberating Paul*; Elliott, *Arrogance of Nations*.
4. Dunn, "New Perspective."
5. Sanders, *Paul and Palestinian Judaism*; Sanders, "On the Question of Fulfilling the Law," 103–26; Sanders, "Paul's Attitude," 175–87; Sanders, *Paul*; and most recently, "Paul between Judaism and Hellenism," 74–90.
6. Neusner, "Comparing Judaisms," 177–91; Neusner, "Use of Later Rabbinic

Reading 1 Corinthians with Philosophically Educated Women

N. T. Wright[7] and James Dunn[8] became the most distinguished proponents and refiners of Sanders's theories, and the "new perspective(s) on Paul" generated a vast amount of literature: scholarly, polemical, and apologetic.[9] The ongoing debate has centered on the nature and construction of Paul's theology including his understanding of law and justification primarily in Romans and Galatians, but also the remainder of the Pauline corpus.[10] Many Christian scholars and theologians continue to expose both real and perceived exegetical and theological weaknesses in the "new perspective(s) on Paul," opting for confessional Catholic, Calvinistic, or Lutheran understandings of Pauline theology and exegesis.[11] Scholars representing the "new perspective(s) on Paul" have consistently argued that we should seek to understand Paul not through later confessions but through his first-century contexts, particularly in light of their reconstructions of the relationships between Paul and Judaism(s). Other scholars have argued against the "new perspective(s) on Paul" on historical, exegetical, and theological grounds.[12]

With the discussion of Paul's Jewish contexts in full force, it has become a methodological concern to broaden the horizons on Pauline studies to include his imperial and Hellenistic contexts. Significant changes in understanding brought about a new perspective on the construction of Paul and his contexts. The questions concerning Paul's use of Greco-Roman rhetorical conventions and epistolary form, moral philosophy, and his interaction with the Roman Empire (including Hellenistic religions, patronage,

---

Evidence," 2:43–63; Neusner, "Mr. Sanders' Pharisees," 73–95; Neusner, *Judaic Law*; Neusner, "E. P. Sanders"; Neusner and Chilton, *In Quest of the Historical Pharisees*.

7. Wright, "Paul of History," 61–68; Wright, *Climax of the Covenant*; Wright, "Gospel and Theology in Galatians," 222–39; Wright, "Romans and the Theology of Paul," 30–67; Wright, "New Exodus," 26–35; Wright, "Gospel and Theology in Galatians," 205–36; Wright, "Redemption," 69–100; Wright, *Paul: In Fresh Perspective*; Wright, *Justification*.

8. Dunn, "New Perspective on Paul," 95–122; Dunn, "Did Paul have a Covenant Theology," 287–307.

9. For bibliography and review of scholarship on the New Perspective, see Swanson, "Bibliography," 317–24; Garlington, "New Perspective," 17–38; Smith, "New Perspective," 91–111; Thompson, *New Perspective*; Meek, "New Perspective," 208–33.

10. Matera, *Galatians*; Thielman, *Paul and the Law*; Dunn, *Epistle to the Galatians*; Dunn, *Romans 1–8*; Dunn, *Romans 9–16*; Rapa, *Meaning of "Works of the Law"*; Stuhlmacher and Hagner, *Revisiting Paul's Doctrine of Justification*; Karris, *Galatians and Romans*.

11. Schreiner, *Law and Its Fulfillment*; Thielman, *Paul and the Law*; Westerholm, *Israel's Law*; Elliott, *Survivors of Israel*; Westerholm, *Perspectives*; Waters, *Justification*; Vlachos, *Law and the Knowledge of Good and Evil*.

12. Note reviews and criticisms in Das, *Paul, the Law*; Das, *Paul and the Jews*; Watson, *Paul, Judaism, and the Gentiles*; Visscher, *Romans 4*.

family structures, and politics) needed to be revisited in light of these "new perspective(s) on Paul" debates. Many scholars sought to view Paul as subversive to the Roman imperial order, criticizing its politics, economics, and family structures. John Elliott's works on social-science criticism[13] and Richard Horsley's *Paul and Empire* sparked interest specifically in how Paul accepts, rejects, or adapts contemporary Roman political ideologies and especially how Christians can use Paul's political ideas today. The work of scholars who use social-scientific methods to study the NT usually attempts to frame Paul's viewpoints within Mediterranean social and anthropological frameworks (such as patronage, honor/shame, family structures, magic and ritual). These valuable studies often focus on reading Paul with a concern for applying his thought to contemporary ideologies such as feminism, social and economic justice, libertarianism, and sexual equality.[14]

Others have sought to foreground Hellenistic contexts and locate Paul primarily in these milieus employing historical methods such as philology, rhetorical criticism, and the situating of Paul within popular moral philosophy. Scholars who study Paul's ideas only within his Jewish and Imperial contexts run the risk of obscuring his place within rhetorical, literary, philosophical and political conventions, and within greater Hellenistic culture. Studies of Paul's use of Greco-Roman rhetoric and philosophy have spanned all the major movements in Pauline studies—from the writings of Justin Martyr and the apologists to Augustine to the Reformers to Bultmann, through the New Perspective to feminist and post-colonial studies.[15] The greatest achievements of modern rhetorical criticism, which began in earnest in the 1960s, comprise the analyses of Paul's epistles as speeches and the identification of various rhetorical devices using ancient rhetorical handbooks and instructions from philosophers, rhetoricians, and other ancient witnesses concerning the art of persuasion.[16] Paul's usage of the diatribe has

---

13. Elliott, *Home for the Homeless*; Elliott, *What is Social-Scientific Criticism?*

14. The Context Group has many significant contributors to this field of study. A regularly updated bibliography of their works is available on their website http://www.contextgroup.org; cf. Blasi, *Handbook of Early Christianity*.

15. For the church fathers, see Rankin, *From Clement to Origen*; for Augustine, see Watson, *Rhetorical Criticism*, 101–2; for the Reformers, see Classen, "St. Paul's Epistles"; for feminist studies and rhetoric, see Schüssler Fiorenza, *Rhetoric and Ethic*, 83–102; Ehrensperger, *That We May Be Mutually Encouraged*; Pui-lan, "Making the Connections," 45–65; cf. Anderson, *Ancient Rhetorical Theory and Paul*; Sampley and Lampe, *Paul and Rhetoric*.

16. E.g., Kennedy, *Art of Persuasion in Greece*; Kennedy, *Art of Rhetoric in the Roman World*; Betz, *Galatians*; Stanley, "Paul and Homer," 48–78; Stowers, *Handbook of Classical Rhetoric*; Anderson, *Ancient Rhetorical Theory and Paul*.

received the most attention,[17] but rhetorical critics have scrutinized the New Testament using rhetorical methods with both historical and contemporary interests.[18] The challenges of rhetorical criticism concern identifying form[19] (epistles are not speeches) and adopting a methodology[20] (while there are ancient works that describe how to construct a speech, there are none that instruct us how to analyze a speech).

Scholars have also contextualized Paul within popular Hellenistic moral philosophy and religion, and it is within this scholarly tradition that I situate my study of the reception of 1 Corinthians by philosophically educated women. I will review the scholarly tradition, beginning with the contributions to the *Corpus Hellenisticum*,[21] the publications of the Hellenistic Moral Philosophy and Early Christianity Section of the SBL, and related conversations regarding Greco-Roman moral philosophy and Paul. Finally, I will situate my study in the current conversation regarding the participation of women in philosophy.

Paul within the Corpus Hellenisticum

The systematic collection of Greco-Roman writings for the interpretation of early Christian writings begins with the work of J. J. Wettstein, who collected parallels from Jewish and classical writers for forty years.[22] Following decades of disinterest, the search for parallels was renewed in the nineteenth century by C. F. Georg Heinrici (1844–1915), Ernst von Dobschütz (1870–1934), Hans Windish (1881–1935), Adolf Deissmann (1866–1937), and

17. For history and bibliography, see Bultmann, *Der stil der paulinischen Predigt*; Malherbe, "MH ΓΕΝΟΙΤΟ," 231–40. Note that page 236 is reprinted as it should have appeared in *HTR* 74, no. 1, as "Erratum: MH ΓΕΝΟΙΤΟ"; Stowers, *Diatribe and Paul's Letters*; Song, *Reading Romans*.

18. For bibliography, see Watson, "Rhetorical Criticism," 232–34; Watson, *Rhetoric of the New Testament*.

19. Meecham, *Light from Ancient Letters*; Stowers, *Letter Writing*; White, *Light from Ancient Letters*; Malherbe, *Ancient Epistolary Theorists*; Stirewalt, *Paul, the Letter Writer*; Richards, *Paul and First-Century Letter Writers*; Stowers and Adams, *Paul and the Ancient Letter Form*.

20. See, e.g., the methodological reflections in Porter, *Rhetorical Interpretation of Scriptures*; Olbricht, "Classical Rhetorical Criticism," 108–24; Watson, "Contributions and Limitations," 123–51; and Porter, "Paul as an Epistolographer *and* Rhetorician?," 222–48.

21. The *Corpus Hellenisticum* is an international research project whose objective is to collect all of the parallels to the New Testament that appear in Greek and Latin literature.

22. Wettstein, *Novum Testamentum Graecum*.

Hans Lietzmann (1875–1942), who influenced NT scholarship concerning the nature of early Christianity and its relationships with Judaism and Hellenism. Heinrici argued that Paul's *concept* of self-awareness has its roots (οἰκείωσις appetitus societatis) in Socratic, Stoic, and Philonic thought, that early Christian groups resemble Roman associations, and that Paul used the form of the Cynic-Stoic diatribe.[23] Ernst von Dobschütz was critical of the methods of the history of religions school that emphasized the similarities of Christianity with Greco-Roman thought and sought to bring out its distinctiveness, arguing that Paul goes beyond the requirements of popular Hellenistic morality.[24] Windisch is best known for his argument concerning the θεῖος ἀνηρ: by providing examples from classical writers, he extended the nature of its usage in John's Gospel for Jesus to how Paul describes himself.[25] Windisch further postulated that Paul's opponents in Corinth are gnostic pneumatics and Jewish preachers.[26] Deissmann famously concluded that the Greek of the NT is that of the lower classes, defined Paul's corpus as letters (non-literary, real communications to real people) instead of epistles (moral essays in the form of a letter), and argued that Pauline Christianity was a movement exclusively of the lower class.[27] Lietzmann argued that Paul's opponents simply adopted the Platonic anthropology of the immortality of the soul and therefore rejected Paul's teachings concerning the resurrection.[28] These scholars made important contributions to what would later become the *Corpus Hellenisticum* project and to related studies. Death and war continually interrupted the project until Kurt Aland suggested in his review of the project in 1955 that an international team of scholars systematically review the *Corpus Hellenisticum*.[29]

The first publication of the *Corpus Hellenisticum* preceded Aland's call by nine years, appearing in 1946. Helge Almqvist's *Plutarch und Das Neue Testament: Ein Beitrag zum Corpus Hellenisticum Novi Testamenti* begins with a detailed outline of the shared culture of Plutarch and the writers of the NT.[30] Almqvist selected the parallels himself (instead of simply reviewing Wettstein's collection) according to the following categories:

23. Heinrici, "Die christengemeinden Koinths," 465–509; Kieran J. O'Mahony interacts with Heinrici's understanding of rhetoric at length in *Pauline Persuasion*.
24. Dobschütz, *Christian Life*, 1–10.
25. Windisch, *Paulus und Christus*, 143.
26. Windisch, *Der zweite Korintherbrief*.
27. Deissmann, *Bible Studies*; Deissmann, *Licht vom Osten*.
28. Lietzmann and Kümmel, *Korinther*, 9.
29. Aland, "Corpus Hellenisticum," 217–21.
30. Almqvist, *Plutarch und Das Neue Testament*, 18–29.

> Those which show cultural-historical reference, those which throw light on religion, on ethics, those which belong to the area of literary style—further subdivided into style of narration, diatribe or dialogue, minor features of rhetorical emphasis, phrases or turns of expression, and major figures of speech.[31]

For example, Almqvist finds a parallel with the cosmology of Plutarch (*Mor.* 282b) and Paul (Rom 1:20), both referring to the seen and unseen nature of elements in the cosmos. He also identifies a parallel between Paul (Rom 2:1) and Plutarch's (*Mor.* 863a) ethical rule not to judge others. Elements of the diatribe occur throughout; one example being Romans 9:19 that parallels *Mor.* 101c, 958e, and 1055a.

Hans D. Betz made his first contribution to the *Corpus Hellenisticum* in 1961 with his revised dissertation, which briefly identifies parallels of a religious nature between the NT and Lucian.[32] He gives much attention to the θεῖος ἀνηρ, the strongest parallels being in Lucian's description of Heracles in *Cynic* 13 and the *Death of Peregrinus* 6.[33] Lucian describes Heracles as the divine man, one who had self-control and helped the poor, and he laments Peregrinus not as the loss of a Pythagoras or a Socrates, but as a god who had had died.[34]

The first methodological essay and very detailed history of the project in English appears in 1964 by W. C. van Unnik.[35] Van Unnik calls for a systematic and historical/scientific review of all Greek and Latin literature, noting that Wettstein's vast collection in his *Novum Testamentum Graecum* is incomplete and arbitrary, necessitating original research. Van Unnik gives particular attention to the problem of defining and identifying parallels. He writes that scholars must not look for parallels only in the contemporaries of Paul because many formative writers and philosophers shaped the contemporary ethos, and later writers preserve this material as well. The evaluations should be done with an historical outlook:

---

31. Andrews, Review of *Plutarch und Das Neue Testament*, 343; cf. Martin Rist, who also notes Almqvist's historical sensitivity, in Review of *Plutarch und Das Neue Testament*, 301–2.

32. Betz, *Lukian von Samosata*, 102, 125; cf. Bartelink, Review of *Lukian von Samosata*, 312–14; Schoedel, Review of *Lukian von Samosata*, 318–21; for more on the divine man, see Betz, "Göttmensch (II)," 234–312.

33. Cf. Betz, "Lukian von Samosata," 226–37.

34. For the problematic scholarly discussion on the divine man, see Flinterman, "Ubiquitous 'Divine Man,'" 82–98; Betz, "Divine Human Being," 243–52.

35. Van Unnik, "Corpus Hellenisticum," 17–33. Van Unnik mentions the methodology of Bonhöffer, *Epiktet* and Sevenster, *Paul and Seneca*. Cf. van Unnik, "Second Report," 254–59.

> Of course in the evaluation of data one must reckon with the fluctuations and currents in the religious, social, and political realms, but in general it must be stated that everything preserved to us from the classical world ought to be investigated for its eventual contribution to this Corpus.[36]

Furthermore, a "parallel" need not be the usage of a particular word or its cognates and various forms,[37] because a parallel idea can be expressed with different words (and in different languages). However, a supposed parallel is stronger with more exact word order, form, and historical situation. Van Unnik later describes this strength: "There must be a relation in substance with the N.T."[38] This "relation in substance" means applying a hermeneutic to both passages that comprises "reading in 'context,'" which is not only the immediate passage from which the words are taken, but also the whole fabric of thought."[39]

Following van Unnik's call for methodological reflection, several volumes in the monograph series *Studia ad corpus hellenisticum Novi Testamenti* reflect deeply on the relationships between classical sources and Paul. G. Petzke made the first contribution, writing on Apollonius of Tyana. Petzke's work includes scant parallels to Paul's writings, being more concerned with stories concerning Jesus and Apollonius and the "divine man" concept in Hellenism.[40] Reimer criticized Petzke for not offering much interpretation of the significance of the data,[41] but Petzke's arguments concerning the contact between Jesus as the Son of God and the "divine man" in Hellenistic traditions remain convincing.

In the second volume of the *Studia ad corpus hellenisticum Novi Testamenti*, G. Mussies in *Dio Chrysostom and the New Testament* briefly introduces Dio and then presents parallels with little or no comment, although his notes give a rationale for the identification of a parallel when present. Mussies's focus is to provide parallels of a religious or philosophical nature, and leave out lexical or grammatical notes. Despite Unnik's call for a more

---

36. Van Unnik, "Corpus Hellenisticum," 28.

37. This project had already been done in the work of the BGAD and *TDNT*.

38. Van Unnik, "Words Come to Life," 203. Van Unnik provides several examples. Regrettably, van Unnik writes, "It is not possible to give a clear-cut definition of a parallel" (206). Some "parallels" are just lexical, some have cultural value, and it is the judgment of the interpreter that determines the significance of the "parallel." See also the use of this method in van Unnik, "Den Geist löschet nicht," 255–69; van Unnik, "Tiefer Friede," 261–79.

39. Van Unnik, "Words Come to Life," 206.

40. Tiede, Review of *Die Traditionen über Apollonius von Tyana*, 465–67.

41. Reimer, *Miracle and Magic*, 17.

substantive discussion of the parallels, Mussies does not give explanation and interpretation of his parallels, claiming that the parallels themselves need to be a part of scholarly discourse. The number of parallels in this volume is quite massive, and a detailed interpretation of each parallel would call for a multivolume work with several contributing scholars. Among various parallels, Mussies finds parallels in 1 Corinthians 1:22 and Cass. Dio 11.39, where Dio says that the Greeks are leaders seeking philosophy and educating their people, and in 37.26 where Favorinus lauds the Corinthians specifically for their learning and other important accomplishments. Elsewhere Dio says that to win a war, soldiers must be saved but at the same time good men have to die, which is similar to what Paul says in Romans 5:7.

The third volume, *Plutarch's Theological Writings and Early Christian Literature*, comprising ten different essays on various treatises in the *Moralia*, broke new ground in 1975 with its ambitious scope. Many of the parallels found in this work are important for highlighting the significance of philosophical terms in Paul's writings, but with the notable exceptions of Morton Smith and David Aune, the contributors do little to elaborate on these themes.[42] Morton Smith finds similarity between the knowledge of God and lack of it in *Mor.* 164e and Galatians 4:8–9; 1 Corinthians 8:2, 15:34; but Paul differs from Plutarch in that he believed pagan belief leads to destruction (2 Thess 2:2–12).[43] David Aune focuses on the diatribe style of Paul and its use in 1 Corinthians 15:29–34, noting the extensive use of poets and sages in Plutarch's treatise and Paul's quotation of Menander in 1 Corinthians 15:33. Aune further argues that both Paul and the early Christian writers who favored the diatribe style used quotations from the Old Testament instead of the appeals to the sages and poets in the Cynic-Stoic diatribe.[44]

Volume 4, *Plutarch's Ethical Writings and Early Christian Literature*, followed in 1978, finally adding substantial discourse with wider scholarship, as the contributors included classicists, historians, and NT interpreters.[45] The articles in this volume include detailed descriptions of parallels between several essays in the *Moralia* and early Christian thought followed by a list of less important parallels with little or no explanation. As a whole, it appreciates the methodological concerns raised by van Unnik, describing substantive parallels in an historical background.

---

42. O'Neil, Review of *Plutarch's Theological Writings*, 631–33.

43. Assuming, of course, Pauline authorship of 2 Thessalonians. Morton Smith, "De Superstitione," 8.

44. Aune, "De esu carnium orationes," 305.

45. Robbins, Review of *Plutarch's Ethical Writings*, 666; Malherbe, Review of *Plutarch's Ethical Writings*, 140–42.

Volume 5 appeared in 1979, being *Corpus Hermeticum XIII and Early Christian Literature*, a revised dissertation by W. C. Grese directed by H. D. Betz.[46] *CH XIII* is unique in Hermetic literature because it focuses on regeneration, the change from humanity to divinity. Dated between the middle of the second century to late third century CE, *CH XIII* possibly carries both Jewish and Christian influences. Grese provides a detailed analysis of *CH XIII*, noting many parallels to Paul. Interestingly, there are two negative parallels: the early Christian communities were open to outsiders (unlike the Hermetic mysteries) and the transition from human to divine (e.g., Jesus) was not as smooth as in *CH XIII*.[47] Paul's use of the term "father" is similar to the widespread use of "father/son" terminology used to indicate a teacher/student relationship and used in mystery religions for the initiator/initiated.[48] Grese observes that in both *CH XIII* and Pauline thought, regeneration occurs through God's initiative.[49]

P. W. van der Horst contributed volume 6 with *Aelius Aristides and the New Testament* in 1980.[50] Van der Horst very briefly introduces Aristides and lists parallels between the writings of Aristides and various NT writings. In his opinion the most significant parallels to Paul are in the hymn to Athena and 1 Corinthians 1.24. Aristides (37, 28) calls Athena δύναμιν τοῦ Διός and Paul says of Christ: Χριστὸν θεοῦ δύναμιν. Aristides (50, 71–93) describes in some length letters of recommendation (2 Cor 3:1; Philemon). Van der Horst finds parallels between 1 Corinthians 1.22 "the Greeks seek wisdom" and with the Athenians "being leaders of all education and learning" in Arist. 330; and between the crown metaphor of the *agon* motif (1 Cor 9:25) and Arist. 402.

In their 1971 article "Contributions to the Corpus Hellenisticum Novi Testamenti: I: plutarch, de e apud delphos," Hans D. Betz and Edgar Smith outline many parallels between Plutarch and 1 Corinthians.[51] The

---

46. William R. Schoedel reviews volumes 3, 4, and 5 in "Three Recent Works," 345–46. Grese's work is in two parts: analysis and text. The analysis is referenced as *Corpus Hermeticum*, and the text is referenced by the abbreviation *CH XIII*.

47. Grese, *Corpus Hermeticum*, 64–65.

48. Ibid., 67. Cf. *CH XIII* 1.1; 1 Cor 4:14, 15, 17; 2 Cor 6:13.

49. Grese, *Corpus Hermeticum*, 84. *CH XIII* 3.1.7–3.1.8.3.2; Rom 8:29–30; 9:6–29; Gal 1:15–16; 1 Thess 5:9; 2 Thess 2:13–14.

50. See the very useful reviews by John Turner, Review of *Aelius Aristides*, 116–17, and David Aune, Review of *Aelius Aristides*, 349–50.

51. Betz and Smith, "Contributions," 217–35. The most significant parallels from 384e to 1 Corinthians include the contrast of "spiritual" and "material" gifts in 1 Cor 9:11; the combination of λόγος and σοφία in 1:17; the metaphorical use of ἀπαρχή, the technical term for sacrificial cults in 1 Cor 15:20, 23 and 16:15; and the usage of ἀπορίαι in 1 Cor 7:32–35. Equally significant are the parallels in Plutarch's theology in 384; Paul's use ὄρεξις in Rom 1:27 and φύσει in Rom 1:27; 2:14, 27; 11.21, 24; and Gal

Reading 1 Corinthians with Philosophically Educated Women

entire discourse concerns γνῶθι σαυτόν (know thyself) which Betz and Smith interpret in light of its companion maxim μηδὲν ἄγαν (in nothing to excess).[52] For example, in 385d the phrase γνῶθι σαυτόν appears, which has a parallel in 1 Corinthians 3:4, with Betz and Smith writing of μηδὲν ἄγαν:

> The maxim is not expressly reflected in [Early Christian Literature]. However, cf. Ro xii 3; 2 Cor x I2f; Eph iv 7, 13, 16. In the Pauline tradition there is a clear opposition to any tendency by man to overextend himself, e.g., Paul's opposition to the θεῖος ἀνηρ of Christianity, and to the gnostics (I Cor iv 8; 2 Cor xii 1–4, 7).[53]

Pieter van der Horst's essays on the neo-Platonist Macrobius (1973) and the Stoic philosophers Musonius Rufus (1974), Hierocles (1975),[54] Cornutus (1981), and the novelist Chariton (1983) provide a list of parallels and briefly introduce the authors but do not offer extensive discussion.[55] Like other contributors to the *Corpus Hellenisticum*, van der Horst finds substantial parallels between Paul and these ancient authors. Macrobius, for example, notes in *Commentary* 1.1.5–6 that Plato argued in *Phaedo* and *Georgias* that there is divine justice, which can be parallel to Romans 2:6. There is a parallel in Romans 8:14 and Macrobius's comment in *Saturnalia* 1.23.13 that the spirit of the god led men bearing the images of the gods in the procession to the Circensian Games. Paul's description of his pursuance of Christ in 1 Corinthians 2:2 is parallel to Macrobius's description of the wise man who seeks wisdom in Commentary 1.8.3. And 1 Corinthians 7:4; 32–34 is also similar to Musonius's essay on the "Chief End of Marriage," when he explains that a marriage must have mutual love between husband and wife.[56] Both

---

2:15. From 385a, αἰνίγματα "riddle" appears only in ECL in 1 Cor 13:12, where it has to do with revelation.

52. Cf. Betz, "ΓΝΩΘΙ ΣΑΥΤΟΝ," 465–84; Betz, "Delphic Maxim," 156–71.

53. Betz and Smith, "Contributions," 223.

54. Ramelli and Konstan, *Hierocles the Stoic*.

55. Van der Horst, "Macrobius," 220–32; van der Horst, "Musonius Rufus," 306–15; van der Horst, "Hierocles the Stoic," 156–60; van der Horst, "Cornutus," 165–72; van der Horst, "Chariton," 348–55. Macrobius notes in *Commentary* 1.1.5–6 that Plato argued in *Pheado* and *Georgias* that there is divine justice, which can be parallel to Rom 2:6.

56. Lutz, 89. Furthermore, Musonius and Paul agree that men's hair should be cut short. Musonius actually uses the beauty of women in cutting their hair as an example for men; however, unlike Paul, Musonius applies the argument from nature to men and not women. Other parallels are Musonius's notion of self-control of an ideal king and Paul's sense of order in worship and Musonius's treatment of the question of the wise-person persecuting those who treat her with contempt and Paul's fighting the wild beasts in Ephesus. Paul's appeal to nature in 1 Cor 11:14 is parallel to Hierocles (p. 15 col 2, 51). A fragment of Hierocles (Stob. 4.27.20) parallels Paul's command not to

Hierocles and Paul agree that man exists in the image of god (1 Cor 11:7 / Stob. 4.25.23). Cornutus (Corn. 20 p. 39, 15) has the phrase τούς . . . πρῶτος ἐκ γῆς γενομένους ἀνθρώπους, similar to Paul's ὁ πρῶτος ἄνθρωπος ἐκ γῆς (1 Cor 15:47). Van der Horst suggests that Dionysus's presence in his absence in Char. 8.4–5 is parallel to 1 Corinthians 5:3. Furthermore, God's mercy in Philippians 2:27 is comparable to the mercy of Aphrodite in Char. 8.1.3. The phrase γνῶθι σαυτόν has parallel in Char. 6.1.10: μηδὲν ἄγαν.

David L. Balch contributed an article to the *Corpus Hellenisticum* in 1992 that begins with an excellent introduction to Pythagoreanism and neo-Pythagoreanism. Balch translates and interprets many neo-Pythagorean texts that reference household codes.[57] Balch finds neo-Pythagorean parallels to the Pauline idea that wives should submit to their husbands.[58] Significantly, Balch concludes that the neo-Pythagorean household codes are more similar to the NT codes in Colossians 3:18—14:1 and Ephesians 5:21—26:9 than are the Stoic and Hellenistic Jewish parallels that NT scholars usually cite.[59]

The scope and depth of the two volumes of the *Neuen Wettstein*, first published in 1996 and edited by Udo Schnelle, update and revise the parallels that Wettstein collected. The first volume appears in two parts: the first covering the epistles of the NT in canonical order to 1 Timothy, and the second covering the remainder of the epistles and the Apocalypse. The second volume is dedicated to the Gospel of John. Matthew and Acts are planned, but the publication date has not been announced. The parallels in the *Neuen Wettstein* are chosen primarily on the similarity in style, and include Hellenistic, Jewish (both Greek and Hebrew), and early Christian texts. The parallels appear in German with a few notes on their significance with relevant Greek phrases.

While the *Neuen Wettstein* was being compiled and edited, Klaus Berger and Carsten Colpe were working with Eugene M. Boring to translate and update a similar project, the *Religionsgeschichtliches Textbuch zum*

---

repay evil with evil in Rom 12:17.

57. David Balch, "Neopythagorean Moralists," 380–411; Balch, "Household Ethical Codes," 397–404; E. W. Smith Jr.'s dissertation did not make it into the series, *Joseph and Asenath*. I presume that this contribution was not published because it is incomplete, covering only the first two parts of *Joseph and Asenath*. Smith provides an excellent introduction to *Joseph and Asenath* and follows with parallels that focus on religion and literary phenomena.

58. Balch presents parallels between 1 Cor 14:34 and Iamblichus 29.26–30.5; Perictione, *De mul. harm.* 144, 8–18; cf. Callicratidas, *De. dom. felic.* 107, 111. Balch's citation of Perictione and Callicratidas is from Thesleff, *Pythagorean Texts*. Iamblichus is cited from *Iamblichi*, ed. Deubner and Klein.

59. Balch, "Neopythagorean Moralists," 409.

Neuen Testament.⁶⁰ The *Hellenistic Commentary to the New Testament* added about three hundred parallels to the original work, and unlike the *Neuen Wettstein,* this project focused on locating and briefly explaining parallels to the NT that are from Greco-Roman literature rather than early Christian or Jewish literature, with an interest in cultural backgrounds (usually focused on religious and philosophical ideas) instead of style. The NT text and Greco-Roman parallels appear in English, almost exclusively by translations cited in the bibliography, with very brief explanations of the significance of the parallel and relevant untranslated Greek.

By their nature, both the *Neuen Wettstein* and the *Hellenistic Commentary of the New Testament* are incomplete and somewhat arbitrary because both works almost never situate parallels within their own literary and historical contexts. Similar phrases from the author of a parallel are almost never referenced, and parallels from other Greco-Roman authors are not presented. A significant point of the *Hellenistic Commentary of the New Testament* project is to demonstrate that the NT writings do not appear in a vacuum, but the parallels themselves are not set within any kind of framework other than the criteria used to select them. This leaves a wide gap for scholars to locate other parallels in both the author that is cited in either work or in another author's work that fits the same criteria. Therefore, there will be a need to continue to identify and review parallels to the New Testament and Greco-Roman literature with fresh research.⁶¹

Hellenistic and Moral Philosophy and Early Christianity Section of the SBL

Also concerned with the relationship between Paul and Hellenistic morality is the work produced by the Hellenistic Moral Philosophy and Early Christianity Section of the Society of Biblical Literature (HMPECS). This work has been particularly concerned with connections between moral philosophy and the Pauline communities. Abraham Malherbe and E. A. Judge played a significant role in developing this line of inquiry and mentored

---

60. Berger and Colpe, *Religionsgeschichtliches Textbuch*; Boring et al., *Hellenistic Commentary.*

61. See the bibliography and discussion in Thom, "To Show Difference by Comparison," 81–100. Cf. Porter, *Handbook to the Exegesis of the New Testament.*

A History of Research

many of the contributors.⁶² Malherbe and Judge,⁶³ among others (such as Helmut Koester, Hans D. Betz, and Wayne Meeks)⁶⁴ laid the groundwork for the significant contemporary argument that the Christian community at Corinth was socially diverse and that Paul's opponents there had beliefs that were not necessarily "gnostic."⁶⁵

The Hellenistic Moral Philosophy and Early Christianity Section of the Society of Biblical Literature (HMPECS) has produced seven monographs, most of which discuss friendship and patronage as important dynamics in Pauline communities. The group published its first collection of essays in 1996 on friendship and flattery in the ancient world, with another volume on friendship in 1997, both edited by John T. Fitzgerald.⁶⁶ *Greco-Roman Perspectives on Friendship* (1996) is a collection of essays that examines friendship from before Aristotle to such near contemporaries of Paul as Cicero, Plutarch, Lucian, the neo-Pythagoreans, Chariton, and Philo, as well as epigraphic evidence such as honorary inscriptions and documentary papyri. *Friendship, Flattery, and Frankness of Speech* (1997) follows an entirely different format, first presenting three essays that define friendship, frankness, and flattery principally in Philodemus and Plutarch. A detailed examination of friendship language in Philippians 4 follows, identifying this chapter as a friendship letter, the function of friendship language in Philippians 4:10–20, and specifically the significance of self-sufficiency in Philippians 4:11. The volume concludes with discussions concerning the usage of frank speech in the Pauline epistles, Acts, and the Johannine Corpus. In 1998, David Konstan led a team of contributors that produced the sourcebook *Philodemus on Frank Criticism: Introduction, Translation, and Notes*, which introduces a critical source that these contributors to the HMPECS

---

62. For a comprehensive bibliography, see Judge, *Social Distinctives*; Judge, *First Christians*. Malherbe directed the dissertations for many students that published in this field: Ronald Hock (1980), David Balch (1981), Stanley Stowers (1981), Benjamin Fiore (1986), and John Fitzgerald (1988).

63. Judge, *Social Pattern*; Judge, "Social Identity," 201–17; Judge, *Rank and Status*; Judge, "Cultural Conformity." Malherbe, *World of the New Testament*; Malherbe, *Social Aspects*; Malherbe, *Cynic Epistles*.

64. Koester and Robinson, *Entwicklungslinien*; Betz, *Der Apostel Paulus*; Meeks, *Zur Soziologie des Urchristentums*.

65. Contra Adolf Deissmann (1895, 1923) on one hand and Walter Schmithals (1956) on the other. Deismann had argued that Christianity was exclusively a movement of the lowest social class based on his review of newly discovered documentary papyri, and Schmithals had characterized Paul's opponents as exclusively gnostic. Cf. Deissmann, *Bibelstudien*; Deissmann, *Licht vom Osten*; and Schmithals, *Die Gnosis in Korinth*. For history and bibliography of the problem of Paul's opponents, see Stanley E. Porter, *Paul and His Opponents*.

66. Fitzgerald, *Friendship*; Fitzgerald, *Greco-Roman Perspectives on Friendship*.

13

regularly utilize when studying Epicureanism and ancient ideas concerning friendship.[67]

A volume of comparative studies in honor of Abraham J. Malherbe appeared in 2003, and revisits several issues related to previous work.[68] The editors organized the essays according to *graphos* (semantics), *ethos* (ethics and moral characterization), *logos* (rhetoric and literary expression), *ethnos* (self-definition and acculturation), and *nomos* (law and normative values).[69] In their methodological essay, White and Fitzgerald present a detailed history of *Corpus Hellenisticum* and the HMPECS, and review the criticisms from scholars that highlight the weaknesses of "parallels," emphasizing instead the unique nature of the Christian message rather than its similarity to popular philosophy and other Hellenistic literature.[70] Such criticisms have been theological, lexical, and methodological in nature.[71] In response to these criticisms, White and Fitzgerald suggest the studies of parallels should critically engage debates concerning backgrounds and contexts. The backgrounds include studies on culture, social interactions, and history. The contexts include the focus on Hellenistic religions and Judaisms, philosophical and intellectual traditions (specifically Philo, Hellenistic moralists, and the Second Sophistic), and "social world" studies.

A further volume, *Philodemus in the New Testament World*, appeared in 2004, with essays directed towards friendship and rhetoric.[72] J. Paul Sampley argues that Paul uses frank speech according to the conventions set forth by Plutarch and Philodemus, varying the degree of his frankness according to how he perceives the situation.[73] Similarly, Bruce Winter argues that Paul denounces the rhetorical delivery (as described by Philodemus) of "megastar orators" in Corinth that distracted the Corinthian church.[74] While the volumes produced by the HMPECS are useful in identifying and interpreting Paul's usage of friendship and patronage language, the con-

---

67. Fragment nine includes a reference to the female Epicurean philosopher Leontion without comment. *Philodemus*, ed. Konstan; Konstan, *Friendship*.

68. Fitzgerald et al., *Early Christianity*.

69. Olbricht, preface to *Early Christianity*, 3.

70. Fitzgerald and Olbricht, "Quod est comparandum," 13–39.

71. See for example, see Filson, *New Testament*; *TDNT* 1:vii; Sandmel, "Parallelomania," 1–13; Aune, "Problem of the Genre," 9; Danker, *Benefactor*, 7.

72. Fitzgerald et al., *Philodemus*.

73. Sampley, "Paul's Frank Speech," 317.

74. Winter, "Philodemus," 340–41. The group also published a volume on Heraclitus that does not address Paul: *Heraclitus*, ed. Russell and Konstan. The forthcoming work on Cornutus was unavailable to me at the time this book was written. David Armstrong et al., *Cornutus*.

versation concerning contextualization of Paul within popular Hellenistic philosophy has a much wider scope.

Popular Hellenistic Philosophy and Paul

There is much conversation on the relationship between Paul and the popular philosophies of the first century, and interest in this topic spans every generation of Pauline scholarship, from the earliest interpreters to today. These studies help to reconstruct the philosophical and rhetorical milieu of Paul and his audiences. These popular philosophies include Cynicism, Stoicism, Epicureanism, Platonism, and neo-Pythagoreanism.

It may not be immediately obvious why it is useful to compare Paul and philosophers beginning with figures which predate Paul by hundreds of years such as the pre-Socratics, Pythagoras, Socrates, the Academy, and other Greek schools, such as the Cynics, Stoics, and Epicureans. The popularity of these schools rose and fell in the course of history—and mostly were unpopular—until the rise of rhetoric and education in the first century BCE. These schools become especially important when NT scholars use writers such as Cicero, Plutarch, and Seneca and other later witnesses to interpret Paul. The ancient writers most often used to interpret Paul knew not only Greek philosophies but also their Roman incarnations, poets, historians, and mythologies. When interpreting Paul in light of Cicero, Seneca, and Plutarch, we are also interpreting Paul in light of the more ancient traditions that have influenced these writers.

On this point, NT scholars have traced Paul's usage of common elements of moral philosophies such as the household codes,[75] the wise-person,[76] suicide,[77] the image of God,[78] self-definition,[79] divine inspiration,[80]

---

75. See the works of David Balch listed above; Malherbe, "Hellenistic Moralists," 267–333.

76. Malherbe, "Hellenistic Moralists," 293–301.

77. Arthur J. Droge argues that Paul's attitude towards life and death can be traced back through various schools of philosophy to Socrates: he is willing to commit a noble suicide if he must, but he would consider it a martyrdom. "Mori Lucrum," 263–86.

78. McCasland, "Image of God," 85–100.

79. Betz, "Christianity as Religion," 315–44.

80. Cf. Freeman, "Plato: The Use of Inspiration," 137–49; Murray, "Poetic Inspiration," 87–100. A very detailed discussion of the divine nature of poetry in Greek thought and its development in Roman thought is available in an article by Sperduti, "Divine Nature of Poetry," 209–40. A few notes are useful here. Sperduti observes that Homer uses the same words (διοῖ, θεῖοι, διοτρεφεές and διογενεές) to describe poets, seers, and kings: Hom. *Il.* 1.176; 2.196, 445; Hom. *Od.* 1.65, 196, 284; 2.27, 233, 394; 3.121; 4.17; 621, 691; 8.87, 539; 16.252; 17.359; 23.133; 143. "As the scepter of the king

Reading 1 Corinthians with Philosophically Educated Women

divorce and remarriage[81] through the history of philosophy (from Paul's contemporaries back to ancient schools) and examined the relationship of Paul's views with several different schools. This process raises some very important questions: what did Paul know and how did he learn it? What about his audiences? If we determine that either Paul or his audiences were educated, what does this imply about their social status?

Rhetorical critics generally assume that Paul and his audiences would have been aware of rhetorical conventions and popular moral philosophy due to the social contexts and conventions that they identify in his letters. Historians usually classify Greek and Latin education during the first century—at least for elite boys—as primary and secondary.[82] Primary education would include basic grammar and the memorization of some definitive philosophical sentences and poetry. Secondary education would include a more advanced study of style, rhetoric, and important Greek and Latin traditions.[83] Stanley Stowers has suggested that "Paul's Greek educational level roughly equals that of someone who had primary instruction with a *grammaticus*, or teacher of letters, and then had studied letter writing and some rhetorical exercises."[84] However, other scholars have reviewed the same body of evidence and conclude on the basis of Paul's extensive use of Greek philosophy and rhetoric that his education must be more extensive than Stowers suggests. Udo Schnelle, Ronald Hock, and Troels Engberg-Pedersen have argued that Paul had a full Greek education.[85] E. P. Sanders has most recently argued that Paul had an excellent education in the LXX, memorizing most of it at an early age, and a basic education in Greek language and the classics.[86] The strongest argument for Paul's education is his competent use of ancient rhetorical methods. However, Paul only quotes three fragments of Greek poets—which he may have learned without a Greek education—and instead he quotes traditions from Jewish heritage. Loveday Alexander argues that Paul cites the Greek

---

comes from Zeus and fillets are conferred upon holy men by Apollo, so, too, the words of the poets come from the gods." Sperduti, "Divine Nature," 209.

81. Mathews, "Social Teaching," 123–33.

82. The availability of education to women is largely ignored and will be discussed below.

83. Marrou, *History of Education*; Bonner, *Education*. Education for elite women is less studied but reflected in ancient monuments, letters, and other literary sources that will be examined in detail in chapter 2.

84. Stowers, *Rereading of Romans*, 17.

85. Engberg-Pedersen, "Stoicism in Philippians," 256–90; Hock, "Paul and Greco-Roman Education," 198; See also Udo Schnelle's discussion of Paul's background in *Apostle Paul*, 57–83.

86. Sanders, "Paul between Judaism and Hellenism," 80.

poets and Jewish traditions in the manner taught on the secondary level.[87] At the same time, Paul's grammar and style do not demonstrate more advanced knowledge in Greek. For this reason, I am skeptical that Paul received a full Greek education. It seems most likely to me that Paul memorized the LXX at an early age, was exposed to rhetoric and popular philosophy in the forums, and applied his Jewish theological insights in the manner that he understood to be most persuasive.[88]

This assessment of Paul differs from two earlier trends in Pauline scholarship. First, if Paul's knowledge of Greco-Roman philosophy came from a rudimentary education and exposure in the forums, his usage of philosophical concepts does not require an introduction of these ideas from his exposure to "gnostic"[89] ideas or other Corinthian opponents.[90] Second, Paul's Hellenism does not need to be mediated through contact with Philo or other constructions of Hellenized Judaism.[91]

Then we come to the problem of the educational level of Paul's audiences, and we rely on similar arguments and assumptions. Many NT scholars assume that at least some people in Paul's audiences would have picked up on his usage of popular morality and rhetorical devices. This does not mean that the Pauline community at Corinth was a philosophical school, although it did have some resemblance to Hellenistic schools.[92] Rather it suggests some degree of social stratification of Paul and his audiences because formal education was mostly reserved for the elite. It is possible that the elite were not in the Pauline community; however, they would be the most likely candidates to receive some education. What is critical, however, is some contact with the patronage system within the city.[93] The access of

---

87. Alexander, "IPSE DIXIT," 103-27; cf. *Plutarch's Quotations*, ed. Helmbold and O'Neil.

88. Hellenistic Jewish schools taught both Jewish and non-Jewish content. Leo G. Purdue, *Wisdom Literature*, 280-82, discusses Hellenistic Jewish schools in a discussion of Philo; cf. van der Horst, "Pseudo-Phocylides Revisited," 3-30.

89. For the debates concerning "gnosticism" and early Christianity, see King, *What is Gnosticism?*

90. For emphasis on "gnostic" ideas, see *TDNT* 1:364-67; Bultmann, *Der zweite Brief an die Korinther*, 126-29.

91. U. Duchrow argues in *Christenheit und Weltverantwortung* that Paul's usage of Platonic ideas comes from his knowledge of Philo.

92. Judge, "Early Christians as a Scholastic Community," 5-15; Stowers, "Does Pauline Christianity Resemble a Hellenistic Philosophy?," 81-102.

93. MacMullen, *Roman Social Relations*; Saller, *Personal Patronage*; Eisenstadt and Roniger, *Partons, Clients, and Friends*; Cynthia Damon examines the negative depiction of the client in Latin literature in *Mask of the Parasite*; Wallace-Hadrill, *Patronage in Ancient Society*; Eilers, *Roman Patrons*.

Reading 1 Corinthians with Philosophically Educated Women

Christians to homes in Galatia, Corinth, Philippi, and Rome evidences sustained interaction between elites and non-elites. The significance of this access to a home means that Paul's audiences had access to all the benefits that the home provides: some measure of access to goods and services like legal protection, food, health care, art, music, and education, regardless of social status.[94] Because several of Paul's churches had access to these necessities, NT scholars generally consider that Paul could have been from a wealthier family and the early churches were economically diverse.[95] At the same time, there is no small debate about Paul's background.

The ongoing debate between Justin Meggitt, Dale Martin, Gerd Theissen, and others demonstrates that Meggitt has not been successful in defeating previous thinking about Paul's social status. He did, however, initiate a need for much clarification.[96] It is worth noting that Balch has recently argued against Meggitt's idea that the elite "1% lived entirely different lives than the other 99%" of the population based on the housing situation in Pompeii and Herculaneum.[97] Bruce Winter has argued that the usage of οἶκος for the meeting places itself suggests an inner room of the home of an elite.[98] However, it is not the simple mentioning of households in the Pauline literature that sustains the theory that the Pauline communities were socially stratified. Paul's household management and structure reflects the management and structure of elite homes (father, wife, children, slaves heirarchy).[99] The usage of καλέω in an invitation formula in 1 Corinthians 10:27 parallels the elites' invitations to dinner as preserved in papyri.[100] G. R. Horsely pointedly summarizes the importance of these papyri:

---

94. Filson, "Significance of the Early House Churches," 109-12; Judge, *Social Pattern*; White, "Social Authority," 216; Witherington, *Conflict and Community*, 30-32; Balch and Osiek, *Families*, 54; Elliott, "Elders," 77-82; Osiek and MacDonald, *Woman's Place*, 146; Gehring, *House Church*, 135, 140, 150.

95. Here I do not specify Paul's or the Corinthian community's social position because the sources that I am reviewing do not agree on these specifics, but generally do agree that Paul and some members of the community are not without some means. Cf. Marshall, *Enmity in Corinth*; Schowalter and Friesen, *Urban Religion*.

96. Meggitt, "Response," 85-94; Martin, "Review Essay," 51-64; Theissen, "Social Structure," 65-84; Meggitt, "First Churches," 137-56; Theissen, " Social Conflicts," 371-91; Meggitt, "Sources," 241-54.

97. Balch, "Rich Pompeiian Houses," 27-46. Balch also notes that women owned some *domūs*. Cf. DeSilva, "Re-writing 'Household,'" 85-89; cf. Métraux, "Ancient Housing," 392-405.

98. Winter, *After Paul Left Corinth*, 206-11.

99. Stambaugh and Balch, *Social Environment*, 140. Furthermore, Stambaugh and Balch note that the household structure that Paul demands is that of the upper class, with marriage and slaves, 124.

100. Kim, "Papyrus Invitation," 398-402; Terry, "Anlaysis," 25.

An interesting verbal affinity in the NT is 1 Cor. 10:27 εἴ τις καλεῖ ὑμας τῶν ἀπίστοων (εἰς δεῖπνον—these words only in D* G) κτλ. Further, the situation in 1 Cor. 8:10 may be seen in illuminating the perspective when the *kline* invitations are taken into account. The latter, too, may be brought to bear on the elucidation of 1 Cor. 11:17-22. The papyrus invitations, then, document in quite a striking manner the situation which would have been known as normal and everyday by the recipients of Paul's letters at Corinth, and no doubt elsewhere.[101]

In fact, connection to some wealthy patron in various cities may have been an important part of Paul's missionary strategy. As Paul moved from city to city, he attempted to secure patrons who could provide various services to the young community of Christ believers.[102] These patronesses include Euodia and Syntyche (Phil 2:2-3) in Philippi, as well as the tradition of Lydia, who while she may not be historical, is a testament to the memory of patronal support of Paul (Acts 16:14-15). The household contexts that indicate some connection with wealth are referenced in the letters to Galatia, Corinth, and Rome but contrast with the absence of households in the Thessalonian correspondence, a city in which Paul failed to secure a patron.[103]

The book of Acts presents a level of support for Paul that is completely foreign to the Thessalonian epistles but comparable to the Corinthian correspondence. While not historically valuable in reconstructing Paul's experiences, Acts does present an important scenario in which Paul's mission could thrive: the critical support of benefactors. Acts indicates that wealthier women in Thessalonica and Jason (Acts 17:5-7) supported the church there, Beroea enjoyed the support of men and women, and Dionysius and Damaris were among Paul's benefactors in Athens (Acts 17:4, 12, 34).

Paul was especially fortunate in Corinth: Phoebe of Cenchrae (Rom 16:1-2), Gaius (Rom 16:23; 1 Cor 1:14), and Stephanus (1 Cor 1:16; 16:15-17). Because the elite household—which included women, children, clients, slaves, and freedpersons—was just as much a source of education as the forum, we should not imagine that Paul's audiences knew of popular morality and rhetoric only from the public interaction of the male heads of the

---

101. *New Docs* 1:9.

102. Meeks, *Urban Christians*, 77; see esp. the portraits of Chloe and Phoebe, 58-59. Meeks and Fitzgerald, *Writings of St. Paul*; MacDonald and Harrington, *Colossians and Ephesians*, 166. The issues related to patronage and Paul will be discussed in more detail in chapter 5.

103. Barclay, "Thessalonica and Corinth," 49-74. The lack of support from an elite in Thessalonica would leave the Pauline community vulnerable to the persecution that they suffered.

households. The οἶκος provided a medium by which everyone connected to it (wife, son, daughter, slaves, and freedpersons) could have access to its benefits, among these being listening to philosophical discussions at the *symposium*, learning from a tutor, or being a tutor oneself. These discussions and teachings were most likely eclectic, drawing from a wide variety of philosophical traditions (Plato, Aristotle, Epicurean, Stoic, neo-Pythagorean) that have had an impact on New Testament studies. New Testament research has considered the importance of Pythagorean texts, Platonism, Cynicism, Stoicism, and Epicureanism in interpreting Paul. I will consider each of these briefly in turn.

Pythagoreanism

The history of the Pythagoreans is the most difficult and fragmentary in the history of philosophy due to its antiquity and the nature of the available sources.[104] According to tradition, the original school consisted of Pythagoras and his family, and he forbade the teaching of his philosophy to outsiders, which eventually led to the important tradition of mothers passing on writings to their daughters. In the first century, interest in Pythagoras revived with the availability of Pythagorean sentences, the ἄκουσμα or αἰνίγματα.[105] The most important sources for these sentences are the now lost commentaries by Aristotle and Androcydes the Pythagorean, hinting at both their antiquity and genuine association with Pythagoras or his followers. The writings of the Pythagorean pseudepigraphon are impossible to date,[106] but many of the Pythagorean ἄκουσμα or αἰνίγματα which appear in the NT[107] (only by parallel) and in many other first-century and later writers such as Alexander Polyhistor, Plutarch, Clement of Alexandria, Hippolytus of Rome, Porphyry, and Iamblichus may be genuinely

---

104. The most important works in English are Holger Thesleff, *Introduction to the Pythagorean Writings*; Philip, *Pythagoras*; Burket, *Lore and Science*; for texts, see Thesleff, *Pythagorean Texts*; for translations of the Pythagorean corpus, see Kenneth Gutherie, *Pythagorean Sourcebook*.

105. Some important studies in the Pythagorean sentences are Boehm, "De symbolis pythagoreis;" Delatte, *Études*; Nilsson, *Geschichte der griechischen Religion*, 703–8; chapters on the sentences are available in Philip, *Pythagoras*, 134–50, and Burket, *Lore and Science*, 166–92.

106. For a discussion of the problems related to date, see Balch, "Neopythagorean Moralists," 380–411.

107. Robert Grant's review of Pythagoreanism in the NT is reduced to parallels only and no direct Pythagorean sentences appear, "Dietary Laws," 299–310. See also the studies referenced below. Cf. Burket who demonstrates that the curious Pythagorean diet is in the oldest traditions, *Lore and Science*, 180–85.

Pythagorean and indicate a renewal of Pythagorean traditions.[108] This developing Pythagorean tradition may have had an impact on first-century thought. It seems to me, that the pre-Socratic Pythagoreanism, Hellenistic neo-Pythagoreanism,[109] and Christianities and Judaisms[110] all had complex—albeit *very* slight—interweaving influences on one another. Johan Thom calls the Pythagorean influence on Hellenistic Judaisms "tangential," and the references are slim.[111] Philo attributes the saying "Do not walk on the highways" to "that saintly community of the Pythagoreans."[112] Louis Feldman suggests that Josephus makes Abraham parallel to Pythagoras, but the parallel does not have much force:[113] like Pythagoras, Abraham goes to Egypt, but this is a familiar schema in traditions related to wise-persons.[114] Robert Grant also notes that Josephus thought that Jewish dietary regulations came from Egypt.[115] With regards to parallels, David Balch's studies in the neo-Pythagorean writings and the NT household codes are the most important.[116] On this point, it is necessary to emphasize that the neo-Pythagorean writings are "Pythagorean" only in the sense that they bear

---

108. Thom, "Don't Walk on the Highways," 95; cf. Thom, "Golden Verses."

109. There is widespread consensus that the Pythagorean pseudepigraphon—that is, the collection of Hellenistic of writings which are attributed to classical Pythagorean philosophers—is evidence for a revived interested in Pythagoreanism in the first to second centuries. All related details, including the precise dating of the documents and whether or not there were neo-Pythagorean communities, are widely disputed. For examples, see De Vogel, *Greek Philosophy*, 340–53. It is critical here to distinguish between the neo-Pythagorean movement and the Pythagorean pseudepigraphon. The neo-Pythagorean movement was a movement in philosophy in the first century with renewed interest in genuine Pythagoreanism, and the Pythagorean pseudepigraphon arose out of this renewed interest but does not share a connection with Pythagorean philosophy.

110. See, e.g., the similarities and differences between genuine Pythagorean communities and the Essenes established, in Justin Taylor, *Pythagoreans and Essenes*.

111. Thom, "Pythagoreanism," in *ABD* 5:564.

112. Philo, *Quod omn. prob.* 2. See the study by Goodenough, *Neo-Pythagorean Source*. Eduard Schweizer, "Slaves of the Elements," 459, discusses Pythagorean influences in Philo, Josephus, and Plutarch and argues that these elements have an impact on how we should interpret Galatians and Colossians. Schweizer suggests that Paul in Galatians and whoever wrote Colossians were responding to neo-Pythagorean influences (466).

113. Feldman, "Abraham the Greek Philosopher," 151.

114. Murray, "Hecataeus of Abdera," 141–71; nevertheless the historical question of whether or not Pythagoras travelled to Egypt is explored by Kingsly, "From Pythagoras to the Turba Philosophorum," 1–13.

115. Joseph. *AJ* 2.282; Grant, "Dietary Laws," 304.

116. Balch, "Neopythagorean Moralists," 380–411; Balch, "Household Ethical Codes," 397–404.

the names of known and unknown ancient Pythagoreans but contain no Pythagorean philosophy (such as music theory, geometry, doctrine of the soul and reincarnation, dietary restrictions) other than popular morality.

Platonism

Most of the conversation regarding Platonic influence on Paul centers on anthropological viewpoints expressed in Paul and his contemporaries. Precisely how Paul adopts Platonic divisions of the soul has significant impact on how interpreters approach Paul's understanding of the human condition, the effects of sin, the meaning of salvation, the resurrection of the body, and freewill. Methodological problems arise from the fact that both Pauline and Platonic interpretations are constantly in flux, and the writings of both of these writers express developments on almost every important concept. Plato contradicts himself on almost everything (reflecting both his dialogical style and development of thought),[117] and the development of Paul's theologies and anthropologies are not without dispute in NT scholarship.[118] Nevertheless, some scholars trace some of Paul's concepts to Plato. For example, Roy Bowen Ward argues that Paul's view of homosexual contact as being "unnatural" in Romans 1:26-27 has its roots in *Timaeus* rather than *Laws*, and Ward concludes that Paul is arguing that sex κατὰ φύσιν is only heterosexual and for procreation only.[119] Navigating through the differing interpretations of both the apostle and Plato, several scholars have argued that Paul's concept of the inner human being (ὁ ἔσω ἄνθρωπος) has its origins in Plato. Betz argues that Paul's anthropology has its origins in Plato, but it was most likely developed in conversation with his collaborators rather than with his opponents (gnostic or otherwise) or by interaction with ideas present in Philo.[120] Emma Wassermann demonstrates that Paul's

---

117. Contradiction becomes paradox in Demos, "Paradoxes," 164-74; for *Lysis*, see Annas, "Plato and Aristotle on Friendship," 532-54; Owen, "Place of the Timaeus," 87; Peck, "Plato's Parmenides," 126-50; Cook, "Dialectic," 440; Ferrar, *Plato's Republic*, 437.

118. For review of the issues related to this problem, arguments, and bibliography, see Jewett, *Paul's Anthropological Terms* and van Kooten, *Paul's Anthropology*.

119. Ward, "Why Unnatural?," 263-84. Ward further demonstrates that Philo and the *Sentences of Pseudo-Phoclides* use similar arguments. For more recent discussions and bibliography on Paul's use of Platonic anthology (as mediated through Stoicism or Hellenstic Judaism), see Winkler, *Constraints of Desire*, 20-23; Martin, "Heterosexism," 332-55; Brooten, *Love between Women*, 271-80; Jewett, "Homoerotic References," 223-41; Swancutt, "Disease of Effemination," 193-235.

120. For a history of this issue, see Betz, "Inner Human Being," 315-41.

notion of sin in Romans 6–8 is an appropriation of apocalyptic thought to a notion of Platonic immortality.[121]

In contrast to scholars who have found concepts in Paul's thought which may have originated in Plato, Athenagoras Ch. Zakopoulos reviews the supposed relationships between Plato and Paul and concludes that Paul has a monistic view of humanity that is completely uninfluenced by Plato. Instead, Paul embraces a Hebraic view that he expressed in Greek philosophical terms without adhering to their traditional philosophical meanings.[122] Therefore, Paul could utilize and/or modify philosophical terms without commitment to a philosophical tradition and use them according to his specific needs.

The importance of Aristotle for the interpretation of Paul comes into play with his influence on later writers such as Cicero, Plutarch, and Seneca. Aristotle's works on ethics are the starting point of discussions regarding popular moral attitudes such as slavery, marriage and family life, and friendship.[123] Similarly, Aristotle's works on poetics and rhetoric are the starting point for rhetorical studies, being influential in later sources such as Cicero and Quintilian.[124]

Cynicism

Abraham Malherbe has consistently argued for locating Paul within Cynicism, concluding that Paul more closely aligned himself with moderate Cynics in his ethics and with the Epicureans in his concern for community. Malherbe situates Paul's description of himself in 1 Thessalonians as a specific type of ideal Cynic (a moderate rather than a highly ascetic) as described by Dio Chrysostom and pseudo-Diogenes.[125] Dio says that some Cynics do not really enter the struggle (*agon*) of life that Cynicism claims, preaching for money or self-gratification, using flattery and frank speech inappropriately. Like Paul's, Dio's ideal Cynic, such as Musonius or Demonax, is frank but gentle as a nurse. Malherbe further notes that many New Testament scholars use the problematic term "Cynic-Stoic" when re-

121. Wassermann, "Paul among the Philosophers," 387–415.

122. Zakopoulos, *Plato and Saint Paul*, 151–57.

123. Jacobs, *Aristotle's Virtues*; Stern-Gillet and Corrigan, *Reading Ancient Texts*; Rorty, *Essays on Aristotle's Rhetoric*; Ierodiakonou, *Topics in Stoic Philosophy*; Reale, *History of Ancient Philosophy*; Algra and Koenen, *Lucretius*; Sandbach, *Aristotle*.

124. See the essays in Porter, *Rhetorical Interpretation*; Olbricht, "Classical Rhetorical Criticism," 108–24; Watson, "Contributions and Limitations," 123–51; Anderson, *Ancient Rhetorical Theory*.

125. Malherbe, "Gentle as a Nurse," 203–17.

ferring to elements of Greco-Roman philosophy. He more clearly defines self-sufficiency as moderately Cynic when he describes Paul's notion of it in Philippians 4.[126] Using the Cynic epistles, Malherbe again argues that the Cynics themselves did not hold to a unified canon of doctrine, but adjusted their behavior to suit their context, strengthening his position that Paul represents a more moderate view.[127] Ronald Hock has suggested that Paul's references to work and his refusal to accept payment from the Corinthians has Cynic connotations.[128]

Stoicism

Early Christian interest in Stoicism is enduring. Marcia Colish has surveyed early Christian scholarship (from the fathers through scholasticism) on Stoicism and Paul, demonstrating early Christian affinity for Stoicism and how it complements Paul.[129] Benjamin Fiore situates 1 Corinthians 5–6 in philosophical discussion with Plutarch's *Dialogue on Love*.[130] Fiore compares Paul's indifference to life and death (with respect to their impact on virtue and devotion to Christ) to the Stoic ἀδιάφορα[131]—the external things that do not matter to the Stoic for happiness. Dale B. Martin has demonstrated that Paul's idea of "the [Corinthian] body" embraces a Stoic anthropology.[132] Troels Engberg-Pedersen is the leading scholar on the relationship between Paul and the Stoics, arguing historical, exegetical, hermeneutical, and theological relationships between Paul and the Stoics. His primary focus is Paul's usage of Stoic argumentation, concluding that Paul uses a distinctly Stoic form to implement his theology.[133] Albert V. Garcilazo recently argued that the problems in Corinth are rooted in Stoic influences exerted by the higher status members of the community who adopted Stoic views concerning dualistic anthropology and cosmology.[134] Engberg-Pedersen has more recently argued that Paul's cosmology of body and spirit (the *pneuma* is tied directly

---

126. Malherbe, "Paul's Self-Sufficiency," 125–39.
127. Malherbe, "Self Definition," 11–24.
128. Hock, "Paul's Tentmaking," 558; Hock, *Social Context*, 29.
129. Cornish, "Stoicism and the New Testament," 334–79; cf. Cornish, "Pauline Theology," 129; Colish, *Stoic Tradition*.
130. Fiore, "Passion in Paul," 135–43.
131. Jaquette, "Life and Death," 30–54.
132. Martin, *Corinthian Body*, 66.
133. Engberg-Pedersen, *Paul and the Stoics*; Lee, *Paul, the Stoics, and the Body of Christ*.
134. Garcilazo, *Corinthian Dissenters*, 77–78.

to heaven) finds a parallel in Stoicism (the idea that reason, heaven, and body are interconnected) and nowhere else.¹³⁵

Paul and Seneca

The relationship between Paul and Seneca in particular has been a favorite topic of conversation because of the striking similarities between the two and the historical connection whereby Acts 12:18 places Paul before Seneca's brother, Gallio.¹³⁶ Linus, Augustine, and Jerome wrote of correspondence between Seneca and Paul. Thirteen epistles exist that appear to document such correspondence, but the overwhelming consensus is that these epistles are forgeries. Kreyher has suggested that early Christian scholars knew of other letters that are now lost.¹³⁷ The recent conversation on Seneca and Paul has focused on the similarities and differences in their theology, anthropology, and ethics. J. N. Sevenster structures his monograph around these questions.¹³⁸ Engberg-Pedersen has demonstrated that Paul uses the structures set out in Seneca's system of benefaction in *De Beneficiis*.¹³⁹

Epicureanism

The discussion of Paul and Epicurean thought mostly relates to his anti-Epicurean tendencies.¹⁴⁰ Abraham Malherbe situated Paul's rhetoric in 1 Corinthians 15:32 within anti-Epicurean polemic, which characterizes the Epicureans as "beasts."¹⁴¹ Malherbe also understands the command to "work with your hands" as a correction to Epicurean and Cynic distaste for manual labor.¹⁴² Norman DeWitt is the leading authority on Epicurus

135. Engberg-Pedersen, "Material Spirit," 179-97.
136. Fluery, *Saint Paul et Sénèque*; Aubertin, *Sénèque et Saint Paul*; Baur, "Seneca und Paulus"; Kreyer, *L. Annaeus Seneca*; Lightfoot, *Philippians*, 270-333; Deissner, *Paulus und Seneca*; Schreiner, *Seneca*; Benoit, "Sénèque et Saint Paul," 7-35; Kurfess, "Zu dem apokryphen Breifwechsel," 42-48; Paul Berry, in *Correspondence*, is convinced that the correspondence between Paul and Seneca, consisting of thirteen letters, is genuine; see also Berry, *Encounter*.
137. Kreyer, *Seneca*, 178.
138. Sevenster, *Seneca*, 196-99.
139. Engberg-Pedersen, "Gift-Giving and Friendship," 15-44.
140. However, there is a strong tradition in earlier Christian writers who approve of Epicurean philosophies and practices. See Jungkutz, "Epicureanism"; Jungkutz "Christian Approval," 279-93; Jungkutz, *Christian Approval*.
141. Malherbe, "Beasts at Ephesus," 71-80.
142. Malherbe, *Paul and the Thessalonians*, 96.

and Paul, and consistently argues that Paul is Epicurean in theory and anti-Epicurean in practice.[143] It is critical to note that DeWitt insists that Paul knew of the "Canon of Epicurus" (the basic tenants of Epicureanism) and accepted several of their theories but guided his audiences away from Epicurean philosophy.[144] For example, the Epicurean teaching that one can trust the senses to learn of reality appears in Paul's notion of face to face knowledge (1 Cor 13:12) but in Colossians Paul warns the reader against the one who is "taking his stand on what he has seen."[145] Polemicists often ridiculed the Epicureans as a group that based their entire system of philosophy on their understanding of the ἄτομος: their entire cosmology and ethics rested on the smallest indivisible unit, giving the appearance of great weakness. Paul likewise directs his attention to "the weak and beggardly elements" but describes the resurrection with ἄτομος, which DeWitt notes that several scholars translate "in a moment."[146] Clarence Glad has produced a study on psychagogy (moral guidance for neophytes) in Paul and Philodemus. Like DeWitt, Clarence Glad suggests that Paul may have known about Epicurean principles of friendship and frankness as described in Philodemus and applied them in varying degrees to the "weak" and "strong" character types in 1 Corinthians and Romans.[147] Malherbe argues that Paul's ideas in 1 Thessalonians are anti-Epicurean in many ways: Paul emphasized brotherly love rather than friendship language, the apostles are God-taught rather than self-taught, and his exhortation to live a quiet life is exclusive of the Epicurean ideal community.[148] Paul Holloway argues that Paul's consolations in Philippians 4:6–9 constitute a single consultation in the Epicurean style described by Cicero and implemented often by Plutarch.[149]

Evaluation

I have briefly discussed the *Corpus Hellenisticum*, the publications of the Hellenistic Moral Philosophy and Early Christianity section of SBL and current conversations regarding Paul and popular Hellenistic moral

---

143. DeWitt, *Epicurus*; DeWitt, *St. Paul and Epicurus*, 77, 86, 89.

144. DeWitt, *St. Paul and Epicurus*, 10.

145. The translation and assumption that both Corinthians and Colossians are genuinely Pauline belong to DeWitt, *St. Paul and Epicurus*, 10.

146. DeWitt, *St. Paul and Epicurus*, 12. Gal 4:9.

147. Glad, *Paul and Philodemus*.

148. Malherbe, "Anti-Epicurean Rhetoric," 136–52; cf. Malherbe, *Paul and the Thessalonians*.

149. Holloway, "Bona Cogitare," 89–96.

philosophy. Wettstein's collection of Jewish, Greek, and Latin parallels to the New Testament inspired later scholars to review systematically Hellenistic references in the *Corpus Hellenisticum*. Contributions to the *Corpus Hellenisticum* have focused on bringing to light parallels regarding style as well as religious and political ideas. Most of the contributions to this project briefly but critically introduce a writer that is a near contemporary of Paul and then list parallels. W. C. van Unnik suggested in 1964 that contributors work to provide both clear criteria for choosing a parallel and explanation of it in light of various contexts. This call for methodological reflection was not substantially observed until the volumes on Plutarch edited by Hans D. Betz appeared more than ten years later. In many ways, the work of the *Corpus Hellenisticum* culminated in the *Neuen Wettstein* and related studies, but scholars are continually working to discover and interpret similarities between Hellenistic writings and Paul. The great achievement of these studies is that they serve as one starting point for situating Paul within Hellenistic culture.

The Hellenistic Moral Philosophy and Early Christianity Section of the Society of Biblical Literature has produced four volumes of essays that describe the nature friendship and patronage in the Pauline communities. These essays offer critical descriptions of friendship and patronage from the writings of Aristotle, Cicero, Plutarch, Seneca, and Philodemus that are invaluable in interpreting Paul's writings. The group also published a collection of articles in honor of Abraham Malherbe which offers methodological insights and further exegesis of the New Testament in its Hellenistic contexts.

Further conversation concerning Paul and popular Hellenistic philosophy has produced important resources for identifying similarities and differences between Paul and all of the popular schools. The ancient Greek schools are important because Paul's near contemporaries used these earlier schools to shape their thinking. Therefore, works on rhetoric and epistolary theory that use Quintilian, Cicero, and pseudo-Libanius begin with Aristotle's *Rhetoric* and *Poetics*. Studies of Pauline ethics identify parallels in Cicero, Seneca, and Plutarch that have their roots in earlier Stoic, Epicurean, Cynic, Aristotelian, and Platonic ethics. The great achievement of these studies is the placement of Paul in contemporary moral conversations that have both precedence and antecedence in Greek and Roman thought.

While as a whole these approaches are invaluable, nevertheless, these conversations pay little attention to matters of gender, particularly the participation of women in these philosophical traditions. There is little consideration of the traditions of philosophically educated women in the ancient world and the possible involvement of such women in the Pauline communities as interpreters of Paul. With few exceptions, interest in such questions has been tangential at best in both New Testament and classical scholarship.

The Conversation Concerning Women in Greco-Roman Philosophy

The conversation regarding the history of scholarship on women in ancient philosophy is quite limited.[150] The histories of the female teachers and students—as well as the wives, sisters, and daughters of male philosophers and women philosophers—are a neglected topic. The standard histories of philosophy, for example, are often silent regarding philosophically educated women. Alfred Weber shows no interest in the history of women in ancient philosophy, and neither do Alexander, Thilly, Webb, Durant, Alpern, Bréhier, Fuller, and Mascia.[151] Copleston dismisses the lives of Pythagoras in his biographers (who indicate that the early Pythagoreans passed on their teachings from mother to daughter), saying that they "can hardly be said to afford us reliable testimony, and it is doubtless right to call them romances."[152] Even works produced during the rise of feminism and onwards do not mention the most famous female philosophers (Theano, Diotima, and Hipparchia) or poets (Sappho, Erinna, and Nossis).[153] Bertrand Russell mentions Hypatia but takes no interest in the ancient female philosophers.[154] Ralph M. McInerny intimates that all of the biographical information concerning Pythagoras is legend (but seems to accept traditions related to the community from the same sources) and that Xanthippe is also a rhetorical figure.[155] Stephen R. L. Clark mentions parenthetically that Crates's wife Hipparchia accompanied him, but other than this note makes no mention of the involvement of women in ancient philosophy.[156]

---

150. There was not even an attempt to recover the ancient history of philosophically educated women in the 1989 *Hypatia* issue dedicated to the history of women in philosophy. Instead, see Waithe, "On Not Teaching," 132–38.

151. Weber, *History of Philosophy*; Alexander, *Short History of Philosophy*; Thilly, *History of Philosophy*; Webb, *History of Philosophy*; Durant, *Story of Philosophy*; Alpern, *March of Philosophy*; Bréhier, *Histoire de la Philosophie*; Fuller, *History of Philosophy*; Carmin Mascia, *History of Philosophy*.

152. Copleston, *History of Philosophy*, 29.

153. Parker, *Story of Western Philosophy*; Popkin, *Columbia History of Western Philosophy*.

154. Russell, *History of Western Philosophy*, 368.

155. McInerny, *History of Western Philosophy*, 40–42, 111.

156. Clark, "Ancient Philosophy," 39.

A History of Research

Disinterest limits scholarly discussion and consideration of the roles of women in the history of philosophy. Historians of philosophy know their sources well and therefore have read about the mothers, female teachers, students, wives, sisters, and daughters of the philosophers—and about the traditions of intense female involvement in Pythagoreanism, Epicureanism, or Stoicism—so it does not appear to be ignorance that accounts for the silence of historians concerning philosophically educated women. The scope of most histories of Hellenistic philosophies is limited to important shifts in Greek thinking, and because these historians have identified no woman who founded a school or made a significant contribution to shaping Greek thought, the activity of women in philosophy is ignored.[157] Nevertheless, the sources that historians have used to reconstruct the thinking of ancient philosophers contain witness to the activity of women that is useful for reconstructing the history of philosophically educated women.

There are, however, a few scholars who have directed their attention to the question of the history of women's involvement in philosophy. The interest in the topic begins in our time with Mary Beard's germinal work, which inspired later generations of scholars to begin to recover the roles of women in ancient history.[158] However, most studies on women and the history of philosophy deal with the idea of woman in philosophy, the ideology of women's liberation, or women who were active after the third century CE (e.g., Hypatia and beyond).[159] Aegidius Menagius's seventeenth-century work *Historia Mulierum Philosopharum*, translated by Beatrice Zeller, in 1984 caused renewed interest in the topic of philosophically educated women.[160] Sarah B. Pomeroy has reviewed the literary and archeological evidence for the education of women in the ancient world, but her work seems completely ignored by historians of philosophy.[161] Richard Hawley wrote a brief article on the problems related to reconstructing the histories of women in ancient philosophy, noting the challenges presented by the close association of female philosophers with men—either they are the wives, daughters, or lovers of the philosophers and all of the traditions are preserved by male writers.[162]

---

157. Indian and Chinese histories of philosophy do pay attention to the importance of women philosophers. See Raphals, *Sharing the Light*, 243–46; Majumbar, *Ancient India*, 91.

158. Beard, *Woman as Force in History*.

159. Tuana, *Woman and the History of Philosophy*; McAlister, *Hypatia's Daughters*; Ward, *Feminism and Ancient Philosophy*; Allen, *Concept of Woman*; Lloyd, *Feminism and History of Philosophy*.

160. Ménage, *History of Women Philosophers*.

161. Pomery, "*Technikai kai mousikai*," 51–68.

162. Hawley, "Problem of Women Philosophers," 70–87; cf. Hawley, "Ancient

Reading 1 Corinthians with Philosophically Educated Women

Kathleen Wilder produced an article on ancient women philosophers, but her work does not improve on that of Ménage.[163] Mary Ellen Waithe is uncritical in her identification of many philosophers and their teachings in her *Ancient Women Philosophers, 600 B.C.–500 A.D.*, which, being little more than a translation of neo-Pythagorean pseudepigraphon, has not been well received because of its unreliability.[164] Ethel M. Kersey produced a sourcebook of women philosophers that is almost exclusively reliant on Ménage and Waithe for ancient sources, and Kersey offers minimal critical notes.[165] Sarah B. Pomeroy's review of the status of research on women in the ancient world mentions none of these studies, nor any other that specifically addresses the history of philosophically educated women.[166] Kate Lindemann owns and operates a website that has a credible list of female philosophers from all over the world with minimal critical notes.[167] Another collaborative bibliography on women in philosophy with a corresponding website that posts updates to the work appears to be abandoned.[168] Ancient papyri, monuments, and other literary sources indicate the education of women from various social status during our time period.[169] As a whole, modern critical review of the history of women in philosophy and scholarly dialogue

---

Collections," 161–69.

163. Wilder, "Women Philosophers," 21–62.

164. Waite, *Ancient Women Philosophers*. Waithe is a bit more enthusiastic in identifying female philosophers and speculating on the authenticity of documents attributed to women than she is in critically verifying and interpreting her sources. Reviews include: Dancy, "On A History of Women Philosophers," 160–71; Green, Review of *A History of Women Philosophers*, 178–79; and Clarke, Review of *A History of Women Philosophers*, 429–30.

165. Kersey, *Women Philosophers*. Unfortunately, Kersey does not expand on the social characteristics of women in the ancient world farther than the seclusion of Athenian women in fifth century BCE.

166. Pomeroy, "Study of Women in Antiquity," 263–68.

167. Lindemann, *Women Philosophers Web Site*, online: http://www.women-philosophers.com.

168. Barth, *Women Philosophers*; Hutchings and Rumsey, *Collaborative Bibliography*. The vision of the *Collaborative Bibliography* was broad: to create an international bibliography of female philosophers together with a list of their works. Unfortunately this project seems to be abandoned. The online database http://billyboy.ius.indiana.edu/WomeninPhilosophy/WomeninPhilo.html is no longer accessible (last attempted Feb 6, 2012), and no further editions of the bibliography have been produced.

169. Pleket, *Epigraphica*. I will cite Pleket by the number of the entry and not page numbers unless otherwise noted. Cf. van Bremen, *Limits of Participation*; Plant, *Women Writers*; Green, *Women Poets*; Lefkowitz and Fant, *Women's Life*; Bagnell, *Women's Letters*.

on the topic are limited to a smattering of articles and a few monographs.[170] The most recent study of the history of women in philosophy appears in a chapter of Joan E. Taylor's *Jewish Women Philosophers of First Century Alexandria*. Taylor reviews the primary sources of Menagius and Waithe and concludes that the traditions of women in philosophy are encased in misogynistic rhetoric.[171] Nevertheless, misogynistic rhetoric of ancient philosophers does not nullify the usefulness of these sources concerning historicity of philosophically educated women because archaeological and papryologial evidence supports the methods of education found in these literary sources. Furthermore, there is evidence of woman-to-woman sharing of philosophical reflections and female heads of households bringing into the home whatever they desire—be it slaves, art, poetry, or philosophers.[172]

Philosophically Educated Women Reading Paul: A Neglected Topic

Some contributors to the *Corpus Hellensticum* and the Hellenistic Moral Philosophy and Early Christianity section of the SBL have highlighted similarities between ancient literature and Paul that have some relevance to the question of educated women in the community. Where the contributors have demonstrated some important similarities between Paul and important sources for reconstructing ancient philosophically educated women, scholars typically neglect interpreting Paul in light of this important context. For example, *Plutarch's Ethical Writings and Early Christian Literature* contains Plutarch's essays "On Consolation to his Wife," "The Virtues of Women," and the "Dinner of the Seven Sages." These dialogs offer rich insight as to how women had access to philosophy and the nature of dinner parties in the ancient world. Hubert Martin Jr. and Jane E. Philips situate Plutarch's consolation to his wife within Greco-Roman rhetoric and philosophy, concluding that he follows pseudo-Dionysius's *Rhetoric* for its form and common philosophical themes for its content.[173] In her review of "The Virtues of Women," Kathleen O'Brien Wicker does not consider the social status of

---

170. Bicknell, "Sokrates' Mistress Xanthippe," 1–5; Nais, "Shrewish Wife of Socrates," 97–99; Eisenberger, *Sokrates*, 83–218; Halperin, "Why Is Diotima a Woman?," 257–308; Frede, "Out of the Cave," 397–422; Hawley, "Problem of Women Philosophers," 70–87; Helleman, "Penelope," 283–302; Helleman, "Homer's Penelope," 227–50; Lambropoulou, "Some Pythagorean Female Virtues," 122–35; Dyson, "Dido the Epicurean," 203–21; Mauch, *Senecas Frauenbild*; Dover, "Two Women of Samos," 222–82.

171. Taylor, *Jewish Women Philosophers*, 173–226.

172. This evidence will be presented and evaluated in chapter 3.

173. Martin and Phillips, "Consolatio ad uxorem," 410–13.

Reading 1 Corinthians with Philosophically Educated Women

women when interpreting Paul's instructions, as does Plutarch in his "Advice to the Bride and Groom," where wealthier women are exempt from moral norms associated with women of lower status.[174] David Aune observes that Plutarch in "Dinner of the Seven Sages" and Paul in 1 Corinthians share the same interest in behavior at the *symposium*.[175] Related to the silence of women and order in the church, Betz and Smith note that in 1 Corinthians 14:33–34 there are two parallels to Plutarch, *Moralia* 385c which includes: πανταχοῦ τριῶν νομιζομένων ([the Muses] are understood as three) and τὸ μηδεμιᾷ γυναικὶ πρὸς τὸ χρηστήριον εἶναι προσελθεῖν (no woman is allowed to approach the oracle)—the argument for unity (1 Cor 4:14; 7:17) and sacred law (cf. 1 Clem 23:1; 29:1).[176] Finally, Balch's articles concerning the neo-Pythagoreans often address writings attributed to women, but he does not imagine philosophically educated women encountering Paul.

The publications of the Hellenistic Moral Philosophy and Early Christianity section of SBL occasionally address issues related to ancient women. *Philodemus in the New Testament World* has an essay devoted to women in the Garden of Epicurus. In it, Pamela Gordon argues that most of the women that we know of were in the first generation of the Garden, although the practice survived for hundreds of years.[177] Unfortunately, she does not consider how this tradition relates to Diogenes of Oenoanda, who wrote a letter to his mother explaining how she should practice Epicurean philosophy.[178] Fragment nine of David Konstan's translation of *Philodemus: On Frank Criticism* preserves a teaching of Leontion without comment.

Recent examples that specifically address popular Hellenistic philosophy in 1 Corinthians do not fare better than classical studies.[179] For example, John T. Fitzgerald's study of the quite popular teaching concerning hardships that the ideal teacher overcomes (fear of death, loss of wealth, exile, loss of honor, etc.) gives attention to Stoic elements in 1 Corinthians 4:7–13 but does not address how philosophically educated women would respond to this content.[180] Stanley Stowers discusses Paul's usage of self-mastery (1 Cor

---

174. Wicker, "Mulierum Virtues," 117.

175. Aune, "Septem Sapientium Convivium," 76.

176. Betz and Smith, "Delphic Maxim," 223.

177. Gordon, "Remembering the Garden," 241.

178. Fragment 52 preserves a letter of Epicurus to his mother, in which he asks her to interact with his philosophy. See Chilton, *Diogenes*, 19; 108–13; see especially 130, "The author is emphasizing the necessity of pursuing philosophy in order to dispel fear (of death and/or the gods?) and attain perfect happiness."

179. Dutch, *Educated Elite*.

180. The importance of self-sufficiency in the Corinthian correspondence is made evident by Fitzgerald, *Cracks in an Earthen Vessel*, 117–84.

7:9; 9:25) and the lack of it (1 Cor 7:5), without reference to how the same principles are applied to women in Seneca and Musonius Rufus.[181] The nature of Paul's application of self-control in his usage of the *agon* motif (1 Cor 9:24–27) has received attention by Pfitzner and Brändl, and again women's interpretation of the text is not addressed.[182] Robert Grant has identified some philosophical terms in 1 Corinthians that pertain to women: the use of "shameful" and "beneficial" in 1 Corinthians 11:5–6 (head coverings and the participation of women in worship) and 14:35 (women speaking in church). Grant, however, does not consider how philosophically educated women might engage 1 Corinthians 11–14. He does note that the form and content of the marriage regulations in 1 Corinthians 7 have important parallels to Diogenes Laertius 6.29 and Epictetus, *Diss* 3.24.60; 6.1.159. Grant also concludes that Paul's use of "conscious scruples" in 1 Corinthians 10:27–29 is not specifically Stoic, "but it is part of the baggage carried by an ordinary educated Greco-Roman *man*."[183] Jeffery Asher has traced the concept of the anthropogenic metaphor (sowing as the origin of humanity) in 1 Corinthians 15:42–44 through Greco-Roman thought, concluding that Paul's *male* readers would have been familiar with the metaphor that is common in mythology and philosophy.[184] While these studies make significant contributions to understanding Paul and his sources in their Hellenistic context, the question of how philosophically educated women would interact with these texts remains unasked. One possible reason for this unasked question may be due to the disinterest in philosophically educated women in classical scholarship. However, another important work on women in the Corinthian church requires special attention.

The Corinthian Women Prophets and the Philosophically Educated Women

Antoinette Wire's valuable work *The Corinthian Women Prophets: A Reconstruction through Paul's Rhetoric* addresses the activity of women prophets in the Corinthian church. Wire describes the women prophets as poor, uneducated, and low born, but rising in status and builds an interpretation of 1 Corinthians with an interest in these women. In contrast to the women prophets, Paul held a higher status before he preached the gospel; however, at the time of writing 1 Corinthians, he was in a state

---

181. Stowers, "Paul and Self-Mastery," 534.
182. Pfitzner, *Paul and the Agon Motif*; Brändl, *Der Agon bei Paulus*.
183. Grant, "Hellenistic Elements," 62.
184. Asher, "ΣΠΕΙΡΕΤΑΙ," 101–22.

of status loss. The rising status of the Corinthian women stems from the wisdom and power attributed to them by the community because of their roles as prophets in the church.[185] Wire argues that the women prophets are among "the many" that Paul refers to in 1 Corinthians 1:26, and those that Paul mentions as owning homes were most likely artisans. Wire also writes, "A society where women are not found in schools, courts, or councils could not have produce many learned or politically powerful women for religious recruitment."[186] I will argue that there indeed were women found in schools, courts, and active in poetry, philosophy, and other intellectual arts. Furthermore, philosophical schools that were traditionally open to the involvement of women were active in Corinth in the first century, and were available for religious recruitment. Because of these contexts, we should consider how such women would read the text.

The most important departure from Wire is that this book examines 1 Corinthians with an interest in how two philosophically educated patronesses would read the text. All of our texts overlap: this book interprets 1 Corinthians 1–4, Paul's teachings on divorce and marriage in chapter 7, and the *agon* motif in chapter 9. As a secondary focus, other issues in 1 Corinthians will be examined for what they can say about philosophically educated women and their contexts: the situation relating to the stepmother and stepson in chapter 5, lawsuits in chapter 6, the nature of household worship, and head coverings. These texts of couse say different things about women prophets. When Wire examines these issues, she does so with an interest in what these texts have to say about her women prophets within their social contexts. Our interest will be in how higher status philosophically educated women would read the same texts, and what is true for women prophets may not be true for philosophically educated women: they are two different groups of women who experience and interact with the text differently. Therefore, there are many points of agreement and disagreement between this book and Wire's work because they both address women in 1 Corinthians, the most significant of which will be noted as they appear below in chapters 5, 6, and 7.

In this book, I identify "philosophically educated women" as women who have come into contact with enough philosophical teaching from any school to identify and interact with components of 1 Corinthians which have points of connection with basic tenants of Greco-Roman philosophy. "Women philosophers" were of course "philosophically educated women,"

---

185. Wire, *Corinthian Women Prophets*, 71.

186. Wire, *Corinthian Women Prophets*, 63; she goes on to say that the appearance of women in courts is rare (76).

but male philosophers were obviously not. That is the only distinction that I make between "philosophically educated women" and male philosophers. I use the term "philosophically educated women" because they are the topic of the book and the focus of my argument. That is, I am not arguing that women philosophers were in the Corinthian community, and if that were the case, the term "women philosophers" would replace "philosophically educated women." On that note, it is very important to clarify that the New Testament was ridiculed by many Roman thinkers: the philosopher Celsus (2nd CE),[187] Porphyry the neo-Platonist, Macarius Magnes the neo-Platonist (4th CE), Sossianus Hierocles (a Roman aristocrat, fl. early 4th CE), and Julian the neo-Platonist (emperor, 331–63). Christianity was also criticized by Pliny the Younger (61–112 CE), Lucian (125–80 CE), and Galen (ca. 129–217 CE).[188] Because these thinkers rejected Christianity based on their understanding of Greek and Roman philosophy, we can expect women philosophers representing these schools would also be hostile to Paul's message. It is safe to assume that a woman philosopher would not be attracted to Christianity, but a philosophically educated woman who has broad intellectual interests could identify with and engage popular philosophical teachings embedded in Paul's teachings and letters.

Moving Forward

I will show that the history of the involvement of women in philosophy, according to a variety of important sources, indicates that a wide variety of women could have received some degree of philosophical education: elite women, freedwomen, wives and daughters of traveling philosophers, and slaves. I will argue that the least that we could expect these women to know well comprises three themes: patronage, marriage and family, and self-sufficiency. First, I will demonstrate that friendship and patronage are common in philosophical writings addressed to and written by women and are important for the interpretation of 1 Corinthians. Second, each philosophical school had teachings related to family life. Finally, each school had some concept of the ideal teacher that was characterized by some level of self-control. The Cynic-Stoic doctrine of self-sufficiency, along with its most common usage in the *agon* motif, stands at the intersection of the most popular philosophies in the first century. The *agon* motif is the common athletic metaphor that philosophers used to explain the importance

---

187. Precise school is unclear, see Cook, *Greco-Roman Paganism*, 17–26.
188. Wilken, *Christians as the Romans Saw Them*; Cook, *Roman Attitudes*.

of training oneself to have adequate mental and physical self-control to live the good life that is marked by self-sufficiency. I will address the question of how philosophically educated women familiar with these four themes would interact with 1 Corinthians concerning the presentation of Paul as ideal teacher, self-sufficiency and Paul's apostleship, Paul's use of friendship language, and his teachings on marriage and family life.

In chapters 2 and 3, I will review the history of women in philosophy as described in ancient sources and reconstruct what education we could expect such women to have. Chapter 4 will describe the state of philosophy in Corinth in the early part of the first century and its significance for understanding 1 Corinthians as well as discuss and evaluate the place of women among the Corinthian believers. Chapters 5, 6, and 7 will address the results of chapters 2, 3, and 4 in light of how philosophically educated women might engage Paul's material that has parallels in the most popular philosophical teachings: (1) friendship and patronage and Paul's relationships with people who were connected to the patronage systems in Corinth, (2) teachings concerning marriage that Paul applies to worship regulations, and (3) self-sufficiency and Paul's usage of the *agon* motif. The final chapter will review the work as a whole, illustrating the significance of philosophically women interacting with certain elements of popular moral philosophy employed by Paul in 1 Corinthians.

2

Educated Women in the Ancient World

MANY NEW TESTAMENT SCHOLARS have already identified strong relationships and parallels between Pauline thought and ancient philosophies. The ongoing *Corpus Hellenisticum* project has focused on the Stoic Hierocles and the neo-Pythagorean pseudepigraphon, but its contributors have not considered how philosophically educated women would have read 1 Corinthians. Similarly, the members of the Hellenistic Moral Philosophy and Early Christianity section of SBL and other scholars who have found parallels to Paul in Pythagorean, Platonism, Cynicism, Stoicism, and Epicureanism have not addressed this question. The histories of philosophically educated women are severely marginalized in classical scholarship.

In chapters 2 and 3, I will review the histories of philosophically educated women in both Greece and Rome. It is important to consider the women philosophers of the classical period because thinkers of the Roman period refer to these women as examples and inspiration for women of their time. I will argue that the histories of philosophically educated women indicate a strong tradition of the involvement of women in every school of popular philosophy which NT scholars have found useful for interpreting Paul: (neo-)Pythagoreanism, Platonism, Cynicism, Stoicism, and Epicureanism. I will also argue that the tradition indicates that women from a broad social background had access to philosophy: female teachers who were poor, women who were married or related to poor teachers, elite women who were educated as girls, and elite patronesses who supported philosophers and could bring teachers into their homes. In this chapter, I will discuss the education of women; in chapter 3 the active involvement of women in philosophy.

Educated Women in the Ancient Greece and Rome

The evidence for the education of women needs to be addressed in the context of education in general, and the scope of this chapter requires a brief discussion of early Greek education as well as education during the Roman period.[1] These next two chapters will prepare for the subsequent discussion of 1 Corinthians by examining the education of women in the ancient world. Considering that women were involved in all other aspects of Greek and Roman education, we can expect that some women would receive some education in philosophy. The female students and teachers of Pythagoras, Socrates, Plato, and Aristotle for example, should be contextualized in the early Greek art and papyri that testify to the education of women during those time periods. Similarly, the later traditions of the involvement of women in philosophy as students and teachers can be contextualized in monuments, statues, and letters written to and by women during the Roman period. In this chapter, I will discuss the involvement of women in every form of education: primarily medicine, writing, and poetry [which may require literacy], and secondarily dance, athletics, oratory, and music [which does not require literacy], and finally their participation in philosophy. A word of caution is needed at this juncture: the historical record is partial and frequently more interested in men than women. Of necessity, our approach will therefore be wide ranging and eclectic. Nevertheless, a picture emerges of women educated in various disciplines and for a range of tasks.

I will ask several questions of this large body of research. First, what is the reliability of the historical existence of philosophically educated women? In other words, how historically reliable are the ancient witnesses, both epigraphic and in some cases, portraits and depictions of education concerning philosophically educated women? Secondly, what did these women know and how did they learn? The questions, of course, overlap, and I will attempt to untangle it in such a way that demonstrates that philosophically educated women would have heard and interacted with 1 Corinthians.

---

1. Bower, "Technical Terms," 462–77; Booth, "Litterator," 371–78; Eyre, "Roman Education," 47–59; Reichmann, "Book Trade," 40–47; Kaster, "'Primary' and 'Secondary' Schools," 323–46.

The Educated Woman at Work: Doctors, Scribes, and Merchants

Education during the Greek and Roman periods can be measured in two interwoven ways: evidence for literacy, and evidence of learning and teaching.[2] We know that the ability to read and write may not include education in science, logic, mathematics, and philosophy. Some philosophers and other thinkers could not read or write, having memorized texts that were read to them, and employed literate slaves or freedpersons to read and write for them.

William Harris argues, along with several other scholars, that literacy in the Greek and Roman worlds can be divided into three types: literacy, semi-literacy, and illiteracy.[3] Literacy is described as the full literacy of a portion of the (typically) elite—they were able to read literature and philosophy. An example of a fully literate woman is the first-century historian Pamphila of Epidaurus. She is a scholar who is said to have produced 33 books on Greek history (of which 11 fragments remain), and showed an interest in Greek historians, philosophers, and politicians.[4] Like other philosophically educated women, she learned from a family member and then practiced philosophy herself. One fragment of her writing indicates that she learned from her husband, but Plant points out that she must have also had access to a great library, and produced much of her work on her own.[5] Semi-literacy is a quite broad category into which most literate people in the ancient world fit: it was the level of literacy that was required of artisans to do their jobs, including but not limited to accounting, recording inventory, and writing receipts, and even the person who could read graffiti or make a single letter on an ostraca to vote. The great majority of people in the ancient world were illiterate.

Literacy is most clearly associated with occupations that required some literacy.[6] Some level of literacy is required of scribes, medical practitioners (doctors, midwives, and nurses), and merchants; women served in all of these capacities.[7] Female scribes in the ancient world were mostly

---

2. Cole, "Could Greek Women Read," 219–45; Hemelrijk, *Matrona Docta*; Hanson, "Ancient Illiteracy," 159–98, elaborates on this point, also made by Harris, *Ancient Literacy*, 32–33; Pomeroy, *Women in Hellenistic Egypt*, 59–72.

3. For bibliography, see Harris, *Ancient Literacy*, 7–8, 327–28. These levels of literacy are a common theme in the book, and Harris provides many examples. Cf. Hornfall, "Statistics or State of Mind," 59–76.

4. Diog. Laert. 1.24, 68, 76, 90, 98, 2.24; 3.23, 5.36; Aul. Gell. 15.23 and Phot. Bibl. *Library*, cod. 175, 119.

5. Plant, *Women Writers*, 127.

6. See Johnson and Parker, *Ancient Literacies*; Johnson, *Readers and Reading*.

7. For women in the workplace, see Susan Treggiari, "Jobs for Women," 76–104; Treggiari, "Lower Class," 65–86; Kampen, *Image and Status*; van Bremen, "Images of

Reading 1 Corinthians with Philosophically Educated Women

of the lower class, serving as slaves or freedpersons in a household or in a public setting.[8] K. Haines-Eitzen has found eleven female scribes in CIL, all of them dated 1st BCE to 2nd CE. Some examples are useful to mention:

> In these inscriptions we meet with Hapate, a shorthand writer of Greek (*notariae Grece*) who lived twenty-five years (CIL 6.33892); Corinna, who was a storeroom clerk or scribe, *cell(ariae) libr(ariae)* (CIL 6.3979); and Tyche, Herma, and Plaetoriae, all three of whom are identified as *amanuenses* (CIL 6.9541; CIL 6.7373; CIL 6.9542). We also find four women who are identified by the title *libraria*, a term that not only denoted a clerk or secretary, but also more specifically a literary copyist.[9]

These scribes were not mindless copyists:[10] they interacted with the text, correcting grammatical and syntactical errors, and sometimes even revising the texts to their liking.[11] Furthermore, female scribes sometimes worked for female patrons:

> A certain Grapte is identified in one inscription as the amanuensis of Egnatia Maximilla—a woman who, according to Tacitus, accompanied her husband, Glitius Gallus, when he was exiled by Nero. Furthermore, we know that this Egnatia Maximilla had a substantial personal fortune; it should not be surprising, therefore, that she had her own personal amanuensis.[12]

Haines-Eitzen's analysis of the inscriptions brings several important points to light. Most of the female scribes were lower class slaves or freedpersons, all of them were in urban contexts, were educated at home or from an apprenticeship, and were typically supported by patrons or patronesses who were wealthy.

Rebecca Fleming has recently analyzed the evidence relating to female physicians in the ancient world, concluding that several female physicians from all around the Mediterranean were literate and contributed to medical

---

Women and Antiquity," 223–41.

8. Quinn, "Poet and His Audience," 75–180; Dix, "Private and Public Libraries"; Bruce, "Palace and Villa Libraries," 510–52. For a helpful summary of the literary evidence for bookshops in Roman antiquity, see Starr, "Circulation of Literary," 213–23; Haines-Eitzen, "Literacy"; Haines-Eitzen, "Girls Trained in Beautiful Writing," 629–46.

9. Her list is 6.3979, 7373, 8882, 9301, 9525, 9540, 9541, 9542, 33892, 37757, 37802 ("Scribes," 634n16). Cf. Kampen, *Image and Status*, 118; Lefkowitz and Fant, *Woman's Life*, 223; Treggiari, "Jobs," 76–104.

10. Goudsmit, "Illiterate Scribe," 78.

11. McDonnell, "Writing," 469–91.

12. Haines-Eitzen, "Scribes," 635; Tac. *Ann*. 15.71

knowledge through writing in the Roman period.[13] Two examples are instructive of the role that educated women played in the practice of medicine:

> The funerary stele of "Mousa, physician, daughter of Agathocles," from Hellenistic Byzantium, for example, shows her holding a book-roll (as do a handful of representations of male physicians); and, in early imperial Rome, the freedwoman Naevia Clara is labeled "physician and scholar" (*medica philologa*) on the stele that commemorates both her and her husband L. Naevius, also a freedman, and "physician and surgeon" (*medicus chirurgus*).[14]

There are a few monuments that attest to female doctors:

> Ἀντιοχὶς Διοδότου | Τλωὶς μαρτυρηθεῖ-
> σα ὑπὸ τῆς Τλωέων | Βοθλῆς καὶ τοῦ δή-
> μου ἐπὶ τῇ περὶ | τὴν ἰατρικὴν τε-
> χνην ἐνπειρίᾳ | ἔστησεν τὸν ἀν-
> δριάντα ἑαυτῆς.

> Antiochis, daughter of Diodotus, of Tlos, marked by the council and people of Tlos for her achievement in the medical art, erected this statue of herself.[15]

The Empiricist Heraclides of Taras addresses Antiochis as a colleague in a letter.[16] Soranus of Ephesus (1st century CE) writes that the midwife should be trained in theory by reading books and by practice.[17] How these women learned medicine is important to my argument. Antiochis is referenced in Galen as an authority for various remedies (12.691 and 13.250, 13.341).[18]

13. Flemming, "Women," 257-79.

14. Flemming, "Women," 260. Cf. Pfuhl and Möbius, *Die ostgriechischen Grabreliefs*, 1.151 (no. 467): Μοῦσά Ἀγαθοκλέους ἰατρείνη (Samama [n. 2], no. 310); and for Naevia, see Flemming, "Women," (no. 2), 386 (no. 9). Cf. Hillert, *Antike Ärztedarstellungen*.

15. Greek text in Pleket, *Epigraphica*, no. 12; cf. no. 20. Translation by Parker, who gives a long interpretation of this inscription in the context of other female patrons in "Women Doctors," 131-50. Parker says that there are forty such inscriptions dedicated to female doctors. Cf. Nutton, *Ancient Medicine*, 197-98. An alternative translation is in Lefkowitz and Fant, "Women's Life," 369.

16. Deichgräber, *Die griechische Empirikerschule*; Kudlien, "Medical Education," 34n70.

17. Sor. *Gyn.* 1.3-4. Hanson and Green, "Soranus," *ANRW* 2.37.2, 968-1075, and also Flemming, "Women," 257n2.

18. The 1st century CE doctor Cleopatra the Physician was also used extensively by Galen, 12.235, 381, 405, 446. Plant notes that she is known to Titus Statilius Crito (2nd CE), Galen (3rd CE), Aëtus of Amida, 8.6 (6th CE), Paulus of Aegina 3.2.1 (7th CE), and John Tzetes (17th CE). Nothing is known concerning her biography.

Reading 1 Corinthians with Philosophically Educated Women

Most likely, her father taught her the art of medicine. Antiochis's father, Diodotus, is almost certainly the notable physician Diodotus mentioned in Dioscorides.[19] The father teaching sons or daughters his craft could be indicative of the poor artisan, whereas the wealthier doctors could learn from books, slaves, or famous doctors.

Soranas describes the qualifications of an ideal midwife, which includes literacy and a quick intellect:

> ἐπιτήδειος δέ ἐστιν ἡ γραμμάτων ἐντός, ἀγχίνους, μνήων, φιλόπονος, κόσμιος καὶ κατὰ τὸ κοινὸν ἀπαρεμπόδιστος ταῖς αἰσθήσεσιν, ἀρτιμελής, εὔτονος, ὡς δ' ἔνιοι λέγουσιν γουσιν καὶ μακροὺς καὶ λεπτοὺς ἔχουσα καὶ τοὺς τῶν χειρῶν δακτύλους καὶ ὑπεσταλκότας ταῖς ῥαξὶν τοὺς ὄνυχας. γραμμάτων μὲν ἐντός εἶναι, ἵνα καὶ διὰ θεωρί ας τὴν τέχνην ἰσχύσῃ παραλαβεῖν· ἀγχίνοθς δὲ πρὸς τὸ ῥᾳδίως τοῖς λεγομένοις καὶ γινομένοις παρακολουθεῖν· μνήμων δέ, ἵνα καὶ τῶν παραδιδομένων ἀποκρατῇ μαθημάτων· μάθησις γὰρ ἐκ μνήμης γίνεται καὶ καταλήψεως.

> A suitable person will be literate, have her wits about her, possessed of a good memory, loving work, respectable and generally not unduly handicapped as regards her senses, sound of limb, robust, and according to some people, endowed with long slim fingers and short nails at her fingertips. She must be literate in order to be able to comprehend the art through theory too; she must have her wits about her so that she may easily follow what is said and what is happening; she must have a good memory to retain the imparted instructions (for knowledge arises from memory of what has been grasped).[20]

Generally speaking, most ancient medical practitioners were of lower social status, and doctors were often viewed as untrustworthy and unreliable.[21] However, some higher status writers remember women doctors who were, at least in their opinion, gifted healers. Galen (ca. 129–217 CE) attributes many remedies to women, some of which were written by women.[22]

---

19. Dioscorides, 1Pr.5; Scarborough and Nutton, "Preface," 187–227.

20. Temkin, *Gynecology*, 5.

21. Amundsen, "Liability," 17–31, presents several well-known references from Greek and Roman writers concerning the mistrust for doctors in ancient times, famous for killing or extorting people using the knife or poisons. Mohler, "Slave Education," 265n6, suggests that most doctors in the ancient world were freedmen, and slave boys were their apprentices. Laws concerning doctors were often combined with superticions concerning magic. Pharr, "Interdiction of Magic," 269–95.

22. From Fleming, "Writing," 265: Gal. *Comp. med. loc.* 7.2, 4 and 8.3 (13.58, 85

Educated Women in the Ancient World

Other writers refer to the contributions of women for their understanding of medicine: Pliny the Elder (*NH* 28.38, 28.83, 28.81, 20.226), pseudo-Galen (19.767), and Aetius (16.12).[23] Other women doctors are attested in ancient sources: Philinna of Thessaly, Salpe of Lesbos (Plin. *HN* 28.7), Laïs of Corinth (late 1st CE, Plin. *HN* 28.23; Plut. *Nic.* 15), Olympias of Thebes (1st CE, Plin. *HN* 28.77), and Sotira (1st CE, Plin. *HN* 28.23); and Elephantine (1st CE, Mart. 12.43.4; Suet. *Tib.* 43.2; Gal. 12:416; Plin. *HN* 28.81).

Women learning medicine from a family member (at least in part) reflects the fact that while there were "ancient medical schools" in Cos, Cnidus, Alexandria, Rome, Pergamon, Symrna, and Ephesus, most doctors learned medicine in an apprenticeship to a member of the family (a father or spouse) or one's master (whether the student is a male or female slave). The physician Glycon honored his wife Panthea, also a physician, with the inscription, "[You] raised high our common fame in healing—though you were a woman you were not behind me in skill."[24] Restituta (Rome, 1st CE) learned medicine as a freedwoman or slave under her patron,[25] and Aurelia Alexandria Zosime and Auguste most likely learned from their husbands (who are mentioned in their inscriptions). There may even be an example of a woman teaching another woman medicine. Terentia Prima is known as a *medica* in Rome in the first or second century CE, and she perhaps had a freedwoman apprentice.[26] Minucia Asste, also a *medica*, may have learned medicine from her matron.[27] This is not unlike how women and men would learn philosophy (and indeed, the histories of medicine and philosophy significantly overlap). The medical historian Plino Prioreschi writes, "medicine

---

and 143 K): Origenia's remedies for coughs, bringing up blood, and for the stomach; *Comp. med. loc.* 9.2 (13.244 K): Eugerasia's remedy for the spleen; *Comp. med. loc.* 9.6 (13.310 and 311 K): Samithra's anal application and Xanthite's very useful hemorrhoids remedy; *Comp. med. gen.* 5.13 (13.840): Maia's excellent dry application for callused and cracked skin, Scrib. Larg. *Comp.* 59, 60, 70, 271.

23. Plant, *Women Writers*, 110–24.

24. Lefkowitz and Fant, *Women's Life*, no. 175; Pleket, *Epigraphica*, no. 20. Arlandson situates this inscription with other roles that lesser class women served which required some level of literacy, *Women, Class, and Society*, 48.

25. *IG* 14.1751 = *CIG* 6604 = *IGRR* 1.283 = *IGUR* 645. Gummerus, *Der Ärztestand*, no. 146; Korpela, *Das Medizinalpersonal*, 166.

26. *CIL* VI.9616; Gummerus, *Ärztestand*, no.113; Korpela, *Medizinalpersonal*, no. 203; Lefkowitz and Fant, *Women's Life*, no. 371. For interpretation, see de Senancour, *Libres méditations*, 128n3, and Kampen, *Image and Status*, 116n40.

27. Rome 1st BCE or 1st CE. *CIL* 6.9615 (33812); Gummerus, *Ärztestand*, no. 112; Korpela, *Medizinalpersonal*, no. 43.

did not develop by itself, in a vacuum, on the basis of purely empirical evidence, but was first an integral part of philosophy."[28]

In both the Greek[29] and Roman[30] periods, women served other vocations that required some level of literacy and education. Three fourth-century BCE inscriptions mention female grocers: Mania,[31] Thraitta,[32] and Parthenia.[33] A mid-second-century CE relief shows a butcher at work, with his wife seated, keeping the books.[34] Two late second-century CE reliefs found at Ostia depict women selling a wide variety of items.[35] A grocer in Greek or Roman times would have to manage several relationships: their many wholesalers, customers, and their patron who may lease a place to sell at the markets. Some sizable transactions would likely have been written for bookkeeping and legal reasons.[36]

The Educated Woman: Greek and Roman Poets

The education of women in the ancient world is demonstrated most clearly in poetry.[37] Greek and Roman female poets were quite popular in ancient life, and the traditions related to female poets are as old as Homer.[38] Sappho of Lesbos is perhaps most intriguing because she is the most ancient female poet and enjoys enduring popularity.[39] In her lifetime, it is likely

---

28. Prioreschi, *History of Medicine*, 2:204; van der Eijk, *Medicine and Philosophy*.

29. Rotroff and Lamberton, *Women in the Agora*.

30. Bernstein, "Pompeian Women," 526–37.

31. *IG* 3.387.G. Lefkowitz and Fant, *Women's Life*, 324.

32. Lewis, "Attic Manumissions," 329.

33. *IG* 3.3.68, 69; Lefkowitz and Fant, *Women's Life*, 337; cf. Lefkowitz, "Wives and Husbands," 44.

34. Dresden, *Staatliche Kuntstsammlungen*, Inv. ZV 44; D'Ambra, *Roman Women*, 137.

35. Ostia, Museo Ostiense, inv. 134 and 198. There is also a relief of a successful shoemaker in Ostia, CIL 14.supp.4698. Cf. Fantham, *Women*, 378.

36. Harris, *Ancient Literacy*, 200.

37. For text, translation, and critical commentary on many of the poets mentioned in this section, see Gutzwiller, *Poetic Garlands*; for the general context of poetry without a focus on women, particularly the competitive and symposium contexts, see Collins, *Master of the Game*.

38. Barnard, "Hellenistic Women Poets," 204–13; Bowman, "Women's Tradition," 1–27.

39. Sappho's biographical information is preserved in P. Oxy. 1800 and the *Suda*, "Sappho"; cf. OCD, "Sappho." Aelian reckons Sappho among the Sages, *Var. hist.* 12.19.

that she ran a school of poetry for girls.[40] Her poetry was cited by a wide variety of ancient poets, philosophers, and thinkers.[41] Maximus of Tyre says that Socrates learned of love from a foreigner: either Sappho of Lesbos (the poet = Pl. *Phaedr.* 230e, 235c) or from a woman from Mantinea (the philosopher Diotima = Pl. *Symp.* 201d).[42] Ancient tradition links Sappho with Corinth: the first-century BCE poet Antipater of Sidon tells us that Sappho died there (EG 3448).[43]

Sappho's popularity is demonstrated by her early and frequent depictions in art. She is found on ancient vases, coins, and mosaics.[44] Christodorus of Thebes (late 5th BCE, gymnasium Zuexippos, Constantinople), Cicero (Sialion, 4th BCE, Syracuse), Antipater (1st BCE, Pergamon), indicate that statues were made of Sappho though none survive.[45] There are three painted vases from the fifth century BCE that depict Sappho in action, reciting her poetry or playing the lyre. Some coins dated in the first through the third centuries CE from Mytilene and Eresos are stamped with a likeness of Sappho, sometimes with an inscription.[46]

While the context of most early Greek poetry was in competitions, Sappho's performances were mostly restricted to the *symposia*.[47] Although Sappho's poems were compiled into nine books in antiquity, only one poem survives intact, and like so many other early figures, the remainder of our information comes from secondary sources that offer conflicting information.[48] Sappho's poetry is important for our understanding of ancient female

---

40. Lefkowitz, *Lives*, 36–37, 61–64, gives a thorough tradition of the life of Sappho as preserved in literary sources; Dover critically analyzes the sources in *Greek Homosexuality*, 174–75; Snyder uncovers the various approaches in Sappho's poetry in "Public Occasion," 1–19.

41. Robinson, *Sappho*; Greenberg, "Erotion," 79–87.

42. Maximus of Tyre, 18.7.

43. Richter, *Portraits of the Greeks*, 194–96.

44. For art depicting Sappho, I am following Richter, *Potraits of the Greeks*, 194–96.

45. Christodorus in *Anth. Pal.* 2.69; Cic. *Verr.* 2.4.126; for Antipater, see Fränkel and Habicht, *Die Inschriften von Pergamon*, no. 198.

46. Richter, *Portraits of the Greeks*, 194.

47. Henderson, "Criteria," 28; cf. Page, *Sappho*, 133–40.

48. While Sappho wrote in the sixth to seventh century BCE, the popularity of her work is endearing. Plutarch comments on the value of her poetry in *Mor.* 397a and 406a. Several of the famous first-century Latin poets either mention Sappho explicitly or rely on her work. Martial alludes to Sappho in *Epigrams* 7.69.9 and 10.35.15; Catullus 11.21–24, 51, 62, and 65.19–24, and his usage of Lesbia rely on Sappho. Ovid applauds her in *Ars amatoria* 3.331; cf. the pseudo-Ovidian *Epistle of Sappho to Phaon* is available in English in Miller and Moore, *Songs of Sappho*. Edwards argues for her influence on Juvenal, "Quotation of Sappho," 255–57. Given the context of the *Satire* as seething with hatred for women, we should not consider this quotation as a compliment. Juvenal

sexualities,⁴⁹ but is especially valuable due to her clear distinction between the loved and beloved.⁵⁰ Sappho portrays a woman that is different from Aristotle's view which would later become dominant in Western philosophy: women are only able to participate in life as a human being as a mutilated male striving for maleness.⁵¹

According to Pausanias, Telesilla was a fifth-century BCE warrior-poetess who was renowned for her lyric poetry and military prowess. Her military might is mentioned in Plutarch (46–120 BCE/CE, *Mor.* 245d-e) and Pausanias (fl. 2nd CE, 2.9-11), and her poetry is remembered also by several other writers. Eight tiny fragments of her poetry are extant.⁵² Snyder suggests that her poetry was composed for the singing by girls at festivals.⁵³ The popularity of Telesilla's poetry is enduring—she is known from Eusebius of Caesarea (263–309 BCE, *Chronicon*, Olympiad 82.4), Antipater of Thessaloniki (fl. 15th CE, *Anth. Pal.* 9. 26), Apollodoros (fl. late 1st BCE, *Biblioteka* 3.5.5), and of course Plutarch (46–120 BCE/CE, *Mor.* 245d-e), Pausanias (fl. 2nd CE, 2.9-11), Maximus of Tyre (fl. 2nd CE, *Anth. Pal.* 37.5), and the Christian apologists Tatian (120–180 CE, *Ad. Gr.* 33) and Clement of Alexandria (150–215 CE, *Strom.* 4.19). Plutarch compliments the accomplishments of Telesilla:

> Οὐδενὸς δ' ἧττον ἔνδοξόν ἐστι τῶν κοινῇ διαπεπραγμένων γυναιξὶν ἔργων ὁ πρὸς Κελομένη περὶ Ἄργους ἀγών, ὃν ἠγωνίσαντο Τελεσίλλης τῆς ποιητρίας προτρεψαμένης. ταύτην δέ φασιν οἰκίας οὖσαν ἐνδόξου τῷ δὲ σώματι νοσηματικὴν εἰς θεοῦ μέμψαι περὶ ὑγιείας· καὶ χρησθὲν αὐτῇ Μούσας θεραπεύειν, πειθομένην τῷ θεῷ καὶ ἐπιθεμένην ᾠδῇ καὶ ἁρμονίᾳ τοῦ τε πάθους ἀπαλλαγῆναι ταχὺ καὶ θαυμάζεσθαι διὰ ποιητικὴν ὑπὸ τῶν γυναικῶν.

> Of all the deeds performed by women for the community none is more famous than the struggle against Cleomenes for Argos,

---

complains about the education of women in *Satire* 6: those conversant in Homer, Virgil, and many others.

49. The interpretation that Sappho addressed female sexualities may be a forced reconstruction. Her poetry was not interpreted as such in the classical period. Hallett, "Sappho," 447–64; Greene, "Apostrophe," 41–56.

50. Rayor, *Sappho's Lyre*.

51. Allen, *Concept of Woman*.

52. Euseb. *Chron.* 82. 4 [449 BC]; Maximus of Tyre, *Dissertations* 37.5; Heph. 11.2; Ath. 11. 437; 14.619b; Hesychius, *Glossary*, "beltiotas"; Julius Pollux, *Onomastikon*, 2.223; Scholiast on the *Od.* 13.289. The classical references are collected in translation by Professor John Paul Adams, online: www.csun.edu/~hcfll004/telesilla.html.

53. Snyder, *Lyre*, 60.

which the women carried out at the instigation of Telesilla the poetess. She, as they say, was the daughter of a famous house but sickly in body, and so she sent to the god to ask about health; and when an oracle was given her to cultivate the Muses, she followed the god's advice, and by devoting herself to poetry and music she was quickly relieved of her trouble, and was greatly admired by the women for her poetic art.[54]

Pausanias writes that on top of Mount Coryphum there is a sanctuary of Artemis Coryphea, which Telesilla mentions in a poem. Pausanias relates the tradition concerning Telesilla that corresponds with Herodotus:

ὑπὲρ δὲ τὸ θέατρον Ἀφροδίτης ἐστὶν ἱερόν, ἔμπροσθεν δὲ τοῦ ἕδους Τελέσιλλα ἡ ποιήσασα τὰ ᾄσματα ἐπείργασται στήλῃ· καὶ Βιβλία μὲν ἐκεῖνα ἔρριπται οἱ πρὸς τοῖς ποσίν, αὐτὴ δὲ ἐς κράνος ὁρᾷ κατέχουσα τῇ χειρὶ καὶ ἐπιτίθεσθαι τῇ κεφαλῇ μέλλουσα.

Above the theater is a sanctuary of Aphrodite, and before the image is a slab with a representation wrought on it in relief of Telesilla, the lyric poetess. Her books lie scattered at her feet, and she herself holds in her hand an helmet, which she is looking at and is about to place on her head.[55]

Pausanius tells us that there was a monument to Telesilla that memorializes her intellect with a book and her military accomplishments with a helmet.[56] We should note, I think, that the educated woman and her military conquests are done in the guise of men. Like the female philosophers who come later, the female poets and their soldiers acting in the domain of men wear the clothing of men.

Many female poets were active in the fourth century BCE, the most influential being Corinna, Erinna, and Nossis. Corinna of Tanagra enjoyed popularity in the ancient world, but she is notoriously difficult to date. The arguments have been for the late fifth century BCE (following Plutarch, Pausanias, and Aelian)[57] or the early third century (following critical examinations of the extant poetry). It is attractive to conclude that the early third century is more appropriate based on the nature of Corinna's usage of what may be considered third-century BCE Greek morphology and syntax.[58]

---

54. Plut. *Mor.* 245c–e (Babbitt, LCL).

55. Paus. 2.20.8 (Jones and Ormerod, LCL). Reference to Herodotus 6.77.

56. For a discussion of the legendary nature of Telesilla's military victory, see Piérart, "Common Oracle," 275–96.

57. Plut., *Mor.* 347f–348a; Paus. 9.22.3. Ael. *Var. hist.* 13.25. Cf. also Eust. *Il.* 326.43; Pind. *Ol.* 6.90.

58. West, "Corinna," 277–87; Clayman, "Meaning," 396–97. West convincingly

Reading 1 Corinthians with Philosophically Educated Women

This would mean that Corrina's claim to fame—her defeat of Pindar—is most likely not historical but a later tradition from readers who thought that her poetry was technically superior.[59] Citing the vocabulary, meter, style, and the fact that no fifth-century writer mentions her, D. L. Page takes an agnostic approach for an exact date that is followed by Skinner and others.[60] However, there survives a 48cm tall marble statuette of a woman reading from an open scroll with KOPINNA inscribed on the base. Richter believes that the statuette has features that indicate it may be a copy from a fourth-century piece, but it does not reflect the quality expected from a Silanion (as Tatian says in *Oratorio ad Graecos* 34.16).[61]

The counterargument to the late dating for Corinna depends on the reliability of ancient sources. Pausanias (fl. 2nd CE) preserves contemporary traditions concerning Corinna that were popular in Tangra, and Plutarch those of Boeotia (being from there), and it seems unlikely that these witnesses would be so mistaken in such a short time after her supposed death, so the fifth-century date seems more likely.[62] Pausanias tells us that he saw a memorial in the gymnasium depicting Corinna crowning herself in victory over Pindar, attributing the victory to her usage of the Doric dialect and her beauty (9.22.3).[63] Corinna is remembered in the second-century CE P.Oxy 2438.1-4 (Gallo 1968, 49), "according to Corinna and other poetesses [Pindar] was the son of Scopelinus; according to most poets he was the son of Daiphantus."[64] The Roman poets Propertius (b. between 54 and 47 BCE, d. 2 BCE), and Statius (ca. 45–83 CE) were also aware of Corinna.

In praise of his beloved, Propertius (ca. 50–15 BCE) compares her beauty to the beloved, referring to the poetry of Sappho, Corinna, and Erinna:

> nec me tam facies, quamvis sit candida, cepit (lilia non domina sint magis alba mea; ut Maeotica nix minio si certet Hibero, utque rosae puro lacte natant folia), nec de more comae per levia colla fluentes, non oculi, geminae, sidera nostra, faces, nec si qua Arabio lucet bombyce puella (non sum de nihilo blandus

---

answers his opponents in "Dating Corinna," 553–57.

59. Clark, "Roman Women," 193–212; 48cm high marble statue of Corinna in Richter, *Portraits*, pl.116. Pausanius (9.22.3) says that there was a portrait of her made; Tatian (*Oratio ad Graecos* 33) refers to a sculpture by Silanion. P. Oxy. 2438.1-4 mentions Corinna who gives biographical info concerning Pindar; cf. Ael. *Var. hist.* 13.25.

60. Page, "Note on Corinna," 109–12; Skinner, "Corinna," 9–20.

61. Richter, *Portraits*, 156.

62. Allen and Frel, "Date for Corinna," 26–30.

63. For women competing in poetry, see Lefkowitz, *Greek Poets*, 64–65.

64. Lefkowitz, *Greek Poets*, 62; Gallo, *Una nuova biografia di Pindaro*.

amator ego): quantum quod posito formose saltat Iaccho, egit ut euhantis dux Ariadna choros, et quantum, Aeolio cum temptat carmina plectro, par Aganippeae ludere docta lyrae; et sua cum antiquae committit scripta Corinnae, carmina quae quivis non putat aequa suis.

It was not her face, bright as it is, that won me (lilies are not more white than my lady; as if Maeotic snows contended with the reds of Spain, or rose-petals swam in purest milk) nor her hair, ordered, flowing down her smooth neck, nor her eyes, twin fires, that are my starlight, nor the girl shining in Arabian silk (I am no lover flattering for nothing): but how beautifully she dances when the wine is set aside, like Ariadne taking the lead among the ecstatic cries of the Maenads, and how when she sets herself to sing in the Sapphic style, she plays with the skill of Aganippe's lyre, and joins her verse to that of ancient Corinna, and thinks Erinna's songs inferior to her own.[65]

The second most famous poetess from ancient Greece is Erinna, dated 353 BCE,[66] at about the time that Socrates defined the goal of poetry as that which makes the soul of all people better:

νῦν ἄρα ἡμεῖς ηὑρήκαμεν ῥητορικήν τινα πρὸς δῆμον τοιοῦτον οἷον παίδων τε ὁμοῦ καὶ γυναικῶν καὶ ἀνδρῶν, καὶ δούλων καὶ ἐλευθέρων, ἣν οὐ πάνυ ἀγάμεθα· κολακικὴν γὰρ αὐτὴν φαμεν εἶναι.

So now we have found a kind of rhetoric addressed to such a public as is compounded of children and women and men, and slaves as well as free; an art that we do not quite approve of, since we call it a flattering one.[67]

Antipater of Thessalonica (fl. 20 BC) listed her along with Sappho as one of the nine "early Muses."[68] Antipater writes, "Sappho exceeded Erinna in lyric poetry by just so much as Erinna exceeded Sappho in hexameters."[69] Her fame is a bit curious, because all traditions point to a low output: only one composition of 300 lines, the *Distaff*, and perhaps a few epigrams. Erinna is the subject of epigrams by Asclepiades of Amos (fl. 270 BCE, *Anth.*

---

65. Prop. 2.3.1–54 (Goold, LCL); Stat. *Silv.* 5.3.158 (his father taught the poetry of Corinna at Naples).

66. West, "Erinna," 95–119. An excellent reconstruction of her text is available in Edmonds, "P. S. I. 1090," 195–203.

67. Pl. *Gorg.* 502d (Lamb, LCL).

68. *Anth. Pal.* 9.26.

69. *Anth. Pal.* 9.190 (Paton, LCL).

Reading 1 Corinthians with Philosophically Educated Women

Pal. 7.11), Leonidas of Tarentum (ca. 3rd BCE, *Anth. Pal.* 7.13), and Antipater of Sidon (fl. 2nd BCE, *Anth. Pal.* 7.713), and she is associated with Callimachus (ca. 305–240 BCE) by Aristophanes (446–386 BCE):

> ἐπ' Ἠρίννῃ δὲ κομῶντες,
> πικροὶ καὶ ξηροὶ Καλλιμάχου προκύνες
>
> proud of your Erinna
> bitter and harsh barkers at Callimachus's command[70]

Errina's "distaff" is the "spindle of the Fates," and this imagery could speak to her life as a woman: the expected doing of domestic duties and lamenting the early death of her beloved, and in the case of the inspired, the writing of poetry. However, it should be noted that the two common metaphors for the doing of poetry are carpentry and weaving.[71] For Erinna, her inspiration was the spindle of the Fates; for others it was the Muses or the Ἔρωτες.[72]

Like Corinna, the date of Erinna is in dispute.[73] The sources used to date Erinna are the traditions in the *Anthology*, Eusebius, Tatian, and the *Suda* as well as the critical analyses of poetry attributed to her.[74] West has argued that a girl on an island in the fourth century BCE could not have had the education to write such sophisticated poetry, and concludes that she did not even exist.[75] The analyses of Gow and Page date Erinna in the third century, and Donado dates her in the late fifth or early fourth century.[76] The poetry of Errina is indeed complex: Marilyn Skinner has demonstrated that Erinna used a prototype from the *Iliad*. Erinna's frequent cries of misery follow a specific type:

> The impassioned wailing of Briseis over the fallen Patroclus, of Hector's wife seeing his corpse dragged by Achilles, and of Andromache, Hecuba and Helen at Hector's wake are all artistic recreations of the *goos*, the dirge ordinarily chanted at the *prothesis* by the nearest female relations of the deceased.[77]

---

70. *Anth. Pal.* 2.322.3–4. Greek text from Paton, LCL. Translation is from another source, Gow, and Page, *Greek Anthology*, 1:91. Cf. Snyder, *Women and the Lyre*, 86–91.

71. For carpentry, see Pind. *Pyth.* 3.113, Paus. 10.5.8; for weaving, see Bacchyl. 5.9–10, 19.8. Cf. Nagy, "Professional Muse," 133–43.

72. Cameron and Cameron, "Erinna's Distaff," 286.

73. Giangrande, "Epigram of Erinna," 1–3.

74. She is also known in Plin. *HN* 34.57–58 and Meleager of Gadara in *Anth. Pal.* 4.1.12.

75. West, "Erinna," 117–18.

76. Gow and Page, *Hellenistic Epigrams*, 2.281. Donado, "Cronologia de Erinna," 349–76.

77. Skinner, "Briseis," 265–69.

While West has argued that Erinna is a literary construct, Sarah Pomeroy has demonstrated from terracotta and inscriptions that the education of women in fourth-century Greece was improving, providing an historical plausibility of her existence.[78] Furthermore, Pomeroy notes that Errina's hometown of Teos has epigraphic evidence of educated women.[79] Pomeroy surmises that the emphasis on the distaff is rooted in the historical fact that wealthier educated women of this time period were expected to spend at least a little time weaving. She compares the tradition of Erinna with the story of Hipparchia, who when she studied Cynicism, was asked why she was not spending a little time weaving.[80] Marilyn B. Arthur notes that while Erinna claims in her poem that she was nineteen years old when she composed it, she could have cast herself as a young woman when actually she could have been much older.[81] Arthur also notes that Greek vases of the period depict girls reading from scrolls.[82]

Anyte of Tegea also wrote at the beginning of the third century BCE, and is recognized as the creator of the pastoral epigram. The *Greek Anthology* preserves about twenty of her epigrams that have mostly women, children, or animal subjects. I. M. Plant suggests that Anyte herself published a book of her poetry.[83]

Nossis of Locri in Italy lived about the same time and imitated Sappho, writing to women concerning women.[84] Marilyn B. Skinner convincingly suggested that Nossis is from an aristocratic family.[85] In one of her poems (*Anth. Pal.* 6.265), Nossis claims to be part of the elite women who present linen to Hera, which could be parallel to the elite women in Athens who present Athena with a woven *peplos*. Like other educated women, Nossis gives us a clue as to her education: she names her mother as her teacher.[86] As a whole, these women poets may portray women in a kinder light than their male counterparts.[87]

78. Pomeroy, "*Technikai kai mousikai*," 51–68.

79. Citing *SIG*³ 578 (2nd BCE). M. M. Austin notes that despite Pomeroy's point, *SIG*³ 578 does not explicitly exclude girls, but neither does it explicitly include the education of girls. *Hellenistic World*, 262.

80. Pomeroy, "Supplementary Notes," 20; Diog. Laert. 6.97–98.

81. Arthur, "Tortoise," 53–65.

82. Immerwahr, "Book Rolls," 27; and cf. Immerwahr, "More Book Rolls," 143–47.

83. Plant, *Women Writers*, 56.

84. Snyder, *Woman and the Lyre*, 77–84.

85. Skinner, "Nossis *Thēlyglōssos*," 23.

86. Skinner, "Sapphic Nossis," 5–6.

87. Skinner, "Ladies' Day," 201–22. Herodas wrote an epigram, *Mime* 6, which seems to parody some female poets of his day. In it, some women comment favorably

Reading 1 Corinthians with Philosophically Educated Women

In times closer to Paul, there are several examples of well-known female poets.[88] Pompey the Great (106–48 BCE) decorated his garden with almost all the known statues of Greek poetesses, many of whom are preserved in the *Greek Anthology*.[89] The list of female poets in Pompey's Garden that Tatian (ca. 120–180 CE) provides in *Address to the Greeks* 33 is quite comprehensive:

> Πράξιλλαν μὲν γὰρ Λύσιππος ἐχαλκούργησεν μηδὲν εἰποῦσαν διὰ τῶν ποιημάτων χρήσιμον, Δεαρχίδα δὲ Μενέστρατος, Σιλανίων δὲ Σαπφὼ τὴν ἑταίραν, Ἤρινναν τὴν Λεσβίαν Ναυκύδης, Βοΐσκος Μυρτίδα, Μυρὼ τὴν Βυζαντίαν Κηφισόδοτος, Γόμφος Πραξαγορίδα καὶ Ἀμφίστρατος Κλειτώ. τί γάρ μοι περὶ Ἀνύτης λέγειν Τελεσίλλης τε καὶ Νοσσίδος; τῆς μὲν γὰρ Εὐθκράτης τε καὶ Κηφισόδοτος, τῆς δὲ Νικήρατος, τῆς δὲ Ἀριστόδοτός εἰσιν οἱ δημιουργοί· Μνησαχίδος τῆς Ἐφεσίας Εὐθυκράτης, Κορίννης Σιλανίων, Θαλιαρχίδος τῆς Ἀργείας.

> For Lysippus cast a statue of Praxilla, whose poems contain nothing useful, and Menestratus one of Learchis, and Selanion one of Sappho the courtezan, and Naucydes one of Erinna the Lesbian, and Boiscus one of Myrtis, and Cephisodotus one of Myro of Byzantium, and Gomphus one of Praxigoris, and Amphistratus one of Clito. And what shall I say about Anyta, Telesilla, and Mystis? Of the first Euthycrates and Cephisodotus made a statue, and of the second Niceratus, and of the third Aristodotus; Euthycrates made one of Mnesiarchis the Ephesian, Selanion one of Corinna, and Euthycrates one of Thalarchis the Argive.[90]

Tatian's description of Pompey's Garden[91] preserves the memory of several female poets and philosophers. Many of the female poets that he mentions are discussed above, and other poets are attested only here (and therefore dates are unknown): Learchis, Praxigoris, Clito, Mnesiarchis the Ephesian, Mystis, and Thalarchis the Argive. Three poets mentioned above have only

---

concerning a dildo made by a shoemaker and the female poets Errinas and Nossis are mentioned. A translation is available in Lefkowitz and Fant, *Women's Life*, and an alternative translation is provided by Davenport, "Private Talk," 32n3.

88. Ridgway, "Issue of Methodology," 717–38; Booth, "Elementary and Secondary Education," 1–14.

89. Kuttner, "Culture and History," 343–73.

90. Translation by J. E. Ryland, *ANF*². For ancient descriptions of the portico, see Goldberg, "Plautus," 12n36.

91. The first to argue that Tatian was describing Pompey's Garden was Coarelli, "Il complesso pompeiano," 99–122; other important works include Gleason, "Garden Portico," 99–122; Gleason, "Porticus Pompeiana," 13–27; Kuttner, "Culture and History," 343–73.

a handful of fragments from the fifth century BCE: Praxilla (8 frgs) and Myrtis (summary of views in Plut. *Mor.* 300d-f), Anyta (fragments in *Carmina novem poetarum foeminarum*, Antwerp, 1565, repr. Hamburg, 1734). Most of the sculptors listed above were well known in the ancient world: Lysippus,[92] Selanion,[93] Naucydes,[94] Euthycrates,[95] and Cephisodotus.[96] While these sculptors were known for their other works, only Tatian knew of their statue of a female poet with the notable exception of Selanion that is mentioned by Cicero (*Verr.* 4, 57, 125). Other sculptors are only attested here: Boiscus, Menestratus, and Gomphus. Tatain continues his description of Pompey's Garden by listing statues of coutezans, lyre players, and women from Greek mythology.[97] His description concludes with Melanippe the Wise woman whose statue was made by Lysistratus (Plin. *HN* 35.44).[98]

Antipater of Thessalonica (fl. 1st CE) gives a very similar list of female poets:

Τάσδε θεογλώσσουσ Ἑλικὼν ἔθρεψε γυναῖκας
ὕμνοις καὶ Μακεδὼν Πιερίας σκόπελος,
Πρήξιλλαν Μοιρώ, Ἀνύτης στόμα, θῆλυν Ὅμηρον,
Λεσβιάδων Σαπφὼ κόσμον ἐυπλοκάμων,
Ἤρινναν, Τελέσιλλαν ἀγακλέα καὶ σέ, Κόριννα,
θοῦριν Ἀθηναίης ἀσπίδα μελψαμέναν,
Νοσσίδα θηλύγλωσσον ἰδὲ γλυκυαχέα Μύρτιν,
πάσας ἀενάων ἐργάτιδας σελίδων.
ἐννέα μὲν Μούσας μέγας Οὐρανός, ἐννέα δ᾽ αὐτὰς
Γαῖα τέκεν θνατοῖς ἄφθιτον εὐφροσύναν.

These god-tongued women were with song supplied
From Helicon to steep Pieria's side:
Prexilla, Myro, Anyte's grand voice –

---

92. Lysippus flourished in the 4th century BCE. Plin. *HN* 34.51, 36.41; Mart. 9.44; Statius *Silv.* 4.6.32; Plut. *Alex.* 4; Paus. 6.1.4; Quint. 12.10.1-10; Ath. 2.784; Strabo 6.3.1; cf. Wilson, *Encyclopedia*, 437-38.

93. Cic. *Verr.* 4, 57, 125 (Sappho); Plut. *Mor.* 674a (Jocasta); Paus. 6.14.11, Favorinus Frag. 36.5 (Muses) = Diog. Laert. 3.25. Mitchell, *Ancient Sculpture*, 2: 482.

94. Naucydes was a fifth-century BCE sculptor known for athletic statues according to Gardner, *Greek Sculpture*, 338. Plin. *HN* 34.19; Paus. 2.17.5, 2.22.7, 6.1.3, 6.6.2, 6.8.4, 6.9.3.

95. Plin. *HN* 134.

96. Paus. 9.30.1 (Muses); Plin. *HN* 34.8.19 (Minerva), 36.4.6; Plut. *Phoc.* 19.

97. Glaucippe (myth, Herodotus, *Library* 2.1.5) by Niceratus, Phryne the courtesan (Plin. *HN* 34.71) by Praxiteles and Herodotus; Panteuchis by Euthycrates, Besantis by Dinomenes; Gycera the courtesan and Argeia the lyre player by Herodotus; Pasiphae by Bryaxis.

98. From Euripides, *Melanippe the Wise*.

Reading 1 Corinthians with Philosophically Educated Women

> The female Homer; Sappho, pride and choice
> Of Lesbian dames, whose locks have earned a name,
> Erinna, Telesilla known to fame.
> And thou, Corinna, whose bright numbers yield
> A vivid image of Athene's shield.
> Soft-sounding Nossis, Myrtis of sweet song,
> Work-women all whose books will last full long.
> Nine Muses owe to Uranus their birth,
> And nine—and endless joy for man—to Earth.[99]

There is a tendency in the commentaries on Tatian to approach this section with disinterest. However, Jane DeRose Evans argues, mostly on the basis that courtesans would not be celebrated in Pompey's Garden during Tatian's time, that the statues in the Garden consisted of famous poets and comedic heroines. Evans is almost certainly correct when she concludes that most of the statues in the Garden would have been loot from Pompey's conquests. As was common practice during this period, most of them would have been renamed, attested to famous sculptors, and possibly even repainted and restored to carry the names of the women that Pompey wanted to memorialize.[100] In their former lives, many of these statues may have been Muses, goddesses, or patronesses. As people walked through Pompey's Garden, they could be inspired by the educated women of ancient Greece—which was lamented by the poets in their misogynistic interpretations of the statues.[101] Several other poets referenced the inspiration and possible allure of the Garden.[102]

Sulpicia is the only Roman female poet who wrote in Latin whose work is extant, and she was active during the reign of Augustus (31 BCE–14 CE).[103] Plant identifies her as the granddaughter of the orator Servius Sulpicius Rufus (106–43 BCE), the friend of Cicero (106–43 BCE). Sulpicia was apparently in the patronage of her uncle Marcus Valerius Messalla Corvinus (64–68 BCE), who also supported Ovid (ca. 43–18 BC) and Tibullus (55–19 BCE).[104] Her education compliments Cicero's witness for the process

---

99. Antipater of Thessalonica, *Anth. Pal.* 9.26. Translation from Neaves, *Anthology*, 128. Cf. Whittaker, *Taitian's Oratio*, 61–62.

100. Pompey's intentions for the statues in the Garden are unclear, particularly because the earliest connection between Tatian and the Garden was not made in ancient times.

101. Evans, "Prostitutes," 123–45; cf. James, *Learned Girls*, 40.

102. Mart. 11.47; Ov. *Am.* 1.67, 3.387; Prop. 2.32.11–12; cf. Plin. *Ep.* 35.59.

103. Plant, *Women Writers*, 106.

104. Parker, "Sulpicia," 39–62; cf. Merriam, "Sulpicia," 11; Keith, "Critical Trends," 3–10; Hallett, "Martial's Sulpicia," 99–123; Roessel, "Significance," 243–45; Hubbard,

Educated Women in the Ancient World

of education of Roman women, which included instruction by parents before marriage and by the husband after marriage.[105] There were also women writing poetry in Greek during this period. In first-century Ephesus, the priestess Claudia Trophime dedicated some lines to Hestia in a prominently placed inscription.[106]

Some women were itinerant poets in the ancient world.[107] The clearest examples of such poetess are Aristodama of Smyrna (ca. 218 CE) and Alcione of Thronion (3rd c. BCE).[108] Two honorary inscriptions dedicated to Aristodama have been analyzed by Ian Rutherford. The following inscription allows us to date Aristodama between 218 and 71 BCE because of the mention of Agetas of Kallipois, who appears in Polybius (200–118 BCE) 5.91.1:

> When Agetas of Kallipois was general (*strategos*) of the Aetolians. With good fortune. Resolved by [the city] of Lamia. Since Aristodama, daughter of Amytas, of Smyrna, an epic poetess from [Ionia], came to the city and gave several [readings] / of her own poems, in which she made worthy mention of the Aetolian people [and] of the ancestors of the nation, delivering her performance with zeal, that she should be made [*proexenos*] and benefactor (*euergetes*) of the city and that she should be granted citizenship, the right to acquire land and [property], the right of grazing (*epinomia*); immunity (*asylia*) and security by land and by [sea] / both in war and in peace, for herself, her children and possessions for [all] time, as well as all the rights which are granted to other *proxenoi* and benefactors. Let *proxenia*, citizenship, and *asylia* be granted also to O . . . her brother and his children. In the archonship of Python, Neon, and Antigenes, when Epigenes was general (*strategos*) and Cylus the hipparch. Guarantor of the *proxenia* was / Python son of Athenaeus.[109]

"Invention," 177–94; Richlin, "Sulpicia the Satirist," 125–40.

105. Best, "Cicero," 199–204; Adcock, "Women in Roman Life," 1–11; Gunhild, *Women in Roman Literature*; Churchill, *Women Writing Latin*.

106. *Inscr. Eph.* 1062. Translation available in Lefkowitz and Fant, *Women's Life*, 9; cf. Gutzwiller, "Gender and Inscribed Epigram," 383–418.

107. Rutherford, "Aristodama," 237–48.

108. There are many parallels to Aristodama's dedicatory inscription in the ancient world. For examples, see Schachter and Slater, "Proxeny Decree from Koroneia," 81–95; see also Skinner, "Homer's Mother," 98. For an excellent discussion of the use of ποιητής, see Ahuvia, *Diachronic Dialogues*, 212n103.

109. IG 9.2.62, 9.12.740, first published by Daux, "Inscriptions de Delphes," 439–66. Translation in Austin, *Hellenistic World*, no. 142; alternative translation in Burstein, *Hellenistic Age*, 64. Dated 218/17 BCE.

Reading 1 Corinthians with Philosophically Educated Women

SEG 2 also tells us that Aristodama received honors from Chalasios: a proxeny and 100 drachmas.

> Aristodama daughter of Amyntas from Smyrna in Ionia, epic poetess, arrived here and commemorated [our city]. So that we are seen to honor her appropriately, (it is resolved) to praise her for the piety which she has to the god and for her good-will to the city and to crown her with a garland of sacred laurel from the god, as is traditional for Khalion. The proclamation about the garland is to be made at the Poitropia. And there should be sent to her from our city a prerogative from Apollo's sacrifice, a share of [meat to the hearth] of Smyrna. She should be *proxenos* and benefactor of the city. And there should be given to her and her offspring from the city possession of land, immunity, inviolability by war and peace by land and sea and everything else that goes to other *proxenoi* and benefactors. And there should be sent to her one hundred drachmas as a guest-gift. Her brother Dionysius should have *proxenia*, citizenship, and immunity. So that it is manifest to all who arrive in the sanctuary that Khaleion values highly those who choose to speak or write about the god, the decree is to be set up in the shrine of Apollo Nasiōtas, the other in Delphi.[110]

Both Burstein and Austin suggest that Aristodama was a travelling poetess perhaps accompanied by her brother.[111] Alcinoe of Thronion received similar honors from the city of Tenos.[112] Rutherford argues that there are few female poets in the Roman period: Hedea of Tralles,[113] an unknown woman of Alexandria and Cos,[114] and Auphria of unknown city, and Damo[115] and Julia Balbilla[116] are weaker examples.

There are further examples of vases, cups,[117] and other plastic arts depicting the education of women and girls in every facet of Greek education:

---

110. FD 3.2.145. Translation in Rutherford, "Aristodama," 239.

111. Burstein, *Hellenistic Age*, 87. Austin, *Hellenistic World*, 295.

112. Ael. *NA* 8.20.2; cf. Parth. *Amat. narr.* 27.1.1.

113. FD 3.1.533–34.

114. She won several competitions, apparently as an Alexandrian competing in Cos. Bosnakis, "Zwei Dichterinnen aus Kos," 99–107.

115. Brennan, "Poets Julia Balbilla and Damo," 215–34.

116. Balbilla is a rare example of a Roman woman writing poetry in Greek. She was commissioned by Hadrian to memorialize a visit to Colossi and the activity of Memnon there. Her text was reconstructed in 1925 by J. M. Edmonds, "Epigrams of Balbilla," 107–10.

117. Venit, "Women in Their Cups," 117–30.

Educated Women in the Ancient World

discussion,[118] reading and/or writing,[119] music,[120] dance,[121] and athletics.[122] To illustrate the activity of women in reading and discussing, the best example is the Sarcophagus of Lucius Publius Peregrinus, where a woman is holding a scroll, listening and looking at an open scroll held by the philosopher.[123] The sarcophagus of Plotinus is very similar, with two women looking on (very close to the philosopher), one holding a scroll, and the other intently listening.[124] A fifth-century BCE Attic hydra in the kalpis shape shows a woman reading, a tablet with stylus, a chest full of scrolls, and a music contest.[125] There are several other examples of women reading that decorate Greek vases.[126] A Roman copy of a third-century BCE original depicts Klio with a stylus and a scroll.[127] Several fifth-century Greek hydrias and calyx-craters also show girls dancing and playing musical instruments.[128] A third-century BCE terracotta female dancer called the Baker Dancer after her donor to the New York Metropolitan Museum of Art is an exquisite piece from this period.[129] Two terracotta depicting literacy include a third-century BCE girl reading from a scroll on her lap and a girl from the late Hellenistic period carrying some writing tablets.[130] Another third-century BCE terracotta depicts two dancing girls holding hands.[131] Examples from the fourth and fifth century BCE of girls in athletics are rare. Beck preserves

---

118. Lullies, *Greek Sculpture*, 219; Stewart, *Greek Sculpture*, 586; Bieber, *Ancient Copies*, 889–90, see also the school scene in 902.

119. Klio holds a scroll and stylus in Stewart, *Greek Sculpture*, 766 (Roman copy); Kleiner, *Roman Sculpture*, 250 (man and wife with scroll); Beck, "Schooling of Girls," 399b (woman with scroll).

120. Beck, "Schooling of Girls," 396–405 (women playing the flute, lyre, and cithara).

121. Ridgway, *Hellenistic Sculpture*, 1:219, pl. 102; cf. 3:160–61, pls. 66a–d, 67a, and 68a–d, the five bronze "Dancers" from the Villa of the Papyri at Herculaneum, 1st CE.

122. Beck, *Greek Education*, 56; Beck, "Schooling," 1–9; Booth, "Douris' Cup," 274–80.

123. Rome, Museo Torlonia, inv. 424.

124. Vatican Museo Gregoriano Profano 9504.

125. Beck, *Greek Education*, pl. 399b, cf. 60.

126. Beck, *Greek Education*, pls. 353–56, 360a–b.

127. Stewart, *Greek Sculpture*, pl. 766.

128. Beck, *Greek Education*, dancing: pl. 391a–b; 392a–b; 393; 395a–b: music: pls. 396–405.

129. Ridgway, *Hellenistic Sculpture*, 1:219, pl. 102.

130. Beck, *Greek Education*, pl. 358. Several more examples of girls and women reading are provided in plates 349–734.

131. Beck, *Greek Education*, pl. 394.

three examples: two vases depict girls in the gymnasium, and there is one statue of a female Olympic runner.[132]

Most of these aspects of education were put to the test in the pan-Hellenic games[133]—including the Isthmian games in Corinth—in which girls participated. Plutarch writes that Aristomache of Erythrae competed in poetry at Isthmia, twice winning first prize.[134] There are further examples of girls winning prizes in the pan-Hellenic games for poetry, and a vase depicts a woman in a reading contest.[135] Girls also participated in ritual, athletics, music, and dance in and around the Isthmian games.[136] There are examples of women learning, teaching, and referenced as authorities in medicine in the Greek and Roman periods. This evidence provides the context for women learning philosophy. Like poetry, medicine, liberal education, and literacy, philosophically educated women learned from family members or tutors in a household context.[137]

Women's Interest in Education: Papyri and Beyond

Roger S. Bagnall, Raffaella Cribiore, and Evie Ahtaridis have compiled several letters attributed to women in their book *Women's Letters from Ancient Egypt*.[138] Their critical notes support premises that are central to my argument: some women were positioned to control the education of themselves and their children, and education was available to lower class slaves and freedpersons who functioned as scribes and teachers.[139] The home, as men-

132. Beck, *Greek Education*, pls. 421–24.

133. Beck, *Greek Education*, pls. 223–60.

134. Plut. *Mor.* 675b; Ath. 6.234d; 10.436d. Cf. Plut. *Mor.* 645a, a girl won a poetry contest at funeral games held in honor of Pelias.

135. "Girls' names appear in the victory-lists from Pergamon of the third–second-century B.C.: one gained a prize in recitation of epic, elegiac and lyric poetry and in reading; the other was victorious in orthography (Inschrift.v.Perg. II 315 no. 463B)," Arthur, "Tortoise and the Mirror," 56n18. See the lists of female victors in Wissowa, "Zur Geschichte des kapitolinischen Agons," 276–82; West, "Notes on Achaean Prosopography," 258–69; Dillon, "Parthenoi," 457–80 (for the death penalty for some women attending the Olympic games, see 457); Barringer, "Temple of Zeus," 211–41.

136. Wayne B. Ingalls argues that choral training in Greece was a central aspect of education in the ancient world. "Ritual Performance," 1–20. For dance, drama, music, and poetry at the Isthmian games, see Jordan, "Isthmian Amusements," 32–67; Brownlee, "Attic Black Figure," 337–82.

137. Monroe, *Source Book*; Snyder, *Teachers and Texts*; Cribiore, *Gymnastics of the Mind*.

138. Bagnall and Cribiore, *Women's Letters*.

139. Robinson, "Roman School Teacher," 57–61; McNelis, "Greek Grammarians,"

tioned above, is the epicenter of education, but one may have to leave the house to follow a well-known rhetor, philosopher, or talented grammarian. BGU 1.332 (dated 2nd to 3rd century) indicates the presence of a household teacher as a mother sends a letter to her children.

> Σεραπιὰς τοῖς τέκνοις Πτολεμαίῳ καὶ Ἀπολιναρίᾳ καὶ Πτολεμαίῳ πλεῖστα χαίρειν.
> πρὸ μὲν πάντων εὔχομαι ὑμᾶς ὑγιαίνειν, ὅ μοι πάντων ἐστὶν ἀναγκαιότερον. τὸ προ[κ]ύνημα ὑμῶν ποιῶ παρὰ τῷ κυρίῳ Σεράπιδι, εὐχομένη ὑμᾶς ὑγιαίνοντας ἀπολαβεῖν, ὡς εὔχομαι ἐπιτετυχότας ἐχάρην κομισαμένη γραμματα, ὅτι καλῶς διεσώθητε. ἀσπάζου Ἀμμώνοῦν σὺν τέκνοις καὶ συνβίῳ καὶ τοὺς φιλοῦτάς σε πάντας. ἀσπάζεταί ὑμᾶς Κυρίλλα καὶ ἡ θυγάτηρ Ἑρμίας, Ἑρμίας, Ἑρ[μ]ανοῦβις ἡ τροφός, Ἀθηναῒς ἡ δέσκαλος, Κυρίλλα, Κασία, [...]μ νιζ, Σ [...]ανος, Ἔμπις, οἱ ἐνθάδε πάτες ἐρωτηθεὶς οὖν πε[ρὶ σ]ὲ ὃ πράσσεις γρ [ἄφ]ε μοι, εἰδὼς, ἐὰν γράμματά σου λάβω, ἱλαρά εἰμι περὶ τῆς σωτηρίας ὑμῶν ἐρρῶσθαι ῾ὑμᾶς εὔχομαι.
> (hand 2) ἀπόδ(ος) Πτολεμαίῳ ἀδ ε(λ) Ἀπολινα[ρί]ας.
> (hand 1) ἀπόδος Πτολεμαίῳ(*) τῷ τέκνῳ.
> ἀσπάζου . . .
>
> Serapias to her children Ptolemaios and Apolinaria and Ptolemaios, many greetings.
> Before all I pray that you are well, which is the most important of all for me. I make your obeisance before the lord Serapis, praying to find you well, as I pray that (you) have been successful. I was delighted to receive a letter to the effect that you have come through well. Greet Ammonous with her children and husband, and those who love you. Kyrilla greets you, and the daughter of Hermias, Hermias, Hermanoubis the nurse, Athenais the teacher, Kyrilla, Kasia, . . . , S-anos, Empis, all those here. Please write me about what you're doing, knowing that if I receive a letter from you I am happy about your well-being. I pray for your health.
> (Address in second hand): Deliver to Ptolemaios the brother of Apolinaria.
> (Address in first hand): Deliver to Ptolemaios her son. Greet . . .[140]

67–94.

140. BGU 1.332. Translation from Bagnall and Cribiore, *Women's Letters*. For the use of δέσκαλος (δέσκαλή) for female teachers, see Cribiore, *Writing*, 23–24, who traces the use of the word from antiquity to modern use; Cf. BL 1.39 (on lines 1, 11, and 12–13); 5.11 (on δέσκαλος); see also Rowlandson, *Women and Society*.

Reading 1 Corinthians with Philosophically Educated Women

Specifically for literacy and education, the editors of *Women's Letters* compile P.Athen. 60, P.Oxy. 6.930, P.Oxy. 56.3860, but many other papyri cited in the book demonstrate interest in education.[141]

P.Brem. 63 (July 117 CE) is a letter from a mother to a daughter, and refers to an educated girl.[142] Also from the second century is the letter from Diogenis to Kronion, instructing Isidora to go to a woman teacher.

> Διωγενὶς Κρονίωι τῶι φιλτάτωι χαίρειν.
> Καμὲ ἀνελθοῦσαν πρὸς ὑμᾶς ἐν Ταλεὶ προσδέχεσθε· ἀλλ' εὔχομαι παραγενομένη ἐν μηδενὶ ὑμᾶς μέμψασθαι, ὅπερ ἐλπίζω μηδὲν τούτων γενήσεσθαι. πάντα δὲ τὰ κατ' ἐμὲ Λούριος ὁ ἀδελφὸς μεταδώσει ὑμεῖν. ἐρρῶσθαί σε βούλ(ομαι). (hand 2) ἀσπάζου πάντας τοὺς ἐμοὺς καὶ Ἰσιδώραν καὶ ὑπαγέτωι εἰς δεσυ (hand 1) ἐὰν Διδυμᾶς ἀντιλέγηι τῇ ἀποδόσει Λουρίωι, προένεγκον τὴν κίστην μου καὶ σφραγίσας αὐτοῦ τὰ γραμματεῖα πέμψον.

> Diogenis to her dearest Kronion, greeting.
> Be expecting me when I come up to you at Tali. But I pray that once I am there I will not find you at fault in anything: I hope that none of these things will happen. My brother Lourios will communicate to you everything concerning me.
> (second hand) I hope that you are well. Salute all my relatives and Isidora, and let her go to a woman teacher.[143]

Further letters exemplify that mothers are concerned with the education of their children. In P.Oxy 6.930 (2nd-3rd CE), a mother expresses concern that her son's *paidgagos* Diogenes had found better work (presumably in Alexandria?) and her child was in need of a new teacher, which Diogenes should arrange. It is very interesting that the mother learns of this from Diogenes's daughter, who had access to his learning. Diogenes's dependence on the author's patronage and his need for more support indicate his lower status and that of his daughter.

> [. . .]υ μὴ ὄκνει ὄκνι μοι [γ]ράφειν καὶ περὶ ὧν ἐ[ὰν] χρείαν ἔχῃς ἐντεῦθεν ἐλοιπήθη ἐπιγνοῦσα παρὰ τῆς θυγατρὸς τοῦ καθηγητοῦ ἡμῶν Διογένους καταπεπλευκέναι αὐτόν· ἡμερίμνουν γὰρ περὶ αὐτοῦ εἰδυῖα ὅτι κατὰ δύν[α]μιν μέλλει σοι προσέχειν. ἐμέλησε δέ μοι πέμψαι καὶ πυθέσθαι περὶ τῆς ὑγίας σου καὶ ἐπιγνῶναι τί ἀναγεινώσκεις. καὶ ἔλεγεν τὸ ζῆτα, ἐμαρτύρει δὲ πολλὰ περὶ τοῦ παιδαγωγοῦ σου. ὥστε οὖν, τέκνον,

---

141. Bagnall and Cribiore, *Letters*, 266–69.

142. Bagnall and Cribiore, *Letters*, 41.

143. P. Mil. Vogl. 2.76. The girl may also be mentioned in P. Mil. Vogl. 2.77. Cf. P. Mil. Vogl. 6.297 and 298.

Educated Women in the Ancient World

μελησάτω σοί τε καὶ τῷ παιδαγωγῷ σου καθήκοντι καθηγητῇ σε παραβάλλειν. ἀσπάζονταί σε πολλὰ αἱ ἀδελφαί σου καὶ τὰ ἀβάσκαντα παιδία Θεωνίδος καὶ οἱ ἡμέτεροι πάντες κατ' ὄνομα. ἄσπασαι τὸν τειμιώτατον παιδαγω γόν σου Ἔρωτα . . .

. . . do not hesitate to write to me also about whatever you need from here. I was grieved to learn from the daughter of our teacher Diogenes that he had sailed downriver, for I was free from care about him, knowing that he would look after you as far as possible. I took care to send and inquire about your health and to learn what you were reading. And he said the 6th book, and he testified a great deal concerning your paidagogos. So now, child, you and your paidagogos must take care to place you with a suitable teacher. Your sisters and the children of Theonis, whom the evil eye does not touch, and all our people greet you individually. Greet your esteemed paidagogos Eros . . .[144]

The editors note that the author of this letter is female because of the participle use, and she demonstrates her education by referring to the *Iliad* simply by *zeta* according to common practice.

Teachers and Students

While what we may call "formal education" was reserved for the elite boys[145] in all time periods relevant to this study,[146] the teacher was usually a slave[147] or a person of low status.[148] In the Roman period, elite boys and sometimes girls would attend a grammar school for elementary education (basic reading, writing, and mathematics). Higher education such as advanced mathematics, astronomy, music, dance, athletics, rhetoric or philosophy would require the tutelage of a teacher who has mastered one or many of these disciplines. For both the grammar school and the advanced teaching, the teacher was almost always a slave or freedperson brought into the home, and a more famous teacher may instruct the children of his patron's friends at the same time. P. Mich 1.77.5 (3rd BCE) is a letter in which the writer Apollonios consoles Zenon for receiving a slave who was older than he thought he would be—he is a φίλον διδάσκαλος—and therefore had some worth

---

144. P. Oxy. 6.930 = Bagnall and Cribiore, *Letters*, 267.
145. Bloomer, "Schooling in Persona," 57–78.
146. Howe, "Three Days," 1–4; Poynton, "Roman Education," 1–12.
147. Mohler, "Slave Education," 262–80; Houston, "Slave and Freedman Personnel," 139–76; Harris, *Ancient Literacy*, 255–59.
148. Kaster, "Social Status," 99–134.

Reading 1 Corinthians with Philosophically Educated Women

because he was a talented teacher. Sometimes teachers were viewed with a lack of respect (Demosthenes, 384–22 BCE, *On the Crown* 285). Aeschines (389–14 BCE) writes that there is a law for when students should come and go to school because no one trusts the schoolmaster to be alone with the pupils after dark (*Against Timarchus*, 9). Teachers of the sort that Gellius railed against, however, do not seem to be the norm.[149] The balance of the literature concerning teachers seems to point in the direction of respect.

There is some evidence for both male and female teachers teaching girls. In a private letter (P. Giss. 1.80, 2nd c. CE), a man requests that the καθηγητής of his daughter is to be paid in some leftover pigeons and birds so that he will pay attention to her. There is a letter to Theon in which the καθηγητής of a girl is paid in oil and grapes (P. Oslo. 3.156, 2nd c. CE). Some scholars have presented the famous painted inscription, "Ἑρμιόνη γραμματική," as evidence a female teacher, but it is possible that the 19 year old woman was an avid student rather than a teacher.[150]

In most cases, the home is the center of education, and girls were typically educated in subjects that were useful in domestic life: spinning and household management. Xenophon (430–354 BCE) records the story where Ischomachus discusses the education of his wife in the manner that her parents should have, and he should learn from her in matters that she knows more about (*Oec.* 7.42).[151] She was only fourteen years old when they married, and Ischomachus says that she barely knew how to spin but she had excellent control over her appetites (*Oec.* 7.6). Ischomachus then says that he instructed her on the household duties that he expected and encouraged her to teach those who know less than her and learn from those who know more (*Oec.* 7.41, 10.10). Aside from the husband teaching his wife, Aristophanes (ca. 446–386 BCE) describes how a girl in Athens could receive some education:

ἐγὼ γυνή εἰμι, νοῦς δ'ἔνεστί μοι,
αὐτὴ δ'ἐμαυτῆς οὐ κακῶς γνώμης ἔχω,
τοὺς δ'ἐκ πατρός τε καὶ γεραιτέρων λόγους

149. *SB* 1.5753.3, Arsinoite, 1st CE. Vardi, "Gellius," 41–54.

150. Turner suggests that we should translate γραμματική as "literary lady" rather than "teacher." *Greek Papyri*, 77. A copy of the *Iliad* was "found rolled up and placed under the mummy of a lady." She may have been literate and this was her most prized possession, or it could be a tool in the afterlife. It seems more convincing to me that she was literate, because why would they expect her to be illiterate in this life and literate in the next? Dominic Montserrat argues that it is praise for the young woman's learning. "Heron," 223–26.

151. Xen. *Oec.* 7.1–10.1. Shero, "Xenophon's Portrait," 17–21; Murnaghan, "How a Woman Can Be More Like a Man," 9–22; Gini, "Manly Intellect," 483–86.

πολλοὺς ἀκούσασ᾽ οὐ μεμούσωμαι κακῶς.

I am a woman, but I'm not a fool.
And what of natural intelligence I own
Has been filled out with the remembered precepts
My father and the city-elders taught me.[152]

Sparta did have a full course of education for girls that Plato and others admired—and the goal of this program was the same as for boys—to produce hearty citizens to defend and preserve the state. This educational program may be one of the reasons why most Pythagorizing women are from Sparta.[153] Women in Athens learned at home, but both in Athens and in other parts of the ancient world, women were students and teachers in every major school of philosophy, as both Tatian[154] (120–180 CE) and Clement of Alexandria[155] (150–215 CE) remember.

We receive a glimpse of education of elite boys in the Roman period when Plutarch (46–120 CE) describes the education of Cato's son. Cato (234–149 BCE) taught him how to read at home, and he also used Chilo to teach his son, a slave that was an exemplary grammarian.[156] In pseudo-Plutarch's essay on the education of free-born children, the focus is on elite boys, and he emphasizes the need for fathers to find competent teachers rather than entrusting the education of a son to an unqualified friend.[157]

Nevertheless, pseudo-Plutarch begins and ends the essay on education with the importance of women in the education. At the end of his essay, pseudo-Plutarch writes that parents should emulate the practice of Eurydice of Hierapolis (Alexander the Great's grandmother), whose inscription[158] reads:

Εὐρυδίκη Ἱεραπολιῆτις τόνδ᾽ ἀνέθηκε
Μούσαις εὔιστον ψυχῇ ἑλοῦσα πόθον

---

152. Ar. *Lys.* 1124–25. Translation in Lindsay, *Lysistrata*, 1926.
153. Pomeroy, *Spartan Women*, 10–11.
154. Tat. *Ad Gr.* 33.
155. Clem. Al. *Strom.* 4.7.
156. Plut. *Cat.* 20.3.
157. Plut. *Mor.* 4c–5a. Berry, "De Liberis Educandis," 387–99.
158. There are two other interesting inscriptions related to Eurydice. In 1992, at the Eucleia temple site in Vergina, a statue base was found with the inscription "Eurydice, daughter of Sirras, to Eucleia." Eight years later, a similar inscription was found. See Oikonomedes, "New Inscription," 52–54; Andronicos, *Verghina*, 49–51; Saatsoglou-Paliadeli, "In the Shadow of History," 353–67, Saatsoglou-Paliadeli, "Εὐρυδίκα Σιρρα Εὐκλεία," 733–44; AR 1983: fig. 84; AR 1990: fig. 91; Ergon 1990: 83–85; Ergon 1991: 65–68. A headless statue of Eucleia was discovered near the second inscription. Carney, *Women and Monarchy*, 41n10; 44n28.

Reading 1 Corinthians with Philosophically Educated Women

γράμματα γὰρ μνημεῖα λόγων μήτηρ γεγαυῖα
παίδων ἡβώντων ἐξεπόνησε μαθεῖν.

Eurydice of Hierapolis
Made to the Muses this her offering
When she had gained her soul's desire to learn.
Mother of young and lusty sons was she,
And by her diligence attained to learn
Letters, wherein lies buried all our lore.[159]

Of course in order for a mother to be able to teach her sons letters,[160] she herself would need to know them, thus daughters would need to be instructed also. Plutarch and pseudo-Plutarch's instructions and thoughts fit within the works of thinkers such as Cicero, Seneca, Musonius Rufus, Heirocles, and others between 100 BCE and 200 CE who valued the education of women and used traditions regarding the involvement of women in medicine, poetry, and philosophy to make their case.[161] These writings will be considered in chapter 3, where our discussion will especially focus on women educated in philosophical traditions.

---

159. Plut. *Mor.* 14c (Babbitt, LCL); *Anth. Pal.*, 128.1. For alternative translation, see Lefkowitz and Fant, *Women's Life*, 213. Cf. Berry, "De Liberis Educandis," 387–99. For the history of Eurydice, see Hammond, *History of Macedonia*, 3:119, 138; Carney, *Women and Monarchy*, 41–50. Eurydice's son Philip was a student of the Pythagorean philosopher in Thebes in the 380s BCE according to Diod. Sic. 16.2.2. Speusippus, successor of Plato wrote Philip a letter in 342 BCE, text and translation in Bickermann and Sykutris, *Speusippus*.

160. Her sons: Alexander II, Perdiccas, and Philip of Macedon. She also had a daughter: Eurynoe.

161. Cornelia was also used by Plutarch and others as an exemplary educated women who cared deeply about the education of her sons, see Plut. *Tib. Gracch.* 1; Tat. *Or.*, 28. Plant, *Women Writers*, 101; Hemelrijk, *Educated Women*, 64–68.

3

Women in Philosophy

IN CHAPTER 2, I surveyed evidence that attests to the education of women and girls in a wide range of disciplines and tasks. In this chapter, I will argue that women were active in almost every ancient philosophical tradition. But these women philosophers are typically not considered in classical or New Testament studies. New Testament scholars have recognized the importance of a wide variety of ancient thought but have not considered how philosophically educated women might have interacted with Paul's epistles. In this chapter, I will explore traditions that bear witness to the activity of women in philosophy in every major school that is considered important to New Testament studies. It is true that the evidence is varied and scattered over many time periods, but several constants emerge. I will argue that women could learn philosophy in a wide variety of contexts. We will see that philosophical education was most available to women who were connected to a wealthy household. Slaves and freedpersons who were connected to a wealthy household were sometimes encouraged to learn philosophy. Wealthy women were educated as girls by a tutor that was brought into the home, and participate in philosophical debate and discussion as young women and adults.

Women in the History of Philosophy

In the late seventeenth century, the French scholar Gilles Ménage scoured classical literature searching for women remembered as philosophers, women who were disciples or relatives of known philosophers, and women who contributed to intellectual interests similar to philosophy.[1] A woman would be a philosopher if she met any one of these criteria, and Ménage found sixty-six women philosophers.[2] This number may become less impressive, though, when one considers that at least seventeen of these women come from one list in Iamblichus (ca. 245–325 CE, *VP* 36.267), another is the daughter of a Centaur, and a few others are simply known associates of philosophers. The following table lists Ménage's women philosophers and the ancient sources that he used.

Table 1. Ménage's Women Philosophers[3]

Philosopher	Era	Location	Family	Criteria	Sources
1. Hippo	12th c. BCE	unknown	daughter of Chiron (or Cheiron) the Centaur	practiced astronomy // prophetess	Clem. Al. *Strom.* 4.15; Cyril against Julian 4; cf. Plut. *Mor.* 1145e–1146b (does not mention Hippo)
2. Cleobulina	fl. 570 BCE	unknown	daughter of Cleobulus	composer of riddles	Arist. *Rh.* 3.2; Plut. *Mor.* 148d, 150e; Clem. *Strom.* 4.19; Ath. 4.21, 10.448b; Diog. Laert. 1.89; Pollux 7.11
3. Diotima	5th c. BCE	Mantenia	unknown	taught philosophy of love to Socrates	Plato, *Sym.* 201d; Lucian, *Images* 18.2, [*Eunuchus* 7.7]

---

1. Ménage's work, published in 1690 in Latin, first appeared in English in 1702 in the anonymous *Lives of the Ancient Philosophers*, 535–64.

2. Zedler, introduction to *History of Women*, vii.

3. The content of this table was taken from Ménage's book. I have updated the references to make it easier for the reader to locate sources from modern editions.

Philosopher	Era	Location	Family	Criteria	Sources
4. Aspasia	470–410 BCE	Milesia	daughter of Axiochus	taught rhetoric to Pericles and philosophy to Socrates	Plato, *Men.* 235e, 235e, 236a–b, 249d; Plut. *Lives* 124.23–25 ["Pericles"]; Diog. Laert. 6.9 ["Antisthenes"]; Clem. *Strom.* 4.19; Ath. 5.61.10, 29, 5.63.7, 13.23.4, 13.25.28, 13.37.16, Epitome vol. 2,1.82.24, vol. 2,2.107.26, vol. 2,2.117.7; 2,2.110.27
5. Beronice	unknown	unknown	unknown	philosopher	Phot. *Bibl.* 144a
6. Pamphila	1st c. CE	Epidaurian from Egypt	daughter of Soteridas, grammarian	philosopher	Phot. *Bibl.*, "Sopater" and "Pamphila"; Sudias "Pamphila" and "Soteridas"; Diog. Laert. often uses her works 1.24.11, 1.68.7, 1.76.1, 1.98.11, 2.24.9, 3.23.4, 5.36.9; Aul. Gell. *NA* 15.17, 23.
7. Clea	1st–2nd c. CE	unknown	unknown	philosopher	Plut. *Mor.* 242e ["On the Bravery of Women"]
8. Eurydice	1st–2nd c. CE	unknown	wife of Pollianus	philosophically educated // taught her children	Plut. *Mor.* 138a [Conjugal Precepts] and *Mor.* 14c [On the Education of Children].
9. Julia Domna	170–217 CE	Rome	wife of Emperor Severus	philosopher	Dio Cass. 76, 78; Philostr. *VS*, 30 (Philiscus the Thessalian), *V A* 1.3.

Philosopher	Era	Location	Family	Criteria	Sources
10. Myro	unknown	Rhodesian	unknown	philosopher	Sudias, "Myro" and Athen. 2.70.
11. Anthusa	5th c. CE	unknown	unknown	contemplation of clouds (physics = philosophy)	Phot. *Bibl.* "Damascius."
12. Aganice (Aglaonice)	unknown	unknown	daughter of Hegetor the Thessalian	successfully calculated times of eclipse	Plut. *Mor.* 145d ["Conjugal Precepts"]
13. Eudocia (Athenais)	401–60 CE	Athens	daughter of Heraclitus or Leontius, wife of Theodosius the Younger	philosopher	*Paschal Chronicle*, Olympiad CCC; Socrates, *Ecc. Hist.* 7.21
14. St. Catherine	d. 307 CE	unknown	unknown	scholar / philosopher	Simeon Metaphrastes, Nov. 25th entry [Gentien Harvet]
15. Anna Comnena	1083–1148 CE	Alexandria	daughter of Emperor Alexius, wife of Nicephorus Brynnius Caesar	scholar / philosopher	Simeon Metaphrastes
16. Eudocia	11th c. CE	Constantinople	wife of despot Constantine Palaeologus	philosopher	Nicephorus Gregoras, *History* 8.5
17. Panypersebasta	14th c. CE	Constantinople	wife of Emperor's nephew John Panypersebastus	scholar / philosopher	Nicephorus Gregoras, *History* 8.5
18. Novella	14th c. CE		daughter of philosopher John Andrea	lawyer	Christine Pisan, *City of Women*, part 2 ch. 16.

Philosopher	Era	Location	Family	Criteria	Sources
19. Heloise	1101–1164 CE	Notre Dame	wife of Peter Abelard, theologian	instructed by husband in philosophy	Francis Ambrosius, *Apologetic Preface for Abelard*
Platonists					
20. Lasthenia	4th c. BCE	unknown	unknown	disciple of Plato	Diog. Laert. 3.31 ["Plato"]; Clem. Al. *Strom.* 4.19; Them. *Or.* 12
21. Axiothia	4th c. BCE	unknown	unknown	disciple of Plato	Diog. Laert. 3.31 ["Plato"]; Clem. Al. *Strom.* 4.19; Them. *Or.* 12
22. Geminae	3rd c. CE	unknown	mother and daughter	disciples of Plotinus	Porph. *Plot.* 9.2–3.
23. Amphilia	4th c. CE	unknown	Daughter of Aristo, wife of the son of Iamblichus	family relationship?	Porph. *Phot.* 9.2–3.
24. Hypatia	370–415 CE	Alexandria	daughter of Theon of Alexandria	philosopher	Eunapis, "Ionicus" (for Theon); Socrates, *Ecclesiastical History* 7.15
Academicians					
25. Caerellia	1st c. CE	unknown	unknown	scholar / philosopher	Cic. *Att.* 12.51; *Letters to His Friends* 13.72; Cass. Dio 46
Dialecticians					
26. Argia 27. Theognida 28. Artemisia 29. Pantaclea	4th–3rd c. BCE		daughters of the rhetorician Diodorus Cronus (Megarian)	philosopher / rhetorician	Clem. Al. *Strom.* 4.19; Jerome, *Against Jovinianus* 1 (cites Philo the Dialectician, disciple of Diodorus Cronus and Zeno of Citium—who said that there were five daughters and he wrote a history of them

Philosopher	Era	Location	Family	Criteria	Sources
Cyrenaics					
30. Arete	4th c. BCE	Cyrene	daughter of Aristippus of Cyrene	philosopher	Clem. Al. *Strom.* 4.19; Diog. Laert. "Aristippus"
Megarians					
31. Nicarete	4th c. BCE	Megara?	friend and disciple of Stilpo	disciple of Stilpo	Ath. 8.596e; Diog. Laert. 2.114.
Cynics					
32. Hipparchia	300 BCE	Maroneia	wife of Crates	philosopher	Antipater *Anth. Pal.* book 3; Clem. Al. *Strom.* 4; Diog. Laert. "Hipparchia"
Peripatetics					
33. Unnamed Daughter of Olympiodorus	5th c. CE		Daughter of Olympiodorus; wife of (his disciple) Proclus of Lycia	taught philosophy by her father	Marinus of Naples "Proclus"; Suidas.
34. Theodora	6th c. CE	unkown	unknown	scholar / philosopher	Photius Codex 118 Bekker page 125b line 33
Epicureans					
35. Themiste	4th–3rd c. BCE	Lampascus	wife of Leontius of Lampascus, daughter of Zoilus of Lampascus	philosopher	Clem. Al. *Strom.* 4; Lactant. 3.25.
36. Leontium	4th–3rd c. BCE	Athens	friend of Epicurus and Metrodorus	philosopher	Cic. *Nat. D.* 1; Plin. *Ep.* 35.11; Diog. Laert., "Epicurus"; Ath. 13
37. Theophila	4th–3rd c. BCE	unknown	unknown	scholar / philosopher	Martial book 8 [7.69]

Philosopher	Era	Location	Family	Criteria	Sources
Stoics					
38. Porcia	42 BCE	Rome	daughter of Cato, wife of Brutus	philosopher	Plut. "Brutus," 13.3.
39. Arria 40. Arria 41. Fannia	42 BCE; fl. 66 CE; d. ca.108 CE	unknown	mother, daughter, granddaughter	philosophers	Plin. *Ep.* 31, 34, 101; Dio Cass. 60.16.4
Pythagoreans					
42. Themistoclea	6th c. BCE		sister of Pythagoras	taught Pythagoras morals	Diog. Laert. "Pythagoras" = Theoclea in Suidas = Aristoclea in Porphyry
43. Theano	6th c. BCE		wife of Pythagoras	philsopher	Hermesianax Frg. 7.85; Plut. *Mor.* 145e ["Nuptial Precepts"], Lucian, Images 19.6; Porph. *Plot.* 4.2, 19.4, Diog. Laert. 8.43.4–6 ["Pythagoras"], Photius codex 177, Bekker page 114b.1; Libanius to Aristaenetus; Theodoritus, Therapeutica 2.23.2, 12.73.7; Clem. Al. *Strom.* 4.19; cf. Herodotus, *Persian*, book 1; Iamblichus 28.146.13; *Anth. Pal.* 14.138.4; Athen. 13.71; Pollux 10.21.7
44. Myia	6th–5th c. BCE		daughter of Pythagoras and Theano	philosopher	Clem. Al. *Strom.* 4, Diog. Laert., Porphyry, Iamblichus [wife of Milo of Crotona], Sudias "Pythagoras"

Philosopher	Era	Location	Family	Criteria	Sources
45. Damo	6th–5th BCE		daughter of Pythagoras	keeper of the sacred Pythagorean writings	Porphyry; Diog. Laert.
46. Sara	6th–5th BCE		daughter of Pythagoras	family relation?	anonymous author of Life of Pythagoras
47. Timycha	ca. 4th c. BCE	Lacedemonian	wife of Myllias of Crotona	philosopher	Iamblichus
48. Philtatis	unknown	Crotona	daughter of Theophis of Crotona, sister of Bynthanichus	philosopher	Iamblichus
49. Occello	unknown	Lucania	unknown	philosopher	Iamblichus; cf. Censorinus, *Natal Day*, ch. 3
50. Ecello	unknown	Lucania	unknown	philosopher	Iamblichus
51. Chilonis	6th c. BCE	Lacedemonia	daughter of Chilo of Lacedemonia	philosopher	Iamclichus
52. Theano	6th c. BCE	Metapontium	wife of Brontius of Metapontium	philosopher	Iamblichus
53. Lasthenia	4th c. BCE	Arcadia	may be the same woman mentioned in Plato	philosopher	Iamblichus
54. Abrotella	unknown	Tarentum	daughter of Arboteles of Tarentum	philosopher	Iamblichus
55. Echecratia	3rd c. BCE	Philasia	unknown	philosopher	Iamblichus
56. Tyrsene	unknown	Sybaris	unknown	philosopher	Iamblichus
57. Bisorronde	unknown	Tarentum	unknown	philosopher	Iamblichus
58. Nestheadusa	unknown	Lacedemonia	unknown	philosopher	Iamblichus

Philosopher	Era	Location	Family	Criteria	Sources
59. Byo	unknown	Argus	unknown	philosopher	Iamblichus
60. Babelyma	unknown	Argos	unknown	philosopher	Iamblichus
61. Cleachma	unknown	Lacedemonia	sister of Autocharidas of Lacedemonia	philosopher	Iamblichus
62. Phintys	3rd c. BCE	Athens?	daughter of Callicrates	philosopher	Stobaeus 72
63. Perictione	unknown	unknown	unknown	philosopher	Sobaeus; Photius (Pierectiones)
64. Melissa	unknown	unknown	unknown	philosopher	letter Melissa to Clareta
65. Rhodope	unknown	unknown	unknown	philosopher	letter from Theano to her "the philosopher"
66. Ptolemais	2nd–3rd c. CE	Cyrene	unknown	philosopher	Porphyry *Commentary on the Harmony of Ptolemy*

As a whole, Ménage's work is still a useful starting point as a sourcebook for classical references to women philosophers. At the same time, there are some significant oversights in Ménage. He completely ignores the epistles of Seneca (ca. 8–65 BCE/CE) to Helvia and Marcia, and does not fully explore Plutarch's (ca. 46–120 BCE) exhortations to Eurydice. This is puzzling because he does acknowledge Cicero's (106–43 BCE) admiration of Caerellia.[4]

More recent examinations of women in philosophy are incomplete and do not significantly improve on Ménage. In 1987, Mary Ellen Waithe published a history of women in philosophy. The following table illustrates the few philosophers that are addressed by the contributors to Waithe's history.

---

4. Ménage, *Philosophers*, 7, 31; Cicero favorably mentions Caerellia in *Fam.* 13.72; and less favorably in *Att.* 13.21.5, 14.19, and 15.1.4. Cicero was not happy that Caerellia was able to obtain a copy of *De Finibus* before it was published (but he said that she was inspired by a love of philosophy to do so), and frustrated by her attempt to heal the rift between Cicero and Publilia. Some fragments of his letters to her are preserved by Quint. 6.3.112.

Table 2. Wathie's Philosophers[5]

Philosopher	Era	Location	Family	Criteria	School	Sources
1. Thesistoclea	600 BCE		Pythagoras's sister	taught Pythagoras morals	Pythagorean	Diog. Laert. "Pythagoras"
2. Theano	600 BCE	Crotona	Pythagoras's wife	philosopher	Pythagorean	wrote "On Pity" [Hesleff]; Stob. 268
3. Arignote	550 BCE		Pythagoras's daughter	philosopher	Pythagorean	Peter Gorman, *Pythagoras*, 90.
4. Myia	550 BCE		Pythagoras's daughter	philosopher = harmonia	Pythagorean	Letter to Phyllis [Thesleff / Hercher]
5. Damo	550 BCE		Pythagoras's daughter	entrusted with writings	Pythagorean	
6. Aesara	3rd c. BCE– 1st c. CE?	Lucania	unknown	philosopher	Pythagorean	book on Human Nature [Thesleff]
7. Phyntis	300 BCE	Sparta	daughter of Kallicrates the Pythagoran	philosopher	Pythagorean	
8. Pericitione I	300 BCE		unknown	philosopher	Pythagorean	On the Harmony of Women [Thesleff]

5. This table was created from data presented in Waithe's book. All dates are her own, and where no location was listed I left the entry blank. The term "philosopher" indicates that Waithe claims that the person engaged in philosophy or was philosophically educated.

Philosopher	Era	Location	Family	Criteria	School	Sources
9. Theano II	3rd c. BCE–1st c. CE?			philosopher	Pythagorean	Theano to Eubole; Theano to Nikostrate; Theano to Kallisto. Spurious: T. to Rhodophe; to Eukleides, to Euridike.
10. Pericitione II	3rd c. BCE–1st c. CE?			philosopher	Pythagorean	On the Moderation of Women frgs 1 and 2 [Thesleff]
11. Aspasia	450 BCE	Miletus		philosopher	Periclean	speech in Plato *Menexus* 241c; Pericles funeral oration
12. Diotima	450 BCE	Matinea	not an historical person	ficticious creation by Plato		speech in Plato *Syposium* 205a–206a
13. Julia Domina	b. 170 CE		wife of Septimius Severus	philosopher	scholar	Dio Cassius 76, 78; Philost. *Lives*, 30 (Philiscus the Thessalian), *Apollonius of Tyana* 1.3.
14. Makrina	300 CE		sister of Gregory of Nyssa	philosopher		P.G. 46, 29b
15. Hypatia	400 CE	Alexandria	daughter of aristocrats Basilius and Emmelia	philosopher	Christian Neo-Platonist	well documented

75

Philosopher	Era	Location	Family	Criteria	School	Sources
16. Arete	300 BCE	Cyrene	daughter of Aristippus	philosopher		Strabo 17.3.22; Clem. Al. *Strom.* 4.19; Diog. Laert. "Aristippus"; Eusebius 18.32.764a; Them. *Or.* 21.44
17. Asclepeigenia	400 CE	Athens	daughter of Plutarch the Younger	philosopher	Syncretism	Marinus, *Life of Proclus* 18–29
18. Axiothea	350 BCE	Philesia	student of Plato	philosopher		Themistius *Or.* 23.295c; Dicaerchus, frg. 44
19. Cleobulina	500 BCE		daughter of Cleobulus	philosopher		Diog. Laert. "Cleobulus"; Aristotle, *Poetics* 1458a24; Plut. *Mor.* 148.
20. Hipparchia	350 BCE		wife of Crates	philosopher		Antipater of Sidon 3.12.52; Clem. *Strom.* 4.19; Diog. Laert. "Hipparchia"; Suda "Hipparchia."
21. Lasthenia	350 BCE		student of Plato	Philosopher		Diog. Laert. "Plato" and "Speusippus"

Waithe's work is heavily concentrated on philosophically educated women in Pythagorean traditions, and is useful for its translations of Thesleff's Pythagorean texts,[6] but it is overshadowed by Guthrie's work in 1920.[7] There are some notes on the historical situation of these women, but

---

6. Thesleff, *Pythagorean Texts*, and its companion volume, *Introduction to the Pythagorean Writings*.

7. Guthrie, *Pythagoras*.

these notes have not been well received in scholarship. For example, Mary Anne Warren complains of the lack of critical notes and transitions from one philosopher to the next.[8] Gillian Clarke posits that Waithe's understanding of the ancient world lacks an historical method, and Waithe ignored recent scholarship.[9] R. M. Dancy writes in his critique, "apart from a few displays of thorough and competent research, it is generally based on substandard scholarship."[10] Monica Green is troubled by the complete lack of reference to the immense amount of scholarship both on the historical and conceptual context of the subject, concluding that Waithe's book is a compilation of translations rather than a history of women in philosophy.[11]

Many other scholars have critically addressed topics that relate to philosophically educated women, but the most important work that critiques Waithe and Ménage is Ethel M. Kersey. Kersey's work is the only modern comprehensive review of ancient female philosophers, but her focus is on the rhetorical portrayal of philosophically educated women in ancient sources rather than establishing reconstructions of the history of educated women.[12] I. M. Plant has collected many writings of women in the ancient world, including many philosophers that will be very useful for this study due to the depth of study and quality of scholarship.[13] I will again review the original sources for the best evidence for philosophically educated women and identify their social contexts. I will attempt to show the strength of traditions concerning philosophically educated women in a variety of schools, from the founding of the schools through the second century CE.

Women in the Pre-Socratics

It is said that in the sixth century BCE, Bias of Priene ransomed some young women from Messina, educated them like they were his own daughters, and sent them back to their fathers (Diog. Laert. 1.82). Diogenes Laertius (fl. 3rd CE) also says that Cleobulus of Lindus (6th BCE) had a daughter named Cleobulina, who wrote enigmas in hexameter verse and is mentioned in a play by Cratinus (518–422 BCE).[14] "[Cleobulus] used to say that men ought to give their daughters in marriage while they were girls in age, but women

8. Warren, "Feminist Archeology," 155–59.
9. Clark, Review of *A History of Women Philosophers*, 429–30.
10. Dancy, "On *A History of Women Philosophers*," 160–71.
11. Green, Review of *A History of Women Philosophers*, 178–79.
12. Kersey, *Women Philosophers*.
13. Plant, *Women Writers*.
14. Diog. Laert. 1.89; cf. Plut. *Mor.* 148d.3; Clem. Al. *Strom.* 4.19.

in sense; as indicating that girls ought to be well educated."[15] The riddles of his daughter Cleobulina (fl. early 7th BCE) are preserved in Aristotle (384–322 BCE, *Poetics* 1458a, not explicitly attributed to Cleobulina), Plutarch (fl. 46–120 CE, *Mor.* 150e), the *Greek Anthology*, and Athenaeus (fl. late 2nd CE, 10.448b).[16] Her riddles were most likely used as subjects of discussion at dinner parties.[17] Because the fragment in Aristotle is spurious, it is best to regard these women as non-historical predecessors of later philosophically educated women.

The First Philosophically Educated Women: The Pythagorizing Women

Like some other later philosophers, it is said that Pythagoras was taught by a woman. In his case, Diogenes Laertius (fl. 3rd CE) says that Pythagoras (570–495 BCE) learned ethics from the priestess Themistoclea.[18] Women were important in Pythagorianism from its beginnings and these traditions were remembered hundreds of years later.

The traditions concerning Pythagoras's wife Theano are very early. Three fragments from ancient poets mention her: Euripides (480–406 BCE, frag. 823 = Stob. 4.23.32 [53] *TLG*) mentions her simply as Θεανὼ ἡ Πυθαγόρειος; in Hermesianax she is Theano of Thebes who speaks in riddles (fl. 330 BCE, frag. 7.85 = Athen.13.10.6); and Empedocles (490–430 BCE, frag. 155.5 = Diog. Laert. 8.43) says she is the wife of Pythagoras. While Cicero (106–43 BCE)[19] and Seneca

---

15. Diog. Laert. 1.91.

16. Plant, *Women Writers*, 29–32. The biographical information concerning Cleobulina is contradictory, but Plant argues that we should not entirely dismiss her historicity.

17. Martin, "Enigmas," 62–63; Martin, "Ancient Collections," 161–69. cf. Martin, "Seven Sages," 108–28.

18. Diog. Laert. 8.1.

19. To my knowledge, Cicero does not mention any traditions of women in Pythagoreanism. Pythagoras was important to Cicero due to his interest in friendship (*Off.* 1.56). He mentions persecution of Pythagoreans but nothing of their families (*Off.* 3.10.45). Cicero knows of the tradition of Pythagoras' remarkable memory (*Sen.* 78, cf. 92). He says that he is irritated with Pythagoreans who quote the philosopher as "the master" (*Nat. D.* 1.26). He argues against the Pythagorean dogma concerning the unity of the human soul with God (*Nat. D.* 1.40, cf. 3.314), he knows of their tradition of secrecy (1.74), and he follows the tradition of Pythagoras sacrificing a goat when he made a discovery in geometry (3.339). In *Orat.* 9.31, he sarcastically asks if a woman had read Plato or Pythagoras (otherwise she would be free from her lusts). In *Rep.* there is a musing about Plato learning from the Pythagoreans (3.301); Pythagoras is dated in the 63rd Olympiad in 2.560.

(1–65 CE)[20] knew about many Pythagorean traditions, they do not mention any traditions concerning women in Pythagoreanism. The biographers of Pythagoras, who may be relying on a lost work of Aristotle, trace the origins of some of his teachings to women. Plutarch (ca. 46–120 CE) mentions Theano in using her teachings to instruct Eurydice in the womanly virtues of modesty, silence, and learning.[21] Julius Pollox (2nd CE) mentions Theano as the author of the epistle to Timaretan.[22] Athenaeus (fl. late 2nd CE) has an interest in Theano due to the association of Pythagoreans with an odd diet.[23] Lucian of Samosata (125–80 CE), in his *Dialogue on Male and Female Love* briefly mentions Theano as the daughter of Pythagoras.[24] Photius (810–893 CE) preserves an anonymous biography of Pythagoras which indicates that Theano was a disciple who was *like* a daughter.[25] Theano's entry in the Suda (10th CE) identifies her as a Pythagorean philosopher who authored a few lost works.[26]

There are seven letters attributed to Theano in the neo-Pythagorean pseudepigraphon which are all addressed to women. However, these letters do not contain any meaningful continuity with the doctrines of Pythagoreanism, none has the preserved teachings of Theano, and some have no contact with any other known philosophy.[27] The letters are considered

20. Seneca knows of Pythagorean reincarnation, *Ben.* 7.20.5; silence for five years, *Ep.* 52; Pythagorean spiritual teachings in *Ep.* 94; Sotion's Pythagorean teachings inspired him to be a vegetarian (even though he did not adopt a Pythagorean rationale), *Ep.* 108. Cf. Inwood, "Seneca," 69–70.

21. Plut. *Mor.* 142c. For detailed discussion and bibliography, see Pomeroy, *Advice*.

22. Julius Pollox, *Onomasticon*, 10.21.7. This letter is preserved in Thesleff, but is certainly not the Pythagorean Theano.

23. Ath. 8.21.36; 13.6.31; 13.10.6; 2.2.102.8; 2.2.102.17.

24. Lucian, *Erotes*, 30.

25. Thesleff, *Pythagorean Texts*, 237.15.

26. Burkert explains that the different roles of Theano as wife, daughter, or student of Pythagoras is related to the conflicting theories of whether or not he was celibate, in *Lore and Science*, 114. I will note here that Robert Garland suggests that there was not much room in antiquity for women with brains, in *Celebrity in Antiquity*, 127. Within Pythagorean families, as well as within the families of Seneca, Plutarch, and Pliny, intelligent women were highly valued.

27. The text of the letters is preserved in Thesleff, *Pythagorean Texts*, 195–201. An English translation and some very brief commentary is available by Vicki Lynn Harper in Waithe, *Ancient Women Philosophers*, 41–55. Discussion of this letter is available in *New Docs* 6:18–23; Pomeroy, *Women in Hellenistic Egypt*, 64–68; Treggiari, *Roman Marriage*, 193. English translation available in Malherbe, *Moral Exhortation*, 82–85. I do not exclude the possibility that these were written by neo-Pythagorean women who may have taken names of early Pythagorean philosophers because they reinforce traditional misogynistic ideals. Therefore, we may need to consider that these writings were not liberating for women. For later traditions, see Rosenmeyer, *Ancient Epistolary Fictions*, 201–2, 206–8.

"neo-Pythagorean" only because some letters are written by or addressed to names traditionally associated with Pythagoreanism. It is important that these letters appear at about the time of Paul: it was feasible for women to be active in philosophy, even if it was restricted to popular morality concerning patronage, marriage and family, and self-sufficiency as I will demonstrate in chapters 5–8.

Pythagoreanism and Early Christianity

Justin Martyr (103–65 CE) is the first Christian apologist to mention Pythagoras, but it is almost in passing and includes no specific reference to his teachings or traditions concerning women.[28] Justin tells us that he tried to be a student of an illustrious Pythagorean but was not qualified; in fact, this is the only instance in Justin where Pythagoras or Pythagoreans are not lumped together with Plato or other schools.[29] Tatian (120–180 CE) uses Pythagoras's teaching concerning reincarnation as part of a polemic against the various teachings of Greek philosophers concerning the doctrine of the soul.[30]

Theophilus of Antioch (d. 181 CE) briefly mentions Pythagoras, but similarly to Tatian it is soundly within his polemic against other philosophers; Pythagoras is attacked for teaching that no god should be worshipped.[31] Hippolytus of Rome (170–235 CE) identifies Valentinus (d. 150 CE) as a Pythagorean, tracing his views back to Timaeus's method in Plato's *Timaeus*.[32]

Being the first Christian apologist to have a knowledgeable and somewhat favorable disposition to the philosopher, Clement of Alexandria (150–215 CE) preserves twelve Pythagorean ἄκουσμα and considered Philo a Pythagorean.[33] Clement is of course not always favorable in his references

---

28. Just. *Apol.* 18.5. For Justin's use of philosophy, see Droge, "Justin Martyr," 303–19.

29. Just. *Dial.* 2; cf. 5 and 6. To modern scholars, Justin's teacher would be considered a neo-Pythagorean.

30. Tat. *Ad. Gr.* 25. Tatian dates Pythagoras in the 62nd Olympaid in ch. 41; Diog. Laert. 8.45 places him in the 60th. Diogenes Laertius says that Pythagoras thought that he was the reincarnated Aethalides, the son of Hermes who could remember everything. Diog. Laert. 8.4. For the theological method of Tatian, see Grant, "Studies in the Apologists," 123–28.

31. Theophilus to Autolychus 3.7. Grant dismisses Theophilus' statement about Pythagoras as incorrect, in "Theophilus," 243.

32. Hippol. *Haer.* 6.26. For bibliography on the methods in *Timaeus*, see Aryeh Finkelberg, "Plato's Method," 391–409.

33. Lilla, *Clement*, 9–59; Runia, "Phythagorean," 1–22; Cf. Witt, "Hellenism of Clement," 195–204; Osborn, "Arguments," 11. Clement favorably mentions Pythagorean practices and teachings in *Strom.* 1.1.10; 1.10.6 referring to Muses and Sirens;

to Pythagoreanism and Platonism, comparing both schools to Marcion in their hatred for being born into the world and decrying marriage.[34] In addition to this, Clement contrasts the way that humans acquire knowledge of the divine in Christianity and philosophy.[35] However, keeping with the apologetic tradition of dating Moses before the philosophers, Clement believes that Pythagoras borrowed many teachings from Moses.[36] Clement (150–215 CE) also knows of the secret nature of Pythagorean teachings, citing for example the expulsion of Hipparchus (ca. 380 BCE).[37] It is the secret nature of the Pythagorean teachings which would give an ideal context for the participation of women in Pythagoreanism as preservers and guardians of secret philosophical tradition within families. Some of Clement's references to Pythagoras (and his teachings and followers) touch on issues related to women,[38] culminating in his four references to Theano.[39]

All of Clement's references to Theano are complimentary and most of them are known by other ancient sources that will be discussed below. Clement mentions, as do other writers, that Theano was the first woman to philosophize:

1.14.62–63 includes important biographical information for Pythagoras but is lacking mention of women (cf. 6.2.27); 1.15.69–70 continues biographical information; 4.3.9 God alone is wise; 4.22.144 hope after death; 4.26.144 the Christian makes use of the Pythagorean teaching of threefold good things and their method of prayer (two references); 5.8.50 Clement sees value in the symbolic interpretation of some words by Androcydes the Pythagorean; 5.11.67 silent reflection applauded; cf. *Paed.* 1.10.94; 2.1.11.

34. *Strom.* 3.3.12–24.

35. *Strom.* 5.13.88 and 6.7.57; cf. 6.8.1. In 5.14.89 Clement challenges Pythagoras and other philosophers on their concept of matter. Pythagoras' concept of the transmigration of the soul is discarded in 2.20.114; 7.6.32.

36. *Strom.* 1.21 has some biographical information as Clement argues for the primacy of Moses; cf. 1.22.3; 2.18.79.

37. *Strom.* 5.9.57; the expulsion of Hipparchus is also known to Iambl. 17.75. Iamblichus quotes part of the letter by Lysis to Hipparchus; Diogenes Laertius also knows of this letter. Michel Tardieu demonstrates that Clement and the letter of Lysis (in Thesleff, *Pythagorean Texts*, 111–14) quote from the same source, "La Lettre à Hipparque et les réminiscences pythagoriciennes de Clément d'Alexandrie," 241–47. Cf., Burkert, *Lore and Science*, for the secret nature of the original Pythagoreans (from Aristotle), 178–79; cf., further discussion in 219–24; for the letter of Lysis, 459.

38. Clement uses Pythagoras and the Hebrew Bible to argue against the practice of exposure in 2.18.92–93 and compares the care of animal mothers to their offspring as a calling for human mothers to care for theirs; cf. 5.1.8; 5.14.

39. Clement seems to mark the beginning of a long tradition of Christian writers mentioning Theano. Eusebius writes that Pythagoras was succeeded by his wife Theano, *PE* 10.14.14; Gregory of Nazianzus, *Contra Julianum imperatorem*, 35.592.19; possibly in John of Damascus, *Passo magni martyris Artemii*, 29.14.

Reading 1 Corinthians with Philosophically Educated Women

> Δίδθμος δ' ἐν τῷ περὶ Πυθαγορικῆς φιλοσοφίας Θεανὼ τὴν Κροτωνιᾶτιν πρώτην γυνακῶν φιλοσοφῆσαι καί ποιήματα γράψαι ἱστορεῖ. Ἡμὲν οὖν Ἑλληνικὴ φιλοσοφία, ὡς μέν τινες, κατὰ περίπτωσιν ἐπήβολος τὴν ἀληθείας ἀμῇ γέ πῃ, ἀμυδρῶς δὲ καὶ οὐ πάσης, γίνεται· ὡς δὲ ἄλλοι Βούλονται, ἐκ τοῦ διαβόλου τὴν κίνησιν ἴσχει. ἔνιοι δὲ δυνάμεις τινὰς ὑποβεβηκυίας ἐμπνεῦσαι τὴν πᾶσαν φιλοσοφίαν ὑπειλήσιν.

> Didymus, however, in his work On the Pythagorean Philosophy, relates that Theano of Crotona was the first woman who cultivated philosophy and composed poems. The Hellenic philosophy then, according to some, apprehended the truth accidentally, dimly, partially; as others will have it, was set a-going by the devil. Several suppose that certain powers, descending from heaven, inspired the whole of philosophy.[40]

Clement (150–215 CE) appeals to Theano alongside several other philosophers as having a grasp on the truth of the afterlife in 4.7.44, "Θεανὼ γὰρ ἡ Πυθαγορικὴ γράφει· ἣν γὰρ <ἂν> τῷ ὄντι τοῖς κακοῖς εὐωχία ὁ βίος πονηρευσαμένοις· ἔπειτα τελευῶσιν, εἰή ψυχή, ἕρμαιον ὁ θάνατο," "For the Pythagorean Theano writes, 'Life were indeed a feast to the wicked, who, having done evil, then die; were not the soul immortal, death would be a godsend.'"[41]

In his third reference to Theano, Clement points to many great women who were popular in Christian traditions—Judith and Esther—as well as Greek (female) philosophers, poets, and artists:

> οὐχὶ Θεανὼ μὲν ἡ Πυθαγορικὴ εἰς τοσοῦτον ἧκεν φιλοσοφίας ὡς πρὸς τὸν περιέργως ἀπιδόντα καὶ εἰπόντα "καλὸς ὁ πῆχυσ" "ἀλλ' οὐ δημόσιος" ἀποκρίνασθαι τῆς αὐτῆς φέρεται σεμνότητος κἀκεῖνο τὸ ἀπόφθεγμα· ἐρωτηθεῖσα γάρ, ποσταία γυνὴ ἀπὸ ἀνδρὸς εἰς τὸ θεσμοφόριον κάτεισιν, "ἀπὸ μὲν ἰδίου μὲν ἰδίου καὶ παραχρῆμα" ἔφη, ἀπὸ δὲ τοῦ ἀλλοτρίου οὐδεπώποτε." ναὶ μὴν καὶ Θεμιστὼ ἡ Ζωΐλου ἡ Λαμψακηνὴ ἡ Λεοντέως γυνὴ τοῦ Λαμψακηνοῦ τὰ Ἐπικούρεια ἐφιλοσόφει

---

40. *Strom.* 1.16.80 (*ANF*, Roberts-Donaldson). Diogenes Laertius, Porphyry, and Iamblichus also use Didymus of Alexandria—a first-century writer—as a source for Pythagoras and Pythagoreans. For the fragments, see Schmidt, *Didymi Chalcenteri*. Cf. Mansfeld and Runia, *Aetiana*; Dickey, *Ancient Greek Scholarship*; Pfeiffer, *History of Classical Scholarship*, 274–79.

41. I have been unable to locate another ancient author who preserves this tradition. Cf. *Strom.* 4.8 (translation from *ANF*), where Clement argues that women should philosophize just like men, although he asserts the superiority of men in all things. Clement mentions two exemplary Pythagoreans in his introduction to this section.

καθάπερ Μυῖα ἡ Θεανοῦς θυγάτηρ τὰ Πυθαγόρεια καὶ Ἀριγώτη ἡ τὰ περὶ Διονύσου γραψαμένη.

Did not Theano the Pythagorean make such progress in philosophy, that to him who looked intently at her, and said, "Your arm is beautiful," she answered "Yes, but it is not public." Characterized by the same propriety, there is also reported the following reply. When asked when a woman after being with her husband attends the Thesmophoria, said, "From her own husband at once, from a stranger never." Themisto too, of Lampsacus, the daughter of Zoilus, the wife of Leontes of Lampsacus, studied the Epicurean philosophy, as Myia the daughter of Theano the Pythagorean, and Arignote, who wrote the history of Dionysius.[42]

Theano's exposed arm, her wit, and her modesty were previously highlighted by Plutarch (46–120 CE). He uses the first teaching to exhort Eurydice to remain silent outside of the home, having her speech modestly covered like her body in *Advice to the Bride and Groom*:

Ἡ Θεανὼ παρέφηνε τὴν χεῖρα περιβαλλομένη τὸ ἱμάτιον. εἰπόντος δέ τινος "καλὸς ὁ πῆχυς," "ἀλλ' οὐ δημόσιος," ἔφη. δεῖ δὲ μὴ μόνον τὸν πῆχυν ἀλλὰ μηδὲ τὸν λόγον δημόσιον εἶναι τῆς σώφρονος, καὶ τὴν φωνὴν ὡς ἀπογύμνωσιν αἰδεῖσθαι καὶ φυλάττεσθαι πρὸς τοὺς ἐκτός· ἐνορᾶται γὰρ αὐτῇ καὶ πάθος καὶ ἦθος καὶ διάθεσις λαλούσης.

Theano, in putting on her cloak about her, exposed her arm. Somebody exclaimed, "A lovely arm." "But not for public," said she. Not only the arm of the virtuous woman, but her speech as well, ought to be not for the public, and she ought to be modest and guarded about saying anything in the hearing of outsiders, since it is an exposure of herself; for in her talk can be seen her feelings, character, and disposition.[43]

For Plutarch (ca. 46–120 CE), the use of philosophy by women is understood as both pragmatic (for modesty and practical living), as well as for the enrichment of the soul (e.g., philosophical reflection). Her husband,

---

42. *Strom.* 4.19.122 (ANF, Roberts-Donaldson).

43. Plut. *Mor.* 142c (Babbitt, LCL). The shortening of the quote is insignificant. Plutarch usually relied on his imperfect memory for quoting sources; Helmbold and O'Neil, *Plutarch's Quotations*, ix; John Ferguson knows that it appears in Plutarch, but offers no further reflection, in *Clement*, 89. None of Clement's quotations of Theano receive treatment in Lilla, *Clement*. I could not find detailed treatment of it in John Patrick, although he does mention Clement's attitude towards women in *Clement*, 170.

Reading 1 Corinthians with Philosophically Educated Women

Pollianus is to seek teachers outside of the home and to bring to his wife both what he thinks that she needs *and* what interests *her*.[44]

> Καὶ σὺ μὲν ὥραν ἔχων ἤδη φιλοσοφεῖν τοῖς μετ' ἀποδείξεως καὶ κατασκευῆς λεγομένοις ἐπικόσμει τὸ ἦθος, ἐντυγχάνων καὶ πλησιάζων τοῖς ὠφελοῦσι· τῇ δὲ γυναικὶ πανταχόθεν τὸ χρήσιμον συνάγω ὥσπερ αἱ μέλιτται καὶ φέρων αὐτὸς ἐν σεαυτῷ μεταδίδου καὶ προσδιαλέγου, φίλους αὐτῇ ποιῶν καὶ συνήθεις τῶν λόγων τοὺς ἀρίστους. πατὴρ μὲν γάρ ἐσσι αὐτῇ καὶ πότνια μήτηρ ἠδὲ κασίγνητος οὐχ ἧττον δὲ σεμνὸν ἀκοῦσαι γαμετῆς λεγούσης ἄνερ. ἀτὰρ σύ μοί ἐσσι καθηγητὴς καὶ φιλόσοφος καὶ διδάσκαλος τῶν καλλίστων καὶ θειοτάτων. τὰ τοιαῦτα μαθήματα πρῶτον ἀφίστησι τῶν ἀτόπων τὰς γυναῖκας: αἰσχυνθήσεται γὰρ ὀρχεῖσθαι γυνὴ γεωμετρεῖν μανθάνουσα, καὶ φαρμάκων ἐπῳδὰς οὐ προσδέξεται τοῖς Πλάτωνος ἐπᾳδομένη λόγοις καὶ τοῖς Ξενοφῶντος. ἂν δέ τις ἐπαγγέληται καθαιρεῖν τὴν σελήνην, γελάσεται τὴν ἀμαθίαν καὶ τὴν ἀβελτερίαν τῶν ταῦτα πειθομένων ἀγυναικῶν, ἀστρολογίας μὴ ἀνηκόως ἔχουσα καὶ περὶ Ἀγλαονίκης ἀκηκουῖα τῆς Ἡγήτορος τοῦ Θεσσαλοῦ θυγατρὸς ὅτι τῶν ἐκλειπτικῶν ἔμπειρος οὖσα πανσελήνων καὶ προειδυῖα τὸν χρόνον, ἐν ᾧ συμβαίνει τὴν σελήνην ὑπὸ τῆς σκιᾶς ἁλίσκεσθαι, παρεκρούετο καὶ συνέπειθε τὰς γυναῖκας ὡς αὐτὴ καθαιροῦσα τὴν σελήνην.

> Besides, Pollianus, you already possess sufficient maturity to study philosophy, and I beg that you will beautify your character with the aid of discourses which are attended by logical demonstration and mature deliberation, seeking the company and instruction of teachers who will help you. And for your wife you must collect from every source what is useful, as do the bees, and carrying it within your own self impart it to her, and then discuss it with her, and make the best of these doctrines her favourite and familiar themes. For to her, *"Thou art a father and precious-loved mother, Yea, and a brother as well."* No less ennobling is it for a man among other things hear his wife say, "My dear husband, Nay, *but thou art to me* guide, philosopher, and teacher in all that is most lovely and divine." Studies of this sort, in the first place, divert women from all untoward conduct; for a woman studying geometry will be ashamed to be a dancer, and she will not swallow any beliefs in magic charms while she is under the charm of Plato's or Xenophon's words. And if anybody professes power to pull down the moon from the sky, she will laugh at the ignorance and stupidity

---

44. In the case that the husband is younger and marries an older, more educated woman, she is to teach him, *Mor.* 754d; cf. Clark, "Roman Women," 193–212.

of women who believe these things, inasmuch as she herself is not unschooled in astronomy, and has read in the books about Aglaonice, the daughter of Hegetor of Thessaly, and how she, through being thoroughly acquainted with the periods of the full moon when it is subject to eclipse, and, knowing beforehand the time when the moon was due to be overtaken by the earth's shadow, imposed upon the women, and made them all believe that she was drawing down the moon.[45]

After citing a number of exemplary women, Plutarch (ca. 46–120 CE) asserts that she is to learn Plato and Xenophon in order to help her live according to reason instead of being attracted to dancing or magic (145c). Plutarch indicates that Eurydice learned some philosophy at home from her parents before she was married and she is to continue that education under the direction of her husband. As a married woman, she is to adorn herself with the teachings of Theano, heroic women, and Cornelia (who educated her sons) rather than with jewels (145e).[46]

The fourth reference in Clement (ca. 150–217 CE) is very well known. It is extant only as its *chreia* form and could have as its source an original moral teaching from Theano herself.[47] This teaching was identified as a *chreia* by the ancient rhetorician Aelius Theon (early 2nd CE).

> ἡ δὲ πυσματικὴ τοιαύτη ἐστίν, οἷον Θεανὼ ἡ Πυθαγορικὴ φιλόσοφος ἐρωτηθεῖσα ὑπό τινος, ποσταία γυνὴ ἀπ' ἀνδρὸς καθαρὰ εἰς τὸ θεσμοφορῖον κάτεισιν, εἶπεν, ἀπὸ μὲν τοῦ ἰδίου παραχρῆμα, ἀπὸ δὲ τοῦ ἀλλοτρίου οὐδέποτε.
>
> The chreia with an inquiry is like this, for example: Theano, the Pythagorean philosopher, on being asked by someone how long after intercourse with a man does a woman go in purity to the Thesmorphorion, said: "With your own, immediately; with another's, never."[48]

---

45. Plut. *Mor.* 145b–c (Babbitt, LCL).

46. The picture painted here—that women learned philosophy from their fathers or husbands—is not intended to be one sided. It is my understanding that wealthy women, particularly widows, were well positioned in the first century to do whatever they wanted and were therefore certainly able to find teachers (whether male or female) willing to come into their home and teach them and their children.

47. For a detailed study on *chreia*, see Hock and O'Neil, *Chreia*; for the conversion of quotes into *chreia* in ancient epistles, see the excellent discussion and examples in Stirewalt, *Ancient Greek Epistolography*, 43–64.

48. Text and translation is from Hock and O'Neil, *Chreia*. Cf. James Butts' dissertation, "Progymnasmata," 190–92; another critical text is available in Spengel, *Rhetores Graeci*, 2:59–130.

Reading 1 Corinthians with Philosophically Educated Women

Significantly, everywhere the quotation appears in antiquity except for Iamblichus, a question is part of the formula. In Clement (150–215 CE, *Stom.* 4.19.122), Aelius Theon (fl. mid 1st CE, 98.3), and Diogenes Laertius (fl. 3rd c. CE, Diog. Laert. 8.22) this teaching of Theano always is in the form of the question. The teaching appears in Iamblichus *VP* 132,[49] but he is uncertain who said it, which may explain why there is no question. This consistency demonstrates the role of Theano as a wise-person: one to whom questions are asked and wisdom is derived. In Aelius Theon, Theano is quoted along with the renowned Greek philosophers Plato, Socrates, and Diogenes the Cynic, not to mention Pythagoras himself (the quote from Pythagoras is not in close proximity to Theano). Aelius Theon remembers Theano not as the student, wife, or daughter of Pythagoras, but simply as a Pythagorean philosopher.

Biographers of Pythagoras: More Teachings of Theano

The first-century and Pythagorean[50] and neo-Pythagorean[51] traditions concerning women in Pythagoreanism are certainly related to the memory of Pythagoras himself as reflected both in his biographers and other ancient references. Pythagoras had many biographers, but only three are largely extant: the biographies of Diogenes Laertius (fl.c. 3rd c. CE); Iamblichus (280–333 CE), Porphry (233–306 CE).[52] Many other biographies existed in ancient times and all extant biographers preserve important traditions related to women in Pythagoreanism and obviously depend on more ancient sources. Most important is Aristotle's lost work on Pythagoras. J. A. Philip argues from the fragments that Aristotle actually wrote two monographs on Pythagoras.[53] Philip also introduces the possibility that the root material concerning Pythagoras in the biographers could have Aristotle's monographs as their ultimate source.

Pythagorean women were leading characters in Old Comedy due to peculiar dietary habits according to Athenaeus (fl. late 2nd CE).[54] Diogenes Laertius (fl. 3rd CE) preserves several traditions regarding Pythagorean

---

49. Text and translation for Iamblichus is from John Dillon, *De Vita Pythagorica*.

50. As previously identified and discussed above in Cicero (106–43 BCE), Seneca (1–65 CE), and Plutarch (46–120 CE).

51. As preserved in the neo-Pythagorean corpus which includes letters attributed to women.

52. Photius (ca. 820–c. 891 CE) is also available but much later than our time period.

53. Philip, "Aristotle's Monograph," 194; cf. Philip, "Aristotle's Sources," 251–65.

54. Burkett, *Lore and Science*, 198.

women. He notes that the involvement of women in Pythagoreanism was satirized by Cratinus in the *Pythagorizing Woman* (the only extant fragment of this play is Diog. Laert. 8.37).[55] Diogenes (fl. 3rd c. CE) says that Pythagoras entrusted his teachings to his daughter Damo, exhorting her not to make the teachings public (Diog. Laert. 8.42), citing the letter of Lysis to Hipparchus as his source. Damo said that she was faithful to her father's wishes because "she was only a woman." This tradition is apparently ancient and popular. An extant letter of Lysis to Hipparchus in Thesleff does not mention Theano, but says that Pythagoras entrusted his teachings to Damo and she in turn taught them to her daughter Bistala.[56] According to Diogenes, Pythagoras's son Telauges succeeded his father but wrote nothing. Pythagoras's wife Theano, on the other hand, did write and is remembered by her philosophy with the familiar teaching:

> Ἦν καὶ Τηλαύγης υἱὸς αὐτοῖς, ὃς καὶ διεδέξατο τὸν πατέρα καὶ κατά τινας Ἐμπεδοκλέους καθηγήσατο· Ἱππόβοτός γέ τοί φησι λέγειν Ἐμπεδοκλέα, Τήλαυγες, κλυτὲ κοῦρε Θεανοῦς Πυθαγόρεώ τε. σύγγραμμα δὲ [φέρεται] τοῦ Τηλαύγους οὐδέν, τῆς δὲ μητρὸς αὐτοῦ Θεανοῦς τινα. ἀλλὰ καί φασιν αὐτὴν ἐρωτηθεῖσαν ποσταία γυνὴ ἀπ' ἀνδρὸς καθαρεύει, φάναι, ἀπὸ δὲ τοῦ ἰδίου παραχρῆμα, ἀπὸ δὲ τοῦ ἀλλοτρίου οὐδέποτε. τῇ δὲ πρὸς τὸν ἴδιον ἄνδρα μελλούσῃ πορεύεσθαι παῄνει ἅμα τοῖς ἐνδύμασι καὶ τὴν αἰσχύνην ἀποτίθεσθαι, ἀνισταμένην τε ἅμ' αὐτοῖσιν ἀναλαμβάνειν. ἐρωτηθεῖσα, ποῖα; ἔφη, ταῦτα δι' ἃ γυνὴ κέκλημαι.

> They also had a son Telauges, who succeeded his father and, according to some, was Empedocles's instructor. At all events Hippobotus makes Empedocles say: *Telauges, famed son of Theano and Pythagoras*. Telauges wrote nothing, so far as we know, but his mother Theano wrote a few things. Further, a story is told that being asked how many days it was before a woman becomes pure after intercourse, she replied, "With her own husband at once, with another man never." And she advised a woman going in to her own husband to put off her shame with her clothes, and

---

55. There were two plays in the classical period, both are not extant, entitled *Pythagorizousa*, one by Cratinus (see in *TLG* Kock frag. 6; Mieneke Pyth. 1) and one by Alexis (pokes fun at the Pythagorean diet, cf. frags. 196–99 Kock; Pyth. 1–3 in Mieneke). Taylor also writes that Philochorus also dedicated a work to Pythagorean women according to FGrHist 328 T 1, *Pythagoreans*, 33. However, I think that Taylor has confused his citation because I cannot verify from *FGrHist* 328 T 1 that it has anything to do with Pythagorean women; cf. Bliquez, "Didymus Papyrus," 356.

56. Lysis, *Ep.* 114.5.

on leaving him to put it on again along with them. Asked, "Put on what?" she replied, "What makes me to be called a woman."[57]

Diogenes also says that Hermippus writes that as Pythagoras was dying, men sent their wives to him to learn his philosophy and they were known as the "Pythagorean women" (Diog. Laert. 8.1.41).

Iamblichus (245–325 CE) presents a Pythagoras who is persuaded by his wife Theano (or another woman) to end marital infidelity in Croton.

> ἀπαλλάξαι δὲ λέγεται τοὺς Κροτωνιάτας καὶ τῶν παλλακίδων καὶ καθόλου τῆς πρὸς τὰς ἀνεγγύους γυναῖκας ὁμιλίας. πρὸς Δεινὼ γὰρ τὴν Βροντίνου γυναῖκα, τῶν Πυθαγορείων ἑνός, οὖσαν σοφήν τε καὶ περιττὴν τὴν ψυχήν, ἧς ἐστὶ καὶ τὸ καλὸν καὶ περίβλεπτον ῥῆμα, τὸ τὴν γυναῖκα δεῖν θύειν αὐθημερὸν ἀνισταμένην ἀπὸ τοῦ ἑαυτῆς ἀνδρός, ὅ τινες εἰς Θεανὼ ἀναφέρουσι, πρὸς δὴ ταύτην παρελθούσας τὰς τῶν Κροτωνιατῶν γυναῖκας παρακαλέσαι περὶ τοῦ συμπεῖσαι τὸν Πυθαγόραν διαλεχθῆναι παρὶ τῆς πρὸς αὐτὰς σωφροσύνης τοῖς ἀνδράσιν αὐτῶν. ὃ δὴ καὶ συμβῆναι, καὶ τῆς γυναικὸς ἐπαγγειλαμένης καὶ τοῦ Πυθαγόρου διαλεχθέντος καὶ τῶν Κροτωνιατῶν πισθέντων ἀναιρεθῆναι παντάπασι τὴν τότε ἐπιπολάζουσαν ἀκολασίαν.

> He is said also to have freed the Crotoniates entirely from concubines and from intercourse with unwedded women. For to Deino, wife of Brontinus, one of the Pythagoreans, a woman of wise and exceptional spirit, to whom also belongs a saying noble and admired by all: "the wife ought to sacrifice on the very day she arose from sleep with her own husband." (which saying some ascribe to Theano); to her, then, the wives of the Crotoniates came, and requested her to join them in persuading Pythagoras to talk about the chastity due them for their own husbands. This, in fact, came about: the women passed on the message, Pythagoras spoke to the Crotoniates, and the were persuaded to altogether abolish the licentiousness then prevalent.[58]

It is important that Iamblichus has Pythagoras teach marital fidelity, something that philosophers, ancient law, and practice are divided on according to time period and geography. It is well known that the prevailing view in the ancient world from the point of view of law and some moralists was that

---

57. Diog. Laert. 8.43 (Hicks, LCL). The shame of a married woman appearing naked before a man other than her husband is discussed in Cairns, "Off with Her ΑΙΔΩΣ," 78–83.

58. *VP* 27.132.

Women in Philosophy

the wife had to be chaste in a marriage, but the husband could be free in his sexual activity.[59] Indeed, the so-called neo-Pythagoreans present separate views on this issue.[60]

Iamblichus (245–325 CE) preserves the tradition mentioned above that Pythagoras left his writings to his daughter Damo who entrusted the writings to her daughter Bitale.[61] Telauges is unknown to Iamblichus's source.[62] Iamblichus tells us that due to persecutions, Pythagorean philosophy was passed on from parents to children, and daughters and wives were crucial to this process.[63] Iamblichus also remarks on the education of Pythagoras's daughter:

> γήμαντα δὲ τὴν γεννηθεῖσαν αὐτῷ θυγατέρα, μετὰ ταῦτα δὲ Μένωνι τῷ Κροτωνιάτῃ συνοικήσασσαν, ἀγαεῖν οὕτως, ὥστε παρθένον μὲν οὖσαν ἡγεῖσθαι τῶν χορῶν, γυναῖκα δὲ γενομένην πρώτην προσέναι τοῖς βωμοῖς.

> "Also when he married, he so educated the daughter that was born to him, and who afterwards married the Crotonian Meno, that while unmarried she was a choir-leader, while as wife she held the first place among those who worshipped at altars."[64]

Iamblichus crowns his *De Vita Pythagorica* with a list of 218 male and 17 female Pythagorean philosophers.[65]

> Πυθαγορίδες δὲ γυναῖκες αἱ ἐπιφανέσταται· Τιμύχα γυνὴ ἡ Μυλλία τοῦ Κροτωνιάτου, Φιλτὺς θυγάτηρ Θεόφριος τοῦ Κροτωνιάτου, Βυνδάκου ἀδελφή, Ὀκκελὼ καὶ Ἐκκελὼ ἀδελφαὶ Ὀκκέλω καὶ Ὀκκίλω τῶν Λευκανῶν, Χειλωνὶς θυγάτηρ Χείλωνος τοῦ Λακεδαιμονίου, Κρατησίκλεια Λάκαινα γυνὴ Κλεάνορος τοῦ Λακεδαιμονίου Θεανὼ γυνὴ τοῦ Μεταποντίνου Βροτίνου, Μυῖα γυνὴ Μίλωνος τοῦ Κροτωνιάτου, Λασθένεια Ἀρκάδισσα,

---

59. See the extensive treatment for ancient Greece in Sue Blundell, *Women in Ancient Greece*; cf. Moore, *Sex and the Second-Best City*, 133–36; for generalizations of the Roman period, see Foley and Fantham, *Women in the Classical World*, 294–306; some detailed interpretation of Roman law is available in Rousselle, *Porneia*, 78–92; the double standard for adultery is explored in Roman literature by Langlands, *Sexual Morality*, 237–46; cf. the punishments for adultery in Rome by Skinner, *Sexuality*, 208.

60. Balch, "Neopythagorean Moralists," 380–411.

61. *VP* 28.146.

62. *VP* 163n23.

63. *VP* 253. Cf. Hallett, *Fathers and Daughters*; Setälä and Berg, *Women, Wealth and Power*; Gardner, *Women in Roman Law*; Rawson, *Family*.

64. Iambl. *VP* 30.170.5 (Dillon and Hershbell, 185).

65. For notes and bibliography on this list, see Burkett, *Lore and Science*, 105n40; Pomery, *Spartan Women*, 11. Iamblichus's student Sopater has a similar list in *Photius*, 161; Walz, *Rhetores Graeci*, vol. 8.

Reading 1 Corinthians with Philosophically Educated Women

Ἀβροτέλεια Ἀβροτέλους θυγάτηρ τοῦ Ταραντίινου, Ἐχεκράτεια Φλιασία, Τυρσηνὶς Συβαρῖτις, Πεισιρρόδη Ταραντινίς, Θεάδουσα Λάκαινα, Βοιὼ Ἀργεία, Βαβελύκα Ἀργεία, Κλεαίχμα ἀδελφὴ Αὐτοχαρὶ δα τοῦ Λάκωνος.

The most illustrious Pythagorean women are Timycha the wife of Myllias the Crotonian; Phyltis the daughter of Theophrius the Crotonian; Byndacis the sister of Ocellus; Lucanians; Chilonis the daughter of Chilon the Lacedenonian; Cratesiclea the Lacedemonian the wife of the Lacedemonian Cleanor; Theane the wife of Brontinus of Metapontum; Mya, the wife of Milon the Crotonian; Lasthenia the Arcadian; Abrotelia the daughter of Abroteles the Tarentine; Echecratia the Phliasian; Tyrsenis the Sybarite; Pisirrhonde the Tarentine; Nisleadusa, the Lacedemonian; Byro the Argive; Babelyma the Argive, and Cleaechma the sister of Autocharidas the Lacedemonian.[66]

Nine of these women have their husbands or family members listed with them as philosophers: Tmycha, Phyltis, Byndacis, Chilonis, Cratesiclea, Theane, Mya, Abrotelia, and Cleaechma. Six are listed strictly on their own merit: Lucanians, Lasthenia, Echecratia, Tyrsenis, Pisirrhonde, Nisleadusa, Byro, and Babelyma. All of these women are known to us only through Iamblichus. Because he gives nothing more than names, and they are available nowhere else, it is unfortunately impossible to do anything but note that he presents the list. The most Iamblichus (ca. 245–325 BCE) can tell us, in my opinion, is that neo-Pythagoreans of his day and recent memory had been friendly to the idea that women played an important role in the history of that school.

The entrusting of writings to family rather than friends may indicate that Pythagoreans either in the time of Iamblichus in particular or possibly Pythagoras himself were not integrated into their communities. This lack of integration would be caused by the secret nature of Pythagorean teachings, the strange diet,[67] and displacement caused by wars and changing rulers. All of these factors would cause alienation from friends and motivate the Pythagoreans to pass on their teachings strictly to students (i.e., members of the community) and especially family members. The production of texts within families is a deviation from the production of literature in the first century by Cicero, Pliny the Younger, and Maecenas, who were integrated into patronage relationships.[68] We see the alienation

---

66. Iambl. *VP* 36.258 (Dillon and Hershbell, 259).

67. Seneca himself experienced alienation due to his meatless diet which was inspired by Pythagorean teachings, *Ep.* 108.

68. Starr, "Circulation," 213–23.

of Pythagoreans from their communities due to their secrecy and diet in Iamblichus,[69] where an expectant mother, Timycha, bites off her tongue rather than share Pythagorean philosophy. Iamblichus concludes, "οὕτως δυσσυγκατάθετοι πρὸς τὰς ἐξωτερικὰς φιλίας, εἰ καὶ βασιλικαὶ τυγάνοιν," "So slow were they to make friendships outside the school, even if they were friendships with kings."[70]

Porphyry (234–305 CE) indicates that the magistrates of Croton ordered the boys and girls and women to learn from Pythagoras.[71] Theano is particularly noted as an illustrious Crotonian woman, but Porphyry does not include any of her teachings. Porphry writes that an association of women was formed for the purpose of learning from Pythagoras (καὶ γυναικῶν σύλλογος αὐτῷ κατασκευάσθη) and they also learned his philosophy alongside men and children. Pythagoras's teachings concerning reincarnation and the secrecy that he enjoined on his followers is also noted (19).

As late as the sixteenth century CE, the Pythagorizing women are remembered in Holinshed's Chronicles (chapter 10, published 1586):

> But sith those bookes are now perished, and the most of the said Ilands remaine vtterlie vnknowen, euen to our owne selues (for who is able in our time to say where is Glota, Hiucrion, Etta, Iduna, Armia, Aesarea, Barsa, Isiandium, Icdelis, Xantisma, Indelis, Siata, Ga. Andros or Edros, Siambis, Xanthos, Ricnea, Menapia, whose names onelie are left in memorie by ancient writers, but I saie their places not so much as heard of in our daies) I meane (God willing) to set downe so manie of them with their commodities, as I do either know by Leland, or am otherwise instructed of by such as are of credit.

Women Associated with Socrates and the Academy

There are three women that Socrates (469–399 BCE) claims as his teachers: Phaenerete, Diotima, and Aspasia of Miletus.[72] In an argument concerning

---

69. Burkert discusses problems in the earliest Pythagorean communities in *Lore and Science*, 106.

70. *VP* 31.192–94 (Dillon and Hershbell, 201). Note the friendship/patronage language in the passage.

71. Porph. *VP* 18–19.

72. Cheryl Glenn discusses the wide variety of speculations concerning Aspasia's identity in *Rhetoric Retold*, 47–48; Mary Ellen Waithe calls her "a rhetorician and a member of the Periclean philosophic circle" in *Women Philosophers*, 75; and Susan Cole writes only of Aspasia's intellectual influence and measure of literacy in "Could Greek

pregnancy and birth, Socrates claims to have authority based on training in midwifery that he received from his mother, Phaenerete.[73] Unlike other traditions concerning ancient philosophically educated women (such as Perictione[74] in the neo-Pythagorean pseudepigraphon), the teachings of Diotima and Aspasia are connected with their earliest appearance in the tradition.[75] Diotima gained fame in Socrates's representation of her in Plato's *Symposium*.

Aspasia of Miletus is remembered as an apt rhetorician by Plato (429–347 BCE), Xenophon (430–354 BCE), Cicero (106–43 BCE), Plutarch (50–120 CE), and Athenaeus (fl. 200 CE).[76] In Plato's *Menexenus*, Socrates claimed to have learned rhetoric from Aspasia who taught many others, including Pericles (235e). In the first century, Plutarch takes this situation as historical (*Per.* 24.7). The sexual availability of the male philosophers with one another and their students could have contributed to the ideal of the educated *hetaira*.[77] The overwhelming scholarly consensus is that Aspasia was a prostitute and ran a brothel in Athens.[78] However, Anthony J. Podlecki has demonstrated that the evidence for this is not very strong: the argument is based on sources that either "tell the truth in jest" or are openly attacking the Socratic circle by casting it in terms of sexual disrepute.[79] It is significant that Aspasia is not an Athenian subject to the strict ideals of the secluded and chaste wife. Tradition indicates that somehow she read Plato and came to Athens to learn from him and subsequently started her own school for girls, and at the same time the school was considered a brothel. Of equal importance is the Platonic concept that women should be held in common and rule of the city should be done by wise men and women—this sexual avail-

---

Women Read and Write?," 225.

73. Pl. *Tht.* 149a.

74. George Boas discusses the sources regarding the life of Plato, in "Fact and Legend," 439–57; Pomeroy, *Women in Hellenistic Egypt*, 68; Haskins, "Pythagorean Women," 316.

75. Neumann, "Diotima's Concept of Love," 33–59; White, "Love and Beauty," 149–57; Rorty, "Diotima,"147; Pl. *Sym.* 208. Diotima's speech is from 210d–212a. Diotima may be a real person or a rhetorical creation of Plato. Her existence, however, cannot be dismissed on the basis that women did not participate in philosophy. The best explanation in my opinion is that she is a fictional character based on an actual female philosopher, but there is no conclusive evidence for either side of the issue.

76. Xen. *Oec.* 3.14–15; Pl. *Menex.* 235e; Ar. *Ach.* 526; Plut. *Per.* 24; *Suid.* 1.387.2.15–24 (no. 4202) = "Aspasia," PG 117, 1230; Theodoret, *Therapeutike* 1.17.

77. Kurke, "Inventing the 'Hetaira,'" 106–50.

78. Madeline M. Henry is the most ardent champion of the point of view that Aspasia is completely lost in the rhetoric of men (*Prisoner of History*).

79. Podlecki, *Pericles*, 110.

ability can certainly lead to the conceptualization of Aspasia's school as a brothel. The atmosphere of philosophical discussion in Athens encouraged and glorified sexual activity between men and their companions—be they male or female students.[80] The appearance of women in public in classical Athens sexualizes the woman, to the point that Aspasia and her prostitutes were seen as the cause of war. The earliest writer that says Aspasia ran a brothel is in Antisthenes (444–365 BCE), *Acharnians* 524, and he makes a similar accusation of Pericles's son, Xanthipppos, who lived with Archestratos, who "plied a trade similar to that of women in the cheaper brothels."[81] Considering these points, it is best to remember Aspasia as the beloved wife of Pericles, which may conflict with her reputation as a courtesan.[82] Her reputation as a courtesan may well be the result of her public activity in the Socratic circle, which gave men the opportunity to over sexualize her memory. Athenaeus (fl. late 2nd CE) writes of Aspasia:

> καὶ Ἀσπασία δὲ ἡ Σωκρατικὴ ἐνεπορεύετο πλήθη καλῶν γυναικῶν, καὶ ἐπλήθυνεν ἀπὸ τῶν ταύτης ἑταιρίδων ἡ Ἑλλάς, ὡς καὶ ὁ χαρίεις Ἀριστοφάνης παρασημαίνεται, λέγων τὸν [Πελοποννησιακὸν πόλεμον] ὅτι Περικλῆς διὰ τὸν Ἀσπασίας ἔρωτα καὶ τὰς ἁρπασθείσας ἀπ' αὐτῆς θεραπαίνας ὑπὸ Μεγαρέων ἀνερρίπισεν τὸ δεινόν.

> And Aspasia, the friend of Socrates, imported great numbers of beautiful women, and Greece was entirely filled with her courtesans; as that witty writer Aristophanes relates [Acharn 524], saying that the Peloponnesian war was excited by Pericles, [570] on account of his love for Aspasia, and on account of the girls who had been carried away from her by the Megarians.[83]

According to Xenophon (430–354 BCE), Socrates learned about marriage from Aspasia:

> Δι' οὐχ ὥς ποτε ἐγὼ Ἀσπασίας ἤκουσα· ἔφη γὰρ τὰς ἀγαθὰς προμνηστρίδας μετὰ μὲν ἀληθείας τἀγαθὰ διαγγελλύσας δεινὰς

---

80. Cantarella, *Bisexuality*, 17–93; Williams *Roman Homosexuality*, 62–95; Halperin, *History of Homosexuality*; Nussbaum, "Eros and Ethical Norms," 55–87; Sissa, *Sex and Sexuality*, 62–69.

81. Podlecki, *Pericles*.

82. Fornara and Samons, *Athens*; Tracy, *Pericles*, 97.

83. Ath. 13.25.24 (translation in *Deipnosophists*, trans. Yonge). She is also mentioned in Plut. *Per.* 24.2; Arist. *Ach.* 527; Thuc. 3.19; D.S. 12; Pl. *Menex.* 235e. A herm is in the Sala delle Muse, Vatican (inv. 272) with Ἀσπασία inscribed on the lower shaft, and due to the unlikely location of the inscription and the period clothing, the statue is dated in the fifth century BCE. Richer, *Portraits*, pl. 64 (p. 99).

Reading 1 Corinthians with Philosophically Educated Women

εἶναι συνάγειν ἀνθρώπους εἰς κηδείαν, ψευδομένας δ᾽οὐκ ἐθέλειν ἐπαινεῖν· τοὺς γὰρ ἐξαπατηθέντας ἅμα μισεῖν ἀλλήλους τε καὶ τὴν προμησαμένην. ἃ δὴ καὶ ἐγὼ πεισθεὶς ὀρθῶς ἔχειν ἡγοῦμαι οὐκ ἐξεῖναί μοι περὶ σοῦ λέγειν ἐπαινοῦντι οὐδὲν ὅ τι ἂν μὴ ἀληθεύω.

"Not so indeed: I can quote Aspasia against you. She once told me that good matchmakers are successful in making marriages only when the good reports they carry to and fro are true; false reports she would not recommend, for the victims of deception hate one another and the matchmaker too. I am convinced that this is sound, and so I think it is not open to me to say anything in your praise that I can't say truthfully."[84]

And on the relationships between husbands and wives, Socrates says:

Οἷς δὲ σὺ λέγεις ἀγαθὰς εἶναι γυναῖκας, ὦ Σώκρατες, ἦ αὐτοὶ ταύτας ἐπαίδευσσαν; Οὐδὲν οἷον τὸ ἐπισκοπεῖσθαι. συστήσν δέ σοι ἐγὼ καὶ Ἀσπασίαν, ἣ ἐπιστημονέστερον ἐμοῦ σοι ταῦτα πάντα ἐπιδείξει. νομίζω δὲ γυναῖκα κοινωνὸν ἀγαθὴν οἴκου οὖσαν πάνυ ἀντίρροπον εἶναι τῷ ἀνδρὶ ἐπὶ τὸ ἀγαθόν. ἔρχεται μὲν γὰρ εἰς τὴν οἰκίαν διὰ τῶν τοῦ ἀνδρὸς πράξεων τὰ κτήματα ὡς ἐπὶ τὸ πολύ, δαπανᾶται δὲ διὰ τῶω τῆς γυναικὸς ταμιευμάτων τὰ πλεῖστα· καὶ εὖ μὲν τούτων γιγνομένων αὔξονται οἱ οἶκοι, κακῶς δὲ τούτων πραττομένων οἱ οἶκοι μειοῦνται. οἶμαι δέ σοι καὶ τῶν ἄλλων ἐπιστημῶν τοὺς ἀξίως λόγου ἑκάστην ἐργαζομένους ἔχειν ἄω ἐπιδεῖξαί σοι, εἴ τι προσδεῖσθαι νομίζεις.

"But what of the husbands who, as you say, have good wives, Socrates? Did they train them themselves?" "There's nothing like investigation. I will introduce Aspasia to you, and she will explain the whole matter to you with more knowledge than I possess." "I think that the wife who is a good partner in the household contributes just as much as her husband to its good; because the incomings for the most part are the result of the husband's exertions, but the outgoings are controlled mostly by the wife's dispensation. If both do their part well, the estate is increased; if they act incompetently, it is diminished. If you think you want to know about other branches of knowledge, I fancy I can show you people who acquit themselves creditably in any one of them."[85]

---

84. Xen. *Mem.* 2.6.36 (Marchant, LCL).
85. Xen. *Oec.* 3.15 (Marchant, LCL).

Socrates quotes Aspasia here in a discussion with his friends concerning the nature of marriage. Socrates has Aspasia say that the wife is just as important as the husband in a marriage: the wife is in control of the outgoings of the house, and the incoming is the responsibilities of the husband. We should note well:

> The Socratic/Aspasian speech also quotes the proverb, "Nothing in excess" (247e) and urges survivors to practice self-reliance. The speech explains that depending on oneself is the best route to happiness. Be temperate (*sophron*) as well as courageous and wise (*andreios kai phronimos*) it counsels (248a).[86]

The speech in *Menexenus* attributed to Aspasia and Socrates refers to events long after their deaths, and the attribution of the speech to her was seen as a joke, but her reputation as a philosopher and teacher of rhetoric is undeniable.[87] Furthermore, while the rhetorical usage of her tradition is obvious in *Menexenus* (particularly the juxtaposition of philosophy [male] and rhetoric [female]), this does not preclude an historical Aspasia which is closely related to the figure that is so prominent in the conceptualization of the beginnings of philosophy by the ancients.

The other notable woman connected with the Socratic tradition is Diotima of Mantinea. Her speech defines true *eros* in Plato's *Symposium*.[88] Diotima's speech takes such a dominant role in the dialogue that Andrea Nye argues that Diotima was the host of the dinner and not Agathon.[89] The speech climaxes with the description of the philosopher as a type of *Eros*, the *daemion* who brings unity to life:

> Τίνες οὖν ἔφην ἐγώ, ὦ Διοτίμα, οἱ Φιλοσοφοῦντες, εἰ μήτε οἱ σοφοὶ μήτε οἱ ἀμαθεῖς; Δῆλον δή, ἔφη, τοῦτό γε ἤδη καὶ παιδί, ὅτι οἱ μεταξὺ τούτων ἀμφοτέρων, ὧν ἂν εἴη καὶ ὁ Ἔρως. ἔστιν γὰρ δὴ τῶν καλλίστων ἡ σοφία, Ἔρως δ' ἐστὶν ἔρως περὶ τὸ καλίν, ὥστε ἀναγκαῖον Ἔρωτα φιλόσοφον εἶναι, φιλόσοφον δὲ ὄντα μεταξὺ εἶναι σοφοῦ καὶ ἀμαθοῦς. αἰτία δὲ αὐτῷ καὶ τούτων ἡ γένεσις· πατρὸς μὲν γὰρ σοφοῦ ἐστι καὶ εὐπόρου, μητρὸς δὲ οὐ σοφῆς καὶ ἀπόρου. ἡ μὲν οὖν φύσις τοῦ δαίμονος, ὦ φίλε Σώκρατες, αὕτη· ὃν δὲ σὺ ᾠήθης Ἔρωτα εἶναι, θαυμαστὸν οὐδὲν ἔπαθες. ᾠήθης δέ, ὡς ἐμοὶ δοκεῖ τεκμαιρομένη ἐξ ὧν σὺ λέγεις, τὸ ἐρώμενον Ἔρωτα εἶναι, οὐ τὸ ἐρῶν· διὰ ταῦτά σοι οἶμαι

---

86. Monoson, "Remembering Pericles," 489–513.

87. Coventry, "Philosophy and Rhetoric," 5; Collins and Stauffer, "Challenge," 89–90.

88. Warren, *Unconventional History*.

89. Nye, "Hidden Host," 45–61.

πάγκαλος ἐφαίνετο ὁ Ἔρως. καὶ γὰρ ἔστι τὸ ἐραστὸν τὸ τῷ ὄντι καλὸν καὶ ἁβρὸν καὶ τέλεον καὶ μακαριστόν· τὸ δέ ἐρῶν ἄλλην ἰδέαν τοιαύτην ἔχον, οἵαν ἐγὼ διῆλθον.

"But who then, Diotima," I said, "are the lovers of wisdom, if they are neither the wise nor the foolish?" "A child may answer that question," she replied; "they are those who are in a mean between the two; Love is one of them. For wisdom is a most beautiful thing, and Love is of the beautiful; and therefore Love is also a philosopher: or lover of wisdom, and being a lover of wisdom is in a mean between the wise and the ignorant. And of this too his birth is the cause; for his father is wealthy and wise, and his mother poor and foolish. Such, my dear Socrates, is the nature of the spirit Love. The error in your conception of him was very natural, and as I imagine from what you say, has arisen out of a confusion of love and the beloved, which made you think that love was all beautiful. For the beloved is the truly beautiful, and delicate, and perfect, and blessed; but the principle of love is of another nature, and is such as I have described."[90]

Diotima characterizes Eros as the son of Poverty (mother) and Means (father). Eros, as an ideal philosopher, is ever seeking the perfect balance between these two natures.

Luce Igigaray interprets this section of the speech as:

He is barefoot, going out under the stars in search of an encounter with reality, seeking the embrace, the acquaintance [connaissance] (co-birthing) of whatever gentleness of soul, beauty, wisdom might be found there. This incessant quest he inherits from his mother. He is a philosopher through his mother, an adept in invention through his father. But his passion for love, for beauty, for wisdom, comes to him from his mother, and from the date when he was conceived. Desired and wanted, besides, by his mother.[91]

Like Aspasia, Diotima's historical essence is deeply embedded in Plato's rhetoric, so much so that some think that she is entirely fictitious, though most scholars seem to at least assent to some type of historical existence.[92] To these women we should also add Socrates's wives Xanthippe and Myrto, who had ample opportunity to share in Socrates's indefatigable curiosities. In Xenophon (430–354 BCE), Socrates engages Theodote in philosophical

---

90. Pl. *Symp.* 204b–c (Jowett, LCL).
91. Irigaray, "Sorcerer Love," 185.
92. Neumann, "Diotima's Concept of Love," 33–34.

Women in Philosophy

reflection concerning beauty.[93] There are also nameless women that Socrates mentions: he learns from unnamed priestesses as well as priests (*Meno* 81a). Socrates appeals to divine revelation concerning the doctrine of the immortality of the soul:

> Οἱ μὲν λέγοντές εἰσι τῶν ἱερέων τε καὶ τῶν ἱερειῶν ὅσοις μεμέληκε περὶ ὧν μεταχειρίζονται λόγον οἵοις τ᾽ εἶναι διδόναι· λέγει δὲ καὶ Πίνδαρος καὶ ἄλλοι πολλοὶ τῶν ποιητῶν ὅσοι θεῖοί εἰσιν. ἃ δὲ λέγουσιν, ταυτί ἐστιν· ἀλλὰ σκόπει εἴ σοι δοκοῦσιν ἀληθῆ λέγειν. φασὶ γὰρ τὴν ψυχὴν τοῦ ἀνθρώπου εἶναι ἀθάνατον, καὶ τοτὲ μὲν τελευτᾶν—ὃ δὴ ἀποθνῄσκειν καλοῦσι—τοτὲ δὲ πάλιν γίγνεσθαι, ἀπόλλυσθαι δ᾽ οὐδέποτε· δεῖν δὴ διὰ ταῦτα ὡς ὁσιώτατα διαβιῶναι τὸν βίον· οἷσιν γὰρ ἂν—Φερσεφόνα ποινὰν παλαιοῦ πένθεος δέξεται, εἰς τὸν ὕπερθεν ἅλιον κείνων ἐνάτῳ ἔτει ἀνδιδοῖ ψυχὰς πάλιν, ἐκ τᾶν Βασιλῆες ἀγαυσοὶ καὶ σθένει κραιπνοὶ σοφίᾳ τε μέγιστοι ἄνδρες αὔξοντ᾽· ἐς δὲ τὸν λοιπὸν χρόνον ἥρωες ἁγνοὶ πρὸς ἀνθρώπων καλεῦνται.

> They were certain priests and who have studied so as to be able to give a reasoned account of their ministry; and Pindar also and many another poet of heavenly gifts. As to their words, they are these: mark now, if you judge them to be true. They say that the soul of man is immortal, and at one time comes to an end, which is called dying, and at another is born again, but never perishes. Consequently one ought to live all one's life in the utmost holiness. For from whomsoever Persephone shall accept requital for ancient wrong, the souls of these she restores in the ninth year to the upper sun again; from them arise glorious kings and men of splendid might and surpassing wisdom, and for all remaining time are they called holy heroes amongst mankind.[94]

Diotima participated in the reciprocation of *eros* in the philosophical circle and in philosophic thought.[95] There is no shortage of interpretations of the *Symposium*, and to interpret the *Symposium* is to interpret Diotima.

Socrates further claims that there are women in Sparta and Crete that are proud of their education and connects them together to the heritage of the famous Delphic maxims:

> εἰσὶν δὲ ἐν ταύταις ταῖς πόλεσιν οὐ μόνον ἄνδρες ἐπὶ παιδεύσει μέγα φρονοῦντες, ἀλλὰ καὶ γυναῖκες. τούτων ἦν καὶ Θαλῆς

---

93. Xen. *Mem.* 3.11.1–15; Nails, *People of Plato*.
94. Pl. *Men.* 81a–b (Lamb, LCL); Pind. frag. 133.
95. Halperin, "Plato and Erotic Reciprocity," 60–80; Nussbaum and Hursthouse, "Plato on Commensurability," 55–96.

Reading 1 Corinthians with Philosophically Educated Women

ὁ Μιλήσιος καὶ Πιττακὸς ὁ Μυτιληναῖς καὶ Βίας ὁ Πριηνεὺς καὶ Σόλων ὁ ἡμέτερος καὶ Κλεόβουλος ὁ Λίνδιος καὶ Μύσων ὁ Χηνεύς, καὶ ἕβδομος ἐν τούτοις ἐλέγετο Λακεδαιμόνιος Χίλων. οὗτοι πάντες ζηλωταὶ καὶ ἐρασταὶ καὶ μαθηταὶ ἦσαν τῆς Λακεδαιμονίων παιδείας, καὶ καταμάθοι ἄν τις αὐτῶν τὴν σοφίαν τοιαύτην οὖσαν, ῥήματα βραχέα ἀξιομνημόνευτα ἑκάστῳ εἰρημένα· οὗτοι καὶ κοινῇ συνελθόντες ἀπαρχὴν τῆς σοφίας ἀνέθεσαν τῷ Ἀπόλλωνι εἰς τὸν νεὼν τὸν ἐν Δελφοῖς, γράψαντες ταῦτα ἃ δὴ πάντες ὑμνοῦσιν. Γνῶθι σαυτόν καὶ Μηδὲν ἄγαν. τοῦ δὴ ἕνεκαταῦτα λέγω; ὅτι οὗτος ὁ τρόπος ἦν τῶν παλαιῶν τῆς φιλοσοφίας, Βραχυλογία τις Λακωνική· καὶ δὴ καὶ τοῦ Πιττακοῦ ἰδίᾳ περιεφέρετο τοῦτο τὸ ῥῆμα ἐγκωμιαζόμενον ὑπὸ τῶν σοφῶν, τὸ Χαλεπὸν ἐσθλόν ἔμμεναι.

In those two states there are not only men but women also who pride themselves on their education ... Such men were Thales of Miletus, Pittacus of Mytilene, Bias of Priene, Solon of our city, Cleobulus of Lindus, Myson of Chen, and, last of the traditional seven, Chilon of Sparta. All these were enthusiasts, lovers and disciples of the Spartan culture; and you can recognize that character in their wisdom by the short, memorable sayings that fell from each of them they assembled together and dedicated these as the first-fruits of their lore to Apollo in his Delphic temple, inscribing there those maxims which are on every tongue—"Know thyself" and "Nothing overmuch." To what intent do I say this? To show how the ancient philosophy had this style of laconic brevity; and so it was that the saying of Pittacus was privately handed about with high approbation among the sages—that it is hard to be good.[96]

Soctrates says here (through Plato) that both Spartan men and women—who did not engage in philosophical discourse—actually did practice philosophy because of the way that they lived their lives. Socrates argues that in their manner of living, the Spartans followed the Delphic maxims "Know thyself" and "Nothing in excess."

According to early tradition, Plato (ca. 428–347 BCE) had two female students in spite of his complicated views concerning women.[97] Later

---

96. Pl. *Prot.* 342d–343b (Lamb, LCL).

97. For his female students Lasthenia of Mantinea and Axiothea of Phlus, see Diog. Laert. 3.46; Them. *Or.* 295e; Ath. 7.279, 12.546; cf. P.Oxy. 3656. Dorothy Wender examines the contradictory nature of Plato's attitudes toward women in "Plato," 213–28; cf. Allen, "Plato on Women," 131–38. An examination of Plato's contradictory views concerning women may serve as an analogy for some Pauline contradictions.

traditions in the pseudo-Pythagorean corpus attribute writings to Plato's mother, Pericitone.

The Cyrenian School

Aristippus of Cyrene (435-356 BCE), a student of Socrates, founded the Cyrenian school. According to some traditions, his daughter Arete took over as head of the school until her son, Aristippus the Younger (late 4th BCE) took over. Significantly, the tradition of Arete first appears in the first-century CE pseudo-Socratic letters, but most likely has earlier sources.[98] Interestingly, the letters contain some material that corresponds with Diogenes Laertius (fl. ca. 3rd c. CE), writing about 200 years later than the epistles:

> Ἀριστίππου διήκουσεν ἡ θυγάτηρ Ἀρήτη καὶ Αἰθίοψ Πτολεμαεὺς καὶ Ἀντίπατρος Κυρηναῖος· Ἀρήτης δὲ Ἀρίστιππος ὁ μητροδίδακτος ἐπικληθείς, οὗ Θεόδωρος ὁ ἄθεος, εἶτα θεός· Ἀντιπάτρου δ᾽ Ἐπιτιμίδης Κυρναῖος, οὗ Παραιβάτης, οὗ Ἡγησίας ὁ πεισιθάνατος καὶ Ἀννίκερις ὁ Πλάτωνα λυτρωσάμενος.

> "Now the pupils of Aristippus were his own daughter Arete, and Aethiops of Ptolemais, and Antipater of Cyrene. Arete had for her pupil the Aristippus who was surnamed *mêtrodidantos*, whose disciple was Theodorus the atheist, but who was afterwards called theos. Antipater had for a pupil Epitimedes of Cyrene who was the master of Pyraebates, who was the master of Hegesias, who was surnamed peisithanatos (persuading to die), and of Anniceris who ransomed Plato."[99]

Similarly, Diogenes writes, "He gave admirable advice to his daughter Arete, teaching her to despise superfluidity."[100] Diogenes also knew of a letter from Aristippus to his daughter Arete, but he apparently does not quote from the extant version as an authority for his writings. Strabo (ca. 63-24 CE) also writes that Arete was the head of the school, and taught her son Aristippus surnamed μητροδίδαντος, who in turn took his mother's place.[101] Her story is known by Aelius (fl. 1st c. CE, NA 3.40.1), Clement of Alexandria (ca.

---

98. Aristippus to Arete in Malherbe, *Cynic Epistles*, 282-85.
99. Diog. Laert. 2.86 (Hicks, LCL).
100. Diog. Laert. 2.72 (Hicks, LCL). Cf. Aristippus to Arete 27.2 in Malherbe, *Cynic Epistles*, 285.
101. Clem. Al. *Strom.* 3.17.22. Malherbe, *Cynic Episles*, 27. Diog. Laert. 2.72, 83, 86; Eus. *PE* 19.18. Cf. Clem. Al. *Strom.* 4.122; Strabo, 27.3. 22; Ael. *NA* 3.40; Theodoret, *Therapeutike*, 11.1; Them. *Or.* 21.244.

150–215 CE, *Strom.* 4.19.22), Theodoret of Cyrus[102] (393–457 CE, *Graecarum affectionum curatio* 11.1), Strabo, (63–24 BCE/CE, *Geo.* 17.3.22.11), Suda (10th c. CE, Ἀρίστιππος = 3908); Aristocles (fl. 1st c. CE, frg. v.3 line 16 = Euseb. *praep. ev.* 14.18.31–32).

The Epicurean Women

Norman DeWitt speculated, "If the history of Epicureanism were as well understood as the history of Stoicism, we might discover that there is more of Epicureanism than of Stoicism in the New Testament."[103] There is a long history of a qualified Christian acceptance of Epicureanism, but the first mention of a woman Epicurean philosopher does not appear until Clement of Alexandria (ca. 150–217 CE).[104] Clement highly values philosophical education: "Women are therefore to philosophize equally with men, though the males are preferable at everything, unless they have become effeminate."[105] Clement uses Themisto, the student of Epicurus (341–270 BCE), as an example of a woman who studied philosophy, "Themisto too, of Lampsacus, the daughter of Zoilus, the wife of Leontes of Lampsacus, studied the Epicurean philosophy."[106]

The Epicurean Garden freely admitted women as well as rich or poor, and these traditions become important to later writers and philosophers.[107] Leontion (lioness), the companion of Metrodorus, is known to Cicero (106–43 BCE), Pliny the Elder (23–79 CE), and Athenaeus (fl. 250 CE).[108]

Athenaeus (fl. 2nd century) writes:

102. Siniossoglou, *Plato and Theodoret*.

103. DeWitt, "Vergil and Epicureanism," 96. The best resource for source material is Usener, *Epicurea*.

104. Jungkuntz, "Epicureanism;" Jungkuntz, "Christian Approval," 279–93. Clement's affinity for Epicureanism is limited. Highly favoring Platonism, Clement identifies Epicureanism and Stoicism as the schools that Paul rejects in 1 Cor 3:19–20, and it is again rejected by Paul in Acts 15:18 because it "abolishes providence and defies pleasure." Clement argues that Paul indicated that the Stoics taught that "the Deity, being a body, pervades the vilest matter. He calls the jugglery of logic the 'tradition of men,'" *Strom.* 1.11 (ANF).

105. *Strom.* 4.7 (ANF).

106. *Strom.* 4.19.1332a (ANF).

107. DeWitt, "Epicurean Contubernium," 57. DeWitt notes that this resembles early Christian communities. Cf. Snyder, *Woman and the Lyre*, 101–5; Brennan, "Epicurus on Sex," 346–52.

108. Cic. *Nat. D.* 1.33, 93; Plin. *HN* 29, 35.99; Ath. 13.588, 593; cf. Diog. Laert. 10.5, 23; Cf. Laura McClure's study on the cultivated *hetaera*, "Subversive Laughter," 259–94. See also Seneca's description early Epicureanism in *Ep.* 20.9; cf. 6.6; 52.3.

οὗτος οὖν ὁ Ἐπίκουρος οὐ Λεόντιον εἶχεν ἐρωμένην τὴν ἐπὶ ἑταιρείᾳ διαβόητον γενομένην; ἣ δὲ οὐδ' ὅτε φιλοσοφεῖν ἤρξατο ἐπαύσατο ἑταιροῦσα, πᾶσι δὲ τοῖς Ἐπικουρείς συνῆν ἐν τοῖς κήποις, Ἐπικούρῳ δὲ καὶ ἀναφανδόν· ὥστ'ἐκῖον πολλὴν φροντίδα ποιούμενον αὐτῆς τοῦτ'ἐμφανίζειν διὰ τῶν πρὸς Ἕρμαρχον' Ἐπιστολῶν.

Now, had not this very Epicurus Leontium[109] for his mistress, her, I mean, who was so celebrated as a courtesan? But she did not cease to live as a prostitute when she began to learn philosophy, but still prostituted herself to the whole sect of Epicureans in the gardens, and to Epicurus himself, in the most open manner; so that this great philosopher was exceedingly fond of her, though he mentions this fact in his letters to Hermarchus.[110]

There is a traditional list of other women in the Epicurean Garden: Mammarion, Hedeia, Erotion, and Nikidion, and Boidion.[111] Plutarch (ca. 46–120 CE) is critical of Epicurus at every mention of the Epicurean women, including individual references to Leontion (*Mor.* 1129b) and Hedia (*Mor.* 1089c), using their reputation as prostitutes to rhetorically attack the character of Epicureans. A fragment of Philodemus (ca. 110–40 BCE) simply says that what Epicurus learned from Leontion might be ascribed to Colotes (9.3).[112]

... καθ]ολου [δ'ἁμαρτημάτων ἐκείνων τ[ά]δ[ε] καὶ ἄπε[ρ ὁ] Ἐπίκουρος Λεοντίου πυνθά[ν]εται προσυποστήσεται πρὸς Κολώτην. ἐπεὶ καὶ μετάξ ποτ'ἐφ'ἑαυτὸν ὁ σοφός θ'ἁμάρτημ· ἄνετον ἐν τ[ῆι] νεότητι γε[γ]ο[ν]εναι ...

... in general such and such of their (sc. the students') errors and what Epicurus learns from Leontium he will {hypothetically} ascribe to Colotes. Since the wise man will also sometimes transfer to himself an intemperate error, {saying} that it occurred in his youth ...[113]

---

109. In Athenaeus's time, there may have been a collection of letters entitled "Letters to Hemarchus." Athenaeus says of Leontium, "And even before the very eyes of Epicurus; wherefore he, poor devil, was really worried about her, as he makes clear in his *Letters to Hermarchus*" (13.522b). The only extant letter from Epicurus to Hermarchus is preserved in Cic. *Fin.* 2.30.96 and it does not mention Leontium.

110. Ath. 13.53 (Yonge, LCL).

111. Diog. Laert. 10.7; Plut. *Mor.* 1097E; 1089c, 1098b; Plin. *Ep.* 35; 35.144. J. Adam argued that the earliest Epicurean women were "facile with the pen" ("Epicurus and Erotion," 303–4). Cic. *Fin.* 1.25; Erotium the Courtesan appears as a minor character in Plautus's *Menaechmi*; see Packman, "Feminine Role Designations," 245–58; cf. Fantham, "Sex, Status, and Survival," 44–74; McClure, *Courtesans*.

112. Text and translation from Konstan et al., *Philodemus*, 32–33.

113. Philodemus, *On Frank Criticism*, vol. Herc. 1, v. 2, frag. 9.

Reading 1 Corinthians with Philosophically Educated Women

Diogenes Laertius (fl. 3rd CE) says that Epicurus wrote many letters to Leontion, and she wrote back (10.5-7). This tradition continues in Alciphron[114] (between 170 and 350 CE):

> τὴν δὲ Δανάην φασίν, ὡς ᾔσθετο τὸν ἐπηρτημένον αὐτῇ κίνδυνον, ἀνακρινομένην ὑπὸ τῆς Λαοδίκης οὐδ ἀποκρίσεως αὐτὴν ἀξιῶσαι· ἀπαγομένην τε ἐπὶ τὸν κρημνὸν εἰπεῖν ὡς δικαίως οἱ πολλοὶ καταφρονοῦσι τοῦ θείου, ὅτε 'ἐγὼ μὲν τὸν γενόμενόν μοι ἄνδρα σώσασα τοιαύτην χάριτα παρὰ τοῦ δαιμονίου λαμβάνω, Λαοδίκη δὲ τὸν ἴδιον ἀποκτείνασα τηλικαύτης τιμῆς ἀξιοῦται.'

> And they say that Danae, when she perceived the danger which was impending over her, was interrogated by Laodice, and refused to give her any answer; but, when she was dragged to the precipice, then she said, that "many people justly despise the Deity, and they may justify themselves by my case, who having saved a man who was to me as my husband, am requited in this manner by the Deity. But Laodice, who murdered her husband, is thought worthy of such honour."[115]

Leontion is then the most famous Epicurean woman (followed closely by Themista) as we see in the references to her in Philodemus (ca. 110-40 BCE) and Athenaeus (fl. late 2nd c. CE).[116] Some traditions indicate that Leontion had a philosophically educated daughter Danaë, who was executed for attempting to thwart the murder of Sophron the governor of Ephesus by Laodice. In this context, Athenaeus preserves a teaching from Danaë concerning the Divine, a common topic in Epicureanism:

> Δανάην δὲ τὴν Λεοντίου τῆς Ἐπικουρείου θυγατέρα ἑταιριζομένην καὶ αὐτὴν Σώφρων εἶχεν ὁ ἐπὶ τῆς Ἐφέσου· δι' ἣν αὐτὸς μὲν ἐσώθη ἐπιβουλευόμενος ὑπὸ Λαοδίκης, ἡ δὲ κατεκρημνίσθη, ὡς γράφει Φύλαρχος διὰ τῆς δωδεκάτης τάδε· 'ἡ πάρεδος τῆς Λαοδίκης Δανάη, πιστευομένη ὑπ'αὐτῆς τὰ πάντα, Λεοντίου δ'οὖσα τῆς μετ' Ἐπικούρου τοῦ φυσικοῦ σχολασάσης θυγάτηρ, Ζώφρονος δὲ γεγονυῖα πρότερον ἐρωμένη, παρακολουθοῦσα διότι ἀποκτεῖναι βούλεται τὸν Σώφονα ἡ Λαοδίκη διανεύει τῷ Ζώφρονι, μηνύουσα τὴν ἐπιβουλήν. ὁ δὲ συλλαβὼν καὶ προσποιηθεὶς συγχωρεῖν περὶ ὧν λίγει δύ' ἡμέρας παρῃτήσατο εἰς σκέψιν· καὶ συγχωρησάσης

---

114. Benner and Fobes, *Alciphron*.

115. Alciphr. *Ep.* 17.5 (Benner and Fobes, LCL). In this epistle, Leontium depicted writing to Lamia.

116. Seneca, *On Marriage*, frag. 45 (= Jerome, *Against Jovinianus*, 1.48); cf. Clement of Alexandria, *Proof of the Gospels*, 2.23; Theodoretus, *Remedies for the Errors of the Greeks* (in Gaisf, *Theodoreti Episcopi*, 479).

νυκτὸς ἔφυγεν εἰς Ἔφεσον. μαθοῦσα δὲ ἡ Λαοδίκη τὸ ποιηθὲν ὑπὸ τῆς Δανάης κατεκρήμνισεν τὴν ἄνθρωπον, οὐδὲν τῶν προγεγενημένων φιλανθρώπων ἐπὶ νοῦν βαλομένη.

Well, did not this same Epicurus keep Leontium as his mistress, the woman who had become notorious as a courtesan? Why! Even when she began to be a philosopher, she did not cease her courtesan ways, but consorted with all the Epicureans in the Gardens, and even before the very eyes of Epicurus; wherefore he, poor devil, was really worried about her, as he makes clear in his Letters to Hermarchus . . . and they say that Danae, when she perceived the danger which was impending over her, was interrogated by Laodice, and refused to give her any answer; but, when she was dragged to the precipice, then she said, that "many people justly despise the Deity, and they may justify themselves by my case, who having saved a man who was to me as my husband, am requited in this manner by the Deity. But Laodice, who murdered her husband, is thought worthy of such honour."[117]

As can be seen from Athenaeus's criticism of Leontium in the quote above, many of the women in the school were considered courtesans (*hetaerae*) and the school endured a good deal of heckling from polemicists. The Stoic Diotimus, for example, supposedly published fifty letters by Epicurus and his mistresses.[118] Cicero (106–43 CE, *Nat. D.* 1.93) rebuked Leontion for her work against Theophrastus.[119] Pliny (61–112 CE) tells us that Aristides of Thebes painted a portrait of her listing, "Leontium, the mistress of Epicurus, in an attitude of meditation."[120] The sister of Metrodorus,[121] Batis wife of Idomeneus,[122] was a first generation Epicurean and wrote a letter to her niece Apia, and other letter fragments survive as well.[123] Batis of Lampscus was known to Seneca (ca. 4–65 CE),[124] "For this very reason I regard as excellent the saying of Metrodorus, in a letter of consolation to his sister on the

---

117. Ath. 13.64 (Yonge, LCL).

118. Diog. Laert. 10.3.

119. Cicero merely says that while she wrote in excellent Attic, the substance of her work is ridiculous. Pliny the Elder (*Praefatio* 29) indicates simply that a woman wrote against Theophrastus even though he was a respected rhetor.

120. Plin. *HN* 35.99, "Et leontion epicure et anapauomenen propter fratis amorem."

121. Strab. 13; Cic. *Nat. D.* 1.40, *Tusc.* 5.9; *Fin.* 2.28, 92; Plut. *Mor.* 1087a, 1094d; 1117b; Diog. Laert. 10.22; Ath. 12.

122. Vogliano frag. 23 = Usener frag. 176. Alternative translations in Klauck, *Ancient Letters*, 154, and Baily, *Epicurus*, 129.

123. Gigante, *Philodemus*; Sider, *Library of the Villa dei Papiri*.

124. Diog. Laert. 10.23.

loss of her son, a lad of great promise: 'All the Good of mortals is mortal.'"[125] Cleomedes (between 1st and 4th c. CE) remembers Leontion along with Philainis as he criticizes Epicurus for having failed in philosophy.[126]

Epicurus (341–270 BCE) and his followers endured harsh criticism from other schools for admitting women, and this polemic continued throughout the Hellenistic period. Lactanius (ca. 240–320 CE) only remembers Themista:

> Denique nullas unquam mulieres philosophari docuerunt, praeter unam ex omni memoria Themisten.
>
> Finally, they never taught any women to be philosophers except one, from all memory: Themista.[127]

Themista is also remembered in P.Herc. 176, which is considered to be an authentic epistle authored by an early Epicurean.[128] The following is addressed to a child, referencing their "mommy" (μ[ά]μμη[σ]οῦ).

> [ἀ]φείγμεθα εἰς Λάμψακον ὑγιαίνοντες ἐγὼ καὶ Πυθο-
> κλῆς καὶ Ἕρμαρχος καὶ Κτήσιππος καὶ ἐκεῖ κατειλήφα-
> μεν ὑγιαίνοντας Θεμίσταν καὶ τοὺς λοιποὺς φόλους·
> εὖ δὲ ποιεῖς καὶ εἰ σὺ ὑγιαίνεις καὶ ἡ μ[ά]μμη [σ]ου
> καὶ πάπαι καὶ Μάτρωνι πάντα πείθῃ [ὥσπ]ερ καὶ ἔμ-
> προσθεν·
>
> Pythocles, Hermarchus and I have reached Lampascus safe and sound. We found Themista and the rest of our friends there in good health. I hope you are well too, and your mummy, and that you are obedient to them in all things.[129]

Epicureanism gained some influence in Lycia. In the second century CE, Diogenes of Oenoanda erected a huge monument there with inscriptions of Epicurean philosophy. It is currently preserved in 224 fragments. Some fragments were discovered that are part of a *Letter to Mother*.[130] C. W. Chilton renewed interest in Diogenes of Oenoanda with a germinal article in 1963, inspiring Martin Ferguson Smith to search for more fragments at

---

125. Sen. *Ep.* 98.9 (Gummere, LCL).
126. Cleom. 2.1.
127. Lactant. *Div. inst.* 3.25.4.
128. Rist, *Epicurus*, 12.
129. Rist, *Epicurus*, 12; for text, see Vogliano, *Epicuri*, 23–55; Angeli, "La scuola epicurea," 27–51.
130. Chilton frag. 52–53.

the original site.[131] Smith produced several articles and books as the fragments were discovered and edited, and repeatedly argues that the *Letter to Mother* is written by Epicurus rather than Diogenes.[132] Smith writes, "To sum up: the *Letter to Mother* is almost certainly addressed to Epicurus's mother; it is possible that it is either a genuine letter, or an adaptation of a genuine letter, of Epicurus."[133] Chilton suggests that "the author is emphasizing the necessity of pursuing philosophy in order to dispel fear (of death and/or the gods?) and attain perfect happiness."[134]

The exhortation for women to utilize Epicurean philosophy is clear in the *Letter to Mother* in the Diogenes inscription, which will be presented in total:

> [--- δεῖ σε πε]ρὶ αὐτῶν [ἀκριβῆ τι καὶ] πιστὴν [σκέψιν ποιεῖ]
> θαι. αἱ μὲν γ[ὰρ φαντασίαι] τῶν ἀπόν[των ἀπὸ τῆςς ὄψ]εως
> ἐπι[οῦσαι τῇ ψυχῇ] τὸν μέ[γιστον τραχ]ον παρέ[χουσιν. ἂν
> δὲ τὸ ὅ]λον [πρᾶγμα ἀκριβῶ]ς διαθεᾶ, μαθήσει ὅτι διαθε[ᾶ,
> μαθήσει ὅτι ἀν]τικρὺς εἰσι τοιαῦται καὶ μὴ παρόντων οἷαι καὶ
> παρόντων. ἁπταὶ γὰρ οὐκ οὖσαι, διανοηταὶ δέ, τὴν αὐτὴν, ὅσον
> ἐφ᾽ ἑαυτα[ῖ]ης, ἔχουσι δύαμιν πρὸς τοὺς παρόντας τῇ ὅτε καὶ
> παρόντων ἐκείνων ὑφειστήκεσαν. [θάρρει· μ]ὴ γὰρ ἐπιλ[ογίσῃ
> τ]ὰ φάζματα ἡμ[ων κακά.] τίθει δ᾽ αὐτ[ὰ ὀρῶσα] καθ᾽ ἡμέρα[ν
> ἀγαθ]όν τι ἡμᾶς π[ροσκ]τωμέρω εἰς [τὸ μακρ]οτέρω τῆς
> εὐδαιμ‹ο›νίας προβαίνειν. ο]ὐ γὰρ μεικρὰ οὐδέν [τ᾽ ἀνύ]τοντα
> περιγείνεται ἡ[μ] εἶν τάδ᾽ οἷα τὴν διάθεσιν ἡμῶν ἰσόθεον ποιεῖ
> καὶ μακαρίας φυσεως λειπομένους ἡμας δείκνυσιν. μὲν γὰρ
> ζῶμεν, ὁμοίως τοῖς θεοῖς χαίρομεν.
>
> (to cause the greatest concern about them. For the appearance of those who are absent, independent from sight, instills very great fear, whereas if they are present with us it causes not the least of dread. But if you carefully examine their nature the appearances) of the absent are exactly the same as those of the present.

---

131. Chilton, "Inscription," 285–86. See also the monographs by Gordon, *Epicurus*; and Chilton, *Diogenes of Oenoanda*; A. S. Hall examines the possibilities of which Diogenes in Oenoanda was the Epicurean, in "Who Was Diogenes?," 160–63.

132. Smith, "Fragments," 51–62; "New Fragments," 357–89; "Fifty-Five New Fragments," 39–92; "Two New Fragments," 147–55; "New Readings," 159–62; "New Fragment 24," 329–31; "Eight New Fragments," 69–89; "New Fragments 122–24," 43–57; "Demostheneia Inscription," 59–64; "Excavations at Oinoanda 1997," 125–70; "ΝΗΣΣΟΣ at Oinoanda in Lycia," 127–30; "Fresh Thoughts," 51–55; "Physics," 238–46; "Elementary, My Dear Lycians," 133–37; "In Praise of the Simple Life," 35–46.

133. Smith, "Discovered and Rediscovered," 60n60; Smith, *Diongenes of Oinoanda*, 558.

134. Chilton, *Diogenes*, 130.

Reading 1 Corinthians with Philosophically Educated Women

> For being not tangible but intelligible they have in themselves the same capacity towards those present when they arose, their subjects being present also. Therefore, Mother, take heart; you must not regard visions of me as evil. Rather consider that I am daily aquiring useful help towards advancing happiness. Not slight or of no avail are the advantages that accrue to me, such that they make my condition equal to the divine and show that not even mortality can make me inferior to the indestructible and blessed nature. For as long as I live I rejoice even as do the gods . . .[135]

> [ἕκαστος γὰρ στερηθεὶς τῶν ἀγαθῶν λυπήν λυ]πήσ[ετα]ι τὴν ἴση[ν, ἄν] [γ'] ἀντιλάβηται τῆς ἐλαττώσεως· ἂν μὴ αἰσθάνηται δέ, πῶς ἐλαττοῦται; μετὰ δὴ τοιούτων ἡμᾶς ἀγαθῶν προσδόκα, μῆτερ, χαίροντας αἰεὶ καὶ ἔπαιρε σεαυτὴν ἐφ' οἷς πράττομεν. των μεντοι χορηγιῶν φείδου, πρὸς Διός, ὧν συνεχῶς ἡμεῖν ἀποστέλλεις. οὐ γὰρ σοί τι Βούλομαι λείπειν, ἵν' ἐμοὶ περιτεύῃ, λείπειν δ' μᾶλλον, ἵνα μὴ σοί, καίτοι γε ἀφθόνως κἀμοῦ διάγ[ον]τος ἐω πᾶσιν, διὰ τ[οὺς] φίλους καὶ τὸ συνεχῶ[ς] τὸν πατέρα ἡμεῖν πέμπειν ἀργύειν ἀργύριον, πεοσφάτως δὲ δὴ καὶ διὰ τοῦ Κλέωνος τὰς ἐννέα ημᾶς ἀπεσταλκότος. οὔκουν ἑκάτερον ὑμῶν ἰδία δεῖ Βαρεῖσθαι δι' ἡμᾶς, συνχρῆσθαι δὲ τῷ ἑτέρῳ τὸν [ἕτερον].

> . . . . the same, if he suffers diminution; but if he has no sensation, how is he diminished? Surrounded by such good things, then, think of me, mother, as rejoicing always and have confidence in how I am faring. But in heaven's name be sparing with the remittances you are constantly sending me. I do not wish you to be in need so that I may have abundance, I would rather suffer need so that you should not; and yet I am living in plenty in every respect thanks to friends and father continually sending me money; indeed only recently Cleon sent me nine minae. So neither one nor other of you should worry about me but enjoy each other's company.[136]

There is general consensus that the fragments that comprise *Letter to Mother* are either authentic Epicurus or from a first generation Epicurean.[137] The first fragment of the *Letter to Mother* (frag. 124) centers on the Epicurean teachings concerning dreams.[138] The author comforts his mother who has visions

---

135. Frag. Ch 52 = Smith frag. 125.
136. Frag. Ch 53 = Smith frag. 126.
137. Smith, *Epicurean Inscription*, 555–58.
138. Clay, "Dreams," 352–55.

or dreams of her son, and tells her that these apparations are a good thing.[139] Pamela Gordon argues that the *Letter to Mother* (frag. 125) is fictional and fits with a common genre of philosophical writing that Gordon calls "philosopher's demurrals," also found in the Cynic epistles. In *Letter to Mother*, Epicurus tells his mother not to send him anything, and in the Cynic Epistles, Crates often requests that the addressee—including his wife Hipparchia—to withhold gifts.[140] Besides Diogenes of Oenoanda, other Roman Epicureans include Amafinius (late 2nd or early 1st c. BCE, Cic., *Acad.* 1.2.5),[141] Rabirius (1st BCE, Cic., *Acad.* 1.2.5), Catius,[142] Pompilius Andronicus (fl. 1st c. CE; Ath. 12.68) Titus Albucius (fl. mid 2nd c. BCE);[143] Gaius Velleius (d. 41 BCE = *Vell. Pat.* 2.26.1, grandfather of the senator Gaius Cassius Paterculus (Cic. *Nat. D.* 1.6.15), Longinus (before 85–42 BCE; Cic. *Fam.* 15.16, 19; Plut., *Brut.* 37.2, 39.6); Demetrius the Laconian (2nd c. CE; Diog. Laert. 10.26; Strabo 14.2.20; Sext. Emp., *Math.*, 10.219–27).[144] The Epicurean Titus Pomponius Atticus (ca. 112–32 BCE), a friend of Cicero, gave his daughter Pomponia Caecilia Attica an excellent liberal education which included philosophical training.[145] Attica's education included elementary training by a slave *paedagogus* (*Att.* 12.33) and the freedman *grammaticus* Q. Caecilius Epirota[146] for advanced grammar. Similarly, Pliny the Younger's (61–112 CE) friend Marcellinus retained a *paedagogus* and a *praeceptores* for the education of his daughter (*Ep.* 5.16). While the early rules of the Garden provided many opportunities for women to learn philosophy, the encouragement to practice philosophy in the household is a guide for later Epicureans:

> Γελᾶν ἅμα δεῖ καὶ φιλοσοφεῖν καὶ οἰκονομεῖν καὶ τοῖς λοιποῖς οἰκειώμασι χρῆσθαι καὶ μηδαμῇ λήγειν τὰς ἐκ τῆς ὀρθῆς φιλοσοφίας φωνὰς ἀφιέντας.
>
> All at the same time we must laugh and practice our philosophy, applying it in our own households, taking advantage of our other intimacies to this end, and under no circumstances

---

139. Epic. *Ed. Hdt.* 49–52; Lucr. 4.29; 722–822, 962–1036; frag. 9–10, 43. Cf. Plut. *Mor.* 1091.

140. Gordon, *Epicurus in Lycia*, 66–93; cf. Gordon, "Remembering the Garden," 76.

141. Cic. *Fam.* 15.19.2; *Acad. Post.* 1.5; cf. *Tusc.* 1.6, 2.7, 6.7.

142. Insubrian Gaul from Ticinum (Pavia). Cic. *Fam.* 15.16; Quint. *Inst.* 10.1.24; Plin. *Ep.* 4.28.

143. Cic. *Brut.* 35.131; *Fin.* 1.3, 8; *Orat.* 3.

144. Castner, "Difficulties," 138–47.

145. Reinhold, "P. Quinctilius Varus," 119–21; Rawson, *Cicero*, 197; Leon, "Caecilia Attica," 35–36; Syme, *Augustan Aristocracy*, 143, 314; Everitt, *Cicero*.

146. Cic. *Att.* 12.1, 6, 13, 33; 13.14, 19, 21, 52; 14.16.11; Quinn, "Poet and His Audience," 110–12.

Reading 1 Corinthians with Philosophically Educated Women

whatever falter in making our utterances consistent with the true philosophy.[147]

The Cynic: Crates and Hipparchia

Hipparchia of Maroneia (ca. 300 BCE), the wife of Crates, the famous student of Diogenes the Cynic (412–323 BCE),[148] is remembered in the following epigram (dated in as early 3rd BCE and as late as 1st BCE):

> Οὐχὶ βαθυστόλμων Ἱππαρχία ἔργα γυναικῶν,
> τῶν δὲ Κυνῶν ἑλόμαν ῥωμαλέον βίοτον·
> οὐδέ μοι ἀμπεχόναι περονήτιδες, οὐ βαθύπελμος
> εὐμαρίς, οὐ λιπόων εὖαδε κεκρύφαλος·
> οὐλὰς δὲ σκίπωνι συνέμπορος, ἅ τε συνωδὸς
> ἄμμι δὲ Μαιναλίας κάρρων ἄμιν Ἀταλάντας.
> τόσσον, ὅσον σοφία κρέσσον ὀριδρομίας.

> I, Hipparchia, chose not the tasks of amply-robed woman, but the manly life of the Cynics. Nor do tunics fastened with brooches and thick-soled slippers, and the hair-caul wet with ointment please me, but rather the wallet and its fellow-traveler the staff and the course double mantle suited to them, and a bed strewn on the ground. I shall have a greater name than that of Archadian Atlanta by so much as wisdom is better than racing over the mountain.[149]

This indicates that Hipparchia has to join the world of men in order to participate in philosophy. Most traditions remember Hipparchia as no longer effeminate, but masculine, and expresses her sexuality in masculine terms: she dresses and speaks like a male Cynic, and there is no more need for her

---

147. *Vatican Sayings*, 41. Translation by DeWitt, "Epicurean Contubernium," 59.
148. Born ca. 404–323 BCE and lived in Corinth near the end of his life.
149. *Anth. Pal.* 7.413.1 (Capps et al., LCL). Lefkowitz and Fant, *Women's Life in Greece and Rome*, 168, date this epigram in third century BCE, and offer an alternative translation: "I, Hipparchia, have no use for the works of deep-robed women; I have chosen the Cynics' virile life. I don't need capes with brooches or deep-soled slippers; I don't like glossy nets for my hair. My wallet is my staff's traveling companion, and the double cloak that goes with them, the cover for my bed on the ground. I'm much stronger than Atlanta from Maenalus, because my wisdom is better than racing over the mountain." This epigram is dated first to second BCE. See also Dudley, *History of Cynicism*.

to be modest, chaste, or quiet in public. Plutarch (ca. 46–120 CE) mentions her as one of the many philosophers that Epicurus slanders in *Mor.* 1086e.[150]

> καὶ ὁ Θέων 'ειτ᾽ οὐκ ἔλεγες᾽ εἶπεν ὅτι τοῖς ἐκείνων ὁ Κωλώτης παραβαλλόμενος εὐφημότατος ἀνδρῶν φαίνεται; τὰ γὰρ ἐν ἀνθρώποις αἴσχιστα ῥήματα, βωμολοχίας ληκυθισμοὺς ἀλαζονείας ἑταιρήσεις ἀνδροφονίας, βαρυστόνους πολυφθόρους βαρυεγκεφάλους συναγαγόντες Ἀριστοτέλους καὶ Σωκράτους καὶ Πυθαγόρου καὶ Πρωταγόρου καὶ Θεοφράστου καὶ Ἡρακείδου καὶ Ἱππαρχίας καὶ τίνος γὰρ οὐχὶ τῶν ἐπιφανῶν κατεσκέδοσαν.

> Here Theon put in: "And you didn't reply that by their standard Colotes looks like a paragon of measured speech? For they made a collection of the most disgraceful terms to be found anywhere—"buffoonery," "hollow booming," "charlatanism," "prostitution," "assassin," "groaner," "hero of many an adventure," "nincompoop,"—and show erred it on Aristotle, Socrates, Pythagoras, Protagoras, Theophrastus, Heraclides, Hipparchia—indeed what eminent name have they spared?[151]

Sextus Empiricus (ca. 160–210 CE) tells us that Hipparchia and Diogenes had sexual intercourse in public, "ἀγωγῇ δὲ ἔθος ἀςτιτίθεται, ὅταν οἱ μὲν πολλοὶ ἄνθρωποι ἀναχωροῦντες μιγνύωνται ταῖς ἑαυτῶν γυναιξίν, ὁ δὲ Κράτες τῇ Ἱππαρχίᾳ δημοσίᾳ, καί ὁ μὲν Διογένης ἀπὸ ἐξωμίδος περιῄει, ἡμεῖς δὲ ὡς εἰώθαμεν," "And habit is opposed to rule of conduct when, whereas most men have intercourse with their own wives in retirement, Crates did it in public with Hipparchia; and Diogenes went about with one shoulder bare, whereas we dress in the customary manner."[152] The Stoic Epictetus (55–135 CE)[153] whose teacher Musonius Rufus (ca. 25–100 CE)[154] believed that women should be philosophically educated, used her as an example for the Cynic lifestyle. Epictetus writes:

> σκόπει, ποῦ κατάγομεν τὸν Κυνικόν, πῶς αὐτοῦ τὴν βασιλείαν ἀφαιρούμεθα. Ναί· ἀλλὰ Κράτης ἔγημεν. Περίστασίν μοι λέγεις ἐξ ἔρωτος γενομένην καὶ γυναῖκα τιθεῖς ἄλλον Κράτητα. ἡμεῖς δὲ περὶ τῶν κοινῶν γάμων καὶ ἀπεριστάτων ζητοῦμεν

---

150. See "Polemic of Plutarch," in *Epicurus Reader*, trans. and ed. by Inwood and Gerson, 68–74.

151. Plut. *Mor.* 1086e.

152. Sext. Emp. *Pyr.* 153.3 (Bury, LCL).

153. Hijmans, Ἄσκησις; Brunt, "Stoicism," 7–35; Roskam, *Path to Virtue*; Boatwright, "Imperial," 513–40.

154. Nussbaum, "Incomplete Feminism," 283–326; Engel, "Women's Role," 267–88.

Reading 1 Corinthians with Philosophically Educated Women

> καὶ οὕτως ζητοῦντες οὐχ εὑρίσκομεν ἐν ταύτῃ τῇ καταστάσει προηγούμενον τῷ Κυνικῷ τὸ πρᾶγμα.
>
> Consider what we are bringing the Cynic down to, how we are taking his royalty from him.—Yes, but Crates took a wife.—You are speaking of a circumstance which arose from love and of a woman who was another Crates. But we are inquiring about ordinary marriages and those which are free from distractions, and making this inquiry we do not find the affair of marriage in this state of the world a thing which is especially suited to the Cynic.[155]

Epictetus provides the one exception to the Cynic opposition to marriage: if both partners in the marriage are Cynic philosophers, then it is possible for both philosophers to still embrace the Cynic lifestyle. And according to the tradition, Hipparchia did embrace the Cynic philosophy and its extreme disconnect from society. The Cynic marriage between Hipparchia and Crates could happen only because they had both achieved the Cynic ideal. In his *Commentary on Epictetus*, Simplicius (6th c. CE) simply writes, "Ἀλλὰ καὶ περὶ οἴκους οὕτως ἔχειν χρή. Κράτητι μὲν ὁ πίθος ἤρκεσεν εἰς οἴκησιν, καὶ γαμετὴν ἔχοντι τὴν καλὴν Ἱππαρχίαν," "Crates was satisfied with a tub for his housing, even though he had a wife, the lovely Hipparchia."[156] According to Diogenes Laertius (fl. 3rd c. CE, who seems more or less reliable in this case),[157] Hipparchia fell in love with Crates and his way of life and married him against her parent's wishes, and Crates married her reluctantly. She attended dinner parties with him and participated in philosophical debate with their colleagues.

Hipparchia is the only philosophically educated woman who received a chapter in Diogenes Laertius (6.7). Diogenes says that Hipparchia was the sister of the Cynic Metrodorus. Both her family and Crates did not want a marriage, but she persisted until finally:

> Καὶ ἤρα τοῦ Κράτητος καὶ τῶν λόγων καὶ τοῦ βίου, οὐδενὸς τῶν μνηστευομένων ἐπιστρεφομένη, οὐ πλούτου, οὐκ εὐγενείας, οὐ κάλλους· ἀλλὰ πάντ' ἦν Κράτης αὐτῇ. καὶ δὴ καὶ ἠπείλει τοῖς γονεῦσιν ἀναιρήσειν αὑτήν, εἰ μὴ τούτῳ δοθείη. Κράτης μὲν οὖν παρακαλούμενος ὑπὸ τῶν γονέων αὐτῆς ἀποτρέψαι τὴν παῖδα, πάντ' ἐποίει, καὶ τέλος μὴ πείθων, ἀναστὰς καὶ ἀποθέμενος τὴν ἑαυτοῦ σκευὴν ἀντικρὺ αὐτῆς ἔφη, "ὁ μὲν νυμφίος οὗτος, ἡ δὲ κτῆσις αὕτη, πρὸς ταῦτα βουλεύου· οὐδὲ γὰρ ἔσεσθαι κοινωνός,

---

155. Epict. *Disc.* 3.22.76.

156. Simpl., *Commentarius in Epicteti enchiridion*, 116.6. Translation in Brennan and Brittain, *On Epictetus' "Handbook 27–33."*

157. On the unreliability of Diogenes Laertius, see Hope, *Book of Diogenes*.

εἰ μὴ καὶ τῶν αὐτων ἐπιτηδευμάτων γενηθείης." Εἴλετο ἡ παῖς καὶ ταὐτὸν ἀναλαβοῦσα σχῆμα συμπεριῄει τἀνδὶ καὶ ἐν τῷ φανερῳ συνεγίνετο καὶ ἐπὶ τὰ δεῖπνα ἀπῄει.

Crates accordingly, being entreated by her parents to dissuade her from this resolution, did all he could; and at last, as he could not persuade her, he rose up, and placing all his furniture before her, he said, "This is the bridegroom whom you are choosing, and this is the whole of his property; consider these facts, for it will not be possible for you to become his partner, if you do not also apply yourself to the same studies, and conform to the same habits that he does." But the girl chose him; and assuming the same dress that he wore, went about with him as her husband, and appeared with him in public everywhere, and went to all entertainments in his company.[158]

Diogenes says that after their marriage, Hipparchia wore the clothing of a male Cynic accompanying Diogenes wherever he went, and participated in philosophic dialog. Interestingly, Diogenes Laertius knew of extant letters to and from Hipparchia, Crates, and other Cynics.[159] From Diogenes (fl. 3rd c. CE), one teaching from Hipparchia is preserved in its context:

ὅτε καὶ πρὸς Λυσίμαχον εἰς τὸ συμπόσιον ἦλθεν, ἔνθα Θεόδωρον τὸν ἐπίκλην Ἄθεον ἐπήλεγξε, σόφισμα προτείνασα τοιοῦτον· ὃ ποιῶν Θεόδωρος οὐκ ἂν ἀδικεῖν λέγοιτο, οὐδ᾽ Ἱππαρχία ποιοῦσα τοῦτο ἀδικεῖν λέγοιτ᾽ ἄν· Θεόδωρος δὲ τύπτων ἑαυτὸν αὐκ ἀδικεῖ, οὐ ἄρα Ἱππαρχία Θεόδωρον τύπτουσα ἀδικεῖ. ὁ δὲ πρὸς μὲν τὸ λεχθὲν οὐδὲν ἀπήντησεν, ἀνέσυρε δ᾽ αὐτῆς θοἰμάτιον· ἀλλ᾽ οὔτε κατεπλάγη Ἱππαρχία οὔτε διεταράχθη ὡς γυνή. ἀλλὰ καὶ εἰπόντος αὐτῇ, αὕτη ἐστὶν ἡ τὰς παρ᾽ ἱστοῖς ἐκλιποῦσα κερκίδας; ἐγώ, φησίν, εἰμί, Θεόδωρε· ἀλλὰ μὴ κακῶς σοι δοκῶ βεβουλεῦσθαι περὶ αὑτῆς, εἰ, τὸν χρόνον ὃν ἔμελλον ἱστοῖς προσαναλώσειν, τοῦτον εἰς παιδείαν κατεχρησάμην; καὶ ταῦτα μὲν καὶ ἄλλα μυρία τῆσ φιλοσόφου.

And once when she went to sup with [king] Lysimachus, she attacked Theodorus, who was surnamed the Atheist; proposing to him the following sophism; "What Theodorus could not be called wrong for doing, that same thing Hipparchia ought not to be called wrong for doing. But Theodorus does no wrong when

---

158. Diog. Laert. 6.96.

159. Cf. Kennedy, "Hipparchia," 48–71; Downing, "Cynical Response," 229–30; Finnegan, "Professional Careers," 67–81. The notion that women wear the same dress as men may be an equalizing factor. Baldry, "Zeno's Ideal State," 10; Burton, "Women's Commensality," 143–65.

he beats himself; therefore Hipparchia does no wrong when she beats Theodorus." He made no reply to what she said, but only pulled her clothes about; but Hipparchia was neither offended nor ashamed, as many a woman would have been; but when he said to her:

> "Who is the woman who has left the shuttle
> So near the warp?"
>
> "I, Theodorus, am that person," she replied; "but do I appear to you to have come to a wrong decision, if I devote that time to philosophy, which I otherwise should have spent at the loom?" And these and many other sayings are reported of this female philosopher.[160]

It is interesting that in this text, Theodorus the Atheist is silent. Hipparchia, in true Cynic form, sharply rebuked Theodorus without provocation. Diogenes Laertius (fl. 3rd c. CE) refers to two reliable sources for Hipparchia: Eratosthenes of Cyrene (276–194 BCE)[161] and Diocles of Peparethus (fl. late 4th c. BCE).[162]

The Roman Tradition

Having discussed Greek traditions about women in various philosophical traditions, we move on to Roman traditions. Many of the notable Roman philosophers had close interwoven relationships. For example, in late second-century Rome, Gaius Laelius was a disciple of Diodes and Panaetius of Rome[163] (all members of the Scipionic Circle). P. Rutilius Rufus, Ae-

---

160. Diog. Laert. 6.98 (Hicks, LCL).

161. Eratosthenes was an imminent librarian of Alexandria who produced (now lost) works including poetry, philosophy, and mathematics. He is most known by his calculation of the circumference of the earth. See his article in the Suda and OCD.

162. Diocles of Peparethus was most likely a third-century BCE historian. OCD sources FGrHist 820; Momigliano, *Secundo contributo*, 403; and Crook, *Cambridge Ancient History*, 89. Fraiser, *Ptol. Alex.* 2.1076n373. See also van der Eijk, *Diocles of Carystus*. Theano is mentioned in fragment 48d, sourced from Censorinus, *DN* 7.2–6 (p. 15, 13–16, 20 Rapisarda). "Nam septimo mense parere mulerium posse plurimi adfirmant, ut Theano Pythagorica, Aristoteles peripateticus, Diocles, Euenor, Straton, Empedocles, Epigenes, multique praeterea, quorum omnium consensus Eurphonem Cnidium non deterret id ipsum intrepide pernegantem." "Most of them affirm that a woman can give birth in the seventh month, as do Theano the Pythagorean, Aristotle the Peripatetic, Diocles, Evenor, Strato, Empedocles, Epigenes and many others; the agreement of all these does not deter Euryphon of Cnidus from intrepidly denying this very [statement]." Text and commentary from Diels and Krantz, *Die Fragmente der Vorsokratiker*, 58a (p. 448), and Rapisarda, *Censorini*.

163. 185–89 BCE. Son of Nicagoras from Rhodes preserved in van Straaten,

lius Stilo,[164] and Quintus Mucius Scaevola Augur[165] were also students of Panaetius of Rome and produced the notable students Cicero and Atticus. Scaevola himself married Laelia, the daughter of Lelius, and his wife, daughters, and granddaughters were famous for their excellent Latin. Quintillian (ca. 35–100 CE) tells us that Cornelia, the mother of the Gracchi, was well educated and skillful in rhetoric. Laelia[166] and Hortensia[167] were accomplished rhetors who learned the art from their fathers:

> Nec de patribus tantum loquor: nam Gracchorum eloquentiae multum contulisse accepimus Corneliam matrem, cuius doctissimus sermo in posteros quoque est epistulis traditus, et Laelia C. filia reddidisse in loquendo paternam elegantiam dicitur, et Hortensiae Q. filiae oratio apud triumviros habita legitur non tantum in sexus honorem.

> We are told that the eloquence of the Gracchi owed much to their mother Cornelia, whose letters even to this day testify to the cultivation of her style. Laelia, the daughter of Gaius Laelius, is said to have reproduced the elegance of her father's language in her own speech, while the oration delivered before the triumvirs by Hortensia, the daughter of Quintus Hortensius, is still read and not merely as a compliment to her sex.[168]

The practice of philosophers teaching their daughters has a long precedence. For example, Quintilian (ca. 35–100 CE) tells us that Chrysippus (279–79 BCE) believed that ideally a girl should be trained in philosophy (1.1.4–5). Diodorus Cronus (d. ca. 284 BCE), the Megarian philosopher, taught his five daughters Menexene, Argia, Theognis, Artemesia, and Pantaclea, who were known as skilled dialecticians.[169] Diogenes of Babylon[170] (ca.

Panaetti Rhodii Fragmenta. Succeeded Antipater as the head of the school in 129 BCE; student was Hecaton.

164. Cic. *Brut.* 205–7, *Leg.* 2.23, 59; Suet. *Gram.* 2; Gell. 3.1.12; Quint. 10.1.99.

165. Frier, *Roman Jurists*; Robinson, *Sources of Roman Laws*; Tellegen-Couperus, *Roman Law*.

166. Cf. Cic. *Brut.* 101, 211.

167. Val. Max. *Fact. dict. mem.* 8.3.3; Appian, *Civil Wars* 2.32–34. Notably missing from OCD. See Plant, *Women Writers*, 104–5. Hortensia is famous for her speech against the taxes levied on the 1400 richest women in Rome in 42 BCE (Liv. 34.1). Cf. Bauman, *Women and Politics*, 81–83; Fowler, *Social Life*. A similar incident, the Oppian Law, occurred in 195 BCE. The situation was parodied by Poenulus, see Johnston, "Poenulus," 143–59.

168. Quint. 1.1.6.

169. Clem. Al. *Strom.* 4.19; OCD, 472; Sedley, "Diodorus Cronus," 74.

170. Known only from the Herculaneum papyri. OCD, 474.

240–152 BCE) the teacher of Laelius,[171] the teacher of Quintus Lucilius Balbus (100 CE)[172] followed Zeno of Tarsus (fl. 200 BCE) as head of the Stoa. Diogenes of Babylon and Crates of Mallus at Pergamum taught Panaetius (ca. 185–89 BCE), who taught Hecaton. The Stoic Diodotus lived in the house of Cicero, who no doubt taught his daughter Tullia (*Att.* 2.20.6). Areus Didymus (fl. late 1st c. BCE / 1st c. CE) taught in the household of Augustus, and comforted the Empress Livia at the death of her son.[173] Several elite Roman women in the first century BCE and CE oversaw their sons' education: Cornelia for Tiberius and Caius Gracchus (Cic. *Brut.* 104), Aurelia for Caesar (Tac. *Dial.* 28), Atia for Octavius (Tac. *Dial.* 28) and Iulia Procilla for Iulius Agricola (Tac. *Agr.* 4.2–3).

Pliny the Younger

In the first century CE, Pliny the Younger praises the education and abilities of a young female relative and relishes in discourse with his wife.[174] In one of these letters, Pliny praises Calpurnia Hispulla for her excellent job in educating his third wife, Calpurnia. Pliny rejoices in his wife's continued participation in education: reading his books and speeches listening to philosophical discussions.[175]

> Accedit his studium litterarum, quod ex mei caritate concepit. Meos libellos habet, lectitat, ediscit etiam. Qua illa sollicitudine, cum, videor acturus, quanto, cum egi, gaudio adficitur! Disponit qui nuntient sibi, quem adsensum, quos clamores excitarim, quem eventum iudicii tulerim. Eadem, si quando recito, in proximo discreta velo sedet laudesque nostras avidissimis auribus excipit. Versus quidem meos cantat etiam formatque cithara non artifice aliquo docente, sed amore, qui magister est optimus.
>
> Her affection to me has given her a turn to books; and my compositions, which she takes a pleasure in reading, and even getting by heart, are continually in her hands. How full of solicitude is she when I am entering upon any cause! How kindly does

---

171. RE 12, "Laelius," 3; Scullard, "Scipio Aemilianus," 62; Astin, *Scipio Aemilianus*; Erskine, *Hellenistic Stoa*; Broughton, *Magistrates*, 116.

172. Cic. *Nat. D.* 1.6, 3.40; *Div.* 1.5.

173. Sen. *Marc.* 3.4; Barrett, *Livia*, 122.

174. Plin. *Ep.* 6.4 and 7.5. For commentary and historical value, see Sherwin-White, *Letters of Pliny*, 259, 407.

175. Pliny's description of his wife's education seems more or less historical. See Hemelrijk, *Matrona docta*, 33; cf. Rawson, *Children*, 242–43.

she rejoice with me when it is over! When I am pleading, she stations messengers to inform her from time to time how I am heard, what applauses I receive, and what success attends the cause. When at any time I recite my works, she sits close at hand, concealed behind a curtain, and greedily overhears my praises. She sings my verses and sets them to her lyre, with no other master but Love, the best instructor.[176]

This is a rare and important instance of a wealthy woman educating another woman, but the pattern of being educated in a wealthy household and furthering that education in her husband's home is familiar. Elsewhere, Pliny eulogizes the patroness Quadratilla for her continued interest in the education of her grandson, which reflects that of the papyri listed above.[177]

Seneca

Seneca (ca. 4–65 CE)[178] cites philosophically educated women as he writes to his mother Helvia and close friend Marcia advising them not to neglect the study of philosophy because of their gender.[179] He encourages both women to apply Stoic philosophy to their lives, notably applying well-known qualities self-control and self-sufficiency, the defining characteristics of the ideal wise-person and student of philosophy.[180] Seneca writes to

---

176. Plin. *Ep.* 4.19 (Gummere, LCL). In his commentary on Pliny, Sherwin-White treats this letter of Pliny as historical. *Letters of Pliny*, 296–97.

177. Plin. *Ep.* 7.24.

178. Inwood, "Seneca," 63–76; Reydams-Schils, *Roman Stoics*; Oates, *Stoic and Epicurean Philosophers*; Toynbee, "Dictators," 43–58; Motto, "Seneca on Women's Liberation," 155–57; for the wealth of Pliny, see Duncan-Jones, *Economy*, 17–32.

179. Seneca, *De Consulatione ad Helvium* and *De Consulatione ad Marcium*. Rebecca Langlands analyzes the manner in which Seneca adapts to his female audience in "A Woman's Influence," 115–26. We can read this in contrast to *On Mercy* 1.5.4, where he writes, "Muliebre est furere in ira, ferarum vero nec generosarum quidem preamordere et urguere proiectos." "It is for women to rage in anger, for wild beasts doubtless—and not even the noble sort of these—to bite and worry their prostrate victims" (Basore, LCL).

180. Some defining qualities of self-sufficiency are fearlessness of death and poverty, able to renounce a good reputation, and invincibility. Teles, Περὶ αὐταρκείας 5H–20H; Cic. *Off.* 1.90, *Tusc.* 5.10.30; Epict. *Disc.* 4.5.4; and Sen. *Const.* 8–18. Cf. Diog. Laert. 2.27. The importance of self-sufficiency in the writings of Paul is made evident by Fitzgerald, *Cracks in an Earthen Vessel*, 117–84; in the Thessalonian letters by Malherbe, "Gentle as a Nurse," 203–17; and in Philippians by Malherbe, "Paul's Self-Sufficiency," 125–39. Musonius Rufus also applies the essential qualities of self-sufficiency to women in 3, 4, 13a.

Reading 1 Corinthians with Philosophically Educated Women

Marcia,[181] the daughter of the late historian Cremutius Cordus, consoling her on the death of her son:

> Non dubito quin Iuliae Augustae, quam familiariter coluisti, magis tibi placeat exemplum: illa te ad suum consilium uocat. Illa in primo feruore, cum maxime inpatientes ferocesque sunt miseriae, consolandam se Areo, philosopho uiri sui, praebuit et multum eam rem profuisse sibi confessa est, plus quam populum Romanum, quem nolebat tristem tristitia sua facere, plus quam Augustum, qui subducto altero adminiculo titubabat nec luctu suorum inclinandus erat, plus quam Tiberium filium, cuius pietas efficiebat ut in illo acerbo et defleto gentibus funere nihil sibi nisi numerum deesse sentiret.
>
> I doubt not that the example of Julia Augusta, whom you regarded as an intimate friend, will seem more to your taste than the other; she summons you to follow her. She, during the first passion of grief, when its victims are most unsubmissive and most violent, made herself accessible to the philosopher Areus, the friend of her husband, and later confessed that she had gained much help from that source—more than from the Roman people, whom she was unwilling to sadden with this sadness of hers; more than from Augustus, who was staggering under the loss of one of his main supports, and was in no condition to be further bowed down by the grief of his dear ones; more than from her son Tiberius, whose devotion at that untimely funeral that made the nations weep kept her from feeling that she had suffered any loss except in the number of her sons.[182]

Seneca then imagines what Areus would have said to Julia Augusta and urges Marcia to follow the same advice, "It was your trouble, Marcia, that was dealt with there, it was at your side that Areus sat; change the role—it was you that he tried to comfort."[183] Seneca goes on to explain that the meaning of the oracle "Know Thyself" is realizing one's mortality, and therefore philosophy will prepare her for any type of hardship.

When Seneca was exiled by Caligula in 41 CE, he wrote a consolatory letter to his mother using similar arguments. He writes that Helvia had some philosophical education, and she should take refuge in what she knows as well as what she can still learn:

---

181. On Marica, see Manning, *On Seneca's "Ad Marciam."*
182. Sen. *Marc.* 3.4.2 (Basore, LCL).
183. Sen. *Marc.* 3.4.2 (Basore, LCL).

> Vtinam quidem uirorum optimus, pater meus, minus maiorum consuetudini deditus uoluisset te praeceptis sapientiae erudiri potius quam inbui! non parandum tibi nunc esset auxilium contra fortunam sed proferendum. Propter istas quae litteris non ad sapientiam utuntur sed ad luxuriam instruuntur minus te indulgere studiis passus est. Beneficio tamen rapacis ingenii plus quam pro tempore hausisti; iacta sunt disciplinarum omnium fundamenta: nunc ad illas reuertere; tutam te praestabunt.

> Would that my father, truly the best of men, had surrendered less to the practice of his forefathers, and had been willing to have you acquire a thorough knowledge of the teachings of philosophy instead of a mere smattering! In that case you would now have, not to devise, but merely to display, your protection against Fortune. But he did not suffer you to pursue your studies because of those women who do not employ learning as a means to wisdom, but equip themselves with it for the purpose of display. Yet, thanks to your acquiring mind, you imbibed more than might have been expected in the time you had; the foundations of all systematic knowledge have been laid. Do you return now to these studies; they will render you safe.[184]

Helvia is also instructed to teach the principles of Stoicism to her granddaughter Novatilla, who was an adult who had just lost her mother.[185]

Seneca (ca. 4–65 CE) assures his mother that he is approaching his exile with Stoic resolve, but he indicates elsewhere that he failed in this regard. Arther Ferrill writes:

> Seneca hated Corsica. He referred to it as *Corsica terribilis* and spoke of himself as though he were among the living dead. His loneliness was overpowering: "*Hic sola haec duo sunt: exul et exilium.*" It was in this atmosphere that Seneca wrote the *Ad Helviam*, and every word of it was written with an eye to recall.[186]

Ferrill goes on to argue that Seneca wrote *Ad Helviam* not to comfort his mother, but in order to promote his feigned disinterest in politics so that he could be recalled from exile. Ferrill's argument excludes the fact that many writers, including Seneca, wrote letters that were intended to be published. Pliny the Younger published his letters written from 95–108 CE up to ten

---

184. Sen. *Helv.* 17.5 (Basore, LCL).
185. Sen. *Helv.* 18.7–8 (Basore, LCL).
186. Ferrill, "Seneca's Exile," 253–57.

years after they were written. Unlike the letters of Cicero, which were spontaneous in nature, Pliny utilized a literary form that could be published later.[187]

Musonius Rufus and Heirocles

The Stoics Musonius Rufus (fl. 1st c. CE) and Hierocles (fl. 2nd c. CE) both share a similar attitude towards a woman learning philosophy. Together, these thinkers give theoretical justification for what philosophers had been practicing for hundreds of years. Musonius Rufus writes that there is no significant difference between a woman and a man, at least in as much as gender does not hinder philosophical reflection: "Women as well as men have received from the gods the gift of reason, which we use in our dealings with one another and by which we judge whether a thing is good or bad, right or wrong."[188] In fact, Musonius (fl. 1st c. CE) exhorts women to learn philosophy so that they can better carry out their duties at home.[189]

> καὶ τίς ἂν μᾶλλον τῆς φιλοσόφου τοιαύτη γένοιτο ἥν γε ἀνάγη πᾶσα, εἴπερ εἴη τῷ ὄντι φιλόσοφος, τὸ μὲν ἀδικεῖν τοῦ ἀδικεῖσθαι χεῖρον νομίζειν, ὅσωπερ αἴσχιον, τὸ δὲ ἐλαττοῦσθαι τοῦ πλεονεκτεῖν κρεῖττον ὑπολαμβάνειν, ἔτι δὲ καὶ τέκνα μᾶλλον ἀγαπᾶν ἢ τὸ ζῆν; τῆς δ'ἐχούσης οὕτω τίς ἂν εἴη γυνὴ δικαιοτέρα; καὶ μὴμ καὶ ἀνδρειοτέραν εἶναι προσήκει γυναῖκα τῆς ἀπαιδεύτου τὴν πεπαιδευμένην καὶ τὴν φιλόσοφον τῆς ἰδιώτιδος· ὡς μήτε θανάτου φόβῳ μήτε ὄκνῳ τῳ πρὸς πόνον ὑπομεῖναί τι αἰσχρόν, μηδ' ὑποπτῆξαι μηδενὶ ὅτι εὐγενὴς ὅτι δυνατὸς ἢ ὅτι πλούσιος ἢ καὶ νὴ Δία ὅτι τύραννος.

> And who better than the woman trained in philosophy—and she certainly of necessity if she has really acquired philosophy—would be disposed to look upon doing a wrong as worse then suffering one (as much as it is the baser), and to regard being worsted as better than gaining an unjust advantage? Moreover, who better than she would love her children more than life itself? What woman would be more just than such a one? Now as for courage, certainly it is to be expected that the educated woman will be more courageous than the uneducated, and one who has studied philosophy than one who has not; and she will not therefore submit to anything shameful because of fear of death or unwillingness to face hardship, and she will not be

---

187. Sherwin-White, "Pliny," 76–90.
188. Muson. 3.36 (Lutz, 34, §That Women Too Should Study Philosophy).
189. Manning, "Seneca," 170–77.

intimidated by anyone of noble birth, or powerful, or weathly, no, not even if he be the tyrant of the city.[190]

Musonius argues that the philosophically educated woman will be more mild tempered, self-controlled, courageous, and chaste than an uneducated woman. This argument uncovers his bias that Stoic philosophy is most useful for anyone, but also that a woman could learn it and apply it to the common situation of women in the ancient world: the household. Apparently, philosophically educated women were such a common occurrence that Musonius goes on to address related questions:

> ἀλλὰ νὴ Δία, φασί τινες, ὅτι αὐθάδεις ὡς ἐπὶ πολὺ καὶ θρασείας εἶναι ἀνάγκη τὰς προσιούσας τοῖς φιλοσόφοις γυναῖκας, ὅταν ἀφέμεναι τοῦ οἰκουρεῖν ἐν μέσοις ἀναστπέφωνται τοῖς ἀνδράσι καὶ μελετῶσι λόγους καὶ σοφίζωνται καὶ ἀναλύωσι συλλογισμούς, δέον οἴκοι καθημένας ταλασιουργεῖν. ἐγὼ δὲ οὐχ ὅπως τὰς γυναῖκας τὰς φιλοσοφούσας ἀλλ'οὐδὲ τοὺς ἄνδρας ἀξιώσαιμ' ἄν ἀφεμένους τῶν προσηκόντων ἔργων εἶωαι παρὶ λόγους μόνον· ἀλλὰ καὶ ὅσους μεταχειρίζονται λόγους, τῶν ἔργων φημὶ δεῖν ἕνεκα μεταχειρίζεσθαι αὐτους.

> Yes, but I assure you, some will say, that women who associate themselves with philosophers are bound to be arrogant for the most part and presumptuous, in that abandoning their own households and turning to the company of men they practice speeches, talk like sophists, and analyze syllogisms, when they should be at home spinning. I should not expect women to study philosophy to shirk their appointed tasks for mere talk any more than men, but I maintain that their discussions should be conducted for the sake of personal application.[191]

Musonius Rufus assures his readers that he does not think that women should abandon their traditional roles in the household and practice philosophical discourse with men in the forums, debate in the symposia, and public teaching. This idea is related to the expectation that the poetess still do her household chores, the negative tradition that Hipparchia completely refused to be a common housewife, and the depiction of women philosophers in Epicureanism as prostitutes. An underlying theme in Musonius Rufus is that philosophically educated women—like other educated women—have the tools to be liberated from the inhuman position of women idealized by Roman society.

---

190. Muson. 3.30 (Lutz, 43).
191. Muson. 3.56 (Lutz, 43).

Reading 1 Corinthians with Philosophically Educated Women

Like Musonius Rufus (fl. 1st c. CE), Hierocles the Stoic (fl. 2nd c. CE) believed that the wise-man should marry and be one with his wife in the pursuit of virtue. Illaria Ramelli writes:

> Hierocles touches on his most important point: marriage is not only a duty but it is also a beautiful thing, of καλόν, since it is orientated toward the pursuit of virtue. This idea of sharing the path of virtue is no longer the privledge only of philosophers who are friends with one another but also of wives and husbands, in communion that, for Hierocles as well as for Musonius, is not just one of bodies with a view to procreation but still more one of souls, carrying with it a moral commitment: marriage becomes a spiritual bond in the pursuit of virtue, which is the goal of philosophy itself, according to the Stoics.[192]

Musonius Rufus and Hierocles have similar views on the role of philosophy in the lives of women. They both appear to have a somewhat egalitarian view of education, but both relegate men and women to their traditional roles. The redeeming quality of their application of Stoicism to family life is their shared belief that philosophy helps people to live the best possible life, whether in traditional male or female roles.

Summary of Conclusions: Women in the History of Philosophy

In chapter 3, I presented evidence for the activity of women in the history of philosophy. All of the popular schools that were active in the first century had a rich history of the participation of women in their philosophical heritage. There were different levels of philosophical education. Some women were remembered as influential philosophers in their own right: Theano the Pythagorean, Hipparchia the Cynic, Laodice the Epicurean, and Arete the Cyrenian. These earlier traditions were alive in the first century BCE/CE. Several pseudo-Pythagorean letters present themselves as authored by and written to philosophically educated women. The Socratic and Cynic epistles also include writings from philosophers to their female colleagues. Seneca, Musonius Rufus, and Heirocles—Paul's Stoic contemporaries—supported the philosophical education of women so that they could most effectively live as women in their first-century social constructs.

A few notable examples indicate that philosophically educated women taught other women, and others criticized their male counterparts. The

---

192. Ramelli, *Hierocles*, 115n23. See Hierocles, *On Marriage* = Stob. 4.67.22–24, 4.75.14.

Pythagorean philosopher Damo taught the secret tenents of Pythagoreanism to her daughter Bistala. While only a fragment remains, Batis the Epicurean wrote a letter to her niece Apia. Seneca encouraged Helvia to teach Stoic principles to her granddaughter Novatilla to help her greive properly for the loss of her mother. Calpurnia Hispulla was responsible for educating her neice, Calpurnia, and Pliny the Younger is thankful for her preparedness to participate in philosophical discussions with him.

Most philosophically educated women learned from family members in a wealthy household. This is especially true in the sources contemporary to Paul: Pliny the Younger, Seneca, Musonius Rufus, and Heirocles describe the educational activities of women near the top of the social strata. Seneca, who was a friend to emperors and their families, encouraged his mother Helvia and the daughter of a historian of senatorial rank to ulitilze Stoic philosophy to overcome loss. Pliny the Younger, a senator, rejoices in his wife's company. Musonius Rufus and Heirocles provide instructions for how wealthy women could use Stoic principles to best manage their households. Similarly, the pseudo-Pythagorean letters present themseleves as instructions for the management of a wealthy household.

Most philosophically educated women were educated by their fathers, and sometimes their learning was continued with their husbands. However, there are three examples of philosophically edcated women who taught their sons and other men. Theano teaches both Pythgoras and their son; Diotima and Aspasia teach Socrates and his associates; and Arete the Cyrenian taught her son. Some women philosophers argued against male thinkers. Hipparchia the Cynic sharply rebuked Theodorus the Atheist for criticizing her participation in philosophical discourse. Leontion the Epicurean wrote a book criticizing Theophrastus.

When Paul wrote his epistles to the Corinthians, philosophical education was available to many different types of women. They could be educated by a female relative or her father, husband, son, a tutor, or a philosopher that she brings into the household herself. These women were typically connected to a wealthy household: either the woman is a member of a wealthy family or attached to one as the relative of someone dependent such a household. She could learn from any combination of schools that were active in the Roman world: neo-Pythagoreanism, middle-Platonism, Cynicism, Epicureanism, and Stoicism. In chapter 4, I will discuss the many contacts of these schools to Corinth to build an argument for the presense of philosophically educated women there.

4

Corinth and Its Philosophers

IN CHAPTERS 2 AND 3, I reviewed the evidence for educated women and girls, and specifically, in chapter 3, of philosophically educated women. I have argued that such women learned philosophy from a variety of media: they attended schools, learned from their husbands or fathers, or received teaching from a tutor in the household. I have also shown that philosophy was not the only education that women received. The archeological and literary records indicated that women were involved in the full spectrum of Greek education, including athletics and dance. Women were also involved in occupations which required some literacy: poetry, medicine, and being a scribe or grocer. Establishing the existence of philosophically educated women has been a necessary step toward considering how women in Corinth might have engaged 1 Corinthians.

In this chapter, our focus centers on Corinth and the community of Jesus-believers in the city. I will discuss the history of the city of Corinth, giving some attention to its social structures and to the existence and roles of philosophically educated women. Then, I will review the nature of philosophy at Corinth as described by ancient writers. Corinth has a heritage of being a refuge where philosophers and orators could engage in open debate without fear of persecution. Before its destruction in 146 BCE by the Romans, deposed tyrants and exiled philosophers who faced death for their views in other cities were able to live peacefully in Corinth. After Corinth was refounded in 46 BCE as a Roman colony, the popular schools continued to maintain representation. It is significant that the history of philosophy in

Corinth and Its Philosophers

Corinth has contact with all the schools that have strong traditions of philosophically educated women. The Corinthian church is situated within these contexts. In order to establish the likelihood of philosophically educated women engaging the writing we know as 1 Corinthians, I will examine the presence of women in the community, issues of social status, and the importance of households in locating philosophically educated women. Considering the nature of some of the problems that Paul faced in Corinth, it is likely that women indeed had access to philosophical education.

Classical Corinth

The city of Corinth was founded in the 900s BCE, and the area had been inhabited since 5200 BCE.[1] The area of land that Corinth controlled in classical times was 559.234m2 (900km2). The land was fertile, and the earth produced enough wealth so that the early Corinth was known for its wealth before the city was known for both land and sea trade.[2] Trade from the north and south of Greece had to pass through Corinth, and the Isthmus connected Asia to Italy.[3] Because of the abundance of natural resources from which the Corinthians fashioned their legendary bronze, the control over trade routes added to Corinthian wealth.[4] The Corinthians participated in a number of wars, with its final mistake being aggression towards Sparta which resulted in its destruction in 146 BCE by Mimmius.[5] While the destruction was proverbial, it is likely that there were people living amoung the ruins throughout its 100 years of desolation.[6] The Isthmus was still being used for both private and military[7] purposes, and the Isthmian games were kept alive by nearby Sikyon.[8]

Classical Corinth was very accommodating to religious worship, having numerous santuaries or temples dedicated to various gods.[9] The most

---

1. Hopper, "Ancient Corinth," 4; Dunbabin, "Early History," 59–69.
2. Salmon, *Wealthy Corinth*, 19–36; Roebuck, "Aspects of Urbanization," 96–127.
3. Strab. 8.6.20.
4. Jacobson and Weitzman, "Corinthian Bronze," 237–47.
5. Plb. 38.3–11; Strab. 8.6.23; Cass. Dio 21.72. Cf. App. *Hisp.* 56.153.
6. Romano, "Hellenistic Deposit," 57–104; Millis, "Miserable Huts," 397–404.
7. Taylor and West, *Corinth*, 1 no. 1.
8. McMurtry, "Excavations," 267–86.
9. Bookidis, "Sanctuaries of Corinth," 247–59; Broneer, "Twenty-Five Years Ago," 158–59; Broneer, "Paul and the Pagan Cults," 169–87; Broneer, "Paul's Missionary Work," 77–96.

Reading 1 Corinthians with Philosophically Educated Women

prominent religions in Corinth consisted of hero[10] and heroine worship,[11] the usual gods of the Pantheon,[12] and their patron gods Demeter[13] and Poseidon.[14] The Isthmian games as religious celebrations were dedicated to Poseidon, but the heroes and other gods played a prominent part in worship and entertainment.[15] These biennial games included sometimes fatal combat sports such as wrestling and boxing,[16] foot races, chariot races, the pancration, pentathalon,[17] and perhaps a ship race.[18] Prizes included not only first place (typically celery or pine crowns),[19] but second place and lower (prizes ranged from honors to monetary rewards, as it was with other Pan-Hellenic games).[20] Slaves and freedmen were a part of the games, either as trainers, attendants, or (rarely) as athletes [typically associated with the household of a weathly person].[21] Women and girls competed in a parallel festival, which included poetry contests. "Aristomache of Erythra had been twice victorious in epic poetry at the Isthmia in the third century BCE."[22] Festivities at the Isthmian games included choral singing, poetry and musical contests, and philosophical debates.

Roman Corinth

The Corinth that Paul saw was a Roman Corinth, founded as *Colonia Laus Iulia Corinthiensis* in 46 BCE.[23] The process of Roman colonization

---

10. Broneer, "Hero Cults," 128–61; Salapata, "Hero Warriors," 245–60.

11. Larson, *Greek Heroine Cults*, 91, 124, 129–30, 138–39, 141–42.

12. Bookidis and Stroud, *Sanctuary of Demeter*, iii–v, vii, ix–xxiii, xxv, 1–11, 13–17, 19–51, 53–83, 85–151, 153–301, 303–91, 393–421, 423–81, 483–97, 499–505, 507–10.

13. Bookidis et al., "Dining in the Sanctuary," 1–54.

14. Gebhard, "Early Sanctuary," 475–76; Williams, "City of Corinth," 408–21; DeMaris, "Demeter," 105–17.

15. Hawthorne, "Myth of Palaemon," 92–98.

16. Brophy and Brophy, "Deaths in the Pan-Hellenic Games," 171–98; cf. Poliakoff, *Combat Sports*; Forbes, "Crime and Punishment," 169–73, 202–3.

17. A five-contest event including the long jump, javelin throw, and discus throw, the stadion, and wrestling.

18. Gardner, "Boat-Races," 90–97; Jordan, "Ithmian Amusements," 38; cf. Geagan, "Agonistic Institutions," 69–76.

19. Broneer, "Isthmian Victory Crown," 259.

20. Crowther, "Second-Place," 97–102. This continued through the Roman period.

21. Crowther, "Slaves and Greek Athletics," 35–42.

22. Plut. *Mor.* 675b (Minar et al., LCL). Dillon, "Parthenoi," 457–80.

23. Broneer, "Colonia Laus Iulia Corinthiensis," 388–90; Walbank, "Corinth under the Flavians," 251–64; Murphy-O'Connor, "Corinth," 147–59.

in Corinth is important to consider because it sets the background for the organization and population of the city when Paul arrives 100 years later.[24] Like the *curiae* in Spain, Roman Corinth was organized according to tribes usually associated with the ruling class in Rome.[25] L. R. Dean has found in the inscriptions at Corinth that the "names which have been preserved are Aelia, Antonia, Antoniniana, Augusta, Aurelia, Caelestia, Commoda, Iovia, Iulia felix, Papiria, Sabina, Saturnia, Severiana, and Traiana."[26] Strabo (ca. 63–24 BCE/CE) tells us that most of the colonists were freedmen, many of whom gained wealth through digging up pottery, brass, and other valuables and selling them back to Rome.[27] The sons of these freedmen would have become Roman citizens[28] and perhaps a few of these Corinthians moved up through the ranks of public office, status, and wealth. The expulsions of some Jews from Rome in 19 CE by the Roman Senate and by Claudius in 49 CE may have supplied the new Roman colony with the majority of its early Jewish inhabitants.[29]

Roman Corinth continued to worship the same gods as the pre-Roman Corinthians.[30] The Romans worshipped both the Greek pantheon as well as the Roman gods, and continued the worship of Demeter and Poesidon as patron gods.[31] The Roman games were integrated, as were all things, into the patronage system.[32] The Isthmian games were revived at about the time that Corinth was founded as a colony.[33]

---

24. Yeo, "Roman Colonies," 104–7, 129–30; MacKendrick, "Roman Colonization," 139–46; Romano, "Roman Surveyors," 62–85; Weigel, "Roman Colonial Commissioners," 224–31.

25. Romano, "City Planning," 279–301; Broneer, "Colonia Laus Iulia Corinthiensis," 388–90; Jones, "Civic Organization," 161–93; Jones, "Corinth Again," 49–56.

26. Dean, "Latin Inscriptions," 189–97.

27. Strab. 8.6.23. Strabo does not mention how Caesar chose the colonists. Cf. Treggiari, *Roman Freedmen*; Weaver, "Social Mobility," 3–20; Barja de Quiroga, "Freedmen," 326–48; Lintott, "Freedmen," 555–65.

28. Treggiari, *Roman Freedmen*, 229; Gardner, *Being a Roman Citizen*; Frier, *Casebook*.

29. Rutgers, "Roman Policy," 56–74.

30. Bookidis, "Religion in Corinth," 141–64.

31. Broneer, "Paul and the Pagan Cults," 169–87.

32. Geagan, "Isthmian Dossier," 349–60.

33. Kajava, "Isthmian Games," 168–78; cf. Broneer, "Apostle Paul and the Isthmian Games," 1–31.

Reading 1 Corinthians with Philosophically Educated Women

Philosophers in Corinth

Philosophers were active in both classical and Roman Corinth, and unfortunately the evidence concerning their lives and teachings is fragmentary. While it was nowhere near the stature of Athens, the hub of ancient philosophy, Corinth served as a place where ideas could be exchanged freely. Perhaps the earliest sources are legends regarding the wisdom of Periander, a seventh-century BCE tyrant of Corinth.[34] Cicero tells us that Dicaearchus (fl. 320–300 BCE), a pupil of Aristotle, held a philosophical discussion on the soul in Corinth:

> Dicaearchus autem in eo sermone, quem Corinthi habitum tribus libris exponit, doctorum hominum disputantium primo libro multos loquentes facit; duobus Pherecratem quendam Phthiotam senem, quem ait a Deucalione ortum, disserentem inducit nihil esse omnino animum, et hoc esse nomen totum inane, frustraque animalia et animantis appellari, neque in homine inesse animum vel animam nec in bestia, vimque omnem eam, qua vel agamus quid vel sentiamus, in omnibus corporibus vivis aequabiliter esse fusam nec separabilem a corpore esse, quippe quae nulla sit, nec sit quicquam nisi corpus unum et simplex, ita figuratum ut temperatione naturae vigeat et sentiat.

> But Dicæarchus, in that discourse of some learned disputants, held at Corinth, which he details to us in three books—in the first book introduces many speakers; and in the other two he introduces a certain Pherecrates, an old man of Phthia, who, as he said, was descended from Deucalion; asserting, that there is in fact no such thing at all as a soul, but that it is a name without a meaning; and that it is idle to use the expression "animals," or "animated beings;" that neither men nor beasts have minds or souls, but that all that power by which we act or perceive is equally infused into every living creature, and is inseparable from the body, for if it were not, it would be nothing; nor is there anything whatever really existing except body, which is a single and simple thing, so fashioned as to live and have its sensations in consequence of the regulations of nature.[35]

Unfortunately, this episode is only mentioned here in ancient literature.[36] The most important thing that this passage tells us is that Cicero thinks it

---

34. Diod. Sic. 9.7 tells us that Periander was removed from the Seven Wise Men because he had become a tyrant.

35. Cic. *Tusc.* 1.21 (Yonge, LCL).

36. It appears that this work is lost and no other writer in the ancient world mentions

Corinth and Its Philosophers

appropriate to place a well-known student of Aristotle in Corinth with other debating learned people concerning the nature of the soul.[37]

Themistius, quoting a lost work of Aristotle, tells us that a Corinthian farmer was so impressed with *Gorgias* that after reading it, he went to Athens to be a student of Plato.[38] Several sources suggest that Dionysius, the tyrant of Syracuse, fled to Corinth to become a school teacher. For example, Philo, a contemporary of Paul, writes:

> ἀρχαὶ βασιλέων αἱ μέγισται καθηρέθησαν βραχείᾳ καιροῦ ῥοπῇ. ἐγγυᾶταί μου τὸν λόγον Διονύσιος ὁ ἐν Κορίωθῳ, ὃς Σικελίας μὲν τύραννος ἦν, ἐκπεσὼν δὲ τῆς ἡγεμονίας εἰς Κόρινθον καταφεύγει καὶ γραμματιστὴς ὁ τοσοῦτος ἡγεμὼν γίνεται.

> The most mighty powers and authority of kings have been overthrown, and have disappeared in a very brief moment of time. There is an example to testify to the truth of my argument in Dionysius, who lived at Corinth, who had been tyrant of Sicily, and who, after he was expelled from his dominions, took refuge in Corinth; and though he had been so mighty a sovereign, became a schoolmaster.[39]

P. Oxy. 12 is a chronology of various events during the fourth century CE, and this papyrus contains a similar history of Dionysius:

> [ὀλυμπιάδι ἐνάτηι καὶ ἑ]κα[τοστῆι | ἐνίκα στάδιον Ἀριστ[ό]λυκος | [Ἀθηναῖο]ς, ἦρχον δ᾽ Ἀθήνησι | Λυκίσκος Πυθόδοτος Σωσι | γ[ένη]ς Νικόμαχος. ταύτης | κατὰ δὲ τὸ δεύτερον ἔτος Διονύσιος ὁ δεύτερος τῆς Σικελίας | τύραννος\ ἐκπεσὼν τῆς ἀρχῆς κατέπλευσεν εἰς Κό | ρινθον καὶ ἐκεῖ κατέμειωε | γράμματα διδάσκων. κατὰ δὲ | τὸν τέταρον βαγώας | εὐνοῦχος Ὤχον τὸν βασιλέ | α τῶν Περσῶν δολοφονή | σας τὸν νεώτατον αὐτοῦ τῶν | υἱῶν Ἄρσην κατέστησε βασιλέα, αὐτὸς πάντα διοκῶν.

> [In the 109th Olympiad] [344 BC] Aristolycus [of Athens won the stadion race], and the archons at Athens were [Lyciscus], Pythodotus, Sosigenes and Nicomachus. In the second year Dionysius II, tyrant of Sicily, fell from power and sailed off to Corinth, where he survived as a schoolteacher. In the fourth year the eunuch Bagoas murdered Ochus, the king of the Persians,

---

it; cf. Fortenbaugh and Schütrumpf, *Dicaearchus*, 19.

37. For details concerning the nature of the soul in this reference, see Sharples, "Dicaearchus," 146.

38. Them. *Or.* 295c–d; Ross, *Aristotle*, 23–24; Rose, *Aristotelis*, frag. 64. Greek text appears in Grote, *Plato*, 2:317.

39. Philo, *On Joseph* 132 (Yonge, *Works of Philo*).

and set up Arses who was the youngest of Ochus' sons as king, while he himself controlled the whole government.⁴⁰

Plutarch (ca. 46–120 CE) associates Dionysius with Plato, " Ἐκπεσὼν δὲ τῆς ἀρχῆς πρὸς μὲν τὸν εἰπόντα 'τί σε Πλάτων καὶ φιλοσοφία ὠφέλησε; τὸ τηλικαύτην' ἔφη 'τύχης μεταβολὴν ῥᾳδίως ὑπομένειν,'" "When he was deposed from his government, and one asked him what he got by Plato and philosophy, he answered, 'That I may bear so great a change of fortune patiently.'"⁴¹ There are even some unreliable traditions that Plato himself wrestled at the Isthmian games, winning twice.⁴² Athenaeus (fl. late 2nd CE) writes that Dionysius participated in some attacks on the school at Athens, notably using Lastheneia against them.

> Διονύσιος γοῦν ὁ τῆς Σικλίας τύραννος ἐν τῇ πρὸς αὐτὸν Ἐπιστολῇ κατὰτῆς φιληδονίας αὐτοῦ εἰπὼν καὶ φιλαργυρίαν αὐτῷ ὀνειδίζει καὶ τὸν Λασθεωενίας τῆς Ἀρκαδικῆς ἔρωτα, ἥτις καὶ Πλάτωνος ἠκηκόει.

> At all events Dionysius, the tyrant of Sicily, in his letter to [Speusippus] blaming him for his fondness for pleasure, reproaches him also for his covetousness, and for his love of Lastheneia the Arcadian, who had been a pupil of Plato.⁴³

Corinth produced many Cynic philosophers. In the fourth century BCE, Xeniades of Corinth purchased Diogenes of Sinope and later convinced Monimus, another slave, to follow his Cynic teachings. There is a tradition recorded by Diogenes Laertius (fl. 3rd c. CE) that Aristippus of Cyrene (ca. 435–ca. 356 BCE), whose grandson was taught by his mother, Arete, visited Corinth twice:

> Τοιοῦτος μὲν ὁ Θεόδβρος κἄν τούτοις. τελευταῖον δ' εἰς Κυρήνην ἀπελθὼν καὶ Μάγᾳ συμβιοὺς ἐν πάσῃ τιμῇ διετέλει τυχάνων. ἔνθεν τὸ πρῶτον ἐκβαλλόμενος λέγερται χάριέν τι εἰπεῖν· φησὶ γάρ, "καλῶς ποιεῖτε, ἄνδρες Κυρηναῖοι, ἐκ τῆς Λιβύης εἰς τὴν Ἑλλάδα με ἐξορίζοντες."

---

40. P. Oxy 12.4 = FGrHist 255.4.

41. Plut. *Mor.* 176.

42. Diog. Laert. 3.4. Alice Swift Riginos notes that the earliest tradition of Plato's competing in the pan-Hellenic games places him at Isthmia. Later traditions place him in one or more of the three other games, and his winning is also a later development, *Platonica*, 41. David C. Young asserts that there is no record anywhere in ancient literature of a person being both a superior intellectual and athlete. *Olympic Games*, 81.

43. Ath. 12.66.15. See also 7.10.9.

Corinth and Its Philosophers

They say also that on one occasion he came to Corinth, bringing with him a great many disciples; and that Metrocles the Cynic, who was washing leeks said to him, "You, who are a Sophist, would not have wanted so many pupils, if you had washed vegetables." And Theodorus, taking him up, replied, "And if you had known how to associate with men, you would not have cared about those vegetables."[44]

Εἰς Κόρινθον αὐτῷ πλέοντί ποτε καὶ χειμαζομένῳ συνέβη ταραχθῆαι. πρὸς οὖν τὸν εἰπόντα, "ἡμεῖς μὲν οἱ ἰδιῶται οὐ δεδοίκαμεν, ὑμεῖς δ᾽ οἱ φιλόσοφοι δειλιᾶτε," "οὐ γὰρ περὶ ὁμοίας," ἔφη, "ψυχῆς ἀγωνιῶμεν ἕκαστοι."

Once it happened, that when he was sailing to Corinth, he was overtaken by a violent storm; and somebody said, "We common individuals are not afraid, but you philosophers are behaving like cowards;" he said, "Very likely, for we have not both us the same kind of souls at stake."[45]

The same Theodorus who challenges Metrocles the Cynic in Corinth also criticized his sister Hipparchia the Cynic.[46]

Corinth was a safe haven for Xenophon of Athens and his children (ca. 394 BCE), and he remained there until his death. Antipater of Sidon (fl. 2nd c. BCE) preserves this event:

Εἰ καὶ σέ, Ξενοφων, Κραναοῦ Κέκροπός τε πολῖται φεύγειν κατέγνων τοῦ φίλου χάριν Κύρου, ἀλλὰ Κόρινθος ἔδεκτο φιλόξενος, ἢ σὐφιληδῶν οὕτως ἀρέσῃ κεῖθι καὶ μένερν ἔγνως.

If the citizens of Cranaus and Cecrops condemned you, Xenophon, to exile because of your friend Cyrus, yet hospitable Corinth received you, with which you were so pleased and content, and decided to remain there.[47]

In the first century, Demetrius of Corinth was a well-known Cynic and friend of Seneca the Younger.[48] Demetrius was born in Corinth and edu-

---

44. Diog. Laert. 2.103.

45. Diog. Laert. 2.71.

46. In both traditions he is referred to as Theodorus the Atheist (Diog. Laert. 2.85; 6.97).

47. *Anth. Pal.* 7.98.

48. Sen. *Ep.* 20.9; 62.3; 91.19; *Ben.* 7.8–11; Tac. *Ann.* 16.34; *Hist.* 4.40 (not a favorable reference—he says that Demetrius plead the cause of a criminal by avoiding fair argument); Dio Cass. 65; Lucian, *Toxaris*; Suet. *Vesp.* 13 (More on Vespasian's explusion of Demetrius); Philostr. *V A* 4.2. Cf. Goulet-Cazé, "Comprehensive Catalouge," 393.

cated in Athens (fl. 37–71 CE)—he was considered the ideal philosopher by Seneca[49] and Epictetus.[50]

Demetrius of Corinth was also friends with the famous senator Thrasea, a Stoic. There are many traditions that associate Demetrius with philosophically educated women. The story of Thrasea's death, a forced suicide by Nero, was quite popular in the ancient world. When one of his closest friends, Domitius Caecilianus, brought Thrasea the news of his condemnation by Nero, he found him in philosophical discussion with Demetrius in the presence of many hearers.

> Tum ad Thraseam in hortis agentem quaestor consulis missus vesperascente iam die. inlustrium virorum feminarumque coetus frequentis egerat, maxime intentus Demetrio Cynicae institutionis doctori.

> Then, as evening approached, the consul's quaestor was sent to Thrasea, who was passing his time in his garden. He had had a crowded gathering of distinguished men and women, giving special attention to Demetrius, a professor of the Cynic philosophy.[51]

Tacitus makes it clear that Thrasea knew he was going to die, so it is appropriate that he he gathered his friends together to discuss with Demetrius the nature of the soul and the separation of spirit and body.[52] Because Thrasea was a senator,[53] it is likely that the discussion group consisted of his elite ("distinguished") friends and their wives, but widows and unaccompanied wives could have attended as well. As for what Thrasea himself may have taught, it certainly aligns with his Stoic outlook:

> ἔλεγε γὰρ ὅτι "εἰ μὲν ἐμὲ μόνον ὁ Νέρων φονεύσειν ἔμελλε, πολλὴν ἂν εἶχον τοῖς ἄλλοις ὑπερκολακεύουσιν αὐτὸν συγγνώμην· εἰ δὲ καὶ ἐκείνων τῶν σφόδρα αὐτὸν ἐπαινούντων πολλοὺς τοὺς μὲν ἀνάλωκε τοὺς δὲ καὶ ἀπολέσει, τί χρὴ μάτην ἀσχημονοῦντα δοθλοπρεπῶς φθαρῆναι, ἐξὸν ἐλευθερίως ἀποδοῦναι τῇ φύσει τὸ ὀφριλάμενον; ἐμοῦ μὲν γὰρ πέρι καὶ ἔπριτα λόγος τις ἔσται, τούτων δέ, πλήνκατ' αὐτὸ τοῦτο ὅτι ἐσφάγησαν, οὐδείς."

---

49. Sen. *Ben.* 7.8.

50. Epict. *Disc.* 1.25.3. Cf. Eunap. *VS* 2.1.5; Philostr. *V A* 4.25.

51. Tac. *Ann.* 16.35. Thrasea continually aggravated Nero, which led to his death. Cf. Tac. *Ann.* 13.49; 14.12 (walked out of the Senate during Agrippina's case); 15.20–22 (short speech to the senate); 16.21–35 (Nero kills him for the Agrippina incident and not supporting the Juvenile games); *Hist.* 2.91, 5.5; Dio Cass. 62.15; cf. Juv. 5.36. Toynbee, "Dictators and Philosophers," 49–58.

52. Tact. *Ann.* 16.34.

53. Oswyn Murray provides a detailed review of Thrasea's career in "Quinquennium Neronis," 41–61.

τοιοῦτος μὲν ὁ Θρασέας ἐγένετο, καὶ τοῦτο ἀεὶ πρὸς ἑαυτὸν ἔλεγεν "ἐμὲ Νέρων ἀποκτεῖναι μὲν δύναται, Βλάψαι δὲ οὔ."

He used to say, for example: "If I were the only one that Nero was going to put to death, I could easily pardon the rest who load him with flatteries. But since even among those who praise him to excess there are many whom he has either already disposed of or will yet destroy, why should one degrade oneself to no purpose and then perish like a slave, when one may pay the debt to nature like a freeman? As for me, men will talk of me hereafter, but of them never, except only to record the fact that they were put to death." Such was the man that Thrasea showed himself to be; and he was always saying to himself: "Nero can kill me, but he cannot harm me."[54]

Thrasea would not indulge Nero by supporting his games, or listening to him at the theatre, and he had a bad habit of walking out of the Senate—or not appearing at all—demonstrating that he did not like the laws which were passed to flatter Nero. For these reasons Dio Cassius tells us that Nero killed him.[55] Pliny the Younger took care of Thrasea's wife and daughter after his death.[56] Thrasea's stepson Helvidius Priscus[57] was also an outspoken Stoic senator and at least one scholar thinks that he led Thrasea's "philosophical band"[58] after his execution.

Demetrius of Corinth was criticized by Dio Cassius:

ὡς δ'οὖν καὶ ἄλλοι πολλοὶ ἐκ τῶν στωικῶν καλουμένων λόγων προαχθέντες, μεθ' ὧν καὶ Δημήτριος ὁ κυνικός, συχνὰ καὶ οὐκ ἐπιτήδεια τοῖς παροῦσι δημοσίᾳ, τῷ τῆς φιλοσοφίας προσχήματι καταχρώμενοι, διελέγοντο, κἀκ τούτου καὶ ὑποδιέφθειρόν τινας, ἔρεισεν ὁ Μινουκιανὸς τὸν Οὐεσπασιανὸν πάντας τοὺς τοιούτους ἐκ τῆς πόλεως ἐκβαλεῖν, εἰπὼν ὀργῇ μᾶλλον ἢ φιλολογίᾳ τινὶ πολλὰ κατ' αὐτῶν.

Inasmuch as many others, too, including Demetrius the Cynic, actuated by the Stoic principles, were taking advantage of the name of philosophy to teach publicly many doctrines inappropriate to the times, and in this way were subtly corrupting some of

---

54. Dio Cass. 62.15.3–4.
55. Dio Cass. 62.26.3.
56. Plin. *Ep.* 3.11.3; Sherwin-White, *Letters of Pliny*, 243.
57. On Helvidius Priscus, see Wirszubski, *Libertas*, 148; Brunt, "Stoicism and the Principate," 28–31; Chilver and Townend, *Historical Commentary*, 6–8.
58. Tac. *Hist.* 4.5, *Dial.* 5; Suet. *Vesp.* 15; Plin. *Ep.* 7. 19 (eulogy for his wife). Epict. *Disc.* 1.2; Malitz, "Helvidius Priscus," 231–46.

their hearers, Mucianus, prompted rather by anger than by any passion for philosophy, inveighed at length against them and persuaded Vespasian to expel all such persons from the city . . .[59]

καὶ πάντας αὐτίκα τοὺς φιλοσόφους ὁ Οὐεσπασιανός, πλὴν τοῦ Μουσωνίου, ἐκ τῆς Ῥώμης ἐξέμαλε, τὸν δὲ δὴ Δημήτριον καὶ τὸν Ὁστιλιανὸν καὶ ἐς νήσους κατέκλεισε. καὶ ὁ μὲω Ὁστίλιος εἰ καὶ τὰ μάλιστα μὴ ἐπαύσατο περὶ τῆς φυγῆς ἀκούσας ἔτυχε γὰρ διαλεγόμενός τινι ἀλλὰ καὶ πολλῷ πλείω κατὰ τῆς μοναρχίας κατέδραμεν, ὅμως παραχρῆμα μετέστη· τῷ δὲ Δημητρίῳ μηδ' ὣς ὑπείκοντι λευσεν ὁ Οὐεσπασιανὸς λεχθῆναι ὅτι σὺ μὲν πάντα ποιεῖς ἵνα σε ἀποκτείνω, ἐγὼ δὲ κύνα ὑλακτοῦντα οὐ φονεύω."

And Vespasian immediately expelled from Rome all the philosophers except Musonius; Demetrius and Hostilianus he even deported to islands. Hostilianus, though he decidedly would not desist when he was told about the sentence of exile (he happened to be conversing with somebody), but merely inveighed all the more strongly against monarchy, nevertheless straightway withdrew. Demetrius, on the contrary, would not yield even then, and Vespasian commanded that this message should be given to him: "You are doing everything to force me to kill you, but I do not slay a barking dog."[60]

Philostratus says that Pancrates the Cynic taught philosophy at the Isthmus in the early second century.[61] Nothing is known about Pancrates other than he lived in Athens for a while and escaped stoning by stunning the crowd with the saying, "Lollianus does not sell bread but words."[62]

Stoicism was well represented in Corinth. At least one tradition indicates that the Megarian philosopher, Thrasymachus of Corinth (fl. 4th c. BCE), taught Stilpo (ca. 360–ca. 280 BC) who taught Zeno of Citium (334 BC–262 BC), the founder of Stoicism.[63] The destruction of Corinth and the subsequent rise in value of Corinthian bronze became proverbial in the writings of Cicero, Servius Sulpicius Rufus (106–43 BCE), and Seneca. Cicero gives a testimony concerning his visit in 77 BCE before the city was rebuilt, "at Corinth the sudden sight of the ruins had more effect on me that upon the actual inhabitants, for long contemplation had the harden-

---

59. Dio Cass. 66.13.
60. Dio Cass. *Xiphilini Epitome* 65.13.1.
61. Philostr. *VS* 1.23.
62. Goulet-Cazé, "Comprehensive Catalouge," 400.
63. Diog. Laert. 2.113 (*Life of Stilpo* 1.1).

Corinth and Its Philosophers

ing effect of length of time upon their souls."[64] Several years later, Servius Sulpicius wrote to Cicero, "As I sailed across, I began to look at the places roundabout; behind me was Aegina, before me Megara, on the right Piraeus, on the left Corinth: they were once flourishing towns, now they lie in ruins, flattened (45 BCE)."[65] Seneca uses the following metaphor, "Therefore, let just as many books be acquired as are enough, but not for mere show. 'It is more respectable,' you say, 'to squander money on these than on Corinthian bronzes and on pictures.'"[66]

The well-known Stoic Musonius Rufus (25-101 CE) was exiled to the island of Gyaros by Nero in 65 CE, and according to Philostratus he was sent to work along with the aforementioned Demetrius the Cynic on the canal of the Isthmus of Corinth two years later.[67] Arrian addresses the discourses of Epictetus to the Corinthian aristocrat Lucius Gellius Menander.[68]

The Stoic/eclectic philosopher and orator Dio Chrysostom (40-120 CE) gives us a view of philosophical debates among the pandemonium of the crowds during the Isthmian Games.[69]

ἐπεὶ δὲ ἧκεν ὁ τῶν Ἰσθμίων χρόνος καὶ πάντες ἦσαν ἐν Ἰσθμῷ, κατέβη καὶ αὐτός . . . καὶ δὴ καὶ τότε ἦν περὶ τὸν νεὼν τοῦ Ποσειδῶνος κούειν πολλῶν μὲν σοφιστῶν κακοδαιμόνων βοώντων καὶ λοιδορουμένων ἀλλήλοις, καὶ τῶν λεγομένων μαθητῶν ἄλλου ἄλλῳ μαχομένων, πολλῶν δὲ συγγραφέων ἀναγιγνωσκόντων ἀναίσθητα συγγράμματα, πολλῶν δὲ ποιητῶν

---

64. Cic. *Tusc.* 3.53. He says elsewhere that the city was completely razed because the Romans feared that the people would one day recover from their defeat, *Off.* 1.9.35.

65. Cic. *Fam.* 4.5.4. Gebhard and Dickie argue that the descriptions of Cicero and Servius should not be taken as eyewitness accounts, "View from the Isthmus," 263.

66. Sen. *Tran.* 9.5. Cf. *On the Shortness of Life*, 12.2. In *Polyb.* 1.1, Seneca argues that it is folly to mourn over the loss of cities when the entire universe will eventually perish.

67. Apollon. v. 19, p. 178; Parker, "Musonius the Etruscan," 123-37. For Musonius at the Isthmus, see Philostratus (Pseudo-Lucian), *Nero*; Whitmarsh, "Pseudo-Lucianic *Nero*," 142-60. For exile, see Braginton, "Exile," 391-407.

68. Kent, *Inscriptions*, no. 124, pp. 55-56 is an inscription honoring Arrian by the Gelli family. Cf. Oliver, "Gellii of Corinth," 335-37.

69. The earlier Greek philosophers appeared at many pan-Hellenic games. The Olympic games were especially important: Pythagoras revealed his golden thigh at the Olympic games (Ael. *Hist.* 2.21), Plato won some disciples in Olympia (Ael. *Hist.* 4.9), Empedocles recruited disciples there, Gorgias was often invited to speak at the Olympic games, and Ion (at Isthmia, Plut. *Mor.* 79d), Antisthenes gave an oration at Isthmia (Diog. Laert. 6.1), Lysias gave an Olympic oration (Plut. *Mor.* 836d), Isocrates gave a lecture there (*Isoc.* 4), Hippias (Pl. *Hip. mai.* 363c) frequented the games to engage in philosophical debate. Håkan Tell examines the role of intellectual pursuits at the games in "Sages at the Games," 249-52; Guthrie, *Sophists*, 44-45; Jennings, *World of Ion of Chios*, 338.

Reading 1 Corinthians with Philosophically Educated Women

> ποιήματα ᾀδόντων, καὶ τούτους ἐπαινούντων ἑτέρων ... εὐθὺς οὖν καὶ αὐτῷ τινες προσῆλθον, τῶν μὲν Κορινθίων οὐδείς· οὐδὲ γὰρ ᾤοντο οὐδὲν ὠφεληθήσεσθαι, ὅτι καθ' ἡμέραν ἑώρων αὐτὸν ἐν Κορίθῳ· τῶν δὲ ξένων ἦσαν οἱ προσιόντες ...
>
> So, when the time for the Isthmian games had arrived, and everybody was at the Isthmus ... That was the time when one could hear Poseidon's temple shouting and reviling one another, and their disciples, as they were called, fighting with one another, many writers reading aloud their stupid works, many poets reciting their poems while others applauded them ... Naturally a crowd gathered around him immediately. No Corinthians, however, for they did not think it would at all be worth their while, since they were accustomed to see him every day at Corinth. The crowd that gathered around him were strangers ...[70]

This speech claims to describe the nature of the attendance of Diogenes the Cynic (ca. 420–323 BCE) at the games, but Chrysostom most likely describes his experience in the first century because it compliments monuments and other artifacts found in the area of that time.[71] Bruce Winter argues that Dio chose the figure of Diogenes to criticize the sophists of his time because Diogenes was a volatile character that made a good platform for criticism. Winter suggests that the speech describes Dio's attendance at the games during a visit to Corinth during his exile in 89–96 CE.[72]

Dio Chrysostom provides one of the many contexts in which philosophically educated women would participate in discourse with other philosophers. In the context of the games, there was public discourse—and we know that women were present because they competed in and supported the games. Cicero and his friends preferred to stay indoors to have philosophical discussions during the Pythian games, and that also seems to be the case with Plutarch.

Plutarch visited Corinth at the time of the Isthmian games and participated in a philosophical discourse with other learned guests. Apparently, Plutarch and his associates preferred to gather with fellow intellectuals rather than celebrate the celebrate feasts hosted by Sospis:

> Ἰσθμίων ἀγομένων ἐν τῇ δευτέρᾳ τῶν Σώσπιδος ἀγωνοθεσιῶν τὰς μὲν ἄλλας ἑστιάσεις διεφύγομεν, ἑστιῶντος αὐτοῦ πολλοὺς μέν ἅμα ξένους πάντας δὲ πολλάκις τοὺς πολίτας· ἅπαξ δὲ τοὺς μάλιστα φίλους καὶ φιλολόγους οἴκοι δεχομένου καὶ αὐτοὶ

---

70. Dio Chrys. *Or.* 8.7.6–9.
71. Broneer, "Apostle Paul," 18; see also Murphy-O'Connor, *St. Paul's Corinth*, 97.
72. Winter, *After Paul Left Corinth*, 32.

παρῆμεν. ἀπηρμένων δε τῶν πρώτων τραπεζῶν ἧκέν τις Ἡρώδῃ τῷ ῥήτορι παρὰ γνωρίμου νενικηκότος ἐγκωμίῳ φοίνικα καὶ στέφανόν τινα τῶν πλεκτῶν κομίζων.

The Isthmian games being celebrated, when Sospis was the second time director of the solemnity, we avoided other entertainments,—he treating a great many strangers and often all his fellow-citizens,—but once, when he entertained his nearest and most learned friends at his own house, I was one of the company. After the first course, one coming to Herodes the rhetorician brought a palm and a wreathed crown, which one of his acquaintance, who had won the prize for an encomiastic exercise, sent him.[73]

Borimir Jordan provides several references for gatherings like this one at Isthmia.[74] Cicero (106–43 BCE) and his friends chose to gather outside of Rome for philosophical discussion during the games.[75] Pliny the Younger (ca. 61–112 CE) was delighted when Tacitus (56–117 CE) was mistaken for him by a Roman knight during a conversation at the Circensian games.[76] Reflecting later the same well-established traditions of philosophical discourse at the games, other sophists who were attracted to the pan-Hellenic games in the second century include: Polemo (90–144 CE, Olympic, patron was Herodes Atticus and he interacted with Favorinus, Philostratus 538, 442, 491), Herodes Atticus (101–77 CE, Olympia, Philostratus 557), Herodes's father (fl. late 2nd c. BCE, Olympia, Philostr. V S 1.25, 539) and Antipater of Hierapolis (fl. 200 CE, Olympic and Panathenaic, Philostr. V S 24.1). The games were attractive to many intellectuals and philosophers because they served as a platform for orations and debate. Robert Weir finds in the inscriptions at Delphi two second-century CE intellectuals who travelled to the Pythian games: P. Cornelius Lupus of Nikopolis (ca. 95–100 CE) and Isocrates of Athens (ca. 80–90 CE).[77]

Favorinus was important philosopher with close ties to Corinth. A distinguished student of Dio Chrysostom (ca. 40–120 CE), Favorinus (ca.

---

73. Plut. *Mor.* 723a.

74. Borimir Jordan provides several references for earlier gatherings like this at Isthmia, "Isthmian Amusements," 32–67; Pind. *Pyth.* 4.294; *Nem.* 9.48; *Isthm.* 6.1 and Scholium on *Ol.* 10.55; Dem. 19.195.

75. Cic. *Orat.* 7.

76. Plin. *Ep.* 104.

77. Weir, *Roman Delphi*, 115. P. Cornelius Lupus = *FD* 3.4.114, 115; Isocrates = *FD* 3.2.98; cf. Kokolakis, "Intellectual Activity," 153–58.

Reading 1 Corinthians with Philosophically Educated Women

80–150 CE)[78] authored some discourses which are preserved under his master's name.[79] Favorinus,[80] an Academic philosopher, was also a pupil and friend of Plutarch and a teacher of Herodes Atticus, who was a notable patron in Corinth.[81] Herodes Atticus himself had a notable student, Sceptus of Corinth (fl. 2nd CE).[82] Favorinus has a part in Plutarch's *Table Talk*, which includes a lengthy discussion on love.

Philostratus (ca. 170–247 CE) tells us that a statue of Favorinus (ca. 80–160 CE) was placed in the public library of Corinth to encourage the youth to imitate his eloquence.[83] Some scholars believe that when Favorinus agitated Hadrian, the Corinthians removed the statue.[84] Simon Swain believes that, on the basis of Favorinus's *Corinthian Oration* (32–35), that the Corinthians pulled down the statue because of a rumor that he had committed adultery.[85]

A word on the library at Corinth, where a statue of Favorinus (ca. 80–160 CE) was erected, would be helpful because it may well have been a source of education in Corinth, perhaps for some in the Pauline community. The concept of "public libraries" was developed in the first century BCE. The sources are inconclusive as to who exactly had access to "public libraries." Certainly the wealthy had easier access to these books, but libraries were often attached to very public points such as baths and porticos, suggesting a slightly larger readership than wealthy book collectors.[86] In any case, literary patronage experienced a shift from private—patrons lending books to wealthy friends or clients—to patrons constructing libraries for a wider audience.

Favorinus's (ca. 80–160 CE) learning was praised by Demetrius the Cynic (fl. 1st CE), Cornelius Fronto (ca. 100–170 CE), Cassius Dio (ca.

---

78. Cf. Winter, *Philo and Paul*, 128.

79. In *Disc.* 37, Favorinus addresses the Corinthians concerning a statue of him that was placed in their library. Winter, "Favorinus," 196–205; Gleason, *Making Men*, 3–20. Håkan Tell examines the role of intellectual pursuits at the games in "Sages at the Games," 249–52; cf. Guthrie, *Sophists*, 44–45.

80. For an ancient biography of Favorinus, see Philostr. *V S* 1.8.

81. Paus. 1.7; Moles, "Career and Conversion," 79–100; Rutledge, "Herodes the Great," 97–109.

82. Philostr. *V S* 573, 585.

83. Philostr. *V S* 1.8. [remember "philosophers who were skilled at rhetoric"]. Weinberg, *Corinth*, 11–12.

84. Winter, "Toppling of Favorinus," 291–306.

85. Swain, "Favorinus and Hadrian," 154.

86. Dix, "Public Libraries," 290; Marshall, "Library Resources," 261–62. My sources do not permit me to speculate on the nature of the literacy of readers in public libraries.

155–229 CE; 69.3.6), and Aulus Gellius (125–80 CE; 2.12.15, 16.1.3). Galen (ca. 129–217 CE) wrote two lost treatises against Favorinus: *To Favorinus on the Best Teaching* and *To Favorinus, Concerning Epictetus*.[87] In his oration on Fortune, Favorinus alludes to many educated women:

ἤδη δέ τινα καὶ τῶν ἰδίων παθῶν τῇ τύχῃ προφέρουσιν, ἡ Μήδεια τὸν ἔρωτα, ὁ Μίδας τὴν εὐχήν, ἡ Φαίδρα τὴν διαβολήν, ὁ Ἀλκμαίων, ὅτι ἐπλανᾶτο ὁ Ὀρέστης, ὅτι ἐμαίνετο. ἐρῶ δὲ ὑμῖν τινα καὶ Κύπριον λόγον, εἰ βούλεσθε. νετο. ἐρῶ δὲ ὑμῖν τινα καὶ Κύπριον λόγον, εἰ βούλεσθε. ἤνεγκεν ὁ παλαιὸς βίος καὶ ἐνδόξους γυναῖκας, Ῥοδογούνην πολεμικήν, Σεμίραμιν βασιλικήν, Σαπφὼ μουσικήν, Τιμάνδραν καλήν· οὕτω καὶ ἐν Κύπρῳ Δημώνασσα ἐγένετο, πολιτική τε ὁμοῦ γυνὴ καὶ νομοθετική. τρεῖς ἔθηκεν αὕτη τοῖς Κυπρίοις νόμους· τὴν μοιχευθεῖσαν κειραμένην πορνεύεσθαι· θυγάτηρ αὐτῆς ἐμοιχεύθη καὶ τὴν κόμην ἀπεκείρατο κατὰ τὸν νόμον καὶ ἐπορεύετο. τὸν αὐτὸν ἀποκτείναντα ἄταφον ῥίπτεσθαι· δεύτερος οὗτος Δημωνάσσης νόμος· τρίτος ὥστε μὴ ἀποκτεῖναι βοῦν ἀρότριον.

Furthermore, men even reproach Fortune for some of their own emotional weaknesses—Medea for her passion, Midas for his prayer, Phaedra for her false accusation, Alcmaeon for his wandering, Orestes for his madness. But I will tell you also a certain Cyprian tale if you wish. The days of old produced women of distinction as well as men—Rhodogunê the warrior, Semiramis the queen, Sappho the poetess, Timandra the beauty; just so Cyprus too had its Demonassa, a woman gifted in both statesmanship and law-giving. She gave the people of Cyprus the following three laws: a woman guilty of adultery shall have her hair cut off and be a harlot—her daughter became an adulteress, had her hair cut off according to the law, and practised harlotry; whoever commits suicide shall be cast out without a burial—this was the second law of Demonassa; third, a law forbidding the slaughter of a plough ox.[88]

Some scholars believe that Favorinus is not simply mentioning Sappho but that her poetry influenced him.[89] Sometime in the first century, the Corinthians honored another rhetor with a statue with the inscription: "By decree

---

87. Ioppolo, "Academic Position," 183–213.

88. Dio Chrys 64.2; Ael. *VH* 5.14: "This also was observed by them; A ploughing Oxe, that laboureth under the yoak, either with Plough or Cart, sacrifice not. For he also is a Tiller of the earth, and partakes with men of their labour."

89. Edmonds, "Sappho's Book," 5.

of the city council, Corinth the mother city (set up this monument in honor of) Peducaeus Cestianus the Apollonian orator."[90]

There may be some memory of (neo-)Pythagoreans in Corinth preserved in a biographer of Phythagoras. Iamblichus (ca. 245–325 CE) tells us of the remarkable friendship that the Pythagoreans Phintias and Damon practiced in Corinth (4th c. BCE).[91] Iamblichus also lists Chrysippus of Corinth as a notable Pythagorean.[92]

There is no direct evidence for contact between Epicureanism and Corinth, but the inscriptions of Diogenes of Oneoanda—which includes the *Letter to Mother* (see above chapter 3)—were installed just 50 miles north of the city in the second century CE. There must have been an Epicurean community in Oneoanda, and it is not unreasonable to assume that members of that community travelled to Corinth for the Isthmian games, to visit friends, or conduct business. C. W. Chilton, in the introduction to his translation of the Oneoanda fragments, writes, "one cannot doubt that there were Epicurean communities in many of these towns, communities which Paul might well have hoped to convert."[93]

The work of Norman DeWitt must be addressed due to its wide usage in older scholarship. DeWitt argues that Paul specifically addresses Epicureans in Corinth.[94] DeWitt begins his analysis with the assumption that as Paul made himself a Greek to the Greeks, so he must have made himself an Epicurean to the Epicureans.[95] From such a starting point, there is nowhere to go but deeper into Epicureanism with nothing to temper one's gaze. DeWitt argues that there was no competition from Platonists or Stoics, so the only popular philosophy that the Corinthian church would be exposed to is Epicureanism:

---

90. Kent, *Inscriptions*, no. 269 = Pl. 23. Inv. 1205. As with many other professions, students destined for a career in oratory would undergo an apprenticeship with a successful orator before entering the profession, or of course learn from their father. On Roman orators, see Wooten, *Orator*; Morstein-Marx, *Mass Oratory*; Steel, *Roman Oratory*; Berry and Erskine, *Form and Function*; for rhetorical exercises in Roman education, see Bloomer, "Schooling in Persona," 57–78.

91. Iambl. *VP* 33.3. Iamblichus attributes the story to Aristoxenus (b. 370 BCE), Porphyry (*VP* 59–61) attributes it to Nichomachus. It was known to Cicero, Cic. *Off.* 3.45; *Tusc.* 5.22. Cicero and Diodorus Siculus place the time of the event at the time of Dionysius the Elder in Syracuse, 405–367 BCE. Iamblichus places the event in the time of Dionysius the Younger in Corinth (Oldfather, LCL, 59n8).

92. *VP* 36.267. Unfortunately, Iamblichus gives no indication of date.

93. Chilton, *Diogenes*, xxiv.

94. DeWitt, *St. Paul and Epicurus*, 113.

95. Ibid., 106.

The other Greek philosophies were offering no competition. Platonism was always for the intellectual few. Neither were the followers of Aristotle numerous and their interest was less in human beings than in plants and animals. Stoicism with its high pretentions attracted the "silk cushion" class and disqualified itself for the multitude by its asperity.[96]

DeWitt's analysis, his assumption notwithstanding, is a good starting place inasmuch as he argues that Paul is using Greco-Roman rhetoric and parts of philosophy to argue against rhetoric/philosophy. However, DeWitt's argument concerning the pervasive influence of Epicureanism on Paul is overstated in the extreme. Without support, he argues that Paul was an Epicurean early in life and whatever Paul writes that is not Epicurean, he does so as an ex-Epicurean.[97] DeWitt also assumes that Paul's audience was literate and of higher status.[98] DeWitt has made several contributions to identifying Epicurean elements and parallels in Paul, but his conclusion related to the significance of these parallels do not recognize the eclectic nature of Paul's use of philosophy. The best research concerning Paul and Epicureanism is the work on Philodemus edited and written by David Konstan. This work focuses on friendship and will be discussed as needed in chapters 5–7 when Paul uses or addresses elements of friendship that would be relevant to a philosophically educated woman with Epicurean sympathies.[99]

Corinth produced many philosophers, beginning with the legacy of Diogenes the Cynic (ca. 412–323 BCE). Other Cynics include Monimus (fl. 4th c. BCE), Metrocles (fl. 325 BCE), and Demetrius (fl. 1st c. CE). The Neo-Pythagorean Iamblichus (ca. 245–325 CE) remembers three Pythagoreans from Corinth: Phintias (4th c. BCE), Damon (4th c. BCE), and Chrysippus (date unknown). Representing Epicureanism, fifty miles north of Corinth, the wealthy parton Diogenes of Oneoanda (fl. 2nd c. CE) erected a huge monument to his beloved philosophy, possibly demonstrating that there was an Epicurean community there. The great orator and Skeptic philospher Favorinus (ca. 80–150 CE) was honored with a statue in the Corinthian library, only to have it torn down for political reasons, and possibly restored after a subsequent oration. Favorinus (ca. 80–150 CE) taught the notable Corinthian patron Herodes Atticus (101–77 CE) who himself had a well-known student, Sceptus of Corinth (fl. 2nd c. CE). Some affection for Stoicism was alive in Corinth, because it was to the Corinthian patron

---

96. Ibid., 106.
97. Ibid., 177.
98. Ibid., 168–69.
99. Konstan et al., *Philodemus*; Konstan, *Friendship*.

Reading 1 Corinthians with Philosophically Educated Women

Lucius Gellius Menander that Arrian addressed the works of Epictetus. There is also a legend that Musonius Rufus helped build the Isthmus of Corinth while in exile.

The Isthmian games attacted philosophers and other intellectuals to Corinth for discussion and debate. Dio Chrysostom (ca. 40–120 CE) describes an incident in the life of Diogenes the Cynic (ca. 412–323 BCE) where intellectuals gathered for debate, but this oration seems to more accurately describe a first-century situation. Plutarch (ca. 46–120 CE) also relates a debate at the Isthmian games during the first century, but the setting of his account is a home. A few other records of philosophers attending other Pan-Hellenic games also survive in Cicero (106–43 BCE, Cic. *Orat.* 7) and Pliny the Younger (61–112 CE; Plin. *Ep.* 104.), and in epigraphical evidence.[100]

These traditions are important because most of these philosophical schools have women who are associated with their founding: Theano the Pythagorean; Arete the Cyrenaic; Lasthenia, Diotima, and Aspasia the teachers of Socrates; Hipparchia the Cynic; and Leontion the Epicurean. The tradition of philosophically educated women continues in the Roman period, and it expands to other schools: the female students of the the first-century Stoics Porcia, Arria and her daughter, and Fannia, Julia Domna (170–217 CE), and the scholar and neo-Platonist Plotinus (ca. 204–70 CE). The tradition of women's involvement in Pythagoreanism continues into the Roman period with the Pythagorean pseudepigraphal works which are attributed to the famous Pythagorean women including: Theano, Perictione (in this case, the name of Plato's mother), and Myia. Crowning this list are the philosophically educated women who are celebrated in Paul's near contemporaries Tullia and Caerellia (Cicero), Marcia and Helvia (Seneca), Eurydice (Plutarch), and Pliny the Younger (Calpurnia). In light of the philosophical heritage of Corinth and the long traditions of philosophically educated women in the schools represented there, the possibility that there were such women in the community of Christ believers is quite strong. I will argue in the next section that the various contexts of 1 Corinthians indicate the presence of philosophically educated women.

Philosophically Educated Women in the Corinthian Church

For the purposes of this study, a philosophically educated woman is a woman who has come into contact with enough philosophical teaching from any school to identify and interact with components of 1 Corinthians which have points of connection with Greco-Roman philosophy. In chapter 2, we

100. Weir, *Roman Delphi*, 115.

saw that some women throughout the Greek and Roman periods received the full compliment of ancient education including poetry, medicine, athletics, dance, music, and literacy. In chapter 3, I reviewed the histories of women in philosophy. Women were instrumental in the founding of most major schools of philosophy including Pythagoreanism, Platonism, Cynicism, Epicureanism, and Stoicism. Women were involved in these schools until the first century and beyond. In the first half of chapter 4, I have shown that all of these schools have a long history in Corinth. Several themes develop when we look at the histories of the education of women in general and philosophical education in particular.

It is critical to remember that the ancient wealthy household provides the central conduit for philosophical education. This does not mean that all philosophers were wealthy. It means that most of the traditions indicate that philosophically educated women were taught by their wealthy fathers or husbands. Wealthy people also brought philosophers into their houses to tutor their children and entertain their wealthy guests at dinner parties. These tutors may have been slaves or freedpersons themselves and could have taught slaves in the household who might later be freed. Other philosophers, such many Cynics and some Stoics, chose to live in poverty and taught their wives and daughters to do the same.

Therefore, it makes sense to examine 1 Corinthians for women who share similar circumstances. In this section, I will argue that the social structures of the Corinthian church compliments the historical contexts in which philosophically educated women thrived. Paul's primary focus of address is churches that meet in households which included a diverse cross section of people.[101] Because education is centered on wealthy households in most philosophical traditions (Platonism, Epicureanism, and [neo-] Pythagoreanism) I will examine the women of 1 Corinthians looking for signs of wealthy households and corresponding philosophical content. The best places to start are with the persons whom we know were participants in the Corinthian community.

Some notes on the relationship between 1 Corinthians and Romans are necessary before we begin. Paul wrote the epistle to the Romans from Corinth,[102] and concludes the letter with greetings from several Corinthians, some of whom may indicate the presence of philosophically educated women in the community of Jesus believers there. These names include Tertius, Gaius, Erastus, and Quartus. The entire chapter of Romans 16 is a

---

101. Theissen, *Social Setting*, 69–120, 145–74; Meeks, *Urban Christians*, 75–77.

102. Based on Romans 16:1, Phoebe of Cenchrae brought the letter from Corinth to Rome. Stuhlmacher, *Paul's Letter to the Romans*, 246; Brendan, *Romans*; Witherington and Hyat, *Romans*, 7.

Reading 1 Corinthians with Philosophically Educated Women

letter of recommendation for Phoebe, who is generally considered to be the courier, reader, and theological interpreter of the epistle to the Romans.[103] Aquila and Priscilla, who apparently were in Rome at the time of the delivery of the epistle, also worked with Paul in Corinth.[104]

In addition to the epistle to the Romans, some members of the Corinthian community are mentioned in Acts. This of course presents other challenges related to the questionable historicity of Acts.[105] The description of Paul's activity in Corinth in Acts 18 includes Titus Justus,[106] Crispus, Sosthenes, and Priscilla and Aquila. Because the historicity of Acts is dubious,[107] I will approach its information tentatively and argue that it *may* indicate something about the community at Corinth. The only information relevant to my argument that is unique to Acts is the question of the office of synagogue leader held by Crispus and Sosthenes, and I will therefore argue that this information *could* point to wealthy households in the Corinthian community. All other information concerning Corinthians will be gleaned from 1 Corinthians and Romans. The remainder of this chapter will comprise a review of the names mentioned in 1 Corinthians and the relevant people mentioned in Romans and Acts, with the purpose of looking for indications of wealth and household contexts that signify the possibility of philosophically educated women in the Corinthian community of Jesus believers.

A Corinthian Christian in Public Office: Erastus

In the first chapter of 1 Corinthians, Paul indicates that there were some unspecified Christ believers who were educated, wealthy, and of noble birth (1 Cor 1:26–29).[108] Interpretations of 1 Corinthians 1:26–29 have led several scholars to conclude that the Christian community at Corinth was socially stratified, with most of the people being of low social status and

---

103. A detailed discussion of Phoebe will follow.
104. Aquila and Priscilla will be discussed in detail below.
105. For historicity of Acts, see Mattill, "Value of Acts," 76–98.
106. I will dismiss from the outset all persons named that have no corresponding information.
107. For a bibliography, see Phillip, *Acts*, 46–77; cf. Talbert, *Reading Luke-Acts*, 197–218; Tyson, "Acts Studies," 23–42; Rothschild, *Luke-Acts*.
108. There is an extensive bibliography on the exegetical and theological problems posed by 1 Cor 1:26–29 in Thiselton, *First Epistle to the Corinthians*, 176–78.

some being of a higher social status.[109] Andrew Clarke nicely characterizes this interpretation:

> It is clear from the verse in question, βλέπετε γὰρ τὴν κλῆσιν ὑμῶν, ἀδελφοί, ὅτι οὐ πολλοὶ σοφοὶ κατὰ σάρκα, οὐ πολλοὶ δυνατοί, οὐ πολλοὶ εὐγενεῖ, that these two perspectives are not mutually exclusive. Paul's statement that there are not many wise in human terms, not many powerful and not many of noble birth demonstrates that there were, at the least, some who fitted these categories; equally, however, there were some who could not be classified as wise, influential, or well-born. The Corinthian church, it seems clear, contained a social mix.[110]

Several aspects of 1 Corinthians, confirm this social stratification in a general sense: Paul's affirmation that there were a few wealthy participants in the community (1 Cor 1:26–28), the household context of worship in the form of love feasts, the invitation of Christ believers to eat with outsiders, and participation in courts. Erastus is generally considered to be a wealthy patron of the church, but there are several problems with the identification of his social status.

Erastus (Acts 19:22; Rom 16:23[111]) deserves some discussion because he is the only person mentioned in the Corinthian community who is explicitly identified as holding a public office: οἰκονόμος τῆς πόλεως (city treasurer). If Erastus moved up the social ladder by serving in higher offices throughout his career, he may have been from a wealthy family and able to support the church as a patron. His household would, then, be a leading location for educated and philosophical discourse and the likely presence of philosophically educated women.

The difficulty, though, is a lack of certain information about Erastus. There are few clues about Erastus's position in early Christian writers. Origen (CER 5:278) simply references the office of Erastus with no explanation.[112] However, John Chrysostom expresses his opinion clearly, "Paul mentions the Erastus's title with the purpose that the Gospel had taken hold of the great as well as among the rest of the population."[113]

---

109. Judge, *Social Pattern*, 59; Moule, *Birth of the New Testament*; Thessien, *Social Setting*; Meeks, *Urban Christians*, 191–92; Winter, *Philo and Paul*, 189; Witherington, *Conflict and Community*, 23–24.

110. Clarke, *Secular and Christian Leadership*, 42.

111. Achtemeier, *Romans*, 224. Lampe, *From Paul to Valentinus*, 153–62.

112. *Commentary on the Epistle to the Romans*.

113. *Homilies on Romans* 32; NPNF¹ 11:561.

Reading 1 Corinthians with Philosophically Educated Women

For many scholars, Chrysostom's opinion was substantiated on April 15, 1929, when an inscription was discovered in Corinth indicating that an Erastus served as *aedile*:

> praenomen nomen ERASTVS · PRO · AEDILITaeE
> vac S · P · STRAVIT vac

> [praenomen nomen] Erastus pro aedilit[at]e
> s (ua) p(ecunia) stravit

> [――――] Erastus in return for his aedileship laid the pavement at his own expense.[114]

Many have concluded that the Erastus of Romans 16:23 is the Erastus of the inscription since the name does not appear anywhere else in the Corinthian inscriptions, the pavement can be dated sometime in the first to second century, and Paul's designation of Erastus as οἰκονόμος may describe the office of aedile.[115] The identification of Erastus the οἰκονόμος and Erastus the aedile is not without its challenges.

Several objections have been raised as to the rarity of Erastus's name, the date of the inscription, and the relationship between aedile and οἰκονόμος. The name Erastus is not exceptionally rare as some have claimed. It is common enough in inscriptions, close to the date of the Erastus inscription, and over a wide geographical area.[116] Andrew Clarke has noted that there is another inscription in Corinth, found in 1960, dated in the second century CE:

> Οἱ Βιτέλλιοι
> [Φρον]τεῖνος
> [kai/ · Ἔ]ραστος
> [καί ·Ἔ]ραστος
> τῶ · - -]
> [- - -]ι

> [The] Vitellii
> [Fro]ntinus
> [and E]rastus
> (dedicate this) [to]–

---

114. Kent, *Inscriptions*, 232.

115. Kent, *Inscriptions*, 99–100; Winter, *Seek the Welfare of the City*, 191–92; Chow, *Patronage and Power*; Theissen, *Social Setting*, 82–83; Meeks, *Urban Christians*, 58–59.

116. Clarke and Gill have found the following examples: SEG 11, 622 (Laconia) and 994 (Messenia); SEG 24, 194 (Attica); SEG 25, 194 (Attica); SEG 28, 1010 (Bithynia); CIG 269; 1241 (Sparta); 1249 (Sparta); 6378; Clarke, *Secular and Christian Leadership*, 54.

[---][117]

The two Erastus inscriptions in Corinth do indicate men who were unquestionably wealthy. And of course we know that the inscriptions belong to two different men, chiefly because the second inscription is dated about 100 years later than the *aedile* inscription. But the relative commonality of the name of Erastus precludes a ready identification with the Erastus of Romans 16:23.

Then, there is the challenge of determining a connection between οἰκονόμος and *aedile*. Several attempts have been made to make such a connection, but these attempts have been convincingly rejected. First, the Greek term οἰκονόμος is not the usual term for the Latin *aedile*, probably because the former is a much lower status position than the latter.[118] The position of οἰκονόμος was typically held by a slave or lowly freeman and not a wealthy freedman or citizen.[119] Erastus could have held the office at the beginning of his public career, and moved on to higher and more decorated positions,[120] but the distance between the two offices in the city hierarchy is so great that it seems unlikely. Kent suggests that Paul may have referred to Erastus as οἰκονόμος instead of ἀγορανόμος because the *aedile* in Corinth oversaw local economic affairs.[121] The argument of Kent has been very influential among scholars who have come to similar conclusions. The wealth of Erastus is uncertain because of the low position of οἰκονόμος, and the identification of the Erastus in Romans with the Erastus inscription is tentative at best. In this case, Erastus would have been one of the many Christ believers who were low born, uneducated, and not influential. After considering the weak archaeological evidence concerning the Erastus inscription and a detailed exegesis, Steven Freisen argues that Erastus was not even a believer based on Paul's deliberate refusal to identify him as such in Romans 16.[122]

It has been very attractive for scholars to use Erastus the οἰκονόμος as a starting point for identifying social stratification in the Corinthian community. If indeed Paul's Erastus was a wealthy officeholder in Corinth, he certainly would have been a valuable asset, providing the church with money, a place to meet, a patron for education, and even legal protection. However, the office of οἰκονόμος is simply too low a position for someone

117. Clarke, *Secular and Christian Leadership*, 55; cf. Clarke, "Another Erastus Inscription," 146–51.
118. Mason, *Greek Terms*, 11.
119. Malherbe, *Social Aspects*, 31.
120. Gill, "Erastus," 293–301.
121. Kent, "Inscriptions," iii–vi, 1–25.
122. Freisen, "Wrong Erastus," 231–56.

of wealth and it is not possible to connect Paul's Erastus with the *aedile* of the inscription. Unfortunately, we cannot look to Erastus as a certain proof of the presence of wealthy Christians in the Corinthian church.

Crispus the Corinthian Synagogue Leader

Another type of office which would indicate wealth is that of the synagogue leader. There may have been a few synagogue leaders who participated in the Corinthian church. Acts 18:8 preserves the story of the baptism of Crispus, a synagogue[123] leader:

> Κρίσπος δὲ ὁ ἀρχισυνάγωγος ἐπίστευσεν τῷ κυρίῳ σὺν ὅλῳ τῷ οἴκῳ αὐτοῦ, καὶ πολλοὶ τῶν Κορινθίων ἀκούοντες ἐπίστευον καὶ ἐβαπτίζοντο.
>
> Crispus, the ruler of the synagogue, believed in the Lord, together with his entire household. And many of the Corinthians hearing Paul believed and were baptized.[124]

There are two indicators of wealth in Crispus's single verse in the NT: his entire household believed and many others believed the Gospel because of his influence. It is widely understood that the role of ἀρχισυνάγωγος probably indicates wealth,[125] and Acts indicates that many Corinthians followed Paul after the baptism of Crispus, remembering him as man of some status.

The primary role of the ἀρχισυνάγωγος was to fund or raise funds for the building and restoration of synagogues, and sometimes may have been responsible for the reading of the law to the people when they could not bring in someone else to preach or teach.[126] Several reviews of epigraphic evidence confirm this assessment.[127]

---

123. For discussion concerning inscriptions regarding a synagogue in Corinth, see Levinskaya, *Acts*, 162–66.

124. Translation from the ESV.

125. Chow believes that the status of Crispus is "ambiguous." *Patronage and Power*, 90. Several other scholars also believe ἀρχισυνάγωγος is an indicator of wealth: Theissen, *Social Setting*, 75; Meeks, *Urban Chistians*, 57; Levine, *Ancient Synagogue*, 390–403; Burtchaell, *From Synagogue to Church*, 244.

126. Schürer, *History of the Jewish People*, 2:434; Brooten, *Women Leaders*, 28–29. For more recent opinions, see Kraemer, *Unreliable Witnesses*; Rajak and Noy focus on the patronal nature of the office rather than any kind of spiritual leadersthip, "Archisynagogoi," 75–93; Williams disagrees with T. Rajak, "Structure of Roman Jewry," 135; White, "Synagogue and Society," 23–58; Clarke, *Serve the Community*, 127–31; Rajak, *Jewish Dialogue*.

127. Levine, "Synagogue Officials," 392–400; Levine, "Synagogue Leadership," 195–213. Feldman, *Studies in Ancient Judaism*, 577–600. There is a long treatment of it

If this is the same Crispus as prominently mentioned in 1 Corinthians 1:15, he would likely be a wealthy patron of the church.[128] If this is a credible identification, any women in his household would be the likely recipients of a philosophical education. This would include any woman (wife, daughter, female relative, slave, freedperson) interested in philosophy that the head of the household takes an interest in educating. However, the best way to approach Crispus is that he is remembered as a synagogue leader in Acts. The value of this memory is not in its direct historicity, but in that the writer of Acts places a wealthy synagogue leader in the Corinthian community. This memory raises the question: were there wealthier members of the Corinthian community that we can examine that are more historically reliable?

Christians in Court: The Affair

A very strong indicator of the presence of high status, powerful, wealthy people in the Corinthian church is the activity that Paul refers to in 1 Corinthians 6.[129] There is overwhelming consensus among New Testament scholars that participation in the Roman courts is an indicator of the wealth of at least one of the litigants.[130] The court processes in Roman Corinth, as throughout the empire, were the privilege of the wealthy.[131] The processes are quite clear and differ according to status,[132] but the practice of law in court was almost wholly dictated by wealth and power.[133] Women were permitted to plead their case on their own, but typically had a male accompany them or serve as representation, or even sent letters to magistrates.[134] The letters

---

in *New Docs* 4:213–20; van Henten and van der Horst, *Jewish Epigraphy*, 178.

128. Rajak and Noy found a three-year-old *archisynagogue* from the 5th century CE in Venosa, Italy. This is evidence that in some cases the *archisynagogue* was a non-functional title for a wealthy, high-status person. Rajak and Noy, "*Archisynagogoi*," 87, 90. *CIJ* 587; *JIWE* 1.53. Cf. Wiedemann, "Children and Benefactors," 163–86.

129. Crook, *Law and Life*, 78–79; Garnsey, *Social Status*, 6; Bergmann and Kondoleon, *Art of Ancient Spectacle*; Bablitz, *Actors and Audience*; Riggsby, *Roman Law*, 50.

130. Chow, *Patronage and Power*, 124–29; Clarke, *Secular and Christian Leadership*, 74; Mitchell, "Rich and Poor," 562–86; Witherington, *Conflict and Community*, 163; Kinman, "Appoint the Despised," 353; Collins, *First Corinthians*, 235; Johnson, *1 Corinthians*, 93–94; Dutch, *Educated Elite*, 33; Nguyen, *Christian Identity*, 138–39.

131. Garnsey, "Legal Privilege," 3–24. Bablitz, *Actors and Audience*, 74: "The legal system dealt mainly with disputes between those of at least some wealth; the more downtrodden members of society had less property to disagree over, and little time to struggle through the system."

132. Johnston, *Roman Law*, 113–32.

133. Crook, *Law and Life*.

134. For examples, see Grubbs, *Women and the Law*; Arjava, *Women and Law*, 245.

sent to magistrates by women include affidavits for divorce (BGU 4.1102, 13 BCE; P.Oxy. 2.281, 20–50 CE) and other complaints (P.Oxy. 54.3770, 334 CE). Valerius Maximus (8.1) tells us the story of Maesia of Sentinum, who successfully defended herself from an unmentioned charge in the first century BCE.[135] Valerius also preserves Gaia Afriana whose participation in court as a prosecutor brought about the need for legislators to ban women from such activity.[136] Slaves and children, of course, could not participate in court as a prosecutor or defence lawyer.[137]

Since 1 Corinthians 1:26–29 identifies most of the Corinthian believers as of low status and possibly impoverished, few people in Paul's community at Corinth would have been wealthy enough to risk the loss of what little they had in litigation. Therefore, it was not beneficial for wealthy people to sue the poor because there would be no gain. The Roman "justice" system was designed for the rich and powerful to destroy or severely weaken their comparatively rich and powerful opponents. In order to have a chance at winning, the litigant would need to hire an advocate trained in forensic rhetoric or be educated in this art her/himself. Advocates could gain fortune and status by their ability to capture both the judge and audience and were therefore motivated to represent their clients effectively. It was much more important to be an impressive rhetor than be knowledgeable about the law because a judge can be persuaded by an effective appeal to emotion. Furthermore, the litigant could bribe the judge,[138] hire people to cheer for his advocate at appropriate times,[139] and pay people to testify to his/her good reputation.[140] It was customary for defendants to wear mourning attire from the time they are notified of an accusation until the end of the trial.[141] Enemies were known to bring up an accusation and then leave town, forcing the defendant to be dishonored for an extensive amount of time.[142]

In relation to 1 Corinthians 6, some scholars have suggested that at least part of the motivation for the injunction against participation in Gentile law courts is the result of legal action that was the direct result of

---

135. Marshall, "Roman Ladies on Trial," 46–59.
136. Val. Max. *Fact. dict. mem.* 8.3; *Dig. Just.* 3.1.1.5.
137. Packman, "Undesirable Company," 97.
138. Mart. 2.13; Tac. *Ann.* 1.75.1, 2.34.1; *Juv.* 13.1–4; Suet. *Tib.* 33.1, *Dom.* 8;
139. Plin. *Ep.* 2.14.4–8; hired by an advocate, Mart. 2.27; Quint. 11.3.131. Cf. Bablitz, *Actors and Audience*, 126–32.
140. Quint. 5.10.26.
141. Tac. *Dial.* 12.1; Juv. 15.131–35.
142. Bablitz, *Actors and Audience*, 84–85.

Corinth and Its Philosophers

the affair mentioned in chapter 5.[143] Another member of the community may have taken advantage of the breakup of the household to lay claim to property owned by the woman or her stepson that was passed on to them by the death of her husband.[144] The whole situation could indicate that the unnamed woman who had an affair with her stepson was wealthy and therefore be a candidate for philosophical education.[145] Being a widow, she was able to control whatever wealth her late husband left to her, and perhaps initiated the affair with her late husband's son (being the party of higher status). Such a situation was a part of the *elite* Greek and Roman psyche.[146] This situation would explain why only the son was rebuked by Paul while the widow remained unscathed: she was a powerful patroness that he could not afford to frustrate.

It is likely that this woman was a member of the church. Roman households typically shared the religion of the patriarch, so families typically joined the church together (Stephanas in 1 Cor 1:16 and 16:15, for example). When a person converted to a religion—especially a new foreign one—they could face alienation from their families, unless the entire household converted as well.[147] Marriages between believers and unbelievers were apparently strained: Paul allowed divorce if an unbelieving partner asked for it. The stepson certainly was not alienated from his stepmother, so she must have either been unusually tolerant of her stepson's refusal to participate in the typical Roman religion or she was a member of the church herself. This

---

143. Richardson, "Judgment on Sexual Matters," 37–58; Deming, "1 Corinthians 5–6," 295–96; cf. Ciampa and Rosner, *First Letter to the Corinthians*, 247.

144. Collins, *First Corinthians*, 226; cf. de Vos, "Stepmothers," 104–14; Clarke notes that the motives for the affair may have been financial and rooted in the attraction of a stepmother for her stepson (*Secular and Christian Leadership*, 80–85). A dowry alone might not be worth enough to tempt a thoughtful litigant (Saller, "Roman Dowry," 199–201); but some dowries were substantial, and aristocrats typically payed out the cash in three annual payments (Dixon, "Polybius," 147–70); cf. Gardner, "Recovery of Dowry," 449–53.

145. Wire accepts the possibility that the stepmother is a responsible member of the community, but does not explore the nature of the relationship in detail. *Corinthian Women Prophets*, 74.

146. Watson, *Ancient Stepmothers*, 234–38.

147. Apparently some families did tolerate religious dissention—in 1 Cor 7, Paul instructs believing husbands and wives to remain married to unbelieving partners unless the unbeliever requests divorce. Ancient references for religious ostracization are (1) early Christian persecution in Plin. *Ep.* 10.96; Tac. *Ann.* 15.44, and Suet. *Ner.* 16, (2) Jewish proselytes in Philo, *Leg.* 4.178; Tac. *Hist.* 5.5.2, (3) Alienation from families in Justin Martyr, *Trypho* 2.2–7. Cf. Taylor, "Social Nature," 129–36; Neyrey, "Loss of Wealth," 139–59.

also could indicate that Paul did not mention her part in the affair because he did not want to further irritate a patroness of the church.

As a wealthy widow, the stepmother would most probably have access to philosophical education either in her father's house, from her husband, or she could bring a philosopher into her home after she was widowed. It is likely that when she was younger that she received her education in her father's house before she got married as did other girls of her status. After marriage, her husband could encourage philosophical education in a number of ways: including her in discussions with philosophically educated persons in the household, teaching her himself, or simply not interfering with her intellectual interests. Later in life, as a member of the church, she no doubt heard 1 Corinthians being read aloud in front of the entire church, and was able to interact with it, utilizing the benefit of her education.

Stephanas and Gaius

Paul says in 1 Corinthians 1:16 that he was thankful that he only baptized a few Corinthians himself, one group including the household of Stephanas, who proved to be a valuable asset (1 Cor 16:17). The wealth, status, and power of Stephanas and Gaius is so widely accepted in scholarship that most commentators simply take it for granted rather than presenting a case for it. Raymond Collins concludes on the basis of Paul's description of Gauis's house that it was able to support the "whole church" (Rom 16:23).[148] Alan F. Johnson and others assert that Paul wrote the epistle to the Romans from Gaius's house and of course the church met there.[149] It is the home ownership of Gaius that is the reason for NT scholars to believe that he is wealthy, of high status, and powerful. Likewise, Paul mentions the "τὸν Στεφανᾶ οἶκον" twice (1 Cor 1:16 and 16:15), quite possibly referring to the wealthy, powerful, and high status ancient household that includes wives, children, slaves, and clients.[150] This presumption is supported by the assistance that Stephanas renders in 1 Corinthians 16.16.[151] An assembly of Christians also met in the house of Prisca and Aquila (1 Cor 16:19; Rom 16:3–5). But

---

148. Collins, *First Corinthians*, 98; Byrne, *Romans*, 459; Horsely, *Paul and Empire*, 213; Stuhlmacher, *Paul's Letter to the Romans*, 255; Yeo, *Rhetorical Interaction*, 88; Horrell, *Social Ethos*, 96; cf. Keener, *1–2 Corinthians*, 26; Thiselton, *First Epistle to the Corinthians*, 25–27.

149. Johnson, *1 Corinthians*, 52.

150. Horrell, *Social Ethos*, 96; Thiselton, *First Epistle to the Corinthians*, 140; Welborn, *Politics and Rhetoric*, 26.

151. Hays, *First Corinthians*, 23–24; Collins, *First Corinthians*, 84; Ciampa and Rosner, *First Letter to the Corinthians*, 858.

Corinth and Its Philosophers

in what kind of dwellings did the Corinthians meet? Such characteristics can also assist in identifying the wealth and status of some members of the community.

The ancient wealthy household was organized in a patriarchal fashion that was reinforced by Roman law and custom and included wives, children, and slaves.[152] This type of household afforded the interaction of the entire spectrum of social status, including the wealthy homeowner and his/her friends, clients, freedpersons, and slaves. The Roman home was a place of business for the elite and workshops for the poor.[153] The wealthier Roman home could facilitate a gathering of about forty people or perhaps many more,[154] and the homeowner would be positioned to offer the church legal and financial stability.

In urban conditions, there is an additional structure that could facilitate the worship situation that is laid out in 1 Corinthians, namely the tenement housing rented by the rest of the population.[155] Paul, however, describes a situation that lends itself more towards a household setting, primarily with the communal meal and the problems which arose out of that practice.[156]

The situation in Corinth can be contrasted with that of another Pauline community that was not integrated into a wealthier household and the benefits that such a relationship entails. When Paul arrived at Corinth, he was a seasoned preacher and church founder. Because of this, he was able to connect with at least a few people who had access to wealth who offered their support to his cause.[157]

> The hosts of Christian house churches functioned in a way analogous to that of such patrons. At Corinth, Stephanas seems to have been such a patron (1 Cor. 16:15-18), and at nearby Cenchreae, Phoebe is identified as *diakonos prostates* (Rom.

---

152. Gardner and Wiedemann, *Roman Household*.

153. Balch and Osiek, *Families*, 54; Meyers, "Problems of Gendered Space," 44-72.

154. Murphy-O'Connor, *St. Paul's Corinth*, 161-69, argues for a smaller gathering due to the size of a Roman house in Corinth during the first century and a smaller Pompeiian house. David Balch, "Rich Pompeiian Houses," 41, argues for the possibility of a considerably larger gathering based on the archaeology at Pompeii; cf. Wallace-Hadrill, *Houses and Society*, 4; Wallace-Hadrill, "Domus and Insulae," 3-18.

155. McKay, *Houses*, 84; Sear, *Roman Architecture*, 33-34.

156. Ciampa and Rosner, *First Letter to the Corinthians*, 546 (1 Cor 11:22).

157. Still, *Conflict*, 239. Some type of beneficial relationship would be required to share a house, whether it was provided by a patron directly or indirectly. Balch and Osiek, *Families in the New Testament World*, 54; Meeks, *Urban Christians*, 75-78.

16:1–2). The latter term probably denotes a woman who functions as patroness to some society.[158]

Unlike Paul's experience in Corinth, in Thessalonica he seems to have preached his Gospel without being sensitive to establishing patronal support, agitating wealthy citizens with frank speech rather than attracting them in a more friendly fashion.[159] As a result, the Pauline community suffered persecution and was not protected by anyone with access to wealth. Therefore, Thessalonians had no patron to provide a home and a love feast; instead, they met in their crowded tenement houses and were vulnerable to all external threats.[160] If there was some integration into the Thessalonian community, there would have been mention of some patron in the Thessalonian correspondence as there is in most other Pauline letters (Phil 4.22; Rom 16.1; 1 Cor 1:16; Philm 2). On the other hand in Corinth we do not see any persecution from outsiders, people are taking each other to court (1 Cor 6:1–8),[161] members of the church are being invited to meals (1 Cor 10:27),[162] and worship described in 1 Corinthians 11 is often understood as occurring in the house of a wealthy person.[163]

Several aspects of the Corinthian church point toward the participation of at least some wealthy people who could have facilitated the philosophical education of women. The household contexts of Christian worship, participation in court, serving as synagogue leader, and the intrigue of the affair all indicate there were some households that could have produced philosophically educated women. From what we learn from the histories of women in philosophy, most access to philosophical education is connected to the wealthy household. Philosophical education was provided to some slaves (Epictetus, for example), a tutor could be brought into the household to teach the master's family and teach her own daughters as well, and freed grammarians taught their partners and daughters. The wealthy Roman household provided a variety of contexts in which women in many different conditions could learn some philosophy.

---

158. Stambaugh and Balch, *Social Environment*, 140.

159. Fredrickson, "ΠΑΡΗΣΙΑ," 163–84; Still, *Conflict*.

160. Jewett, "Communal Meals," 23–43: Jewett, "Love Feasts," 43–58.

161. Hays, *First Corinthians*, 94.

162. For review of the issues related to food offered to idols and relevant bibliography, see Fotopoulos, *Food Offered to Idols*; Phua, *Idolatry and Authority*.

163. Horrell, *Social Ethos*, 98; Witherington, *Conflict and Community*, 30; Collins, *First Corinthians*, 74; Hays, *First Corinthians*, 196; Dunn, *1 Corinthians*, 90. Contra Wire, *Corinthian Women Prophets*, 106–7.

Aquila and Prisca

According to 1 Corinthians, Romans, and Acts,[164] Aquila and Prisca[165] moved their tentmaking business and established households in three cities in the ancient world: from Rome to Corinth to Ephesus and back to Rome. Some scholars have argued that this travel indicates that Aquila and Prisca had access to some wealth.[166] In light of the historical evidence, however, these arguments are not convincing. Travel in the ancient world was dangerous for everyone, but particularly so for the wealthy who actually had goods and money for bandits to steal. Even travelers who were able to hire a contingent of bodyguards attracted bandits who would plunder and maybe even kill everyone in the party.[167] Perhaps the most successful travelers were people who were poor—or looked the part—and slipped by danger due to their humble appearance. Because of the dangers associated with travel, a good deal of travel was done only by people who absolutely needed to do so: the military and merchants.[168] Travel was by no means restricted to the elite and therefore it is not a signifier of wealth. Peter Lampe has shown that humble tentmakers' earnings could have easily funded all of the travels of Aquila and Prisca.[169]

Although Ronald Hock's work has focused on Paul in his studies on tentmaking, his researches are applicable to the occupations of Aquila and Prisca.[170] Hock argues that tentmaking can easily be a mobile trade because it only requires few tools to transport.[171] Todd Still has challenged the widely accepted views of Hock, but for the most part his critique finely tunes Hock's

---

164. William O. Walker convincingly argues that virtually all of the information in Acts concerning Aquila and Prisca is in Pauline letters, which possibly served as a source for Acts. "Portrayal of Aquila and Priscilla," 479–95.

165. Keller, *Priscilla and Aquila*.

166. Mount, *Pauline Christianity*, 116–17; Jewett, *Romans*, 955. Opposing views include Schüssler-Fiorenza, "Missionaries, Apostles, Coworkers," 429; Murphy-O'Connor, "Prisca and Aquila," 42. Keller does not take a stand on the issue, in *Priscilla and Aquila*, xiii–xv.

167. Shaw, "Bandits," 3–52; cf. Knapp, "Travel," 281–304; Hunter, "Cicero's Journey," 73–97; Montiglio, "Should the Aspiring Wise Man Travel?," 553–86; Skalitzky, "Horace on Travel," 316–21.

168. Casson, *Travel*; Mooney, *Travel*; Wells, "Trade and Travel," 7–16, 67–78.

169. Lampe, *From Paul to Valentinus*, 187–95.

170. Hock, "Simon the Shoemaker," 41–53. Reprinted in Billerbeck, *Die Kyniker*, 259–71; Hock, "Paul's Tentmaking," 4–13; Hock, "Workshop," 438–50, reprinted in Tentmaking, 14–25; Hock, "Problem of Paul's Social Class," 7–18.

171. Hock, *Social Context*, 24.

work with respect to Paul's social status.¹⁷² Of course, other views about Paul and poverty have further questioned the nature of Paul's social status.¹⁷³ For Paul, one must reconcile the nature of Paul's education with his lowly position as a tentmaker. For Hock and others, this problem is resolved by noting that Paul has an aristocratic view towards work and he chose a profession much like a wise-man would do to demonstrate his self-sufficiency and freedom from the will of a patron. For Aquila and Prisca, there is no hint that they were educated as Paul was, but they did have a church meeting in their home (perhaps a tenement house rented by low-status, poorer people) and traveled extensively. Nevertheless, since we have no indication of wealth in Prisca and Aquila's tenement home, there is no context for education, and nothing else indicates the presence of philosophically educated women. It is likely that Prisca and Aquila did enjoy some status in the community of Christ believers because of their close association with Paul.

Phoebe the Patroness

Because Paul gives two titles to Phoebe in Romans 16:1 which have a wide range of meanings, there is no shortage of views concerning the nature of her roles. In this section I will present the central arguments concerning the nature of Phoebe with a special interest in Paul's description of her as his *prostatis*. The term *prostatis* has been translated "patroness," "helper," or "protector." The current trends point toward Phoebe as a wealthy patroness.¹⁷⁴ R. A. Kearsley has argued on the basis of the careers of Junia Theodora

---

172. Still, "Did Paul Loathe Manual Labor?," 781–95; Agrell, *Work, Toil and Sustenance*, 104, 115.

173. Steven J. Friesen writes the apostle "may have chosen a life of downward mobility," "Poverty in Pauline Studies," 359. With respect to the economic conditions of Paul's converts, John M. G. Barclay comments, "I doubt we will ever be able to reach more than tentative and imprecise conclusions," "Poverty in Pauline Studies," 365. See also Horrell, *Social Ethos*, 203.

174. Meeks, *Urban Chrisitans*, 60, 79; Stambaugh and Balch, *Social Environment*, 140; Witherington, *Conflict and Community*, 35; Roman Garrison, "Phoebe," 63–73. On the other hand, Esther Yue L. Ng argues that Phoebe was not necessarily wealthy or influential and certainly did not have a typical patronal relationship with Paul, who showed contempt for such things, "Phoebe as *Prostatis*," 3–13. Ng is unconvincing because she relies exclusively on Paul's rhetoric in 1 Cor 9:1–18 and 2 Cor 11:9–10 as rationale that Paul could not have entered into a patronal relationship. However, Romans often masked their patronal relationships in such rhetoric to create an air of artistic or academic freedom in spite of the financial support that they received: Hor. *Od.* 3. For the patrons who give a similar view on artistic freedom and the friendship nature of literary patronage, see Cic. *Arch.* and Plin. *Ep.* 3.21.

and Claudia Metrodora (in contrast to Ernst Käsemann[175]) that wealthy women in Kenchreai "could and did hold influential positions in the society of Paul's lifetime, and that the title *prostatis* and cognate words designated such actions."[176] Junia Theodora is by far the most important example of the wealthy *prostatis*/patroness but scholars also point to the wealthy mother charged with providing for her orphaned son as his *prostatis* with parallel examples.[177] In addition to patron and guardian, there is also the usage of the term as president of an association.[178] Ross Shepard Kraemer notes that the association at Aphrodisias may have had a *prostatis*, a woman patron.[179] While the precise shade of meaning might be muddled by the relative rarity of *prostatis* and its apparent wide range of meaning, it is clear that the term denotes someone of either real or attributed wealth or power, and Paul is expressing his social inferiority and reliance on the assistance of Phoebe.[180] In this respect, Paul is acknowledging her as his patron at least in an informal sense, but probably not the legal sense.[181]

Joan Cecelia Campbell has written a monograph on Phoebe, setting her within the many contexts of the wealthy first-century Roman woman.[182] Elizabeth Schüssler-Fiorenza has repeatedly examined the modern interpretations of Phoebe's role in the early church, demonstrating the need for a more balanced approach that does not come from the dominant patriarchal perspectives.[183] Schüssler-Fiorenza's method frees the interpreter

---

175. Käsemann, *Romans*, 411.

176. The nature of the activity of Junia Theodora and Claudia Metrodora will be discussed in detail in chapter 5. Kearsley, "Women in Public Life," 189–211; Kearsley utilizes the work of Horsley, *New Docs* 4:241–44; 5:149; Reynolds and Tannenbaum, *Jews and Godfearers*, 5 l. 9, 8, 101; Williams, "Jews and Godfearers," 300. Cf. Judge, "Cultural Conformity," 3–24.

177. P.Med.Bar. 1 = SBXVI 1270.1–20, 142 BCE. Translation in Rowlandson, *Women and Society*, 125. Judith Evans Grubbs notes that the *prostatis* mother-guardian relationship changed later to *epitropos* in *Women and the Law*, 254. Grubbs's examples include P.Oxy. 7.898, 123 CE and P.Oxy. 3.496, 127 CE. Van Bremen demonstrates that the *epitropoi* usually are the guardians of their own children and always act under the authority of their own *kyrios*: *I.Erythrai* 201; *Milet* 13.147 and *Milet*, no. 151. For comment by New Testament scholars, see Witherington, *Conflict and Community*, 34, and Judge, "Cultural Conformity," 21.

178. Schulz, "Case for 'President,'" 124–27.

179. Kraemer, *Unreliable Witnesses*, 232.

180. Barrett, *Romans*, 283; Cranfield, *Romans 12–13*, 783; Käsemann, *Romans*, 411.

181. Osiek, "Diakonos and Prostatis," 348, 364–65.

182. Campbell, *Phoebe*.

183. Schüssler-Fiorenza, "Pre-Pauline and Pauline Churches," 157–58; Schüssler-Fiorenza, "Missionaries, Apostles, Coworkers," 420–433; Schüssler-Fiorenza, "Phoebe," 162–64; Schüssler-Fiorenza, "Quilting of Women's History," 35–49.

to approach the text concerning Phoebe without the constraints of male-centered assumptions that baselessly exclude the possibilities of Phoebe's leadership roles. Wendy Cotter argues that the service of women in the Pauline churches fits within cultural norms for the wealthy, but the egalitarian description of their service in the church is countercultural.[184] Caroline F. Whelan says of Phoebe:

> [she was] a wealthy and independent woman, likely educated, and patron to one or more clubs, undoubtedly moved in more elite circles than Paul and his church, among those of her social rank. As a member of the upper classes, she was able to secure connections for Paul and his church connections which, in a status-conscious like the Roman world where wealth and power went hand in hand, could only be beneficial.[185]

Robert Jewett goes so far as to argue that Phoebe was essential to establishing the Spanish mission by helping Paul develop relationships with wealthy patrons there.[186] On the basis of being true to the role of women as patronesses in Kenchreai, I will agree with Theissen and many others that *prostatis* is an indicator of wealth for Phoebe, and therefore she would be a good candidate for a philosophical education either as a child or an adult.

Divorce in 1 Corinthians 7:1–16

In 1 Corinthians 7:1–16, Paul gives instructions on marriage and divorce for both men and women. This section will remain focused on the issue of the presence of philosophically educated women in the Corinthian community. The question that I will ask of 1 Corinthians 7:1–16 is simply this: does this material offer any suggestion that households which could facilitate the philosophical education of women were active in the Corinthian community? To address this question, I will examine Paul's instructions concerning marriage and divorce for signs of wealthy households within the church. Some of these signs could include the practices of divorce described in the text, possible interest in the stability of the wealthy Roman home, and parallels to Roman philosophy.

Unfortunately, it is customary for scholars not to address questions of wealth and status when interpreting 1 Corinthians 7:1–16, and no one

---

184. Cotter, "Women's Authority," 350-72. For more on Phoebe, see Judge, "Early Christians as a Scholastic Community," 125-37; Mitchell, "Paul's Letters," 311; Cf. Fitzgerald, "Early Christian Missionary Practice," 24-44.

185. Whelan, "Amica Pauli," 85.

186. Jewett, "Spanish Mission," 142-61.

looks for philosophically educated women.[187] This practice is particularly distressing for two reasons: the widespread consensus among scholars that the Corinthian church was socially stratified (1 Cor 1:26) and what we know about marriage and divorce in the Roman period. It is common for scholars who argue that 1 Corinthians 1:26 indicates that there were at least some wealthy people in the Corinthian community to not consider this interpretation when they examine 1 Corinthians 7:1-16.[188] It is also common for scholars who contextualize the social setting of divorce and remarriage in the Roman period to use materials that are exclusively written by and for the elite and do not address what this context may say about the social setting of women in the church.[189] Most of these scholars do not even ask the question regarding whether or not Paul is addressing at least some wealthier members of the church, even though his instructions and the practices of the church obviously share characteristics of the Roman elite with regard to marriage and divorce as indicated by their studies.

However, some interpreters have indicated that 1 Corinthians 7:1-16 does have something to do with the marriage practices of wealthy women. Divorce was common in the upper classes, and it is very difficult to determine how legal categories of marriage and divorce pertained among the poor.[190] Rodney Stark argues from the patristics and other later evidence that wealthy Christian women had managed to convert their husbands with increasing frequency in the first five centuries.[191] Lynn H. Cohic argues that Paul directs his instructions concerning marriage and divorce to wealthy men and women, who have the most to gain or lose from such actions.[192] With regard to the possibility of philosophically educated women, the

---

187. Beattie, *Women and Marriage*, 15-36.

188. Fitzmyer, *Corinthians*, 162, 273-329; Collins, *First Corinthians*, 98, 251-72, cf. Collins, *Divorce*; Bearslee, *First Corinthians*; Ciampa and Rosner, *First Letter to the Corinthians*, 105, 272-367; Keener, *1-2 Corinthians*, 31, 63-65; Thiselton, *First Epistle to the Corinthians*, 27, 497-543. David zGill believes that there are wealthy people in the church but does not address the issue of marriage and divorce, in "Social Elite," 323-37.

189. Gordon, *Sister or Wife?*; Instone-Brewer, "Graeco-Roman Marriage and Divorce Papyri," 101-15; Instone-Brewer, "Jewish Greek and Aramaic Marriage and Divorce Papyri," 225-43; Instone-Brewer, *Divorce and Remarriage*; Hodge, "Married to an Unbeliever," 1-25.

190. David Instone-Brewer, *Divorce and Remarriage*, 74; Dixon, *Roman Family*, 61; Treggiari, "Divorce Roman Style," 38-39; Bradley, "Remarriage," 79-93; McDonnell, "Divorce Initiated by Women," 54-80; Corbier, "Divorce and Adoption," 47-78; Gardner suggests that poor women may have been more interested in whatever economic advantage there was in keeping the family unit intact, in *Women in Roman Law*, 82.

191. Stark, "Rise of Christianity," 229-44.

192. Cohic, *Women in the World of the Earliest Christians*, 99-112.

Reading 1 Corinthians with Philosophically Educated Women

phrase, "It is good for a man not to touch a woman" is likely an ascetic slogan from those Christians who were "wise" and "strong."[193] This interpretation nicely compliments Wire, who argues that the slogan could have been misapplied to the women prophets, who did not apply the slogan to themselves.[194] Philosophical training might be an influence for this slogan that refers to abstinence from sex, either within or outside of marriage.[195] According to Iamblichus (ca. 245–325 CE), Pythagoras (ca. 570–495 BCE) also required marital faithfulness from men and women:

> λέγεται δὲ καὶ τοιοῦτόν τι διελθεῖν, ὅτι περὶ τὴν χώραν τῶν Κροτωνιατῶν ἀνδρὸς μὲν ἀρετὴ πρὸς γυναῖκα διαβεβόηται, Ὀδυσσέως οὐ δεξαμένου παρὰ τῆς Καλυψοῦς ἀθανασίαν ἐπὶ τῷν Πηνελόπην καταλιπεῖν, ὑπολείποιτο δὲ ταῖς γυναιξὶν εἰς τοὺς ἄνδρας ἀποδείξασθαι τὴν καλοκαγαθίαν, ὅπως εἰς ἴσον καταστήσωσι τὴν εὐλογίαν. ἁπλῶς δὲ μνημονεύεται διὰ τὰς εἰρημένας ἐντεύξεις περὶ Πυθαγόραν οὐ μετρίαν τιμὴν καὶ σπουδὴν καὶ κατὰ τὴν πόλιν τῶν Κροτωνιατῶν γενέσθαι καὶ διὰ τὴν πόλιν περὶ τὴν Ἰταλίαν.

> This discourse had effect also on marital fidelity, to an extent such that in the Crotonan region connubial faithfulness became proverbial; (thus imitating) Ulysses who, rather than abandon Penelope, considered immortality well lost. Pythagoras encouraged the Crotonian women to emulate Ulysses, by exhibiting their probity to their husbands. In short, through these (social) discourses Pythagoras acquired great fame both in Crotona, and in the rest of Italy.[196]

Iamblichus also tells us that the Pythagoreans strictly practiced sexual intercourse within marriage, and then only for reproduction.[197] It is possible that 7.1b may have Cynic connotations that Paul seeks to correct.[198] William Klassen finds parallels between Paul and Epictetus's (55–135 CE) description of the ideal Cynic.[199] Paul also may be expressing Stoic attitudes similar to of Musonius Rufus (fl. 1st c. CE), Epictetus (55–155 CE), and

---

193. Hurd, *Origins*, 67; Phipps, "Paul's Attitude," 125–30.
194. Wire, *Corinthian Women Prophets*, 94.
195. Rosner, *Paul, Scripture, and Ethics*, 151; Clark, *Reading Renunciation*, 264–76; Fee, "1 Corinthians 7.1," 307–14; Fee, "1 Corinthians 7.1–7 Revisited," 197–213; cf. Kraemer, "Conversion of Women," 298–307.
196. Iambl. *VP* 11.57, cf. 27.132.
197. Iambl. *VP* 47–48, 57, 210; Gaca, "Reproductive Technology," 117.
198. Deming, *Paul on Marriage*, 115.
199. Klassen, "Musonius Rufus," 195; Epict. *Disc.* 3.22.70–71, 74.

Corinth and Its Philosophers

Hierocles (fl. 2nd c. CE).[200] The result of Paul's teaching is a religious group that encourages marriage between believers and prohibits divorce: such a practice contains immorality.[201] Paul's advice is therefore precisely opposite of the Epicurean Metrodorus (ca. 331–278 BCE) who wrote to Pythocles (ca. 340–285 BCE):

> Πυνθάνομαί σου τὴν κατὰ σάρκα κίνησιν ἀφθονώτερον διακεῖσθαι πρὸς τὴν τῶν ἀφροδισίων ἔντευξιν. σὺ δὲ ὅταν μήτε τοὺς νόμους καταλύῃς μήτε τῶν πλησίον τινὰ λυπῇς μήτε τὴν σάρκα καταξαίνῃς μήτε τὰ ἀναγκαῖα καταναλίσῃς, χρῶ ὡς βούλει τῇ σεατοῦ προαιέσει· ἀμήχανον μέντοι γε τὸ μὴ οὐχ ἑνέ γέ τινα τούτων συνέ χεσθαι· ἀφροδίσια γὰρ οὐδέποτε ὤνησεν· ἀγαπητὸν δὲ μὴ ἔβλαψεν.

> You tell me that the movement of your flesh is too inclined towards sexual intercourse. So long as you do not break the laws or disturb the established or distress any of your neighbours or ravage your body or sqaunder the necessities of life, act upon your inclination any way you like. Yet it is impossible not to be constrained by at least one of these. For sex is never advantageous, and one should be content if it does not harm.[202]

Metrodorus views sexual intercourse in itself as a natural, morally neutral act. Because sexual intercourse is not inherently harmful, sexual desire can be expressed without any kind of penalty. For Paul, sexual desire is something that must be controlled, and sexual intercourse should only occur with one's husband or wife. Paul's advice to Pythocles would be much different that of the Epicurean Metrodorus: either practice self-control or get married.

Head Coverings and Status, Wealth, and Power

In 1 Corinthians 11:2–16, Paul gives instructions concerning head coverings to both men[203] and women in the Corinthian church, with a special interest in behavior during worship. The issue of head coverings for women proph-

---

200. Balch, "1 Cor 7:32–35 and Stoic Debates," 429–39; Yarborough, *Not Like the Gentiles*; Wimbush, *Paul, the Worldly Ascetic*; Klassen, "Musonius Rufus, 185–206.

201. MacDonald, *Early Christian Women*, 131; cf. MacDonald, "Early Christian Women," 14–28; Kraemer, "Conversion of Women," 298–307.

202. Metrodorus to Pythocles = Epicurus, *Sent. Vat.* 51. Long and Sedley, *Hellenistic Philosophers*, 1:116. Two editions of the text are available: Arrighetti, *Epicuro Opere* and Long and Sedley, *Hellenistic Philosophers*, vol. 2.

203. Winter, *After Paul Left Corinth*, 121–22.

Reading 1 Corinthians with Philosophically Educated Women

ets is naturally an important one in Antionette Wire's *Corinthian Women Prophets*. As I noted above in section 1.8, Wire situates her woman prophets as precisely the social opposite to most philosophically educated women.[204] Beginning from this point of departure, my argument is orientated towards how Paul's instructions would foreground two wealthy philosophically educated women instead of a group of poor uneducated women prophets.

There has been some discussion as to whether or not 1 Corinthians 11:2–16 is Pauline,[205] but multi-disciplinary examinations have demonstrated that this passage is genuine.[206] There is also some debate concerning the nature of the head covering, whether it is a hairstyle[207] or some type of veil.[208] Another debate centers on the question of the meaning and significance of κεφαλή,[209] whether it means "authority/leader,"[210] or "source."[211] What 1 Corinthians 11:2–16 doubtlessly shows is that women were active in worship—along with men—and Paul attempted to regulate their activity according to his own sensibilities.[212] Apparently, the Corinthians were muddling the outer differences between the sexes by switching what Paul considered normal attire for worship: women were not wearing their head coverings and men wore something on their heads.[213] This muddling of the sexes has caused some interpreters to conclude that the issue had something to do with male or female homosexuality.[214] For women, the absence of the

---

204. Wire, *Corinthian Women Prophets*, 65; Wire, "Prophecy and Women," 134–50.

205. Walker, "1 Corinthians 11:2–16," 94–110; Walker, "Vocabulary," 75–88; Cope, "1 Cor 11.2–16," 435–36; Mount, "1 Corinthians 11:3–16," 313–40.

206. Murphy-O'Connor, "Non-Pauline Character of 1 Corinthians 11:2–16?," 615–21. Murphy-O'Connor, "Interpolations," 81–94, argues that 1 Cor 11:2–16 is Pauline and not an interpolation.

207. Derrett, "Religious Hair," 100–103; Padgett, "Paul on Women," 69–86; Murphy-O'Connor, "Sex and Logic," 485; Neyrey, *Paul, in Other Words*, 133.

208. Martin, "Unusual Interpretation," 75–84; Preston T. Massey demonstrates that the interpretation "hairstyle" cannot be sustained lexically. "1 Corinthians 11.2–16," 502–23.

209. Johnson, "Review of the Scholarly Debate," 35–57; Grudem, "Meaning of Kephalē," 25–65.

210. Grudem, "Survey of 2,336 Examples," 38–59; Cervin, "Rebuttal," 85–112; Fitzmyer, "Another Look," 503–11; Fitzmyer argues against "source" for "authority over," "Kephalē," 52–59; A. C. Perriman argues for the authority metaphor, but concludes that in 1 Corinthians it is a matter of reciprocal honor, in "Head of a Woman," 602–22.

211. Wayne A. Grudem reviews this perspective and convincingly argues against it in "Meaning of Kephalē," 3–72; Oster, "Use, Misuse and Neglect," 52–73.

212. Holmyard, "1 Corinthians 11:2–16," 461–72.

213. Richard Oster, "When Men Wore Veils," 481–505; Yeo, "Differentiation and Mutuality," 7–21; Wilson, "Should Women Wear Headcoverings," 442–62.

214. Townsley, "Gender Trouble in Corinth"; MacGregor, "1 Corinthians 11:2–16,"

veil has also been associated with the attire of prostitutes and otherwise sexual availability of women, so one of Paul's motivations for writing this passage is a concern for modesty.[215] While Paul is almost certainly addressing issues related to modesty and sexual differentiation, it is evident from epigraphy and archaeology that Corinthian women wore veils only on certain occasions and were free to appear in public without a veil.[216] However, for Paul, prophesying without a veil is immodest and sexually immoral.[217]

In 1 Corinthians 11:2–16, Paul seeks to correct these behaviors, encouraging the Corinthians to adhere to his views regarding proper attire in a worship setting. At this point, I will ask of 1 Corinthians 11:2–16 simply this: does this material offer any suggestion that wealthy households were active in the Corinthian community? Can head coverings somehow point to wealth? Unfortunately, scholars who interpret this passage normally do not address questions of wealth, status, and power; although many studies focus on sources that are exclusively describe the sensibilities and practices of the elite.[218] Other scholars, however, have realized that the material that informs us about Roman custom, fashion, and moral sensibilities relate only to the elite, so Paul's regulation of this issue must be given to elite women.[219] Some lower class women die not wear veils because such clothing would hinder manual labor.[220] This is significant because if Paul is addressing lower class prophesying women—as Wire imagines—then he could be insulting their plight by demanding that they do something that they could never afford due to their humble circumstance.[221]

The popular moral philosophers in the schools that were associated with Corinth were also concerned with the modesty of women. The teachings of the Pythagorean Theano (fl. 6th c. BCE) are used by Plutarch (*Mor.* 142c; 46–120 CE) and Clement of Alexandria (*Strom.* 4.19.122; ca.150–217 CE) as

---

201–16.

215. Prostitutes and other sexually available or otherwise disgraced women were instantly recognizable not due to the lack of a veil but because they wore the toga. Heskel, "Cicero," 141; Goldman, "Reconstructing Roman Clothing," 228.

216. Fantham, "Covering the Head," 228.

217. Martin, "Veiled Exhortations," 269.

218. Lowery, "Head Covering," 155–63; Collins, *Divorce*, 9–39; Gill, "In Search of the Social Elite," 323–37; cf. Martin, "Tongues of Angels," 347–89.

219. Corrington, "Headless Woman," 223–31; Keener, *Paul, Women, and Wives*, 45; Schottroff, "Holiness and Justice," 51–60; Finney, "Honour, Head-Coverings and Headship," 31–58.

220. Olson, *Dress*, 45–47; For precisely the opposite view, see MacMullen, "Women in Public," 217–18; Kroeger, "Apostle Paul," 37.

221. Wire, *Corinthian Women Prophets*, 65.

Reading 1 Corinthians with Philosophically Educated Women

a model for how women should practice modesty. The Pythagorean pseudipigrapha regularly addresses women's dress, and is mostly orientated towards modesty and self-control. For example, Periictione (ca. 350 BCE?) writes:

> σκῆνος γὰρ ἐθέλει μὴ ῥιγέειν μηδὲ γυμνὸν εἶναι χάριν εὐπρεπείης, ἄλλου δ'οὐδενὸς χρήζει. δόξα δὲ ἀνθρώπων μετὰ ἀμαθίης ἐς τὰ κενεά τε καὶ περισσὰ ἵεται. ὥστ' οὔτε χρυσὸν ἀμφιθήσεται ἢ λίθον Ἰνδικὸν ἢ χώρης ἐόντα ἄλλης, οὐδὲ πλέξεται πολυτεχνίῃσι τρίχας, οὐδ'ἀλείψεται Ἀραβίης ἄλλης, λευκαίνουσα ἢ ἐρυθραίνουσα τοῦτο ἢ μελαίνουσα ὀφρύας τε καὶ ὀφθαλμοὺς καὶ τὴν πολιὴν τρίχα βαφαῖσι τεχνεωμένη, οὐδὲ λούσεται θαμινά. ἡ γὰρ ταῦτα ζητέοθσα θηητῆρα ζητεῖ ἀκρασίης γυναικηίης.

> For the body wants neither to shiver nor to be naked (for the sake of decency), and needs nothing else. But human opinion, with its ignorance, rushes into what is empty and excessive. So she will not wear gold nor Indian stone nor will she plait her hair with great skills, nor anoint herself with Arabian perfumes, nor will she paint her face, whitening or roughing it, nor blacken her eyebrows and eyelashes and treating her gray hair with dyes, nor will she bathe too often. For a woman who seeks these things seeks an admirer of feminine weakness. For beauty from intelligence, and not from these things, pleases women who are well born.[222]

Similarly, Melissa argues that the ideal wife is concerned with how to please her husband and the economy of her household instead of spending money on expensive clothes. Melissa's conclusion is that "She should trust the beauty and richness of her soul rather than that of her appearance and wealth; for envy and illness remove the later, but the former extend right up to her death," "πιστεύεν γὰρ χρὴ τῷ τᾶς ψυχᾶς κάλλει τε καὶ πλούτῳ μᾶλλον ἢ τῷ τᾶς ὄψιος καὶ τῶν χρημάτων· τὰ μὲν γὰρ φθόνος καὶ νοῦσος παραιρέ εται, τὰ δὲ μέχρι θανάτω πάρεντι ἐκτεταμένα."[223] Phyntis also thinks that women should find their fulfillment in virtue and not the various ornamentations of the body.[224] When Iamblichus describes the self-control of the Pythagoreans, he writes that the early communities did not allow free-born women to wear gold (33.187; cf. 11.56).

---

222. Periictione, *On the Harmony of Women* 1 = Stob. 4.28.19. Translation from Plant, *Women Writers*, 77.

223. Melissa to Cleareta in Plant, *Women Writers*, 83.

224. Phyntis, *On Women's Temperance*. Text is Stob. 4.23.61a = Thesleff, *Pythagorean Texts*, 153. Translation from Gutherie, *Complete Pythagoras*.

Cicero (106–43 BCE) often criticized both men and women for wearing inappropriate and immodest clothing.[225] Seneca (4–65 CE) compliments to his philosophically educated mother Helvia for her modesty:
non faciem coloribus ac lenociniis polluisti; numquam tibi placuit vestis, quae nihil amplius nudaret, cum poneretur. Unicum tibi ornamentum, pulcherrima et nulli obnoxia aetati forma, maximum decus visa est pudicitia.

you have not defiled your face with paints and cosmetics; never have you fancied the kind of dress that exposed no greater nakedness by being removed. In you has been seen that peerless ornament, that fairest beauty on which time lays no hand, that chiefest glory which is modesty.[226]

Epictetus (55–135 CE) discusses the importance of dressing appropriately, appealing to nature:

ἀνὴρ εἶ ἢ γυνή;— ἀνήρ.—ἄνδρα οὖν καλλώπιζε, μὴ γυναῖκα. ἐκείνη φύσει λεία γέγονε καὶ τρυφερά· κἂν ἔχῃ τρίχας πολλάς, τέρας ἐστὶ καὶ ἐν τοῖς τέρασιν ἐν Ῥώμῃ δείκνυται. τοῦτο δ᾽ ἐπ᾽ ἀνδρός ἐστι τὸ μὴ ἔχειν· κἂν μὲν φύσει μὴ ἔχῃ, τέρας ἐστίν, ἂν δ᾽ αὐτὸς ἑαυτοῦ ἐκκόπτῃ καὶ ποτίλλῃ, τί αὐτὸν ποιήσωμεν; ποῦ αὐτὸν δείξωμεν καὶ τί προγράψωμεν; 'δείξω ὑμῖν ἄνδρα, ὃς θέλει μᾶλλον γυνὴ εἶναι ἢ ἀνήρ.' . . . ἄνθρωπε, τί ἔχεις ἐγκαλέσαι σου τῇ φύσει; ὅτι σε ἄνδρα ἐγέννησεν; τί οὖν; πάσας ἔδει γυναῖκας γεννῆσαι; καὶ τί ἂν ὄφελος ἦν σοι τοῦ κοσμεῖσθαι; τίνι ἂν ἐκοσμοῦ, εἰ πάντες ἦσαν γυναῖκες; ἀλλ᾽ οὐκ ἀρέσκει σοι τὸ πραγμάτιον· ὅλον δι᾽ ὅλων αὐτὸ ποίησον· ἆρον—τί ποτ᾽ ἐκεῖνο;—τὸ αἴτιον τῶν τριχῶν· ποίησον εἰς ἅπαντα σαυτὸν γυναῖκα, ἵνα μὴ πλανώμεθα, μὴ τὸ μὲν ἥμισυ νδρός, τὸ δ᾽ ἥμισυ γυναικός.

Are you a man or a woman? A man. Then adorn yourself as a man, not as a woman. A woman is naturally smooth and delicate, and if hairy, is a monster, and shown among the monsters at Rome. It is the same thing in a man not to be hairy; and if he is by nature not so, he is a monster. But if he depilates himself, what shall we do with him? . . . Of what have you to accuse your nature, sir, that it has made you a man? Why, were all to be born women, then? In that case what would have been the use of your finery? For whom would you have made yourself fine, if all were women? But the whole affair displeases you. Go to work upon the whole, then. Remove your manhood itself and make yourself a woman entirely, that we may be no longer deceived, nor you be half man, half woman.[227]

225. Dyck, "Dressing to Kill," 119–30.
226. Sen. *Helv.* 16:3–6.
227. Epict. *Disc.* 3.1.

Like Paul in Galatians 5:12, Epictetus suggests that men go all the way and castrate themselves if they want to pretend that they are something that they are not.[228]

Silence in Worship: 1 Corinthians 14:33b–5

It appears that Paul again regulates the activity of women in worship in chapter 14. While Paul affirms in chapter 11 the activity of prophesying women in worship as long as their heads are covered, women are to be silent during the prophetic activity of the church. Several interpreters have attempted to resolve this apparent contradiction. First, interpreters have questioned whether or not this teaching is Pauline and a later interpolation.[229] P. B. Payne has been a consistent voice for text-critical argument that there is a gap in the text from the end of 1 Corinthians 14:33 to verse 36.[230] Payne summarizes the rationale for the exclusion of the text by comparing it to John 7:53—58.1:

1. In both, the doubtful verses occur at different locations in the text.
2. Manuscripts of both display a high concentration of textual variations.
3. Both contain word usage atypical of the book's author.
4. In both, the doubtful verses disrupt the narrative or topic of the passage.
5. In both, marginal symbols or notes indicate scribal awareness of a textual problem. In particular, Vaticanus has a distigme at the beginning of both passages.[231]

Feminist scholars divide over the nature of 1 Corinthians 14:33–35, with a few important scholars convinced by the textual arguments mentioned above.[232] The majority of feminist interpreters approach this text as

---

228. Ivarsson, "Vice Lists," 180.

229. Niccum, "Voice of the Manuscripts," 242–55; Odell-Scott, "Editorial Dilemma," 68–74; Miller, "1 Corinthians 14.34–35," 217–36.

230. Payne, "Fuldensis," 240–62; "Ms 88," 152–58; Payne and Canart, "Originality of Text-Critical Symbols," 105–13; cf. bibliography and discussion in Payne, *Man and Woman*, 234–36.

231. Payne, *Man and Woman*, 235.

232. Munro, *Authority in Peter and Paul*, 67–81. See also Munro, "Patriarchy," 141–59; Munro, "Woman, Text and Canon," 26–31; Munro, "Interpolation," 431–43; Bassler, "1 Corinthians," 327–28.

Corinth and Its Philosophers

Pauline.[233] Wire notes that the textual approaches that critics use to exclude 1 Corinthians 14:34–35 from the original text come from one widely copied family of manuscripts. The Latin traditions, however, include 1 Corinthians 14:34–35 in its canonical position, indicating that it is old enough and strong enough to be what Paul actually wrote.[234]

Once the issue of authenticity is settled, the reading of the text is straightforward. If the text is authentic, the primary issue obviously is the question of its relationship with 1 Corinthians 11. However, the arguments that 1 Corinthians 14:33–35 is a non-Pauline interpolation withstand all counterarguments. The presence of the verses in the manuscripts demonstrates that the scribes knew of the textual problems. Combined with the non-Pauline vocabulary, all other points are secondary and make the central argument all the more convincing. Since the text is not Pauline, it says nothing about the presence or role of philosophically educated women in Corinth.

Summary of Conclusions

In this chapter, I have discussed the philosophical heritage of classical and Roman Corinth and examined the social conditions of the Pauline community there in order to demonstrate that it had ideal conditions for the presence of philosophically educated women. These conditions included the presence of wealthy, powerful, and high status persons in Corinth who supported philosophical schools that had a heritage of philosophically educated women, the wide exchange of philosophical ideas at the Isthmian games, the presence of all the popular schools during the Roman period, and a long history of philosophical interest since the pre-Socratics to long after the first century CE. The city of Corinth had always been a city that was tolerant of the most popular philosophies in the ancient world: Pythagoreanism, Cynicism, Platonism, Stocism, and Epicureanism and their first-century incarnations. The Isthmian games attracted philosophers from all of these schools for oratory and debate, and Corinth produced many Cynics and Stoics. Moreover, I have argued that the Pauline community could sustain the presence of philosophically educated women.

The Christian community in Corinth was socially stratified, having both poor and wealthy participants. This is significant because the strongest signifier of the availability of education and the presence of philosophically

---

233. Pagels, "Paul and Women," 544; Crüsemann, "Irredeemably Hostile," 27; Schüssler Fiorenza, *In Memory of Her*, 230–33; Stichele, "Is Silence Golden?," 241–53.

234. Wire, *Corinthian Women Prophets*, 149–53.

educated women is wealth. To show this social stratification, I examined the Corinthians mentioned in 1 Corinthians, Romans, and Acts for indicators of wealth. These indicators include holding public office, being a public benefactor, participating in the public court system, and owning a household. I dismissed Erastus's office as an indicator of wealth, status, and power, but Crispus's position as a synagogue leader probably does mean that he is wealthy—if Acts is reliable on this point. The situation concerning the unnamed woman who was in a sexual relationship with her stepson may have caused lawsuits with other wealthy members of the community. The householders Gaius and Stephanas, along with Phoebe were most likely patrons of the church. I dismissed the criterion of travel as an indicator of wealth because both elites and non-elites in the Roman world were able to travel, and it was uncomfortable and dangerous for everyone. Finally, the instructions concerning head coverings speak not only to women prophets in their social and theological contexts, but also to philosophically educated patronesses. The higher status women may cover or uncover their heads for differing theological and social reasons, but Paul presents a redemptive, fictive equalizing message: all women should cover their heads and all men should uncover their heads in worship.

    The importance of this chapter is to demonstrate that philosophers in Corinth were active in the first century, and many women in the Pauline community were in the perfect social situation to receive a philosophical education. This would include women in the households of Gaius and Stephanas, Phoebe, and the unnamed stepmother in chapter 5. If one of these householders had an interest in one or more of the various philosophical schools that were active in Corinth in the first century, any members of the household would have had access to a philosophical education. These members would include wives, sisters, daughters, slaves, freedpersons, and clients. In the next three chapters, I will apply these concepts to three important situations that are addressed in 1 Corinthians: self-sufficiency and Paul's usage of the *agon* motif, friendship and patronage and Paul's relationships with people who were connected to the patronage systems in Corinth, and teachings concerning marriage that Paul applies to worship regulations.

5

Patronage and Philosophically Educated Women

IN CHAPTERS 5, 6, and 7, I will shift the focus from the question of context (Does the situation in Corinth support the presence of philosophically educated women?) to reading 1 Corinthians with philosophically educated women. In chapter 1, I discussed the various efforts by New Testament scholars to identify and interpret parallels between Paul and the popular philosophers. While these studies established relationships between Paul and philosophy, they did not expand to philosophically educated women. In chapter 2, I argued that philosophically educated women fit into a broader context of educated and active women including poets, physicians, merchants, and activity in education. Furthermore, these women received their education in the household, learning from their fathers, husbands, or teachers in the home. I reviewed the history of women in philosophy in chapter 3, giving attention also to how these women learned and what they believed. In chapter 4, I discussed the nature of philosophy in Corinth and the social contexts of philosophically educated women in the Corinthian churches.

The household context is of great importance for the education of women because some relationship to wealth is the single most reliable indicator that education was at least available to women. Therefore, I examined the history of philosophy in Corinth and argued that every philosophical school with a history of producing educated women has some connection with that city. Moreover, I identified several households in the Corinthian church that could have facilitated the philosophical education of women:

Reading 1 Corinthians with Philosophically Educated Women

Gaius, Stephanas, and Phoebe. There were also unnamed households that could have supported the education of women: those able to spend money on law suits, divorce, and head coverings. These chapters have established that Paul's writings interacted with the popular philosophies that both produced educated women and were present in Corinth, and the church provided an adequate context in which such women were found. Finally, the question remains, "how do we read 1 Corinthians with philosophically educated women?" To address this question, I have chosen three widely discussed issues in popular moral philosophers that would be basic knowledge for women educated in any popular school and that have some resonance with content in 1 Corinthians: patronage in chapter 5, marriage and family in chapter 6, and the *agon* or contest motif in chapter 7.

In chapter 5, I will examine how two philosophically educated women—Sophia and Fortuna—would interact with Paul's notion of patronage. As wealthy widows, Sophia and Fortuna fit the best historical context for a broad philosophical education and patronesses of the church. Reading selections of 1 Corinthians with these two women will produce both complementary and contrasting understandings according to Paul's persuasiveness and their philosophical sympathies.

As the material above indicates, most philosophically educated women were either wealthy or attached to wealthy households. Because of this history, it is safe to imagine that if philosophically educated women were somehow connected to Paul's Corinthian community, they would be patronesses of the churches. Paul's interaction with philosophically educated women and the men that they influenced could therefore determine possible meeting places for followers, legal representation, monetary support, and the various other benefits that patronesses bestowed on their clients. These patronesses are unmentioned in the epistle because Paul does not want to appear controlled by them or unduly attached to them, but they are not invisible because their presence can be drawn out of the content of the letter. In 1 Corinthians, Paul the apostle interacts with his philosophically educated patronesses like a poet or philosopher who appeals to his inspired divine right to instruct, correct, admonish, and exhort both patronesses and persons in the church that these wealthy women influenced. At the outset, it appears that Paul threatens both sides of the patron/client relationships in Corinth by using his apostleship to instruct both the rich and poor of the community. This kind of behavior is somewhat expected from a Roman who values freedom and friendship, as well as a poet or philosopher who gives sharp rebuke to their patron. However, Paul is also careful to give adequate praise at the appropriate time (1 Cor 1:3-9; 3:21-23). I will argue in this chapter that the philosophically educated patronesses of the

Corinthian church valued Paul for his inspired speech and teaching, which allowed some toleration for frank (corrective) speech, but these patronesses would also value Paul's dutiful praise.

Philosophical Patronage

Patronage was an important economic, legal,[1] and social part of Roman life[2] during the time of Paul.[3] Typically, the patron/client relationship existed between a wealthy, powerful, and influential person and a somewhat inferior person who did not possess the wealth, power, or influence needed to advance or simply exist in the Roman world. Most influential philosophers were a part of this system but their efforts were not always successful. For example, the philosophers Philodemus (ca. 110–35 BCE) and Lucretius (ca. 99–55 BCE) had a difficult time securing patrons. Lucretius had a tenuous relationship with Memmius[4] and Philodemus enjoyed some support from Torquatus and Cicero.[5] However, neither philosopher was able to attach himself to one patron. Such patronage was important, and wealthy philosophically educated women actively supported their intellectual interests.

Two imperial women lavishly supported their philosophical interests. Pompeia Plotina (d. ca. 122 CE), the wife of Trajan, was a well-known patron of the Epicureans.[6] She likely made more than one trip to Athens with Hadrian—or on her own—in which her study of philosophy could have taken place.[7] Plotina may have started out as a neo-Pythagorean due to a

---

1. Hunter, *Systematic and Historical Exposition of Roman Law*, 667–72; Buckland, *Text-Book of Roman Law*, 145–46; Watson, "Roman Private Law," 100–105.

2. Cynthia Damon, "Greek Parasites," 181–95, argues that the "parasites" in Roman literature tells us something about patronage. For Romans discussing patronage and friendship, see Gardner and Wiedemann, *Roman Household*, 166–83; Damon, *Mask of the Parasite*; Longfellow, *Roman Imperialism*.

3. Schmidt, *Friends, Followers, and Factions*; and Gellner and Waterbury, *Patrons and Clients*; Eisenstadt and Roniger, *Patrons, Clients and Friends*; Elliott, "Patronage and Clientage," 142–56; DeSilva, "Patronage and Reciprocity," 32–84; Wheatley, *Patronage*.

4. John Stearns, "Lucretius and Memmius," 67–68, suggested that Lucretius originally was enthusiastic about his patron Memmius when he promised to construct a building for the Epicureans, and later Lucretius had a change of heart when Memmius reneged on his promise. It is also likely that Lucretius viewed his "patron" Memmius with the same kind of derision as everyone else; see Roller, "Gaius Memmius," 246–48.

5. Allen and Delacy, "Patrons of Philodemus," 65.

6. Swan, "Consular Epicurean," 54–60; Ferguson, "Epicureanism," 2257–2327; Hanslik, "Pompeia Plotina," 2293–98; Jones, *Epicurean Tradition*.

7. Hanslik, "Pompeia Plotina," 200.

connection with Nicomachus of Gerasa[8] and probably converted to Epicureanism later in life.[9] The neo-Pythagorean Nicomachus of Gerasa wrote his *Enchiridion* at the request of an unnamed patroness, often identified as Plotina.[10] In 121 CE she petitioned Hadrian, whose education she oversaw, requesting on behalf of the Epicurean Pompillius Theotimus to exempt the school from the government appointment of the head of the school.[11] If Plotina was not a neo-Pythagorean or an Epicurean, she was certainly an important patroness of both schools, with an interest in learning philosophy and championing its causes.

Julia Domna (170–217 CE) was a part of a philosophic circle. The members of this literary/intellectual circle may have included Aelius Antipater (sophist/rhetorician), Philostratus (sophist/biographer), Serenus Sammonicus (polymath), Dio Cassius (historian), Asinius Quadratus (historian), and perhaps Philiscus (sophist), Papinian (jurist), Ulpian (jurist), Paulist (jurist), and Galen (physician/philosopher).[12] Julia herself enjoyed participating in the learned discussions with these intellectuals.[13] She commissioned the sophist Philostratus (ca. 170–250 CE) to write the biography of the neo-Pythagorean Apollonius of Tyana (ca. 15–100 CE).[14] Philostratus tells us the story of how a certain Damis came to be supported by Julia Domna:

> ἐγένετο Δάμις ἀνὴρ οὐκ ἄσοφος τὴν ἀρχαίαν ποτὲ οἰκῶν Νῖνον· οὗτος τῷ Ἀπολλωνίῳ προσφιλοσοφήσας ἀποδημίας τε αὐτοῦ ἀναγέγραφεν, ὧν κοιωνῆσαι καὶ αὐτός φησι, καὶ γνώμας καὶ λόγους καὶ ὁπόσα ἐς πρόγνωσιν εἶπε. καὶ προσήκων τις τῷ Δάμιδι τὰς δέλτους τῶν ὑπομνημάτων τούτων οὔπω γιγνωσκομένας ἐς γνῶσιν ἤγαγεν Ἰουλίᾳ τῇ Βασιλίδι. μετέχοντι δέ μοι τοῦ περὶ

---

8. Hemelrijk suggests that Plotina employed Nicomachus as a teacher before he wrote his *Enchiridion*, "τὴν δὲ ἀρχὴν ἐκεῖθέν ποθεν ποιήσομαι ῥᾴονος ἕνεκα παρακολουθήσεως, ὅθεν καὶ ἡνίκα ἐξηγούμην σοι περὶ αὐτῶν τούτων τὴν τῆς διδασκαλίας ἐποιησάμην ἀρχή," "But now, to make my exposition easier to follow, I shall begin from the same place where I began my instruction to you in person." MSG 238.12–15; translation in Barker, *Greek Musical Writings*.

9. Oliver, "Empress Plotina," 125–28; cf. Swan, "Consular Epicurean," 57; Boatwright, "Imperial Women," 513–40.

10. McDermott, "Plotina Augusta," 192–203.

11. CIL 3.12283 (stele found at Athens in 1890). For the Greek letter, see *SIG*² 834. For a full text, see Smallwood, *Documents*, no. 442. All three are translated in Henderson, *Life and Principate*, 50–52.

12. Levick, *Julia Domna*, 114; cf. Bowersock, who thinks that the letter is inauthentic but provides valuable interpretative insights, in "Circle of Julia Domna," 101–9.

13. Bowerstock, "Julia Domna," 103.

14. Dio Cass. 77.18.4; cf. *Vita Alexandri* 29.2; Dzielska, *Apollonius of Tyana*, 56–60, 174.

αὐτὴν κύκλου—καὶ γὰρ τοὺς ῥητορικοὺς πάντας λόγους ἐπῄνει καὶ ἠσπάζετομεταγράψαι τε προσέταξε τὰς διατριβὰς ταύτας καὶ τῆς ἀπαγγελίας αὐτῶν ἐπιμεληθῆναι . . .

There was a man, Damis, by no means stupid, who formerly dwelt in the ancient city of Nineveh. He resorted to Apollonius in order to study wisdom, and having shared, by his own account, his wanderings abroad, wrote an account of them. And he records his opinions and discourses and all his prophesies. And a certain kinsman of Damis drew the attention of the empress Julia to the documents hitherto unknown. Now I belonged to the circle of the empress, for she was a devoted admirer of all rhetorical exercises; and she commanded me to recast and edit these essays . . .[15]

Philostratus also wrote a letter to Julia Domna that reveals her interest in Plutarch and possibly Platonism (*Ep.* 73).[16] In this letter, Philostratus exhorts Julia Domna (170-217 CE) to persuade Plutarch (46-120 CE) not to be angry with the sophists, perhaps in response to her reading of Plutarch's *Gorgias* or another lost work. Obviously, she could not persuade Plutarch of anything because he had died half a century before she was born. Philostratus's lack of concern for chronology does not threaten the letter's authenticity. Philostratus would not choose a friend of Julia's to express this idea because "it is part of a strategy to establish a communality of feeling and opinion between Julia, himself, and his readers."[17] Philostratus is responding to a work by Plutarch that threatened to sway her against sophists, which comprised a good portion of her intellectual friends. The best reading of this exhortation is "Do not let Plutarch persuade you to be angry with the sophists."[18] If this interpretation is correct, then Philostratus's statement seems to be in jest or sarcastic because of Julia's consistent favor towards the great sophists of her time.

In this section, we looked at the philosophical support of women at the very top of Roman society: the wife of the Emperor Trajan (53-117 CE), Pompeia Plotina (d. ca. 122 CE), and the wife of the Emperor Septimius Severus (145-211 CE), Julia Domna (170-217 CE). Pompeia supported both neo-Pythagorean and Epicurean causes. Julia Domna's interests were very broad: she participated in a philosophical circle that included the

15. Philostr. *VS* 1.3.
16. Penella, "Philostratus' Letter," 161-68; cf. Anderson, "Putting Pressure on Plutarch, 43-45. Philostratus also wrote a letter to Epictetus, no. 65 (in *Alciphron, Aelian and Philostratus: The Letters*).
17. Van der Stockt, "Never the Twain Shall Meet?," 191.
18. Bowersock, *Greek Sophists*, 101-9.

brightest minds of her day. These two women serve as a starting point for the examination of non-imperials in and near Corinth who supported their intellectual and political interests.

Patronage in 1 Corinthians

Just as a young aristocrat can gain wealth and power through moving up to more distinguishing offices of the city, the city of Corinth itself moved from "colony" to "free city"[19] with astonishing speed. The close relationship with Rome doubtlessly helped both the city itself and its elite move up through the ranks. Many dedicatory inscriptions in Corinth indicate some relationship to the imperial family.[20] Patrons in first-century Corinth[21] include (but are not limited to) Erastus the *aedile* (discussed above in 4.6.5), Gn. Babbius Philinus,[22] Tiberius Claudius Dinippus,[23] L. Castricius Regulus,[24] T. Manlius Juvencus,[25] Herodes Atticus (mentioned above), Lucius Gellius Menander,[26] and Junia Theodora (discussed below).

John K. Chow's analysis of 1 Corinthians indicates that patron/client relationships may be behind many problems in the Christian community at Corinth, including Paul's apostleship, eating meat sacrificed to idols, Paul's clarification of his relationship to patronage, and the problem of unity in the church.[27] Paul's presentation of himself as apostle asserts the divine authority that he needs to admonish the church's patrons (1 Cor 1:1, 16:22). The civic rites in which some of the Corinthians participated, and which sacrificial

---

19. Paul A. Gallivan dates the liberation of Corinth to 67 CE, in "Nero's Liberation," 230-34.

20. Chow, *Patronage and Power*, 44.

21. Spawforth, "Roman Corinth," 167-82.

22. Dean, "Latin Inscriptions," 168-70. Babbius most likely is the patron who reconstructed the Southeast Building, and his son refurbished it. Broneer, "Investigations at Corinth, 1946-1947," 233-47. Gn. Babbius Philinus also payed for a building in the western forum. Sturgeon, "Dedications of Roman Theaters," 27, 28, 123; Scranton, "Corinth," 73.

23. Dean, "Latin Inscriptions," 189-97; Standing, "Claudian Invasion," 281-88; Danylak, "Tiberius Claudius Dinippus," 231-70.

24. Strabo 8.6.22; Kent, *Inscriptions*, 70-72, nos. 152, 153; Gebhard, "Isthmian Games," 78-94, Walbank, "Corinthian Coinage," 337-49.

25. Arrian 1.1; West, *Latin Inscriptions*, iii-v, vii-ix, xi, xiii-xiv, 1-141, 143-45, 147-171.

26. Wiseman, "Gymnasium Area, 1967-1968," 64-106.

27. Bruce Winter focuses on the civil litigation in 1 Cor 6.1-11, social mobility in 1 Cor 7.17, civic rights 1 Cor 8-11.1. *Seek the Welfare of the City*, 105-18, 145-63, 165-74; Neyrey, *Render to God*, 144-90; Tucker, "Baths, Baptism, and Patronage," 173-88.

Patronage and Philosophically Educated Women

meat was likely offered could have been dedicated to the Roman emperor, the ultimate patron (1 Cor 10). Paul defends his apostleship against patrons who may have been investigating him, claiming that he serves God alone—not the Corinthians or himself (1 Cor 4:1–5). Paul further defends himself in 1 Corinthians 9:1–23, refusing to accept payment (μισθός) that patrons normally owe their inferiors.[28] Yet Paul's teaching that the church is a body (1 Cor 12:18–29) supports the patronage system because it reinforces the current social and economic makeup of the community.[29] The metaphor of the unity of the body and its parts was often used by ancient writers to support the extreme social distance between the rich and the poor.[30] In 1 Corinthians 16:22, Paul utilizes friendship language that has patronal overtones,[31] and perhaps this is intentional as φιλεῖν appears only here in the Pauline corpus. Chow goes on to argue that many of the problems in the Corinthian church are rooted in strained patronal relationships. Paul's refusal to accept money (1 Cor 9:1–27), the possible wealth of the litigants in court (1 Cor 6:1–8), the issue with the stepmother (the man was seeking power and influence through the sexual relationship in 1 Cor 5:1–5), and the situation with disunity related to the problem of idol food (8:1—11:1) all point to disruptions in relationships between patrons and the church.

There is another factor to consider with respect to the relationships between Paul and his patronesses: the organization of the church. If the church can be somewhat likened to a *collegia*,[32] then the support of the *collegia* by patronesses might provide some understanding for the dynamics between the patronesses of the church and Paul. The Corinthian community shares several similarities with the *collegia*: patronal support, a high population of freedmen, and high ranking offices held by long-term members.[33] Robert Wilken has noted that Pliny the Younger (ca. 61–112 CE, *Ep.* 10.96)

---

28. Chow, *Patronage and Power*, 173. Cf. Hock, *Social Context*, 61; Winter, "Christian Benefactors," 87–103.

29. Lee, *Paul, the Stoics, and the Body of Christ*, 143–50.

30. Chow, *Patronage and Power*, 176; Sen. *Clem.* 1.3.5; 1.4.3; 1.5.1 (the Emperor is the head); cf. Plut. *Mor.* 478d, 797e; Philo. *Praem.* 125; Dio Chrys. *Or.* 3.104–7; Dion. Hal. *Ant. Rom.* 6.86.2.

31. John 19:12; Marshall, *Emnity*, 131; Garnsey and Saller, *Roman Empire*, 148–50, 154–56.

32. Mihaila, *Paul-Apollos Relationship*, 101; cf. Wilken, "Collegia," 268–91; Richardson, "Early Synagogues," 90–109; Kwon, "Discovering the Characteristics of *Collegia*," 166–82; Kloppenborg, "Edwin Hatch," 212–38; McLean, "Agripinilla Inscription," 239–70; Kloppenborg, "*Collegia* and *Thiasoi*," 16–30; Clarke, *Serve the Community*, 154–57.

33. Holmberg, "Methods," 266.

interpreted the early Christian groups as voluntary associations.[34] Similarly, Celsus (fl. 2nd c. CE) asserted that Christianity had no right to exist as a voluntary association because of its secret nature.[35] In chapters 38–39 of his *Apologeticum*, Tertullian (ca. 160–225 CE) argued that churches of his time should be regarded as *collegia*, indicating that there was still a struggle for Christians to be accepted by their peers.[36] However, in my opinion, the earliest churches lacked the organizational structure of the *collegia*:

> (1) they often incorporated persons who shared a common trade or craft being thus more homogeneous in terms of status; (2) they engaged in common meals which were graced with the oratory of guest rhetors and provided the necessary context trade for socio-economic advancement; (3) they participated in rituals and cultic activities; and (4) they were able to function because of the beneficence of wealthier persons who acted as patrons.[37]

While Christian practices and organization had not yet solidified, the wealthy women of the church who supported other *collegia* may have interacted with Paul and the church within a similar framework.

Junia Theodora and Claudia Metrodora

Junia Theodora, doubtless a Corinthian of higher status and greater wealth than anyone in the early church, served as patroness for many cities in Lycia in the first century. She is significant for this study because Junia is the only woman from first-century Corinth that is honored as *prostatis*, the same term that Paul uses for Phoebe (Rom 16:2). A similar patroness, Claudia Metrodora, is important because she serves as a parallel to Junia's influence; however, the term *prostatis* does not appear in her dedicatory inscriptions. While these two women are of higher status than any woman that we would expect to find in the Pauline churches, their behavior as patronesses greatly illuminates our understanding of the situation in Corinth. These women were in control of their wealth and used it according to their political, intellectual, and economic interests.

In 1954, a French archaeological team discovered a reused stele in a late Roman tomb near Corinth with five inscriptions on it concerning the

---

34. Wilken, *Christians as the Romans Saw Them*, 32.
35. Origen, *Contra Celsus* 1.1; 8.17, 47. Cf. Wilken, "Collegia," 282.
36. Wilken, "Collegia," 283–86.
37. Mihaila, *Paul-Apollos Relationship*, 101.

benefactions of Junia Theodora.[38] Despite its importance in illuminating the world of Paul as a very intriguing piece of epigraphy, it has not received the scholarly attention or popular fame of other familiar inscriptions regarding important males such as Gallio,[39] Erastus the *aedile*, and the possible epigraphic evidence of a synagogue[40] in Corinth. R. A. Kearsley has provided the most recent edition of the text of the Junia Theodora inscriptions with several germinal comments regarding its importance for the study of women in the first century and its impact on New Testament studies.[41]

Junia Theodora received high honors from several Lycian cities: two from a federal assembly of the Lycian cities, Myra, Patara, and Telmessos. Junia protected the Lycians when they rebelled against their governor. During this time of political transition, Junia's home served as a safe haven for important Lycians. Junia also assisted several citizens of Myra, Patara, and Telmessos when they visited Corinth. We find in Junia Theodora a woman controlling her resources, interested in the political aspirations of the wealthy citizens of several Lycian cities, and willing to serve as their patroness.[42]

It is significant that the Lycian cities that honor Junia are no strangers to honoring their female athletes, physicians, wives, officeholders, and patronesses.[43] Junia Theodora is not to be placed among the mothers, wives, or concubines of the Emperors and Senators who famously (or infamously) influenced Roman history, but with her sisters who contributed to provincial Greek life by serving in the provinces as patrons (here we place priestesses and various officeholders), athletes, philosophers, and physicians.[44] Herodotus and other early witnesses tell us that Lycians were a matrilineal

---

38. Pallas, "Inscriptions," 496–508. In their original publication, the team does not offer a detailed interpretation of the importance of the find. SEG 18.143; Robert, *Opera Minora Selecta*, 2:840–48; Picard, "Junia Theodora," 95–97.

39. Murphy-O'Connor, *St. Paul's Corinth*, commentary 149–60, text 179–82.

40. Wiseman, "Corinth and Rome," 2.7.1:438–548 (pl. 5, no. 8).

41. Kearsley, "Women in Public Life," 189–211; cf. the summary and bibliography listed by Winter, *Roman Wives, Roman Widows*, 183; van Bremen, *Limits of Participation*, 164n73; 165n78; 198n11. Cf. Klauck, "Junia Theodora," 42–57.

42. Murphy-O'Connor, *St. Paul's Corinth*, 82.

43. Pleket presents other inscriptions that concern the social activity of women in Lycia, several of which are presented above. E.g., the physician Antiochis, mentioned above, is from Lycia (Pleket, *Epigraphica*, no. 12), then there is the chase Asë (Pleket, *Epigraphica*, no. 15) and the gymnasiarch Lalla of Arneae (Pleket, *Epigraphica*, no. 14).

44. The point that women of a more "normal" vein functioned as patrons in the Greek East and throughout the Empire is carefully argued by van Bremen, "Images of Women," 223–42, and MacMullen, "Women's Power," 169–76.

society.⁴⁵ However, the matrilineal nature of the Lycian cities does not indicate that they were matriarchal or that women there enjoyed more freedoms from abuse and neglect.⁴⁶

One of the curiosities of the Junia Theodora inscription is its *apotheosis* motif:

> Τοῦ γεγονότος ψηφίσματος φιλανθρώπου καὶ στεφανώσεως χρυσῷ καὶ ἀναθέσεως εἰκόνος εἰς ἀποθέωσιν μετὰ τὴν [ἀπ]αλ[λ] αγὴν Ἰουνία Θεοδώρα κατοικούσῃ παρ' ὑμεῖν ἐξαπεστάλκαμεν ὑμεῖν τὸ ἀντιγισάμενοι τῇ δημοσία σφραγεῖδι ὅπως ε[ἴ]δητε τ[αῦτα].

> By an honorific decree made in favor of Junia Theodora, living among you, it is voted to grant her both the crowning with a golden crown and the offering of a portrait for her deification after her death, and we have sent you a copy (of the decree) sealed with the public seal so as to inform you at the same time.⁴⁷

The *apotheosis* motif was originally used to honor patronesses and patrons associated with the imperial cult, but the term became so popular in funerary inscriptions that it means simply "buried."⁴⁸ However, in Junia Theodora's case, the *apotheotic* formula is clearly an honor intended to persuade her to continue her many benefactions. The inscription from Telmessos reads "and invite her, living with the same intentions, to always be the author of some benefit towards us, well knowing that in return our city recognises and will acknowledge the evidence of her goodwill," "παρακαλεῖν τε αὐτὴν μένουσαν ἐπ[ὶ] τῆς αὐτῆς ὑποσ[τάεως] ἀεί τινος ἀγαθοῦ παραιτίαν γείεσθαι πᾶσιν ἡμεῖν εἰδυῖαν ὅτ[ι καὶ ἡ πόλις) ἡμῶν εὐχάριστος ἀποδώσι αὐτῇ πάλιν τὰς καθηκο[ύσας] μαρτυρίας."⁴⁹ These inscriptions were presented to Junia and her heir, both are explicitly said to be living: Junia (from Lycian cities, no. 1 *ll.* 1–2; the second Lycian inscription "living among you," "κατοικούσῃ παρ' ὑμεῖν ἐξαπεστα," no. 4, *l.* 45) and Sextus Iulius (who will receive one of the inscriptions from the Lycian federal assembly, no. 4 *l.* 53). One important parallel to this honor is the *apotheotic* image on the Arch of the Sergii.

---

45. Herodotus 1.173; Plut. *Mor.* 428d; Pembroke, "List of the Matriarchs," 217; cf. Plut. *Lyc.* 14–16.

46. Pembroke, "Women in Charge," 5.

47. *A Letter of the Federal Assembly to Corinth Introducing a Second Decree in Favor of Junia Theodora*, *ll.* 43–46. Text and translation in Winter, *Roman Wives, Roman Widows*, 208.

48. Radin, "Apotheosis," 44–46.

49. *A Decree of the Lycian City of Telmessos*, no. 5 *ll.* 83–85. Text and translation from Winter, *Roman Wives, Roman Widows*, 209–10.

Patronage and Philosophically Educated Women

The Roman patroness Salvia Postuma funded the building of an arch in Pula, Croatia in the first century BCE. Scholars still debate the significance of the monument.[50] Importantly for our purposes, Magaret Woodhull discusses the scene of *apotheosis* on Salvia Postuma's arch and the significance of her patronage. Woodhull's basic argument is intriguing:

> By inclusion on the Arch of the Sergii, the panel implied for its viewer that the Sergii deserved to be honored with apotheosis for lifetime accomplishments marked by their civic and military deeds noted in the inscriptions. They were, in effect, heros of the town. Moreover, the apotheotic iconography functioned kinetically within the monument's design to activate a theatrical dramatization of this event: approaching the arch, the viewer would first see the portraits; then, moving in closer, she would read the inscriptions accrediting civic and military valour; finally, passing under the arch, she would look up and note the eagle in the soffit, wings spread, "bearing" the figures just seen on the arch's attic heavenwards. The arch's continual use recreated the moment of apotheosis each time a person passed through the arch. Much as Augustus had joined the tutelary gods at Rimini, here Salvia made her family, now members of a heavenly realm, perpetual guardians of her fellow citizens.[51]

Woodhull argues that Salvia Postuma's *apotheosis* is implied by the *apotheotic* symbolism and her dedication of the arch, which makes the explicit *apotheosis* of Junia Theodora even more impressive.

Claudia Metrodora was an influential patroness in Asia Minor. R. A. Kearsley presents text, translation, and commentary along with discussion of Metrodora's importance to the Pauline community via Phoebe.[52] Like Junia Theorda, Metrodora received honors from various cities for her patronage: three inscriptions in six fragments are extant from Chios,[53] another honorific inscription made by a private group,[54] and a building in Ephesus preserves her memory.[55] Metrodora held the office of *stephanephros* twice, *gymnasiarch* four times, *agonothete* three times, named queen of the thirteen

---

50. This debate is presented in detail with photographs by Magaret L. Woodhull, "Matronly Patrons," 75–91.

51. Woodhull, "Matronly Patrons," 89.

52. Kearsley, "Women in Public Life," 189–211. Text and translation for Junia Theodora and Claudia Metrodora also appear in Winter, *Roman Wives, Roman Widows*, 205–11.

53. Robert, "Inscriptions de Chios," 128–33.

54. Robert, "Bulletin épigraphique," 152–53, no. 213.

55. Meriç, *Die Inschriften von Ephesos*, 7.1, no. 3003.

cities of the Ionian federation, and priestess for life of Aphrodite Livia.[56] She gave oil to the city twice for the Heraclean games and erected and dedicated a building along with her husband (whose name does not survive in the inscription).[57] Kearsley convincingly argues that the various offices and gifts to the city are credited to Metrodora herself—and not to her tutor or male relatives—indicates that Metrodora controlled her property and used it to advance her interests.[58]

The epigraphic evidence indicates that some women in the Greek East were active and influential in urban life. Junia Theodora's inscriptions indicate that several cities in Lycia had a positive relationship with Corinth and that the Lycians were no strangers to honoring important women for their various contributions. A woman of Junia Theodora's wealth, power, and influence is by no means singular: Claudia Metrodora is a parallel example from Chios.

Pleasing the Patroness: Literary Patronage as Pattern

We have seen in the patronesses of philosophy that their philosopher-clients often wrote and dedicated works to them. These philosophers did not fill their works with excessive praise for the patroness and there is no indication that the patroness, while very rich and powerful, controlled the philosopher's every word and thought. It is possible then that Paul could be dependent on one or more patron/patroness for both himself and the churches and still retain his apostolic authority and freedom. In this section, I will explore literary patronage as a clue for understanding Paul's relationship with his named and unnamed patrons. I will argue that the interpretative key for this issue lies in what Paul's patroness expects from him and the liberalities he can take (such as corrective, frank speech) as an apostle without jeopardizing the relationship.

A writer—especially a good one—possessed the unique ability to immortalize their patrons in either a positive or a negative light.[59] The most important similarity between Paul and the poets is they both understand

---

56. Winter, *Roman Wives, Roman Widows*, 210.

57. Winter, *Roman Wives, Roman Widows*, 211.

58. Kearsley, *Women in Public Life*, 200–201. Cf. Winter, *Roman Wives, Roman Widows*, 182; Dutch, *Educated Elite*, 143; Økland, *Women in their Place*, 293.

59. Direct eulogy was not necessary to immortalize patrons and fulfill this obligation. A favorite technique of the Roman writers was to pass the task of praise on to someone else. Clarke, "Poets and Patrons," 48. For Paul, see John K. Chow, where he discusses the special nature of literary patronage, in "Patronage in Roman Corinth," 121; and his discussion of what patrons would provide churches, 124.

themselves to be inspired by the divine. However, despite the declaration of independence due to inspiration, both the poet and Paul give the obligatory praise and thanksgivings to their patrons in return for services rendered and desired (1 Cor 1:3-9; 3:21-23).[60] Paul's divine inspiration is expressed in his roles as a genuine apostle: preaching the word of God, correcting loose morals, being a model for imitation, and giving instructions from God for the community.[61] In the following subsections, I will argue that if a patron was to delve too deeply into the business of the apostle or of writing (in the case of the poet), both Paul and the poets would declare freedom by means of the written word—a power that few other clients were fortunate enough to possess.

The Poet and the Apostle

As an apostle, Paul participates in reciprocal friendships. While Paul did not normally ask for gifts for himself, he did maintain relationships with benefactors and patrons of many cities as part of his missionary strategy.[62] Unlike many philosophers and poets, and indeed other apostles, Paul did not attach himself to the house of any of his patrons or the patrons of the house—churches, instead choosing to work with his hands, doing the work of a tentmaker.[63] What Paul did expect in return for his work as an apostle was faithfulness to his message (1 Cor 1:21, 2:11-16; 3:1-3, 16-17; 9:24-27; 14:36-38; especially 15:2) and the imitation of his character (1 Cor 4:15-21; 11:1) from the entire believing community as well as other critical benefits from those of higher status (support of himself, which he did not accept, 1 Cor 9:1-19; a place to meet for the Lord's Supper, provision of food and drink, 1 Cor 11:17-34; giving money 1 Cor 16:1-3).

---

60. Dio Chrys. 1.30; 13.21; 31.14, 65. "Dio Chrysostom is especially indignant at people being ungrateful towards benefactors." Mussies, *Dio Chrysostom*, 41. Sen. *Ben.* 23: "The ungrateful [person] tortures and torments [her or] himself; [she or] he hates the gifts which [she or] he has received. And what is more wretched than a [person] who forgets [her or] his benefits and clings to [her or] his injuries?"

61. Schnelle, *Apostle Paul*, 262-63; Sandnes, *Paul, One of the Prophets?*, 115; Forbes, *Prophecy and Inspired Speech*; cf. de Vos, "Rhetoric and Theology," 176.

62. Meeks, *Urban Christians*, 58-59; MacDonald and Harrington, *Colossians and Ephesians*, 166.

63. Lampe's study confirms that Paul and others could support themselves as tentmakers (*From Paul to Valentinus*, 187), and therefore Paul and his coworkers could work independently of personal patrons. Cf. Hock, *Tentmaking and Apostleship*, 29, 65; Hock, "Paul's Tentmaking," 558.

Reading 1 Corinthians with Philosophically Educated Women

Most poets needed patrons in order to survive,[64] and the relationships they had with their patrons are similar to Paul. Literary clients needed resources, defense in court and from other forms of attack, and the means needed to pursue their art. One of the features that make Paul's writings unique is that he maintained relationships with several newly founded groups by utilizing the epistle.[65] He used this common tool in an uncommon way, writing to create and maintain identity[66] within these new groups which needed patrons in order to survive.[67] Paul expected patrons to provide a meeting place for the house churches, read the letters to the community, defend Paul's integrity and teaching,[68] and provide financial support for the church (1 Cor 16:1–3; the support is not for himself, according to Paul in 1 Cor 9:11–18 and 2 Cor 11:7–10). Patrons expected, and indeed *needed* praise, flattery, and/or otherwise have their beneficence reciprocated by the apostle.

Despite the fact that the church could not survive without patrons, Paul exercised his power to punish patrons that overstepped their role or otherwise failed in their duty to provide for the church and for Paul's needs. One tool used by literary clients and Paul was the written curse.[69] Paul utilizes

---

64. Dalzell, "Maecenas and the Poets," 151; cf. Gold, *Literary Patronage*, 3.

65. Abraham Malherbe concludes that there is no exact analogy for Paul's use of the epistle as maintaining a newly created community (*Social Aspects*, 48). The closest analogy in my opinion is the administration of the Roman army and interests, which in part used letters as illustrated by Ael. *Ep.* 30: "There is therefore no need for [the Emperor] to wear himself out by journeying over the whole empire, nor by visiting different people at different times to confirm individual matters, whenever he enters their land. But it is very easy for him to govern the whole inhabited world by dispatching letters without moving from the spot. And the letters are almost no sooner written than they arrive, as if borne by winged messengers" (translation from Behr, *Complete Works*, 80). Aristides describes in detail some of these letters (noting that he received special treatment due to his practice in oration) in 50.71–93, which van der Horst identifies as parallel to Romans 16 in *Aelius Aristides*, 51. Aristides uses his special relationship with the gods to compose poetry (50.31) and because of his recognized skill in oratory he is able to persuade benefactors to give him what he wants (50.80–87). Cf. Wells, *Roman Empire*, 234.

66. Philip Esler states that Paul by writing the epistle to the Romans is an "entrepreneur of identity," *Conflict and Identity*, 109.

67. Malherbe, *Social Aspects*, 61–91; Stowers, "Social Status," 66–68.

68. Rom 16:17–18; 1 Cor 1:10–16; Gal 1:6–9; 1 Thess 2:1–13.

69. Mary Beard argues that the power of a written curse adds to its potency, in "Function of the Written Word," 37. Paul wrote several of them: 1 Cor 5:1–5; 16:22; Gal 1:8; 3:10; cf. 2 Thess 1:5–12. Cf. *TDNT* 1:354. It is interesting that the curse in 1 Cor 16:22 is in close proximity to the commendation of several patrons. Whether or not Paul actually cursed former benefactors of the church is not explicitly clear, although Chow identifies the sexually deviant man in 1 Cor 5 as a patron (*Patronage and Power*, 123–30). Paul's cursing activity certainly serves as a warning to the entire church to remain faithful to his message and character.

the curse twice in 1 Corinthians (1 Cor 5:1–5; 16:22).[70] In 1 Corinthians 5:5, Paul instructs the Corinthians to eject the sinful man from the community, delivering his flesh over to Satan to be destroyed so that his soul might be saved. While the use of the curse in 1 Corinthians 5:5 is not directed at a patron, it certainly demonstrates that Paul has the authority to call down a type of divine judgment on someone in the community. Furthermore, if the man had a relationship with a wealthy widow as I argued above, the curse does affect a patroness by proxy and other wealthy persons in the community would have taken note.

The other curse appears near the conclusion of the letter, where Paul marks unbelievers as enemies, plainly saying that they are cursed (1 Cor 16:22). In both 1 Corinthians 5:5 and 16:22, Paul utilizes the ancient generic curse form found in other curses at Corinth, which are characterized by a person invoking divine judgment or punishment on an enemy.[71] As such, the enemies are excluded from fellowship in the community. If Paul really did have the authority to cause the community to withdraw fellowship from a member, that indeed would be a powerful weapon to discipline patrons. As stated above, the two most important features of writers[72] that gave them special standing with their patrons is their divine inspiration and ability to immortalize their patrons. Both the poets[73] and Paul[74] openly claimed both of these powers, and used them decisively.

70. Wiles, *Paul's Intercessory Prayers*, 142–55.

71. Although Bruce Winter focuses his discussion on Corinthian curses on 1 Cor 12:3, he has a very useful bibliography and review of the archaeological evidence in *After Paul Left Corinth*, 164–79.

72. M. L. Clarke notes that Vitruvius' work on architecture is dedicated to Augustus in response to being appointed to an important post and Quntilian's *Institutio* is dedicated to his friend Marcellus Victorius. While Quintilian was writing the *Insitutio*, he was appointed to a post and inserted some adulatory remarks to Domitian in book 4, "Poets and Patrons," n12.

73. The tradition of poetic inspiration is at least as old as Homer, who describes poets as he does kings and princes in the *Iliad*. A very detailed discussion of the divine nature of poetry in Greek thought and its development in Roman thought is available in an article by Sperduti, "Divine Nature," 209–40. A few notes are useful here. Sperduti observes that Homer uses the same words (διοῖ, θεῖοι, διοτρεφεές, and διογενεές) to describe poets, seers, and kings: Hom. *Il.* 1.176; 2.196, 445; Hom. *Od.* 1.65, 196, 284; 2.27, 233, 394; 3.121; 4.17; 621, 691; 8.87, 539; 16.252; 17.359; 23.133; 143. "As the sceptre of the king comes from Zeus and fillets are conferred upon holy men by Apollo, so, too, the words of the poets come from the gods." Sperduti, "Divine Nature," 209. Cf. Freeman, "Plato," 137–49, and Murray, "Poetic Inspiration," 87–100.

74. The tradition of Pauline inspiration is evident in but not limited to the nature of his description of his apostolic calling, the practice of blessing and cursing, apostolic prayers, the exercising of his apostolic office as giving the words of God, and the reading of the Pauline letters in worship. Udo Schnelle, *Paul*, 159, writes that Paul understood

Reading 1 Corinthians with Philosophically Educated Women

Horace: A Client like Paul

I will now examine the relationship between Horace and Maecenas, which will serve as an example for how Paul might interact with his supporters. An important pattern will emerge: the value of the poet to his patron is the poet's inspiration and this quality serves as an equalizing force, allowing the poet to be a friend and engage in corrective or frank speech. Horace is one of the many Roman poets of the Augustan age who were clients of Maecenas,[75] an ideal literary patron.[76] While Maecenas had many poets in his retinue, Horace is most attractive for this study because he garners more scholarly attention with regard to the relationship between Maecenas and his literary clients.

All of Horace's works are dedicated to Maecenas; the first book of the *Sermones*, *Odes*, and *Poems* include a statement of praise to him. Horace *wanted* Maecenas to be pleased with his work, which is indicative of the friendship that he sought to maintain.[77] This desire is explicit in *Satire* 1.10.81, "Plotius et Varius, Maecenas Vergiliusque/ Valgius et probet haec Octavius optimus atque/ Fuscus et haec utinam Viscorum laudet uterque/ ambitione relegata," "Let but Plotius and Varius approve of these verses; let Maecenas, Virgil, and Valgius; let Octavius and Fuscus, best of men; and let but the Viscus brothers give their praise!" According to Suetonius, who preserves the verses from Maecenas dedicated to Horace, he was successful in this venture:

> Ni te visceribus meis, Horati,
> Plus iam diligo, tu tuum sodalem
> Ninnio videas strigosiorem

---

himself to be "one grasped by the πνεῦμα" like the First Testament prophets. Cf. Longenecker, *Galatians*, 30. The reading of the Pauline epistles likely takes the place of the reading of poetry or the discussion of philosophy in the Greco-Roman symposium after which the early Christian worship services are patterned. Cf. Dennis Smith, *Symposium*, 138–39.

75. Details about the life of Maecenas are available in Reckford, "Horace and Maecenas," 195; Dalzell, "Maecenas," 151–53; and Holland, *Seneca*. The power of Maecenas is illustrated by his friendship with Augustus. Maecenas was an extravagant man, flirting with the wife of his host at dinner in Plut. *Mor.* 760A. Seutonius writes about Maecenas' literary patronage, 10.93. Maecenas is widely mentioned in literature: Dio Cass. 49.6, 55.7; Vell. Pat. 2.88; Sen. *Ep.* 14.4, 114.6, and Theognis, *Elegiae* 1.27 and 114; Tac. *Ann.* 1.51. Cf. Purnell, *Roman Literary Patronage*; Bowditch, *Horace*.

76. Dalzell, "Maecenas," 151. Dalzell notes here the many other literary clients of Maecenas.

77. Aristotle affirms that true friends are very intimate: "καὶ μίαν ψυχὴ εἶναι τοῖς ἀληθῶς φίλος," "True friends are one spirit," *Eth. Eud.* 7.1240b.3 (Rackham, LCL). Aristotle goes on to say that in such closeness two people want to both live and die together, not ever wanting to separate. Cf. Pl. *Lysis* 207c; Sen. *Ep.* 3.2; Cic. *Amic.* 80.

If that I do not love you, my own Horace, more than life itself, behold your comrade leaner than Ninnius.[78]

The tone of Horace's references to Maecenas is almost always positive and cordial. Horace was critical of Maecenas before becoming his client, but his new patron allowed the criticisms to remain: "Wickham[79] thought that *Sermones* 1.2 must then have been written before Horace made the acquaintance of Maecenas and suggests that it was the express request of Maecenas himself that the lines were left unchanged, in order, one may suppose, to avoid the odium of exercising improper influence on his friend's literary product."[80] We should note that Horace never explicitly thanks his patron.[81]

Matthew Santirocco argues that in the *Odes*, the relationship of Horace to Maecenas develops from one of dependence to a declaration of independence.[82] This theory is sustained by references and allusions to the relationship in the *Sermones, Poems,* and *Epistles*. Santirocco notes that book one of the *Odes* emphasizes the vast material difference between patron[83] and poet.[84] Then, in book two, Horace outlines a spiritual dimension, as Horace's poverty is symbolic of his artistic inspiration that sets him apart from others, including Maecenas. In book three, Santirocco suggests that Horace is superior to Maecenas in his independence from the anxieties of wealth and Horace therefore becomes a spiritual patron of Maecenas. As a whole, Santirocco's conclusions suggest that the poet can express both de-

---

78. Suet. *Vita Hor.*

79. Horace, *Satires*, ed. Wickham, 12.

80. Hewitt, "Gratitude," 464. The veiled criticism of Maecenas is in *Serm.* 1.2.25. See *Ep.* 1.7 for a letter to Maecenas; criticisms of his sex life in *Epod.* 3. Cf. Campbell, *Horace* (London: Methuen, 1924), 141. Horace in 2.6.58 is accused of being a puppet of Maecenas, but he says that it is his pleasure to be his client.

81. Hewitt, "Horace," 466. Maecenas gives Horace a farm, e.g., for which Horace is grateful but does not express explicit thanks, in *Serm.* 2.6.1; *Ep.* 1.14.1; 1.16.5. This is reminiscent of Paul's "thankless thank-you" in Philippians 4. See Briones, "Philippians 4:10–20," 47–49; Peterman, "Thankless Thanks," 261–70.

82. Santirocco, "Maecenas Odes," 241–53. The development of Horace as a client as portrayed in the *Satires* is noted in Baker, "Maecenas and Horace," 213.

83. On the wealth of Maecenas, see Reckford, "Horace and Maecenas," 195; Dalzell, "Maecenas," 151–53.

84. The social position of Horace is explored by Taylor, "Equestrian Career," 164–70. Taylor examines the writings of Horace and concludes that as a son of a freedman he was disqualified for equestrian service and thus well below the social position of Maecenas, 164. As the scribe of a powerful knight, he enjoyed several privileges: he attended the *ludi* with Maecenas, sitting in seats in the theater reserved for knights (*Serm.* 2.6.48; Taylor, "Equestrian Career," 163); and Horace wore the knight's ring and garb (*Serm.* 2.7.53–55; Taylor, "Equestrian Career," 166).

pendence on a patron and literary independence at the same time because of their (both the patron and the poet) understanding of inspiration. Santirocco concludes, "While consistently affirming Horace's sincere affection for Maecenas, these odes, by their dynamic disposition, also create a certain distance and enable their author to maintain a high degree of personal and artistic freedom."[85]

Horace declares independence by virtue of his inspiration. This claim is evident in *Ode* 3, where Horace expresses his close friendship with Maecenas, their economic separation, as well as Horace's immortality.

> Cur me querellis exanimas tuis? nec dis amicum est nec mihi te pruis
> obire, Maecenas, mearum grande decus columenque rerum.
> a! te meae si partem animae rapit maturior vis, quid moror altera,
> nec carus aeque nec superstes integer? ille dies utramque
> ducet ruinam. non ego perfidumdixi sacramentum: ibimus, ibimus,
> utcumque praecedes, supermum carpere iter comites parati.
> me nec Chimaerae spiritus igneae nec, si resurgat, centimanus Gyas
> divellet umquam: sic potenti Iustitiae placitumque Parcis.
> seu Libra seu me Scorpios adspicit formidolosus pars violentior
> natalis horae seu tyrannis Hesperiae Capricornus undae,
> utrumque nostrum incredibili modo consentit astrum. te Iovis impio
> tutela Saturno refulgens eripuit volueriusque Fati
> tardavit alas, cum populus frequens laetum theatris ter erepuit sonum;
> me truncus inlapsus cerebo sustulerant, nisi Faunus ictum
> dextra levasset, Mercurialium custos virorum. reddere victimas
> aedemque votivam memento; nos humilem feriemus agnam.

Why doest thou crush my life out of complaints? 'Tis the will neither of the gods nor of myself that I should pass away before thee, Maecenas, the great glory and prop of my own existence. Alas, if some untimely blow snatches thee, the half of my own life, away, why do I, the other half, still linger on, neither so dear as before nor surviving whole? That fatal day shall bring the doom of both of us. No false oath have I taken; both, both together, we will go, whene'er thou leadest the way, prepared as comrades to travel the final journey. Me no firey breath of the Chimaera, nor hundred-handed Gyas, should he rise against me, shall ever tear from thee. Such is the will of mighty Justice and the Fates. Whether Libra or dread Scorpio or Capricornus, lord of the Hesperian wave, dominates my horoscope

---

85. Santirocco, "Maecenas," 253. Santirocco does not believe that Maecenas is a poet, but I think that his argument and conclusions are still important. Horace interacted with Maecenas as a poet, albeit not a one as gifted as himself. For Maecenas described as a poet—and indeed not a good one—see Dalzell, "Maecenas," 161.

as the more potent influence of my natal hour, the stars of us twain are wonderously linked together. To thee the protecting power of Jove, outshining that of baleful Saturn, brought rescue, and stayed the wings of swift Fate what time the thronging people thrice broke into glad applause at the theatre. Me the trunk of a tree, descending on my head, had snatched away, had not Faunus, the protector of poets, with his right hand warded off the stroke. Remember then to off the victims due and to build a votive shrine! I will sacrifice a humble lamb.[86]

Horace expresses his dependence on Maecenas in no uncertain terms. He declares that Maecenas will die before him, and it will destroy Horace because they are true friends: Maecenas is half of Horace. While Maecenas will be honored greatly when he dies, unlike his wealthy friends, Horace will only be able to sacrifice a lamb. This declaration of affection demonstrates to Maecenas that Horace will be faithful to his obligation to reciprocate his many gifts.

The independence of Horace is clearly expressed in his refusal to acquiesce to the requests of Maecenas. Horace refuses to publish the *Epods* when asked (*Epod.* 14) or to celebrate Augustus's victories (*Carm.* 2.12).[87] Horace discusses literary patronage:

> Multa quidem nobis facimus mala saepe poetae
> (ut vineta egomet caedam mea), cum tibi librum
> sollicito damus aut fesso; cum laedimur, unum
> si quis amicorum est ausus reprehendere versum;
> cum loca iam recitata revolvimus irrevocati;
> cum lamentamur non apprare labores
> nosotros et tuni deducta poema filo;
> cum speramus eo rem venturam ut, simul atque
> carmina rescieris nos fingere, commodus ultro
> arcessas et egere vetes et scribere cogas.

> We poets doubtless often do much mischief to our own cause—
> let me hack at my own vines—when you are anxious or weary
> and we offer you our book; when we are hurt if a friend has

---

86. In this ode, Horace is encouraging Maecenas to commit to the present and celebrate it due to the uncertainness of the future. Commager, "Function of Wine," 71. Horace speaks only of Maecenas with tender affection: *Ode* 3.16.20, with the possible exception of *Epod.* 3, where he playfully criticizes Maecenas's sexual appetite, and *Ode* 3.19.1, a criticism of the extravagance that we know Maecenas to enjoy. A celebration of Maecenas's birthday with poetry and divine blessings, which the poet honors almost more than his own, *Ode* 4.11. Support and praise for Maecenas' military valor and a vow to support him, *Epod.* 1 and 9.

87. Cf. Reckford, "Horace and Maecenas,," 202.

dared to censure a single verse; when, unasked, we turn back to passages already read; when we complain that men loose sight of our labours, and of our poems so finely spun; when we hope it will come to this, that, as soon as you hear we are composing verses, you will go so far as kindly to send for us, banish our poverty, and compel us to write.[88]

Here Horace describes a literary patron/client relationship. The poet appreciates patronage but shields himself from censure. The reciprocation of patronage is the literary work itself, and the writer is the best person to shape it according to their talents. The writer does desire a patronal relationship, but like a friend seeking a friend, the poet wants the patron to actually enjoy (rather than shape) their literary work for what it is.

Horace's expresses his independence, by defining the nature of his relationship with his patron. In *Satire* 1.9, Horace praises Maecenas for his literary taste and suggestions that the attention of a man of his stature should not be easily earned: he should not allow just anyone to be a literary client.[89] Horace goes on to criticize Alexander the Great for paying an unskilled poet.[90] Alexander presented money to the poet Chœrilus as a *gratia* (*Ep.* 2.1.232) for his poetry, as well as requiring Lyssipus to only cast bronze sculptures of Alexander, and ordering that Apelles paint no one but him. Horace then writes that it is foolish to support ungifted poets because their poems will soon become useless slips of paper (*Ep.* 2.1.270). Talented poets such as Virgil, Varius, and himself instead should be supported (*Ep.* 2.1.245–70).

Despite his claim to independence, Horace's dependence on Maecenas is clearly displayed in the description of his servitude in *Satire* 1.6.

The critical question then arises, what was the *quid pro quo*? Horace did not live in Maecenas' house, nor did he pay him the *salutationes* in the early morning. But comparison of *Satires* 2.6, in praise of the Sabine farm, with the earlier city-idyll of 1.6

---

88. Hor. *Ep.* 2.1.219–28.

89. In this satire, Horace is harassed in the market by a less gifted poet who wishes to be introduced to Maecenas. The pest says that Horace is lucky to have this friendship, which Horace denies in 1.6.52 and 2.6.49—it is because of Horace's talent and relationship with the gods combined with Maecenas' ability to recognize and enjoy such gifts that is the cause of the friendship. Cf. Courtney, "Horace and the Pest," 4. There is a long tradition of testing a friend before entrusting one's soul to them, particularly when one is superior to another. Cf. Arist. *Eth. Eud.* 7.1237b.19; 7.12.39a.20; Cic. *Amic.* 63; Sen. *Ep.* 3.2; Plut. *Mor.* 48e–74e (*How to Tell a Flatterer from a Friend*).

90. Clyde Murley notes interesting parallel vocabulary in this epistle and Cicero's defense of his literary patronage, in "Cicero, *Pro Archia*," 533. Cicero, too, contrasts Alexander's patronage with his own practice of supporting a gifted poet.

shows that in time life in Rome became more complicated for the friend of Maecenas. Horace's days began to be wasted, as he says, *in officia*, and most of these revolved around Maecenas. He was forced to commute to Rome even in the malarial season, to visit the Esquiline, to carry letters for Maecenas to sign and to perform various other commissions for his patron. He was jostled in the crowded streets, he was pounced upon by ambitious flatterers and envious gossips, and all the time he longed to be back on the Sabine farm. By fulfilling his social duties in the face of these annoying inconveniences, he paid part of his debt. At the same time, however, as he was bitterly satirizing the irritations of the city, he was also endowing Maecenas and his circle with ideal attributes.[91]

Horace eventually received a farm from Maecenas, which provided for some of his needs, but he still was required to serve his friend as a client in the marketplace and morning salute. Furthermore, despite any claim to superiority to his patron, the wealth, status and power clearly elevated Maecenas. He writes in *Satire* 6.1, "Though all of the Lydians that are settled in the Tuscan lands none is of nobler birth than you, and though grandsires of yours, on your mother's and father's side alike, commanded mighty legions in the days of old, yet you, Maecenas, do not, like most of the world, curl up your nose at men of unknown birth, men like myself, a freedman's son."[92] This separation in status is also evident when Horace refers to Maecenas as *rex paterque* to refer to Maecenas in *Ep.* 1.7.37.[93] Perhaps late in his career Horace was free from the menial servitude that he resented.[94]

The very intimate connection between Horace and Maecenas is complimented by the Greco-Roman friendship literature. Horace writes that

91. Reckford, "Horace and Maecenas," 201. Cf. Hor. *Sat.* 1.9, where an aspiring poet wants Horace to introduce him to Maecenas, and the hecklers who harass Horace, accusing him of being the literary puppet of his client. Cf. Hor. *Ep.* 2.1.245–70, where Horace describes the patronage of a talentless poet.

92. Hor. *Sat.* 1.6.1; cf. 1.1.1. Horace mentions his low status again as he predicts his own immortality in *Ode* 2.20.

93. Juvenal often uses *rex* or *dominus* to refer to patrons. *Sat.* 5.14, 130, 137, 161; 7.45; 10.161. With Mayor, *Thirteen Satires*, 265, we can compare this use of *rex* in Martial 2.18.5–8 and *orbus* in Plin. *Ep.* 4.15.3. Horace is not a burden to Maecenas because he provides reciprocity in friendship and poetry.

94. Richard Saller writes in "Martial on Patronage," 448, that "every time Martial mentions Maecenas as an ideal patron, the reason is that his support gave Horace and Virgil *otium* in the form of an estate large enough to provide an adequate income." See Mart. 1.107; 8.56; 11.3; 12.4. Francis L. Jones provides an excellent selection of citations from Martial highlighting his aversion to services rendered by clients in "Martial, the Client," 355.

Maecenas is his other half and this is the very definition of a friend: someone with whom one can share one's soul.[95] Horace refers to their relationship as friendship in *Epod.* 1.2; *Serm.* 1.6.50, 53, 62; *Carm.* 2.18.12; *Ep.* 1.7.12. There is also a tradition of testing a person's integrity before entrusting them with intimacy much as a literary patron should test the integrity of a poet's work before rewarding him with patronage.[96]

Two applications to 1 Corinthians are apparent. First, the nature of Paul's apostleship is comparable to poetic inspiration,[97] in the sense that both the apostle and the poet were allowed the freedom to criticize their patrons because of the nature of the services that they provide. The ideal patronal relationship with the poet allows for some artistic license and freedom, which allows the poet to criticize and attempt to correct their patron's bad habits which may include complaints concerning the level of support that the patron is giving the client. So Paul can give very high praises to the Corinthian patrons (Stephanas in 1 Cor 16:15–17; Phoebe in Rom 16:2) while disciplining their beliefs and behaviors along with everyone else (1 Cor 1:17–31; 2:6–8, 18–20; 4:17–21; 5:1–13; 6:1–11, 19; 10:27; 11:1–16). Paul can also discipline his patrons by declaring his freedom from the usual reciprocity that their gifts entail (1 Cor 9:1–23). At the same time, poetic inspiration is what the patron values most of all: if the poet is truly inspired, the patron will be immortalized in the client's writing. In this case, Maecenas and Phoebe got an excellent return on their investments.

Secondly, other artistic clients were clamoring for the support of Maecenas, and Horace was quick to attack his competition and urge Maecenas to continue his level of support for the truly talented poet. After discussing this artistic patron/client relationship, I will discuss what patrons said of the institution, and present some expectations and disappointments that patrons and clients had in their "friendships." I will then discuss how in the first four chapters of 1 Corinthians, Paul defends his apostleship and Gospel against the ideal qualities of the travelling sophist—a person that some

---

95. The definition of a friend is being of one mind (φρονέω), Hom. *Il.* 4.359–61; it is used as a contrast in 22.262–65; cf. Hom. *Od.* 6.180–85; 15.195–98; Arist. *Eth. Nic.* 1166a "ἔστι γὰρ ὁ φίλος ἄλλος αὐτός," "for the friend is another self"; cf. Phld. frag. 8; Cic. *Amic.* 6.1–7.23; Sen. *Ep.* 3; the reason why the flatterer is so dangerous is his counterfeiting such closeness, Plut. *Mor.* 51c; cf. *Alc.* 203c. In a letter to another friend, he may be referring to himself and Maecenas in a story about a client and a parton, *Ep.* 1.7.46–95, see especially 75 and 92.

96. Arist. *Eth. Eud.* 7.1237b.19; 7.1239a; cf. Phild. frag. 88; Cic. *Amic.* 63; Sen. *Ep.* 3.2; Plut. *Mor.* 49e.

97. This description of the nature of Paul's apostleship is not to the exclusion of Christopher Mount's notion of Paul's "spirit possession" ("1 Corinthians 11:3–16," 313–40).

Patronage and Philosophically Educated Women

philosophically educated women may support if they are impressed with his rhetoric. The sophists worked as public lawyers (using forensic rhetoric),[98] competed[99] publicly in rhetorical contest for disciples, students, and patronal support, and honors from cities.[100] I will also examine how Paul positions himself against the sophist, places his knowledge of God outside of philosophical inquiry, and embodies the true nature of the ideal wise-person (a concept that receives more elaboration in chapter 7). However, I will first address the nature of patronage as described by literary patrons themselves.

The Patrons Speak

The review of Horace and Maecenas relies mostly on the point of view of the literary client. We are also fortunate enough to have the perspective of literary patrons Cicero and Pliny the Younger. In these two literary patrons, the same pattern emerges as above, but from a different perspective. The patron expects pleasure from the client in the form of a good literary product and provides the usual critical support of gifts, legal protection, and other benefits of friendship.

Cicero defends both the practice of literary patronage and practices it as he defends his client, the gifted poet Archias in his speech *Pro Archia*.[101] In this forensic speech, Cicero defends the Roman citizenship of his friend on the basis of his lineage and inspiration as a poet.[102]

> Qua re quis tandem me reprehendat, aut quis mihi iure suscenseat, si, quantum ceteris ad suas res obeundas, quantum ad festos dies ludorum celebrandos, quantum ad alias voluptates et ad ipsam requiem animi et corporis conceditur temporum, quantum alii tribuunt tempestivis conviviis, quantum denique alveolo, quantum pilae, tantum mihi egomet ad haec studia recolenda sumpsero? Atque hoc ideo mihi concedendum est magis, quod ex his studiis haec quoque crescit oratio et facultas; quae, quantacumque in me est, numquam amicorum periculis defuit. Quae si cui levior videtur, illa quidem certe, quae summa sunt, ex quo fonte hauriam sentio. Nam nisi multorum praeceptis multisque litteris mihi ab adulescentia suasissem, nihil esse in

---

98. Dio Chrys. *Or.* 8.9; cf. Winter, *After Paul Left Corinth*, 37.

99. Russell, *Greek Declamations*, 75–80; Bowerstock, *Greek Sophists*, 588.

100. Winter, *Seek the Welfare of the City*, 26–33. One honor includes a golden crown.

101. Martial likewise needed defense, but for a different reason: poets published works in his name; see 7.72.12–16. Saller, "Martial," 247.

102. Murphy, "Cicero's *Pro Archia*," 100.

189

Reading 1 Corinthians with Philosophically Educated Women

> vita magno opere expetendum nisi laudem atque honestatem, in ea autem persequenda omnis cruciatus corporis, omnia pericula mortis atque exsili parvi esse ducenda, numquam me pro salute vestra in tot ac tantas dimicationes atque in hos profligatorum hominum cotidianos impetus obiecissem. Sed pleni omnes sunt libri, plenae sapientium voces, plena exemplorum vetustas: quae iacerent in tenebris omnia, nisi litterarum lumen accederet.
>
> How then can I justly be blamed or censured, if it shall be found that I have devoted to literature a portion of my leisure hours no longer than others without blame devote to the pursuit of material gain, to the celebration of festivals or games, to pleasure and the repose of mind and body, to protracted banqueting, or perhaps to the gaming board or to ball-playing? I have the better right to indulge herein, because my devotion to letters strengthens my oratorical powers, and these, such as they are, have never failed my friends in their hour of peril. Yet insignificant though these powers seem to be, I fully realize from what source I draw all that is highest in them. Had I not persuaded myself from my youth up, thanks to the moral lessons derived from a wide reading, that nothing is to be greatly sought after in this life save glory and honour, and that in their quest all bodily pains and dangers of death or exile should be lightly accounted, I should never have borne for the safety of you all the brunt of many a bitter encounter, or bared my breast to the daily onsets of abandoned persons. All literature, all philosophy, all history, all abounds with incentives to noble action which would be buried in black darkness were the light of the written word not flashed upon them.[103]

In his apology for literary patronage, he emphasizes the practical nature of the Roman interest in moral lessons. Cicero claims that people do not criticize each other for supporting ventures from which they enjoy some type of material gain. No one can look down on his support of the arts which produces an abundance of virtue. Cicero goes on to write that there is no shame in supporting an inspired poet because engaging in literary study and its moral lessons shaped and strengthened him for his successful career. Cicero therefore supports literacy due to its moral value while defending his participation in literary patronage as well as encouraging his audience to do the same.

> Quae vero accurate cogitateque scripsisset, ea sic vidi probari, ut ad veterum scriptorum laudem perveniret. Hunc go non

103. Cic. Arch. 6.13–14.

> diligam, non admirer, non omni ratione defendendum putem? Atqui sic a summis hominibus eruditissimisqu accepimus, ceterarum rerum studia et doctrina et praeceptis et arte constare, poëtam natura ipsa valere et mentis viribus excitari et quasi divino quodam spiritu inflari.

> To his finished and studied work I have known such approval accorded that his glory rivalled that of the great writers of antiquity. Does not such a man deserve my affection and admiration? Should I not count it my duty to strain every nerve in his defense? And yet we have it on the highest and most learned authority that while other arts are matters of science and formula and technique, poetry depends solely upon an inborn faculty, is evoked by a purely mental activity, and is infused with a strange supernatural inspiration.[104]

Inspiration of the poet is evident in the quality of the work and not in an experiential affirmation of divine presence when reading the poetry. Incidentally, the quality of the poetry is what gives it enduring life and therefore immortality to the patrons who support it. Because of the inspired work that Archia in particular has produced, Cicero feels obliged to defend him:

> Sit igitur, iudices, sanctum apud vos, humanissimos homiens, hoc poëtae nomen, quod nulla umquam barbaria violavit. Saxa et solitudines voci respondent, bestiae saepe immanes cantu flectuntur atque consistunt: nos institui rebus optimis non poëtarum voce moveamur?

> Holy then, [ladies and] gentlemen, in your eyes let the name of the poet be, inviolate hitherto by the most benighted of races! The very rocks of the wilderness give back a sympathetic echo to the voice; savage beasts have sometimes been charmed into stillness by song; and shall we, who are nurtured upon all that is highest, be deaf to the appeal of poetry?[105]

Cicero goes on to submit that poets should be called "sanctum," holy because of their special relationship with God.

Cicero reasons that while many potential patrons have the desire to study for themselves, not everyone is gifted with poetic inspiration.[106] Cicero

---

104. Cic. *Arch*. 8.18. Perhaps Cicero is referring to Plato or Aristotle's views on poetic inspiration.

105. Cic. *Arch*. 8.19.

106. Cicero, like Maecenas after him, not only enjoyed poetry but dabbled in it a bit himself. If Cicero could claim divine inspiration for himself, other writers did not attribute it to him. Cf. Cic. *Div*. 1.17–22. Plutarch writes, "His fame for oratory abides to

Reading 1 Corinthians with Philosophically Educated Women

argues that a patron should support artistic talent when the patron cannot do it himself / herself (Quod si ipsi haec neque attingere neque sensu nostro gustare possemus, ta- men ea mirari deberemus, etiam quum in aliis videremus) [But it may happen that we ourselves were without literary tastes or attainments; yet even so, it would be incumbent on ourselves to reverence their manifestation in others].[107] As a literary patron, Cicero longed for a poet to immortalize his consulship in Rome in 63 BCE something that he ended up doing himself in Greek.[108] Cicero highly praises the eternal reward for such patronage (Neque enim quisquam est tam aversus a Musis qui non mandari versibus aeternum suorum laborum facile praeconium patiatur) [For indeed that is no man to whom the Muses are so distasteful that he will not be glad to entrust to poetry the eternal emblazonment of his achievements].[109]

In a letter to his friend Cornelius Priscus (dated around 104 CE), the younger Pliny writes of an exchange with Martial.[110] In exchange for Martial's verses, Pliny funds his journey from Rome to Bilbilis in Spain. Even after Martial's death, Pliny shows off his prize to another friend and reasons:

> Meritone eum qui haec de me scripsit et tunc dimisi amicissime et nunc ut amicissimum defunctum esse doleo? Dedit enim mihi quantum maximum potuit, daturus ampilus si potuisset. Tamestsi quid homini potest dari maius, quam gloria et laus et aeternitas? At non erunt aeterna quae scripsit: non erunt fortasse, ille tamen scriptsit tamquam essent futura.

> Was I right then to part on such friendly terms from the author of these verses about me? Am I right to mourn his death of one of my dearest friends? He gave me of his best, and would have given me more had he been able, though surely nothing more can be given to a man than a tribute which will bring him fame and immortality. You may object that his verses will not be immortal; perhaps not, but he wrote them with that intention.[111]

---

this day, although there have been great innovations in style; but his poetry, since many gifted poets have followed him, has altogether fallen into neglect and disrepute" (*Cic.* 2.4). Cf. Spaeth, "Cicero the Poet," 500, and the many more contemporary references, 510. An analysis of the literary activity of Maecenas is available in Dalzell, "Maecenas," 157.

107. Cic. *Arch.* 7.17.

108. Cic. *Att.* 1.19.10; and in 2.1.1 he confesses that the poem is rather amateurish. Cf. Spaeth, "Cicero the Poet," 507.

109. Cic. *Arch.* 9.19; Cf. 9.22 and 26, where Cicero claims that Metellus sought to have his deeds immortalized by Archias.

110. For more on this episode, see White, "Friends of Martial," 265–300; Saller, "Martial on Patronage," 253; Hershkowitz, "Pliny the Poet," 168–81; Pitcher, "Hole in the Hypothesis," 554–61.

111. Plin. *Ep.* 3.21 (Radice, LCL). Peter White, "Amicitia," 84, notes that Martial

Pliny supposes that since Martial wrote verses about him with the intent that the words last forever, Martial was reciprocating Pliny's patronage adequately.[112] Of course, Pliny knew that Martial was quite talented and his verses would most likely endure, and he made certain of that because he published it in his own epistles. Martial's gift was nothing less than an invocation for the Muse to approach Pliny's house on the Esquiline with respect:

> Sed ne tempore non tuo desertam
> Pulses ebria januam vide to.
> Totos dat tetricse dies Minerva?
> Dum centum studet auribus virorum
> Hoc quod ssecula posterique possint
> Arpinis quoque comparere chartis;
> Seras tutior ibis ad lucernas:
> Hac hora est tua dum furit Lyaeus,
> Dum regnat rosa, dum madent capilli,
> Turn me vel rigidi legant Catones.

> But take heed you give no drunken knock on Eloquence's [Pliny's] door at a time that is not yours; all the day he devotes to serious study, while he prepares for the ears of the Hundred Court that which time and posterity may compare even with Arpinum's [Cicero's] pages. Safer will you go at the time of the late-kindled lamps; that hour is yours when Lyaeus is in revel, when the rose is queen, when locks are drenched. Then let even unbending Catos read me.[113]

We should note that Pliny was not interested in an ongoing relationship with Martial—he simply recognized the poet's ability to write and paid him for a poem that honored him.[114]

---

receives less attention than other necrologies; compare Silius Italicus in 3.7 and Domitius Tullus in 8.18.

112. Garthwaite, "Patronage," 161–75.

113. Mart. 10.19 (Bailey, LCL). Pliny is also favorably mentioned in 5.81.13 and 7.84.1.

114. There are some other letters of Pliny that tell us of the patron's interpretation of his role. Pliny knew of Cicero's generosity in supporting poetry and he committed himself to the criticism of a friend's poetry (3.15). Pliny exchanged his works with Cornelius Tacitus, whom he considered to be his friend and social equal, so that they could critique one another's work (7.20 and 6.6.3). Pliny also passes literary works on to his friends (1.16 and 4.27.5).

Reading 1 Corinthians with Philosophically Educated Women

Expectations and Disappointments

From his philosophically educated patronesses,[115] Paul would expect one simple thing first: faithfulness to himself and his teachings before any other teacher or philosophical idea. Faithfulness to Paul's message and specific imitation of his character are a major theme in 1 Corinthians (1 Cor 4:16; 11:1) and in the other undisputed epistles.[116] This imitation is a direct result of receiving Paul as an apostle who gives the words of God (1 Cor 4:15).[117] If the audience is faithful to Paul's message, then it is evidence that Paul did not do this work in vain (κενός in 1 Cor 15:10).[118] In all of these instances, Paul is addressing the entire audience, motivated by a variety of reasons to reaffirm the nature of his apostleship so as to obligate his hearers to do what he wants them to do. Paul's insistence on faithfulness rather than personal benefits (1 Cor 4:12–13), like attaching himself to a household, likely caused some confusion and frustration from the wealthier people in the community who felt obligated to reciprocate his ministries (1 Cor 9:12).[119]

Despite his refusal to participate in personal patronage, Paul did expect critical benefits from people of higher status, and philosophically educated women would be connected to wealth in some way, whether directly or by means of influence within their household. Monetary gifts to the churches, defense in court,[120] providing a place for the church to meet,[121] and exchanging and reading his letters to the churches are benefits that would normally require higher class benefactors.

Another benefit that Paul expected from higher status community members was the facilitation of letter exchange, which a philosophically educated woman could frustrate if she were unhappy with its content. There is one such

---

115. As indicated above, I will be exploring the most likely candidates for a philosophical education: the wealthy widow. Certainly such women (wealthy widows) existed in the Pauline community at Corinth. My research affirms that women of a variety of social status could have received a philosophical education: women with philosophers in the immediate family who may or may not be attached to a wealthy household. This would include wives and slaves of philosophers. At the same time, however, the overwhelming amount of existing evidence speaks to women of higher status.

116. 1 Thess 1:5–6; 2:14–16; Gal 4:12; Phil 3:17; 4:9.

117. See also 1 Thess 1:5; Gal 4:13–14; Phil 3:1–16; and Fiore, "Paul, Exemplification, and Imitation," 240.

118. Cf. κενός in 1 Thess 2.1; Phil 2.16, and εἰκῇ in Gal 4.11.

119. Hock, *Tentmaking*, 65. Because Paul did not attach himself to a household, he may have encountered resistance, frustration, or confusion; Chow, *Patronage and Power*, 109.

120. Jewett, "Phoebe," 152.

121. Cf. Stowers, "Social Status," 68; Chow, *Patronage and Power*, 16–27.

Patronage and Philosophically Educated Women

exchange in the New Testament: the churches of Colossae and Laodicea were instructed to circulate their epistles (Col 4:16), a role that Horace expected from his patron Maecenas[122] and that Cicero[123] and Pliny[124] practiced. Nympha was perhaps responsible for having it read in Laodicea, providing a house in which the church met (Col 4:15). Paul expected the largest audience possible for all of his letters, consistently addressing the widest cross section of potential hearers within the churches. This is significant because the epistle, with its thanksgivings, blessings, praises, and curses, would be read aloud repeatedly to the largest audiences possible, which greatly enhances the power and severity of both positive and negative speech.

One source of the fragility between Paul and a philosophically educated patroness would be the confusing and non-standardized methods of ascertaining a fictional equality of status. In the Roman world, the patron is always superior, but the parton/client relationship can express the superiority of the client by means of virtue and the patron by means of service. Because of this dynamic, the ancients could describe the patron/client relationship as "friendship." Aristotle theorizes that friendship only exists between equals, but superiors and inferiors can compensate the difference in status.[125] In order for "true" friendship between unequals to occur, fictive equality must be established, and an inferior can rise to the status of the superior on the basis of the inferior's goodness.[126] So if there is any inequality, as there is between a god and a human being or a ruler and a subject, the inferior one compensates for inferiority by honoring the superior. The superior then reciprocates the honor received by giving a benefit that she reckons equal to the honor received. There is no set scale by which a person can determine proportional equity, which will cause disruption in friendships and perhaps even lawsuits if the persons involved do not base their relationship on goodness.[127]

Paul's calling as teacher/apostle—at least in his mind—set him in a higher status than anyone in the church: he is uniquely called by God to do

---

122. Hor. *Ep.* 2.1.245–70.

123. Cic. *Arch.* 6.13–14.

124. Plin. *Ep.* 3.21.

125. Arist. *Eth. Eud.* 7.1241b.12–13.

126. This can be seen in the claims of certain poets or philosophers as rising to the status of their patrons, kings, or gods on the basis of their relationship or commission by the god(s) or muse(s).

127. Arist. *Eth. Eud.* 7.1243b.25 and following. Occasionally, the reciprocal relationship may be violated, especially when monetary transactions are involved, and friends may sue one another in court. The moral way to resolve a conflict, according to Aristotle, is to solve issues voluntarily instead of in a court of law, *Eth. Eud.* 7.1243a.7–14.

everything that he does (sometimes one gets the feeling that Paul is making it up as he goes along). This unique calling is emphasized especially in his record of his divine calling and subsequent correction of Peter in Galatians,[128] the patterning of his self-description after the Christ-hymn in Philippians,[129] and his consistent self-sufficiency.[130] Paul often compensates for his assertions of superiority[131] with terms like coworker (1 Cor 3:9; 2 Cor 1:24), coprisoner (Rom 16:7),[132] and king (1 Cor 4:8) by honoring and praising the community and individuals who would otherwise be disqualified for friendship due to inequality. In 1 Corinthians 3:9, Paul equates himself with Apollos as coworkers of God, so that there can be unity between those who claim to follow both teachers. Paul humbles himself to the level of Andronicus and Junia, his fellow prisoners in Romans 16:7. Elsewhere, Paul uses βασιλεύω similarly to *rex*, the client's word for a rich patron (1 Cor 4:8).[133] Similarly, Paul humbles himself by referencing his voluntary poverty, compensating for the inferiority of his patrons (their wealth has made them inferior to Paul because they have become proud and indulgent) and general audience (1 Cor 4:9–13).[134] Because Paul compensates for his superiority by referencing the foolishness of his Gospel and the sufferings that he has to endure, he is able to practice corrective speech, frankness that is only possible after friendship is established. Paul reminds the Corinthians of his established friendship with them by referencing his previous visits. Paul's frank, corrective speech manifests itself in his disapproval of their human wisdom (1 Cor 1:17–31; 2:1–5, 7–10; 3:18–20), moral failures (1 Cor 5:1–5; 6:1–11), disunity (1 Cor 1:10–16; 3:3–4 11:17–20), and the inferiority of their calling (1 Cor 1:16–19). Paul will always be superior to the community by way of his calling as apostle (2:12–16; 3:10; 4:9–13; 9:1–27). It is these issues that Paul addresses with corrective, frank speech.

128. Hay, "Paul's Indifference to Authority," 42; Gaventa, "Galatians," 309; Hall, "Rhetorical Outline," 285; cf. Joubert, *Paul as Benefactor*, 80.

129. Cf. Fiore, "Paul, Exemplification, and Imitation," 240.

130. According to Malherbe's analysis, Paul associates himself with the Cynic ideal philosopher in both 1 Thess 2 and in Phil 4. Cf. Malherbe, "Gentle as a Nurse," 203–17; Malherbe "Paul's Self-sufficiency," 125–39.

131. Joubert, *Paul as Benefactor*, 216.

132. Cf. Col 4:10 and Phlm 23.

133. Horace uses *rex paterque* to refer to Maecenas in *Ep.* 1.7.37. Gilbert Highet also demonstrates that Juvenal often uses *rex* or its attributes to refer to patrons Juvenal *Sat.* 5.14, 130, 137, 161; 7.45; 10.161; "Libertino patre natus," 279; Cf. Morford, "Juvenal's Fifth *Satire*," 219–45; cf. Garland, *1 Corinthians*, 137; Malherbe, *Social Aspects*, 72–73; Matin, *Corinthian Body*, 66.

134. Hock, *Tentmaking*, 60; Harrison, *Paul's Language of Grace*, 325. His self-description as a slave of Christ fits here, as well. Joubert, *Paul as Benefactor*, 81.

Patronage and Philosophically Educated Women

To understand better Paul's use of frank speech, the corrective words of a friend, we must look to the writings of his contemporaries. The most useful insights into frank/corrective speech are in the fragments of Philodemus's Περὶ παρρησίας and Plutarch's *How to Tell a Flatterer from a Friend*.[135] These documents demonstrate without doubt that frank speech is corrective speech. Because false friends of inferior status or character could compensate for their inferiority by flattering/praising/honoring their superiors, and indeed many people of superior status enjoyed this attention, the moralists taught that the true character of a friend was corrective speech. And in this spirit of correction, school, kinship and medical terms are often used.[136]

The fragments of Philodemus preserve for us the remains of the only known work by any author entitled Περὶ παρρησίας (*Conerning Frank Speech*).

> τῶν γὰρ ἀγαθῶν ἕνεκα μεταποιήσομεν [τὸν] ὁμιλία <ι> γενσο[μενον] φίλ[ων] τρόπον· ιἐ δὲ [ἀγαθ]ῶν, πῶς οὐχὶ καὶ τῶν κακῶν; ὡς γὰρ ἐνείνων, οὕτω καὶ τούτων προσήκει συνπαθίας χάριν, δὶ ἣν βοηθούμεθα. καὶ γὰρ εἰ μὲν ἔσ[τι παρ]ρησ[ι]άσαντα μεῖναι ἐπὶ τῶν αὐτῶν, εἰ μηθὲν ἔξα[ις], σωσ[εις] ἄνδ[ρα φίλον·]
>
> ... <[for, on account] of {our} good qualities, we shall [reform the] character of [friends]> as it will come to be <by means of {our} conversation>. But if {on account} of [{our} good {qualities}], how not also of {our} bad ones? For, just as it is suitable on account of the good cheer of the former, so too is thanks to sympathy for the latter, through which we are helped. <For in fact if it is possible for you, having spoken frankly, to stay in the same {condition}—if you withhold nothing—[you will] save a man [who is a friend]>...[137]

Sharp frank speech may offend (frag. 60) because it could appear to be an insult. Frank speech properly applied is like the work of a doctor (frag. 63, 64, 69, cf. 67; cf. Plutarch *Mor.* 66a), a metaphor that Philodemus uses both positively and negatively. Many of Philodemus's fragments are in the context of the wise-person correcting students or the general public with the proper use of frank speech. Paul's frank speech in 1 Corinthians could certainly be taken as insults: their inability to unify (1 Cor 1:10-13), Paul had to feed

---

135. Cf. Fitzgerald, "Paul and Friendship," 319–43, and the compilations of essays edited by Fitzgerald, *Friendship, Flattery, and Frankness of Speech* and *Greco-Roman Perspectives on Friendship*. The text and translation of Philodemus is from *On Frank Criticism*. See also Obbink, *Philodemus*.

136. Philodemus uses medical terminology in frag. 63, 64, 69, and 67; cf. Plut. *Mor.* 69c–e.

137. Phld. frag. 43.

them "milk" due to their immaturity (3:1–4), they did not have the foresight to handle judgment properly (5:1–5; 6:1–11), and had disunity in worship (11:17–34). Like Philodemus (*On Frank Criticism* XXIa), Paul states that is not his intention to offend and grieves over the possible strain that his corrective speech would put on their relationship (7:8–9). It may be painful, like a medical procedure, but frank speech is intended to improve one's friend (Plut. *Mor.* 51c; Phld. frag. 32, col. 17b; Dio Chrys. *Or.* 32.5, 7, 11).[138]

So far in this chapter, I have examined philosophical patronage, the question of patronage in 1 Corinthians, the possibility of wealthy members of the Pauline community in Corinth, and the similarities of the literary patron/client relationship and what that could mean for Paul's interaction with his wealthy supporters. Most philosophers in the Roman period participated in patronage relationships (whether or not they praised the institution itself), and many patrons and patronesses enjoyed supporting them. Supporting philosophy was one of the means by which a wealthy woman could secure a philosophical education for herself and her children. Some of the members of the Pauline community—both named and unnamed—could have had some wealth and supported their artistic/philosophical interests as well as Paul and the church as they would a voluntary association or a philosophical school. Literary/artistic clients enjoyed some measure of artistic freedom: philosophers, poets, rhetors, and other artists were somewhat free to criticize their patrons and even show contempt for the patron/client relationship in general. This is important for Pauline studies because while he claims to be completely self-reliant, he may indeed participate in some informal reciprocal relationship with a wealthy member of the Corinthian community.[139]

All of this is meant to bring two characters into focus: Sophia and Fortuna, philosophically educated women who read 1 Corinthians from their unique point of view. Both are wealthy, widowed, and have the broad philosophical education of a woman who has participated in many philosophical discussions in her home. These women represent the *most likely* type of philosophically educated women that Paul would encounter in first-century Corinth. The wealthier widows had more control of their own property and therefore were able to support and bring philosophers and thinkers into their home as they pleased, and when they encountered Paul they evaluated him based on their philosophical preference and possibly even on the opportunity to secure or improve their standing with their friends. Because

138. Sampley, "Paul and Frank Speech," 293–318.
139. I have no interest here in describing the Christ cult as an artistic movement, but merely to show how a client can lay claim to freedom to criticize their patron and the patronage system while participating in patron/client relationships.

Patronage and Philosophically Educated Women

these women are wealthy, there is much at stake for Paul. It is in his best interest to persuade them without alienating them or otherwise frustrating their sympathies. With that being said, we are ready to begin reading 1 Corinthians with two philosophically educated women.

Reading 1 Corinthians 1–4 with Sophia and Fortuna

In the following section, we will read 1 Corinthians chapters 1–4 with two philosophically educated women.[140] This specific type of woman is a wealthy patroness of the church who was fortunate enough to be familiar with the popular philosophical schools of her day. Wealthier women were much more likely to be educated and financially able to pursue their philosophical interests, which could be quite broad. At the same time, there are simply too many known and unknown variables to anticipate *exactly* how a given person would read a text, because a person can inexplicably choose to break conventions at any time. For example, a woman educated by an Epicurean could choose to break away from the basic tenants of Epicureanism when she hears Paul's epistle read to the church. A Stoic could suddenly turn neo-Pythagorean or Platonist, and then inexplicably accept Paul's teaching at the same time. But our philosophically educated women, having a broad philosophical experience and no commitment to a specific school, interact with Paul from this liberal perspective, valuing Paul according to these interests.

Another element that should be discussed at the outset is the method of reading. We will read 1 Corinthians in a somewhat strict canonical order, the divisions being 1:18—12:5; 2:6—3:4; 3:5—4:5; 4:6-21.[141] That is, modern interpreters read 1 Corinthians 1–4 with the entire Corinthian correspondence in mind, sometimes in a highly creative chronological order, with the various interpretative tools in mind such as textual criticism, letter form, rhetorical criticism, etc. We will read 1 Corinthians 1–4 with philosophically educated women as they would have heard the epistle being read for the first time, trying to understand with each woman the meaning as she would have heard it from her various contexts.

---

140. For rhetorical devices in these chapters, see Fiore, "Covert Allusion," 85–102.

141. Of course the divisions of the text are similar but not uniform. My division matches Collins, *First Corinthians*, 30; cf. Thiselton, *Fist Epistle to the Corinthians*, vii. Some interpreters vary slightly, varying on transitional verses: Ciampa and Rosner, *First Letter to the Corinthians*, vi–viii; Hays, *First Corinthians*, vii; Keener, *1–2 Corinthians*, viii.

Reading 1 Corinthians with Philosophically Educated Women

There are, of course, limits to this discussion. This book is not written from the perspective of Antoinette Wire:[142] she addresses women prophets who are of low social status, and I am examining women philosophically educated women of higher status, so my interpretations will start from these points of departure. My work does not seek to correct or challenge Wire's work, but to offer a complimentary study that focuses on *two* wealthy philosophically educated women rather than *a group* of poor women prophets. There were few people in the Corinthian community who were the same status as Sophia and Fortuna, which is why I am not arguing that philosophically educated women were some kind of dynamic group like Wire's women prophets. While it is entirely possible that some of the Corinthian women prophets were philosophically educated because such education was available to women of lower status, this study will focus on wealthier women because most of the evidence for philosophically educated women is concentrated on higher status women. Because Wire's work and my own both address women in the Corinthian community, there is significant overlap in the texts that we interpret. However, we should expect that philosophically educated women and Wire's women prophets would experience the text in quite different ways.

Another significant limitation is the subjectivity of the interpreter, myself. I can attempt to set aside myself and my contexts as far as possible to try and understand the world of the Corinthian church using the fragmentary evidence from the past, but I will always be present in an alien culture with everything that defines me as a person and a scholar. I cannot stop being a twenty-first-century male, indoctrinated my entire life by the ideals of my cultures, and educated in religion and historical methods for my entire adult life. While I imagine the past, the positive and negative elements of my contexts will always be either in the foreground or background. So my subjectivity is defined by my limited understanding of myself and my contexts: I do not assume that I can know myself well enough to proclaim a grasp of positive knowledge, especially of people of the past. However, having observed the philosophical education of women in the ancient world the best that I can, it is appropriate to apply that knowledge to similar women in the Corinthian community and how they would interpret the New Testament. An important underlying interpretative theory behind this work is an awareness that the author exists only in his present contexts, and any access that the author has to his subject is provided by a wide range of ancient and modern primary and secondary sources.

142. See above, chapter 1.

Patronage and Philosophically Educated Women

Because there is no record of philosophically educated women reading the New Testament, if we want to read 1 Corinthians with them, we must use some historical imagination. It is historically plausible that there were such women in the church—they simply need to be brought to the foreground with a reading that is as true as possible to their historical contexts. The following sections will not be a full exegesis of 1 Corinthians, but an imaginative exploration of how a specific type of woman would read certain portions of the text which might apply or appeal to, puzzle, or offend her because of her education and social status. I will attempt to read selections from 1 Corinthians from the perspectives of two hypothetical philosophically educated women: Sophia and Fortuna. I have constructed these perspectives by situating them in the context of ancient education (connection to a wealthy household), the schools with traditions of women in philosophy and the social status that are associated with Corinth (neo-Pythagoreans, Stoics, Cynics, Epicureans, and [middle-] Platonism), and read 1 Corinthians from that location.

Amidst all uncertainties, I am constructing two specific women, using the evidence gathered in the first four and a half chapters of this book. I have written above that a philosophically educated woman is a woman who has come into contact with enough philosophical teaching from any school to identify and interact with components of 1 Corinthians which have points of connection with Greco-Roman philosophy. This woman does not have to adhere to a particular school or even remember everything that she learned from her teachers or friends (or whatever circumstances that she came in contact with philosophy). Because a philosophically educated woman would typically have been connected to a wealthy household or be wealthy herself, we will read 1 Corinthians with a wealthy woman who has broad intellectual interests like Julia Domna and can give patronal support for the Paul and the church, like Phoebe. We will look at 1 Corinthians 1–4 with two hypothetical patronesses. Our first philosophically educated woman will be named Sophia, who is generally sympathetic to Paul's message. Alongside Sophia, we will read with Fortuna, a philosophically educated woman who is generally unsympathetic to Paul's message. Both Sophia and Fortuna are best described as "municipal elites" in Bruce Longenecker's scale, which includes most decurial families, wealthy men and women who do not hold office, and some freedpersons, retainers, veterans, and merchants.[143] I refer to Sophia and Fortuna as "wealthier," "wealthy," or of "higher status" with respect to their status relative to most other members of the church, who were ES 5, 6, and 7 (just above, at, and below sustenance level). Paul was

143. Longenecker, *Remember the Poor*, 44–53, 317–32.

Reading 1 Corinthians with Philosophically Educated Women

most likely from the "municipal elite" before he willingly (to serve as an apostle) or unwillingly (because he served as an apostle) lost his status.[144] The similar backgrounds of Paul, Sophia, and Fortuna facilitate an environment for understanding, particularly regarding Paul's usage of popular philosophy and patron/client relationships.

Like other literary clients, Paul appears indifferent to personal patronal support; however, patronage was needed for the church to thrive in Corinth and wealthier women were active in the community. Eager to participate in or support the latest artistic/intellectual trend, the patroness was financially able to support both Paul and his opponents. But the pressure to keep the support secure was evidently too much for Paul to bear: he could no longer risk losing support due to the threat of his opponents, who his patronesses could chose to exclusively support at any time.

In 1 Corinthians 1–4, Paul gets right to the point and distinguishes himself from his perceived competition by elevating himself and his message far beyond what a mere sophist[145] or wise-person could do.[146] Paul begins by distinguishing himself as the apostle called by God.[147] Paul was sent by Christ to preach the good news as opposed to sophistic discourse (1 Cor 1:17), he is the founder of the church in Corinth (1 Cor 3:5, 10, 9:1) and as the apostle, he has the highest calling in the church (1 Cor 12:28). Furthermore, Paul renounces his right as apostle to payment (and his sophist opponents also should?).[148] Paul therefore never demands payment for himself, but he does expect wealthier members of the community to support the church, providing a place for the church to meet, monetary gifts, and legal protection. Positioning himself against his opponents, Paul asserts that the God who called him to be an apostle, has made the wise foolish.[149] These comments are directed specifically toward his opponents and address whatever views they may have held, and make no comment on any other school or beliefs, regardless of who holds them. That is, a sympathetic

---

144. Cf. Wire, *Corinthian Women Prophets*, 66–67.

145. Timothy H. Lim notes the lack of clarity here: a "sophist" can be either a professional speaker or one who picked up the sensibilities of a travelling orator ("Not in Persuasive Words," 145). What is not in dispute is that Paul's opponents did embrace sophistic tendencies, however they came by them.

146. This sort of polemic is common in the ancient world. See Harrison, *Paul's Language of Grace*, 338–39; Barnett, "Opponents of Paul," 644–53; Sumney, *Identifying Paul's Opponents*.

147. Selby, "Paul, the Seer," 351–73.

148. Taylor, "Conflict as Context," 933–45.

149. This is reminiscent of the Socratic denial of knowledge. Cf. Vlastos, "Socrates' Disavowal of Knowledge," 1–31.

philosophically educated woman may well hold to the same teachings that Paul opposes, but in courting her favor Paul feels it necessary to distinguish himself from other sophists in the church. An unsympathetic philosophically educated woman would be constantly frustrated throughout the first four chapters of 1 Corinthians, particularly by Paul's artificial separation of the wisdom that she identifies with and his divine wisdom.

Both Sophia and Fortuna were initially attracted to Paul because of the theology of freedom embodied in his message of the cross. Paul's teachings concerning the cross were liberating both in theological and social dimensions.[150] Through the cross, God brought all people to the same fictive social level, and freed everyone—male and female, rich and poor, Greek and Jew, powerful and powerless, educated and illiterate—to experience God and the community without normative social constraints (at least in theory). Paul embraced what may have already been a familiar social message in some voluntary associations: that within the community, social patterns can be reversed or achieve a kind of fictive equality.[151] Paul's teachings on this concept, however, were a bit more aggressive and comprehensive than other *collegia*.[152] The difference between Paul's community and other voluntary associations[153] and religious cults in Corinth was that it was more open to the public participation of women who were not priestesses. Following the pattern of self-sacrificing love exemplified in the cross,[154] Sophia and Fortuna expressed their freedom by participating with other men and women in worship, prophesy, hosting meals, supporting the church financially, engaging in intellectual interests, and by means of their philosophical education choose for themselves how to interpret Paul's teachings concerning patronage, instructions regarding marriage and divorce, and the *agon* motif.

150. Cf. Shi, *Paul's Message*, 106; Picket, *Cross in Corinth*.

151. A list of members in a cultic association in Attica (135 BCE?) includes men, women, and slaves of different social status. Kloppenborg and Ascough, *Greco-Roman Associations*, no. 40 = IG II2 2358; cf. no. 43, 52, 53, 68, and 72. There was a household-based association led by a certain Dionysios, who established rules for the association that allowed for the participation of "men, women, free people and slaves" (*ILydiaKP* III 18 = SIG^3 985). For notes and bibliography, see Philip Harland, *Associations, Synagogues, and Congregations*, 30–31. For more on gender and social rank in the associations, see Ascough, *Paul's Macedonian Associations*, 47–59.

152. McGready, "EKKLĒSIA and Voluntary Associations," 59–78; Comeron and Miller, "Redescribing Paul," 287–89.

153. *ILS* 4203 and 4215 (slave and free). R. H. Barrow, *Slavery in the Roman Empire*, 166, does argue that most slaves only participated in the collegia that consisted of slaves and freedpersons.

154. Cf. Witherington, *Conflict and Community*, 196; Garland, *1 Corinthians*, 299–30, 404; Hays, *First Corinthians*, 101–7; Ciampa and Rosner, *First Letter to the Corinthians*, 120–24.

Reading 1 Corinthians with Philosophically Educated Women

Reading 1 Corinthians 1:18—12:5 with Sophia

In this section and throughout chapters 1–4, Paul distinguishes himself from his opponents, "those of Apollos."[155] These "opponents" may well only be opponents to Paul in his mind and not aware that their thinking and practices go against Paul's teaching. Paul's critique of *sophia* in 1 Corinthians 1:18–31 goes directly against many common sophistic and philosophical ideals concerning wisdom, but that does not need to complicate his relationship with a philosophically educated patroness such as Sophia, who sees little difference between her wisdom and Paul's divine wisdom.[156] Paul declares that human wisdom[157] (σοφίαν τοῦ κόσμου) is insufficient for the knowledge of God (1 Cor 1:18–19).[158] Moreover, it is something that God destroys and confuses (1 Cor 1:19–20).[159] Paul goes on to assert that God's wisdom is different from this human wisdom (1 Cor 1:21) and human wisdom approaches Paul's message as foolishness (1 Cor 1:18, 1:23). Furthermore, the lowly things of the world will shame the wise (1 Cor 1:27). This Christ whose message and work appear foolish is actually the wisdom of God (1 Cor 1:30). Paul specifically identifies this wisdom as Greek wisdom ("Ἕλληες σοφίαν ζητοῦσιν") with a phrase that encompasses not only the sophists but the popular philosophies that also have a distinct Greek heritage and hold similar values.[160]

Despite his critique of human wisdom, Paul nevertheless plays on what a philosophically educated patroness like Sophia would expect from him. The reciprocal relationship would be something like this: Sophia would give Paul and/or his opponents substantial support for substantial teaching. There would be great reward if the teaching is received as substantial, inspired, or if the patroness is convinced that the teaching will memorialize

---

155. Joop F. M. Smit argues that chapters 1–4 are a coherent unit based on their syntax, semantics, and pragmatics, and that Paul is defending himself against the opinions that the followers of Apollos had of him ("What is Apollos? What is Paul?" 231–51); see also Smith, "Paul's Arguments," 255; cf. Mihaila, *Paul-Apollos Relationship*, 181–212.

156. Waters, "Paradoxes," 432; Welborn argues that this wisdom is definitely that of the rhetoricians ("Discord in Corinth," 101–3).

157. This is an interpretation and not a translation. Cf. Thiselton, *First Epistle to the Corinthians*, 155; Ciampa and Rosner, *First Letter to the Corinthians*, 89; Lampe, "Theological Wisdom," 117–31.

158. Cf. Koperski, "Knowledge of Christ," 377–96.

159. Heil, *Rhetorical Role*, 36.

160. Hence the dazzling array of possibilities for how to precisely define *sophia*. For bibliography, see Margaret M. Mitchell, who posits that Paul need not refer to one specific "wisdom" (*Rhetoric of Reconciliation*," 211); see also Taylor, *Paul, Antioch, and Jerusalem*, 207–14; and the essays edited by Stowers in *Paul and His Opponents*.

Patronage and Philosophically Educated Women

her gift in perpetuity. In chapters 1–4, Paul makes it clear that he can accomplish exactly that, and his opponents cannot, no matter how learned or eloquent they are (1 Cor 1:17–21).

In chapter 2:1–5 (and beyond), Paul continues his contrast between human wisdom and divine wisdom. Paul appeals to his previous visit with the Corinthian community: originally Paul proclaimed "the testimony of God" without lofty speech or wisdom (1 Cor 2:1). Evidently, he did impress Sophia and Fortuna with his presentation of his Gospel in spite of whatever sympathies they had with sophism or popular moral philosophy. Again Paul alludes to the cross of Christ, putting it in opposition to the "lofty speech and wisdom," which Paul perceives or characterizes that his audience views as "strength." The repeated appeal to the cross and knowing God through this divine foolishness may simply be a repeat of what Paul taught to Sophia and Fortuna in the first place, so his appeal to this original teaching that attracted them to the church is not so shocking as it would be if they heard this message for the first time upon hearing the epistle.[161] In his opinion, Paul's original message of the cross was delivered to the Corinthians in weakness, fear, and trembling instead of the strong, forceful, and convincing rhetoric of the sophist or moral philosopher who sought wealth, power, or disciples. This means that Paul is distinguishing himself from a certain type of rhetor that the Corinthians knew well: one that used his/her power of speech for wealth and fame. Paul's speech and message was not in "plausible words of wisdom, but as he says, in the demonstration of the Spirit and power—so that their faith might not rest in human wisdom but in the power of God."[162]

Because of the dynamics of a literary/artistic patron/client relationship, Sophia would be able, and possibly willing, to lend support to both Paul and his opponents. When Paul discusses σοφία and the nature of God in 1 Corinthians 1:18–31, Sophia's philosophical education would not be threatened but reinforced. The tension between human σοφία and God's wisdom that Paul describes can be easily overcome if she understands her σοφία to come from God. Pythagoras, with his wife Theano and daughter Damo, was remembered as the founder of a religious sect and the divine was critical to his philophizing.[163] Epicurus, who had in his original school a large circle of women, had high regard for the divine as a foundation for ethics, but did not believe that the gods themselves interfered with the affairs

---

161. Welborn, "Mōros Genesthō," 420–35.

162. Van Roon, "Christ and the Wisdom of God," 207–39.

163. Vlastos, "Theology and Philosophy," 97–123; for the theology of Pythagoras, see Drozdek, *Greek Philosophers*, 53–70.

Reading 1 Corinthians with Philosophically Educated Women

of humans.[164] The Epicurean Diogenes of Oneoanda, who preserved Epicurus's *Letter to Mother*, also affirmed the divine but with great restraint.[165] Cicero, who valued the philosophical education of women, could—at least in some of his writings—hold belief in a god in high regard.[166] Seneca, who encouraged Helvia and Marcia to apply his philosophy to their lives, understood that the role of philosophy is to understand the divine and the human, and the wise-person can only accomplish this with help from the divine.[167] Generally, the authors of the neo-Pythagorean pseudepigraphon (which claimed to be authored by well known women philosophers), carried on the emphasis that Pythagoras had placed on the divine. Iamblichus, however, specifically believed that the wise-person could not achieve *harmonia* unless she had help from the gods.[168]

All that is to say that because Sophia received a general education from the active schools in first-century Corinth, she can quite easily identify with Paul's situation of wisdom and with him see "human wisdom" as at least incomplete for her purposes. Furthermore, if she reads this section as an indictment against Paul's opponents, as he intends, she can congratulate herself by recognizing and appreciating Paul's unique potential and support him and the church accordingly. Despite her sympathy for Paul's message, though, Sophia is likely more than a little shocked at Paul's identification of intolerable division in the church and that the various divisions must unite under Paul's banner. However, as a sympathetic reader, she identifies with Paul's divine wisdom, respects his apostolic authority as founder of the Corinthian church, and at least tolerates his request for his style of unity.

Paul positions himself between followers of divine and human wisdom, Jews and Greeks, and the rich and poor by bringing everyone to the same starting point (1 Cor 1:18–31). Every possible advantageous position: being a non-Jew, a Jew (favor with God), a wealthy and powerful person, and finally even the poor are brought to nothing by the power and wisdom of God. This lack of being—however exactly Paul imagines it and the church interprets it—is the ultimate rhetorical equalizer so that friendship can exist between Paul, philosophically educated women, and the rest of the church. At the very least, despite the fact that Paul has rhetorically aligned

---

164. Mansfeld, "Epicurean Theology," 172–210; Dominic Scott, "Epicurean Illusions," 360–74.

165. Hadzsits, "Epicurean Gods," 318; cf. Summers, "Lucretius," 32–57.

166. Burriss, "Cicero," 524–32; Heibges, "Cicero," 304–12.

167. Burton, "Seneca's Idea of God," 350–69; Setaioli, "Seneca and the Divine," 333–68.

168. Smith, *Porphyry's Place*; for the general history of the neo-Pythagoreans, see Kahn, *Pythagoras and the Pythagoreans*, 94–138.

himself with the futility of both Greek and non-Greek wisdom, he too has to experience divine wisdom from his divine source. Although Paul is nothing and experiences this divine wisdom through his calling as an apostle, the Corinthians are nothing and can experience his divine wisdom by following his teaching. As a sympathetic reader, Sophia is able to balance her philosophical interests and the divine roots of these teachings with Paul's understanding of the nature of his.

Moving on to 1 Corinthians 2:1–5, Sophia is reminded of Paul's visit and the Gospel that he preached. Paul then continues to separate the human wisdom of his opponents from divine wisdom of God that is in the word of the cross.[169] As a student of popular moral philosophy, Sophia recognizes Paul's characterization of his opponents as having the less attractive qualities of the sophists that Corinth knew well. Paul characterizes the sophists by an insatiable lust for fame, influence, and fortune.[170] Their grandiose speech was intended to persuade crowds to do or think anything that is to the speaker's pleasure. It would be easy for a sympathetic reader like Sophia to disassociate herself from Paul's opponents, even if she did not think that they were as bad as Paul makes them out to be.[171] Sophia can recognize the threat that Paul is addressing: if she identifies herself with his opponents, she would be compromising the freedom appropriated to her through the wisdom of the cross. Sophia also detects that Paul is addressing only one offensive practice: the common offenses of the sophists. It makes sense to Sophia that the selfish preaching of the sophists that Paul opposes challenges the concept of selfless love that characterizes the wisdom of the cross.

Reading 1 Corinthians 1:18—12:5 with Fortuna

Another aspect needs to be examined: Paul's opponents could include philosophically educated women. Philosophically educated women openly challenged men of their time. For example, Hipparchia the Cynic opposed Theodorus the Atheist at a dinner party and Leontion the Epicurean composed a work against Theophrastus.[172] In the late second to early third century CE, the sophist Philostratus was concerned about the security of the patronage of the empress Julia Domna for the sophists after she read a treatise by Plutarch.

---

169. Wire offers a similar interpretation, *Corinthian Women Prophets*, 51.
170. Witherington, *Conflict and Community*, 349.
171. Cf. Winter, *Philo and Paul*, 179–202.
172. Cic. *Nat. D.* 1.93; Pliny the Elder (*Praefatio* 29) indicates simply that a woman wrote against Theophrastus even though he was a respected rhetor.

Reading 1 Corinthians with Philosophically Educated Women

For this discussion, I will use Fortuna as a hypothetical example of a philosophically educated woman who is an unsympathetic reader of 1 Corinthians. This is an entirely different interpretative paradigm from that discussed above, because Paul would be pitting himself against a philosophically educated woman rather than attempting to secure their patronage. Paul was opposed from within[173] the church and not from without:[174] at some point Fortuna was sympathetic enough to Paul's message to join Paul's Corinthian community. Therefore, either she has changed her mind or Paul could no longer tolerate her and the opposition that she supported. Before this falling out, Fortuna supported both Paul and his opponents and was later irritated with him for some reason: possibly his lack of commitment to a philosophical school, his inability to get along with his opponents (her allies), or his strange moral teachings.[175] However, all that Paul is willing to admit is that his opponents expect him to be a good sophist/philosopher[176] and question his apostolic authority.[177] Embracing the independent spirit of the philosophically educated woman and asserting her responsibility to think for herself, Fortuna is unimpressed with Paul's separation of himself from the other sophists in the Corinthian church—possibly in person during his earlier visits (1 Cor 2:1–5) and epistles (1 Cor 5:9).[178]

We saw with Sophia in 1 Corinthians 1:18–31 that Paul attempted to separate himself from his opponents by the way that he describes what human wisdom cannot do, and that only the Christ of his message can accomplish what sophists claimed that their philosophy was capable of achieving. Sophia was able to tolerate Paul's message because like Paul, she and those whom she supported also viewed their wisdom to come from a divine source. Fortuna, however, is frustrated by Paul's message in 1 Corinthians 1:18–31 for precisely the same reason. She reads Paul attacking the divine source of her wisdom by exclusively associating his divine source with the message of the cross. In other words, according to Paul the divine power of

---

173. Chow, *Patronage and Power*, 114. Welborn, *Politics and Rhetoric*, 65, calls the opponents' rhetoric as "distinctively Christian."

174. Richard Liong-Seng Phua imagines attempts by outsiders to infiltrate the Corinthian community. *Idolatry and Authority*, 7.

175. Many scholars believe that Paul is dismissing sophistic values. Winter, *Philo and Paul*, 116–44; Sigurd Grindheim, "Wisdom for the Perfect," 689–709.

176. Martin, *Corinthian Body*, 52; Grant, *Paul in the Roman World*, 25–31. Cf. Long, *Ancient Rhetoric*, 2; Stowers, "Kinds of Myth," 116.

177. Welborn, *Politics and Rhetoric*, 83.

178. For a review of the various redaction theories of 1 Corinthians, see Hall, *Corinthian Correspondence*, and Barnett, *Corinthian Question*.

the foolishness of God, the work of the cross, accomplishes what her wisdom cannot do: σῶσαι τοὺς πιστεύοντας (1 Cor 1:21).

Like Sophia, Fortuna considers her wisdom to be "godly wisdom" rather than Paul's "human wisdom." With a broad philosophical education, Fortuna is already aware of several contradictory philosophies that claim divine origin, but Paul's characterization of "Greek wisdom" into one homogenous term is unfair and his claim to an exclusive superiority over all of them is quite alarming. The Cynic, Epicurean, Stoic, Platonic, and Pythagorean wisdom, all with claims of knowledge of the divine to some degree, are not homogenous in their failure to overcome human passion and actualize a relationship with the divine. Fortuna would have a hard time believing that all of these schools has failed so completely, and that Paul could circumvent every means of philosophical enquiry and still attain access to wisdom by means of his calling, bearing the gospel of the crucified Christ (1 Cor 1:23). However, because of her importance in the community and sympathy for Paul's opponents, she is able to receive Paul's hostility with the aloofness of a powerful matron.

The presence of Paul's opponents could actually work in Paul's favor, if his goal is to retain support for the church from their patroness. Fortuna can support Paul's opponents, disagree with his teachings and moral philosophy, and the church can still enjoy the benefits that they would receive if she supported Paul alone (and therefore withdraw her support because of his hostility). The direct benefit for Paul is that he can criticize his opponents and the patroness of the church as sharply as he desires without fear of reprisal. Perhaps his apostolic boldness is rooted in the security of a philosophically educated patroness who supports the church due to her interest in his opponents.

As Paul develops his argument in 1 Corinthians 2:1–5, it can only serve to further alienate Fortuna. She sees it as a great offense that Paul characterizes his "opponents" as people who follow philosophers, rhetoricians, and sophists just because they are captivated by some kind of empty human whim. The moral philosophers condemned the professional rhetoricians much like Paul does in 1 Corinthians, and Fortuna would not appreciate Paul lumping her with a common rhetor. Further, the "weakness" of the cross in itself did not frustrate Fortuna as a philosophically educated woman when she was initially attracted to Paul's Gospel. Fortuna had no issue with the weak of the world triumphing over the strong: this kind of social status / gender / intellectual / religious inversion is welcome and valuable. While she is not the most defenseless or poorest person in the community, she can identify herself with the "weak" because she lives in a world of injustices directed towards her because of her social status (she is not highest in the social pecking order), gender, and intellectual interests.

In Fortuna's theology, the wisdom of the cross was accessible to people who valued what Paul calls "human wisdom" and isolates from "divine wisdom." She was attracted to the community and supported it because of its broad tolerances: the activity of both male and female prophets, the participation of people of different social status, and the coexistence of different theologies and practices. After Paul could no longer tolerate these diversities within the community, she does not appreciate her philosophical sensibilities being contrasted with the the preaching of the cross.

Reading 1 Corinthians 2:6—3:4 with Sophia

Paul continues his distinction between himself and his opponents in 1 Corinthians 2:6—3:4, following the line of thought in 1:18—12:5. Paul again refers to the cross in 2:6-8 in order to distinguish himself from his "opponents." He begins by strongly insinuating that only the mature accept his message (1 Cor 2:6a), and of course his opponents are immature in their enslavement to human passion. Sophia is delighted to be counted among the mature: Paul's designation matches her self-perception. In contrasting the human wisdom that his opponents seek and divine wisdom, he associates their human wisdom with the doomed thinking of the rulers of the age who crucified Jesus (1 Cor 2:6b). We can follow the interpretation of "human wisdom" and interpret "τῶν ἀρχόντων τοῦ αἰῶνος τούτου" as "human rulers of this age." Because these rulers follow doomed human wisdom and not the divine wisdom of God (according to Paul), they did not recognize the divine and crucified the Lord of glory (1 Cor 2:8).

In 1 Corinthians 2:9-11, Paul describes the hidden nature of the wisdom of God, which here is that which "God has prepared for those who love him," who are in this case those who are committed to the gospel of the cross: Paul's teachings. Paul undermines major forms of human discovery—sight, hearing, and imagination (1 Cor 2:9)—as a means by which his audience can access the wisdom of God. And then, Paul discusses the difference between the natural and the spiritual (1 Cor 2:14), on the same line of thought as "human wisdom" (associated with the "natural") and "divine wisdom" (associated with the Spirit of God). Thiselton captures this idea of human wisdom in describing it as "the person who lives on an entirely human level."[179] Paul's wisdom is received and imparted by means of wisdom taught by the Spirit and does not comprise the wisdom gained by human

179. Thiselton, *First Epistle to the Corinthians*, 269.

means and imparted with human rhetoric and sophistry (plausible words of wisdom). The person who values human wisdom is "natural" and cannot receive Paul's wisdom because his message must be spiritually and not naturally evaluated and received. But Paul and his companions have the mind of Christ and therefore can access and proclaim the words of the wisdom of God. Sophia is not threatened by Paul's isolation of divine wisdom from the senses, primarily because she understands that he is clearly addressing those who seek human wisdom and not those (like Sophia) who have divine wisdom.

In 3:1–4, Paul refers again to a previous visit with the Corinthians, saying that he could not address them as spiritual people (except for the mature ones like Sophia who can receive the words of the cross, the wisdom of God) but as "people of the flesh" and "infants in Christ." The "people of the flesh," who apparently can only follow their bodily desires, clarifies nicely the demonization of human wisdom. The moral philosophers often characterized their opponents as people who can only follow their stomachs or passions. The Epicureans (notorious for following their human passions) and sophists (equally notorious for seeking wisdom to fulfill their lust for money) got the brunt of this beating, but of course all was fair in rhetorical polemic.[180] In 1 Corinthians 3:3, Paul declares that this human wisdom is the cause of jealousy and strife that divided the Corinthians into those who followed Paul and those who claimed Apollos. But Sophia was a member of the faith community, apparently valuing Paul's message of the cross while pursuing her other intellectual interests. Just as she associates her divine wisdom with Paul's and she does not affiliate herself with the "rulers of the world" who embraced human wisdom and crucified Jesus, she also understands that her divinely inspired wisdom cannot cause division in the church. In fact, Paul's preaching complimented the wisdom that she already had, containing within it both affirmations and criticisms of popular moral philosophy. With her broad education, Sophia is accustomed to learning a philosophy and hearing a dedicated teacher or educated friend criticize other schools, sometimes perhaps harshly. In spite of this, like other patrons of the arts, she could support a teacher or be friends with a person who criticizes philosophical teachings that she embraces.

---

180. For the anti-Epicurean polemic of the first century BCE, see Phillip DeLacy, "Cicero's Invective," 49–58; cf. Maslowski, "Opponents of Lactantius," 187–213; Vander Waerdt, "Justice of the Epicurean," 402–22; Gordon, "Some Unseen Monster," 86–109; Roskam, *Plutarch's De latenter vivendo*; Dyson, "Pleasure and the Sapiens," 313–18. For sophists, see Winter, *Philo and Paul*, 116–25.

Reading 1 Corinthians with Philosophically Educated Women

Reading 1 Corinthians 2:6—3:4 with Fortuna

Fortuna reads Paul as undermining her philosophical interests. As in 1 Corinthians 1:21, where Paul declares that the knowledge of God is inaccessible to "human wisdom," in 1 Corinthians 2:7, Paul plainly states that the wisdom that he imparts is the secret and hidden wisdom of God. It is not human wisdom, but divine wisdom that apparently only Paul and his companions can impart, and no one can have access to divine wisdom unless Paul mediates it. The sustained disassociation of human wisdom with divine wisdom in 1 Corinthians 2:6—3:4 (and beyond) is infuriating and increasingly nonsensical to Fortuna—who is tolerant of "human" wisdom because of her interest in Epicureanism, but attentive to the gods and the sources of divine wisdom in philosophical schools like Stoic, neo-Pythagoreanism, and Platonic thought. The stark opposition that Paul tries to establish between the "human wisdom" and "divine wisdom" is made even more offensive because of the association of "human wisdom" with the "human rulers" of this word that crucified the Lord of Glory (1 Cor 2:8).

Fortuna possibly detected a glimmer of hope when Paul explains that the divine wisdom that he associates himself with is prepared for the ones that love God in 1 Corinthians 2:9. Fortuna certainly identified herself as lover of wisdom and a lover of God—maybe not in the sense that Paul would prefer—so this passage can cause some confusion because of how Paul applies it in 1 Corinthians 2:12-14. If Fortuna and Paul's "opponents" consider themselves to be lovers of God, why would Paul take issue with them? And Paul takes issue violently, attacking them in familiar fashion: it is symptomatic of human wisdom that those who seek it must live by their base human passions and because of this they do not have access to divine wisdom (1 Cor 2:14). As such, they put themselves at odds with God's wisdom, and are divided because of this weakness (1 Cor 3:3). So not only are Paul's opponents unable to access divine wisdom, they are affiliated with the rulers of this age who crucified Christ and responsible for divisions in the church because of their tendency to follow human wisdom. Paul's isolation of human wisdom from divine wisdom is an unbearable restraint on Fortuna's intellectual and spiritual freedom rooted in her theology of the cross. Paul's teaching here corrects Fortuna's theology of the cross: she does not have the freedom to support his opponents and have a correct relationship with crucified Christ. If so, Paul argues that Fortuna will be more like the rulers of the world that crucified Christ rather than a believer who participates in the freedom of the cross. Fortuna, along with her allies, simply cannot accept the nature of Paul's polemic, other than recognizing that he is denigrating members of the group to increase his own credibility. Although many of them had heard it before, the sting of being on the receiving end of this kind of polemic was an alienating experience.

Reading 1 Corinthians 3:5—4:5 with Sophia

Like most of the epistle, 1 Corinthians 3:5—4:5 was likely viewed quite differently by Paul and those whom he opposed—some may well have better identified with Apollos—but like Paul, understood Apollos and Paul to be unified in such a way that to identify with one is to identify with the other. Sophia (and Fortuna) probably understood the factions as believers that could exist in unity, just as in Paul's mind he and Apollos were workers toiling together with the same divine purpose: to build the Corinthian church, which is a building of God (1 Cor 3:9).

The reception of these two different characters from the Corinthian community's perspective, however, likely could have been quite a bit different than the unity that Paul imagines. Paul uses a familiar Socratic τί . . . construction "what is x (or x-ness)" in 1 Corinthians 3:5, "τί . . . τί οὖν ἐστιν Ἀπολλῶς; τέ δέ ἐστιν Παῦλος."[181] For Paul, he and Apollos are both servants of God with a different role, explained metaphorically as Paul planting, Apollos watering, and God giving growth (1 Cor 3:6-9). This metaphor is extended to clearly reinforce Paul's superior apostolic authority.[182] Paul presents himself as the master builder who lays the foundation and Apollos built on the excellent foundation that Paul laid (1 Cor 3:11-15).[183] This building, the people of the church, is not just any building but a holy temple of God, and the sanctity (or unity) of the church is sealed with the assured destruction for those who are hostile to it (1 Cor 3:16-17), especially those who value a wisdom that Paul does not (1 Cor 3:18-20): his idea of "worldly wisdom" (human wisdom). After all, the Lord has found out the thoughts of the ones who seek worldly wisdom, and their wisdom is futile (1 Cor 3:20).[184]

At first it seems prudent to examine how Sophia would read Paul's usage of the Socratic construct "what is x?" in 1 Corinthians 3:5. Unfortunately, not much can be read into the "what is x" construct because Paul

---

181. Some scholars use the letter F instead of the letter X so as not to confuse the reader who may think of the mathematical x. For bibliography on the "what is x(-ness)" question, see Benson, *Socratic Wisdom*, 100; cf. Thiselton, *First Epistle to the Corinthians*, 299; Robertson and Plummer, *1 Corinthians*, 56.

182. Ker, "Paul and Apollos," 88.

183. Cf. Wire, *Corinthian Women Prophets*, 43.

184. Cf. Pogoloff, *Logos and Sophia*, 146.

does not peer into the heart of a matter using a Socratic query into x-ness (what is good, what is being, etc). Sophia's broad philosophical education would have exposed her to any number of varieties of this type of query.[185] However, by the time Sophia received her philosophical education, the Socratic "what is x" query had been grafted so much into the particular philosophical schools[186] that one can no longer attribute meaning to the construct beyond its rhetorical usage by Paul, which does not carry with it any type of philosophical query.

In the metaphors of the planting, builder // building, and the temple, the roles of Paul, Apollos, and God seamlessly flow together, with Paul explaining that he and Apollos are nothing because only God gives the growth and Jesus is the foundation. While Sophia acknowledges God as the source of wisdom, Paul characterizes these opponents as severely handicapped by human thinking that causes separation from his teaching and therefore they are divorced from whatever interaction with God that one can achieve by receiving his message as he intends it to be received (1 Cor 3:18–21a).

Unity and harmony in the community are not foreign ideas to Sophia. In fact, the concept of unity as described by Paul is likely the most significant point of confusion for her as a philosophically educated patroness. As long as she supported the church, the community would be unified under her care, and she would make certain that no immoral thing would be going on inside of her household. The kind of disunity that Paul speaks of is rooted in human wisdom that is gained by following human passions. In popular moral philosophy, the unbridled following of human passion is what leads to every kind of immorality—the kind of things that could cause unpleasant consequences for Sophia if she continued to support the kind of unruly group that Paul portrays his opponents to be. While Paul's characterization of his opponents is rhetorical, it does seem that at least part of it is true, at least from Paul's point of view. There probably was sexual immorality, boasting, and criticism of Paul because he did not embody sophistic values. Paul did explain that their bad behavior came from their bad thinking, and that correct thinking would help fix the problem. The idea is that correct thinking leads to correct behavior and a correct relationship with the divine (often because correct thinking comes from the divine). The problem is

---

185. Epict. *Disc.* 4.1.41; cf. 2.11.

186. The Socratic formulation does appear in Antisthenes the Cynic, frag. 44b, 47a–b, 60 (Caizzi). Porter, "Philosophy of Aristo of Chios," 185. "There is another allusion to Pythagorean definition, 1078b 21–23, where it appears that they are said to define because they ask 'What is X?,'" Philip, *Pythagoras*, 222. It shows up again in Iambl. *VP* 82; Cic. *Off.* 2.83; 3.55; *Tusc.* 1.64, 1.75 and elsewhere; for full discussion, see Powell, *Cato*, 110.

Patronage and Philosophically Educated Women

that there was wide disagreement as to what correct thinking was, and this struggle is definitely something that makes perfect sense to Sophia.

Paul exhorts the Corinthians not to boast in human beings (1 Cor 3:21), who are at best the source of human wisdom.[187] Interesting is that Cephas is mentioned again without warning, further confirming that Paul is attacking the followers of Apollos in his separation of human wisdom and divine wisdom. Paul's divisions of the Corinthians into followers of himself, Apollos, Cephas, and Christ are almost certainly intentionally artificial. By choosing these labels and then rhetorically unifying these figures in divine purpose, and their product into one temple, Paul is tactfully addressing corresponding issues.[188] However, while the Cephas and Christ groups may not have existed, there were certainly opponents that Paul characterizes as followers of Apollos who valued human wisdom.[189]

Even though Paul mentioned the divisions in 1 Corinthians 1:12, it is a bit late in the epistle to paint his opponents in a positive light by rhetorically uniting hypothetical groups that may follow himself, Christ, and Apollos. If Paul had not spent so much time characterizing the human wisdom of the followers of Apollos so negatively, making it impossible for them to have knowledge of God and access to morality, his tactful arguments for unity might be a bit more convincing. Can it really be said by Paul that his opponents, the followers of Apollos, are so unified with the community that they can be thought of as one temple, one building, and one work of God? Can it really be said that Paul's opponents, who, he argues, are severely handicapped by the follies of human wisdom, comprise the ones for whom Paul laid the foundation, Apollos watered, and God caused to grow, along with everyone else? Sophia can certainly understand the importance of unity and the ability for Paul's "opponents" to coexist with the rest of the community. The confusing aspect is that Paul can engage in polemic with people in the community and then declare that they are indeed unified.

When Paul writes "all things belong to you" in 1 Corinthians 3:21, Sophia could understand him to be employing intentionally the Stoic maxim "all things belong to the wise-person."[190] This maxim is found in Seneca, Ci-

---

187. See the discussion in Winter, *Philo and Paul*, 186–202.

188. Collins, *First Corinthians*, 80, suggests that the early Corinthian Christians knew of Cephas only by reputation and Paul's use of the name to designate a certain person or group was in itself tactful and unifying: there is no difference between Paul and Cephas, so it is an appeal for unity rather than a description of a Petrine group. Cf. Sampley, forward to *Paul and Rhetoric*, xii.

189. Smit, "What Is Apollos, What Is Paul?," 231–51.

190. Conzelmann, *Corinthians*, 80; Lindemann, *Corinthians*, 93; cf. Fitzmyer, *Corinthians*, 208; Collins, *First Corinthians*, 166. For ancient references, Cic. *Fin.* 3.22.75;

Reading 1 Corinthians with Philosophically Educated Women

cero, and Diogenes Laertius—all of whom are important sources for women in philosophy. A critical issue is the question of whom Paul is addressing here. It is possible that Paul is using a maxim from human philosophy in an ironic fashion—those who truly claim Apollos, Cephas, and Christ actually are unified when they follow the teachings of Paul—and it is the one who follows Paul's idea of divine wisdom and not human wisdom who receives the reward and promises of both types of wisdom. Or is Paul addressing all the believers/hearers of the epistle?[191] Whoever Paul is addressing belongs to Christ's and Christ is God's. Paul here extends the idea of the Stoic wise-person "all things belong to you" to the community of believers in general, which is significant because it is the general believer who achieves wisdom and not only the one who seeks worldly wisdom.

The Stoic maxim that Paul uses is unmistakable to Sophia. The most basic philosophical education would include the definition of the person who actualizes wisdom: the wise-person. When a philosopher describes their particular school's wise-person, it is often explained in terms of contrast with the wise-person of another school. According to tradition, Diogenes the Cynic "reasoned that all things belong to the gods; the wise are friends of the gods; since friends have all things in common, all things belong to the wise."[192] The Stoics used the maxim "all things belong to the wise man" as opposed to the Epicurean position. For example, Seneca argues against an unnamed Epicurean who includes the use of prostitutes in "all things that belong to the wise man":

> "Is," inquit, "cuius prostitutae sunt, leno est; omnia autem sapientis sunt; inter omnia et prostitutae sunt; ergo prostitutae sapientis sunt. Leno autem est, cuius prostitutae sunt; ergo sapiens leno est," Sic illum vetant emere, dicunt enim: "Nemo rem suam emit; omnia autem sapientis sunt; ergo sapiens nihil emit." Sic vetant mutuum sumere, quia nemo usuram pro pecunia sua pendat. Innumerabilia sunt, per quae cavillantur, cum pulcherrime, quid a nobis dicatur, intellegant.

> "He to whom courtezans belong," argues our adversary, "must be a procurer: now courtezans are included in all things, therefore courtezans belong to the wise man. But he to whom courtezans belong is a procurer; therefore the wise man is a procurer." Yes! by the same reasoning, our opponents would forbid him to

---

4.27.74; Sen. *Ben.* 7.5 and *Ep.* 109.1; Diog. Laert. 6.37; 7.124–25.

191. So Fitzmyer, *Corinthians*, 208; probably Collins, *First Corinthians*, 166; Ciampa and Rosner, *First Letter to the Corinthians*, 168.

192. Diog. Laert. 6.72 = Diogenes, *Ep.* 9. For notes and bibliography, see Klauk, *Anient Letters*, 74–75.

buy anything, arguing, "No man buys his own property. Now all things are the property of the wise man; therefore the wise man buys nothing." By the same reasoning they object to his borrowing, because no one pays interest for the use of his own money. They raise endless quibbles, although they perfectly well understand what we say.[193]

In 1 Corinthians 4:1–5, Paul dictates to the Corinthians how they should regard him and his associates. Paul and his associates, being bearers of divine wisdom, are "servants (ὑπηρέτας) of Christ and stewards (οἰκονόμους) of the mysteries of God." The idea of stewardship extends the idea of Paul and his associates as planters and builders, and God as the one who causes growth and Jesus Christ is the foundation. As a steward[194] Paul probably has a slave in mind who manages their master's property according to their master's liking.[195] The lowly position of Paul and his associates receives elaboration later in the chapter (1 Cor 4:9–13). Like a slave in the house of God, Paul has intimate access to the wisdom of God and manages its distribution according to God's purpose.[196] As servants of God and Christ, no one in the community or outside of it can judge or challenge the nature of the divine wisdom and practice of Paul and his associates.

Sophia is only slightly insulted that Paul associates himself with the lowest public position in the city, and even on the level of a slave. Yet Paul says that he is the steward of the mysteries of God: he is the teacher of the divine wisdom that his opponents cannot touch. Indeed, because of his access to divine wisdom that he can be indifferent to the worldly power and status. This is a virtue that Sophia can value.

Paul's teachings here set some boundaries to Sophia's freedom. However, the boundaries are tolerable and familiar. Paul's concept of self-control is a familiar and welcome constraint on freedom: the loss of self-control isolates one from divine wisdom. Self-control brought about by philosophical discipline and fellowship with the divine have defined Sophia's intellectual pursuits, so Paul's criticism of the lack of these virtues is welcome.

Reading 1 Corinthains 3:4—4:5 with Fortuna

Paul's discussion of the nature of Apollos, himself, and the divine is confusing for Fortuna. Paul has just said in 1 Corinthians 3:3–4 that the followers

193. Sen. *Ben.* 7.4.
194. The same term that Paul uses with Erastus in Rom 16:23.
195. Byron, "Slave of Christ," 179–98.
196. *TDNT* 8:542.

Reading 1 Corinthians with Philosophically Educated Women

of human wisdom are the cause of division—when in fact it is possible that no division actually exists—and then in 1 Corinthians 3:10–17 he claims that everyone in the community, no matter who they would hypothetically claim as their inspiration, are actually unified because they are one sacred building built on one divine foundation. From Paul's perspective, the metaphors of the field, the building, and the temple in 1 Corinthians 3:5–17 are all in direct response to the jealousy and division brought about by the lack of self-control of the seekers of human wisdom in 1 Corinthians 3:3–4, and he immediately returns to this theme in 1 Corinthians 3:18–21a. Fortuna understands that her wisdom comes from a divine source, but since it is not necessarily Paul's interpretation of divine wisdom, there is plenty of room for an unsympathetic reading here, particularly because Paul has frustrated Fortuna from the beginning of the epistle with his juxtaposition of human and divine wisdom.

It is offensive to Fortuna that Paul uses tidbits of philosophical ideas and constructs, yet claims to have the benefits of mastering a philosophical method while characterizing "human wisdom" as completely different from his "divine wisdom." If Fortuna caught the Socratic construction, it serves as a definite sign that Paul has no intention of pursuing any concept even remotely related to philosophical inquiry. Paul then can declare that "all things belong to you," that is, those who have not followed philosophical inquiry to explore God, themselves, and anything else. It is impossible that those who inquire about God through the popular philosophical schools can actually know God, but Paul uses a Stoic maxim related to the wise-person to describe people in the community whose understanding of wisdom that he can tolerate. Not only can his opponents not know God—they do not have access to the desired outcome of their philosophy—this to Fortuna is deeply divisive and insulting.

Fortuna sees Paul constraining freedom so severely that an entire group of believers who were attracted to the community based on this theology of the cross are now excluded from their method of understanding God and themselves. The exercise that enabled Fortuna to participate in the community while retaining her philosophical heritage was dismissed by Paul. Human wisdom was much more than half of Fortuna's philosophical experience. Her philosophical methods—human wisdom—were the means by which she exercised self-control and became aware of the divine. Because of her intellectual freedom, she was able to value competing philosophies and incorporate Pauline teachings into this experience. This freedom works both ways: her philosophical experience can tolerate her Christian experience, and her Christian experience compliments her philosophical education. Paul chooses to upset this balance by artificially separating divine and human wisdom and philosophical outcomes from philosophical (human/divine) methods.

Reading 1 Corinthians 4:6–21 with Sophia

As a supporter of Paul, Sophia is likely familiar with the ways in which Paul's ministry differs from the values of the sophists. In 1 Corinthians 4:6–13, Paul expands on his lowly status by contrasting it with the status of his opponents. Paul has already associated divine wisdom as appearing foolish to those who value human wisdom, and now the deliverer of this divine wisdom is made low in every way. Paul refers to his opponents as kings and wealthy (1 Cor 4:8), perhaps indicating the wealth of his educated patroness, Sophia. Perhaps a plea for unity with Fortuna—who he knows may well be frustrated by this epistle—is in Paul's wish that his opponents could actually rule so Paul could be elevated from his lowly state and rule with them (1 Cor 4:8b). In contrast to the wealthy and powerful people in the community—especially his opponents who seek human wisdom—Paul presents himself and his associates as publicly humiliated in the extreme, and they are fools for the sake of their audience. The apostles are hungry and thirsty, inadequately clothed, abused and homeless, they work with their hands, they are despised, reviled, persecuted, and slandered (1 Cor 4:11–13).[197] When Paul contrasts himself with the Corinthians as "kings," Sophia[198] can read Paul as saying that the Corinthians are not in reality as powerful as they think they are.[199] Paul would be contrasting a metaphor—the authority, power, and wealth of the Corinthians, the "kings"—with the actual suffering of the apostles. This metaphor brings Paul's loss of status in sharp contrast to the rising status of some of his audience.[200] In spite of Paul's rhetoric and Sophia's sympathies toward Greek philosophy, she recognizes that Paul is focusing his invective on his opponents, not her. Sophia does not think of herself as an all-knowing and all powerful queen while Paul suffers without her help. Paul associates himself with poverty, and his suffering highlights his need for and value of her continued support of the church.

---

197. 1 Cor 4:11–13 has been identified as a Stoic hardship list by Fitzgerald, *Cracks in an Earthen Vessel*; Garcilazo, *Corinthian Dissenters*, 8.

198. It is critical to note once again that the focus here is on how Sophia—a wealthy philosophically educated woman—would read 1 Corinthians. Her reading does not speak for Paul's entire audience, or what this passage says about other readers.

199. Wire's focus on the Corinthian women prophets produces a different reading than Sophia, a wealthy philosophically educated woman.

200. Cf. Wire, *Corinthian Women Prophets*, 188–89.

Reading 1 Corinthians with Philosophically Educated Women

According to Paul, the actual suffering of the apostles and the metaphor of the Corinthians as kings were not meant to shame the Corinthians (however, Paul makes it clear that he is actually mocking them by calling attention to it in 1 Cor 4:14). Paul then presents himself as a kind of idealistic father who lovingly admonishes his children rather than shames them when they need discipline (1 Cor 4:15). So, as their father in Jesus Christ through the Gospel, they are to imitate him (1 Cor 4:16; 11:1).[201] The appeal to the role of the father is an unmistakable appeal to authority, and imitation is as important concept in Paul's apostle as it is in ancient philosophy.[202] At this point, it seems that the love of the father is a very thin veil over an exhortation to follow more closely after Paul's teaching rather than that of his opponents. Paul sent Timothy specifically for the purpose of reminding them of Paul's previous visits, which is what Paul referred to himself earlier in the epistle (1 Cor 4:17). Apparently, Paul was very confident that his presence—whether in person, through Timothy, or by way of rhetoric—is an unstoppable unifying force (1 Cor 4:18–21). Paul argues that if he were present, then his opponents would be reminded of his authority and the power of his gospel would bring everyone into the kind of unity that Paul can tolerate.

Again Paul uses a format that would be familiar to Sophia: the Stoic hardship list in 1 Corinthians 4:9–13. The hardship list points to the prestige of the wise-person, who can withstand any hardship with magnanimity. It is difficult to imagine that Sophia did not know such a basic concept, especially due to its popularity and the debates that the popular schools had concerning the nature of the wise-person.[203] Paul's endurance of hardship is something that she can respect: he is able to achieve the status of a Stoic wise-person without actually being a Stoic sage. His faithfulness to his calling has achieved a truly brilliant outcome, and she and the community have access to the divine power that enabled such an accomplishment if they imitate him. Sophia knows that her wisdom comes from a divine source, and if she actualizes it properly, she too can endure hardship with magnanimity like Paul. If she dares to believe that Paul is a successful pattern, she could value his company as a partner in dialog.

---

201. Clarke, *Serve the Community*, 218–27.

202. Stanley, "Imitation in Paul's Letters," 127–41; Castelli, *Imitating Paul*; Malherbe, "Exhortation," 240–41; Malherbe, "Hellenistic Moralists," 290.

203. See especially Fitzgerald, *Cracks in an Earthen Vessel*.

Reading 1 Corinthians 4:6–21 with Fortuna

Just as Paul can use the Stoic maxim "all things belong to the wise-person" (1 Cor 3:21) to people who have not followed a philosophical method to achieve wisdom, he applies the qualities of the Stoic wise-person to himself (1 Cor 4:9–13), when he had no right. Fortuna knew about Diogenes the Cynic, famous in Corinth, who said that all things belong to the gods, and because the wise-person is friends with the gods and friends hold all things in common, that all things belong to the wise-person. However, Paul is no Diogenes. While Diogenes's reasoning works well with Paul to a point, there is a significant difference in how one becomes friends with God. Fortuna understands that for Paul, it is his calling as an apostle that enables him to preach the word of the Gospel, which is the foolishness of the cross, the wisdom of God (1 Cor 1:21). Because of his calling as apostle, Paul claims that he is able to endure the hardships of the wise-person (1 Cor 4:9). If Paul had not completely alienated Fortuna by this point of the letter, perhaps she could be sympathetic to Paul's rhetorical or actual suffering (1 Cor 4:11–13). But to claim the identity and virtues of the Stoic wise-person without actually following their teachings[204] has no persuasive power for Fortuna.

Paul's reference to his personal visits to Corinth, while they may have been pleasant experience for her, is probably not the most effective rhetorical tactic that he could have used to capture Fortuna's favor. This sentiment is compounded by Paul's reasoning for sending Timothy and his threat of a future visit (1 Cor 4:14–21). After repeatedly devaluing her philosophical experience, positively applying the desired outcome to people who did not even discipline themselves according to a popular school, and then applying qualities of a wise-person to himself, a good memory of Paul's visit or the threat of his coming would have little persuasive effect for Fortuna. She will continue to support the Christian community at Corinth because of the unity that she valued before Paul wrote this epistle and the unity in diversity that the other members of the community enjoy, but Paul's rhetoric was simply unsuccessful with her.

Conclusion: Reading 1 Corinthians 1–4 with Sophia and Fortuna

In chapter 5, we have read the first four chapters of 1 Corinthians with two hypothetical philosophically educated women: Sophia and Fortuna. Their backgrounds share some similarities. First, they are both wealthy widows

---

204. Cf. Malherbe, "Paul: Hellenistic Philosopher or Christian Pastor?," 3–13; Badiou, "Universal Subject," 30–31.

who are patronesses of the church. As such, they are able to control their wealth and more freely engage in philosophical discourse. Second, both women have broad philosophical interests and are aware of the basic teachings of the popular philosophical schools: Cynicism, Stoicism, Epicureanism, Platonism, and neo-Pythagoreanism. Third, both women were attracted to Paul's theology of the cross that brings social and theological freedom to the community.

When Paul distinguishes divine wisdom from human wisdom, and as an expression of freedom to balance philosophical education and a theology of the cross, both Sophia and Fortuna understand that they already possess a balance of human and divine wisdom. However, as Paul further develops his arguments, Sophia continues to identify with Paul's divine wisdom but Fortuna is frustrated by his sustained division of divine and human wisdom. Fortuna is further alienated by Paul as he uses philosophical teachings and claims to have qualities of the ideal wise-person without following a philosophical method. In chapter 6, I will discuss how Sophia and Fortuna would read Paul's teachings concerning marriage and worship.

6

Marriage, Family, and Worship in 1 Corinthians

IN THIS CHAPTER, I will focus on the question of what would Sophia and Fortuna know about marriage if they had the broad philosophical education of a wealthy Corinthian patroness. What might these women be exposed to at the Isthmian games or a dinner party that feature discussion by a variety of people in an intellectual circle? These questions will be addressed by outlining the views of the popular schools regarding marriage. Then, I will read Paul's material related to marriage and family in 1 Corinthians with Sophia and Fortuna, with special emphasis on how Paul uses this material to encourage unity in Christian worship.

This chapter will review Paul's teachings on marriage (1 Cor 5:1–13; 6:9–20; 7:1–40), especially with respect to the nature of household worship (1 Cor 11:1–16).[1] Every time that Paul addresses worship in 1 Corinthians, he does so in the context of teachings concerning marriage and family. In 1 Corinthians 11:3, Paul explains that the head of the wife is the husband; he gives his teaching concerning the role of women prophets in Christian worship. In 1 Corinthians 14:26–40, Paul gives further instructions concerning the role of prophets in Christian worship, followed by a teaching concerning the silence of women in the churches and that husbands should teach their wives at home.

---

1. In chapter 4, I addressed 1 Cor 14:33–35 and argued that it was not Pauline and therefore not an issue for further discussion.

Reading 1 Corinthians with Philosophically Educated Women

Marriage and Family in the Popular Philosophers

Instructions concerning marriage and family were common topics in both the popular philosophers and some philosophically educated women. Teachings concerning the passions played no small role in addressing these issues.[2] There are parallels to Paul's approach in the philosophers who teach and encourage women to practice philosophy but relegate them to their contemporary gender roles. In the following sections, I will address writings of the Pythagoreans and neo-Pythagoreans as well as the Roman Epicureans, Stoics, Cynics, and Platonists.

The Pythagoreans and Neo-Pythagoreans

There is some material in the older Pythagorean writers that address marriage and family and while the neo-Pythagorean corpus has strained connections with the earliest groups, the traditions concerning the importance of marriage is intact. For that reason, I will begin with the older traditions (such as the teachings of Theano which may have their source in Aristotle) and then focus on the writings which may reflect the knowledge or opinions of a first-century follower of the school. The Neo-Pythagoreans inherited a rich tradition of focus on the family from legends concerning Pythagoras and his earliest followers. The legacy of these followers, led by his disciple wife Theano and his daughter Damo, inspired later writers to author works in their name. The precise date of the Pythagorean pseudepigrapha is unknown, but as a whole it reflects popular first-century values. The difficulty with these writings, other than date, is that they contain no relationship with any philosophy except that they are attributed to well-known philosophically educated women. From these writings we can see that Pythagorean women were fondly remembered by some writers and their audiences, and there indeed are some paralells with Paul's moral teachings.[3]

Several writings/sayings are attributed to the Pythagorean Theano, who lived in the sixth century BCE but some of the extant writings are dated as late as second century CE. The works attributed to Theano are *Pythagorean Apophthegms, Female Advice, On Piety, On Pythagoras, Philosophical Commentaries* and *Letters*. Of these, all except the *Letters* survive in a handful of fragments. And it is in the *Letters* that we find the most substantive similarity to Paul, specifically the letter to Eurydice (dated 3rd BCE). In

---

2. Fitzgerald, *Passions and Moral Progress*.
3. Balch, "Neopythagorean Moralists," 380–411.

this epistle, Theano gives instructions regarding how she should handle the problem of her husband sleeping with a prostitute.

In a similar manner, Theano (3rd BCE) says that Eurydice should not be a jealous wife but inspire her husband by her virtue to change his ways. Theano addresses the same issue in her epistle to Nicostrate, using the metaphor of the body:

> γαμετῆς γὰρ ἀρετή ἐστιν οὐχ ἡ παρατήρησις τἀνδρός, ἀλλ' ἡ συμπεριφορά· συμπεριφορὰ δέ ἐστι τὸ φέρειν ἄνοιαν. εἴθ' ἑταίρᾳ μὲν πρὸς ἡδονὴν ὁμιλεῖ, γαμετῇ δὲ πρὸς τὸ συμφέρον· συμφέρον δὲ κακοῖς κακὰ μὴ μίσγειν, μηδὲ παρανοίᾳ παράνοιαν ἐπάγειν . . . ἑαυτὴν δὲ παρεκτέον ἐπιτηδείαν ταῖς διαλλαγαῖς· τὰ γὰρ καλὰ ἤθη καὶ παρ' ἐχθροῖς εὔνοιαν φέρει, φίλη, καὶ μόνης καλοκαγαθίας ἔργον ἐστὶν ἡ τιμή, ταύτῃ δὲ καὶ δυνατὸν ἀνδρὸς ἐξουσίαν καθυπερέχειν γυναικί, καὶ τιμᾶσθαι πλέον ἢ θεραπεύειν τὸν ἐχθρόν.

> For the virtue of a wife is not in watching over her husband, but bearing things in common with him. And bearing things in common with him is to bear his madness. If he mixes with a prostitute for his pleasure, he does so with his wife for his advantage. It is an advantage not to mix evils with evils, nor to add madness with madness . . . prepare yourself for reconciliation. For a fine character and high regard even from enemies, my friend, and honor is the outcome of a true nobility. Through this it is possible for a woman's authority to exceed a man's, and for her to he honoured even more, rather than serve her enemy.[4]

Perictione (3rd c. BCE)—taking the name of Plato's mother—notes that adultery is a pleasure for men only, because women and not men are punished for it.[5]

The importance of marriage and family life in Pythagoreanism is expressed in many ways as Iamblichus (245-325 CE) tells the story of Phythagoras (ca. 570-495 BCE) and his early followers. According to Iamblichus, Pythagoras taught that husbands and wives should be faithful to each other and win the affection of children through affection and not force.[6] It is also relevant to note that Pythagoras successfully persuaded women to dress with humility and assigned divine rank to three parts of a woman's life: "the unmarried woman was called Core, or Proserpine, a

---

4. Theano to Nicostrate (Theano, *Fragmenta*, TLG 198, 199).

5. Perictione, *On the Nature of Women* (Perictione, *Fragmenta* TLG 104 = Stob. 4.28.19).

6. Iambl. *VP* 9.48.

Reading 1 Corinthians with Philosophically Educated Women

bride Nympha, a matron, Mother, in the Doric dialect, *Maia*."[7] Porphyry (284-305 CE) writes that women participated as hearers of Pythagoras's early lecturesin the 6th century BCE (γενομένων δὲ τούτων μεγάλη περὶ αὐτοῦ ηὐξήθη δόξα, καὶ πολλοὺς μὲν ἔλαβεν ἐξ αὐτῆς τῆς πόλεως ὁμιλητὰς οὐ μόνον ἄνδρας ἀλλὰ καὶ γυναῖκας, ὦν μιᾶς γε Θεανος) [Through this he achieved great reputation, he drew great audiences from the city, not only of men, but also of women, among whom was a specially illustrious person named Theano] (6th BCE). "γενομένων δὲ τούτων μεγάλη περὶ αὐτοῦ ηὐξήθη δόξα, καὶ πολλοὺς μὲν ἔλαβεν ἐξ αὐτῆς τῆς πόλεως ὁμιλητὰς οὐ μόνον ἄνδρας ἀλλὰ καὶ γυναῖκας, ὦν μιᾶς γε Θεανος."[8] Ocellus Lucanus, a 5th BCE Pythagorean, wrote that husbands should marry women their age and status—and more importantly—a woman who is not weathlier:

> ἡ μὲν γὰρ ὑπερέχουσα πλούτῳ καὶ γένει καὶ φίλοις ἄρχειν προαιρεῖται τοῦ ἀνδρὸς παρὰ τὸν τῆς φύσεως νόμον, ὁ δέ γε διαμαχόμενος δικαίως καὶ οὐ δεύτερος ἀλλὰ πρῶτος θέλων εἶναι ἀδυνατεῖ τῆς ἡγεμονίας ἐφικέσθαι.

> For the wife who surpasses her husband in wealth, in birth, or in friends, is desirous of ruling over him, contrary to the law of nature. But the husband justly resisting this desire of superiority in his wife, and wishing not to be the second, but the first in domestic sway, is unable, in the management of his family, to take the lead.[9]

A pseudonymous work attributed to Charondas the Catanean (5th BCE, work preceeds Stobaeus) teaches that husbands and wives should be faithful to one another:

> Γυναῖκα δὲ τὴν κατάα νόμους ἕκαστος στεργέτω καὶ ἐκ ταύτης τεκνοποιείσθω, εἰς ἄλλο δὲ μηδὲν προι έσθω τέκνων τῶν αὐτοῦ σποράν· μηδὲ τὸ φύσει καὶ νόμῳ τί μιον ἀνόμως ἀναλισκέω καὶ ὑβριζέτω. ἡ γὰρ φύσις τεκνοποιίας ἕνεκεν, οὐκ ἀκολασίας ἐποίησε τὴν σποράν. Γυναῖκα δὲ σωφρονεῖν χρὴ καὶ μὴ προσδέχεσθαι συνουσίαν ἀσεβῆ παρ' ἄλλων ἀνδρῶν, ὡς ἀπαντώσης νεμέσεως παρὰ δαιμόνων ἐξοικιστῶν καὶ ἐχθροποιῶν.

> Let every one dearly love his lawful wife and beget children by her. But let none shed the seed due his children into any other

---

7. Iambl. *VP* 9.49; cf. Diog. Laert. 8.10 = Timaeus *FGrH* 566 F 13b.

8. Porph. *VP* 19.4.

9. Ocell. *De universi natura*, 4.6; cf. Callicratidas frag. 106. Translation in Balch, "Neo-Pythagorean Moralists," 398; cf. Thomas Taylor, *Ocellus*, 24.

person, and let him not disgrace that which is honorable by both nature and law. For nature produced the seed for the sake of producing the children, and not for the sake of lust. A wife should be chaste, and refuse impious connection with other men, as by so doing she will subject herself to the vengeance of the geniuses, whose office it is to expel those to they are hostile from their houses, and to produce hatred.[10]

Charondas is mentioned here because of his later association with Pythagoreanism which appears rather thin because it was common practice for the ancients to associate the famous law-givers with Pythagoreanism.[11] However, the writer who attributed this writing to him as a Pythagorean preserves common Pythagorean traditions.

As Pythagoras taught his daughter philosophy, the neo-Pythagorean Callicratidas (date unknown)[12] wrote that husbands—as a duty of managing their wives—should teach their wives:

ποτὶ λόγον δὲ μναστευσάμενον τὸν γάμον δεῖ καὶ ἐπίτοπον καὶ κύριον ἐπιστάταν τᾶς αὐτῶ γυναικὸς εἶμεν ἐπίτροπον μὲν τῷ φροντίζειν τῶν ἐκείνας, κύριον δὲ τῷ ἄρχεν καὶ κυριεύειν, διδάσκαλοι δὲ τῷ διδάσκειν τὰ δέοντα.

The husband should be his wife's regulator, master and preceptor. Regulator, in paying diligent attention to his wife's affairs; master, in governing, and exercising authority over her, and preceptor in teaching her such things as are fitting for her to know.[13]

The importance of harmony in the state and the home is critical to Callicratidas (Stob. 4.28.17 = *TLG* 106). This concept is expressed again in Polus the Pythagorean:

ἐν κόσμῳ μὲν ὦν αὐτὰ τὰν ὅλαν ἀρχὰν διστραταγοῦσα πρόνιά τε καὶ ἁρμονία καὶ δίκα καὶ νῶς τινὸς θεῶν οὕτω ψαφιξαμένω· ἐν πόλει δὲ εἰράνα τε καὶ εὐνομία δικαίως κέκληται· ἐν οἴκῳ δ' ἔστι ἀνδρὸς μὲν καὶ γυναικὸς ποτ' ἀλλάλως ὁμοφροσύνα. οἰκετᾶν δὲ ποτὶ δεσπότας εὔνοια, δεσποτᾶν δὲ ποτὶ θεράποντας καδεμονία.

---

10. Charondas, *frag.* 62. Translation in Gutherie, *Iamblichus*, 112.

11. Kahn, *Pythagoras and the Pythagoreans*, 70; cf. Morrison, "Pythagoras of Samos," 143.

12. Balch, "Neopythagorean Moralists," 391.

13. Callicratidas in Stob. 4.28.18 = *TLG* 107. Translation in Gutherie, *Iamblichus*, 116.

It conducts the whole world government and is called providence, harmony, and vengeance, by the decrees of a certain kind of geniuses. In a city it is justly called peace, and equitable legislation. In a house, it is the concord between husband and wife; the kindliness of the servant towards his master, and the anxious care of the master for his servant.[14]

The Pythagoreans and neo-Pythagoreans do not always teach exactly the same thing about marriage, but they are unified in the worth of marriage and its preservation. The family is very important to the preservation of Pythagorean teachings because they were originally kept in the family, passed from father to son or even mother to daughter. Iamblichus writes that Pythagoras persuaded the inhabitants of Croton to give up adultery and prostitution, and works that are attributed to Pythagorean women encourage faithfulness in marriage. Neo-Pythagoreans may have been rare in Corinth in the first century, but their morality parallels other schools that were prevalent that taught self-control and applied it to the marriage relationship. Epicureans, of course, were the exception to this rule.

Epicureans and Marriage

Epicurus (341–270 BCE) did not encourage marriage because it threatened his idea of αὐτάρκεια (self-sufficiency).[15] Casual sex, however, was permissible and encouraged because it was a natural pleasure—without the marital commitment that put αὐτάρκεια in jeopardy.[16] This teaching can explain popularity of courtesans in the history of Epicureanism. The ideal Epicurean wise-person should not marry but can engage in as many sexual encounters as he or she wants because it is an act according to nature, as long as he remains unconnected to anyone or anything.[17] This may sound Cynic on the outset, but while Epicureans did not participate intimately in the livelihood of the city by establishing a household or serving the city, they were free to

---

14. Stob. 3.9.51. Translation in Gutherie, *Complete Pythagoras*, 205.

15. Martha C. Nussbaum, *Therapy of Desire*, 152. For this section of the paper, Hans-Josef Klauck's work, *Religious Context of Early Christianity*, has been particularly helpful in locating sources and relating ancient philosophical thought to the New Testament (331–416).

16. On Epicurean self-sufficiency, see Epicurus, *Letter to Menoeceus* 130–31; *Sent. Vat.* 36, 44, 77. On necessity, see Diog. Laer. 10.148–49. Cf. Andrew Mitchell, "Friendship"; Eric Brown, "Epicurus on the Value of Friendship," 68–80; Vander Waerdt, "Justice," 402–22.

17. Downing, *Cynics, Paul, and the Pauline Churches*, 109.

exploit existing systems for personal enjoyment.[18] Expressing some form of distaste towards marriage was quite popular in philosophy. Stobaeus collects 38 sayings from 35 different ancient thinkers who opposed marriage including notables such as Menander, Euripides, Soctrates, Plato, and Solon.[19] Pseudo-Diogenes takes up this cause in an epistle addressed to Zeno, teaching that marriage should be avoided as a human weakness.[20]

After Epicurus, not many Epicureans give an opinion about marriage. Philodemus of Gadara (ca. 110–35 BCE) refers to the Epicurean way while he discusses other approaches to household management.[21] Lucretius (ca. 99–55 BCE) continues the Epicurean tradition that the wise-person should not marry, but under certain circumstances he can take a wife and genuine friendship can result from the union.[22] Diogenes of Oenoanda (fl. 2nd c. CE) briefly mentions marriage but gives no opinion on it in what remains as a fragment.[23] Epictetus (ca. 55–135 CE) writes that the Epicurean wise-person will not marry (3.7.19), raise children, or participate in politics (1.23). Similarly, Paul's ideal follower of Christ, following his example, will not marry (1 Cor 7:8). However, just as Paul provides an exception for marriage for those who cannot practice self-control (1 Cor 7:9), a highly disputed text in Diogenes Laertius (10.119) says that Epicurus taught that the wise-person could marry under certain (unknown) circumstances, but this exception is only found here and contradicts all other extant teachings of Epicurus on the subject.[24]

Cynics and Marriage

With the notable exception of Crates and Hipparchia, there is no record of marriage in the history of the Cynics.[25] Marriage goes against the grain of the extreme individualism of Cynicism: the complete freedom from all

18. Asmis, "Epicurean Economics," 167.
19. Stob. *Concerning Marriage* = 4.22 Hense. Translation available in Wibush, *Ascetic Behavior*, 171–72.
20. Ep. 47 in Malherbe, *Cynic Epistles*.
21. Philodemus, *On Household Management* col. 2–3, 9. For Lucretius' view on marriage, see Nussbaum, *Therapy of Desire*, 185–91.
22. Lucretius 4.1283. Betensky, "Lucretius and Love," 291–99; Snyder, "Lucretius and the Status of Women," 17–20; Arkins, "Epicurus and Lucretius," 141–43.
23. Diogenes of Oneoanda, frag. 25.
24. Bailey, *Greek Atomists*; Chilton, "Did Epicurus Approve of Marriage?," 71–74; Fish and Sanders, *Epicurus*, 93.
25. Navia, *Classical Cynicism*, 135; Navia, *Diogenes*; Desmond, *Cynics*, 93; Fitzgerald, *Passions and Moral Progress*, 60.

constraints. Epictetus, for example, writes that the Cynic "ought to be free from distraction, wholly devoted to the service of God, free to be among the people, not tied down by the private duties of men, nor involved in relationships which he cannot violate."[26] The Cynics and Stoics engaged in ongoing debate about marriage.[27]

The Stoics and Marriage

The Stoics supported traditional marriage with the exception of Zeno (ca. 334–262 BCE), who taught that there should be a community of wives for the ideal Stoic community (Diog. Laert. 7.131, following Pl. *Rep.* 423e, 457a–b, 462).[28] Cicero took his own advice and married to his advantage: he was married twice, and relished his interactions with daughter Tullia and his second wife Terentia.[29] Although it may be a fanciful interpretation of the historical data, it is possible Seneca (ca. 4 BCE–65 CE) not only valued marriage, but engaged in philosophical discussion regularly with the sisters of Caligula: Agrippina the Younger,[30] Julia Drusilla, and Julia the Elder.[31] Hierocles and Musonius Rufus[32] supported marriage, but with the careful qualification that women are only superficially equal to men on a theoretical level, but the traditional household duties are actively reinforced.[33]

Plutarch, the "Middle Platonist"

Represented by Plutarch, the so-called "middle Platonists" believed that the philosopher was to be fully integrated into society, taking a wife, establishing a household, and serving the city in public offices. Plutarch is the first-century representative of Middle Platonism, and the primary resources from his writings on this topic are his *Advice to Bride and Groom* and *On*

---

26. Epict. *Disc.* 3.22.69.

27. Deming, *Paul on Marriage*, 48.

28. Epictetus explains that this is another form of marriage, "καὶ ἄλλο τι εἶδος γάμου εἰσφέρων," frag. 15. Elizabeth Asmis believes that this is an indication that the community of wives also participated in philosophical discourse and education ("Stoics on Women," 68–94).

29. Myers, "Cicero's (S)Trumpet," 337–52; Treggiari, *Terentia, Tullia and Publilia*.

30. It was Agrippina who secured Seneca's return from exile so that he could teach Nero, Ginsburg, *Representing Agrippina*, 20.

31. Clarke, "Seneca the Younger," 62–69.

32. Ward, "Musonius Rufus and Paul on Marriage;" Engle, "Women's Role," 267–88.

33. Gaca, *Making of Fornication*, 83.

Consolation to his Wife. In the *Advice to the Bride and Groom*, Plutarch expresses his belief that it was wrong for husbands to irritate their wives with the slight pleasure of adultery.[34] Plutarch writes of his wife: "Every philosopher who has been in our company has been amazed at the simplicity of your person and the unpretentiousness of your life," "εὐτελείᾳ μὲν γὰρ τῇ περὶ τὸ σῶμα καὶ ἀθρυψίᾳ τῇ περὶ δίαιταν οὐδείς ἐστι τῶν φιλοσόφων."[35] The ideal wife, according to Plutarch, is philosophically educated:

> Σὺ δ' ὦ Εὐρυδίκη μάλιστα πειρῶ τοῖς τῶν σοφῶν καὶ ἀγαθῶν ἀποφθέγμασιν ὁμιλεῖν καὶ διὰ στόματος ἀεὶ τὰς φωνὰς ἔχειν ἐκείνας ὧν καὶ παρθένος οὖσα παρ' ἡμῖν ἀνελάμβανες, ὅπως εὐφραίνῃς μὲν τὸν ἄνδρα, θαυμάζῃ δ' ὑπὸ τῶν ἄλλων γυναικῶν, οὕτω κοσμουμένη περιττῶς καὶ σεμνῶς ἀπὸ μηδενός. τοὺς μὲν γὰρ τῆσδε τῆς πλουσίας μαργαρίτας καὶ τὰ τῆσδε τῆς ξένης σηρικὰ λαβεῖν οὐκ ἔστιν οὐδὲ περιθέσθαι μὴ πολλοῦ πριαμένην, τὰ δὲ Θεανοῦς κόσμια καὶ Κλεοβουλίνης καὶ Γοργοῦς τῆς Λεωνίδου γυναικὸς καὶ Τιμοκλείας τῆς ἀδελφῆς καὶ Κλαυδίας τῆς παλαιᾶς καὶ Κορνηλίας τῆς Σκιπίωνος καὶ ὅσαι ἐγένοντο θαυμασταὶ καὶ περιβόητοι, ταῦτα δ' ἔξεστι περικειμένην προῖκα καὶ κοσμουμένην αὐτοῖς ἐνδόξως ἅμα βιοῦν καὶ μακαρίως. Θεαγένους ἀδελφῆς καὶ Κλαυδίας τῆς παλαιᾶς καὶ Κορνηλίας τῆς Σκιπίωνος καὶ ὅσαι ἐγένοντο θαυμασταὶ καὶ περιβόητοι, ταῦτα δ' ἔξεστι περικειμένην προῖκα καὶ κοσμουμένην αὐτοῖς ἐνδόξως ἅμα βιοῦν καὶ μακαρίως.

> And as for you, Eurydice, I beg that you will try to be conversant with the sayings of the wise and good, and always have at your tongue's end those sentiments which you used to cull in your girlhood's days when you were with us, so that you may give joy to your husband, and may be admired by other women, adorned, as you will be, without price, with rare and precious jewels. For you cannot acquire and put upon you this rich woman's pearls or that foreign woman's silks without buying them at a high price, but the ornaments of Theano, Cleobulina, Gorgo the wife of Leonidas, Timocleia, the sister of Theagenes, Claudia of old, Cornelia, daughter of Scipio, and of all other women who have been admired and renowned, you may wear about you without price, and, adorning yourself with these, you may live a life of distinction and happiness.[36]

---

34. Goessler, "Advice to the Bride and Groom," 107.
35. Plut. *Mor.* 609c. Translation by Donald Russell in *Plutarch's Advice*, 59–63.
36. Plut. *Mor.* 145e-f (Babbitt, LCL).

Reading 1 Corinthians with Philosophically Educated Women

Plutarch gives us important information concerning how a woman could gain access to philosophical education. Eurydice learned philosophical maxims when she was a child in Plutarch's house, which included lines from poetesses, stories of female heroes, and sayings of women philosophers. As a wife, she is to remember these lessons and is encouraged to learn more.

Pseudo-Plutarch's essay on love (*Mor.* 748e–771e) is also relevant here, because the author, pretending to be his son, presents Plutarch's view as the writer understands it. The dialog centers on the question of the marriage of a young man, Bacchon, and a wealthy widow that was a bit older. The dialogue embodies Plutarch's views concerning marriage and it is modeled after Plato's *Symposium*, so older traditions are represented in the debate.[37] The dialog reveals that Plutarch thought that the foundation of marriage was love between a man a woman.[38] For these reasons, pseudo-Plutarch will receive more discussion than some of the other ancient works.

Pseudo-Plutarch's *Dialogue on Love* contains many conflicting views about love: its object (whether one can love men or women physically or only inner beauty), when and who one should marry, and how women are to act in relationship to others. While these issues are debated, Ismenodora, a wealthy widow in love with a young man, acts according to her will to achieve her own purposes. She asserts her love for the young man, which causes heated debate among the older male lovers[39] and other men who are involved in his life. While they discuss whether he should marry her or not, Ismendora kidnaps and marries Bacchon in her home. While this kidnapping and forced marriage is intended as playful and the men are willing participants, there is definitely an undercurrent of Ismendora's power over Bacchon and the other men of the group. Perhaps the activities of Ismenodora in pseudo-Plutarch's *Dialogue on Love* can serve as a model of how wealthy women in the Pauline churches could have moved and acted according to their will while the idealistic views of the activity and role of women in the church was subject to debate. At least by analogy, it shows us the activity of a wealthy woman in the lives of men outside of the royal circle.

Ismendora's character is considered excellent by everyone present, and she fell in love with Bacchon when she was trying to introduce him to one of her friends (749d–e). More importantly, she is the aggressor in the relationship, seeking him as her husband. Bacchon's friends of the same age make a joke of the idea of him marrying her because of her superiority:

---

37. Rist, "Plutarch's 'Amatorius,'" 557–75; Klotz and Olkonomopoulou, *Philosopher's Banquet*, 1–33; Brenk, "Plutarch's Erotikos," 13–27.

38. Ferguson, *Moral Values*, 97.

39. For the dynamics of friendship and pederasty in the ancient world, see Schachter, *Voluntary Servitude*, 23–38.

Marriage, Family, and Worship in 1 Corinthians

her age, wealth, power, authority, and previous marriage. Because of these concerns, Bacchon's elder friends and family enter into serious debate as to the dynamics of such a marriage. Many people had an opinion about the marriage, but the decision was left up to Anthemion (an elder cousin of Bacchon) and Pisias (the most sober of Bacchon's lovers = ὁ δὲ Πεισίας αὐστηρότατος τῶν ἐραστῶν). Plutarch is nominated as a moderator of this debate, and offers his own views at the close, which is comparable in length to everything that precedes it.

The argument for pederasty/homoerotica as the highest form of love comes principally from Pisias, a man in a pederastic relationship with Bacchon.[40] His argument is not entirely rejected by the others, but he does take more than a little bit of flack for his obvious bias (from Anthemion 749f; from Daphnaeus 750b). Protogenes, however, will agree with him. Protogenes asserts that love has nothing to do with women because a man is only acting according to nature (the desire to produce children, and possibly the force of sexual attraction) when he interacts sexually with women. Protogenes insists that the most noble form of love is the love of boys, which goes against these natural urges and therefore cultivates true friendship and virtue (750d–e).

Protogenes argues that the love of *freeborn* boys is the only genuine love (εἷς Ἔρως ὁ γνήσιος ὁ παιδικός ἐστιν in 751a is qualified in 751b to exclude slave boys). At this point, Daphnaeus interrupts Protogenes and declares (after a jest insinuating that Protogenes himself is bewitched by infatuation) that women's yielding to men sexually is called "favor" by the poets, but the unnatural yielding of boys to men *or adults* to men is violent if involuntary or effeminate if it is voluntary. Daphnaeus does not wholly do away with pederasty as a normative mode of affection, but wants to force Protogenes to admit that if unnatural activity is hailed as such, natural expressions must be accepted as well, particularly because natural intercourse wins immortality for the human race (from 751f–752e).

Pisias then expresses a familiar standard (ἐπεὶ ταῖς γε σώφροσιν οὔτ᾽ ἐρᾶν οὔτ᾽ ἐρᾶσθαι δήπου προσῆκόν ἐστιν) [Decent women cannot, of course, without impropriety either receive or bestow a passionate love] (752c). To this Plutarch interjects with a very interesting rebuttal, placing marriage within the context of friendship:

καὶ νὴ Δία Δαφναίῳ συνδίκους ἡμᾶς προστίθησιν οὐ μετριάζων
ὁ Πεισίας, ἀλλὰ τοῖς γάμοις ἀνέραστον ἐπάγων καὶ ἄμοιρον
ἐνθέου φιλίας κοινωνίαν, ἣν τῆς ἐρωτικῆς πειθοῦς καὶ χάριτος

40. Klabunde, *Boys or Women?*

Reading 1 Corinthians with Philosophically Educated Women

ἀπολιπούσης μονονοῦ ζυγοῖς καὶ 'Δ'. χαλινοῖς ὑπ' αἰσχύνης καὶ φόβου μάλα μόλις συνεχομένην ὁρῶμεν.

"I swear that it is Pisias' lack of moderation that makes me join forces with Daphnaeus. So marriage is to be a loveless union, devoid of its god-given friendship!" Yet we observe that a loveless alliance, once it is deserted by courtship and "favor," can scarcely be held together by such yokes as shame and fear.[41]

Because friendship must be between equals—and several ancient writers of this time want to apply the principals of friendship to many unequal relationships like patronage, kingship, kinship, and marriage—Plutarch must find a way to make husband and wife "equal." Plutarch defends marriage, addressing the two ways that women can often be superior to men in general: in beauty and wealth, and gives examples of how both have destroyed men.

Pisias asserts again that women have no part at all in love, and because of this wealthy and beautiful women are particularly dangerous. He explicitly attacks Ismenodora, saying that she is only seeking to dominate a boy younger and less wealthy than herself (752e–f). Pisias argues that women only feel passion and not true love, being lead only by the baser part of the soul. He restates the position asserted by Protogenes above (ἐρᾶν δὲ φάσκουσαν γυναῖκα φυγεῖν τις ἂν ἔχοι καὶ βδελυχθείη, μήτι γε λάβοι γάμου ποιησάμενος ἀρχὴν τὴν τοιαύτην ἀκρασίαν) [For if a woman makes a declaration of love, a man can only take to his heels in utter disgust, let alone accepting and founding a marriage on such intemperance].[42]

In this case, the age difference also has to be addressed. First, Plutarch submits that not all married men are unhappy with the companionship of women and do not seek to be freed from it (753c). Some women are worthless to men and destroy them with their wealth and beauty, but if a man brings his wife down to his level by degrading her wealth and beauty, he will also demean himself. Plutarch therefore says:

ὁ δὲ συστέλλων τὴν γυναῖκα καὶ συνάγων εἰς μικρόν, ὥσπερ δακτύλιον ἰσχνὸς ὢν μὴ περιρρυῇ δεδιώς, ὅμοιός ἐστι τοῖς ἀποκείρουσι τὰς ἵππους εἶτα πρὸς ποταμὸν ἢ λίμνην ἄγουσι· καθορῶσαω γὰρ ἑκάστην τῆς ὄψεως ἀκαλλῆ καὶ ἄμορφον ἀφιέναι τὰ φρυάγματα λέγεται καὶ προςδέχεσθαι τὰς τῶν ὄνων ἐπιβάσεις.

---

41. Plut. *Mor.* 752c (Minar, Sandbach, and Hemhold, LCL).
42. Plut. *Mor.* 753b (Minar, Sandbach, and Hemhold, LCL).

The man who cramps and diminishes his wife (as a thin man does his ring for fear that it may fall off) is like those who shear their mares and then lead them to a river or a pool: when the poor beast sees how ugly she looks in the reflection, ugly and unsightly, they say that she abandons her haughty airs and allows asses to mount her.[43]

The equality which is requisite to friendship occurs not by the man degrading the wealth and beauty of his wife, but by the enhancement of the husband's character. His character is enhanced not by shunning his wife, or by making her poor or ugly, but by bearing all of her advantages with dignity. It is the husband's own will not to serve his more powerful wife that makes him strong.

> ἀνδὶ δὲ πλουσίας ἢ καλῆς οὐ προσήκει, μηδὲ τὴν γυναῖκα ποιεῖν ἄμορφον ἢ πενιχράν, ἀλλ' ἑαυτὸν ἐγκρατείᾳ καὶ φρονήσει καὶ τῷ μηθὲν ἐκπεπλῆχθαι τῶν περὶ ἐκείνην ἴσον παρέχειν καὶ ἀδούλωτον, ὥσπερ ἐπὶ ζυγοῦ ῥοπὴν τῷ ἤθει προστιθέντα καὶ βάρος, ὑφ' οὗ κρατεῖται καὶ ἄγεται δικαίως ἅμα καὶ συμφερόντως.

The husband, however, of a rich or beautiful woman must not make her unsightly or poor; rather by his own self-possession and prudence, as well as by the refusal to be over-awed by any of her advantages, he must hold to his own without servility. The extra weight of his character must turn the scales; thus his wife is controlled and guided with as much profit as justice.[44]

Perhaps even more remarkable, in light of other passages regarding the education of women in Cicero, Seneca, Plutarch, and Diogenes Laertius, is that the elder wife educates the younger husband. Cicero, Seneca, and Plutarch together bear witness to the education of elite women by their husbands. Yet Plutarch notes that a more educated woman should teach her husband:

> εἰ δ' ἄρχει βρέφους μὲν ἡ τίτθη καὶ παιδὸς ὁ διδάσκαλος ἐφήβου δὲ γυμνασίαρχος ἐραστὴς δὲ μειρακίου γενομένου δ' ἐν ἡλικίᾳ νόμος καὶ στρατηγὸς οὐδεὶς δ' ἄναρκτος οὐδ' αὐτοτελής, τί δεινὸν εἰ γυνὴ νοῦν ἔχουσα πρεσβυτέρα κυβερνήσει νέου βίον ἀνδρός, ὠφέλιμος μὲν οὖσα τῷ φρονεῖν μᾶλλον ἡδεῖα τῷ φιλεῖν καὶ προσηνής.

---

43. Plut. *Mor.* 754a (Minar, Sandbach, and Hemhold, LCL).
44. Plut. *Mor.* 754b (Minar, Sandbach, and Hemhold, LCL).

Reading 1 Corinthians with Philosophically Educated Women

> The nurse rules the infant, the teacher the boy, the gymnasiarch the youth, his admirer the young man who, when he comes of age, is ruled by law and his commanding general. No one is his own master, no one is unrestricted. Since this is so, what is there dreadful about a sensible older woman piloting the life of a young man? She will be useful because of her superior intelligence; she will be sweet because she loves him.[45]

At this point, Ismendora asserts her power by summoning all the young men and young ladies loyal to her to help her to kidnap Bacchus. Apparently, Bacchus was in the habit of walking by her house at a certain time of day, and some other young men brought him in to the house and the party dressed him in wedding clothes and they proceeded with the ceremony. Upon hearing this news, Pisias loses his mind and leaves the debate to call upon the *gymnasiarchs* to settle the matter, and Protogenes follows to calm him down (755c).

It appears to me that the rest of the persons participating in the discussion were amused with Ismendora and end up associating her with other great male and female lovers. With the most passionate defenders of pederasty now out of the debate, Pemptides appeals to the group again to discuss the topic at hand, appealing to the analogy of two people finding an asp and wanting to keep it for good luck: whether love can be found with men or women or both (755e-f). Plutarch was just about to open his mouth to answer when Ismendora again asserts her power: she summons Anthemion, the one other moderator from the debate, to come to her house to help her settle the uproar. Anthemion therefore leaves the group of men at the request of a woman (756a), which is very significant: Ismendora forces her will on Bacchon—the younger, inexperienced man—and then on Athemion, his elder, who may well be her superior in age and wealth.

Plutarch begins his answer with a long sermon (756b-757c) declaring the divinity of Eros and Ares. Plutarch asserts that Eros guides the older male lovers of young boys—when friendship is their goal—and therefore does not undermine pederasty in the slightest (758b-c; again lauded quite a bit in 760e-761e). In this case, one should guard against following one's lust, because pederasty is criticized when the object of the elder man's affection is not beauty of soul and the enjoyment of the body. It is in this balance that Plutarch can argue both for pederasty, adult male homoeroticism, and then the expression of love with women/wives (759f-760b). Women in general have done courageous deeds in the name of love, he declares (761e).

---

45. Plut. Mor. 754d (Minar, Sandbach, and Hemhold, LCL).

Pederasty again seems to be the type of love praised by in 762b–f. It makes the slow-witted man clever, every man generous, and happy to give (examples are given of pederastic men who change while in love with boys). Zeuxippus continued this point by offering his own example, and then appealed to Sappho who gives an example of the same thing happening to women when they see their beloved (763a).

In the midst of another long speech by Plutarch, he mentions Plato's doctrine of love (764a; as mentioned in the *Symposium*). In Plato's doctrine of love, the object of affection is the soul. For Plutarch, the object of affection is also the beauty of the soul, but there is appreciation for physical beauty. As a god, Eros graciously leads the person to love the soul while the lover longs to be united sexually with the beloved, be they male or female (765a–b). This concept is elucidated by the following quote:

> εὐφυοῦς δ'ἐραστοῦ καὶ σώφρονος ἄλλος τρόπος· ἐκεῖ γὰρ ἀνακλᾶται πρὸς τὸ θεῖον καὶ νοητὸν καλόν· ὁρατοῦ δὲ σώματος ἐντυχὼν κάλλει καὶ χρώμενος οἷον ὀργάνῳ τινὶ τῆς μνήμης ἀσπάζεται καὶ ἀγαπᾷ, καὶ συνὼν καὶ γεγηθὼς ἔτι μᾶλλον ἐκφλέγεται τὴν διάνοιαν.

> But the noble and self-controlled lover [of either men or women] has a different bent. His regard is refracted to the other world, to Beauty divine and intelligible. When he encounters beauty in a visible body, he treats it as an instrument to memory. He welcomes and delights in it, yet the pleasure of its company only serves the more to inflame his spirit.[46]

Pseudo-Plutarch has received much attention in this section because of its value for understanding the historical, cultural milieu, and the philosophical landscape. The dialog presents us with a limited variety of first-century views concerning pederasty, love, and marriage. Some considered love between males as the ideal because only males were equipped to be free from their natural impulses and cultivate virtue. Others considered love between men and women as expressed in marriage to be ideal. Isomendora, an older and wealthier woman exerts her will on a younger man as well as an older and wealthier man. Like an empress, she appears to be perfectly in control of her destiny in this episode. She is a threat to the younger Bacchon because the older men know from experience that wealthier women can control their husbands. In the end, Plutarch gives the final judgment: love between men and women, even between social "unequals" is not only possible, but can be successful and foster virtue. Finally, we can highlight Plutarch's suggestion that

---

46. Plut. *Mor.* 766a (Minar, Sandbach, and Hemhold, LCL).

Reading 1 Corinthians with Philosophically Educated Women

a more educated wife should teach her husband, and the husband therefore should consider her greater education to be an advantage.

Paul and Marriage

After discussing the opinions on the various popular philosophers on marriage, we move on to Paul. All of these schools had a history of teaching women, and all of them had some kind of presence in Corinth. Therefore, we should expect that some women in the Corinthian community would understand Paul's teachings in light of what they had learned in their philosophical education. In this section, I will review Paul's teachings concerning marriage in 1 Corinthians and then examine how two philosophically educated women would read his teachings.

How Not to Do Marriage: Improper Union with the Stepmother (1 Cor 5:1–5) and Prostitutes (6:12–16)

I addressed this issue in chapter 4 because Paul is most likely speaking to a somewhat common problem of a wealthy widow cohabitating with her stepson. Paul completely rejects this situation as an appropriate expression of Christian love or marriage, and it disrupts Christian fellowship so severely that the stepson must be expelled from the community. Nothing is said of the woman—most readers of 1 Corinthians take this silence to mean that she is not a member of the community—if she is considered at all.[47] If so, Paul could be risking the alienation of wealthier members of the Christian community with their higher status friends—something that Paul does not seem interested in at all in 1 Corinthians.[48] Paul's teachings in 1 Corinthians 10:27 allow for the wealthier members of the community to continue their relationships with their "unbelieving" friends because they can invite and be invited to dinner parties without dietary restrictions.[49] These teachings also allow the wealthier members to host the community in their households without censure from their wealthy friends because of the strange dietary

---

47. Robertson and Plummer, *Corinthians*, 96; Barrett, *Corinthians*, 121; Witherington, *Conflict and Community*, 158; Fitzmyer, *Corinthians*, 234; Chow, *Patronage and Power*, 114.

48. Cf. Ciampa and Rosner, *First Letter to the Corinthians*, 203.

49. For discussion, see Horrell, *Social Ethos*, 108. Hays, *First Corinthians*, 142–43, writes that Paul prefers that the "strong" join him with the "weak" and avoid meat altogether if necessary. However, if no one at the table is offended, it seems that the "strong" can eat meat as they please. Cf. Fotopoulos, *Food Offered to Idols*, 253; Chow, *Patronage and Power*, 156–57.

restrictions of the community.⁵⁰ It was the secretive nature of early Christian meetings that later brought criticism from their polemicists, who let their imaginations run wild with assumptions as to what the Christians might be doing behind closed doors.⁵¹ If Paul can convince his followers to be above suspicion, that is one less thing for the patrons of the church to worry about. It would be an incentive for the wealthy members of the community—both insiders and outsiders—to begin or continue supporting the church.

However, if the stepmother in 1 Corinthians 5:1–5 is a member of the community, she would have more sympathetic relationship to Paul than an outsider, and the expulsion of her stepson from the community may have been to her advantage and perhaps beneficial for the rest of the community. The questions surrounding the death of a wealthy man and the precise division of that wealth and settlements of debt is a time of tremendous vulnerability, and other members of the Christian community perhaps could not resist such a temptation. The expulsion of the stepson in 1 Corinthians 5:1–5 combined with forbidding lawsuits in public courts nicely solves these problems. The public shaming of the stepmother may cause more problems that it solves, unless the separation works out to her advantage (discourages lawsuits, publically dissolves a problematic relationship, and secures her claim to her husband's wealth).

Paul addresses the problem of the union of men and women⁵² in the Christian community with prostitutes in 1 Corinthians 6:12–16. Paul focuses on the unity of the Christian body, utilizing the "one body many parts" metaphor. The metaphor is deceptive in its simplicity: the strength of the body is determined by the unity of the members, which are useless if they stand alone. That is simple enough, but the metaphor is exclusively used in antiquity to explain that the rich and poor are unified in one body, and the poor should continue happily in their servile position.⁵³ Because the Christians are unified with one another and with Christ, sexual intercourse with a prostitute is much more than simply one person indulging himself or

50. Martin, *Corinthian Body*, 75; cf. Witherington calls it a "qualified endorsement" of both positions (*Conflict and Community*, 191–92); Lull and Beardslee, *Corinthians*, 81, 89–92.

51. Men. Fel. *Oct.* 9.5; Tertullian, *Apol.* 7–8; Origen, *Celsus*, 6.40. See also Rives, "Human Sacrifice," 65–85; Lanzillotta, "Early Christians," 81–102; Wilken, *Remembering the Christian Past*, 27–46.

52. In the Roman world, both men and women exploited prostitutes who were typically slaves (both adults and children). There is no reason to assume that Paul is restricting this teaching to men alone, unless Paul does not think that a female can unite the body of Christ with a prostitute. For references and bibliography, see below in chapter 6.

53. Martin, *Corinthian Body*, 95; Mitchell, *Paul and the Rhetoric of Reconciliation*, 157–64.

herself by sexually exploiting another person. The unity that the Christian enjoys with Christ and the community is disrupted when this unity is extended by means of a sexually immoral activity to a prostitute. Paul seeks to motivate his audience to preserve this unity by warning them that they are uniting Christ with the prostitute in sexual immorality.

Paul's Regulations for Marriage: 1 Corinthians 7:1–40

In 1 Corinthians 7:1–40, Paul gives the community his regulations for marriage. Apparently, some members of the community were married but thought that it was best not to engage in sexual acts within that marriage. Paul begins his teaching on marriage with a negative motivation: people should marry because of the temptation to sexual immorality (7:2). Paul goes on to give his understanding of conjugal rights: the husband and wife should not deprive one another sexually (7:3). He seems to reject the idea that sexual union is reserved for procreation, and gives both the male and female over to their natural lusts. Then Paul expresses the ideal to be imitated: to be unmarried and in complete control over the passions (7:9). However, if a person cannot maintain self-control, then they should marry (7:10).

Paul teaches that a man and wife should not divorce one another, and if they do seperate, they should not remarry but reconcile to each other (7:10–11). The prohibition on divorce is unqualified,[54] and supported by the superlative example: even if one has an unbelieving spouse, the believing partner should not initiate divorce and make their partner and their children holy. Remarriage is forbidden for a woman who does leave her husband, the only option that Paul gives is reconciliation. The only divorce that is sanctioned is when an unbelieving spouse asks for one. Paul then gives more justification for remaining unmarried: the present distress (7:26) and the added anxieties of marriage that distract one from serving the Lord (7:32–34). However, marriage and betrothal are not sins in themselves (7:28). Paul concedes that if done properly (ie, with both persons practicing acceptable levels of self-control) marriage and betrothal are good, but remaining unmarried is better (7:38). Paul concludes by giving instruction specifically to women: they should not divorce or remarry as long as their

---

54. Deming, *Paul on Marriage*, 218, suggests that Paul is following a Jesus tradition that prohibits divorce and interprets 1 Cor 7:11 as speaking to separation and not necessarily divorce. However, Paul is not allowing for divorce or qualifying his prohibition on it by recognizing that it will happen in the community (1 Cor 7:11) but gives instructions for what should be done if divorce or separation should occur (reconciliation and no remarriage).

first husband lives, but if he dies, then she can remarry someone in the Christian community.

Paul's Regulations in Worship: 1 Corinthians 11:1–17

In 1 Corinthians 11:1–17, Paul uses his concept of marriage to give instructions concerning the use of head coverings in worship.[55] These instructions comprise the concept of "headship": the head of the wife is the husband, the head of the husband is Christ, and the head of Christ is God (11:2). Paul moves on to the regulation of worship, elaborating on the idea of "headship" with instructions concerning head coverings. Men are to pray and prophesy with their heads uncovered, and women are to pray and prophesy with their heads covered. Men should remain uncovered because men are the image and glory of God, women are the image of men. Paul elaborates further on unity: men and women are made for each other and are interdependent. Paul concludes discussion on the topic of head coverings by an appeal to nature: if a man wears long hair, it is against nature, and if a woman has long hair, it is perfectly natural so she should wear a head covering.

Sophia and Fortuna on Marriage

We have seen in chapter 5 that Sophia and Fortuna have approached Paul from different perspectives. Both readers have difficulties, confusion, and points of departure from his arguments, but they also find that they can appreciate him for their own reasons. Paul's teachings concerning human and wisdom in chapters 1–4 were understandable to both Sophia and Fortuna, who both identify with his teachings concerning divine wisdom. The confusing nature of Paul's understanding of division within the church and the sharp contrast between divine and human wisdom is troublesome to both women. However, Sophia's sympathetic reading allows her to identify with Paul and approach his rhetoric as directed toward the human wisdom of his opponents and not her own. Paul's persistence on the issue and especially his claim to attain self-sufficiency without a philosophical method eventually alienate Fortuna. At the same time, however, the less sympathetic Fortuna intends to continue her support to the church and despite the shortcomings of Paul's arguments. In this chapter, we will explore how Sophia and Fortuna would read Paul's regulations concerning marriage and worship.

---

55. For exegetical questions and bibliography, see chapter 4 above.

Reading 1 Corinthians with Philosophically Educated Women

Reading 1 Corinthians 5:1–5 and 6:12–16 with Sophia

Paul's teachings concerning marriage address the problem of unity. I have argued that the problem of the stepmother and stepson provides the perfect conditions for serious discord in the community. The stepson is usually seen as the person in control of the wealth,[56] but the larger share in the property may well have passed to his stepmother who can leave him disinherited should he leave the house.[57] Even if the consequence is not quite that severe, the property situation could be a powerful motivation to maintain a continued positive relationship with her.[58] Not much needs to be said about this issue except for the threat that it can present to the wealthy patroness: if the church acts according to Paul's command, then he is exerting authority on a very intimate aspect of her household. Paul himself is not ejecting the man from the household, but is calling for the community to remove him from a group that he may care deeply about. The problem that Sophia may encounter is the threat that Paul may attempt to exert the same kind of authority in an area of her life that only she should determine. Paul's evident lack of concern for the goodwill of a wealthy woman demonstrates a gross lack of respect for the people who are providing the church with critical support. However, Sophia can support Paul's expulsion of the stepson on the basis of his promotion of self-control and unity within the community. This episode is not merely one that highlights one woman's home and an improper sexual relationship, but is a matter that affects the entire community. Paul's action could have worked to the benefit of the stepmother, removing the temptation for other people in the community to take advantage of her vulnerability in court by attacking her character. In this case, Sophia can approach Paul's handling of this situation in an entirely appropriate manner: he is teaching self-control and ridding the community of a very real problem.

Paul addresses the problem of the unification of the church in a strange manner: sex with prostitutes. The principle sources for prostitution were exposed children, female and male slaves, and female and male freedpersons who sold themselves into slavery. Most prostitutes were forced into prostitution by their masters or families, which complicate the ethical situation that Paul addresses.[59] From the literary sources, prostitution was rarely practiced by choice. Prostitution was a problem for Roman women and men because by exploiting prostitutes, men could both displease their

---

56. Keener, *1–2 Corinthians*, 49; Garland, *1 Corinthians*, 162–63.
57. Cf. Gardner, *Women in Roman Law*, 163–204.
58. Cf. Clarke, *Secular and Christian Leadership*, 81.
59. Glancy, *Slavery in Early Christianity*, 21–24; cf. Glancy, *Slavery as Moral Problem*.

wives and produce illegitimate heirs that threaten their fortunes. Wealthy Roman women could participate in prostitution as either a buyer or a seller, and that could cause legal problems for her husband and destitution or death for herself, provided that her husband followed the law himself or his friends or enemies see to it that the law is enforced.[60] The first problem is addressed by the neo-Pythagorean philosophers, who encourage women to bear this hardship with magnanimity. The concepts presented in these neo-Pythagorean writers could have been expressed by any Stoic or Middle Platonist. The popular philosophers and other ancient writers also used the metaphor of the body to reinforce social unity. Sophia is glad to hear that Paul prohibits sex with prostitutes because of her experience as a wife and widow and especially because of her philosophical education. For Sophia, it is good that both men and women are taught to practice self-control not only with respect to prostitutes but in every other area of life.[61]

Reading 1 Corinthians 5:1–5 and 6:12–16 with Fortuna

As with Sophia, there is not much to say about Fortuna's reading of the incident concerning the inappropriate relationship between the woman and her stepson. The challenge of the situation for Fortuna would doubtless be Paul's undue influence on one of their peers' household. Like the stepmother, Fortuna is a wealthy patroness of the church. If Paul can impose his will on one of her sisters, showing an unforgivable lack of gratitude and cowardly use of the church to expel the stepson instead of taking a more sublte, private approach to the situation, then someday he could betray her in a similar manner. Fortuna suspects that if Paul can suddenly find fault with her, perhaps she would face a similar embarrassment.

Fortuna is pleased that Paul calls for self-control of men and women with respect to prostitutes. However, she finds it useless to attempt to reform the sexual behaviors of people who for all their lives they had seen nothing wrong with Paul's version of sexual "immorality." For Fortuna, however, self-control is attained by disciplined commitment to a philosophical method. By its nature, the self-control that Paul requires of the entire community

---

60. Cf. McGinn, *Prostitution*. Contra Wire, who suggests that only men solicited male (and female?) prostitutes, so Paul could only be speaking to men (*Corinthian Women Prophets*, 74).

61. Both men and women of various status participated as both consumers and prostitutes. For women paying male prostitutes, see Clarke, *Looking at Lovemaking*, 226; ancient sources in Johnson and Ryan, *Sexuality in Greek and Roman Society*, 87–109. Contra Wire, who asserts that this text cannot apply to women because they never paid male prostitutes (*Corinthian Women Prophets*, 74).

is only available to the disciplined few who have the stamina to follow the rigors of good teachings. Although the prohibition is something of a trite criticism in her opinion, if Paul persuades some people to avoid prostitutes and it does settle some discord in the community, then the prohibition is good for everyone.

Reading Regulations for Marriage in 1 Corinthians 7:1-40 with Sophia

The entire chapter of 1 Corinthians 7 addresses the issue of marriage and divorce.[62] Within this block of text there are many issues and questions. Within 1 Corinthians 7:1-16, there are the implications for women prophets,[63] question of the sayings/views of the Corinthians,[64] spiritual marriage,[65] the nature of Paul's asceticism,[66] the use of archaeological evidence,[67] the issue of self-control,[68] the nature of Paul's usage of a teaching of Jesus,[69] Jewish background,[70] Paul's teachings of slavery and social status (1 Cor 7:17-24),[71]

---

62. Coiner, "Divorce and Remarriage Passages," 367-84; Bartling, "Sexuality, Marriage, and Divorce," 355-66; Boston, "Womanist Reflection," 81-89; Caragounis, "'Fornication' and 'Concession,'" 543-59; Molvaer, "St. Paul's Views on Sex," 45-59; Wanamaker, "Connubial Sex," 839-49; Caragounis, "What Did Paul Mean?," 189-99; Keener, "Interethnic Marriages," 25-43; Hodge, "Married to an Unbeliever," 1-25; Horrell, "Development of Theological Ideology," 224-36.

63. Wire, *Corinthian Women Prophets*, 72-79.

64. Winter, "1 Corinthians 7:6-7," 57-65.

65. Beck, "1 Corinthians 7:36-38," 370-72; O'Rourke, "Hypotheses regarding 1 Corinthians 7:36-38," 292-98; Seboldt, "Spiritual Marriage," 103-19; Seboldt, "Spiritual Marriage in the Early Church," 176-89; Peters, "Spiritual Marriage," 211-24.

66. Dolfe, "1 Cor 7,25 Reconsidered," 115-18; Gundry-Volf, "Celibate Pneumatics and Social Power," 105-26; Hunter, "Reception and Interpretation of Paul," 163-91; Gundry-Volf, "Controlling the Bodies," 519-41.

67. Oster, "Use, Misuse and Neglect of Archaeological Evidence," 52-73.

68. Barré, "To Marry or to Burn," 193-202; Neirynck, "Paul and the Sayings of Jesus," 265-321; Alexander, "Better to Marry," 235-56.

69. Wenham, "Paul's Use of the Jesus Tradition," 7-37; Wong, "Deradicalization of Jesus' Ethical Sayings," 181-94; Neirynck, "Sayings of Jesus in 1 Corinthians," 141-76.

70. Ford, "Hast Thou Tithed Thy Meal?," 71-79; Farla, "Two Shall Become One Flesh," 67-82; Tomson, "Paul's Jewish Background," 251-70; Gillihan, "Jewish Laws on Illicit Marriage," 711-44.

71. Roberts, "Meaning of *Chorizo* and *Douloo*," 179-84; Bartchy, *MALLON CHRESAI*; Dawes, "But If You Can Gain Your Freedom," 681-97; Harrill, "Paul and Slavery," 5-28; Deming, "Diatribe Pattern," 130-37; Braxton, "Role of Ethnicity," 19-32; Byron, *Slavery Metaphors*; Byron, "Slaves and Freed Persons," 91-107.

Marriage, Family, and Worship in 1 Corinthians

Paul's rhetoric,[72] and questions related to the betrothed.[73] Somewhere beneath all of these arguments, interpretations, and readings, are our philosophically educated women, who heard 1 Corinthians being read with as much noise as a modern reader who is aware of all these arguments. Sophia and Fortuna read 1 Corinthians from their multi-valent backgrounds (wealth, status, power, education, sense of style and tradition, etc.), and I will continue to focus on their readings from their perspective as wealthy philosophically educated women.

Paul opens his discussion with a very low view of marriage: it is permissible only because people are weak and cannot control their passions. While he expresses this negative sentiment three times (1 Cor 7:2, 9, 36), Paul qualified it by saying that marriage and betrothal are not sins. Therefore, the ideal is the person who has a self-control that can successfully overcome passion. For everyone else who cannot attain this ideal, marriage is a concession. The regulations concerning marriage are that it is a lifetime commitment for a woman, divorce is forbidden for both men and women who are members of the community, but believers should grant unbelievers a divorce if the unbeliever requests it on account of religion. If a couple within the community does divorce, they are encouraged to reconcile but forbidden to marry anyone else.

These teachings do not apply directly to Sophia because she is a widow. She is unmarried and her husband is dead, so she meets the only explicit criteria for remarriage (perhaps a loophole in Paul's thinking is the question concerning whether or not people who agreed to divorce their partners because they did not want to be married to a Christian could remarry). Of slight interest to Sophia are the parallels in Paul's thinking to other philosophers who prohibit or make marriage a concession for someone who lacks self-control. For Sophia, it is self-control that captures her imagination, not Paul's concept of marriage itself. It is of no consequence to Sophia whether or not the members of the community marry (unless the union somehow effects her), but she can celebrate being a part of community that strives together for the virtue of mastering the self.

Reading Regulations for Marriage in 1 Corinthians 7:1–40 with Fortuna

Fortuna receives Paul's regulations concerning marriage with complete disinterest. Fortuna is slightly amused that Paul offers marriage as a concession

---

72. Ramsaran, "More than an Opinion," 531–41.
73. Beck, "1 Corinthians 7:36–38," 370–372; Kugleman, "1 Cor. 7:36–38," 63–71.

Reading 1 Corinthians with Philosophically Educated Women

to self-control: instead of developing an environment that encourages self-control, Paul allows for a context where people can live a less than ideal life (1 Cor 7:7, 32–34). At least Paul is consistent and teaches that both the husband and wife should willingly participate in sexual relations except for an agreed-upon time of prayer (1 Cor 7:5). That is, marriage is for those who are not self-controlled, and therefore one should not allow their partner to "burn" with passion (7:9). If Paul tells people to marry who lack control of their passions, it would completely defeat the purpose if he did not allow for these passions to be somehow expressed within marriage, his remedy to the problem. This approach to sex and restraint within marriage seems to be an attempt to appease those who said that it was good for a man not to "touch" a woman (a euphemism for sex[74]), but instead of a lifestyle, the mutual choice to refrain from sex should be brief (7:5).

The only possible benefit for Fortuna would be the possibility of the approval of her patronage of the Pauline community from her friends, because of the stability that the prohibition of divorce in 1 Corinthians 7:10–17 could bring to the community. However, this benefit is slight because her friends—should they discover the prohibition—would be more alarmed and amused that than anything else. While we know of several couples from monuments and other sources in the Roman world who were committed to each other for life, no other Greek or Roman teacher had ever prohibited divorce (although some leaders like Augustus in his *lex Iulia* discouraged it).[75] If the prohibition of divorce somehow gained popularity—or perhaps even in Fortuna's circle of Christian friends—it would threaten the ambitions of entire families.[76] As families sought to better their status, secure their estate, and gain wealth and power, divorce and remarriage were simply used as means to that end. Sexual gratification and fulfillment for both elite men and women were found elsewhere: in the exploitation of children, slaves, prostitutes, clients, freed persons, and other unmarried and married people outside of the marriage.[77]

---

74. Ciampa, "Revisiting the Euphemism," 325–38.

75. There were a few other teachings that prohibited divorce (not to mention the Jesus tradition, but Paul makes no indication that he has shared this with the Corinthians before); see Horrell, *Solidarity and Difference*, 156.

76. Cooper, *Roman Household*, xii.

77. For clients and freedpersons, see Oliensis, "Erotics of *Amicitia*," 168; Butrica, "Some Myths," 222–77.

Marriage, Family, and Worship in 1 Corinthians

Reading Regulations for Worship in 1 Corinthians 11:1–17 with Sophia

Like all other sections of 1 Corinthians, there are many exegetical and theological problems in 1 Corinthians 11:1–7. I have already addressed the scholarly debates on 1 Corinthians 11:2–16 above in 4.6.8 concerning the question of Pauline authenticity, the role of the veil in worship, and the nature of the head covering (hairstyle or veil?), and the significance of κεφαλὴ (source or authority?). I am approaching this text from the perspective that it is Pauline, women were active in community worship, Paul wanted the women to wear veils and the men not to wear veils in worship, and Paul used an unusual argument from nature to support his teaching.

As a philosophically educated woman, Sophia is familiar with the various attempts by the philosophers (both male and female) to regulate her dress and every other part of her life. Since she had been a member of the community, no regulation concerning head coverings had been given to her. Before reading this epistle, she could pray, prophesy, or otherwise participate in worship without such restraint, exercising the freedom that defines the theology of the cross. Even after the receipt of this epistle, her own sense of fashion and common practice for women of her status would have much more influence on her choice than Paul's unconvincing theological rationale for the use of head coverings.[78] The dynamics of Sophia's choice on this matter are the same before she hears Paul and after she hears Paul. This is a matter of freedom for women (and men) of her status: she wears what she desires as is appropriate to display wealth and power. Like anyone else of her status, if she allows someone of inferior status to dictate her dress, she would be heroically humbling herself, especially when they are using a weak theology that she had likely never heard before.

As with many other points like eating together and refraining from idol meat, the tangible benefit for uniform dress would be at least the outer expression of economic unity. It is entirely possible that women demonstrated their wealth and style with their hair and head coverings.[79] If by some miracle, all of the women in the community were both convinced by Paul to

---

78. The same can be said of men of her status, who were equally cognizant of style and common practice—and would equally be dismissive of Paul's theological virtues concerning their clothing. Portraits of women with and without head coverings are found in the same context, suggesting that it is a matter of choice rather than social pressure that dictates dress. Schottroff, *Let the Oppressed Go Free*, 109; Olson, "Matrona and Whore," 193.

79. Ruden, *Paul among the People*, 87. Cf. Neil Elliott, *Liberating Paul*, 209; Ciampa and Rosner, *First Letter to the Corinthians*, 541; Murphy-O'Connor, *Keys to 1 Corinthians*, 180.

Reading 1 Corinthians with Philosophically Educated Women

wear a head covering to every worship meeting and they were able to do so, there is the slight possibility that everyone would be enriched by the sense of unity that Paul desires. It is also interesting to note here that some women were prohibited by law from wearing the veil: anyone who had ever been a prostitute and anyone who had ever committed adultery.[80] In that case, Paul's requirement for all women to wear a veil can be read as redemption: all women, no matter what their condition are to enjoy a certain equality and unity with everyone else. However, it is impossible to gloss over the profound economic/power/status differences in the community that will forever be apparent to everyone in the community. No matter what theological justification Paul uses, these differences cannot be veiled.

Reading Regulations for Worship in 1 Corinthians 11:1–17 with Fortuna

Fortuna is a bit confused concerning Paul's regulations concerning head coverings. For Fortuna, these regulations are useless. The argument for unity between men, women, and Christ is easy enough to follow and it is welcome. That this unity depends on what Fortuna and other women wear on their heads as well on what men do not wear is not convincing. Fortuna is aware that temples, associations, and philosophical schools have their own customs concerning dress.[81] However, Paul's introduction of a new theologically based regulation after years of disinterest makes no sense.[82] If their hairstyles had caused such a disruption in worship, how is it that she and other women were able to enjoy fellowship with other believers until now? Paul is not persuasive because his attempt to correct fashion trends with ineffective theology, and his timing did not help. There is no man that is the head of Fortuna. Like many philosophically educated women before her, Fortuna has declared her relative equality with and independence from men. She is quite free to reject Paul's unconvincing arguments and even less inclined to have him dictate to her the virtues of her sense of style.

Furthermore, Paul's argument for head coverings threatened Fortuna's theology, which she adopted from Paul's earlier teachings in Corinth. Fortuna was attracted to the Pauline community because she could express her freedom in a number of ways that Paul would later find intolerable. One way

---

80. Zanker, *Power of Images*; Croom, *Roman Clothing*; McGinn, *Prostitution*, 154.

81. Payne, *Man and Woman*, 155–61; Kloppenborg, *Voluntary Associations*, 64; Edmondson and Keith, *Roman Dress*, 52, 169; van Nijf, *Civic World*, 201; Olson, *Dress and the Roman Woman*, 74.

82. Martin, "Veiled Exhortation," 263.

Marriage, Family, and Worship in 1 Corinthians

that Fortuna expressed her freedom was in her dress, and Paul's theological argument for head coverings is far less important than the theology that attracted her to the community in the first place.

Conclusion: Reading Paul on Marriage with Sophia and Fortuna

Most of the popular moral philosophies celebrated marriage with varying degrees of emphasis. The Epicureans did not encourage marriage because it threatened the disconnection from attachment that characterizes the ideal wise-person, and the wise-person (be they male or female[83]) could indulge in sex acts with anyone—as long as this act broke no law and harmed no one—because sex was natural. With the exception of Crates and Hipparchia, the Cynics did not marry because of their separation from human society unless they marry another Cynic. Stoics celebrated marriage as an enriching union between man and woman that the wise-person uses to better herself, her situation, and society. The neo-Pythagorean Theano and Perictione taught wife should tolerate her husband's use of prostitutes because of her self-control (controlling anger) and in hopes of changing his behavior through her virtue. Plutarch, our first-century Middle-Platonist, celebrates marriage as the best way to express human love.

Paul's teachings on marriage focus on strengthening the unity of the community. Paul gives instructions to the community on how not to do marriage: the stepmother's affair with her stepson, and men using prostitutes. Paul has a view of marriage that is far below the Stoics and Plutarch. He teaches that the ideal Christian does not marry, but if a person cannot control herself/himself then she/he should marry. A consolation—that married persons can practice some small measure of self-control—is that the husband and wife should not withhold their bodies from one another unless they mutually agree for a short period of time. Furthermore, husbands and wives should not initiate divorce for any reason but they can grant a divorce to unbelievers who ask for one, and remarriage is forbidden for everyone but widows who lack self-control. Finally, women should wear head coverings in worship. The rationale for all of these teachings is that no one stands alone: the affair, sex with prostitutes, and divorce all disrupt the unity of the community because everyone is unified with the body of Christ.

Some issues effect Sophia and Fortuna in the same way. With regard to the stepmother, Paul is treating someone of their status with more than a little contempt. Instead of being thankful for patronage, Paul seeks to

---

83. This female sexual activity could be a reason why Epicurean women philosophers are portrayed as prostitutes. See discussion in chapter 3 above.

Reading 1 Corinthians with Philosophically Educated Women

control a wealthy woman by requiring the community to expel her stepson from the fellowship. This is a threat to any other patron: Paul has demonstrated that he is an ungrateful beneficiary. The issue concerning prostitutes is welcome because it encourages self-control, but trite because neither Sophia nor Fortuna is convinced that enough people in the church will submit to this teaching for it to be worth Paul's trouble. Both Sophia and Fortuna are amused with Paul's teaching concerning head coverings, mostly because of Paul's disinterest in it during previous visits and epistle(s).[84] Paul's teaching concerning marriage and divorce is a bit strange, but it does compliment self-control. Paul shares some parallels with philosophical moralists, and if he is able to convince the church to be self-controlled in marriage (1 Cor 7:1–5), divorce (1 Cor 7:10–16), prostitutes (6:13–18), and head coverings (1 Cor 11:2–16), then Sophia and Fortuna can have an easier time supporting the church as patronesses because the church would not bring them shame.

---

84. For the chronology of Paul, see Jewett, *Chronology*; Lüdemann, *Paul*; Riesner, *Paul's Early Period*; for bibliography and analysis of the epistles to Corinth, see Yeo, *Rhetorical Interaction*, 75–80; Ciampa and Rosner, *First Letter to the Corinthians*, 19–21; Fitzmyer, *Corinthians*, 50–53.

7

Self-Sufficiency in Paul and the Popular Philosophers

IN CHAPTER 5, WE explored the ways that Sophia and Fortuna would read 1 Corinthians chapters 1–4. These first chapters of 1 Corinthians separate divine wisdom from human wisdom in such a way that completely alienates Fortuna, but Sophia's understanding of her divine wisdom enhances her sympathy for Paul's arguments. In chapter 6, we explored how Sophia and Fortuna would read Paul's teachings concerning marriage. While Fortuna reads Paul from an increasingly hostile point of view, like Sophia she can appreciate Paul's attempt to unify the church through self-control with respect to the affair, prostitutes, head coverings, and marriage and divorce. In this chapter, we will examine how Sophia and Fortuna would interact with Paul's usage of the defining characteristic of the ideal wise-person in popular philosophy: self-sufficiency in 1 Corinthians 9:24–27. Then, we will read 1 Corinthians 9:24–27 with Sophia and Fortuna in light of their philosophical and social background.

Philosophically educated women like Sophia and Fortuna would be very familiar with the Cynic-Stoic doctrine of self-sufficiency. Its common usage in the *agon* motif stands at the intersection of the most popular philosophies in the first century.[1] The *agon* motif is a common athletic meta-

---

1. For Paul's use of the *agon* motif, see Pfitzner, *Agon Motif*, 76–129. Pfitzer suggests that Paul's usage of the *agon* motif is not limited to an internal struggle (111). I agree with Ronald Hock that Paul's struggles in Corinth were related to patronage. That is, the church desired to bring Paul into their homes like other teachers to reciprocate

phor that philosophers used to explain the importance of training oneself to have adequate mental and physical self-control to successfully live the good life. At the same time, the doctrine of self-sufficiency[2] or self-control is a central component to how popular philosophies approached many other issues such as friendship and patronage,[3] the ideal teacher, and family life. Despite the claim from several philosophers that women can and should possess the qualities of self-sufficiency (which will be discussed below), there is not the slightest hint of this in the works that address self-sufficiency and Paul.

This chapter begins with a discussion concerning Paul's usage of the *agon* motif in 1 Corinthians 9. This discussion is followed by a brief summation of the *agon* motif—the struggle of the wise-person/student for self-control as an athlete struggles for a crown—in Greek and Roman philosophy and its appearance in 1 Corinthians 9:24–27.[4] Then, I will discuss how Sophia and Fortuna would interact with Paul's image of the crown in 1 Corinthians 9 both as philosophically educated women and patronesses. As philosophically educated women, Fortuna and Sophia were equipped to interact with the metaphor. As wealthy patronesses, they were able to interact with the more concrete aspects of *agon* motif. These women helped fund the Isthmian games and were eligible to be rewarded for their patronage with an imperishable crown of gold rather than a perishable crown of celery that they earned in races or poetry competitions when they were girls. Both aspects are important to consider—the philosophical background as well as their social context as patronesses—when imagining how Sophia and Fortuna would read 1 Corinthians 9:24–27. The discussion will be centered

---

his ministry. Because Paul did not accept payment, he suffered by means of his employment, the church suffered some confusion on how to reciprocate his patronage, and some members may have actively sought retribution for this offense. Hock, *Social Context*, 29; Hock, "Paul's Tentmaking," 558.

2. Cf. Abraham Malherbe's works, "Gentle as a Nurse," 203–17; Malherbe, *Popular Philosophers*; Malherbe, "Paul's Self-Sufficiency," 125–39; Stowers, "Paul and Self-Mastery," 524–50. Neither Malherbe nor Stowers mentions female philosophers in their treatment of self-sufficiency, the defining quality of the teacher in many schools. The possibility of women interacting with Paul's presentation of himself as a popular wise-person is even lessened by John T. Fitzgerald's persistent use of "wise man" in his description of the ideal teacher, in *Cracks in an Earthen Vessel*.

3. In the *TNDT* entry for στέφανος there is no indication that women or girls could have interacted with the metaphor, *TDNT* 7:615–36. For Paul's use of στέφανος in conjunction with the *agon* motif, see Pfitzer, *Agon Motif*, 77; for patronage, see 106: "But by their continual faithfulness they ensure for him a crown on the day when the final word will be spoken on his apostolic work."

4. Self-sufficiency is characterized by self-control. Cf. Fitzgerald, *Cracks in an Earthen Vessel*, 139; Stowers, "Paul and Self-Mastery," 524–50.

on the heart of the *agon* motif, the means by which people discipline themselves to win the imperishable crown: self-sufficiency.

Setting Up the Agon Motif: 1 Corinthians 9:1–23

Philosophical traditions that either parallel or influence 1 Corinthians 9:24–27 are widely known and recognized by New Testament scholars.[5] However, before addressing the nature of self-sufficiency in the popular philosophers, its setting in 1 Corinthians chapter 9 needs to be examined.

Paul begins chapter 9 by explaining his relationship to wealthier members of the church, and he does so in a manner that clearly demonstrates an independence from the undue influences of personal patronage (1 Cor 9:1–18). After Paul argues by analogy to a vinedresser, soldier, and a shepherd (1 Cor 9:7) that he has the right to receive all of the benefits of personal patronage from the Corinthians (payment, meals, other material benefits, and perhaps a beneficial marriage), he volunteers his apostolic services for free, and in this service his full freedom is expressed (1 Cor 9:18). Paul's free service is seemingly in contrast to his opponents ("rightful claim" is from their point of view, not Paul's, 1 Cor 9:12), other apostles (1 Cor 9:12),[6] and meant to shame the Corinthian patrons who evidently were taking pride in supporting them. Furthermore, the wealthy Corinthians were taking advantage of their rights by taking other believers to court,[7] eating meat sacrificed to idols,[8] marrying and divorcing to their advantage like other elites, and supporting rhetors that agitated Paul's sensibilities.[9]

Everything that leads up to the *agon* motif in 1 Corinthians 9 serves to present Paul as a self-controlled person in contrast to his opponents and at least some of the wealthy members of the community. Paul is not dependent on a personal patron and corrupted by the influence of a patron's wealth and power.[10] Instead, he is content to survive by working with his hands

---

5. The most notable work in English is Pfitzner, *Agon Motif*, 23–37. The motif is such a recurring one that there are too many examples to list here. I will choose some examples from Pfitzner, who traces the motif from Xenophanes through the Hellenistic and Roman philosophers and Judaism. Cf. Garrison, "Paul's Use of the Athlete Metaphor," 209–17; Thiselton, *First Epistle to the Corinthians*, 710–17; Garland, *1 Corinthians*, 441–45.

6. Smit, "Rhetorical Disposition," 489.

7. Cf. Collins, *First Corinthians*, 330.

8. For bibliography on the identification of the "strong" with higher status and the "weak" with lower status, see Thiselton, *First Epistle to the Corinthians*, 644.

9. Garland, *1 Corinthians*, 398n5.

10. Collins, *First Corinthians*, 331; Ciampa and Rosner, *First Letter to the Corinthians*,

like a poor, powerless person. Moreover, Paul has made himself a servant to "everyone": Jews, Gentiles, and the weak (1 Cor 9:20–22). We should observe that Paul clarifies the Jews as those under the law and the Gentiles as those not under the law—but he does not pair the weak with the strong. Paul identifies himself with Jews and Gentiles as well as the poor (weak) but not the rich (strong).[11] This point cannot be emphasized enough: while Paul does not participate in personal patronage (eg., attach himself to the house of a patron), he never shows discontent with patronage of the community (ie., wealthier people giving to the community). However, his contempt for personal patronage may well discourage people from giving to the community that values his teaching. It is within this framework that Sophia and Fortuna read the important philosophical concept of self-sufficiency and the *agon* motif 1 Corinthians 9.

Self-sufficiency in Popular Philosophy

The concept of self-sufficiency is an important one in popular philosophy because it was used to describe the characteristics of someone who has mastered philosophy: the wise-person. Self-sufficiency is the result of an inner control of the self rather than seclusion from the community, friendship, and inspiration from God. The importance of self-sufficiency in a study of 1 Corinthians is that Paul utilizes this ideal—as he does elsewhere—to assert his authority as apostle (1 Cor 7:4, 9; 9:24–27).[12] From his perspective, Paul has attained the level of self-control that is characteristic of a philosophical sage even though he claims not to have come to the Corinthians "in wisdom." As such, 1 Corinthians 9:24–27 can be an effort by Paul to convince Sophia and Fortuna that he has realized the ideal of being a self-sufficient teacher so that they will recognize his authority to instruct and correct. Before this issue is explored, self-control and its role in the achievement of self-sufficiency needs to be examined.

Self-control (often with the discipline like an athlete in the *agon* motif) is the method by which a person achieves self-sufficiency. While the popular

---

411.

11. Hays, *First Corinthians*, 154; Collins, *First Corinthians*, 325; Ciampa and Rosner, *First Letter to the Corinthians*, 429, offer a description of the "weakness motif" in 1 Corinthians; Malina and Pilch write that in some Hellenistic contexts, "the weak" denotes a person unfamiliar with the sophistication of elite life (*Corinthians*, 94).

12. The importance of self-sufficiency in the Corinthian correspondence is made evident by Fitzgerald, *Cracks in an Earthen Vessel*, 117–84; in the Thessalonian letters by Malherbe, "Gentle as a Nurse," 203–17; and in Philippians by Malherbe, "Paul's Self-sufficiency," 125–39.

philosophers debated the definitions of self-control and self-sufficiency, the discipline that it takes to achieve the desired goal is highly praised. For example, Aristotle (384–322 BCE) teaches that the self-controlled person is the ideal good person, "For it is a fundamental assumption with us, and a general opinion, that wickedness makes men more unrighteous; and lack of self-control seems to be a sort of wickedness."[13]

Already in Aristotle's time (384–22 BCE), the Cynic wise-person was characterized by the ideal of αὐτάρκεια.[14] There are two examples of self-sufficiency from the Cynics that are applicable here. First, there is an epistle attributed to Diogenes the Cynic (of Corinth), who met the champion Cicermus on the road to Olympia. Diogenes convinced Cicermus to disregard his crown and pursue self-sufficiency:

ἧκε δὲ ἐπὶ τὰ ὄντως καλὰ καὶ μάθε μὴ ὑπὸ ἀνθρωπίων τυπτόμενος κατερεῖν, ἀλλ᾽ ὑπὸ τῆς ψυχῆς, μηδ᾽ ἱμᾶσι μηδὲ πυγμαῖς, ἀλλὰ πενία, ἀλλ᾽ ἀδοξία, ἀλλὰ δυσγενεία, ἀλλὰ φυγαδεία. τούτων γὰρ ἀσκήσας καταφρονεῖν μακαρίως μὲν ζήσεις, ἀνεκτῶς δὲ ἀποθάνῃ.

learn to be steadfast under blows, not by puny men, but of the spirit, not under leather straps or fists, but through poverty, disrepute, lowly birth, and exile. For when you have trained to despise these things, you will live happily, and will die in a tolerable way.[15]

The *agon* motif is not directly applied to women when male or female philosophers address women and self-control or self-sufficiency. It is not present in the other Cynic epistles, the Pythagorean letters attributed to women, the works by Seneca addressed to Helvia and Marcia, the Diogenes of Oneoanda inscriptions, the essays by Musonius Rufus concerning the philosophical education of women, nor does Heirocles address it when he writes about marriage. However, in all of these works there is some emphasis on a philosophically motivated self-control that would prepare Sophia and Fortuna to interact with Paul's usage of the *agon* motif in 1 Corinthians.

Second, there is one example in the history of women in philosophy that applies an athletic metaphor to a woman. An epistle attributed to the Cynic Crates (ca. 365–285 BCE) to his wife Hipparchia, "You believe, it seems, that toiling is the cause of your not having to toil. For you would not

---

13. "φαίνεται δὲ καὶ τοῦτο ἀδύνατον. ὑπόκειται γὰρ ἡμῖν καὶ δοκεῖ ἡ μοχθηρία ἀδικωτέρους ποιεῖν ἡ δ᾽ ἀκρασία μοχθηρία τις φαίνεται," Arist. *Eth. Eud.* 1223b (Rackham, LCL).

14. Teles, Περὶ αὐταρκείας 5H–20H.

15. Diogenes to Phaenylus 4; Malherbe, *Cynic Epistles*, 137.

have given birth so easily, unless, while pregnant, you had continued to toil as athletes do," "πέπεισαι ἄρα ὅτι τὸ πονεῖν αἴτιόν ἐστι τοῦ μὴ πονεῖν. οὐδὲ γὰρ ὅτι τὸ πονεῖν αἴτιόν ἐστι τοῦ μὴ πονεῖν· οὐδε γὰρ ἂν ὧδέ γ'εὐμαρῶς ἀπέτεκες, εἰ μὴ κύουσα ἐπόνεις ὥσπερ οἱ ἀγωνισταί."[16]

Self-sufficiency is achieved by the mastery of self-control: the ability to renounce one's reputation, fearlessness of death, the ability to be generous in wealth and content in poverty; and the achievement of these qualities makes the wise-person invincible. Paul's hardship list in 1 Corinthians 4:9–13 nicely matches these qualifications: Paul and the apostles are hungry and thirsty, inadequately clothed, abused and homeless, they work with their hands, they are despised, reviled, persecuted, and slandered, but are able to endure all of these hardships because of their appropriate relationship with divine wisdom.

It is critical to note that in the popular philosophers, the achievement of self-sufficiency is more valuable than the specific methodology that characterizes a particular school. As the popular philosophers describe self-sufficiency, they consistently present one person as their exemplar who pre-dates all of their methods, Socrates.[17] So while the moral philosophers may boast in their Cynic, Stoic, or other methodology, what they truly value is the outcome. This is very useful when Paul claims to be made self-sufficient with the help of Christ: the highly valued outcome has been achieved in him through Christ (cf. Phil 4:11–13). He has not followed a Cynic or Stoic methodology (which did not exclude help from the divine), but has been made self-sufficient and he lives a life without care for his reputation, he is unafraid of death, and he lives a selfless life. It is likely that Seneca (4 BCE—65 CE) and others would have commended Paul for his manner of living.[18] They would value Paul's refusal to accept payment for his preaching, admire his ability to suffer for the sake of his teachings, and appreciate the concern and sacrifice that he made for his friends.

The practice of the self-sufficient life does not preclude friendship: Paul, Sophia, and Fortuna could all practice self-control and a renouncement of the excesses of elite life while also practicing friendship. Because the wise-person claimed self-sufficiency, Aristotle notes that there were some

---

16. Crates to Hipparchia 33.1; Malherbe, *Cynic Epistles*, 83.

17. Xen. *Mem.* 1.3.14; Teles, Περὶ αὐταρκείας 5H–20H; Cic. *Off.* 1.90, *Tusc.* 5.10.30; Epict. *Disc.* 4.5.4; and Sen. *Constan.* 8–18. Cf. Diog. Laert. 2.27. The exception to this practice would be the Epicureans, because their sworn enemies—the Stoics and the Academics, see Long, *Stoic Studies*, 9–10; Riley, "Epicurean Criticism," 55–68; Warren, *Epicurus*.

18. I do not agree with Malherbe ("Exhortation in 1 Thessalonians," 249) that Paul's modifications to the methodology would have been shocking to his audience.

people who thought that such a person would not desire friends nor be able to selflessly practice friendship (7.1244b).

> ἀλλὰ μὴν καὶ τότε φανερὸν ἂν εἶναι δόξειεν ὡς οὐ χρήσεως ἕνεκα ὁ φίλος οὐδ' ὠφελείας, ἀλλὰ δι' ἀρετῆς φίλος μόνος. ὅταν γὰρ μηθενὸς ἐνδεεῖς ὦμεν, τότε τοὺς συναπλαυσομένους ζητοῦσι πάντες, καὶ τοὺς εὖ πεισομένους μᾶλλον ἢ τοὺς ποιήσοντας. ἀμείνω δ' ἔχομεν κρίσιν αὐτάρκεις ὄντες ἢ μετ' ἐνδείας, ὅτε μάλιστα τῶν συνζῆν ἀξίων δεόμεθα φίλων.

> But assuredly even his case would seem to show that a friend is not for the sake of utility or benefit but the only real friend is the one loved on account of goodness. For when we are not in need of something, then we seek all people to share our enjoyments, and beneficiaries rather than benefactors; and we can judge them better when we are self-sufficing than when in need, and we most need friends who are worthy of our society.[19]

Aristotle (384–322 BCE) affirms that the self-sufficient person will not seek a friend for utility or society because she is sufficient to herself for these benefits. Such a person is the best equipped to seek out a friend for the sake of goodness alone. Cicero (106–43 BCE) will insist that the good person alone can be a friend, and this good person is self-controlled.[20] The one who needs nothing—the self-sufficient wise-person[21]—is the only one who can pursue friendship selflessly.[22] Another threat to friendship, because of the supposed lack of participation in the giving and receiving of gifts, is the teaching that the wise-person "lacks nothing that he can receive as a gift" (nihil deest quod accipere possit loco muneris).[23]

In his essay *On the Constancy of the Wise-person*, Seneca explains that self-sufficiency is a matter of self-control. Once a person realizes that death is not an injury, Seneca argues, all other pains and injuries are easier to bear: losses and pains, disgrace, changes of abode, bereavements, and separations (8.3). Seneca discusses the possible injuries that can befall a person: losing a long-chased prize like his legacy or the goodwill of a lucrative house (9.2). To support the commonality of his claim, Seneca writes that even Epicurus assents that the wise-person is invincible (15.4–16.1). The wise-person is unafraid of insult (15.5); Socrates is listed as a general example of how a wise-person can endure the insults of comedies that were written that

---

19. Arist. *Eth. Eud.* 7.1244b.15–20 (Rackham, LCL).
20. Cic. *Off.* 1.90.
21. Cic. *Amic.* 65.
22. Cic. *Amic.* 51.
23. Sen. *Constant.* 8.1 (Basore, LCL).

scoffed at him as well as his wife drenching his head with sewage (18.5). Seneca's conclusion concerning the nature of the wise-person is, "But his virtue has placed him in another region of the universe; he has nothing in common with you" ("Non obruetur eorum coetu et qualis singulis, talis universes obsistet").[24]

According to Seneca, the wise-person seeks friends in order to practice friendship. Epicurus taught that the wise-person seeks friends so that, in the words of Seneca, ""that there may be someone to sit beside him when he is ill, to help him when he is in prison or in want," "ut habeat, qui sibi aergo adsideat, succurrat in vincula coniecto vel inopi."[25] Seneca, however, says that the wise-person has friends so that *he* may have someone to care for: someone to sit by when *they* are ill and free from prison when they are in hostile hands (9.7). Furthermore, the one who enters into friendship only to have someone serve them is practicing friendship for the wrong reason (9.8–9). Such a person is most likely a fair-weather (*temporarias populus*) friend. As a self-sufficient person, Seneca seeks a friend so that he may have someone to die for or follow into exile—not someone with whom he wants to strike a bargain (9.10).

It is critical to note that for Paul his philosophically educated readers, self-sufficiency is a rise above fortune (eg, circumstances) that is not threatened by help from the divine.[26] Although it may seem like self-sufficiency is achieved without any aid, Seneca (ca. 4 BCE–65 CE) writes: "The Supreme Good calls for no practical aids from the outside; it is developed at home, and arises entirely within itself. If the good seeks any portion of itself from without, it begins to be subject to the play of Fortune" ("Summum bonum extrinsecus instrumenta non quaerit. Domi colitur, ex se totum est. Incipit fortunae esse subiectum, si quam partem sui foris quaerit").[27] Seneca clarifies himself a bit further:

> Non sunt ad caelum elevande manus nec exorandus aedituus,
> ut nos ad aurem simulacri, quasi magis exaudiri possimus,

---

24. Sen. *Constant.* 8.2 (Basore, LCL).

25. Sen. *Ep.* 9.7 (Gummere, LCL).

26. There are differences between the Stoic pantheism of Seneca and the theology of Paul, especially as outlined by Lightfoot, *Philippians*, 270–328. However, the distinction between an experimental external reality with a personal Deity and following nature as expressed by the divine seems rather artifical, particularly when one must follow the same general methodology. Paul must deny himself in order to follow Christ, who we are told empowers him. Whether or not that is true is altogether a different issue. I cannot imagine Seneca or Epictetus objecting to Paul receiving help from Christ to maintain his self-sufficiency.

27. *Ep.* 9.15 (Gummere, LCL).

Self-Sufficiency in Paul and the Popular Philosophers

> admittat; prope est a te deus, tecum est, intus est. Ita dico, Lucili: sacer intra nos spiritus sedet, malorum bonorumque nostrorum observator et custos. Hic prout a nobis tractatus est, ita nos ipse tractat. Bonus vero vir sine deo nemo est; an potest aliquis supra fortunam nisi ab illo adiutus exurgere?
>
> We do not need to uplift our hands towards heaven, or beg to the keeper of the temple to let us approach the idol's ear, as if in this way our prayers were more likely to be heard. God is near you, he is with you, he is within you. This is what I mean, Lucilius: a holy spirit indwells within us, one who marks our good and bad deeds, and is our guardian. As we treat this spirit, so we are treated by it. Indeed, no man can be good without the help of God. Can anyone rise superior to fortune unless God helps him to rise?[28]

Seneca believes that the wise-person can only achieve self-sufficiency with the help of God. In *Epistle* 41, Seneca says that if we see a person who is fearless in the face of troubles, not following his desires, and happy and peaceful in a storm, he says (Vis isto divina descendit) [A divine power has descended upon that man].

> Animum excellentem, modernatum, omnia tamquam minora transeuntem, quicquid timemus optamusque ridentem, caelestis potentia agitat. Non potest res tanta sine adminiculo numinis stare.
>
> When a soul rises superior to other souls, when it is under control, when it passes through every experience as if it were a small account, when it smiles at our fears and our prayers, it is stirred by a force from heaven. A thing like this cannot stand upright unless it be propped by the divine.[29]

Not only is self-sufficiency attained with the help of the divine, Seneca concludes that the wise-person can only retain the qualities of self-sufficiency with divine help.

It is significant that other schools such as the Pythagoreans[30] and Epicureans[31] did not reject this ideal of self-control and self-sufficiency as it

---

28. *Ep.* 41.1–2 (Gummere, LCL).

29. *Ep.* 41.5 (Gummere, LCL).

30. Allen, *Concept of Woman*, 142–51; De Vogel, *Pythagoras*, 105–6, 111.

31. See especially Epicurus' section on αὐτάρκεια in *Epistula ad Menoeceum* 130–35, text and translation with commentary available in Bailey, *Epicurus*, 83–93. For differences between Zeno and Epicurus with respect to the ideal wise-person, see Waerdt, "Justice of the Epircurean," 404; for common qualities of self-sufficiency in Stoicism

became popular with the Stoics and Cynics. On the contrary, other schools debated with the Stoics as to precisely what self-sufficiency and its method meant for the sage.[32] Therefore, women who were exposed to the popular philosophies, not just Stoicism and Cynicism, could have interacted with the way that Paul expressed himself using his model of self-control and self-sufficiency. The Pythagorean Ecphantus the Crotonian (ca. 400 BCE) wrote that a king and his subjects should imitate God and seek self-sufficiency for the good of the community.[33] Diogenes Laertius (fl. 3rd c. CE) says that Pythagoras contrasted the crown—along with other rewards—with philosophers, who search for truth and not fame.[34] Philosophically educated women also wrote concerning self-sufficiency. From the pseudo-Pythagorean corpus, Perictione (late 4th c. BCE?) writes:

> Τὴν ἁπμονίην γυναῖκα νώσασθαι δεῖ φρονήσιός τε καὶ σωφροσύνης πλείην· κάρτα γὰρ ψυχὴν πεπνῦσθαι δεῖ εἰς ἀρετήν, ὥστ' ἔσται καὶ δικαίη καὶ φρονέουσα καὶ αὐταρκείη καλλυνομένη καὶ κενὴν δόξην μισέουσα. ἐκ τούτων γὰρ ἔργματα καλὰ γίγερται γυναικὶ ἐς αὐτήν τε καὶ ἄνδρα· καὶ τέκεα καὶ οἶκον· πολλάκις δὲ καὶ πόλει, εἴ γε πόλιας ἢ ἔθνεα ἡ τοίη γε κρατύνοι, ὡς ἐπὶ βασιληίης ὀρέομεν.

> It is necessary to consider the harmonious woman full of intelligence and moderation. For it is necessary for a soul to be extremely brave and intelligent and well decorated with self-sufficiency and hating baseless opinion. For from this comes great benefit for a woman, for herself as well as her husband and children and her house, often too for her city, if such a woman rules cities and peoples, as we see in kingdoms.[35]

Epicurus (341–270 BCE) references the rewards of self-control and self-sufficiency, "The wise man when he has accomodated himself to straits knows better how to give than to receive: so great is the treasure of self-sufficiency which he has discovered."[36]

Cicero and Seneca utilized the metaphor of the crown to express their ideals concerning friendship. Cicero used the metaphor of the crown to typify Stoic friendship:

---

and Epicureanism, see Avontis, "Training in Frugality," 215.

32. Sen. *Constan.* 15.4.
33. Ecphantus, *On Kings*.
34. Diog. Laert. 6.
35. Perictione, *On the Harmony of Women* 1 = Stob. 4.25.50. Translation from Plant, *Women Writers*, 76.
36. Epicurus, *Fragmenta*, 44; cf. 34, 45, 70, 77.

Self-Sufficiency in Paul and the Popular Philosophers

> Nec tamen nostrae nobis utilitates omittendae sunt aliisque tradendae, cum his ipsi egeamus, sed suae cuique utilitati, quod sine alterius iniuria fiat, serviendum est. Scite Chrysippus, ut multa, "qui stadium, inquit, currit, eniti et contendere debet quam maxime possit, ut vincat, supplantare eum, quicum certet, aut manu depellere nullo modo debet; sic in vita sibi quemque petere, quod pertineat ad usum, non iniquum est, alteri deripere ius non est."

> And yet we are not required to sacrifice our own interest and surrender to others what we need for ourselves, but each one should consider his own interests, as far as he may without injury to his neighbour's. "When a man enters the footrace," says Chrysippus with his usual aptness, "it is his duty to put forth all his strength and strive with all his might to win; but he ought never with his foot to trip, or with his hand to foul a competitor. Thus in the stadium of life, it is not unfair for anyone to seek to obtain what is needful for his own advantage, but he has no right to wrest it from his neighbour."[37]

Seneca also uses the metaphor of the crown to teach an important aspect of friendship:

> Qui gratus futurus est, statim, dum accipit, de reddendo cogitet. Chrysippus quidem ait illum uelut in certamen cursus conpositum et carceribus inclusum opperiri debere tempus suum, ad quod uelut dato signo prosiliat; et quidem magna illi contentione opus est, magna celeritate, ut consequatur antecedentem.

> The man who intends to be grateful, immediately, while he is receiving, should turn his thought to repaying. Such a man, declares Chrysippus, like a racer, who is all set for the struggle and remains shut up within the barriers, must await the proper moment to leap forth when, as it were, the signal has been given; and, truly, he will need to show great energy, great swiftness, if he is to overtake the other who has the start of him.[38]

In *On Providence*, Seneca explains that the Olympic crown is worth nothing, but the reward of pursuing philosophy is true strength that can withstand any opponent.[39] Plutarch, when discussing why it is proper to have debates at the dinner table, quotes Strato:

---

37. Cic. *Off.* 3.42 (Miller, LCL).
38. Sen. *Ben.* 2.25 (Basore, LCL).
39. Sen. *Prov.* 3.14–14.4.

Reading 1 Corinthians with Philosophically Educated Women

> καὶ Στράτνω ὁ φυσικός, ἀκούσας ὅτι πολλαπλασίους ἔχει Μενέδημος μαθητάς, τί οὖν ἔφη θαυμαστόν, εἰ πλείονές εἰσιν οἱ λούεσθαι τῶν ἀλείφεσθαι βουλομένων;
>
> And Strato, the natural philosopher, when he heard that Menedemus had many more pupils than he himself had, said, "Why be surprised if there are more who wish to bathe than to be anointed for the contest?"[40]

The concept of self-sufficiency was also applied to women by the philosophers. The earliest application of self-sufficiency to women appears in Teles the Cynic. Teles applies the attributes of self-sufficiency to exemplary women who grieved properly for the loss of their sons in battle.[41] Grieving must not be done in excess but self-controlled and tempered by reason. This kind of application is also found in Seneca when he consoles Helvia and Marcia, encouraging them to approach the contests of life strengthened by the principles of Stocism.[42]

In convincing Marcia to cling to Stoic philosophy in her time of loss, Seneca contrasts two female role models: Octavia, who has no self-control, and Livia, who is self-controlled.[43] We see that he applies the qualities of self-sufficiency as the solution to the problem to excessive grieving: the self-control that allows a person to be fearless of death and exile, able to have success in both wealth and poverty, and so on.[44] According to Seneca, by adopting his Stoic mindset, Marcia will be able to grieve the loss of her son in a healthy, natural way.

Similar reasoning is used in Seneca's letter to his mother. He applies the qualities of self-sufficiency to himself and then advises his mother to adopt the same philosophy.[45] He exempts her from common vices of sexual immorality and encourages her to follow the example of Cornelia and Rustilia, who bore similar loss with his (moderate) Stoic resolve.[46] He reminds his mother that she never participated in several vices and therefore could not

---

40. Plut. *Mor.* 472e (Helmbold, LCL).

41. Teles 57H–60H. Teles does not name the women but contrasts nameless women from Attica, Laconia, and Sparta who all reacted differently to the loss of their sons. It is almost certainly rhetoric against women in Attica who have not lived up, at least in his eyes, to the legendary women of Laconia and Sparta. It is nevertheless intriguing that women are examples of how the philosopher should grieve.

42. Manning, "Consolatory Tradition," 71–81.

43. Sen. *Marc.* 2.2–4.

44. Sen. *Marc.* 9.1–10.5.

45. Sen. *Helv.* 5.2–6.1; 10.3.

46. Sen. *Helv.* 16.6–7.

blame excessive grief on her feminine weakness.⁴⁷ Instead, Helvia should take refuge in philosophy.

> Itaque illo te duco, quo omnibus, qui fortunam fugiunt, confugiendum est, ad liberalia studia. Illa sanabunt vulnus tuum, illa omnem tristitiam tibi evellent. His etiam si numquam adsuesses, nunc utendum erat; sed quantum tibi patris mei antiquus rigor premisit, omnes bonas artes non quidem comprendisti, attigisti tamen.
>
> And so I guide you to that in which all who fly from Fortune must take refuge—to philosophic studies. They will heal your wound; they will uproot your sadness. Even if you had not been acquainted with them before, you would need to use them now; but so far as the old-fashioned strictness of my father permitted you, though you have not indeed fully grasped all the liberal arts, still you had some dealings with them.⁴⁸

Like Seneca, Musonius Rufus teaches that women should learn Stoic philosophy and apply it to their lives. While he does not envision roles for women aside from their roles as wives and mothers, he invites women to enter the struggle of the self-controlled life:

> εἶτα δὲ ἐμποιητέον αἰδῶ πρὸς ἅπαν αἰσχρόν· ὧν ἐγγενομένων ἀνάγκη σώφρονας εἶναι καὶ ἄνδρα καὶ γυναῖκα. καὶ μὴν τὸν παιδευόμενον ὀρθῶς, ὅστις ἂν ᾖ, εἴτε ἄρρην εἴτε θήλεια, ἐθιστέον μὲν ἀνέχεσθαι πόνου, ἐθιστέον δὲ μὴ φοβεῖσθαι θάνατον, ἐθιστέον δὲ μὴ ταπεινοῦσθαι πρὸς συμφορὰν μηδεμίαν· δι' ὅσων ἄν τις εἴη ἀνδρεῖος.
>
> When these two qualities have been created within them, man and woman are of necessity self-controlled. And most of all, the child who is trained properly, whether boy or girl, must be accustomed to endure hardship, not to fear death, not to be disheartened in the face of any misfortune; he must in short be accustomed to every situation which calls for courage.⁴⁹

Musonius concludes that women can draw great benefits from philosophy (ἀλλ' ὅτι ἤθους χρηστότητα καὶ καλοκἀγαθίαν τρόπου κτητέον ταῖς

---

47. Sen. *Helv.* 16.1–5.

48. Sen. *Helv.* 27.3–4 (Basore, LCL). Seneca goes on to say that if his father had been thorough in educating his mother, that she would have been fully equipped to handle anything in life. His father withheld a complete education from her because he thought some women learned only so they could impress others and not to enrich their lives. Cf. Juv. *Sat.* 6.242.

49. Muson. 4.79–82 (Lutz, 48–49).

Reading 1 Corinthians with Philosophically Educated Women

γυναιξίν· ἐπειδὴ καὶ φιλοσοφία καλοκἀγαθίας ἐστὶν ἐπιτήδευσις καὶ οὐδὲν ἕτερον) [I only urge that they [women] should acquire from philosophy goodness in conduct and nobility of character. Now in very truth philosophy is training in nobility of character and nothing else]. [50]

In this section, we have seen that in the popular philosophers, self-sufficiency is highly valued: it is often the defining characteristic of the wise-person. There are several critical parallels to the type of self-sufficiency that Paul practices: the method is self-control in all circumstances in life, the self-sufficient person can practice friendship, and it is achieved and maintained with help from the divine. Paul attributes these qualities to himself throughout 1 Corinthians, but in 1 Corinthians 9:24–27, he utilizes the *agon* motif to compare his struggle for self-control to the successful athlete. Because he has mastered self-control, he has achieved the ideal that is valued by many other teachers: self-sufficiency. An examination of the philosophical traditions of *agon* motif will further explain the importance of its appearance in 1 Corinthians 9:24–27 and how philosophically educated women would read this passage.

Philosophical Traditions of the Agon Motif

According to Plato, Socrates likens the thoughtful life to a contest (agon) (παρακαλῶ δὲ καὶ τοὺς ἄλλους πάντας ἀνθρώπους, καθ' ὅσον δύναμαι, καὶ δὴ καὶ σὲ ἀντιπαρακαλῶ ἐπὶ τοῦτον τὸν βίον καὶ τὸν ἀγῶνα τοῦτον, ὃν ἐγώ φημι ἀντὶ πάντων τῶν ἐνθάδε ἀγώνων εἶναι) [And I invite all other men likewise, to the best of my power, to this life and this contest, which I say is worth all other contests on this earth].[51] This life, of course, is the struggle to train oneself in virtue. According to Plutarch, Epicurus taught that people should strive for the crown of ἀταραξια (impassiveness).[52] Lucretius reflects his struggle to be an Epicurean poet:

> tu mihi supremae praescripta ad candida callis
> currenti spatium praemonstra, callida musa
> Calliope, requies hominum divomque voluptas,
> te duce ut insigni capiam cum laude coronam.
>
> As I race toward the white line that marks the end of my course, do you, clever Muse Calliope, repose of human beings and

---

50. Muson. 4.98–100 (Lutz, 49).
51. Pl. *Grg.* 526d (Lamb, LCL).
52. Plut. *Mor.* 1125c.

delight of the gods, point out the track to me, and under your guidance I may win the garland of victory with glorious praise.[53]

The reward for the athlete who undergoes hardship and gains the victor's crown is often contrasted with the philosopher and student who discipline themselves for a more beneficial reward. Seneca the Younger, Musonius Rufus, and Epictetus represent first-century Stoic philosophers who followed this ancient tradition. Seneca writes that athletes punish their bodies only to receive a crown, but the Stoic who punishes it for philosophy receives everlasting peace.

> Athletae quantum plagarum ore, quantum toto corpore excipiunt! ferunt tamen omne tormentum gloriae cupiditate nec tantum quia pugnant ista patiuntur, sed ut pugnent: exercitatio ipsa tormentum est. Nos quoque evincamus omnia, quorum praemium non corona nec palma est nec tubicen praedicationi nominis nostri silentium faciens, sed virtus et firmitas animi et pax in ceterum parta, si semel in aliquo certamine debellata fortuna est.

> What blows do athletes receive on their faces and all over their bodies! Nevertheless, through their desire for fame they endure every torture, and they undergo these things not only because they are fighting but in order to be able to fight. Their very training means torture. So let us also win the way to victory in all our struggles,—for the reward is not a garland or a palm or a trumpeter who calls for silence at the proclamation of our names, but rather virtue, steadfastness of soul, and a peace that is won for all time, if fortune has once been utterly vanquished in any combat.[54]

In his description of the Stoic wise-person in his essay *On Firmness*, Seneca again utilizes the *agon* motif. Because the wise-person practices the self-control in virtue like an athlete, the wise-person is seeking to be free from the vanity that would cause distress over misfortune:

> Nam si tangit illum iniuria, et mouet et inpellit; caret autem ira sapiens, quam excitat iniuriae species, nec aliter careret ira nisi et iniuria, quam scit sibi non posse fieri. Inde tam erectus laetusque est, inde continuo gaudio elatus; adeo autem ad offensiones rerum hominumque non contrahitur ut ipsa illi iniuria usui sit, per quam experimentum sui capit et uirtutem temptat.

---

53. Lucretius 6.94 (Smith, *Lucretius*, 91).
54. Sen. *Ep.* 78.16 (Gummere, LCL).

Reading 1 Corinthians with Philosophically Educated Women

> Our aim is not that you may be prevented from doing injury, but that the wise man may cast all injuries far from him, and by his endurance and his greatness of soul protect himself from them. Just so in the sacred games many have won the victory by wearing out the hands of their assailants through stubborn endurance.[55]

Musonius Rufus (fl. 1st c. CE) laments that some athletes risk their lives in contest but do not train their bodies and minds in philosophy.[56] Epictetus (55–135 CE), a student of Musonius Rufus, is also fond of the metaphor.[57]

In light of the evidence presented above, Sophia and Fortuna were well positioned to interact with an idea as basic as self-control—the point of the athletic metaphor in 1 Corinthians 9:24–27—and determine for themselves how Paul adopts, modifies, or challenges the precise view that they hold. The metaphor may call to mind specific challenges which were relative to their lives: the loss of friends and family, the embarrassment of lawsuits, or whether to continue to support Paul's ministry. The question arises, then, how would Sophia and Fortuna interact Paul's usage of this popular motif?

Sophia and the Philosophical Tradition

The most important concept to glean from popular philosophy is that the outcome of self-sufficiency is more important than the method. However, the self-control of a champion athlete in training is a good metaphor for the self-discipline that achieves and characterizes self-sufficiency. Self-sufficiency is not only the defining characteristic of the wise-person, it prepares someone to be a selfless friend and patron. Sophia or Fortuna would not need to isolate themselves from the community both in personal fellowship and patronage because they valued or attempted to achieve a sort of self-sufficiency.

Self-sufficiency is also not prohibitive of participation in the divine nature of Paul's wisdom. Sophia can embrace both the qualities of the self-controlled wise-person without being overly concentrated on herself that she cannot attribute some credit to God for helping her attain wisdom. As such, she can accept Paul's claim to the attainment of the qualities of the Stoic wise-person because of his calling as an apostle. It naturally follows that if Paul has a unique relationship with the divine, he has a unique relationship with divine wisdom, which produces an outstanding result: the realization

---

55. Sen. *Constant.* 10.1 (Basore, LCL).
56. Cf. Valantasis, "Roman Asceticism," 553; Garland, *1 Corinthians*, 445.
57. Epict. *Disc.* 3.22.57; 3.26.31; 4.10.10.

of self-sufficiency. However, it would be difficult for any patroness to read about Paul's independence from patronage. It certainly appears that Paul is utterly ungrateful for any support that Sophia might give or want to give him for his valued services.

Fortuna and the Philosophical Tradition

Fortuna's frustration with Paul is further aggravated by his outright claim to something that he intimated before: the realization of the qualities of the ideal wise-person. And at this point it's a double insult: Paul appears to show no appreciation for her sustained support for himself or the church. Paul declares in 1 Corinthians 9:2-6 that as apostles, he and his associates have the right to food and drink without working for a living. Despite this basic right (continued with many examples in 1 Cor 9:6-18)—not unlike any other client who would attach him/herself to a household—Paul and his associates instead choose the high road and reject personal support from wealthier members of the Corinthian community. In fact, Paul claims that he is not writing to secure such support (1 Cor 9:15). Quite the contrary: he associates his Gospel with his independence from personal patronage, and he is bound to preach the Gospel (1 Cor 9:16). Instead, Paul's reward is not in the support of patronesses but in boasting that he preaches the Gospel both free of charge and free from undue influence from an outside source.

Reading 1 Corinthians in this light—from the perspective of Fortuna, a distanced philosophically educated woman—it may seem as if Paul is sharing with the struggles of the poor instead of enjoying the gifts of the wealthy. Paul writes that he became a servant of everyone: those outside the law, the Jews, and the weak, and everyone else (1 Cor 9:19-22) except for people like Fortuna who could provide support (the strong). And he makes this sacrifice for the Gospel so that he can share with them its blessings (1 Cor 9:23). The sharing in the blessings of the Gospel with everyone but the strong (1 Cor 9:19-22) can be contrasted with Paul's metaphor of the wealthy Corinthians as kings so that he can rule with them (1 Cor 4:8). If Paul cannot personally appreciate her support, Fortuna finds no motivation to continue supporting the church according to *his* interests.

Paul then has opportunity to withstand all of the sufferings due to poor patronal support that he claims to have willingly refused. He then gives the means by which he endures every trial: he "runs" like the champion who wins the race, seeking the imperishable rather than the perishable crown. Fortuna can appreciate that Paul encourages the community to practice self-control. If the more serious offenses of the

Christian community (or even rumors of it) were made known to Fortuna's friends, she could suffer some embarrassment. These offenses would include strange sexual practices, mysterious and rowdy religious practices, and lawsuits between group members. Fortuna is relieved to hear that a philosophical discipline of self-control is being taught by Paul as a noble act, earning the self-controlled person an imperishable crown. The problem is, Paul is claiming to realize this ideal.

The Agon Motif and Female Athletes in the Greek East

In the epigraphic evidence, victories of female athletes and the terminology of the "crown" that they contain is important evidence that wealthier women like Paul's patronesses could relate to Paul's athletic metaphors. From the earliest pan-Hellenic games, women participated as competitors, and the imperial period saw women as patrons and presidents of the games as well. Pausanius says that there was a hero shrine to Cynisca along with several others in Laconia, and that she bred the horses that led her to victory.[58] Also in Olympia there was a crown, bronze horses, a statue made by Apelles, and the epigram by an unknown poet to celebrate her victories.[59]

> Σπάρτας μὲν βασιλῆες ἐμοὶ πατέρες καὶ ἀδελφοί. ἅρμασι δ'ὠκυπόδων ἵππων νικῶσα Κυνίσκα εἰκόνα τάνδ' ἔστησα. μόναν δέ με φαμὶ γυναικῶν Ἑλλάδος ἐκ πάσας τόνδε λαβεῖν στέφανον.
>
> Kings of Sparta were my fathers and bothers, and I, Cynisca[60], winning the race with my chariot of swift-footed horses,[61] erected this statue. I assert that I am the only woman in all Greece who won this crown.[62]

---

58. Paus. 3.15.1.

59. Paus. 5.12.5; cf. 6.1.6.

60. Cynisca is mentioned by Xen. *Ages.* 9.6 and Paus. 3.8.1, 15.1; 5.12.5; 6.1.6. The name Cynisca, "little hound," may be a nickname for a tomboyish woman. Sarah Pomeroy suggests that Cyniska may have been as old as 50 when she won the race, in *Spartan Women*, 21. For studies on the unique position of women in Sparta, see Scanlon, "Virgineum Gymnasium," 185–216; Kunstler, "Family Dynamics," 31–48; Mosse, "Women in the Spartan Revolutions," 138–53; Foley and Fantham, *Women in the Classical World*, 56–67.

61. Cf, Ath. 13.567e-f.

62. *Anth. Pal.* 13.16 (Paton, LCL). Juvenal shows more than a little contempt for female athletes—and women in general—in *Satire* 6.242. There has been some attempt to free Juvenal from misogyny by Braund, "Juvenal," 71–86.

Self-Sufficiency in Paul and the Popular Philosophers

Pausanius identifies Cynisca as the daughter of king Archidamas and her epigram as one of only two poems that celebrate royal Spartans.[63] Xenophon and Plutarch attribute Cynisca's victory to the influence of her powerful family, while Pausanius seems to indicate that she won on her own merit.[64] The victory of Cynisca belongs to the games of old,[65] whereas the inscription found at Delphi honoring three other female victors in the Isthmain games—Tryphosa, Hedea, and Dionysia—belongs to Paul's day.[66]

> Ἑρμησιάναξ Διονυσίου Καισαρεύς Τραλ[λιαν]ὸς ὁ καὶ Κο[ρίνθιος] τὰς ἑαυτοῦ θυγατέτας ἐχούσας καὶ α[ὐτ]ὰς τὰς αὐτὰς πο[λειτείας.] Τρυφῶσαν νεικήσασαν Πύθια ἐπὶ ἀγωνοθετῶν Ἀντιγόνου καὶ Κλεομαχίδα· καὶ Ἴσθμια ἐπὶ ἀγωνοθέτου Ἰουβεντίου Πρόκλου· στάδιον κατὰ τὸ ἑξῆς πρώτη παρθένων. Ἡδέαν νεικήσασαν. Ἴσθμια ἐπὶ ἀγωνοθέτου Κορνηλίου Πούλχρου ἐνόπλιον ἅρματι, καὶ Νέμεα στάδιον ἐπὶ ἀγωνοθέτου Ἀντιγόνου, καὶ ἐν Σικυῶνι ἐπὶ ἀγωνοθέτου Μενοίτα· ἐνείκα δὲ καὶ παῖδας κιθαρῳδοὺς Ἀθήνησι Σεβάστεια ἐπὶ ἀγωνοθέτου Νουίου τοῦ Φιλείνο<υ>· πρώ[τη ἀπ'αἰῶ]νος ἐγένετο πολεῖ[τις... πρώ(τη) παρθένος. Διονυσίαν νεικ[ήσασαν...] ἐπὶ ἀγωνοθέτου Ἀν[τιγ]ό[νου]· καὶ Ἀσκλάπεια ἐν Ἐπιδαύρῳ τῇ ἱερᾷ ἐπὶ ἀγων[ο]θέτου Νεικοτέλου στάδι[ον]. Ἀπόλλωνι Πυθίῳ.

Hermesianax, son of Dionysius, of Caesarea in Tralles and of Corinth, for his daughters, who also have the same citizenships. Tryphosa each time was first in the girls' single-course race at the Pythian Games with Antigonus and Cleomachus as judges, and at the Isthmian Games with Juventius Proculus as president. Hedea won the race in armor and the chariot race at the Isthmian Games with Cornelius Pulcher as judge; she won the single-course race at the Nemean Games with Antigonus as president, likewise in Sicyon with Menoites as president. She also won the children's lyre contest at the Augustan games in

---

63. Paus. 3.8.1.

64. Xen. *Ages.* 9.6; Plut. *Ages.* 20.1.

65. Paus. in 5.16.1 writes that the women competed with the right breast exposed, which archaeological finds compliment. The well-known statue of a running Spartan woman belonging to Cynisca's era (about 520 BCE) fits this description; cf. Swaddling, *Ancient Olympic Games*, 42–43. The tradition of women competing with the right breast exposed is also preserved in the mosaics in Piazza Armerina, Villa del Casale (4th c. CE). Photographs of the mosaics are available online in McManus, "Index of Images, Part III." It is interesting that women of a later time period are shown crowing one another and themselves, and one female giving a crown has her right breast exposed.

66. Kajava, "Isthmian Games," 168–78.

Athens with Nuvius son of Philinus as president. She was first in her age group ... Dionysia won ... the single-course race at the Asclepian Games at the sanctuary of Epidaurus with Nicoteles as president. To the Pythian Apollo.[67]

Female athletes such as these were not the only women crowned at the games; the Greeks were fond of crowning their poets and musicians at their agonistic festivals.[68] In Delphi in 86 BCE, the Theban harpist Polygonta was crowned and awarded several other honors for her services to the city.[69] I do not know of a poetess receiving a crown in the festivals, but there are certainly some famous Greek poetesses who would have been candidates.[70] As we have seen above, Greek women poets were widely read in the first century: Sappho, Nossis, and Erinna. Sulpicia, mentioned in Martial, *Epigrams* 10.35 is an example of a first-century Roman poet. In first-century Ephesus, the priestess Claudia Trophime dedicated some lines to Hestia in a prominently placed inscription.[71]

Paul's usage of the metaphor of the crown is not strictly limited to athletic imagery, but is connected simultaneously to patronage and the concept of the ideal wise-person or teacher in popular philosophies. The games themselves in the imperial period were inextricably tied to patronage: patrons and patronesses were needed to provide oil, maintain the facilities, and preside over the games.[72] Both the male and female athletes competed for perishable crowns of *withered* celery (more precisely, *already perished*),[73] but patronesses of the Greek East competed with one another for the imperishable crown of the reciprocated honor due them upon the completion of their liturgies.

Many women in the Greek East received honors for their patronage. Phyle of Priene tells us in her inscription that she is first female *stephanephorus* of her city, an office that allows the wearing of the crown while the person is in service.[74] This office was bestowed on other generous patronesses

---

67. Pleket, *Epigraphica*, 9. Translation by Lewis and Reinhold, *Roman Civilization*, 2:368. Alternative translation in Lefkowitz and Fant, *Women's Life*, 206.

68. Irene Ringwood Arnold discusses the importance of poetry in the games of the imperial period, "Agonistic Festivals," 248.

69. Pleket, *Epigraphica*, 6.

70. Barnard, "Hellenistic Women Poets," 204–13.

71. *Inscr. Eph.* 1062. Translation available in Mary Lefkowitz and Fant, *Women's Life*, 9.

72. The bond of the games with patronage is quite obvious with the infamous victories of Nero at the games; see Suet. *Ner.*12.3; 22.3.

73. Oscar Broneer, "Crown," 260; cf. Broneer, "Apostle Paul," 1–31.

74. Pleket, *Epigraphica*, 5.

and their husbands.⁷⁵ We saw above that the honorary inscriptions to Junia Theodora in Corinth, an illustrious patron living in Paul's day, indicates that she received a golden crown and a portrait for her apotheosis in return for her services to several cities in the Lycian League.

The significance of wearing a crown is the designation of leadership; the one who wears it is the pattern which others are encouraged to follow. In the fourth inscription to Junia Theodora, her heir is said to mimic her excellent qualities. "Σέκτον Ἰούλιον Ῥωμαῖον ἄνδρα ἀγαθὸν ὄντα καὶ τῇ ὑπερβαλλούσῃ εὐνοίᾳ κρατέ οντα καὶ σπουδῇ πρὸς τὸ ἔνθος ἡμῶν στοιχοῦτα τῇ ἄνωθεν Ἰουωίας πρὸς εὐνοί," "Sextus Iulius, a Roman, a good man also behaving with surpassing goodwill and zeal towards our nation, imitating the devotion of Junia towards us which was mentioned above."⁷⁶ The verb στοιχέω, which usually is used in the sense of "falling in line," certainly also calls to mind a student following a teacher. It does not appear in its verbal form in many important philosophical writings (such as Plato, Aristotle, Xenophon—who does use it twice outside of a philosophical context—Epictetus) or poets (Homer, Hesiod, Euripides, Pindar). However, it does appear in the context of philosophy by the time of Musonius Rufus,⁷⁷ the first-century Roman Stoic who advocated teaching philosophy to women. We also see it in Sextus Empiricus, "ἐν φιλοσοφίᾳ μὲν τῇ τῶν φιλοσόφων στοιζχήσομεν," "in philosophy we will follow the philosophers."⁷⁸ It is used in the New Testament five times as a synonym for the often used περιπατέω, which appears 95 times.⁷⁹ In Romans 4:12, Paul uses στοιχέω to refer to following Abraham, and in Galatians 5:25, it refers to the Holy Spirit. In Philippians 3:17, Paul uses it to prepare for the audience's imitation of himself. Paul uses the popular *agon* motif both to bolster his claims of apostleship—he has realized the self-sufficiency of the wise-person—and to encourage his audience to imitate his success.

Reading 1 Corinthians 9:24–27 with Sophia

Paul begins his usage of the *agon* motif by encouraging his audience to run as if they were the only one who would win the race: the only one in the race who will receive a crown. If Paul has in mind that the outcome of such

---

75. For a detailed discussion, see van Bremen, *Limits of Participation*, 31.

76. Lines 54–56. Text and translation from Kearsley, "Women in Public," 206.

77. Musonius Rufus, with reference to following the words of Socrates, *Dissertationum a Lucio digestarum reliquiae*, 18b, line 48; cf. 8 line 5; *Fragmenta minora* 42.5.

78. Sext. Emp. *Math.* 11.59 (Bury, LCL).

79. *TDNT* 7:667.

Reading 1 Corinthians with Philosophically Educated Women

discipline would result in self-sufficiency without following a philosophical method, this statement is an affront to the philosophical schools. However, since self-discipline is the method and self-sufficiency is the goal, Paul's admonition for the community to practice self-discipline would be familiar and welcome to both Sophia and Fortuna. As patronesses who supported the churches and Paul himself, they may well have previously competed in the Isthmian games as children and were competing for honors and crowns as adult patronesses. As such, both Fortuna and Sophia could certainly understand in a very intimate way the contrast between struggling for a perishable and imperishable crown.

Part of growing up in a wealthy family in first-century Corinth included participation in the Isthmian games. One aspect of the games included the races that won a perishable crown of celery. Another important aspect of participation was patronage of the games that could help the patroness earn an imperishable golden crown in gradituse of her gifts. Before she met Paul, Sophia could participate in philosophical learning and support that and her other interests, enjoying reciprocating patronal relationships with these persons and groups according to her interests. Now, in Paul's usage of the *agon* motif, Sophia again sees Paul's claim to have realized the distinction of an ideal self-controlled philosopher. His language of the crown may have reminded her of her competitions in the Isthmian games as a little girl, and certainly of the competitive nature of patronage: the race to give the best benefactions to the people of Corinth. Sophia could understand in a very intimate way the contrast between struggling for a perishable and imperishable crown.

Reading 1 Corinthians 9:24–27 with Fortuna

Paul then applies the *agon* motif to himself (1 Cor 9:26–27): his work is not aimless because he disciplines his body so he will not be disqualified and win the race. It seems that as he presents himself in contrast to his audience, Paul has actually achieved the level of self-discipline that he needs to qualify for the race and only needs to persevere. This is where Sophia and Fortuna part company. As a sympathetic reader, Sophia is not disturbed by Paul claiming the qualities of the wise-person without devoting himself to a particular school. Fortuna, however, remains unconvinced that Paul's apostleship escorts him to the most desired outcome of moral philosophy: to be a wise-person like Socrates, a person who is in complete control of their passions and able to withstand any challenge or hardship with magnanimity.

In light of Paul's apparent lack of concern for personal patronage, perhaps Fortuna can read Paul as contrasting his reward (imperishable reward from God) and her reward (the reciprocation of her patronage). In this regard, Paul's writing is very divisive. Paul's opponents are at least thankful for Fortuna's benefactions: she allows them to meet in her home, provides food for the meetings, and risks her relationships with outsiders who may suspect her of supporting a foreign religion. Fortuna's two major problems with Paul: his repeated claims concerning wisdom and the ideal wise-person and his ingraditude are more than enough to completely alienate Fortuna.

Conclusion: Reading the Agon Motif with Sophia and Fortuna

Sophia and Fortuna approach Paul's usage of the *agon* motif with more than enough philosophical education and life experience to be able to interact with what Paul is trying to communicate. They knew what it meant to train for athletic competitions, and the meanings of self-sufficiency in different schools from participation in philosophical debates, and can appreciate the rewards of both endeavors. Furthermore, both Sophia and Fortuna could receive a crown because of their patronage to the city, whether it is the temporary crown of the *stephanephorus* or the permanent golden crown for her *apotheosis*. Paul's plea for the church to practice self-control is appreciated by Sophia, but Fortuna cannot overcome Paul's claim to have actually achieved the ideal quality of the wise-person without following any philosophical method.

8

Summary of Conclusions

I HAVE RECONSTRUCTED a reading of selected passages of 1 Corinthians with philosophically educated women: 1 Corinthians 1–4 with an emphasis on patronage, Paul's regulations concerning marriage and divorce in 1 Corinthians 7, and finally the *agon* motif in 1 Corinthians 9. This project is situated in Pauline studies that examine his many Hellenistic contexts that include his relationship to expressions used in other ancient writings (parallels), the ancient rhetorical and epistolary theorists, and especially popular moral philosophy. The popular schools included in this argument are (neo-)Pythagoreanism, Cynicism, Epicureanism, Stoicism, and Middle Platonism, and all of these schools have a substantial history of including women. Furthermore, all of these schools had some connection with Corinth.

In reconstructing the philosophically educated women, I have discussed other areas of ancient intellectual life that women contributed to: poetry, medicine, music, and oratory. In the other areas of intellectual life as well as in philosophy, women learned their art as a member of or someone connected to a wealthy household. Therefore, I chose to reconstruct a philosophically educated woman who was a wealthy widow who was in control of her own property and who could more easily participate in intellectual life.

A wealthy widow would naturally serve as a patroness of the church, so I reviewed patronage in Corinth and argued that because the women honored for patronage in the ancient world were more wealthy and powerful than their male counterparts, there is much at stake for Paul in the presentation of himself and his arguments. After a review of patronage in

Summary of Conclusions

Corinth, I examined the nature of the patronal relationship between the poet Horace and his patron Maecenas. I argued that as the poet's inspiration gives him the ability to criticize his patron and patronage, Paul's calling as apostle gives him similar privileges. This dynamic prepares us for Paul's apparent refusal to participate in personal patronage in 1 Corinthians 9. We should not imagine that wealthier members of the community would be unwilling to support him or the church because of Paul's attitude—provided that at some point he appeals to their sympathies (need for praise or other reciprocation). So after foregrounding Sophia and Fortuna within the historical traditions of philosophically educated women and in their social status as wealthy women I move on to address how they would read 1 Corinthians.

Reading 1 Corinthians with Sophia and Fortuna

I chose to read 1 Corinthians with two reconstructions of philosophically educated women: Sophia and Fortuna. Both of these women are wealthy widows and patronesses of the church, so there is much to gain or lose if Paul manages to balance his teachings with their philosophical sympathies. Sophia and Fortuna both have a broad philosophical education in the popular schools and are of the same social status. The difference between the two women is that Sophia reads 1 Corinthians with a perspective that is sympathetic to Paul's argument. Fortuna, however, upon reading 1 Corinthians 1–4, becomes unsympathetic to Paul's argument and is increasingly distanced and frustrated as Paul develops his presentation of himself in contrast to his opponents. Sophia identifies herself as a follower of a divine wisdom like Paul, and is able to listen to what he has to say in the rest of the epistle. While Sophia is the more sympathetic reader, she is still confused with some of Paul's teachings and mildly annoyed at times. Similarly, Fortuna is consistently frustrated by Paul, beginning with his distinction between human and divine wisdom which culminates in his characterization of himself as a wise-person without using a method from any philosophical school.

Some of Paul's teachings are read similarly by both Sophia and Fortuna. A large portion of 1 Corinthians is dedicated to moral teachings such as lawsuits, dietary issues, usage of prostitutes, and regulations concerning marriage and divorce. Sophia and Fortuna would be equally confused that Paul prohibits divorce and remarriage, which was typically essential to the security of wealth and status. Both women can value Paul's emphasis on self-control. Furthermore, Sophia and Fortuna may have issue with Paul's method or be confused by the uselessness of prohibiting the use of prostitutes (1 Cor 6:12–16) and divorce/remarriage (1 Cor 7:1–40), if the community can be united and reasonably moral, it would reflect well on its patronesses if their friends have a high moral standard.

Sophia is able to connect with precisely the concept that seals Fortuna's alienation from him, his claim to the actualization of self-sufficiency. This self-sufficiency is best expressed in Paul's usage of the *agon* motif in 1 Corinthians 9:24–27. I explored two perspectives that could impact Sophia and Fortuna's reading of the *agon* motif: their philosophical education concerning self-control, and their familiarity with the games. I argued that in popular philosophy, self-control is the common method to achieve self-sufficiency, and the struggle to attain this virtue is often compared to the athlete's effort to win the crown, the *agon* motif. While the *agon* motif is rarely applied directly to women, self-control and self-sufficiency are quite commonly attributed to women, so Sophia and Fortuna are well prepared to read 1 Cor 9:24–27. Another context that prepares Sophia and Fortuna to read the *agon* motif is their proximity to the Isthmian games and their involvement in patronage: two fields in which these women competed for crowns. These women knew what it meant to struggle for material and philosophical rewards, and Paul's claim to the mastery of self-control is either laudable or offensively arrogant. Despite both of their frustrations with Paul, Sophia and Fortuna both continue to support the church because of their ongoing commitment to the community.

Suggestions for Further Research

This project calls for further studies because of its many limitations due to its scope and methods. I read portions of 1 Corinthians with two constructions of philosophically educated women: Sophia and Fortuna. Both were wealthy widows who were patronesses of the church, and the nature of their philosophical education is broad. These two constructs cannot possibly represent the depth of the histories of women in philosophy. There were women in the ancient world, perhaps even in Corinth, who were committed to one philosophical school and were hostile to all other schools of thought. There were also women of lower status who had access to philosophical teachings, namely the wives and children of Cynics who idealized the life of poverty, other wandering philosophers, and those women somehow connected to tutors in wealthy households. From these variables, there are many different ways to read 1 Corinthians—there are five popular schools and even more social settings—and from these choices we can construct many different philosophically educated women and even more readings.

Summary of Conclusions

The other limitation is the text. I did not examine all of the philosophical parallels in 1 Corinthians, but I did choose issues that are most common in the histories of women in philosophy. So 1 Corinthians can be examined more broadly and read in total by Sophia and Fortuna and other philosophically educated women. Of course, 1 Corinthians is not the only Pauline epistle that has important passages that would attract the attention of philosophically educated women. By the same token, the philosophical texts written by and attributed to women can be examined thoroughly for important issues that are unique to a single text rather than concepts related to the balance of the sources. There is much to explore related to the question: how would philosophically educated women read Paul?

Works Cited

BIBLIOGRAPHIC RESOURCES AND SOURCEBOOKS

Berry, Paul. *Correspondence between Paul and Seneca*. Ancient Near Eastern Texts and Studies 12. Lewiston, NY: Edwin Mellen, 1999.

Cribiore, Raffaella. *Writing, Teachers, and Students in Graeco-Roman Egypt*. Atlanta: Scholars, 1996.

Epicurus. *The Epicurus Reader: Selected Writings and Testimonia*. Translated and edited by Brad Inwood and L. P. Gerson. Indianapolis: Hackett, 1994.

Gallo, I. *Una nuova biografia di Pindaro (P. Oxy. 2438)*. Salerno, Italy: Di Giacomo, 1968.

Grubbs, Judith Evans. *Women and the Law in the Roman Empire: A Sourcebook on Marriage, Divorce, and Widowhood*. New York: Routledge, 2002.

Hutchings, Noël, and William D. Rumsey, editors. *The Collaborative Bibliography of Women in Philosophy*. Bowling Green, Ohio: Philosophy Documentation Center, 1997.

Kersey, Ethel M. *Women Philosophers: A Bio-Critical Source Book*. New York: Greenwood, 1989.

Kloppenborg, John S., and Richard Ascough. *Greco-Roman Associations: Texts, Translations, and Commentary: I Attica, Central Greece, Macedonia, Thrace*. Berlin: de Gruyter, 2011.

Lefkowitz, Mary R., and Maureen B. Fant. *Women's Life in Greece and Rome: A Sourcebook in Translation*. Baltimore: Johns Hopkins University Press, 2005.

Lewis, Naphthali, and Meyer Reinhold, editors. *Roman Civilization*. 3rd ed. Vol. 2, *The Empire*. New York: Columbia University Press, 1990.

Lindemann, Kate. *Women Philosophers Web Site*. Online: http://www.women-philosophers.com.

Llewelyn, S. R., editor. *New Documents Illustrating Early Christianity*. 9 vols. North Ryde, Australia: Ancient History Documentary Research Center, Macquarie University, 1981–.

Malherbe, Abraham. *Ancient Epistolary Theorists*. Atlanta: Scholars, 1988.

———. *The Cynic Epistles*. Missoula, MT: Scholars, 1977.

Works Cited

———. *Moral Exhortation: A Greco-Roman Sourcebook*. Philadelphia: Westminster, 1986.
Monroe, Paul. *Source Book of the History of Education for the Greek and Roman Period* New York: Macmillan, 1932.
Plant, I. M. *Women Writers of Ancient Greece and Rome: An Anthology*. Norman: University of Oklahoma Press, 2004.
Pleket, H. W., editor. *Epigraphica II: Texts on the Social History of the Greek World*. Leiden: Brill, 1964.
Samama, Evelyne. *Les médecins dans le monde grec: Sources épigraphiques sur la naissance d'un corps médical*. Geneva: Librairie Droz, 2003.
Smith, Jay E. "The New Perspective on Paul: A Select and Annotated Bibliography." *Criswell Theological Review* 2 (2005) 91–111.
Snyder, Jane McIntosh. *The Woman and the Lyre: Women Writers in Classical Greece and Rome*. Edwardsville: Southern Illinois University Press, 1989.
Swanson, Dennis M. "Bibliography of Works on the New Perspective on Paul." *Master's Seminary Journal* 16 (2005) 317–24.
Vogliano, A. *Epicuri et Epicureorum scripta in Herculanensibus papyris servata*. Berlin: Weidmann, 1928.
Watson, Duane. *The Rhetoric of the New Testament: A Bibliographic Survey*. Blandford Forum, UK: Deo, 2006.
———. "Rhetorical Criticism of the Pauline Epistles since 1975." *Currents in Research: Biblical Studies* 3 (1995) 219–48.

ARTWORK

Beck, F. A. *Album of Greek Education: The Greeks at School and at Play*. Sydney: Cheiron, 1975.
Bieber, Margarete. *Ancient Copies: Contributions to the History of Greek and Roman Art*. New York: New York University Press, 1977.
———. *The Sculpture of the Hellenistic Age*. New York: Columbia University Press, 1955.
Capasso, Mario. *Manuale di papirologia ercolanese*. Testi e Studi 3. Lecce, Italy: Università degli Studi di Lecce, Dipartmento di Filologia Classica e Medioevale, 1991.
Clarke, John. *Looking at Lovemaking: Constructions of Sexuality in Roman Art 100 BC–AD 250*. Berkeley: University of California Press, 2001.
Die Antiken im Albertinum: Staatliche Kunstsammlungen Dresden. Skulpturensammlung. Kordelia Knoll et al., eds. Mainz Am Rhein: Philip van Zabern, 1993.
Gardner, Ernest Arthur. *A Handbook of Greek Sculpture*. 2 vols. London: Macmillan, 1896.
Kleiner, Diana E. E. *Roman Sculpture*. New Haven: Yale University Press, 1992.
Lullies, Reinhard. *Greek Sculpture*. Photos by Max Hirmer. Translated by Michael Bullock. New York: Abrams, 1957.
Mitchell, Lucy Myers Wright. *A History of Ancient Sculpture*. New York: Dodd, Mead, 1883.
Richter, Gisela M. A. *The Portraits of the Greeks: Abridged and Revised by R. R. R. Smith*. Ithaca, NY: Cornell University Press, 1984.

Ridgway, Brunilde Sismondo. *Hellenistic Sculpture*. 3 vols. Madison: University of Wisconsin Press, 1990-2002.
Stewart, Andrew F. *Greek Sculpture: An Exploration*. New Haven: Yale University Press, 1990.

INSCRIPTIONS AND PAPYRI

Ägyptische Urkunden aus den Museen zu Berlin. Griechische Urkunden. Berlin, 1863-.
Arnim, H. von. *Stoicorum Veterum Fragmenta*. Vol. 3. Leipzig: Teubner, 1903.
Astin, A. E. *Scipio Aemilianus*. Oxford: Clarendon University Press, 1967.
Bagnall, Roger S., and Raffaella Cribiore. *Women's Letters from Ancient Egypt, 300 BC-AD 800*. Translated and edited by Evie Ahtaridis. Ann Arbor: University of Michigan Press, 2006.
Böckh, August, et al., editors. *Inscriptiones Graecae*. 49 vols. Berlin, 1825-.
Cagnat, René, et al., editors. *Inscriptiones Graecae ad res Romanas pertinentes*. Paris: Leroux, 1906-1928.
Cribiore, Raffaella, editor. *Gymnastics of the Mind: Greek Education in Hellenistic and Roman Egypt*. Princeton: Princeton University Press, 2005.
Diels, H., and W. Krantz. *Die Fragmente der Vorsokratiker*. 3 vols. Berlin: Weidmann, 1964.
Dittenberger, W., editor. *Sylloge Inscriptionum Graecarum*. 3rd ed. 4 vols. Hildesheim, Germany: Olms, 1960.
Edwards, I. E. S. *Cambridge Ancient History*. 2nd ed. 19 vols. New York: Cambridge University Press, 1970.
Eijk, P. J. van der. *Diocles of Carystus: A Collection of the Fragments with Translation and Commentary*. Vol. 1. Studies in Ancient Medicine 22. Leiden: Brill, 2000.
Engelmann, H., et al., editors. *Die Inschriften von Ephesos*. Bonn, Germany: Habelt, 1980.
Fraser, P. M. *Ptolemaic Alexandria*. New York: Dutton, 1968.
Gigante, M. *Catalogo dei Papiri Ercolanesi*. Naples: Centro Internazionale per lo Studio dei Papiri Ercolanesi, 1979.
Grenfell, Bernard P., et al., editors. *The Oxyrhynchus Papyri*. London: Egypt Exploration Fund, 1898-.
Gummerus, Herman. *Der Ärztestand im Römischen Reiche nach den Inschriften*. Helsinki: Akademische Buchhandlung, 1992.
Homolle, Théophile, editor. *Fouilles de Delphes, École française d'Athène*. 3 vols. Paris: Fontemoing, 1905.
Jacoby, E. *Fragmente der griechischen Historiker*. Berlin: Weidmann, 1923.
Kampen, Natalie. *Image and Status: Women Working in Ostia*. Berlin: Mann, 1981.
Kent, John Harvey. *The Inscriptions, 1926-1950*. Corinth series 8.3. Princeton, NJ: American School of Classical Studies at Athens, 1966.
———. "The Inscriptions, 1926-1950." *Corinth* 8 (1966) iii-vi, 1-25.
Korpela, Jukka. *Das Medizinalpersonal im antiken Rom: eine sozialgeschichte Untersuchung*. Helsinki: Suomalainen Tiedeakatemia, 1987.
Llewelyn, S. R., editor. *New Documents Illustrating Early Christianity*. 9 vols. North Ryde, Australia: Ancient History Documentary Research Center, Macquarie University, 1981-.

Works Cited

Mattusch, Carol C., editor. *The Villa dei Papiri at Herculaneum: Life and Afterlife of a Sculpture Collection.* Los Angeles: Getty Museum, 2005.
Pauly, August Friedrich. *Paulys Real-Encyclopädie der classischen Altertumswissenschaft: Neue Bearbeitung.* Stuttgart: Metzler, 1894–1963.
Plant, I. M. *Women Writers of Ancient Greece and Rome.* London: Equinox, 2001.
Ramelli, Ilaria, and David Konstan. *Hierocles the Stoic: Elements of Ethics, Fragments, and Excerpts.* Atlanta: SBL, 2009.
Rowlandson, Jane, editor. *Women and Society in Greek and Roman Egypt: A Sourcebook.* Cambridge: Cambridge University Press, 1998.
Schmidt, M. *Didymi Chalcenteri grammatici Alexandrini fragmente.* Leipzig, 1854. Reprint, Amsterdam: Hakkert, 1964.
Senancour, Étienne Pivert de. *Libres méditations.* 3rd ed. Textes littéraires français 172. Geneva: Droz, 1970.
Spengel, Leonardus. *Rhetores Graeci.* 3 vols. Leipzig, 1854–56. Reprint, Frankfurt: Minerva, 1966.
Sprague, Rosamond Kent, editor. *The Older Sophists: A Complete Translation by Several Hands of the Fragments in Die Fragmente der Vorsokratiker, edited by Diels-Kranz; With a New Edition of Antiphon and Euthydemus.* Columbia: University of South Carolina Press, 1972.
Straaten, Modestus van. *Panaetii Rhodii Fragmenta.* Leiden: Brill, 1962.
Tracy, Stephen V. *Pericles: A Sourcebook and Reader.* Berkeley: University of California Press, 2009.
Vogliano, Achille. *Epicuri et Epicureorum scripta in Herculanensibus papyris servata.* Berlin, 1928.
——— . *Il nuovo Alceo, da un papiro di Oxyrhynchus.* Rome: Ra Istituto grafico tiberino, 1952.
Vogliano, Achille, et al., editors. *Papiri della R. Università di Milano.* 7 vols. Milan: Università di Milano, 1937–81.

ANCIENT SOURCES

Aelian. *Historical Miscellany.* Translated by Nigel G. Wilson. Loeb Classical Library. Cambridge: Harvard University Press, 1997.
Aelian. *On Animals.* Translated by A. F. Scholfield. Loeb Classical Library. 3 vols. Cambridge: Harvard University Press, 1958–1959.
Alciphron, Aelian, and Philostratus. *Alciphron, Aelian and Philostratus: The Letters.* Translated and edited by Allen R. Benner and Francis H. Fobes. Loeb Classical Library. Cambridge: Harvard University Press, 1949.
Ante-Nicene Fathers. Edited by Alexander Roberts and James Donaldson. 10 vols. Peabody, MA: Hendrickson, 1994.
Appian. *Roman History.* Translated by Horace White. 4 vols. Loeb Classical Library. Cambridge: Harvard University Press, 1912–1913.
Aristides. *The Complete Works.* Translated by Charles A. Behr. Leiden: Brill, 1981.
Aristophanes. *Works.* Edited and translated by Jeffery Henderson. Loeb Classical Library. 6 vols. Cambridge: Harvard University Press, 1936–1998.
Aristotle. *Aristotelis qui ferebantur librorum fragmenta.* Edited by Valentin Rose. Leipzig: Teubneri, 1886.

———. *The Works of Aristotle*. Vol. 12, *Selected Fragments*. Edited by William David Ross. Oxford: Clarendon University Press, 1952.

Athenaeus. *The Deipnosophists*. Translated by Olson S. Douglas. 7 vols. Loeb Classical Library. Cambridge: Harvard University Press, 2007-2011.

———. *The Deipnosophists; or, Banquet of the Learned of Athenaeus*. Translated by C. D. Yonge. 3 vols. London: Bohn, 1853-1854.

Bacchylides. *Bacchylides*. Translated by David A. Cambell. Loeb Classical Library. Cambridge: Harvard University Press, 1992.

Bickermann, E. J., and J. Sykutris. *Speusippus Breif an König Philipp*. Verhandlung der süchsischen Akademie der Wussenschaften 80.3. Leipzig: Hirzel, 1928.

Cassius Dio. *Works*. Translation by Earnest Cary. Loeb Classical Library. 9 vols. Cambridge: Harvard University Press, 1914-1927.

Catling, H. W. "Archaeology in Greece, 1983-84." *Archaeological Reports* 30 (1983-1984) 3-70.

Catullus, Gaius Valerius. *Works*. Edited and translated by Francis Warre Cornish et al. Loeb Classical Library. Cambridge: Harvard University Press, 1988.

Censorinus. *The Birthday Book*. Translated by Holt N. Parker. Chicago: University of Chicago Press, 2007.

———. *De die natali*. Edited by William C. Maude. New York: Cambridge Encyclopedia Co., 1900.

Cicero. *Brutus: Orator*. Translated by G. Hendrickson and H. M. Hubbel. Loeb Classical Library. Cambridge: Harvard University Press, 1939.

———. *Letters to Atticus*. Translated by D. R. Shackelton Bailey. 4 vols. Loeb Classical Library. Cambridge: Harvard University Press, 1988.

———. *On Duties*. Translated by H. Rackham. Loeb Classical Library. Cambridge: Harvard University Press, 1914.

———. *On the Nature of the Gods: Academics*. Translated by H. Rackham. Loeb Classical Library. Cambridge: Harvard University Press, 1933.

———. *On Old Oge. On Friendship. On Divination*. Translated by W. A. Falconer. Loeb Classical Library. Cambridge: Harvard University Press, 1923.

———. *On the Republic. On the Laws*. Translated by Clinton W. Keys. Loeb Classical Library. Cambridge: Harvard University Press, 1933.

Cleomedes. *Cleomedes' Lectures on Astronomy: A Translation of The Heavens*. Translated by Alan C. Bowen and Robert B. Todd. Berkeley: University of California Press, 2004.

Cornutus. *Cornutus: A Cursory Examination of the Traditions of Greek Theology (Theologiae Graecae Compendium), with Text, Translation, and Commentary*. Edited and translated by David Armstrong et al. New York: Routledge, forthcoming.

Diodorus, Siculus. *Library of History*. Translated by C. H. Oldfather et al. 12 vols. Loeb Classical Library. Cambridge: Harvard University Press, 1933-1950.

Diogenes Laertius. *Lives of the Eminent Philosophers*. Edited and translated by R. D. Hicks. 2 vols. Loeb Classical Library. Cambridge: Harvard University Press, 1925.

Diogenes of Oenoanda. *Diogenes of Oenoanda: The Fragments*. Edited and translated by C. W. Chilton. London: Oxford University Press, 1971.

Epictetus. *Discourses: The Encheiridion*. Translated by W. A. Oldfather. 2 vols. Loeb Classical Library. Cambridge: Harvard University Press, 1925-1928.

Works Cited

———. *Epicurea*. Edited by Hermannus Usener. Dubuque, Iowa: Brown Reprint Library, 1887.

———. *Epicurus: The Extant Remains*. Edited by Cyril Bailey. Oxford: Clarendon University Press, 1926.

Erler, M. "Epikur, Die Schule Epikurs, Lukrez." In *Die Philosophie der Antike*, vol. 4, *Die hellenistische Philosophie*, edited by H. Flashar, 29–430. Basel: Schwabe, 1994.

Eunapius. *Eunapius: Lives of the Philosophers and Sophists*. Translated by Wilmer C. Wright. Loeb Classical Library. New York: Putnam, 1921.

Eusebius of Caesarea. *The Eccleastical History*. Edited and translated by Kirsopp Lake and John Oulton. Loeb Classical Library. Cambridge: Harvard University Press, 1980.

———. *Preparation for the Gospel*. Translated by E. H. Gifford. Oxford: Clarendon University Press, 1903.

Eustathius. *Eustathii Archiepiscopi Thessalonicensis Commentarii ad Homeri Odysseam*. Edited and translated by J. G. Stallbaum. 2 vols. Cambridge Library Collection Classics. Leipzig: Weigel, 1827–1830.

———. *Eustathii Commentarii ad Homeri Iliadem*. Edited and translated by J. Stallbaum. Cambridge Library Collection Classics. Cambridge: Cambridge University Press, 2010.

Foraboschi, D., editor. *L'Archivio di Kronion*. Milan: Università di Milano, 1971.

Galen. *On the Natural Faculties*. Edited and translated by A. J. Brock. Loeb Classical Library. Cambridge: Harvard University Press, 1916.

———. "Quod optimus medicus sit quoque philosophus." In *Claudii Galeni Opera Omnia*, edited by Karl Gottlob Kühn, 53–63. Cambridge: Cambridge University Press, 2011.

Gaisford, Thomas. *Theodoreti Episcopi Cyrensis Graecarum Affectionum Curatio*. Oxonii, 1839.

Gellius, Aulus. *Attic Nights*. Edited and translated by J. C. Rolfe. 3 vols. Loeb Classical Library. Cambridge: Harvard University Press, 1927.

Gerber, Douglas E. *Greek Elegiac Poetry*. Loeb Classical Library. Cambridge: Cambridge University Press, 1999.

Gow, A. S. F., and D. L. Page, editors. *The Greek Anthology: The Garland of Philip and Some Contemporary Epigrams*. 2 vols. London: Cambridge University Press, 1968.

Gregory of Nazianzus. *Julian the Emperor, Containing Gregory Nazianzen's Two Invectives and Libanius' Monody with Julian's Extant Theosophical Works*. Compiled and translated by C. W. King. London: Bell and Sons, 1888.

Grese, William. *Corpus Hermeticum XIII and Early Christian Literature*. Studia ad corpus Hellenisticum Novi Testamenti 5. Edited by H. D. Betz. Leiden: Brill, 1979.

Guthrie, Kenneth Sylvan. *Pythagoras: Sourcebook and Library*. Yonkers, NY: Platonist, 1920.

Hephaestion. *Hephaestion On Metre*. Translated by J. M. van Ophuijsen. New York: Brill, 1987.

Heraclitus. *Heraclitus: Homeric Problems*. Edited and translated by Donald A. Russell and David Konstan. Writings from the Greco-Roman World 14. Atlanta: SBL, 2005.

Herodotus. *The Persian Wars*. Translated by A. D. Godley. 4 vols. New York: Putnam's Sons, 1920–24.

Works Cited

Latte, Kurt, editor. *Hesychii Alexandrini Lexicon*. 2 vols. Copenhagen: Munksgaard, 1953, 1956.
Horace. *The Satires, Epistles, Ars Poetica*. Translated and edited by Edward Wickham. New York: Oxford University Press, 1903.
Iamblichus. *Iamblichi De vita Pythagorica liber*. Edited by Ludwig Deubner and Ulrich Klein. Stuttgart: Teubner, 1975.
———. *De Vita Pythagorica*. Translated by John Dillon and Jackson Hershbell. Atlanta: Scholars, 1991.
John of Damascus. *Die Schriften des Johannes von Damaskos*. Vol. 5. Edited by P. B. Kotter. Patristische Texte und Studien 29. Berlin: de Gruyter, 1988.
Julius Pollux. *Onomastikon*. Edited and translated by Immanuel Bekker. Berlin: Friderici Nicolai, 1846.
Juvenal. *Satires*. Translated by G. G. Ramsay. Cambridge: Harvard University Press, 1999.
Lefkowitz, Mary. "Scolium on Pindar." *American Journal of Philology* 106 (1985) 269-82.
Livy. *History of Rome*. Translated by B. O. Foster et al. 14 vols. Loeb Classical Library. Cambridge: Harvard University Press, 1919-1959.
Lucian of Samasota. *Works*. Edited and translated by A. M. Harmon et al. 8 vols. Loeb Classical Library. Cambridge: Harvard University Press, 1913-1967.
Lutz, Cora E. *Musonius Rufus: "The Roman Socrates."* Yale Classical Studies 10. New Haven: Yale University Press, 1947.
Martial. *Epigrams*. Edited and translated by D. R. Shackleton Bailey. Loeb Classical Library. Cambridge: Harvard University Press, 1993.
Maximus of Tyre. *The Philosophical Orations*. Translated by M. B. Trapp. Oxford: Oxford University Press, 1997.
Nicene and Post-Nicene Fathers. Edited by Philip Schaff. 14 vols. Peabody, MA: Hendrickson, 1994.
Ovid. *Ars amatoria*. Translated and edited by J. H. Mozley. Loeb Classical Library. Cambridge: Harvard University Press, 1929.
Parthenius. *Parthenius*. Translated by J. L. Lightfoot. Loeb Classical Library. Cambridge: Harvard University Press, 2010.
Pausanias. *Description of Greece*. Edited and translated by W. H. S. Jones et al. 5 vols. Loeb Classical Library. Cambridge: Harvard University Press, 1918-1935.
Philo. *The Works of Philo Judaeus*. Translated by C. D. Yonge. London: Bohn, 1854-55.
Philodemus. *Philodemus: On Frank Criticism*. Translated and edited by David Konstan et al. Texts and Translations 43. Atlanta: Scholars, 1998.
Philostratus. *The Life of Apollonius of Tyana, the Epistles of Apollonius, and the Treatise of Eusebius*. Translated by F. C. Conybeare. Cambridge: Harvard University Press, 1969.
Photius. *Plotini opera*. Edited by P. Henry and H.-R. Schwyzer. 3 vols. Leiden: Brill, 1951-1973.
Pindar. *Olympian Odes and Pythian Odes*. Translated by William H. Race. Loeb Classical Library. Cambridge: Harvard University Press, 1997.
Plato. *Lysis, Symposium, and Gorgias*. Translated by W. R. M. Lamb. Loeb Classical Library. Cambridge: Harvard University Press, 1925.
———. *Republic*. Translated by Paul Shorey. Loeb Classical Library. Cambridge: Harvard University Press, 1930-1935.

Works Cited

Pliny the Elder. *Natural History*. Translated by H. Rackham and W. H. S. Jones. 10 vols. Loeb Classical Library. Cambridge: Harvard University Press, 1925.

Plotinus. *Plotinus*. Translated by A. H. Armstrong and Paul Henry. Loeb Classical Library. London: Heinemann, 1966–1988.

Plutarch. *Lives*. Edited and translated by Bernadotte Perrin. 11 vols. Loeb Classical Library. Cambridge: Harvard University Press, 1914–1936.

———. *Plutarch's Quotations*. Compiled by William C. Helmbold and Edward N. O'Neil. Baltimore: American Philological Association, 1959.

Polybius. *Histories*. Translated by W. R. Paton. Translated by H. Rackham and W. H. S. Jones. 10 vols. Loeb Classical Library. Cambridge: Harvard University Press, 1923–1927.

Porphory. *Plotini opera*. Vol. 1. Edited by P. Henry and H. R. Schwyzer. Leiden: Brill, 1951.

———. *Porphyrii philosophi Platonici opuscula selecta*. 2nd ed. Edited by A. Nauck. Leipzig, 1886. Reprint, Hildesheim, Germany: Olms, 1963.

Pseudo-Ovid. *The Songs of Sappho*. Translated by Marion Mills Miller and David Moore Robinson. New York: Frank-Maurice, 1925.

Quintilian. *The Orator's Education*. Translated by Donald A. Russell. 5 vols. Loeb Classical Library. Cambridge: Harvard University Press, 2002.

Rupprecht, Hans-Albert, editor. *Sammelbuch griechischer Urkunden aus Äegypten*. 20 vols. Berlin: de Gruyter, 1913–2001.

Scarborough, John, and Vivian Nutton. "The Preface of Discorides' Materia Medica: Introducion, Translation, and Commentary." *Transactions and Studies of the College of Physicians of Philadelphia* 4 (1982) 187–227.

Scholiast. *Scholia Graeca in Homeri Odysseam*. 2 vols. Edited by W. Dindorff. Oxford, 1855. Reprint, Amsterdam: Hakkert, 1962.

———. *Scholia in Homeri Odysseae: A 1–309 Auctiora et Emendatiora*. Edited by A. Ludwich. Königsberg, 1888–1890. Reprint, Hildesheim, Germany: Olms, 1966.

———. *Scholia metrica vetera in Pindari Carmina*. Leipzig: Teubner, 1989.

Seneca. *Fragments*. Edited by Friedrich G. Haase. Leipzig: Teubner, 1897.

———. *Works*. Translated by Michael Heseltine et al. 13 vols. Loeb Classical Library. Cambridge: Harvard University Press, 1913–2004.

Simplicius. *On Epictetus' "Handbook 27–33."* Translated by Tad Brennan and Charles Brittain. Ithaca, NY: Cornell University Press, 2002.

Spengel, Leonhard von. *Rhetores Graeci*. Vol. 2. Leipzig: Teubner, 1854.

Statius. *Silvae*. Translated by D. R. Shackleton. Loeb Classical Library. Cambridge: Harvard University Press, 2003.

Strabo. *Geography*. Translated by Horace Leonard Jones. 8 vols. Loeb Classical Library. Cambridge: Harvard University Press, 1917–1932.

Suetonius. *The Lives of the Caesars*. Edited by J. C. Rolfe. 2 vols. Loeb Classical Library. New York: Putnam's Sons, 1928.

Tacitus. *Annals*. Translated by John Jackson. 2 vols. Loeb Classical Library. Cambridge: Harvard University Press, 1937.

———. *Dialogus. Agricola. Germania*. New York: Putnam's Sons, 1925.

Themistius. *The Private Orations of Themistius*. Translated, annotated, and introduced by Robert J. Penella. Berkeley: University of California Press, 2000.

Thesleff, Holger, editor. *The Pythagorean Texts of the Hellenistic Period*. Turku, Sweden: Åbo Akademi, 1965.

Thucydides. *History of the Peloponnesian War*. Translated by C. F. Smith. 4 vols. Loeb Classical Library. Cambridge: Harvard University Press, 1917-1932.
Valerius Maximus. *Memorable Sayings and Doings*. Translated by D. R. Shackleton Baily. 2 vols. Loeb Classical Library. Cambridge: Harvard University Press, 2000.
Velleius Paterculus. *Compendium of Roman History*. Translated by F. W. Shipley. Loeb Classical Library. Cambridge: Harvard University Press, 1924.
Xenophon. *Works*. Translated and edited by Carleton Lewis Brownson et al. 7 vols. Loeb Classical Library. Cambridge: Harvard University Press, 1914-1998.

MODERN SOURCES

Achtemeier, Paul J. *Romans*. Atlanta: John Knox, 1985.
Adam, J. "Epicurus and Erotion." *Classical Review* 7 (1893) 303-4.
Adcock, F. E. "Women in Roman Life and Letters." *Greece & Rome* 14 (1945) 1-11.
Agrell, Goran. *Work, Toil and Sustenance: An Examination of the View of Work in the New Testament*. Lund: Ohlssons, 1976.
Asher, Jeffrey R. "ΣΠΕΙΡΕΤΑΙ: Paul's Anthropogenic Metaphor in 1 Corinthians 4:42-44." *Journal of Biblical Literature* 120 (2001) 101-22.
Badiou, Alain. "Paul, the Founder of the Universal Subject." In *St. Paul among the Philosophers*, edited by John D. Caputo and Linda Martin Alcoff, 30-31. Bloomington: Indiana University Press, 2009.
Aland, Kurt. "The Corpus Hellenisticum." *New Testament Studies* 2 (1955-56) 217-21.
Alexander, A. B. D. *A Short History of Philosophy*. Glasgow: James Maclehose, 1908.
Alexander, Loveday. "IPSE DIXIT: Citation of Authority in Paul and Hellenistic Schools." In *Paul Beyond the Judaism/ Hellenism Divide*, edited by Troels Engberg-Pedersen, 103-27. Louisville: Westminster, 2001.
Algra, Keimpe, and M. H. Koenen. *Lucretius and His Intellectual Background: Proceedings of the Colloquium, Amsterdam, 26-28 June 1996*. Amsterdam: North-Holland, 1997.
Allen, Christine Garside. "Plato on Women." *Feminist Studies* 2 (1975) 131-38.
Allen, Prudence. *The Concept of Woman*. Grand Rapids: Eerdmans, 1997.
Allen, Walter, Jr., and Phillip H. Delacy. "The Patrons of Philodemus." *Classical Philology* 34 (1939) 59-65.
Almqvist, Helge. *Plutarch und Das Neue Testament: Ein Beitrag zum Corpus Hellenisticum*. Novi Testamenti. Uppsala, Sweden: Appelbergs, 1946.
Alpern, Henry. *The March of Philosophy*. New York: Dial, 1933.
Amundsen, Darrell W. "The Liability of the Physician in Roman Law." In *International Symposium on Society, Medicine, and the Law*, edited by H. Karplus, 17-31. Amsterdam: Elsevier, 1973.
Anchor Bible Dictionary. Edited by David N. Freedman. 6 vols. New York: Doubleday, 1992.
Anderson, Graham. "Putting Pressure on Plutarch: Philostratus Epistle 73." *Classical Philology* 72 (1977) 43-45.
Anderson, R. Dean, Jr. *Ancient Rhetorical Theory and Paul*. Contributions to Biblical Exegesis and Theology 18. Leuven: Peeters, 1999.

Works Cited

Andrews, Mary E. Review of *Plutarch und Das Neue Testament: Ein Beitrag zum Corpus Hellenisticum Novi Testamenti*, by Helge Almqvist. *Journal of Biblical Literature* 66 (1947) 343.

Andronicos, Manolis. *Verghina, the Royal Tombs and the Ancient City*. Athens: Ekdotike Athenon, 1984.

Annas, Julia. "Plato and Aristotle on Friendship and Altruism." *Mind*, n.s., 86 (1977) 532–54.

Arjava, Antti. *Women and Law in Late Antiquity*. Oxford: Clarendon University Press, 1996.

Arkins, B. "Epicurus and Lucretius on Sex, Love, and Marriage." *Apeiron: A Journal for Ancient Philosophy and Science* 18 (1984) 141–43.

Arlandson, James Malcolm. *Women, Class, and Society in Early Christianity: Models from Luke-Acts*. Peabody, MA: Hendrickson, 1997.

Arnold, Irene Ringwood. "Agonistic Festivals in Italy and Sicily." *American Journal of Archaeology* (1960) 245–51.

Arrighetti, Graziano. *Epicuro Opere*. Torino: Einaudi, 1960.

Arthur, Marylin B. "The Tortoise and the Mirror: Erinna PSI 1090." *Classical World* 74 (1980) 53–65.

Ascough, Richard S. *Paul's Macedonian Associations*. Wissenschaftliche Untersuchungen zum Neuen Testament 2.161. Tübingen: Mohr/Siebeck, 2003.

Asmis, Elizabeth. "Epicurean Economics." In *Philodemus and the New Testament World*, edited by John T. Fitzgerald et al., 133–76. Novum Testamentum Supplement 111. Leiden: Brill, 2004.

———. "The Stoics on Women." In *Ancient Philosophy and Feminism*, edited by J. Ward, 68–94. New York: Routledge, 1996.

Aune, David E. "De esu carnium orationes I and II (Moralia 993a–999b)." In *Plutarch's Ethical Writings and Early Christian Literature*, edited by Hans Dieter Betz, 301–7. Leiden: Brill, 1975.

———. "The Problem of the Genre of the Gospels: A Critique of C. H. Talbert's What Is a Gospel?" In *Gospel Perspectives: Studies of History and Tradition in the Four Gospels*, edited by David Wenham and R. T. France, 2:9–60. Sheffield, UK: Journal for the Study of the New Testament, 1981.

———. Review of *Aelius Aristides and the New Testament*, by Pieter W. van der Horst. *Journal of Biblical Literature* 99 (1980) 641–44.

———. Review of *Corpus Hermeticum XIII and Early Christian Literature*, by William C. Grese. *Journal of Biblical Literature* 102 (1983) 349–50.

———. "Septem Sapientium Convivium." In *Plutarch's Ethical Writings and the New Testament*, edited by Hans D. Betz, 51–105. Studia ad Corpus Hellenisticum Novi Testamenti 4. Leiden: Brill, 1978.

Austin, Michel M. *The Hellenistic World from Alexander to the Roman Conquest: A Selection of Ancient Sources in Translation*. 2nd ed. Cambridge: Cambridge University Press, 2006.

Avontis, Ivars. "Training in Frugality in Epicurus and Seneca." *Phoenix* 31 (1977) 214–17.

Bablitz, Leanne E. *Actors and Audience in the Roman Courtroom*. New York: Routledge, 2007.

Bailey, Cyril. *The Greek Atomists and Epicurus*. Oxford: Clarendon University Press, 1928.

Works Cited

Baker, Robert J. "Maecenas and Horace 'Satires 2.8.'" *Classical Journal* 83 (1988) 212–33.
Balch, David L. "1 Cor 7:32–35 and Stoic Debates about Marriage Anxiety, and Distraction." *Journal of Biblical Literature* 102 (1983) 429–39.
———. "Household Ethical Codes in Peripatetic, Neopythagorean, and Early Christian Literature." SBL Seminar Papers 11 (1977) 397–104.
———. "Neopythagorean Moralists and the New Testament Household Codes." In *Aufstieg und Niedergang der römischen Welt: Geschichte und Kultur Roms im Spiegel der neueren Forschung*, vol. 2.26.1, edited by Hildegard Temporini and Wolfgang Haase, 380–411. New York: de Gruyter, 1991.
———. "Rich Pompeiian Houses, Shops for Rent, and the Huge Apartment Building in Herculaneum as Typical Spaces for Pauline House Churches." *Journal for the Study of the New Testament* 27 (2004) 27–46.
Balch, David L., and Carolyn Osiek. *Families in the New Testament World: Households and House Churches*. Louisville: Westminster John Knox, 1997.
Baldry, H. C. "Zeno's Ideal State." *Journal of Hellenic Studies* 79 (1959) 3–15.
Baily, Cyril. *Epicurus: The Extant Remains*. Oxford: Oxford Unversity Press, 1926.
Ballif, Michelle, and Michael G. Moran, editors. *Classical Rhetorics and Rhetoricians: Critical Studies and Sources*. Westport, CT: Praeger, 2005.
Barclay, J. M. G. "Poverty in Pauline Studies: A Response to Steven Friesen." *Journal for the Study of the New Testament* 26 (2004) 363–66.
———. "Thessalonica and Corinth: Social Contrasts in Pauline Christianity." *Journal for the Study of the New Testament* 47 (1992) 49–74.
Barker, A. *Greek Musical Writings*. Vol. 2, *Harmonic and Acoustic Theory*. Cambridge: Cambridge University Press, 1989.
Barnard, Sylvia. "Hellenistic Women Poets." *Classical Journal* 73 (1978) 204–13.
Barnett, P. W. "Opponents of Paul." In *Dictionary of Paul and His Letters: Compendium of Contemporary Biblical Scholarship*, edited by Gerald F. Hawthorne et al., 644–53. Downers Grove, IL: InterVarsity, 1993.
Barré, Michael L. "To Marry or to Burn: *Pyrousthai* in I Cor 7:9." *Catholic Biblical Quarterly* 36 (1974) 193–202.
Barrett, Anthony. *Livia: The First Lady of Rome*. New Haven: Yale University Press, 2002.
Barrett, C. K. *A Commentary on the Epistle to the Romans*. New York: Harper, 1957.
Barringer, Judith M. "The Temple of Zeus at Olympia, Heroes, and Athletes." *Hesperia* 74 (2005) 211–41.
Bartchy, Scott. *MALLON CHRESAI: First Century Slavery and the Interpretation of 1 Corinthians 7:21*. SBL Dissertation Series 11. Missoula, MT: Scholars, 1973.
Bartelink, G. J. M. Review of *Lukian von Samosata und das Neue Testament. Religionsgeschichtliche und paränetische Parallelen. Ein Beitrag zum Corpus Hellenisticum Novi Testamenti*, by Hans D. Betz. *Mnemosyne*, 4th ser., 16 (1963) 190–91.
Barth, E. M. *Women Philosophers: A Bibliography of Books Through 1990*. Bowling Green, OH: Philosophy Documentation Center, 1992.
Bartling, Walter J. "Sexuality, Marriage, and Divorce in 1 Corinthians 6:12—17:16." *Concordia Theological Monthly* 39 (1968) 355–66.
Bassler, Jouette M. "1 Corinthians." In *The Women's Bible Commentary*, edited by Carol A. Newsom and Sharon H. Ringe, 557–65. London: Westminster John Knox, 1992.

Works Cited

Bauer, Walter, et at. *A Greek-English Lexicon of the New Testament and Other Early Christian Literature*. 3rd ed. Chicago: University of Chicago Press, 2000.

Bauman, Richard A. *Women and Politics in Ancient Rome*. London: Routledge, 1992.

Baur, F. C. "Seneca und Paulus, Das Verhaltnis des Stoicismus zum Christentum nach den Schriften Seneca." *Zeitschrift für wissenschafliche Theologie* 1 (1858) 161–246, 441–70.

Beard, Mary R. "The Function of the Written Word in Roman Religion." In *Literacy in the Greco-Roman World*, edited by Mary Beard et al., 35–58. Ann Arbor, MI: Journal of Roman Archaeology, 1991.

———. *Woman as Force in History: A Study in Traditions and Realities*. New York: Macmillan, 1946.

Bearslee, William. *First Corinthians: A Commentary for Today*. St. Louis: Chalice, 1994.

Beattie, Gillian. *Women and Marriage in Paul and His Early Interpreters*. Journal for the Study of the New Testament Supplement 296. London: T. & T. Clark, 2005.

Beck, F. A. "The Schooling of Girls in Ancient Greece." *Classicum* 9 (1978) 1–9.

Beck, William F. "1 Corinthians 7:36–38." *Concordia Theological Monthly* 25 (1954) 370–72.

Bellemore, Jane. "The Dating of Seneca's Ad Marciam De Consolatione." *Classical Quarterly*, n.s., 42 (1992) 219–34.

Benoit, Pierre. "Sénèque et Saint Paul." *Revue biblique* (1946) 7–35.

Berger, Klaus, and Carsten Colpe. *Religionsgeschichtliches Textbuch zum Neuen Testament*. Göttingen: Vandenhoeck & Ruprecht, 1987.

Bergmann, Bettina, and Christine Kondoleon. *The Art of Ancient Spectacle*. New Haven: Yale University Press, 1999.

Bernstein, Francis. "Pompeian Women." In *The World of Pompeii*, edited by John J. Dobbins and Pedar W. Foss, 526–37. London: Routledge, 2007.

Berry, D. H., and Andrew Erskine. *Form and Function in Roman Oratory*. Cambridge: Cambridge University Press, 2010.

Berry, Edmund G. "The De Liberis Educandis of Pseudo-Plutarch." *Harvard Studies in Classical Philology* 63 (1958) 387–99.

Berry, Paul. *The Encounter between Seneca and Christianity*. Lewiston, NY: Edwin Mellen, 2002.

Best, Edward E., Jr. "Cicero, Livy and Educated Roman Women." *Classical Journal* 65 (1970) 199–204.

Betensky, Aya. "Lucretius and Love." *Classical World* 73 (1980) 291–99.

Betz, Hans D. "Christianity as Religion: Paul's Attempt at Definition in Romans." *The Journal of Religion* 71 (1991) 315–44.

———. "The Concept of the 'Inner Human Being' (ὁ ἔσω ἄνθρωπος) in the Anthropology of Paul." *New Testament Studies* 46 (2000) 315–41.

———. "De Fraterno Amore." In *Plutarch's Ethical Writings and the New Testament*, edited by Hans D. Betz, 231–63. Leiden: Brill, 1978.

———. "The Delphic Maxim ΓΝΩΘΙ ΣΑΥΤΟΝ in Hermetic Interpretation." *Harvard Theological Review* 63 (1970) 465–84.

———. "The Delphic Maxim 'Know Yourself' in the Greek Magical Papyri." *History of Religions* 21 (1981) 156–71.

———. *Der Apostel Paulus und die sokratische Tradition: eine exegetische Untersuchung zu seiner Apologie 2 Korinther 10–13*. Tübingen: Mohr, 1972.

———. "The Divine Human Being." *Harvard Theological Review* 78 (1985) 243–52.

———. *Galatians*. Philadelphia: Fortress, 1979.

———. "Göttmensch II (Griechisch-römische Antike und Urchristentum)." In *Reallexikon für Antike und Christentum*, edited by T. Klauser et al, 12:234–312. Stuttgart: Hiersmeann, 1983.

———. "Lukian von Samosata und das Christentum." *Novum Testamentum* 3 (1959) 226–37.

———. *Lukian von Samosata und das Neue Testament*. Religionsgeschichtliche und paränetische Parallelen. Ein Beitrag zum Corpus Hellenisticum Novi Testamenti. Berlin: Akademie, 1961.

Betz, Hans D., and Edgar W. Smith Jr. "Contributions to the Corpus Hellenisticum Novi Testamenti: I: Plutarch, de e apud delphos." *Novum Testamentum* 13 (1971) 217–35.

Bicknell, P. J. "Sokrates' Mistress Xanthippe." *Apeiron* 8 (1974) 1–5.

Blasi, Anthony J., et al. *Handbook of Early Christianity: Social Science Approaches*. Walnut Creek, CA: AltaMira, 2002.

Bliquez, Lawrence J. "A Note on the Didymus Papyrus XII.35." *Classical Journal* 67 (1972) 356.

Bloomer, W. Martin. "Schooling in Persona: Imagination and Subordination in Roman Education." *Classical Antiquity* 16 (1997) 57–78.

Blundell, Sue. *Women in Ancient Greece*. Cambridge: Harvard, 1995.

Boas, George. "Fact and Legend in the Biography of Plato." *Philosophical Review* 57 (1948) 439–57.

Boatwright, Mary T. "The Imperial Women of the Early Second Century A.C." *American Journal of Philology* 112 (1991) 513–40.

Boccaccini, Gabriele. "Multiple Judaisms: A New Understanding of the Context of Earliest Christianity." *Biblical Research* 11 (1995) 38–41.

Boehm, F. "De symbolis pythagoreis." PhD diss., Friedrich-Wilhelms-Universität, Berlin, 1905.

———."Elementary and Secondary Education in the Roman Empire." *Florilegium* 1 (1979) 1–14.

———. "Litterator." *Hermes* 109 (1981) 371–78.

Bonhöffer, A. *Epiktet und das Neue Testament*. Giessen, Germany: Töpelmann, 1911.

Bonner, Stanley F. *Education in Ancient Rome from the Elder Cato to the Younger Pliny*. London: Methuen, 1977.

Bookidis, Nancy. "Religion in Corinth: 146 B.C.E to 100 C.E." In *Urban Religion in Roman Corinth: Interdisciplinary Approaches*, edited by D. Schowalter and S. Freisen, 141–64. Harvard Theological Studies 53. Cambridge: Cambridge University Press, 2005.

———. "The Sanctuaries of Corinth." *Corinth* 20 (2003) 247–59.

Bookidis, Nancy, Julie Hansen, Lynn Snyder, and Paul Goldberg. "Dining in the Sanctuary of Demeter and Kore at Corinth." *Hesperia* 68 (1999) 1–54.

Bookidis, Nancy, and Ronald S. Stroud. *The Sanctuary of Demeter and Kore: Topography and Architecture*. Corinth 18. Princeton, NJ: American School of Classical Studies in Athens, 1997.

Booth, A. D. "Douris' Cup and the Stages of Schooling in Classical Athens." *Echos du Monde Classique* 29 (1985) 274–80.

Borimir, Jordan. "Isthmian Amusements." *Classics Ireland* 8 (2001) 32–67.

Works Cited

Boring, Eugene M., et al. *Hellenistic Commentary to the New Testament*. Nashville: Abington, 1995.

Bosnakis, D. "Zwei Dichterinnen aus Kos: Ein neues inschriftliches Zeugnis über das öffentliche Auftreten von Frauen." In *The Hellenistic Polis of Kos: State, Economy and Culture*, edited by K. Höhgmmar, 99–108. Uppsala, Sweden: Uppsala University Press, 2004.

Boston, Linda. "A Womanist Reflection on 1 Corinthians 7:21–24 and 1 Corinthians 14:33–35." *Journal of Women and Religion* 9–10 (1990–1991) 81–89.

Bowditch, Phebe Lowell. *Horace and the Gift Economy of Patronage*. Berkely: University of California Press, 2001.

Bower, E. W. "Some Technical Terms in Roman Education." *Hermes* 89 (1961) 462–77.

Bowersock, G. W. *Greek Sophists in the Roman Empire*. Oxford: Oxford University Press, 1969.

Bowman, Laurel. "The 'Women's Tradition' in Greek Poetry." *Phoenix* 58 (2004) 1–27.

Boys-Stontes, G. R., et al., editors. *The Oxford Handbook of Hellenic Studies*. Oxford: Oxford University Press, 2009.

Bradley, K. R. "Remarriage and the Structure of the Upper Class Roman Family." In *Marriage, Divorce and Children in Ancient Rome*, edited by Beryl Rawson, 79–93. Oxford: Clarendon University Press, 1991.

Braginton, M. V. "Exile under the Roman Emperors." *Classical Journal* 39 (1944) 391–407.

Brändl, Martin. *Der Agon bei Paulus: Herkunft und Profil paulinischer Agonmetaphorik*. Tübingen: Mohr/Siebeck, 2006.

Braund, S. H. "Juvenal—Misogynist or Misogamist?" *Journal of Roman Studies* 82 (1992) 71–86.

Braxton, Brad Ronnell. "The Role of Ethnicity in the Social Location of 1 Corinthians 7:17–24." In *Yet with a Steady Beat: The African-American Struggle for Recognition in the Episcopal Church*, edited by Harold T. Lewis, 19–32. Leiden: Brill, 2003.

Bréhier, Émile. *Histoire de la Philosophie*. L'Antiquite et le Moyen Age. Paris: Presses Universitaires de France, 1960.

Bremen, Reit van. "Images of Women and Antiquity." In *Women and Wealth*, edited by Averil Cameron and Amelie Kuhrt, 223–42. Detroit: Wayne State University Press, 1983.

———. *The Limits of Participation: Women and Life in the Greek East in the Hellenistic and Roman Periods*. Amsterdam: Gieben, 1996.

Brenk, Frederick E. "Plutarch's Erotikos: The Drag Down Pulled Up." In *Relighting the Souls: Studies in Plutarch, in Greek Literature*, edited by Frederick E. Brenk, 13–27. Stuttgart: Steiner, 1998.

Brennan, T. C. "The Poets Julia Balbilla and Damo at the Colossus of Memnon." *Classical World* 91 (1997) 215–34.

Broneer, Oscar. "The Apostle Paul and the Isthmian Games." *Biblical Archaeologist* 25 (1962) 1–31.

———. "Colonia Laus Iulia Corinthiensis." *Hesperia* 10 (1941) 388–90.

———. "Hero Cults in the Corinthian Agora." *Hesperia* 11 (1942) 128–61.

———. "Investigations at Corinth, 1946–1947." *Hesperia* 16 (1947) 233–47.

———. "The Isthmian Victory Crown." *American Journal of Archaeology* 66 (1962) 259–63.

———. "Paul and the Pagan Cults at Isthmia." *Harvard Theological Review* 64 (1971) 169–87.

———. "Paul's Missionary Work in Greece." *Biblical Archaeologist* 14 (1951) 77–96.

———. "Twenty-Five Years Ago: Cults at St. Paul's Corinth." *Biblical Archaeologist* 39 (1976) 158–59.

Brooten, Bernadette J. *Love between Women: Early Christian Responses to Female Homoeroticism.* Chicago: University of Chicago Press, 1996.

———. *Women Leaders in the Ancient Synagogue: Inscriptional Evidence and Background Issues.* Chico, CA: Scholars, 1982.

Brophy, Robert, and Mary Brophy. "Deaths in the Pan-Hellenic Games II: All Combative Sports." *American Journal of Philology* 106 (1985) 171–98.

Broughton, Robert S. *The Magistrates of the Roman Republic.* Vol. 3 supplement. New York: American Philological Association, 1951–52.

Brown, Eric. "Epicurus on the Value of Friendship ("Sententia Vaticana" 23)." *Classical Philology* 97 (2002) 68–80.

Brownlee, Ann Blair. "Attic Black Figure from Corinth: III." *Hesperia* 64 (1995) 337–82.

Brunt, P. A. "Stoicism and the Principate." *Papers of the British School at Rome* 43 (1975) 7–35.

Buckland, W. W. *A Text-Book of Roman Law: From Augustus to Justinian.* Cambridge: Cambridge University Press, 1921.

Bultmann, Rudolf. *Der stil der paulinischen Predigt und die kynisch-stoische Diatribe.* Göttingen: Vanderhoek, 1910.

———. *Der zweite Brief an die Korinther.* Edited by E. Dinkler. Göttingen: Vandenhoek & Ruprecht, 1976.

Burkert, Walter. *Lore and Science in Ancient Pythagoreanism.* Cambridge: Harvard, University Press, 1972.

Burnstein, S. M. *The Hellenistic Age from the Battle of Ipsos to the Death of Cleopatra VII.* Cambridge: Cambridge University Press, 1985.

Burriss, E. "Cicero and the Religion of His Day." *Classical Journal* 21 (1926) 524–32.

Burton, Henry F. "Seneca's Idea of God." *American Journal of Theology* 13 (1909) 350–69.

Burton, Joan. "Women's Commensality in the Ancient Greek World." *Greece & Rome*, 2nd ser., 45 (1998) 143–46.

Butrica, James L. "Some Myths and Anomalies in the Study." In *Same-Sex Desire and Love in Greco-Roman Antiquity and in the Classical Tradition of the West*, edited by Beert C. Verstraete and Vernon Provencal, 209–70. Binghamton, NY: Harrington Park, 2005.

Butts, James. "The 'Progymnasmata' of Theon." PhD diss., Claremont Graduate School, 1986.

Byrne, Brendan. *Romans.* Edited by Daniel Harrington. Sacred pagina. Collegeville: Liturgical, 1999.

Byron, John. "Slave of Christ or Willing Servant? Paul's Self-Description in 1 Corinthians 4:1–2 and 9:16–18." *Neotestamentica* 37 (2003) 179–98.

———. *Slavery Metaphors in Early Judaism and Pauline Christianity: A Traditio-Historical and Exegetical Examination.* Tübingen: Mohr/Siebeck, 2003.

———. "Slaves and Freed Persons: Self-Made Success and Social Climbing in the Corinthian Congregation." *Jian Dao* (2008) 91–107.

Works Cited

Cairns, Douglas L. "'Off with Her AIDWS': Herodotus 1.8.3–4." *Classical Quarterly* 46 (1996) 78–83.

Cameron, Averil, and Alan Cameron. "Erinna's Distaff." *Classical Quarterly*, n.s., 19 (1969) 285–88.

Cameron, Ron, and Merrill P. Miller. "Redescribing Paul and the Corinthians." In *Redescribing Paul and the Corinthians*, edited by Ron Comeron and Merrill P. Miller, 245–302. Atlanta: SBL, 2011.

Campbell, Archibald. *Horace: A New Interpretation*. London: Methuen, 1924.

Campbell, Joan Cecelia. *Phoebe: Patron and Emissary*. Collegeville: Liturgical, 2009.

Cantarella, Eva. *Bisexuality in the Ancient World*. Translated by Cormac Ó Cuilleanáin New Haven: Yale University Press, 1992.

Caragounis, Chrys C. "'Fornication' and 'Concession:' Interpreting 1 Cor 7,1–7." In *The Corinthian Correspondence*, edited by R. Bieringer, 543–59. Leuven: Leuven University Press, 1996.

———. "What Did Paul Mean? The Debate on 1 Cor. 7:1–7." *Ephemerides theologicae Lovanienses* 82 (2006) 189–99.

Carney, Elizabeth Donnelly. *Women and Monarchy in Macedonia*. Norman: University of Oklahoma Press, 2000.

Castner, Catherine J. "Difficulties in Identifying Roman Epicureans: Orata in Cicero De Fin. 2.22.70." *Classical Journal* 81 (1986) 138–47.

———. *Prosopography of Roman Epicureans from the Second Century B.C. to the Second Century A.D.* Frankfurt: Lang, 1991.

Casson, Lionel. *Travel in the Ancient World*. Toronto: Hakkert, 1974.

Cervin, Richard S. "Does *Kephalē* Mean 'Source' or 'Authority Over' in Greek Literature: A Rebuttal." *Trinity Journal*, n.s., 10 (1989) 85–112.

Chilton, C. W. "Did Epicurus Approve of Marriage? A Study of Diogenes Laertius X, 119." *Phronesis* 5 (1960) 71–74.

———. "The Inscription of Diogenes of Oenoanda." *American Journal of Archaeology* 67 (1963) 285–86.

Chilver, G. E. R., and G. B. Townend. *An Historical Commentary on Tacitus Histories IV and V*. Oxford: Clarendon University Press, 1985.

Chow, John K. *Patronage and Power: A Study of Social Networks in Corinth*. Journal for the Study of the New Testament 75. Sheffield, UK: JSOT, 1992.

———. "Patronage in Roman Corinth." In *Paul and Empire: Religion and Power in Roman Imperial Society*, edited by Richard Horsley, 104–26. Harrisburg, PA: Trinity Press International, 1997.

Churchill, Laurie J., et al., editors. *Women Writing Latin: From Roman Antiquity to Early Modern Europe*. New York: Routledge, 2002.

Ciampa, Roy. "Revisiting the Euphemisim in 1 Corinthians 7.1." *Journal for the Study of the New Testament* 31 (2009) 325–38.

Ciampa, Roy, and Brian S. Rosner. *The First Letter to the Corinthians*. Grand Rapids: Eerdmans, 2010.

Clark, Elizabeth A. *Reading Renunciation: Asceticism and Scripture in Early Christianity*. Princeton: Princeton University Press, 1999.

Clark, Gillian. "Roman Women." *Greece & Rome*, 2nd ser., 28 (1981) 193–212.

Clark, Stephen R. L. "Ancient Philosophy." In *The Oxford History of Western Philosophy*, edited by Anthony Kenny, 1–54. New York: Oxford University Press, 1994.

Clarke, Andrew D. "Another Corinthian Erastus Inscription." *Tyndale Bulletin* 42 (1991) 146-51.

———. *Secular and Christian Leadership in Corinth: A Socio-Historical and Exegetical Study of 1 Corinthians 1-6*. New York: Brill, 1993.

———. *Serve the Community of the Church: Chrisitans as Leaders and Ministers*. Grand Rapids: Eerdmans, 2000.

Clarke, G. W. Review of *A History of Women Philosophers. Volume I: Ancient Women Philosophers, 600 B.C.-500 A.D.*, by Mary Ellen Waithe. *Classical Review*, n.s., 38 (1988) 429-30.

———. "Seneca the Younger under Caligula." *Latomus* 24 (1965) 62-69.

Clarke, M. L. "Poets and Patrons at Rome." *Greece and Rome*, 2nd ser., 51 (1978) 46-54.

Classen, C. Joachim. "St. Paul's Epistles and Ancient Greek and Roman Rhetoric." *Rhetorica* 10 (1992) 319-44.

Clay, Diskin. "An Epicurean Interpretation of Dreams." *American Journal of Philology* 101 (1980) 342-65.

Clayman, Dee Lesser. "The Meaning of Corinna's Ϝεροῖα." *Classical Quarterly*, n.s., 28 (1978) 396-97.

Coarelli, F. "Il complesso pompeiano del Campo Marzio e la sua decorazione scultorea." In *Atti della Pontificia Accademia Romana di Archeologia, Rendiconti* 44 (1970-1971) 99-122.

Cohic, Lynn H. *Christians: Illuminating Ancient Ways of Life*. Grand Rapids: Baker Academic, 2009.

———. *Women in the World of the Earliest Christians: Illuminating Ancient Ways of Life*. Grand Rapids: Baker Academic, 2009.

Coiner, Harry G. "Those Divorce and Remarriage Passages." *Concordia Theological Monthly* 39 (1968) 367-84.

Cole, Susan. "Could Greek Women Read and Write?" In *Reflections of Women in Antiquity*, edited by Helene P. Foley, 219-45. New York: Gordon & Breach Science Publishers, 1981.

Collins, Derek. *Master of the Game: Competition and Performance in Greek Poetry*. Cambridge: Harvard University Press, 2004.

Collins, Raymond F. *Divorce in the New Testament*. Collegeville: Liturgical, 1992.

———. *First Corinthians*. Edited by Daniel J. Harrington. Collegeville: Order of St. Benedict, 1999.

Collins, Susan D., and Devin Stauffer. "The Challenge of Plato's 'Menexenus.'" *Review of Politics* 61 (1999) 85-115.

Commager, Steele. "The Function of Wine in Horace's Odes." *Transactions and Proceedings of the American Philological Association* 88 (1957) 68-80.

Conzelmann, Hans. *First Corinthians: A Commentary on the First Epistle to the Corinthians*. Hermeneia. Minneapolis: Fortress, 1988.

Cook, Albert. "Dialectic, Irony, and Myth in Plato's Phaedrus." *American Journal of Philology* 106 (1985) 427-41.

Cook, John Granger. *Interpretation of the New Testament in Greco-Roman Paganism*. Tübingen: Mohr/Siebeck, 2000.

———. *Roman Attitudes toward the Christians from Claudius to Hadrian*. Wissenschaftliche Untersuchungen zum Neuen Testament 261. Tübingen: Mohr/Siebeck, 2010.

Works Cited

Cooper, Kate. *The Fall of the Roman Household*. Cambridge: Cambridge University Press, 2007.
Cope, L. "1 Cor 11.2-16: One Step Further." *Journal Biblical Literature* 97 (1978) 435-36.
Copleston, Frederick. *A History of Philosophy: Greece and Rome*. New Haven: Westminster, 1955.
Corbier, Mireille. "Divorce and Adoption as Roman Familial Strategies." In *Marriage, Divorce, and Children in Ancient Rome*, edited by Beryl Rawson, 47-78. New York: Oxford University Press, 1991.
Cornish, Marcia. "Pauline Theology and Stoic Philosophy: An Historical Study." *Journal of the American Academy of Religion* 47 (1979) 1-21.
———. *The Stoic Tradition from Antiquity to the Early Middle Ages*. New Haven: Yale University Press, 1985.
———. "Stoicism and the New Testament: An Essay in Historiography." In *Aufstieg und Niedergang der römischen Welt: Geschichte und Kultur Roms im Spiegel der neueren Forschung*, vol. 2.26.1, edited by Wolfgang Haase and Hildegard Temporini, 334-79. New York: de Gruyter, 1982.
Corrington, Gail P. "The 'Headless Woman': Paul and the Language of the Body in 1 Cor 11:2-16." *Perspectives in Religious Studies* 18 (1991) 223-31.
Cotter, Wendy. "Women's Authority Roles in Paul's Churches: Countercultural or Conventional?" *Novum Testamentum* 36 (1994) 350-72.
Courtney, E. "Horace and the Pest." *Classical Journal* (1994) 1-8.
Coventry, Lucinda. "Philosophy and Rhetoric in the Menexenus." *Journal of Hellenistic Studies* 109 (1989) 1-15.
Cranfield, C. E. B. *A Commentary on Romans 12-13*. Edinburgh: Oliver & Boyd, 1965.
Crook, J. A., et al., editors. *Cambridge Ancient History 7.2*. 2nd ed. Cambridge: Cambridge University Press, 1989.
———. *Law and Life of Rome*. New York: Cornell University Press, 1967.
Croom, Alexandra T. *Roman Clothing and Fashion*. Stroud, UK: Tempus, 2010.
Crowther, Nigel B. "Second-Place Finishes and Lower in Greek Athletics (Including the Pentathlon)." *Zeitschrift für Papyrologie Epigrapik* 90 (1992) 97-102.
———. "Slaves and Greek Athletics." *Quaderni Urbinati di Cultura Classica*, n.s., 40 (1992) 35-42.
Crüsemann, Marlene. "Irredeemably Hostile to Women: Anti-Jewish Elements in the Exegesis of the Dispute about Women's Right to Speak (1 Cor. 14.34-35)." Translated by Brian McNeil. *Journal for the Study of the New Testament* 79 (2000) 19-36.
Cunningham, I. C. "Herodas 6 and 7." *Classical Quarterly*, n.s., 14 (1964) 32-35.
Dalzell, A. "Maecenas and the Poets." *Phoenix* 10 (1956) 151-62.
D'Ambra, Eve. *Roman Women*. Cambridge: Cambridge University Press, 2007.
Damon, Cynthia. "Greek Parasites and Roman Patronage." *Harvard Studies in Classical Philology* 97 (1995) 181-95.
———. *The Mask of the Parasite: A Pathology of Roman Patronage*. Ann Arbor: University of Michigan Press, 1997.
Dancy, Russell M. "On *A History of Women Philosophers*, Vol. 1." Review of *A History of Women Philosophers. Volume I: Ancient Women Philosophers, 600 B.C.-500 A.D.*, by Mary Ellen Waithe. *Hypatia* 1 (1986) 160-71.

Works Cited

Danker, Frederick W. *Benefactor: Epigraphic Study of a Graeco-Roman and New Testament Semantic Field*. St. Louis: Clayton, 1982.
Danylak, Barry N. "Tiberius Claudius Dinippus and the Food Shortages in Corinth." *Tyndale Bulletin* 59 (2008) 231-70.
Das, Andrew A. *Paul and the Jews*. Peabody, MA: Hendrickson, 2003.
———. *Paul, the Law, and the Covenant*. Peabody, MA: Hendrickson, 2001.
Daux, G. "Inscriptions de Delphes." *Bulletin de Correspondance Hellénique* 46 (1922) 439-66.
Davenport, Guy. "A Private Talk among Friends." *Grand Street* 53, Fetishes (1995) 53-58.
Dawes, Gregory W. "'But If You Can Gain Your Freedom' (1 Corinthians 7:17-24)." *Catholic Biblical Quarterly* 52 (1990) 681-97.
De Vogel, C. J. *Greek Philosophy*. Vol. 3, *The Hellenistic-Roman Period*. Leiden: Brill, 1959.
———. *Pythagoras and Early Pythagoreanism*. Assen: Van Gorcum, 1956.
De Vos, Craig Steven. "Stepmothers, Concubines and the Case of Πορνεία in 1 Corinthians 5." *New Testament Studies* 44 (1998) 104-14.
De Witt, Norman W. *Epicurus and His Philosophy*. Minneapolis: University of Minnesota Press, 1954.
———. *St. Paul and Epicurus*. Minneapolis: University of Minnesota Press, 1954.
Dean, L. R. "Latin Inscriptions from Corinth." *American Journal of Archaeology* 22 (1918) 189-97.
———. "Latin Inscriptions from Corinth II." *American Journal of Archaeology* 23 (1919) 163-74.
Deichgräber, Karl. *Die griechische Empirikerschule*. Berlin: Weidmann, 1930.
Deissmann, Adolf. *Bibelstudien: Beiträge, zumeist aus den Papyri und Inschriften, zur Geschichte der Sprache, des Schrifttums und der Religion des hellenistischen Judentums und des Urchristentums*. Marburg, Germany: Elwert, 1895.
———. *Bible Studies: Contributions Chiefly from Papyri and Inscriptions to the Hisory of Language, the Literature, and the Religion of Hellenistic Judaism and Primative Christianity*. Translated by Alexander Grieve. Edinburg: T. & T. Clark, 1901.
———. *Licht vom Osten. Das Neue Testament und die neuentdeckten Texte der hellenistisch-römischen Welt*. Tübingen: Mohr, 1923.
———. *Light from the Ancient East: The New Testament Illustrated by Recently Discovered Texts of the Graeco-Roman World*. Translated by Lionel R. M. Strachan. New York: Hodder & Stoughton, 1911.
Deissner, Kurt. *Paulus und Seneca*. Edited by D. A. Schlatter and D. W. Lütgert. Fördung christlicher Theologie 21. Gütersloh: Bertelsmann, 1917.
Delatte, Armand. *Études sur la littérature pythagoricienne*. Paris: Champion, 1915.
DeMaris, Richard E. "Demeter in Roman Corinth: Local Development in a Mediterranean Religion." *Numen* 42 (1995) 105-17.
Deming, Will. "A Diatribe Pattern in 1 Cor 7:21-22: A New Perspective on Paul's Directions to Slaves." *Novum Testamentum* 37 (1995) 130-37.
———. *Paul on Marriage and Celibacy: The Hellenistic Background of 1 Corinthians 7*. Cambridge: Cambridge University Press, 1995.
———. "The Unity of 1 Corinthians 5-6." *Journal of Biblical Literature* 115 (1996) 289-312.

Works Cited

Demos, Raphael. "Paradoxes in Plato's Doctrine of the Ideal State." *Classical Quarterly*, n.s., 7 (1957) 164–74.

Derrett, J. Duncan M. "Religious Hair." *Man*, n.s., 8 (1973) 100–103.

DeSilva, David. "Patronage and Reciprocity: The Context of Grace in the New Testament." *Ashland Theological Journal* 31 (1999) 32–84.

―――. "Re-writing 'Household' in the Early Church." *Ashland Theological Journal* 36 (2004) 85–89.

Desmond, William D. *Cynics*. Berkeley: University of California Press, 2008.

DeWitt, Norman W. "Epicurean Contubernium." *Transactions and Proceedings of the American Philological Association* 67 (1936) 55–63.

―――. "Vergil and Epicureanism." *Classical Weekly* 25 (1932) 89–96.

Dickey, Eleanor. *Ancient Greek Scholarship: A Guide to Finding, Reading, and Understanding*. New York: Oxford, 2006.

Dillon, Mattthew. "Did Parthenoi Attend the Olympic Games? Girls and Women Competing, Spectating, and Carrying Out Cult Roles at Greek Religious Festivals." *Hermes* 128 (2000) 457–80.

Dix, Thomas Keith. "Private and Public Libraries at Rome in the First Century B.C.: A Preliminary Study in the History of Roman Libraries." PhD diss., University of Michigan, 1986.

Dixon, Suzanne. "Polybius on Roman Women and Property." *American Journal of Philology* 106 (1985) 147–70.

―――. "'Public Libraries' in Ancient Rome: Ideology and Reality." *Libraries & Culture* 29 (1994) 282–96.

―――. *The Roman Family*. Baltimore: Johns Hopkins Press, 1992.

Dobschütz, Ernst von. *Christian Life in the Primative Church*. Boston: American Unitarian Association, 1904.

Donado, Vara. "Cronologia de Erinna." *Emerita* 41 (1973) 349–46.

Donfried, Karl P. "The Cults of Thessalonica and the Thessalonian Correspondence." *New Testament Studies* (1985) 336–56.

―――. "The Imperial Cults of Thessalonica." In *Paul and Empire: Religion and Power in Roman Imperial Society*, edited by Richard Horsely, 215–23. Harrisburg, PA: Trinity Press International, 1997.

Dover, Kenneth J. *Greek Homosexuality*. Cambridge: Harvard University Press, 1978.

―――. "Two Women of Samos." In *The Sleep of Reason: Erotic Experience and Sexual Ethics in Ancient Greece and Rome*, edited by Martha C. Nussbaum and Juha Sihvola, 222–82. Chicago: University of Chicago Press, 2002.

Downing, Francis Gerald. "A Cynical Response to the Subjection of Women." *Philosophy* 69 (1994) 229–30.

―――. *Cynics, Paul, and the Pauline Churches: Cynics and Christian Origin*. London: Routledge, 1988.

Droge, Arthur J. "Justin Martyr and the Restoration of Philosophy." *Church History* 56 (1987) 303–19.

―――. "Mori Lucrum: Paul and Ancient Theories of Suicide." *Novum Testamentum* 30 (1988) 263–86.

Duchrow, U. *Christenheit und Weltverantwortung. Traditionsgeschichte und systematische Struktur der Zweireichelehre*. Forschungen und Berichte der Evangelischen Studienge-meinschaft 25. Stuttgart: Klett, 1970.

Works Cited

Dudley, D. R. *A History of Cynicism from Diogenes to the Sixth Century.* London: Methuen, 1937.

Dunbabin, T. J. "The Early History of Corinth." *Journal of Hellenistic Studies* 68 (1948) 59–69.

Dunn, James D. G. "Did Paul Have a Covenant Theology? Reflections on Romans 9.4 and 11.27." In *Concept of the Covenant in the Second Temple Period*, edited by Stanley E. Porter and Jacqueline De-Roo, 287–307. Journal for the Study of Judaism Supplement 71. Leiden: Brill, 2003.

———. *The Epistle to the Galatians.* Black's New Testament Commentaries 9. Peabody, MA: Hendrickson, 1995.

———. *1 Corinthians.* New York: T. & T. Clark International, 2003.

———. "The New Perspective on Paul." *Bulletin of the John Rylands Library* 65 (1983) 95–122.

———. *Romans 1–8.* Word Biblical Commentary 38a. Dallas: Word, 1988.

———. *Romans 9–16.* Word Biblical Commentary 38b. Dallas: Word, 1988.

Durant, William. *The Story of Philosophy: The Lives and Opinions of the Greater Philosophers.* New York: Simon & Schuster, 1926.

Dutch, Robert S. *The Educated Elite in 1 Corinthians: Education and Community Conflict in Graeco-Roman Context.* London: T. & T. Clark, 2005.

Dyck, Andrew R. "Dressing to Kill: Attire as a Proof and Means of Characterization in Cicero's Speeches." *Arethusa* 34 (2001) 119–30.

Dyson, J. T. "Dido the Epicurean." *Classical Antiquity* 15 (1996) 203–21.

Dzielska, Maria. *Apollonius of Tyana in Legend and History.* Translated by Pior Pieńkowski. Rome: L'Erma di Bretschneider, 1986.

Edmonds, J. M. "The Epigrams of Balbilla." *Classical Review* 39 (1925) 107–10.

———. "P. S. I. 1090." *Mnemosyne*, 3rd ser., 6 (1938) 195–203.

———. "A Quotation of Sappho in Juvenal Satire 6." *Phoenix* 45 (1991) 255–57.

———. "Sappho's Book as Depicted on an Attic Vase." *Classical Quarterly* 16 (1922) 1–14.

Ehrensperger, Kathy. *That We May Be Mutually Encouraged: Feminism and the New Perspective in Pauline Studies.* New York: T. & T. Clark, 2004.

Eijk, Philip J. van der. *Medicine and Philosophy: Doctors and Philosophers on Nature, the Soul, Health and Disease.* Cambridge: Cambridge University Press, 2005.

Eilers, Claude. *Roman Patrons of Greek Cities.* Oxford: Oxford University Press, 2002.

Eisenberger, H. "Sokrates, Diotima und die 'Wahrheit' über 'eros.'" In *AINIΓMA: Festschrift für Helmut Rahn*, edited by Freyr Roland Varwig, 183–218. Heidelberg: Winter, 1987.

Eisenstadt, S. N., and L. Roniger. *Partons, Clients, and Friends: Interpersonal Relations and the Structure of Trust in Society.* Cambridge: Cambridge University Press, 1984.

Elliot, Neil. *The Arrogance of Nations: Reading Romans in the Shadow of Empire.* Minneapolis: Fortress, 2010.

———. *Liberating Paul: The Justice of God and the Politics of the Apostle.* Minneapolis: Fortress, 2006.

Elliott, John H. "Elders as Honored Household Heads and Not Holders of 'Office' in Earliest Christianity." Review of *The Elders: Seniority within Earliest Christianity*, by Alastair Campbell. *Biblical Theology Bulletin* 33 (2003) 77–82.

Works Cited

———. *A Home for the Homeless. A Sociological Exegesis of 1 Peter, Its Situation and Strategy*. Philadelphia: Fortress, 1981.

———. "Patronage and Clientage." In *The Social Sciences and New Testament Interpretation*, edited by Richard L. Rohrbaugh, 142–56. Peabody, MA: Hendrickson, 1996.

———. *What Is Social-Scientific Criticism? Guides to Biblical Scholarship*. Minneapolis: Fortress, 1993.

Elliott, Mark A. *The Survivors of Israel: A Reconsideration of the Theology of Pre-Christian Judaism*. Grand Rapids: Eerdmans, 2000.

Engberg-Pedersen, Troels. "Gift-Giving and Friendship: Seneca and Paul in Romans 1–8 on the Logic of God's Χάρις and Its Human Response." *Harvard Theological Review* 101 (2008) 15–44.

———. "The Material Spirit: Cosmology and Ethics in Paul." *New Testament Studies* 55 (2009) 179–97.

———. *Paul and the Stoics*. Louisville: Westminster, 2000.

———. "Stoicism in Philippians." In *Paul in His Hellenistic Context*, edited by Troels Engberg-Pederson, 256–90. Minneapolis: Fortress Press, 1995.

Engel, David M. "Women's Role in the Home and the State: Stoic Theory Reconsidered." *Harvard Studies in Classical Philology* 101 (2003) 267–88.

Erskine, W. *The Hellenistic Stoa*. Ithaca, NY: Cornell University Press, 1990.

Esler, Philip. *Conflict and Identity in Romans: The Social Setting of Paul's Letter*. Minneapolis: Fortress, 2003.

Evans, Jane DeRose. "Prostitutes in the Portico of Pompey? A Reconsideration." *Transactions of the American Philological Association* 139 (2009) 123–45.

Everitt, Anthony. *Cicero: A Turbulent Life*. London: John Murray, 2001.

Eyre, J. J. "Roman Education in the Late Republic and Early Empire." *Greece & Rome*, 2nd ser., 10 (1963) 47–59.

Fantham, Elaine. "Covering the Head at Rome." In *Roman Dress and the Fabrics of Roman Culture*, edited by Jonathan Edmondson and Allison Keith, 213–37. Toronto: University of Toronto Press, 2008.

Fantham, Elaine, et al. *Women in the Classical World*. New York: Oxford University Press, 1994.

Farla, Piet. "'The Two Shall Become One Flesh': Gen 1.27 and 2.24 in the New Testament Marriage Texts." In *Intertextuality in Biblical Writings: Essays in Honour of Bas van Iersel*, edited by S. Draisma, 67–82. Kampen, Netherlands: Kok, 1989.

Fee, Gordon D. "1 Corinthians 7.1 in the NIV." *Journal of the Evangelical Theological Society* 23 (1980) 307–14.

———. "1 Corinthians 7.1–7 Revisited." In *Paul and the Corinthians: Studies on a Community in Conflict*, edited by Trevor J. Burke and J. Keith Elliot, 197–213. Leiden: Brill, 2003.

Feldman, Louis H. "Abraham the Greek Philosopher in Josephus." *Transactions of the American Philological Association* 99 (1968) 143–56.

———. *Studies in Ancient Judaism*. Leiden: Brill, 1996.

Ferguson, John. *Clement of Alexandria*. Edited by Sylvia Bowman. Twayne's World Authors Series 289. New York: Twayne, 1974.

———. "Epicureanism under the Roman Empire." In *Aufstieg und Niedergang der römischen Welt: Geschichte und Kultur Roms im Spiegel der neueren Forschung*, vol. 2.36.4, edited by Wolfgang Haase and Hildegard Temporini, 2257–2327. New York: de Gruyter, 1990.

———. *Moral Values in the Ancient World*. London, Methuen: 1958.

Ferrar, Giovanni R. F. *The Cambridge Companion to Plato's Republic*. New York: Cambridge University Press, 2007.

Ferrill, Arther. "Seneca's Exile and the *Ad Helviam*: A Reinterpretation." *Classical Philology* 61 (1966) 253–57.

Filson, Floyd. *The New Testament Against Its Environment*. London: SCM, 1950.

———. "The Significance of the Early House Churches." *Journal of Biblical Literature* 58 (1939) 109–12.

Finkelberg, Aryeh. "Plato's Method in Timaeus." *American Journal of Philology* 117 (1996) 391–409.

Finnegan, Rachel. "The Professional Careers: Women Pioneers and the Male Image Seduction." *Classics Ireland* 2 (1995) 67–81.

Finney, Mark. "Honour, Head-Coverings and Headship: 1 Corinthians 11.2–16 in Its Social Context." *Journal for the Study of the New Testament* 33 (2010) 31–58.

Fiore, Benjamin. "Paul, Exemplification, and Imitation." In *Paul in the Greco-Roman World*, edited by J. Paul Sampley, 228–57. New York: Trinity, 2003.

———. "Passion in Paul and Plutarch: 1 Corinthians 5–6 and the Polemic against Epicureans." In *Greeks, Romans, and Christians*, edited by David Balch et al., 135–43. Minneapolis: Fortress, 1990.

Fiorenza, Elizabeth Schüsseler. *Rhetoric and Ethic: The Politics of Biblical Studies*. Minneapolis: Fortress, 1999.

Fish, Jeffrey, and Kirk R. Sanders. *Epicurus and the Epicurean Tradition*. Cambridge, Cambridge University Press, 2011.

Fitzgerald, John T. *Cracks in an Earthen Vessel: An Examination of the Catalogues of Hardships in the Corinthian Correspondence*. Atlanta: Scholars, 1988.

———. "Early Christian Missionary Practice and Pagan Reaction: 1 Peter and Domestic Violence against Slaves and Wives." In *Renewing Tradition: Studies in Texts and Contexts in Honor of James W. Thompson*, edited by M. W. Hamilton et al., 24–44. Princeton Theological Monograph Series. Eugene, OR: Pickwick, 2007.

———, editor. *Friendship, Flattery, and Frankness of Speech: Studies on Friendship in the New Testament World*. Novum Testamentum Supplement 82. Leiden: Brill, 1996.

———. *Greco-Roman Perspectives on Friendship*. Atlanta: SBL, 1997.

———, editor. *Passions and Moral Progress in Greco-Roman Thought*. Routledge Monographs in Classical Studies. London: Routledge, 2008.

Fitzgerald, John T., Dirk Obbink, and Glenn S. Holland. *Philodemus and the New Testament World*. Novum Testamentum Supplement 111. Leiden: Brill, 2004.

Fitzgerald, John T., and Thomas H. Olbricht. "Quod est comparandum: The Problem of Parallels." In *Early Christianity and Classical Culture: Comparative Studies in Honor of Abraham J. Malherbe*, edited by John T. Fitzgerald et al., 13–39. Leiden: Brill, 2003.

Fitzgerald, John T., Thomas H. Olbricht, and L. Michael White, editors. *Early Christianity and Classical Culture: Comparative Studies in Honor of Abraham J. Malherbe*. Novum Testamentum Supplement 110. Leiden: Brill, 2003.

Fitzmyer, Joseph A. "Another Look at Kephale in 1 Corinthians 11:3." *New Testament Studies* 35 (1989) 503–11.

Works Cited

———. *1 Corinthians: A New Translation with Introduction and Commentary.* The Anchor Yale Bible. New Haven: Yale University Press, 2008.

———. "Kephalē in I Corinthians 11:3." *Interpretation* 47 (1993) 52–59.

Flemming, Rebecca. "Women, Writing and Medicine in the Classical World." *Classical Quarterly* 57 (2007) 257–79.

Fleury, Amédée. *Saint Paul et Sénèque: Recherches sur les rapports du philosophe avec l'apôtre et sur l'infiltration du Christianisme naissant à travers le paganisme.* Paris: Ladrange, 1853.

Flinterman, Jaap-Jan. "The Ubiquitous 'Divine Man.'" Review of *Apollonius von Tyana in der neutestamentlichen Exegese: Forschungsbericht und Weiterführung der Diskussion,* by Erkki Koskenniemi and *Sage, Saint, and Sophist: Holy Men and Their Associates in the Early Roman Empire,* by Graham Anderson. *Numen* 43 (1996) 82–98.

Foley, Helene Peet, et al., editors. *Women in the Classical World.* New York: Oxford, 1994.

Forbes, Christopher. *Prophecy and Inspired Speech in Early Christianity and Its Hellenistic Environment.* Wissenschaftliche Untersuchungen zum Neuen Testament 2.75. Tübingen: Mohr, 1995.

Forbes, Clarence A. "Crime and Punishment in Greek Athletics." *Classical Journal* 47 (1952) 169–73, 202–3.

Ford, J. Massyngberde. "'Hast Thou Tithed Thy Meal?' and 'Is Thy Child Kosher?' (1 Cor 10:27ff and 1 Cor 7:14)." *Journal of Theological Studies,* n.s., 17 (1966) 71–79.

Fornara, Charles W., and Loren J. Samons II. *Athens from Cleisthenes to Pericles.* Berkeley: University of California Press, 1991.

Fortenbaugh, William, and Eckart Schütrumpf, editors. *Dicaearchus of Messana: Text, Translation, and Discussion.* New Brunswick, NJ: Transaction, 2001.

Fotopoulos, John. *Food Offered to Idols in Roman Corinth: A Social-Rhetorical Reconsideration of 1 Corinthians 8:1—11:1.* Tübingen: Mohr/Siebeck, 2003.

Fowler, W. Warde. *Social Life at Rome in the Age of Cicero.* New York: Macmillan, 1909.

Fränkel, Max, and Christian Habicht, editors. *Die Inschriften von Pergamon.* Altertümer von Pergamonn. Berlin: Spemann, 1890–95.

Frede, D. "Out of the Cave: What Socrates Learned from Diotima." In *Nomodeiktes: Greek Studies in Honor of Martin Ostwald,* edited by Ralph M. Rosen and Joseph Farrell, 397–422. Ann Anbor: University of Michigan Press, 1993.

Fredrickson, David E. "ΠΑΡΗΣΙΑ in the Pauline Epistles." In *Friendship, Flattery, and Frankness of Speech,* edited by John T. Fitzgerald, 613–84. New York: Brill, 1996.

Freeman, Kathleen. "Plato: The Use of Inspiration." *Greece & Rome* 49 (1940) 137–49.

Freisen, Steven J. "The Wrong Erastus: Ideology, Archaeology, and Exegesis." In *Corinth in Context: Comparative Studies on Religion and Society,* edited by Steven J. Freisen et al., 231–56. Leiden: Brill, 2010.

French, E. B. "Archaeology in Greece 1990–91." *Archaeological Reports* 37 (1990–1991) 3–78.

Frier, Bruce W. *A Casebook on Roman Family Law.* Oxford: Oxford University Press, 2004.

———. *The Rise of the Roman Jurists: Studies in Cicero's "Pro Caecina."* Princeton: Princeton University Press, 1985.

Friesen, Steven J. "Poverty in Pauline Studies: Beyond the So-Called New Consensus." *Journal for the Study of the New Testament* 26 (2004) 323–61.

Fuller, Benjamin A. G. *A History of Philosophy*. Translated by Sterling M. McMurrin. New York: Holt, 1960.

Furst, Lilian R. *Women Healers and Physicians: Climbing a Long Hill*. Lexington: University of Kentucky Press, 1999.

Gaca, Kathy L. *The Making of Fornication: Eros, Ethics, and Politial Reform in Greek Philosophy and Early Christainity*. Berkeley: University of California Press, 2003.

———. "The Reproductive Technology of the Pythagoreans." *Classical Philology* 95 (2000) 113–32.

Gallivan, Paul A. "Nero's Liberation of Greece." *Hermes* 101 (1973) 230–34.

Garcilazo, Albert V. *The Corinthian Dissenters and the Stoics*. Studies in Biblical Literature 106. New York: Peter Lang, 2007.

Gardner, Jane F. *Being a Roman Citizen*. New York: Routledge, 2002.

———. "The Recovery of Dowry in Roman Law." *Classical Quarterly*, n.s., 35 (1985) 449–53.

———. *Women in Roman Law and Society*. Bloomington: Indiana University Press, 1991.

Gardner, Jane F., and Thomas Wiedemann, editors. *The Roman Household: A Sourcebook*. London: Routledge, 1991.

Gardner, Percy. "Boat-Races among the Greeks." *Journal of Hellenistic Studies* 2 (1881) 90–97.

Garland, David. *1 Corinthians*. Baker Exegetical Commentary on the New Testament. Grand Rapids: Baker Academic, 2003.

Garland, Robert. *Celebrity in Antiquity: From Media Tarts to Tabloid Queens*. London: Duckworth, 2006.

Garlington, Don B. "The New Perspective on Paul: An Appraisal Two Decades Later." *Criswell Theological Review* 2 (2005) 17–38.

Garnsey, Peter. "Legal Privilege in the Roman Empire." *Past & Present* 41 (1968) 3–24.

———. *Social Status and Legal Privilege*. Oxford: Clarendon University Press, 1970.

Garrison, Roman. "Paul's Use of the Athlete Metaphor in 1 Corinthians 9." *Studies in Religion / Sciences Religieuses* 22 (1993) 209–17.

———. "Phoebe, the Servant-Benefactor and Gospel Traditions." In *Text and Artifact in the Religions of Mediterranean Antiquity: Essays in Honor of Peter Richardson*, edited by Stephen G. Wilson and Michel Robert Desjardins, 63–73. Studies in Christianity and Judaism 9. Ontario: Wilfrid University Press, 2000.

Garthwaite, John. "Patronage and Poetic Immortality in Martial, Book 9." *Mnemosyne*, 4th ser., 51 (1998) 161–75.

Gaventa, B. R. "Galatians 1 and 2: Autobiography as Paradigm." *Novum Testamentum* 28 (1986) 309–26.

Geagan, Daniel J. "The Isthmian Dossier of P. Licinius Priscus Juventianus." *Hesperia* 58 (1989) 349–60.

———. "Notes on the Agonistic Institutions of Roman Corinth." *Greek, Roman, and Byzantine Studies* 9 (1968) 69–76.

Gebhard, Elizabeth. "The Isthmian Games and the Sanctuary of Poseidon in the Early Empire." In *The Corinthia in the Roman Period*, edited by Timothy E. Gregory, 78–94. Journal of Roman Archaeology Supplementary Series 8. Ann Arbor, MI: Journal of Roman Archaeology, 1993.

Gehring, Roger W. *House Church and Mission: The Importance of Household Structures in Early Christianity*. Peabody: Hendrickson, 2004.

Works Cited

Gellner, Ernst, and John Waterbury, editors. *Patrons and Clients in Mediterranean Societies*. London: Duckworth, 1977.
Giangrande, Giuseppe. "An Epigram of Erinna." *Classical Review*, n.s., 19 (1969) 1–3.
Giannantoni, Gabriele. *Socratis et Socraticorum Reliquiae*. 4 vols. Napoli: Bibliopolis, 1990–1991.
Gigante, Marcello. *Philodemus in Italy: The Books from Herculaneum*. Translated by Dirk Obbink. Ann Arbor: University of Michigan Press, 1995.
Gill, David W. J. "Erastus." *Tyndale Bulletin* 40 (1989) 293–301.
———. "In Search of the Social Elite in the Corinthian Church." *Tyndale Bulletin* 44 (1993) 323–37.
Gillihan, Yonder Moynihan. "Jewish Laws on Illicit Marriage, the Defilement of Offspring, and the Holiness of the Temple: A New Halakic Interpretation of 1 Corinthians 7:14." *Journal of Biblical Literature* 121 (2002) 711–44.
Gini, Anthony. "The Manly Intellect of His Wife: Xenophon, 'Oeconomicus' Ch. 7." *The Classical World* 86 (1993) 483–86.
Ginsburg, Judith. *Representing Agrippina: Constructions of Female Power in the Early Roman Empire*. Oxford: Oxford University Press, 2006.
Glad, Clarence E. *Paul and Philodemus: Adaptability in Epicurean and Early Christian Psychagogy*. Leiden: Brill, 1995.
Gleason, M. W. *Making Men: Sophists and Self-Presentation in Ancient Rome*. Princeton: Princeton University Press, 1995.
Gleason, Kathryn. "The Garden Portico of Pompey the Great: An Ancient Public Park Preserved in the Layers of Rome." *Expedition* 32 (1990) 4–13.
———. "Porticus Pompeiana: A New Perspective in the First Public Park of Ancient Rome." *Journal of Garden History* 14 (1990) 13–27.
Glenn, Cheryl. *Rhetoric Retold: Regendering the Tradition from Antiquity through the Renaissance*. Carbondale: Southern Illinois University Press, 1997.
Goessler, Lisette. "Advice to the Bride and Groom: Plutarch Gives a Detailed Account of His Views on Marriage." In *Plutarch's Advice to the Bride and Groom and A Consolation to His Wife*, translated by Hazel Harvey, edited by Sarah B. Pomeroy, 97–115. New York: Oxford University Press, 1999.
Gold, Barbara. *Literary Patronage in Greece and Rome*. Chapel Hill: University of North Carolina, 1987.
Goldberg, Sander M. "Plautus on the Palatine." *Journal of Roman Studies* 88 (1998) 1–20.
Goldman, Norma. "Reconstructing Roman Clothing." In *The World of Roman Costume*, edited by Judith Lynn Sebesta and Larissa Bonfante, 213–34. Madison: University of Wisconsin Press, 2001.
Goodenough, Erwin. *A Neo-Pythagorean Source in Philo Judaeus*. New Haven: Yale University Press, 1932.
Gordon, J. Dorcas. *Sister or Wife? 1 Corinthians 7 and Cultural Anthropology*. Sheffield, UK: Sheffield Academic, 1997.
Gordon, Pamela. *Epicurus in Lycia: The Second-Century World of Diogenes of Oenoanda*. Ann Arbor: University of Michigan Press, 1996.
———. "Remembering the Garden: The Trouble with Women in the School of Epicurus." In *Philodemus and the New Testament World*, edited by Dirk Obbink at al., 221–44. Novum Testamentum Supplement 111. Boston: Brill, 2004.
Goudsmit, S. A. "An Illiterate Scribe." *American Journal of Archaeology* 78 (1974) 78.

Works Cited

Goulet-Cazé, Marie-Odile. "A Comprehensive Catalouge of Known Cynic Philosophers." In *The Cynics: The Cynic Movement in Antiquity and Its Legacy*, edited by R. Bracht Branham and Marie-Odile Goulet-Cazé, 389–413. Berkeley: University of California Press, 1996.

Grant, Frederick Clifton. "St. Paul and Stoicism." *Biblical World* 45 (1915) 268–81.

Grant, Robert. "Dietary Laws among the Pythagoreans, Jews, and Christians." *Harvard Theological Review* 73 (1980) 299–310.

———. "Hellenistic Elements in 1 Corinthians." In *Early Christian Origins: Studies in Honor of Harold R. Willoughhy*, edited by A. Wikgren, 60–66. Chicago: Quadrangle, 1961.

———. "ΣΠΕΙΡΕΤΑΙ: Paul's Anthopogenic Metaphor in 1 Corinthians 15:42–44." *Journal of Biblical Literature* 120 (2001) 101–22.

———. "Studies in the Apologists." *Harvard Theological Review* 51 (1958) 123–28.

———. "Theophilus of Antioch to Autolycus." *Harvard Theological Review* 40 (1947) 227–56.

Green, Monica. Review of *A History of Women Philosophers. Volume I: Ancient Women Philosophers, 600 B.C.–500 A.D.*, by Mary Ellen Waithe. *Isis* 80 (1989) 178–79.

Greenberg, Robert A. "'Erotion,' 'Anactoria,' and the Sapphic Passion." *Victorian Poetry* 29 (1991) 79–87.

Greene, Ellen. "Apostrophe and Women's Erotics in the Poetry of Sappho." *Transactions of the American Philological Association* 124 (1994) 41–56.

———. Review of *A History of Women Philosophers. Volume I: Ancient Women Philosophers, 600 B.C.–500 A.D.*, by Mary Ellen Waithe. *Isis* 80 (1989) 178–79.

———, editor. *Women Poets in Ancient Greece and Rome*. Norman: University of Oklahoma Press, 2005.

Grese, William C. "De profectibus in virtute." In *Plutarch's Ethical Writings and the New Testament*, edited by Hans D. Betz, 11–33. Leiden: Brill, 1978.

Griffin, Miriam. "De Beneficiis and Roman Society." *Journal of Roman Studies* 93 (2003) 92–113.

Grindheim, Sigurd. "Wisdom for the Perfect: Paul's Advice to the Corinthian Church (1 Corinthians 2:6–16)." *Journal of Biblical Literature* 121 (2002) 689–709.

Grote, George. *Plato, and the Other Companions of Sokrates*. London: Murray, 1865.

Grubbs, Judith Evans. *Women and the Law in the Roman Empire: A Sourcebook on Marriage, Divorce and Widowhood*. London: Routledge, 2002.

Grudem, Wayne A. "Does ΚΕΦΑΛΗ ("Head") Mean 'Source' or 'Authority Over' in Greek Literature: A Survey of 2,336 Examples." *Trinity Journal*, n.s., 6 (1985) 38–59.

———. "The Meaning of κεφαλή ("Head"): A Response to Recent Studies." *Trinity Journal*, n.s., 11 (1990) 3–72.

———. "The Meaning of Κεφαλή ("Head"): An Evaluation of New Evidence, Real and Alleged." *Journal of the Evangelical Theological Society* 44 (2001) 25–65.

Gundry-Volf, Judith M. "Celibate Pneumatics and Social Power: On the Motivations for Sexual Asceticism in Corinth." *Union Seminary Quarterly Review* 48 (1994) 105–26.

———. "Controlling the Bodies: A Theological Profile of the Corinthian Sexual Ascetics (1 Cor 7)." In *Corinthian Correspondence*, edited by Reimund Bieringer, 519–41. Leuven: Leuven University Press, 1996.

Guthrie, W. K. C. *The Sophists*. Cambridge: Cambridge University Press, 1971.

Works Cited

Gutzwiller, Kathryn J. "Gender and Inscribed Epigram: Herennia Procula and the Thespian Eros." *Transactions of the American Philological Association* 134 (2004) 383–418.

———. *Poetic Garlands: Hellenistic Epigrams in Context*. Berkeley: University of California Press, 1998.

Hall, A. S. "Who Was Diogenes of Oenoanda?" *Journal of Hellenic Studies* 99 (1979) 160–63.

Hall, David R. *The Unity of the Corinthian Correspondence*. New York: T. & T. Clark, 2003.

Hall, Robert G. "The Rhetorical Outline for Galatians: A Reconsideration." *Journal of Biblical Literature* 106 (1987) 277–87.

Hallett, Judith P. *Fathers and Daughters in Roman Society. Women and the Elite Family* Princeton: Princeton University Press, 1984.

———. "Sappho and Her Social Context: Sense and Sensuality." *Signs* 4 (1979) 447–64.

Halperin, David M. *How to Do the History of Homosexuality*. Chicago: University of Chicago Press, 2002.

———. "Plato and Erotic Reciprocity." *Classical Antiquity* 5 (1986) 60–80.

———. "Why Is Diotima a Woman? Platonic Eros and the Figuration of Gender." In *Before Sexuality: The Construction of Erotic Experience in the Ancient World*, edited by D. M. Halperin et al., 257–309. Princeton: Princeton University Press, 1990.

Hammond, N. G. L. *A History of Macedonia*. Oxford: Clarendon University Press, 1972.

Hanslik, R. "Pompeia Plotina." *Pauly-Wissowa, Real-Encyclopädie der classischen Altertumswissenschaft* 21 (1921) 2293–98.

Hanson, Ann Ellis. "Ancient Illiteracy." In *Literacy in the Ancient World*, edited by M. Beard et al., 159–98. Ann Arbor, MI: Journal of Roman Archaeology, 1991.

Hanson, Ann Ellis, and Monica H. Green. "Soranus of Ephesus: Methodicorum princeps." In *Wissenschaften (Medizin und Biologie [Forts.])*, edited by Wolfgang Haase, 968–1065. Aufstieg und Niedergang der römischen Welt 37.2. Berlin: de Gruyter, 1994.

Harland, Philip. *Associations, Synagogues, and Congregations: Claiming a Place in Ancient Mediterranean Society*. Minneapolis: Fortress, 2003.

Harrill, J. Albert. "Paul and Slavery: The Problem of 1 Corinthians 7:21." *Biblical Research* 39 (1994) 5–28.

Harris, W. V. *Ancient Literacy*. Cambridge: Harvard University Press, 1989.

Harrison, James R. *Paul's Language of Grace in Its Graeco-Roman Context*. Wissenschaftliche Untersuchungen zum Neuen Testament 2. Tübingen: Mohr Siebeck, 2003.

Haskins, Ekaterina. "Pythagorean Women." In *Classical Rhetorics and Rhetoricians*, edited by Michelle Ballif and Michael G. Moran, 315–19. Westport, CT: Praeger, 2005.

Hawley, Richard. "Ancient Collections of Women's Sayings." *Bulletin of the Institute of Classical Studies* 50 (2007) 161–69.

———. "The Problem of Women Philosophers in Ancient Greece." In *Women in Ancient Societies: An Illusion of the Night*, edited by Leonie J. Archer et al., 70–87. New York: Routledge, 1994.

Hawthorne, John G. "The Myth of Palaemon." *Transactions of the American Philological Association* 89 (1958) 92–98.

Works Cited

Hay, David M. "Paul's Indifference to Authority." *Journal of Biblical Literature* 88 (1969) 36–44.
Hays, Richard B. *First Corinthians*. Louisville: John Knox, 1997.
Heibges, Ursula. "Cicero, a Hypocrite in Religion?" *American Journal of Philology* 90 (1969) 304–12.
Heil, John Paul. *The Rhetorical Role of Scripture in 1 Corinthians*. Atlanta: SBL, 2005.
Heinrici, Georg C. F. *Das zweite Sendschreiben des Apostel Paulus an die Korinthier*. Berlin: Hertz, 1887.
―――. "Die christengemeinden Korinths und die religiösen Genossenschaften der Griechen." *Zeitschrift für Wissenschaft* 19 (1896) 465–509.
―――. *Paulinische Probleme erörtert*. Leipzig: Durr, 1914.
Helleman, W. E. "Homer's Penelope: A Tale of Feminine Arete." *Echos du Monde Classique* 14 (1995) 227–50.
―――. "Penelope as Lady Philosophy." *Phoenix* 49 (1995) 283–302.
Hemelrijk, Emily Ann. *Matrona Docta: Educated Women in the Roman Élite from Cornelia to Julia Domna*. London: Routledge, 1999.
Henderson, Bernard. *The Life and Principate of the Emperor Hadrian, A.D. 76–138*. London: Methuen, 1903.
Henderson, W. J. "Criteria in the Greek Lyric Contests." *Mnemosyne* 42 (1989) 24–40.
Henry, Madeline M. *Prisoner of History: Aspasia of Miletus and Her Biographical Tradition*. New York: Oxford University Press, 1995.
Henten, Jan Willem van, and Pieter W. van der Horst, editors. *Studies in Early Jewish Epigraphy*. New York: Brill, 1994.
Hershkowitz, Debra. "Pliny the Poet." *Greece & Rome*, 2nd ser., 42 (1995) 168–81.
Heskel, Julia. "Cicero as Evidence for Attitudes to Dress in the Late Republic." In *The World of Roman Costume*, edited by Judith Lynn Sebesta and Larissa Bonfante, 133–45. Madison: University of Wisconsin Press, 2001.
Hewitt, Joseph William. "The Gratitude of Horace to Maecenas." *Classical Journal* 36 (1941) 464–72.
Highet, Gilbert. "Libertino patre natus." *Journal of Philology* 94 (1973) 268–81.
Hijmans, B. L. Ἄσκησις, *Notes on Epictetus' Educational System*. Assen, Netherlands: van Gorcum, 1959.
Hillert, A. *Antike Ärztedarstellungen*. Frankfurt: Lang, 1990.
Hock, Ronald. "Paul and Greco-Roman Education." In *Paul in the Greco-Roman World: A Handbook*, edited by J. Paul Sampley, 198–227. New York: Trinity, 2003.
―――. "Paul's Tentmaking and the Problem of His Social Class." *Journal of Biblical Literature* 97 (1978) 555–64. Reprinted in *Tentmaking: Perspectives on Self-Supporting Ministry*, edited by James M. M. Francis and Leslie J. Francis, 4–13. Leominster: Gracewing, 1998.
―――. "The Problem of Paul's Social Class: Further Reflections." In *Paul's World*, edited by Stanley Porter, 7–18. Pauline Studies 4. Leiden: Brill, 2008.
―――. "Simon the Shoemaker as an Ideal Cynic." *Greek, Roman and Byzantine Studies* 17 (1976) 41–53. Reprinted in *Die Kyniker in der moderne Forschung: Aufsätze mit Einführung und Bibliographie*, edited by Margarethe Billerbeck, 259–71. Bochumer Studien zur Philosophie 15. Amsterdam: Grüner, 1991.
―――. *The Social Context of Paul's Ministry: Tentmaking and Apostleship*. Philadelphia: Fortress, 1980.

Works Cited

———. "The Workshop as a Social Setting for Paul's Missionary Preaching." *Catholic Biblical Quarterly* 41 (1979) 438–50. Reprinted in *Tentmaking: Perspectives on Self-Supporting Ministry*, 14–25.

Hock, Ronald, and Edward O'Neil. *The Chreia in Ancient Rhetoric*, edited by Hans Dieter Betz and Edward O'Neil. SBL Texts and Translation Series 27. Atlanta: Scholars, 1986.

Hodge, Caroline E. Johnson. "Married to an Unbeliever: Households, Hierarchies, and Holiness in 1 Corinthians 7:12–16." *Harvard Theological Review* 103 (2010) 1–25.

Holland, Francis. *Seneca*. London: Books for Libraries, 1969.

Holloway, Paul A. "Bona Cogitare: An Epicurean Consolation in Phil 4:8–9." *Harvard Theological Review* 91 (1998) 89–96.

Holmyard, Harold R., III. "Does 1 Corinthians 11:2–16 Refer to Women Praying and Prophesying in Church." *Biblotheca sacra* 154 (1997) 461–72.

Hope, Richard. *The Book of Diogenes Laertius: Its Spirit and Method*. New York: Columbia University Press, 1930.

Hopper, R. J. "Ancient Corinth." *Greece and Rome*, 2nd ser., 2 (1955) 2–15.

Horrell, David. "The Development of Theological Ideology in Pauline Christianity: A Structuration Theory Perspective." In *Modelling Early Christianity: Social-Scientific Studies of the New Testament and Its Context*, edited by Philip F. Esler, 224–36. London: Routledge, 1995.

———. *The Social Ethos of the Corinthian Correspondence: Interests and Ideology from 1 Corinthians to 1 Clement*. Edinburgh: T. & T. Clark, 1996.

———. *Solidarity and Difference: A Contemporary Reading of Paul's Ethics*. London: T. & T. Clark, 2005.

Horsley, G. H. R. *New Documents Illustrating Early Christianity*. Vol. 4. Sydney: Macquarie University, Ancient History Documentary Research Centre, 1987.

———. *New Documents Illustrating Early Christianity*. Vol. 5. Sydney: Macquarie University, Ancient History Documentary Research Centre, 1989.

———, editor. *Paul and Empire: Religion and Power in Roman Imperial Society*. Harrisburg, PA: Trinity Press International, 1997.

———. *Paul and Politics: Ekklesia, Israel, Imperium, Interpretation: Essays in Honor of Krister Stendahl*. Harrisburg, PA: Trinity Press International, 2000.

———. *Paul and the Roman Imperial Order*. Harrisburg, PA: Trinity Press International, 2004.

Horsley, Richard A., editor. *Hidden Transcripts and the Art of Resistance: Applying the Work of James C. Scott to Jesus and Paul*. Leiden: Brill, 2004.

Houston, George W. "Slave and Freedman Personnel of Public Libraries in Ancient Rome." *Transactions of the American Philological Association* 132 (2002) 139–76.

Howe, Winifred E. "Three Days in the Life of a Roman Prince: Germanicus' First Day at School." *Metropolitan Museum of Art Bulletin* 11 (1916) 1–4.

Hubbard, Thomas K. "The Invention of Sulpicia." *Classical Journal* 100 (2005) 177–94.

Hunter, David G. "The Reception and Interpretation of Paul in Late Antiquity: 1 Corinthians 7 and the Ascetic Debates." In *Reception and Interpretation of the Bible in Late Antiquity: Proceedings of the Montréal Colloquium in Honour of Charles Kannengiesser, 11–13 October 2006*, edited by Lorenzo DiTommaso and Lucian Turcescu, 163–91. Leiden: Brill, 2008.

Hunter, L. W. "Cicero's Journey to His Province of Cilicia in 51 B.C." *Journal of Roman Studies* 3 (1913) 73–97.

Works Cited

Hunter, William Alexander. *A Systematic and Historical Exposition of Roman Law in the Order of a Code.* London: Maxwell & Son, 1885.

Hurd, John C., Jr. *The Origins of 1 Corinthians.* New York: Seabury, 1965.

Hutchings, Noël, and William D. Rumsey, editors. *The Collaborative Bibliography of Women in Philosophy.* Bowling Green, OH: Philosophy Documentation Center, 1997.

Ierodiakonou, Katerina, editor. *Topics in Stoic Philosophy.* New York: Oxford University Press, 2004.

Immerwahr, H. R. "Book Rolls on Attic Vases." In *Festschrift Ullman I,* edited by C. Henderson, 17–41. Rome: Ed. di storia e letteratura, 1964.

———. "More Book Rolls and Attic Vases." *Antike Kunst* 16 (1973) 143–47.

Ingalls, Wayne B. "Ritual Performance as Training for Daughters in Archaic Greece." *Phoenix* 54 (2000) 1–20.

Instone-Brewer, David. *Divorce and Remarriage in the Bible: The Social and Literary Context.* Grand Rapids: Eerdmans, 2002.

———. "1 Corinthians 7 in the Light of the Graeco-Roman Marriage and Divorce Papyri." *Tyndale Bulletin* 52 (2001) 101–15.

———. "1 Corinthians 7 in the Light of the Jewish Greek and Aramaic Marriage and Divorce Papyri." *Tyndale Bulletin* 52 (2001) 225–43.

Inwood, Brad. "Seneca in His Philosophical Milieu." *Harvard Studies in Classical Philology* 97 (1995) 63–76.

Inwood, Brad, and L. P. Gerson. *Hellenistic Philosophy: Introductory Readings.* 2nd ed. Indianapolis: Hackett, 1997.

Ioppolo, Anna Maria. "The Academic Position of Favorinus of Arelate." *Phronesis* 38 (1993) 183–213.

Irigaray, Luce. "Sorcerer Love: A Reading of Plato's Symposium, Diotima's Speech." In *Feminist Interpretations of Plato,* translated by Eleanor H. Kuykendall, edited by Nancy Tuana, 181–96. University Park: Pennsylvania State University Press, 1994.

Ivarsson, Fredrik. "Vice Lists and Deviant Masculinity: The Rhetorical Function of 1 Corinthians 5:10–11 and 6:9–10." In *Mapping Gender in Ancient Religious Discourses,* edited by Todd C. Penner and Caroline Vander Stichele, 163–84. Leiden: Brill, 2006.

Jacobs, Jonathan A. *Aristotle's Virtues: Nature, Knowledge and Human Good.* New York: Lang, 2004.

Jacobson, D. M., and M. P. Weitzman. "What Was Corinthian Bronze?" *American Journal of Archaeology* 96 (1992) 237–47.

James, Sharon L. *Learned Girls and Male Persuasion: Gender and Reading in Roman Love Elegy.* Berkely: University of California Press, 2003.

Jaquette, James L. "Life and Death, 'Adiaphora,' and Paul's Rhetorical Strategies." *Novum Testamentum* 38 (1996) 30–54.

Jennings, Victoria. *The World of Ion of Chios.* Leiden: Brill, 2007.

Jewett, Robert. *A Chronology of Paul's Life.* Philadelphia: Fortress, 1979.

———. "Paul, Phoebe, and the Spanish Mission." In *The Social World of Christianity and Judaism: Essays in Honor of Howard Clark Kee,* edited by Jacob Neusner et al., 142–61. Philadelphia: Fortress, 1988.

———. *Paul's Anthropological Terms: A Study of Their Use in Conflict Settings.* Leiden: Brill, 1971.

———. *Romans: A Commentary.* Hermeneia. Minneapolis: Fortress, 2007.

Works Cited

———. "The Social Context and Implications of Homoerotic References in Romans 1:24-27." In *Homosexuality, Science, and the "Plain Sense" of Scripture*, edited by David L. Balch, 223-41. Grand Rapids: Eerdmans, 2000.

———. "Tenement Churches and Communal Meals in the Early Church: The Implications of a Form-Critical Analysis of 2 Thess 3:10." *Biblical Research* 38 (1993) 23-43.

———. "Tenement Churches and Pauline Love Feasts." *Quarterly Review: A Journal of Theological Resources for Ministry* 14 (1994) 43-58.

———. *The Thessalonian Cooerespondence*. Philadelphia: Fortress, 1986.

Johnson, Alan F. *1 Corinthians*. Edited by Grant R. Osborne. IVP New Testament Commentary Series 7. Downers Grove, IL: InterVarsity, 2004.

———. "A Review of the Scholarly Debate on the Meaning of 'Head' (Κεφαλή) in Paul's Writings." *Ashland Theological Journal* 41 (2009) 35-57.

Johnson, William A. *Readers and Reading Culture in the High Roman Empire: A Study of Elite Communities*. Oxford: Oxford University Press, 2010.

Johnson, William A., and Holt N. Parker, editors. *Ancient Literacies: The Culture of Reading in Greece and Rome*. Oxford: Oxford University Press, 2009.

Johnston, David. *Roman Law in Context*. Cambridge: Cambridge University Press, 1999.

Johnston, Patricia A. "Poenulus I, 2 and Roman Women." *Transactions of the American Philological Association* 110 (1980) 143-59.

Jones, Francis L. "Martial, the Client." *Classical Journal* (1935) 355-61.

Jones, Howard. *The Epicurean Tradition*. London: Routledge, 1989.

Jones, Nicholas F. "The Civic Organization of Corinth." *Transactions of the American Philological Association* 110 (1980) 161-93.

———. "The Organization of Corinth Again." *Zeitschrift für Papyrologie Epigrapik* 120, (1998) 49-56.

Jordan, Borimir. "Isthmian Amusements." *Classics Ireland* 8 (2001) 32-67.

Joubert, Stephan. *Paul as Benefactor: Reciprocity, Strategy and Theological Reflection in Paul's Collection*. Tübingen: Mohr/Siebeck, 2000.

Judge, E. A. "Cultural Conformity and Innovation in Paul: Some Clues from Contemporary Documents." *Tyndale Bulletin* 35 (1984) 3-24.

———. "The Early Christians as a Scholastic Community." *Journal of Religious History* 1 (1961) 5-15.

———. *The First Christians in the Roman World*. Edited by James R. Harrison. Tübingen: Mohr/Siebeck, 2008.

———. *Rank and Status in the World of the Caesars and St. Paul*. Christchurch, NZ: University of Cantebury Press, 1982.

———. *Social Distinctives of the Christians in the First Century: Pivotal Essays*. Edited by David M. Scholer. Peabody, MA: Hendrickson, 2008.

———. "The Social Identity of the First Christians: A Question of Method in Religious History." *Journal of Religious History* 11 (1980) 201-17.

———. *The Social Pattern of the Christian Groups in the First Century*. London: Tyndale, 1960.

Jungkutz, Richard. *Christian Approval of Epicureanism*. Chicago: American Society of Church History, 1962.

———. "Epicureanism and the Church Fathers." PhD diss., University of Wisconsin, 1961.

Works Cited

Kahane, Ahuvia. *Diachronic Dialogues: Authority and Continuity in Homer and the Homeric Tradition.* Lanham, MD: Lexington, 2005.

Kahn, Charles K. *Pythagoras and the Pythagoreans.* Indianapolis: Hackett, 2001.

Kajava, Mika. "When Did the Isthmian Games Return to Corinth? (Reading 'Corinth' 8.3.153)." *Classical Philology* 97 (2002) 168–78.

Kampen, Natalie. *Image and Status: Roman Working Women in Ostia.* Berlin: Mann, 1981.

Karle Gustav Dolfe, *Zeitschrift für die neutestamentliche Wissenschaft und die Kunde der älteren Kirche* 83 (1992) 115–18.

Karris, Robert J. *Galatians and Romans.* New College Bible Commentary. Collegeville: Liturgical, 2005.

Käsemann, Ernest. *Commentary on Romans.* Translated and edited by G. W. Bromiley. Grand Rapids: Eerdmans: 1980.

Kaster, Robert A. "Notes on 'Primary' and 'Secondary' Schools in Late Antiquity." *Transactions of the American Philological Association* 113 (1983) 323–46.

———. "The Social Status of the Grammarians." In *Guardians of Language: The Grammarian and Society in Late Antiquity*, edited by Robert A. Kaster, 99–134. Berkeley: University of California Press, 1988.

Kearsley, R. A. "Women in Public Life in the Roman East: Iunia Theodora, Claudia Metrodora and Phoebe, Benefactress of Paul." *Tyndale Bulletin* 50 (1999) 189–211.

Keener, Craig S. *1–2 Corinthians.* New Cambridge Bible Commentary. Cambridge: Cambridge University Press, 2005.

———. "Interethnic Marriages in the New Testament (Matt 1:3–6; Acts 7:29; 16:1–3; cf. 1 Cor 7:14)." *Criswell Theological Review*, n.s., 6 (2009) 25–43.

———. *Paul, Women, and Wives.* Peabody, MA: Hendrickson, 1992.

Keith, Alison. "Critical Trends in Interpreting Sulpicia." *Classical World* 100 (2006) 3–10.

Keller, Marie Noël. *Priscilla and Aquila: Paul's Coworkers in Christ Jesus.* Paul's Social Network: Brothers and Sisters in Faith. Collegeville: Liturgical, 2010.

Kennedy, George A. *The Art of Persuasion in Greece.* Princeton: Princeton University Press, 1963.

———. *The Art of Rhetoric in the Roman World: 300 B.C.–A.D. 300.* Princeton: Princeton University Press, 1972.

Kennedy, Kristen. "Hipparchia the Cynic: Feminist Rhetoric and the Ethics of Embodiment." *Hypatia* 14 (1999) 48–71.

Ker, Donald P. "Paul and Apollos – Colleagues or Rivals?" *Journal for the Study of the New Testament* 22 (2000) 75–97.

Kersey, Ethel M. *Women Philosophers: A Bio-Critical Source Book.* New York: Greenwood, 1989.

Kidd, R. M. *Wealth and Beneficence in the Pastoral Epistles: A Bourgeois Form of Early Christianity?* Atlanta: Scholars, 1990.

Kim, Chan-Hae. "The Papyrus Invitation." *Journal of Biblical Literature* 34 (1975) 398–402.

King, Karen. *What Is Gnosticism?* Cambridge: Belknap Press of Harvard University Press, 2003.

Kingsley, Peter. "From Pythagoras to the *Turba philosophorum*: Egypt and Pythagorean Tradition." *Journal of the Warburg and Courtauld Institutes* 57 (1994) 1–13.

Works Cited

Kinman, Brent. "Appoint the Despised as Judges! (1 Corinthians 6:4)." *Tyndale Bulletin* 48 (1997) 345–54.

Klabunde, Michael Robert. *Boys or Women? The Rhetoric of Sexual Preference in Achilles Tatius, Plutarch, and Pseudo-Lucian*. PhD diss., University of Cincinnati, 2001.

Klassen, William. "Musonius Rufus, Jesus, and Paul: Three First-Century Feminists." In *From Jesus to Paul: Studies in Honour of Francis Wright Beare*, edited by Peter Richardson and John C. Hurd, 185–206. Waterloo, ON: Wilfrid Laurier University Press, 1984.

Klauck, Hans-Josef. *Ancient Letters and the New Testament: A Guide to Content and Exegesis*. Waco, TX: Baylor University Press, 2006.

———. "Junia Theodora und die Gemeinde von Korinth." In *Kirche und Volk Gottes: Festschrift für Jürgen Roloff zum*, edited by Martin Karrer et al., 42–57. Neukirchen-Vluyn, Germany: Neukirchener, 2000.

———. *The Religious Context of Early Christianity: A Guide to Graeco-Roman Religions*. Translated by Brian McNeil. New York: T. & T. Clark, 2003.

Kloppenborg, John S. "*Collegia* and *Thiasoi*: Issues in Function, Taxonomy and Membership." In *Voluntary Associations in the Graeco-Roman World*, edited by John S. Kloppenborg and Stephen G. Wilson, 16–30. London: Routledge, 1996.

———. "Edwin Hatch, Churches and *Collegia*." In *Origins and Method: Towards a New Understanding of Christianity and Judaism*, edited by B. McLean, 212–38. Sheffield, UK: Sheffield University Press, 1993.

Klotz, Frieda, and Katerina Olkonomopoulou. *Philosopher's Banquet: Plutarch's Table Talk in the Intellectual Culture of the Roman Empire*. Oxford: Oxford University Press, 2011.

Knapp, Charles. "Travel in Ancient Times as Seen Plautus and Terence. II." *Classical Philology* 2 (1907) 281–304.

Koester, Helmut, and James M. Robinson, *Entwicklungslinien durch die Welt des frühen Christentums*. Tübingen: Mohr, 1971.

Kokolakis, Minos. "Intellectual Activity at the Fringes of the Games." In *Proceedings on an International Symposium on the Olympic Games: 5–9 of September, 1988*, edited by William Coulson and Helmut Kyrieleis, 153–58. Athens: Deutsches Archäologisches Institut Athen, 1992.

Konstan, David. *Friendship in the Classical World*. Cambridge: Cambridge University Press, 1997.

Kooten, Geurt Hendrik van. *Paul's Anthropology in Context: The Image of God, Assimilation to God, and Tripartite Man in Ancient Judaism, Ancient Philosophy and Early Christianity*. Tübingen: Mohr Siebeck, 2008.

Koperski, V. "Knowledge of Christ and Knowledge of God in the Corinthian Correspondence." In *The Corinthian Correspondence*, edited by Reimund Bieringer, 377–96. Leuven: Leuven University Press, 1996.

Korpela, Jukka. *Das Medizinalpersonal im antiken Rom: eine sozialgeschichte Untersuchung*. Helsinki: Suomalainen Tiedeakatemia, 1987.

Kraemer, Ross S. "The Conversion of Women to Ascetic Forms of Christianity." *Signs* 6 (1980) 298–307.

———. *Unreliable Witnesses: Religion, Gender, and History in the Greco-Roman Mediterranean*. Oxford: Oxford University Press, 2010.

Kreyer, Johannes. *L. Annaeus Seneca und seine Beziehungen zum Urchristentum*. Berlin: Gaertners, 1887.

Kroeger, Catherine. "The Apostle Paul and the Greco-Roman Cults of Women." *Journal for the Evangelical Theological Society* 30 (1987) 25–38.

Kudlien, Fridolf. "Medical Education in Classical Antiquity." In *The History of Medical Education*, edited by C. D. O'Malley, 3–37. Berkeley: University of California Press, 1970.

Kugleman, Richard. "1 Cor. 7:36-38." *Catholic Biblical Quarterly* 10 (1948) 63–71.

Kunstler, Barton Lee. "Family Dynamics and Female Power in Ancient Sparta." *Helios* 13 (1986) 31–48.

Kurfess, Alfons. "Zu dem apokryphen Breifwechsel zwischen dem Philosophen Seneca und dem Apostel Paulus." *Aevum* 26 (1952) 42–48.

Kurke, Leslie."Inventing the 'Hetaira': Sex, Politics, and Discursive Conflict in Archaic Greece." *Classical Antiquity* 16 (1997) 106–50.

Kuttner, Ann L. "Culture and History at Pompey's Museum." *Transactions of the American Philological Association* 129 (1999) 343–73.

Laes, Christian. *Children in the Roman Empire: Outsiders Within*. Cambridge: Cambridge University Press, 2011.

Lambropoulou, V. "Some Pythagorean Female Virtues." In *Women in Antiquity: New Assessments*, edited by R. Hawley and B. Levick, 122–35. New York: Routledge 1995.

Lampe, Peter. *From Paul to Valentinus: Christians at Rome in the First Two Centuries*. Translated by Michael Steinhauser. Minneapolis: Fortress, 2003.

———. "Theological Wisdom and the 'Word of the Cross': The Rhetorical Scheme in 1 Corinthians 1–4." *Interpretation* 44 (1990) 117–31.

Langlands, Rebecca. *Sexual Morality in Ancient Rome*. Cambridge: Cambridge University Press, 2006.

———. "A Woman's Influence on a Roman Text." In *Women's Influence on Classical Civilization*, edited by F. McHardy and E. Marshall, 115–26. London: Routledge, 2004.

Lanzillotta, L. Roig. "The Early Christians and Human Sacrifice." In *The Strange World of Human Sacrifice*, edited by Jan N. Bremmer, 81–102. Leuven: Peeters, 2007.

Larson, Jennifer. *Greek Heroine Cults*. Madison: University of Wisconsin Press, 1995.

Lee, Michelle V. *Paul, the Stoics, and the Body of Christ*. New York: Cambridge University Press, 2006.

Lefkowitz, Mary. *The Lives of the Greek Poets*. London: Duckworth, 1981.

———. "Wives and Husbands." *Greece and Rome*, 2nd ser., 30 (1983) 31–47.

Leon, E. F. "Note on Caecilia Attica." *Classical Bulletin* 38 (1962) 35–36.

Levick, Barbara. *Julia Domna, Syrian Empress*. London: Routledge, 2007.

Levine, Lee I. *The Ancient Synagogue: The First Two Thousand Years*. New Haven: Yale University Press, 2000.

———. "Synagogue Leadership: The Case of the Archisynagogue." In *Jews in a Greco-Roman World*, edited by M. Goodman, 195–213. New York: Clarendon University Press, 1998.

———. "Synagogue Officials: The Evidence from Caesarea and Its Implications for Palestine and the Diaspora." In *Caesarea Maritima: A Retrospective after Two Millennia*, edited by A. Raban and K. Holum, 392–400. Leiden: Brill, 1996.

Levinskaya, Irina. *The Book of Acts in Its Diaspora Setting*. Grand Rapids: Eerdmans, 1996.

Lewis, D. M. "Attic Manumissions." *Hesperia* 28 (1959) 203–8.

Works Cited

Lietzmann, Hans, and W. G. Kümmel. *An Die Korinther*. 2 vols. Tübingen: Mohr/Siebeck, 1969.
Lightfoot, Joseph B. *St. Paul's Epistle to the Philippians: A Revised Text with Introduction, Notes and Dissertations*. New York: Macmillan, 1903.
Lilla, Salvatore R. C. *Clement of Alexandria*. Oxford: University Press, 1971.
Lim, Timothy H. "Not in Persuasive Words of Wisdom, but in the Demonstration of the Spirit and Power." *Novum Testamentum* 29 (1987) 137–44.
Lintott, Andrew. "Freedmen and Slaves in the Light of Legal Documents from First Century A.D. Campania." *Classical Quarterly*, n.s., 52 (2002) 555–65.
Liong-Seng Phua, Richard. *Idolatry and Authority: A Study of 1 Corinthians 8.1–11.1 in the Light of the Jewish Diaspora*. London: T. & T. Clark, 2005.
Lloyd, Genevieve, editor. *Feminism and History of Philosophy*. New York: Oxford University Press, 2002.
Long, A. A., and D. N. Sedley. *The Hellenistic Philosophers*. Vol. 1, *Translations of the Principal Sources with Philosophical Commentary*. Cambridge: Cambridge University Press, 1987.
———. *The Hellenistic Philosophers*. Vol. 2, *Greek and Latin Texts*. Cambridge: Cambridge University Press, 1987.
Longenecker, Bruce. *Remember the Poor: Paul, Poverty, and the Greco-Roman World*. Grand Rapids: Eerdmans, 2010.
Longenecker, Richard. *Galatians*. Word Biblical Commentary 41. Nashville: Thomas Nelson, 1990.
Longfellow, Brenda. *Roman Imperialism and Civic Patronage: Form, Meaning and Ideology in Monumental Fountain Complexes*. Cambridge: Cambridge University Press, 2011.
Lopez, Davina C. *Apostle to the Conquered: Reimagining Paul's Mission*. Minneapolis: Fortress, 2008.
López Barja, Pedro. "Freedmen Social Mobility in Roman Italy." *Historia* 44 (1995) 326–48.
Lowery, David K. "The Head Covering and Lord's Supper in 1 Cor 11:2–34." *Bibliotheca sacra* 143 (1986) 155–63.
Lüdemann, Gerd. *Paul, Apostle to the Gentiles: Studies in Chronology*. Translated by F. Stanley Jones. Philadelphia: Fortress, 1984.
MacDonald, Margaret. *Early Christian Women and Pagan Opinion: The Power of the Hysterical Woman*. Cambridge: Cambridge University Press, 1996.
———. "Early Christian Women and Unbelievers." In *A Feminist Companion to the Deutero-Pauline Epistles*, edited by Amy-Jill Levine and Marianne Blickenstaff, 14–28. London: T. & T. Clark.
MacGregor, Kirk R. "Is 1 Corinthians 11:2–16 a Prohibition of Homosexuality?" *Bibliotheca sacra* 166 (2009) 201–16.
MacKendrick, P. L. "Roman Colonization." *Phoenix* 6 (1952) 139–46.
MacMullen, Ramsay. *Roman Social Relations, 50 B.C. to A.D. 284*. New Haven: Yale University Press, 1974.
———. "Women in Public." *Historia: Zeitschrift für Alte Geschichte* 29 (1980) 208–18.
———. "Women's Power in the Principate." In *Changes in the Roman Empire: Essays in the Ordinary*, edited by Ramsay MacMullen, 169–76. Princeton: Princeton University Press, 1990.
Majumbar, R. C. *Ancient India*. Delhi: Montilal Banarsidass, 2003.

Malherbe, Abraham. "Anti-Epicurean Rhetoric in 1 Thessalonians." In *Text und Geschichte: Facetten theologischen Arbeitens aus dem Freundes- und Schuleterkreis: Dieter Lubermann zum 60. Geburstag*, edited by Stefan Maser and Egbert Schlarb, 136–42. Marburg, Germany: Elwart, 1999.

———. "The Beasts at Ephesus." *Journal of Biblical Literature* 87 (1968) 71–80.

———. "Exhortation in First Thessalonians." *Novum Testamentum* 25 (1983) 238–56.

———. "'Gentle as a Nurse': The Cynic Background to 1 Thess ii." *Novum Testamentum* 12 (1970) 203–17.

———. "Hellenistic Moralists and the New Testament." In *Aufstieg und Niedergang der römischen Welt: Geschichte und Kultur Roms im Spiegel der neueren Forschung*, vol. 2.26.1, edited by Wolfgang Haase and Hildegard Temporini, 227–333. New York: de Gruyter, 1992.

———. "MH ΓENOITO in the Diatribe and Paul." *Harvard Theological Review* 73 (1980) 231–40; page 236 corrected in "Erratum: MH ΓENOITO in the Diatribe and Paul." *Harvard Theological Review* 74 (1981) 236.

———. *Paul and the Thessalonians: The Philosophic Tradition of Pastoral Care*. Philadelphia: Fortress, 1987.

———. "Paul: Hellenistic Philosopher or Christian Pastor?" *Asbury Theological Journal* 68 (1986) 3–13.

———. "Paul's Self-Sufficiency (Philippians 4:11)." In *The Function of Biblical Texts in Their Textual and Situance Contexts. Fetschrift for Lars Hartman*, edited by Tord Fornberg and David Hellholm, 813–26. Oslo: Scandinavian University Press, 1995.

———. Review of *Plutarch's Ethical Writings and Early Christian Literature*, by Hans Dieter Betz. *Journal of Biblical Literature* 100 (1981) 140–42.

———. "Self Definition among Cynics and Epicureans." In *Paul and the Popular Philosophers*, 11–24. Minneapolis: Fortress, 1988.

———. *Social Aspects of Early Christianity*. Baton Rouge: Louisiana State University Press, 1977.

Malina, Bruce J., and John J. Pilch. *Social-Science Commentary on the Letters of Paul*. Minneapolis: Fortress, 2006.

Malitz, J. "Helvidius Priscus und Vespasian." *Hermes* 113 (1985) 231–46.

Manning, C. E. "The Consolatory Tradition and Seneca's Attitude to the Emotions." *Greece & Rome* 21 (1974) 71–81.

———. *On Seneca's "Ad Marciam."* Leiden: Brill, 1981.

———. "Seneca and the Stoics on the Equality of the Sexes." *Mnemosyne*, 4th ser., 26 (1973) 170–77.

Mansfeld, Jaap, and David T. Runia. *Aetiana: The Method and Intellectual Context of a Doxographer*. Vol. 1, *The Sources*. New York: Brill, 1997.

Marchal, Joseph A. *The Politics of Heaven: Women, Gender, and Empire in the Study of Paul*. Minneapolis: Fortress, 2008.

Marrou, Henri. *A History of Education in Antiquity*. London: Sheed & Ward, 1956.

Marshall, Anthony J. "Library Resources and Creative Writing at Rome." *Phoenix* 30 (1976) 252–64.

Marshall, Peter. *Enmity in Corinth: Social Conventions in Paul's Relations with the Corinthians*. Tübingen: Mohr, 1987.

Martin, Dale B. *The Corinthian Body*. New Haven: Yale University Press, 1995.

Works Cited

———. "Heterosexism and the Interpretation of Romans 1:18–32." *Biblical Interpretation* 3 (1995) 332–55.

———. "Review Essay: Justin J. Meggitt, Paul, Poverty, and Survival." *Journal for the Study of the New Testament* 84 (2001) 51–64.

———. "Tongues of Angels and Other Status Indicators." *Journal of the American Academy of Religion* 59 (1991) 347–89.

Martin, Hubert, Jr., and Jane E. Phillips. "Consolatio ad uxorem." In *Plutarch's Ethical Writings and the New Testament*, edited by Hans Dieter Betz, 394–441. Leiden: Brill, 1978.

Martin, Richard P. "Ancient Collections of Women's Sayings: Form and Function." *Bulletin of the Institute of Classical Studies* 50 (2008) 161–69.

———. "Enigmas of the Lyric Voice." In *Making Silence Speak: Women's Voices in Greek Literature and Society*, edited by André Lardinois and Laura McClure, 55–74. Princeton: Princeton University Press, 2001.

———. "The Seven Sages as Performers of Wisdom." In *Cultural Poetics in Archaic Greece: Cult, Performance, Politics*, edited by Carol Dougherty and Leslie Kurke, 108–28. Cambridge: Cambridge University Press. 1993.

Martin, Troy W. "Paul's Argument from Nature for the Veil in 1 Corinthians 11:13–15: A Testicle Instead of a Head Covering." *Journal of Biblical Literature* 123 (2004) 75–84.

———. "Veiled Exhortations regarding the Veil." In *Rhetoric, Ethic, and Moral Persuasion in Biblical Discourse: Essays from the 2002 Heidelberg Conference*, edited by Thomas H. Olbricht and Anders Ericksson, 255–73. London: T. & T. Clark, 2005.

Mascia, Carmin. *A History of Philosophy*. Paterson, NJ: St. Anthony Guild, 1957.

Mason, H. J. *Greek Terms for Roman Institutions – A Lexicon and Analysis*. Toronto: Hakkert, 1974.

Massey, Preston T. "The Meaning of κατακαλύπτό and κατα κεφαλή εχων in 1 Corinthians 11.2–16." *New Testament Studies* 53 (2007) 502–23.

Matera, Frank J. *Galatians*. Sacra Pagina 9. Collegeville: Liturgical, 1992.

Mathews, Shailer. "The Social Teaching of Paul. VII. The Family." *Biblical World* 2 (1902) 123–33.

Mattill, A. J., Jr. "The Value of Acts as a Source for the Study of Paul." In *Perspectives on Luke-Acts*, edited by C. H. Talbert, 76–98. Danville, VA: Association of Baptist Professors of Religion, 1978.

Mauch, Mercedes. *Senecas Frauenbild in den philosophischen Schriften*. New York: Peter Lang, 1997.

Mayor, John E. B. *Thirteen Satires of Juvenal*. New York: Macmillan, 1889.

McAlister, Linda, editor. *Hypatia's Daughters: 1500 Years of Women Philosophers*. Indiana University Press, 1996.

McCasland, S. Vernon. "'The Image of God' According to Paul." *Journal of Biblical Literature* 69 (1950) 85–100.

McClure, Laura. *Courtesans at Table: Gender and Greek Literary Culture in Athenaeus*. New York: Routledge, 2003.

———. "Subversive Laughter: The Sayings of Courtesans in Book 13 of Athenaeus' Deipnosophistae." *American Journal of Philology* 124 (2003) 259–94.

McDonnell, Myles. "Divorce Initiated by Women in Rome: The Evidence of Plautus." *American Journal of Ancient History* 8 (1983) 54–80.

———. "Writing, Copying, and Autograph Manuscripts in Ancient Rome." *Classical Quarterly* 46 (1996) 469–91.
McDermott, William C. "Plotina Augusta and Nicomachus of Gerasa." *Historia: Zeitschrift für Alte Geschichte* 26 (1977) 192–203.
McGinn, Thomas A. J. *Prostitution, Sexuality, and the Law in Roman Society*. Oxford: Oxford University Press, 1998.
McGready, Wayne O. "EKKLĒSIA and Voluntary Associations." In *Voluntary Associations in the Greco-Roman World*, edited by John S. Kloppenborg and Stephen Wilson, 59–73. New York: Routledge, 1996.
McInerny, Ralph M. *A History of Western Philosophy*. Notre Dame: University of Notre Dame Press, 1963.
McKay, Alexander Gordon. *Houses, Villas, and Palaces in the Roman World*. Baltimore: Johns Hopkins University Press, 1998.
McLean, B. H. "The Agrippinilla Inscription: Religious Associations and Early Church Formation." In *Origins and Method: Towards a New Understanding of Judaism and Christianity; Essays in Honor of John C. Hurd*, edited by B. McLean, 239–70. Journal for the Study of the New Testament Supplement 86. Sheffield, UK: Sheffield University Press, 1993.
McManus, Barbara. "Index Of Images, Part III." *Vroma: A Virtual Community For Teaching And Learning Classics*. Online: www.vroma.org/images/mcmanus_images/index3.html.
McMurtry, W. J. "Excavations by the American School at the Theatre of Sikyon. I. General Report of the Excavations." *American Journal of Archaeology* 5 (1889) 267–86.
McNelis, Charles. "Greek Grammarians and Roman Society during the Early Empire: Statius' Father and His Contemporaries." *Classical Antiquity* 21 (2002) 67–94.
Meecham, Henrey G. *Light from Ancient Letters*. London: Allen & Unwin, 1923.
Meek, James A. "The New Perspective on Paul: An Introduction for the Uninitiated." *Concordia Journal* 27 (2001) 208–33.
Meeks, Wayne. *The First Urban Christians*. New Haven: Yale University Press, 1983.
———. *Zur Soziologie des Urchristentums: ausgew. Beiträge zum frühchristlichen Gemeinschaftsleben in seiner gesellschaftlichen Umwelt*. München: Kaiser, 1979.
Meeks, Wayne, and John T. Fitzgerald, editors. *The Writings of St. Paul: Annotated Texts, Reception, and Criticism*. 2nd ed. Norton Critical Editions in the History of Ideas. New York: Norton, 2007.
Meggitt, Justin J. "The First Churches: Social Life." In *The Biblical World*, edited by John Barton, 157–56. London: Routledge, 2002.
———. "Response to Martin and Theissen." *Journal for the Study of the New Testament* 84 (2001) 85–94.
———. "Sources: Use, Abuse, and Neglect; The Importance of Ancient Popular Culture." In *Christianity at Corinth*, edited by Edward Adams and David Horrell, 241–54. Louisville: Westminster John Knox, 2004.
Ménage, Gilles. *The History of Women Philosophers*. Translated by Beatrice H. Zedler Lanham, MD: University Press of America, 1984.
Meriç, Recep, et al., editors. *Die Inschriften von Ephesos, Inschriften griechischer*. Städte aus Kleinasien 17.1. Bonn: Habelt, 1981.
Merriam, Carol U. "Sulpicia: Just Another Roman Poet." *Classical World* 100 (2006) 11–15.

Works Cited

Métraux, Guy P. R. "Ancient Housing: 'Oikos' and 'Domus' in Greece and Rome." *Journal of Religious History* 58 (1999) 392–405.

Meyers, Eric M. "The Problems of Gendered Space in Syro-Palestinian Domestic Architecture: The Case of Roman-Period Galilee." In *Early Christian Families in Context: An Interdisciplinary Dialogue*, edited by David L. Balch and Carolyn Osiek. Grand Rapids: Eerdmans, 2003.

Mihaila, Corin. *The Paul-Apollos Relationship and Paul's Stance toward Greco-Roman Rhetoric*. New York: T. & T. Clark, 2009.

Miller, J. Edward. "Some Observations on the Text-Critical Function of the Umlauts in Vaticanus, with Special Attention to 1 Corinthians 14.34–35." *Journal for the Study of the New Testament* 26 (2003) 217–36.

Millis, Benjamin W. "'Miserable Huts' in Post-146 B.C. Corinth." *Hesperia* 75 (2006) 397–404.

Mitchell, Alan C. "Rich and Poor in the Courts of Corinth: Litigiousness and Status in 1 Cor 6:11–11." *New Testament Studies* 39 (1993) 562–86.

Mitchell, Andrew. "Friendship amongst the Self-Sufficient: Epicurus." *Essays in Philosophy* 2 (2001). No pages. Online: http://commons.pacificu.edu/eip/vol2/iss2/5.

Mitchell, Margaret M. *Paul and the Rhetoric of Reconciliation: An Exegetical Investigation of the Language and Composition of 1 Corinthians*. Louisville: Westminster John Knox, 1991.

———. "Paul's Letters to Corinth." In *Urban Religion in Roman Corinth*, edited by Daniel Schowalter and Steven Friesen, 307–38. Cambridge: Harvard University Press, 2005.

Mohler, S. L. "Slave Education in the Roman Empire." *Transactions and Proceedings of the American Philological Association* 71 (1940) 262–80.

Moles, J. L. "The Career and Conversion of Dio Chrysostom." *Journal of Hellenistic Studies* 98 (1978) 79–100.

Molvaer, Reidulf K. "St. Paul's Views on Sex according to 1 Corinthians 7:9 & 36–38." *Studia theologica* 58 (2004) 45–59.

Momigliano, Arnaldo. *Secondo contributo alla storia degli studi classici*. Rome: Storia e Letteratura, 1960.

Monoson, S. Sara. "Remembering Pericles: The Political and Theoretical Import of Plato's Menexenus." *Political Theory* 26 (1998) 489–513.

Montiglio, Silvia. "Should the Aspiring Wise Man Travel? A Conflict in Seneca's Thought." *The American Journal of Philology* 127 (2006) 553–86.

Montserrat, Dominic. "Heron 'Bearer of Philosophia' and Hermione 'Grammatike.'" *Journal of Egyptian Archaeology* 83 (1997) 223–26.

Mooney, William West. *Travel among the Ancient Romans*. Boston: Gorham, 1920.

Moore, Kenneth Royce. *Sex and the Second-Best City*. New York: Routledge, 2005.

Morford, Mark. "Juvenal's Fifth *Satire*." *American Journal of Philology* 98 (1977) 219–45.

Morrison, J. S. "Pythagoras of Samos." *Classical Quarterly*, n.s., 6 (1956) 135–56.

Morstein-Marx, Robert. *Mass Oratory and Political Power in the Late Roman Republic*. Cambridge: Cambridge University Press, 2004.

Mosse, Claude. "Women in the Spartan Revolutions of the Third Century BC." In *Women's History and Ancient History*, edited by S. Pomeroy, 138–53. Chapel Hill: University of North Carolina Press, 1991.

Motto, Anna Lydia. "Seneca on Women's Liberation." *Classical World* 65 (1972) 155–57.

Works Cited

Moule, C. D. F. *The Birth of the New Testament*. London: Harper & Row, 1962.
Mount, Christopher. "1 Corinthians 11:3–16: Spirit Possession and Authority in a Non-Pauline Interpolation." *Journal Biblical Literature* 124 (2005) 313–40.
———. *Pauline Christianity: Luke-Acts and the Legacy of Paul*. Leiden: Brill, 2002.
Munro, W. *Authority in Peter and Paul: The Identification of a Pastoral Stratum in the Pauline Corpus and 1 Peter*. Society for New Testament Studies 45. Cambridge: University Press, 1983.
———. "Interpolation in the Epistles: Weighing Probability." *New Testament Studies* 36 (1990) 431–43.
———. "Patriarchy and Charismatic Community in 'Paul.'" In *Women and Religion: 1972 AAR Proceedings*, edited by Judith Plaskow et al., 141–59. Missoula, MT: American Academy of Religion, 1973.
———. "Woman, Text and Canon: The Strange Case of 1 Corinthians 14:33–35." *Biblical Theological Bulletin* 18 (1988) 26–31.
Murley, Clyde. "Cicero, *Pro Archia* and Horace, *Epistles* II, 1,223ff." *The Classical Journal* 21 (1926) 533–34.
Murnaghan, S. "How a Woman Can Be More Like a Man: The Dialogue between Ischomachus and His Wife in Xenophon's Oeconomicus." *Helios* 15 (1988) 9–22.
Murphy, Paul R. "Cicero's *Pro Archia* and the Periclean Epitaphios." *Transactions and Proceedings of the American Philological Association* 89 (1958) 99–101.
Murphy-O'Connor, Jerome. "The Corinth that Saint Paul Saw." *Biblical Archaeologist* 47 (1984) 147–59.
———. "Interpolations in 1 Corinthians." *Catholic Biblical Quarterly* 48 (1986) 81–94.
———. "The Non-Pauline Character of 1 Corinthians 11:2–16?" *Journal Biblical Literature* 95 (1976) 615–21.
———. "Prisca and Aquila: Travleing Tentmakers and Church Builders." *Bible Review* (1992) 40–51.
———. "Sex and Logic in 1 Corinthians 11:3–16." *Classical Biblical Quarterly* 42 (1989) 482–500.
———. *St. Paul's Corinth: Texts and Archaeology*. Wilmington, DE: Glazier, 1983.
Murray, Oswyn. "Hecataeus of Abdera and Pharoic Kingship." *Journal of Egyptian Archaeology* 56 (1970) 141–71.
———. "The 'Quinquennium Neronis' and the Stoics." *Historia: Zeitschrift für Alte Geschichte* 14 (1965) 41–61.
Murray, Penelope. "Poetic Inspiration in Early Greece." *Journal of Hellenic Studies* 101 (1981) 87–100.
Myers, Nancy. "Cicero's (S)Trumpet: Roman Women and the Second Philippic." *Rhetoric Review* 22 (2003) 337–52.
Nagy, Gregory. "The 'Professional Muse' and Models of Prestige in Ancient Greece." *Cultural Critique* 12 (1989) 133–43.
Nails, Debra. *The People of Plato: A Prosopography of Plato and Other Socratics*. Indianapolis: Hackett, 2002.
Nais, D. "The Shrewish Wife of Socrates." *Echos du Monde Classique* 4 (1985) 97–99.
Navia, Luis E. *Classical Cynicism: A Critical Study*. Westport, CT: Greenwood, 1996.
———. *Diogenes the Cynic: The War against the World*. Amherst, NY: Humanity Books, 2005.

Works Cited

Neirynck, Frans. "Paul and the Sayings of Jesus." In *Apôtre Paul: Personnalité, Style et Conception du Ministère*, edited by A. Vanhoy, 265–321. Bibliotheca Ephemeridum theologicarum Lovaniensium 73. Leuven: Uitgeverij Peeters, 1986.

———. "The Sayings of Jesus in 1 Corinthians." In *The Corinthian Correspondence*, edited by Reimund Bieringer, 141–76. Leuven: Leuven University Press, 1996.

Neumann, Harry. "Diotima's Concept of Love." *The American Journal of Philology* 86 (1965) 33–59.

Neusner, Jacob. "Comparing Judaisms." *History of Religions* 18 (1978–79) 177–91.

———. "E. P. Sanders Paul, the Law, and the Jewish People." In *Ancient Judaism: Debates and Disputes*, edited by W. S. Green, 73–95. Brown Judaic Studies 64. Chico, CA: Scholars, 1994.

———. "The Four Approaches to the Description of Ancient Judaism(s): Nominalist, Harmonistic, Theological, and Historical." In *Death, Life-after-Death, Resurrection, and the World to Come in the Judaisms of Antiquity*, edited by A. Avery-Peck and J. Nuesner, 1–34. Vol. 4 of *Judaism in Antiquity*. Leiden: Brill, 2000.

———. *Judaic Law from Jesus to the Mishnah: A Systematic Reply to Professor E. P. Sanders*. Atlanta: Scholars, 1993.

———. "Mr. Sanders' Pharisees and Mine: A Response to E. P. Sanders, Jewish Law from Jesus to the Mishnah." *Scottish Journal of Theology* 44 (1991) 73–95.

———. "The Use of Later Rabbinic Evidence for the Study of Paul." In *Approaches to Ancient Judaism: Theory and Practice*, edited by W. S. Green, 2:43–63. Chico, CA: Scholars, 1980.

Neusner, Jacob, and Bruce Chilton. *In Quest of the Historical Pharisees*. Waco, TX: Baylor University Press, 2007.

Neyrey, Jerome. "Loss of Wealth, Loss of Family and Loss of Honor." In *Modelling Early Christianity*, edited by Philip Esler, 139–59. New York: Routledge, 1995.

———. *Paul, in Other Words: A Cultural Reading of His Letters*. Louisville: Westminster John Knox, 1990.

———. *Render to God: New Testament Understanding of the Divine*. Minneapolis: Fortress, 2004.

Ng, Esther Yue L. "Phoebe as *Prostatis*." *Trinity Journal* 25 (2004) 3–13.

Nguyen, Henry T. *Christian Identity in Corinth: A Comparative Study of 2 Corinthians, Epictetus and Valerius Maximus V*. Tübingen: Mohr/Siebeck, 2008.

Niccum, C. "The Voice of the Manuscripts on the Silence of Women: The External Evidence for 1 Cor. 14.34–35." *New Testament Studies* 43 (1997) 242–55.

Nijf, Onno van. *The Civic World of Professional Associations in the Roman East*. Leiden: Brill, 1997.

Nilsson, Martin. *Geschichte der griechischen Religion*. München: Beck, 1955.

Nussbaum, Martha C. "Eros and Ethical Norms: Philosophers Respond to a Cultural Dilemma." In *The Sleep of Reason: Erotic Experience and Sexual Ethics in Ancient Greece and Rome*, edited by Martha C. Nussbaum and Juha Sihvola, 327–53. Chicago: University of Chicago Press, 2002.

———. "The Incomplete Feminism of Musonius Rufus." In *The Sleep of Reason: Erotic Experience and Sexual Ethics*, edited by Martha C. Nussbaum and Juha Sihvola, 283–326. Chicago: University of Chicago Press, 2002.

———. *The Therapy of Desire: Theory and Practice in Hellenistic Ethics*. Princeton: Princeton University Press, 1994.

Nussbaum, Martha C., and Rosalind Hursthouse. "Plato on Commensurability and Desire." *Proceedings of the Aristotelian Society, Supplementary Volumes* 58 (1984) 55–96.

Nutton, Vivian. *Ancient Medicine*. London: Routledge, 2005.

Nye, Andrea. "The Hidden Host: Irigaray and Diotima at Plato's Symposium." *Hypatia* 3 (1989) 45–61.

Oates, Whitney J. *The Stoic and Epicurean Philosophers: The Complete Extant Writings of Epicurus, Epictetus, Lucretius, Marcus Aurelius*. New York: Modern Library, 1994.

Odell-Scott, D. W. "Editorial Dilemma: The Interpolation of 1 Cor 14.34–35 in the Western Manuscripts of D, G, and 88." *Biblical Theological Bulletin* 30 (2000) 68–74.

Oh-Young, Kwon. "Discovering the Characteristics of *Collegia*: *Colegia Sodalicia* and *Collegia Tenuiorum* in 1 Corinthians 8, 10 and 15." *Horizons in Biblical Theology* 32 (2010) 166–82.

Oikonomedes, A. "A New Inscription from Vergina and Eurydice Mother of Philip II." *Ancient World* 7 (1983) 52–54.

Økland, Jorunn. *Women in Their Place: Paul and the Corinthian Discourse of Gender and Sanctuary Space*. New York: T. & T. Clark International, 2004.

Olbricht, Thomas H. "Classical Rhetorical Criticism and Historical Reconstructions: A Critique." In *The Rhetorical Interpretation of Scripture: Essays from the 1996 Malibu Conference*, edited by Stanley E. Porter, 108–24. Novum Testamentum Supplement 180. Sheffield, UK: Sheffield Academic, 1999.

———. Preface to *Early Christianity and Classical Culture: Comparative Studies in Honor of Abraham J. Malherbe*, edited by John T. Fitzgerald et al., 1–12. Leiden: Brill, 2003.

Oliensis, Ellen. "The Erotics of *Amicitia*: Readings in Tibullus, Propertius, and Horace." In *Roman Sexualities*, edited by Marilynn Skinner and Judith P. Hallett, 151–71. Princeton: Princeton University Press, 1997.

Oliver, James H. "Arrian and the Gellii of Corinth." *Greek, Roman, and Byzantine Studies* 11 (1970) 335–37.

———. "The Empress Plotina and the Sacred Thymelic Synod." *Historia: Zeitschrift für Alte Geschichte* 24 (1975) 125–28.

Olson, Kelly. *Dress and the Roman Woman: Self-Presentation and Society*. London: Routledge, 2008.

———. "*Matrona* and Whore: Clothing and Definition in Roman Antiquity." In *Prostitutes and Courtesans in the Ancient World*, edited by Christopher A. Faraone and Laura K. McClure, 186–206. Madison: University of Wisconsin Press, 2006.

O'Mahony, Kieran J., *Pauline Persuasion: A Sounding in 2 Corinthians 8–9*. Sheffield, UK: Sheffield University Press, 2000.

O'Rourke, John J. "Hypotheses regarding 1 Corinthians 7:36–38." *Catholic Biblical Quarterly* 20 (1958) 292–98.

Osborn, Eric. "Arguments for Faith in Clement of Alexandria." *Vigiliae Christianae* 48 (1994) 1–24.

Osborne, Grant R. *Romans*. Downers Grove, IL: InterVarsity, 2004.

Osiek, Carolyn. "Diakonos and Prostatis: Women's Patronage in Early Christianity." *Hervormde teologiese studies* 61 (2005) 347–70.

Osiek, Carolyn, and Margaret Y. MacDonald. *A Woman's Place: House Churches in Earliest Christianity*. Minneapolis: Fortress, 2006.

Works Cited

Oster, Richard E. "Use, Misuse and Neglect of Archaeological Evidence in Some Modern Works on 1 Corinthians (1 Cor 7,1–5, 8,10, 11,2–16, 12,14–26)." *Zeitschrift für die neuetestamentliche Wissenschaft und die Kunde der älteren Kirche* 83 (1992) 52–73.

———. "When Men Wore Veils to Worship: The Historical Context of 1 Corinthians 11:4." *New Testament Studies* 34 (1988) 481–505.

Owen, G. E. L. "The Place of the Timaeus in Plato's Dialogues." *Classical Quarterly*, n.s., 3 (1953) 79–95.

Packman, Z. M. "Feminine Role Designations in the Comedies of Plautus." *The American Journal of Philology* 120 (1999) 245–58.

———. "Undesirable Company: The Categorisation of Women in Roman Law." *Scholia* 3 (1994) 94–106.

Padgett, A. "Paul on Women in the Church: The Contradictions of Coiffure in 1 Corinthians 11:2–16." *Journal for the Study of the New Testament* 20 (1984) 69–86.

Page, D. L. "A Note on Corinna." *Classical Quarterly*, n.s., 7 (1957) 109–12.

———. *Sappho and Alcaeus*. Oxford: Clarendon University Press, 1955.

Pagels, E. H. "Paul and Women: A Response to Recent Discussion." *Journal of the American Academy of Religion* 42 (1974) 538–49.

Pallas, Demetre I., et al. "Inscriptions." *Bulletin de correspondance hellenique* 83 (1954) 496–508.

Parker, Charles Pomeroy. "Musonius the Etruscan." *Harvard Studies in Classical Philology* 7 (1896) 123–37.

Parker, Francis H. *The Story of Western Philosophy*. Bloomington: Indiana University Press, 1967.

Parker, Holt N. "Sulpicia, the *Auctor de Sulpicia*, and the Authorship of 3.9 and 3.11 of the *Corpus Tibullianum*." *Helios* 21 (1994) 39–62.

———. "Women Doctors in Greece, Rome, and the Byzantine Empire." In *Women Healers and Physicians: Climbing a Long Hill*, edited by Lilian R. Furst, 131–50. Lexington: University of Kentucky Press, 1997.

Paton, W. R., editor. *The Greek Anthology*. London: Heinemann, 1908.

Patrick, John. *Clement of Alexandria*. London: Blackwood, 1914.

Patterson, Orlando. *Slavery and Social Death: A Comparative Study*. Cambridge: Harvard University Press, 1982.

Payne, Philip B. "Fuldensis, Sigla for Variants in Vaticanus, and 1 Cor 14.34–35." *New Testament Studies* 41 (1995) 240–62.

———. *Man and Woman, One in Christ: An Exegetical and Theological Study of Paul's Letters*. Grand Rapids: Zondervan, 2009.

———. "Ms 88 as Evidence for a Text without 1 Cor 14:34–35." *New Testament Studies* 44 (1998) 152–58.

Payne, Philip B., and Paul Canart, "The Originality of Text-Critical Symbols in Codex Vaticanus." *Novum Testametum* 42 (2000) 105–13.

Peck, A. L. "Plato's Parmenides: Some Suggestions for Its Interpretation." *Classical Quarterly*, n.s., 3 (1953) 126–50.

Pembroke, Simon. "List of the Matriarchs: A Study of the Inscriptions of Lycia." *Journal of the Economic and Social History of the Orient* 8 (1965) 217–47.

———. "Women in Charge: The Function of Alternatives in Early Greek Tradition and the Ancient Idea of Matriarchy." *Journal of the Warburg and Courtauld Institutes* 30 (1967) 1–35.

Penella, Robert J. "Philostratus' Letter to Julia Domna." *Hermes* 107 (1979) 161–68.

Perriman, C. "The Head of a Woman: The Meaning of 'Head' in 1 Cor. 11:3." *Journal of Theological Studies* 45 (1994) 602–22.
Peters, Greg. "Spiritual Marriage in Early Christianity: 1 Cor 7:25–38 in Modern Exegesis and the Earliest Church." *Trinity Journal*, n.s., 23 (2002) 211–24.
Pfeiffer, Rudolph. *History of Classical Scholarship: From the Beginnings to the Hellenistic Age*. Oxford: Clarendon University Press, 1968.
Pfitzner, Victor C. *Paul and the Agon Motif: Traditional Athletic Imagery in the Pauline Literature*. Leiden: Brill, 1967.
Pfuhl, Ernst, and Hans Möbius. *Die ostgriechischen Grabreliefs*. Mainz, Germany: von Zabern, 1977.
Pharr, Clyde. "The Interdiction of Magic in Roman Law." *Transactions of the American Phililogical Association* 63 (1932) 269–95.
Philip, J. A. "Aristotle's Monograph on Pythagoras." *Transactions and Proceedings of the American Philological Association* 94 (1963) 185–98.
———. "Aristotle's Sources for Pythagorean Doctrine." *Pheonix* 17 (1963) 251–65.
———. *Pythagoras and the Early Pythagoreanism*. Toronto: University of Toronto Press, 1966.
Phillips, Thomas E. *Acts within Diverse Frames of Reference*. Macon, GA: Mercer University Press, 2009.
Phipps, W. E. "Is Paul's Attitude Towards Sexual Relations Contained in 1 Cor 7:1." *New Testament Studies* 28 (1982) 125–30.
Picard, Ch. "La donation de safran en l'honneur de la Corinthienne Junia Theodora. Décret de la Confédération lycienne." *Revue d'assyriologie et d'archéologie orientale* 2 (1962) 95–97.
Piérart, Michael. "The Common Oracle of the Milesians and the Argives (Hdt. 6.19 and 77)." In *Herodotus and His World*, edited by Peter Derow and Robert Parker, 275–96. Oxford: Oxford University Press, 2003.
Pitcher, R. A. "The Hole in the Hypothesis: Pliny and Martial Reconsidered." *Mnemosyne*, 4th ser., 52 (1999) 554–61.
Podlecki, Anthony J. *Pericles and His Circle*. London: Routledge, 1998.
Pogoloff, Stephen M. *Logos and Sophia: The Rhetorical Situation of 1 Corinthians*. SBL Dissertation Series 134. Atlanta: Scholars, 1992.
Poliakoff, M. B. *Combat Sports in the Ancient World: Competition, Violence and Culture*. New Haven: Yale University Press, 1987.
Pomeroy, Sarah B. *Advice to the Bride and Groom*. Oxford: Oxford University Press, 1999.
———. *Spartan Women*. Oxford: Oxford University Press, 2002.
———. "The Study of Women in Antiquity: Past, Present, and Future." *American Journal of Philosophy* 112 (1991) 263–68.
———. "Supplementary Notes on Erinna." *Zeitschrift für Papyrologie und Epigraphik* 32 (1978) 20.
———. "Technikai kai mousikai: The Education of Women in the Fourth Century and in the Hellenistic Period." *American Journal of Ancient History* 2 (1977) 51–68.
———. *Women in Hellenistic Egypt from Alexandria to Cleopatra*. New York: Schocken, 1984.
Popkin, Richard H., editor. *The Columbia History of Western Philosophy*. New York: Columbia, 1998.

Works Cited

Porter, J. I. "The Philosophy of Aristo of Chios." In *The Cynic Movement in Antiquity and Its Legacy*, edited by Marie-Odile Goulet-Cazé and Robert B. Branham, 156–89. Berkely: University of California Press, 1996.

Porter, Stanley E., editor. *Handbook to the Exegesis of the New Testament*. Boston: Brill, 2002.

———. *Paul and His Opponents*. SBL Pauline Studies 2. Leiden: Brill, 2005.

———. "Paul as an Epistolographer *and* Rhetorician?" In *The Rhetorical Interpretation of Scripture: Essays from the 1996 Malibu Conference*, edited by Stanley E. Porter, 222–48. Novum Testamentum Supplement 180. Sheffield, UK: Sheffield Academic, 1999.

———. *The Rhetorical Interpretation of Scripture: Essays from the 1996 Malibu Conference*. Novum Testamentum Supplement 180. Sheffield, UK: Sheffield Academic, 1999.

Powell, J. G. F. *Cato maior de senectute*. Cambridge: Cambridge University Press, 1988.

Poynton, J. B. "Roman Education." *Greece & Rome* 4 (1934) 1–12.

Prioreschi, Plino. *A History of Medicine*. 2nd ed. Vol. 2. Omaha: Horatius, 1996.

Purdue, Leo G. *Wisdom Literature: A Theological History*. Louisville: Westminster John Knox, 2007.

Purnell, George Roberts. "A Study of Roman Literary Patronage: With Special Reference to the Messalla Circle." PhD diss., Stanford University, 1930.

Quinn, Kenneth. "The Poet and His Audience in the Augustan Age." In *Aufstieg und Niedergang der römischen Welt*, vol. 2.30.1, edited by Wolfgang Haase and Hildegard Temporini, 75–180. New York: de Gruyter, 1982.

Radin, Max. "Apotheosis." *Classical Review* 30 (1916) 44–46.

Rajak, Tessa. *The Jewish Dialogue with Greece and Rome: Studies in Cultural and Social Interaction*. Leiden: Brill, 2001.

Rajak, Tessa, and David Noy. "*Archisynagogoi*: Office, Title and Social Status in the Greco-Jewish Synagogue." *Journal of Roman Studies* 83 (1993) 75–93.

Ramsaran, Rollin A. "More than an Opinion: Paul's Rhetorical Maxim in First Corinthians 7:25–26." *Catholic Biblical Quarterly* 57 (1995) 531–41.

Rankin, David Ivan. *From Clement to Origen: The Social and Historical Context of the Church Fathers*. Aldershot, UK: Ashgate, 2006.

Rapa, Robert Keith. *The Meaning of "Works of the Law" in Galatians and Romans*. Studies in Biblical Literature 31. New York: Lang, 2001.

Raphals, Lisa. *Sharing the Light: Representations of Women and Virtue in Early China*. Chinese Philosophy and Culture. Albany: State University of New York Press, 1998.

Rawson, Beryl. *Children and Childhood in Roman Italy*. Oxford: Oxford University Press.

———. *The Family in Ancient Rome: New Perspectives*. Ithaca, NY: Cornell University Press, 1986.

Rawson, Elizabeth. *Cicero: A Portrait*. London: Allen Lane, 1975.

Rayor, Diane J. *Sappho's Lyre: Archaic Lyric and Women Poets of Ancient Greece*. Berkley: University of California Press, 1991.

Reale, Giovanni. *A History of Ancient Philosophy: The Schools of the Imperial Age*. Edited and translated by John R. Catan. New York: State University of New York Press, 1990.

Reckford, Kenneth J. "Horace and Maecenas." *Transactions and Proceedings of the American Philological Association* 90 (1959) 195–208.
Reichmann, Felix. "The Book Trade at the Time of the Roman Empire." *Library Quarterly* 8 (1938) 40–47.
Reimer, Andy M. *Miracle and Magic: A Study in the Acts of the Apostles and the Life of Apollonius of Tyana*. London: Sheffield, 2002.
Reinhold, Meyer. "Marcus Agrippa's Son-in-Law P. Quinctilius Varus." *Classical Philology* 67 (1972) 119–21.
Reydams-Schils, G. *The Roman Stoics: Self, Responsibility, and Affection*. Chicago: University of Chicago Press, 2005.
Reynolds, Joyce M., and Robert Tannenbaum. *Jews and Godfearers at Aphrodisias*. Proceedings of the Cambridge Philological Society Supplement 12. Cambridge: Cambridge Philological Society, 1987.
Richards, E. Randolph. *Paul and First-Century Letter Writers: Secretaries, Composition and Collection*. Downers Grove, IL: InterVarsity, 2004.
Richardson, Peter. "Early Synagogues as Collegia in the Diaspora and Palestine." In *Voluntary Associations in the Graeco-Roman World*, edited by John Kloppenborg, 90–109. London: Routledge, 1996.
———. "Judgment in Sexual Natters in 1 Corinthians 6:1–11." *Novum Testamentum* 25 (1983) 37–58.
Richlin, Amy. "Sulpicia the Satirist." *Classical World* 86 (1992) 125–40.
Ridgway, Brunilde Sismondo. "An Issue of Methodology: Anakreon, Perikles, Xanthippos." *American Journal of Archaeology* 102 (1998) 717–38.
Riesner, Rainer. *Paul's Early Period: Chronology, Mission Strategy, and Theology*. Grand Rapids: Erdmans, 1998.
Riggsby, Andrew M. *Roman Law and the Legal World of the Romans*. Cambridge: Cambridge University Press, 2010.
Riginos, Alice Swift. *Platonica: The Anecdotes Concerning the Life and Writings of Plato*. Leiden: Brill, 1976.
Riley, Mark T. "The Epicurean Criticism of Socrates." *Phoenix* 34 (1980) 55–68.
Rist, John M. *Epicurus: An Introduction*. Cambridge: Cambridge University Press, 1938.
———. "Plutarch's 'Amatorius': A Commentary on Plato's Theories of Love?" *Classical Quarterly*, n.s., 51 (2001) 557–75.
Rist, Martin. Review of *Plutarch und Das Neue Testament: Ein Beitrag zum Corpus Hellenisticum Novi Testamenti*, by Helge Almqvist. *Journal of Biblical Literature* 66 (1947) 301–2.
Rives, J. "Human Sacrifice among Pagans and Christians." *Journal of Roman Studies* 85 (1995) 65–85.
Robbins, Vernon. Review of *Plutarch's Ethical Writings and Early Christian Literature*, by Hans Dieter Betz. *Journal of the American Academy of Religion* 47 (1979) 666.
Robert, Jeanne, and Louis Robert. "Bulletin épigraphique." *Revue des études grecques* 69 (1956) 152–53.
Robert, Louis. "Inscriptions de Chios du er siècle de notre ère." In *Études épigraphiques et philologiques*, 128–33. Paris: Champion, 1938.
———. *Opera Minora Selecta: Epigraphie et antiquités grecques*. 7 vols. Amsterdam: Hakkert, 1969–1990.
Roberts, R. L. "The Meaning of *Chorizo* and *Douloo* in 1 Corinthians 7:10–17." *Restoration Quarterly* 8 (1965) 179–84.

Works Cited

Robinson, David. *Sappho and Her Influence*. London: Harrap, 1924.
Robinson, Rodney P. "The Roman School Teacher and His Reward." *Classical Weekly* 15 (1921) 57–61.
Robinson, Olivia F. *The Sources of Roman Law: Problems and Methods for Ancient Historians*. London: Routledge, 1997.
Roebuck, Carl. "Some Aspects of Urbanization in Corinth." *Hesperia* 41 (1972) 96–127.
Roessel, David. "The Significance of the Name Cerinthus in the Poems of Sulpicia." *Transactions of the American Philological Association* 120 (1990) 243–50.
Roller, Duane W. "Gaius Memmius: Patron of Lucretius." *Classical Philology* 65 (1970) 246–48.
Romano, David Gilman. "City Planning, Centuriation, and Land Division in Roman Corinth: Colonia Laus Iulia Corinthiensis & Colonia Iulia Flavia Augusta Corinthiensis." *Corinth* 20 (2003) 279–301.
———. "Roman Surveyors in Corinth." *Proceedings of the American Philological Society* 150 (2006) 62–85.
Romano, Irene Bald. "A Hellenistic Deposit from Corinth: Evidence for Interim Period Activity (146–44 B. C.)." *Hesperia* 63 (1994) 57–104.
Roon, A. van. "Relation between Christ and the Wisdom of God according to Paul." *Novum Testamentum* 16 (1974) 207–39.
Rorty, Amélie Oksenberg. "As Diotima Saw Socrates." *Arion* 4 (1997) 147.
———, editor. *Essays on Aristotle's Rhetoric*. Berkeley: University of California Press: 1996.
Rosenmeyer, Patricia A. *Ancient Epistolary Fictions: The Letter in Greek Literature*. Cambridge: Cambridge University Press, 2001.
Roskam, G. *On the Path to Virtue. The Stoic Doctrine of Moral Progress and Its Reception in (Middle-)Platonism*. Leuven: Leuven University Press, 2005.
Rosner, Brian S. *Paul, Scripture, and Ethics: A Study of 1 Corinthians 5–7*. Leiden: Brill, 1994.
Rothschild, Clare K. *Luke-Acts and the Rhetoric of History*. Wissenschaftliche Untersuchungen zum Neuen Testament 2.175. Tübingen: Mohr, 2004.
Rotroff, Susan I., and Robert D. Lamberton. *Women in the Athenian Agora*. Athens: American School of Classical Studies at Athens, 2006.
Rousselle, Aline. *Porneia*. Translated by Felicia Pheasant. New York: Basil Blackwell, 1983.
Ruden, Sarah. *Paul among the People: The Apostle Reinterpreted and Reimagined in His Own Time*. Toronto: Pantheon, 2010.
Runia, David T. "Why Does Clement of Alexandria Call Philo 'The Phythagorean'?'" *Vigiliae Christianae* 49 (1995) 1–22.
Russell, Bertrand. *A History of Western Philosophy*. New York: Simon & Schuster, 1945.
Rutgers, Leonard Victor. "Roman Policy towards the Jews: Expulsions from the City of Rome during the First Century C.E." *Classical Antiquity* 13 (1994) 56–74.
Rutherford, Ian. "Aristodama and the Aetolians: An Itinerant Poetess and Her Agenda." In *Wandering Poets in Ancient Greek Culture: Travel, Locality and Pan-Hellenism*, edited by Richard Hunter and Ian Rutherford, 237–48. Cambridge: Cambridge University Press, 2009.
Rutledge, Harry C. "Herodes the Great: Citizen of the World." *Classical Journal* 56 (1960) 97–109.

Works Cited

Saatsoglou-Paliadeli, Chrysoula. "Εὐρυδίκα Σιρρα Εὐκλεία." In Αμητός τιμητικός για τον καθηγητή Μανόλη Ανδρόνικο. Thessaloniki, 1987.

———. "In the Shadow of History: The Emergence of Archaeology." *Annual of the British School at Athens* 94 (1999) 353–67.

Salapata, Gina. "Hero Warriors from Corinth and Lakonia." *Hesperia* 66 (1997) 245–60.

Saller, Richard. "Martial on Patronage and Literature." *Classical Quarterly* 33 (1983) 246–57.

———. *Personal Patronage under the Early Roman Empire*. Cambridge: Cambridge University Press, 1982.

———. "Roman Dowry and the Devolution of Property in the Principate." *Classical Quarterly*, n.s., 34 (1984) 195–205.

Salmon, J. B. *Wealthy Corinth: A History of the City to 338 B.C.* Oxford: Clarendon University Press, 1997.

Sampley, J. Paul. Foreword to *Paul and Rhetoric*, edited by Sampley and Peter Lampe, ix–xvii. New York: T. & T. Clark, 2010.

———. "Paul's Frank Speech with the Galatians and the Corinthians." In *Philodemus and the New Testament World*, edited by John T. Fitzgerald et al., 295–321. Leiden: Brill, 2004.

Sampley, J. Paul, and Peter Lampe, editors. *Paul and Rhetoric*. New York: T. & T. Clark, 2010.

Sandbach, F. H. *Aristotle and the Stoics*. Cambridge: Cambridge Philological Society, 1985.

Sanders, E. P. "On the Question of Fulfilling the Law in Paul and Rabbinic Judaism." In *Donum Gentilicum: New Testament Studies in Honour of David Daube*, edited by C. K. Barrett et al., 103–26. Oxford: Clarendon University Press, 1978.

———. *Paul*. Oxford: Oxford University Press, 1991.

———. *Paul and Palestinian Judaism: A Comparison in Patters of Religion*. London: SCM, 1977.

———. "Paul between Judaism and Hellenism." In *St. Paul among the Philosophers*, edited by John D. Caputo and Linda Martin Alcoff, 74–90. Bloomington: Indiana University Press.

———. "Paul's Attitude toward the Jewish People." *Union Seminary Quarterly Review* 33 (1978) 175–87.

Sandmel, Samuel. "Parallelomania." *Journal of Biblical Literature* 81 (1962) 1–13.

Sandnes, Karl Olav. *Paul, One of the Prophets? A Contribution to the Apostle's Self-Understanding*. Wissenschaftliche Untersuchungen zum Neuen Testament 2.45. Tübingen: Mohr, 1991.

Santirocco, Matthew. "The Maecenas Odes." *Transactions of the American Philological Association* 114 (1984) 241–53.

Scanlon, Thomas. "Virgineum Gymnasium. Spartan Females and Early Greek Athletics." In *Archaeology of the Olympics*, edited by W. Raschke, 185–216. Madison: University of Wisconsin Press, 1988.

Schachter, Albert, and William J. Slater. "A Proxeny Decree from Koroneia, Boiotia in Honour of Zotion Son of Zotion, of Ephesos." *Zeitschrift für Papyrologie und Epigraphik* 163 (2007) 81–95.

Schachter, Marc D. *Voluntary Servitude and the Erotics of Friendship from Classical Antiquity to Early Modern France*. Burlington, VT: Ashgate, 2008.

Works Cited

Schmidt, Steffen W., et al., editors. *Friends Followers and Factions: A Reader in Political Clientelism*. Berkeley: University of California Press, 1977.

Schnelle, Udo. *Apostle Paul: His Life and Theology*. Grand Rapids: Baker, 2005.

Schoedel, William R. Review of *Lukian von Samosata und das Neue Testament. Religionsgeschichtliche und paränetische Parallelen. Ein Beitrag zum Corpus Hellenisticum Novi Testamenti*, by Hans D. Betz. *Journal of Biblical Literature* 84 (1965) 318–21.

———. "Three Recent Works on Patristics and Early Christian Literature." Review of *Corpus Hermeticum XIII*, by William C. Grese; *Plutarch's Theological Writings*, edited by Hans D. Betz; and *Plutarch's Ethical Writings*, edited by Hans D. Betz. *History of Religions* 20 (1981) 345–46.

Schottroff, Luise. "Holiness and Justice: Exegetical Comments on 1 Corinthians 11.17–34." Translated by Brian McNeil. *Journal for the Study of the New Testament* 23 (2000) 51–60.

———. *Let the Oppressed Go Free: Feminist Perspectives on the New Testament*. Louisville: Westminster John Knox, 1992.

Schowalter, Daniel N., and Steven J. Friesen, editors. *Urban Religion in Roman Corinth: Interdisciplinary Approaches*. Harvard Theological Studies 53. Cambridge: Cambridge University Press, 2005.

Schreiner, Thomas R. *The Law and Its Fulfillment: A Pauline Theology of Law*. Grand Rapids: Baker, 1993.

———. *Seneca in Gegensatz zu Paulus*. Tübingen: Mohr, 1936.

Schulz, Ray R. "A Case for 'President' Phoebe in Romans 16:2." *Lutheran Theological Journal* 24 (1990) 124–27.

Schurer, Emil. *The History of the Jewish People in the Age of Jesus Christ*. 5 vols. Edinburgh: Clark, 1973–1987.

Schüssler Fiorenza, Elisabeth. *In Memory of Her: A Feminist Theological Reconstruction of Christian Origins*. New York: Crossroad, 1983.

———. "Missionaries, Apostles, Coworkers: Romans 16 and the Reconstruction of Women's Early Christian History." *Word and World* 6 (1986) 420–33.

———. "Phoebe." *Bibel Heute* 79 (1984) 162–64.

———. "The Quilting of Women's History: Phoebe of Cenchreae." In *Embodied Love: Sensuality and Relationship as Feminist Values*, edited by Paula M. Cooey et al., 35–49. San Francisco: Harper & Row, 1987.

———. "Women in the Pre-Pauline and Pauline Churches." *Union Seminary Quarterly Review* 33 (1978) 153–66.

Schweizer, Eduard. "Slaves of the Elements and Worshipers of Angels: Gal 4:3, 9 and Col 2:8, 18, 20." *Journal of Biblical Literature* 107 (1989) 455–68.

Scranton, R. L. "The Corinth of the Apostle Paul." *Emory University Quarterly* 5 (1949) 72–75.

Scullard, H. H. "Scipio Aemilianus and Roman Politics." *Journal of Roman Studies* 50 (1960) 59–64.

Sear, Frank. *Roman Architecture*. Ithaca, NY: Cornell University Press, 2005.

Seboldt, Roland H. A. "Spiritual Marriage in the Early Church: A Suggested Interpretation of 1 Corinthians 7:36–38." *Concordia Theological Monthly* 30 (1959) 103–19.

Sedley, D. "Diodorus Cronus and Hellenistic Philosophy." *Proceedings of the Cambridge Philological Society*, n.s., 203 (1977) 74–120.

Works Cited

Setaioli, Aldo. "Seneca and the Divine: Stoic Tradition and Personal Developments." *International Journal of the Classical Tradition* 13 (2007) 333–68.

Setälä, P., et al., editors. *Women, Wealth and Power in the Roman Empire*. Rome: Institutum Romanum Finlandiae, 2002.

Sevenster, Jan N. *Paul and Seneca*. Leiden: Brill, 1962.

Sharples, R. W. "Dicaearchus on the Soul and Divination." In *Dicaearchus of Messana: Text, Translation, and Discussion*, edited by William W. Fortenbaug and Eckhart Schütrumpf, 143–74. Rutgers University Studies in Classical Humanities 10. New Brunswick, NJ: Transaction, 2001.

Shaw, Brent D. "Bandits in the Roman Empire." *Past & Present* 105 (1984) 3–52.

Shero, L. R. "Xenophon's Portrait of a Young Wife." *Classical Weekly* 26 (1932) 17–21.

Sherwin-White, A. N. *The Letters of Pliny: A Historical and Social Commentary*. Oxford: Clarendon University Press, 1985.

———. "Pliny, the Man and His Letters." *Greece & Rome*, 2nd ser., 16 (1969) 76–90.

Shi, Wenhua. *Paul's Message of the Cross as Body Language*. Wissenschaftliche Untersuchungen zum Neuen Testament 2.254. Tübingen: Mohr/Siebeck, 2008.

Sider, David. *The Library of the Villa dei Papiri at Herculaneum*. Los Angeles: Getty Museum, 2005.

Sihvola, Juha. "Two Women of Samos." In *The Sleep of Reason: Erotic Experience and Sexual Ethics in Ancient Greece and Rome*, edited by Martha C. Nussbaum and Juha Sihvola, 222–82. Chicago: University of Chicago Press, 2002.

Siniossoglou, Niketas. *Plato and Theodoret: The Christian Appropriation of Platonic Philosophy and the Hellenic Intellectual Resistance*. Cambridge: Cambridge University Press, 2008.

Sissa, Giulia. *Sex and Sexuality in the Ancient World*. Translated by George Staunton. New Haven: Yale University Press, 2008.

Skalitzky, Rachel I. "Horace on Travel (Epist. 1.11)." *Classical Journal* 68 (1973) 316–21.

Skinner, Marilyn B. "Briseis, the Trojan Women, and Erinna." *Classical World* 75 (1982) 265–69.

———. "Corinna of Tanagra and Her Audience." *Tulsa Studies in Women's Literature* 2 (1983) 9–20.

———. "Homer's Mother." In *Women Poets in Ancient Greece and Rome*, edited by Ellen Greene, 91–111. Norman: University of Oklahoma Press, 2005.

———. "Ladies' Day at the Art Institute: Theocritus, Herodas and the Gendered Gaze." In *Making Silence Speak: Women's Voices in Ancient Greek Literature and Society*, edited by André Lardinois and Laura McClure, 201–22. Princeton: Princeton University Press, 2001.

———. "Nossis *Thēlyglōssos*: The Private Text and the Public Book." In *Women's History and Ancient History*, edited by Sarah B. Pomeroy, 21–47. Chapel Hill: University of North Carolina Press, 1991.

———. "Sapphic Nossis." *Arethusa* 22 (1989) 5–18.

———. *Sexuality in Greece and Roman Culture*. Oxford: Blackwell, 2005.

Smallwood, E. Mary. *Documents Illustrating the Principates of Nerva, Trajan and Hadrian*. Cambridge: Cambridge University Press, 2001.

Smit, Joop F. M. "'What Is Apollos? What Is Paul?': In Search for the Coherence of First Corinthians 1:10—14:21." *Novum Testamentum* 44 (2002) 231–51.

Smith, Dennis. *From Symposium to Eucharist: The Banquet in the Early Christian World*. Minneapolis: Fortress, 2003.

Works Cited

Smith, Andrew. *Porphyry's Place in the Neoplatonic Tradition*. The Hague: Nijhoff, 1974.

Smith, E. W. *Joseph and Asenath and Early Christian Literature: A Contribution to the Corpus Hellenisticum Novi Testamenti*. PhD diss., Claremont Graduate School, 1974.

Smith, Jay E. "The New Perspective on Paul: A Select and Annotated Bibliography." *Criswell Theological Review* 2 (2005) 91–111.

Smith, Martin Ferguson. "Diogenes of Oenoanda, New Fragment 24." *American Journal of Philology* 99 (1978) 329–31.

———. "Diogenes of Oenoanda, New Fragments 122–24." *Anatolian Studies* 34 (1984) 43–57.

———. "Eight New Fragments of Diogenes of Oenoanda." *Anatolian Studies* 29, (1979) 69–89.

———. "Elementary, My Dear Lycians: A Pronouncement on Physics from Diogenes of Oinoanda." *Anatolian Studies* 50 (2000) 133–37.

———. "Excavations at Oinoanda 1997: The New Epicurean Texts." *Anatolian Studies* 48 (1998) 125–70.

———. "Fifty-Five New Fragments of Diogenes of Oenoanda." *Anatolian Studies* 28 (1978) 39–92.

———. "Fragments of Diogenes of Oenoanda: Discovered and Rediscovered." *American Journal of Archaeology* 74 (1971) 51–62.

———. "Fresh Thoughts on Diogenes of Oinoanda fr. 68." *Zeitschrift für Papyrologie und Epigraphik* 133 (2000) 51–55.

———. "The Introduction to Diogenes of Oinoanda's 'Physics.'" *Classical Quartery*, n.s., 50 (2000) 238–46.

———. "New Fragments of Diogenes of Oenoanda." *American Journal of Archaeology* 75 (1971) 357–89.

———. "New Readings in the Demostheneia Inscription from Oinoanda." *Anatolian Studies* 44 (1994) 59–64.

———. "New Readings in the Text of Diogenes of Oenoanda." *Classical Quarterly*, n.s., 22 (1972) 159–62.

———. "ΝΗΣΣΟΣ at Oinoanda in Lycia: Misspelling or Genuine Variant." *Zeitschrift für Papyrologie und Epigraphik* 130 (2000) 127–30.

———. "In Praise of the Simple Life: A New Fragment of Diogenes of Oinoanda." *Anatolian Studies* 54 (2004) 35–46.

———. *Supplement to Diogenes of Oinoanda: The Epicurean Inscription*. La Scuola di Epicuro. Naples: Bibliopolis, 1993.

———. "Two New Fragments of Diogenes of Oenoanda." *Journal of Hellenistic Studies* 92 (1972) 147–55.

Smith, Morton. "Paul's Arguments as Evidence of the Christianity from which He Diverged." *Harvard Theological Review* 79 (1986) 254–60.

———. "De Superstitione." In *Plutarch's Theological Writings and Early Christian Literature*, edited by Hans D. Betz, 1–35. Leiden: Brill, 1975.

Snyder, Jane McIntosh. "Lucretius and the Status of Women." *Classical Bulletin* 53 (1976) 17–20.

———. "Public Occasion and Private Passion in the Lyrics of Sappho of Lesbos." In *Women's History and Ancient History*, edited by Sarah B. Pomeroy, 1–19. Chapel Hill: University of North Carolina Press, 1991.

———. *The Woman and the Lyre: Women Writers in Classical Greece and Rome.* Edwardsville: Southern Illinois University Press, 1989.
Song, Changwon. *Reading Romans as a Diatribe.* New York: Lang, 2004.
Songer, Harold. "Problems Arising from the Worship of Idols: 1 Corinthians 8:1—11:1." *Review & Expositor* 80 (1983) 363–75.
Spaeth, John. "Cicero the Poet." *Classical Journal* (1931) 500–512.
Spawforth, Antony J. S. "Roman Corinth: The Formation of a Colonial Elite." In *Roman Onomastics in the Greek East: Social and Political Aspects*, edited by Athanasios D. Rizakis, 167–82. Athens: Research Centre for Greek and Roman Antiquity, 1996.
Sperduti, Alice. "The Divine Nature of Poetry in Antiquity." *Transactions of the American Philological Association* 81 (1950) 209–40.
Stambaugh, John E., and David Balch. *The New Testament in Its Social Environment.* Edited by Wayne Meeks. Philadelphia: Westminster John Knox, 1986.
Standing, Giles. "The Claudian Invasion of Britain and the Cult of Victoria Britannica." *Britannia* 34 (2003) 281–88.
Stanley, Christopher D. "Paul and Homer: Greco-Roman Citation Practice in the First Century CE." *Novum Testamentum* 32 (1990) 48–78.
Stanley, David. "Imitation in Paul's Letters: Its Significance for His Relationship to Jesus and His Own Christian Foundations." In *From Jesus to Paul: Studies in Honor of Francis Wright Bear*, edited by Peter Richardson and John C. Hurd, 127–41. Waterloo: Wilfrid Laurier University Press, 1984.
Stark, Rodney. "Reconstructing the Rise of Christianity: The Role of Women." *Sociology of Religion* 56 (1995) 229–44.
Starr, Raymond J. "The Circulation of Literary Texts in the Roman World." *Classical Quarterly* 37 (1987) 213–23.
Stearns, John. "Lucretius and Memmius." *Classical Weekly* 25 (1931) 67–68.
Steel, Catherine E. W. *Roman Oratory.* Cambridge: Cambridge University Press for the Classical Association, 2006.
Stern-Gillet, Suzanne, and Kevin Corrigan, editors. *Reading Ancient Texts.* Vol. 2, *Aristotle and Neoplatonism.* Leiden: Brill, 2008.
Stichele, Caroline Vander. "Is Silence Golden? Paul and Women's Speech in Corinth." *Louvain Studies* 20 (1995) 241–53.
Still, Todd D. *Conflict at Thessalonica: A Pauline Church and Its Neighbors.* Edited by Stanley E. Porter. Journal for the Study of the New Testament Supplement Series 183. Sheffield, UK: Sheffield Academic, 1999.
———. "Did Paul Loathe Manual Labor? Revisiting the Work of Ronald F. Hock on the Apostle's Tentmaking and Social Class." *Journal of Biblical Literature* 125 (2006) 781–95.
Stirewalt, M. Luther, Jr. *Paul, the Letter Writer.* Grand Rapids: Eerdmans, 2003.
———. *Studies in Ancient Greek Epistolography.* Edited by Marvin A. Sweeney. Scholars: Atlanta, 1993.
Stowers, Stanley K. *The Diatribe and Paul's Letters to the Romans.* Chicago: Scholars, 1981.
———. "Does Pauline Christianity Resemble a Hellenistic Philosophy." In *Paul Beyond the Judaism/Hellenism Divide*, edited by Troels Engberg-Pedersen, 81–102. Loiusville: Westminster John Knox, 2001.
———, editor. *Handbook of Classical Rhetoric in the Hellenistic Period.* Leiden: Brill, 1997.

Works Cited

———. *Letter Writing in Greco-Roman Antiquity*. Philadelphia: Westminster, 1986.
———, editor. *Paul and His Opponents*. Pauline Studies 2. Leiden: Brill, 2005.
———, editor. *A Rereading of Romans: Justice, Jews, and Gentiles*. New Haven: Yale University Press, 1994.
———. "Social Status, Public Speaking, and Private Teaching: The Circumstances of Paul's Preaching Activity." *Novum Testamentum* 26 (1984) 59–82.
Stowers, Stanley K., and Sean A. Adams, editors. *Paul and the Ancient Letter Form*. Pauline Studies 6. Brill: Leiden, 2009.
Stuhlmacher, Peter. *Paul's Letter to the Romans: A Commentary*. Translated by Scott J. Hafemann. Louisville: Westminster, 1994.
Stuhlmacher, Peter, and Donald Alfred Hagner. *Revisiting Paul's Doctrine of Justification: A Challenge to the New Perspective*. Downers Grove, IL: InterVarsity, 2001.
Sturgeon, Mary C. "Dedications of Roman Theaters." In *ΧΑΡΙΣ: Essays in Honor of Sara A. Immerwahr*, edited by Anne P. Chapin, 411–29. Hesperia Supplement 33, Princeton: Princeton University Press, 2004.
Sumney, Jerry. *Identifying Paul's Opponents: The Question of Method in 2 Corinthians*. Journal for the Study of the New Testament Supplements 40. Shefflield: JSOT, 1990.
Swaddling, J. *The Ancient Olympic Games*. 3rd ed. London: British Museum Press, 2004.
Swan, P. M. "A Consular Epicurean under the Early Principate." *Phoenix* 30 (1976) 54–60.
Swancutt, Diana. "The Disease of Effemination." In *New Testament Masculinities*, edited by Stephen Moore and Janice Anderson, 223–41. Atlanta: SBL, 2003.
Syme, R. *The Augustan Aristocracy*. Oxford: Oxford University Press, 1989.
Talbert, Charles H. *Reading Luke-Acts in Its Mediterranean Milieu*. Novum Testamentum Supplements 107. Leiden: Brill, 2003.
Tardieu, Michel. "La Lettre à Hipparque et les réminiscences pythagoriciennes de Clément d'Alexandrie." *Vigiliae christianae* 28 (1974) 241–47.
Taylor, Joan E. *Jewish Women Philosophers of First Century Alexandria*. New York: Oxford University Press, 2003.
Taylor, Justin. *Pythagoreans and Essenes: Structural Parallels*. Paris: Peeters, 2004.
Taylor, Lily Ross. "The Equestrian Career of Horace." *American Journal of Philology* 46 (1925) 164–70.
Taylor, Nicholas. "The Social Nature of Conversion." In *Modelling Early Christianity*, edited by Philip Esler, 124–32. New York: Routledge, 1995.
Tell, Håkan. "Sages at the Games: Intellectual Displays and Dissemination of Wisdom in Ancient Greece." *Classical Antiquity* 26 (2007) 249–55.
Tellegen-Couperus, Olga. *A Short History of Roman Law*. London: Routledge, 1993.
Terry, Ralph. "An Analysis of Certain Features of the Discourse in the New Testament Book of 1 Corinthians." PhD diss., University of Texas at Arlington, 1993.
Theissen, Gerd. "Social Conflicts in the Corinthian Community: Further Remarks on J. J. Meggitt, Paul, Poverty, and Survival." *Journal for the Study of the New Testament* 25 (2003) 371–91.
———. *The Social Setting of Pauline Christianity: Essays on Corinth*. Philadelphia: Fortress, 1982.
———. "The Social Structure of Pauline Communities: Some Critical Remarks on J. J. Meggitt, Paul, Poverty, and Survival." *Journal for the Study of the New Testament* 84 (2001) 65–84.

Works Cited

Theological Dictionary of the New Testament. Edited by G. Kittel and G. Friedrich. Translated by J. T. Willis et al. 8 vols. Grand Rapids: Eerdmans, 1974–.

Thesleff, Holger. *An Introduction to the Pythagorean Writings of the Hellenistic Period.* Åbo: Åbo Academi, 1961.

Thielman, Frank. *Paul and the Law: A Contextual Approach.* Downers Grove, IL: InterVarsity, 1994.

Thilly, Frank. *A History of Philosophy.* New York: Holt, Rinehart, & Winston, 1957.

Thiselton, Anthony C. *The First Epistle to the Corinthians: A Commentary on the Greek Text.* New International Greek Testament Commentary. Grand Rapids: Eerdmans, 2000.

Thom, Johan. "'Don't Walk on the Highways': The Pythagorean Akousmata and Early Christian Literature." *Journal of Biblical Literature* 113 (1994) 93–112.

———. "The Golden Verses of Pythagoras: Its Literary Composition and Religio-historical Significance." PhD diss., University of Chicago, 1990.

———. "'To Show Difference by Comparison': The Neuen Wettstein and Cleanthes' Hymn." In *Reading Religions in the Ancient World: Essays Presented to Robert McQueen Grant on His 90th Birthday,* edited by David E. Aune and Robert Darling Young, 81–100. Leiden: Brill, 2007.

Thompson, Michael B. *The New Perspective on Paul.* Grove Biblical Studies. Cambridge: Grove, 2002.

Tiede, David L. Review of *Die Traditionen über Apollonius von Tyana und das Neue Testament,* by Gerd Petzke. *Journal of Biblical Literature* 90 (1973) 465–67.

Tomson, Peter J. "Paul's Jewish Background in View of His Law Teaching in 1Cor 7." In *Paul and the Mosaic Law: Tübingen Studies and Earliest Christianity and Judaism,* edited by J. D. G. Dunn, 251–70. Tubingen: Mohr/Siebeck, 1996.

Townsley, Gillian. "Gender Trouble in Corinth: Que(e)rying Constructs of Gender in 1 Corinthians 11:2–16." *Bible & Critical Theory* 2 (2006) 17.1–14.

Toynbee, Jocelyn M. C. "Dictators and Philosophers in the First Century A. D." *Greece & Rome* 13 (1944) 43–58.

Treggiari, Susan. "Divorce Roman Style: How Easy and How Frequent Was It?" In *Marriage, Divorce and Children in Ancient Rome,* edited by Beryl Rawson, 31–46. Oxford: Clarendon University Press, 1991.

———. "Jobs for Women." *American Journal of Ancient History* 1 (1976) 76–104.

———. "Lower Class Women in the Roman Economy." *Florilegium* 1 (1979) 65–86.

———. *Roman Freedmen During the Late Republic.* Oxford: Clarendon University Press, 1969.

———. *Terentia, Tullia and Publilia: The Women of Cicero's Family.* London: Routledge, 2007.

Tuana, Nancy. *Woman and the History of Philosophy.* St. Paul, MN: Paragon House, 1992.

Tucker, J. Brian. "Baths, Baptism, and Patronage: The Continuing Role of Roman Social Identity in Corinth." In *Reading Paul in Context: Explorations in Identity Formation,* edited by Kathy Ehrensperger and J. Brian Tucker, 73–88. Library of New Testament Studies 428. London: T. & T. Clark, 2010.

Turner, E. G. *Greek Papyri: An Introduction.* Princeton: Princeton University Press, 1968.

Turner, John. Review of *Aelius Aristides and the New Testament,* by Pieter W. van der Horst. *Journal of the American Academy of Religion* 48 (1980) 116–17.

Works Cited

Tyson, Joseph B. "From History to Rhetoric and Back: Assessing New Trends in Acts Studies." In *Contextualizing Acts: Lukan Narrative in Greco-Roman Discourse*, edited by Todd C. Penner and Caroline Vander Stichele, 23–42. Atlanta: SBL, 2003.

Unnik, W. C. van. "Corpus Hellenisticum Novi Testamenti." *Journal of Biblical Literature* 83 (1964) 17–33.

———. "'Den Geist löschet nicht aus' I Thessalonicher V 19." *Novum Testamentum* 10 (1968) 255–69.

———. "Second Report on the Corpus Hellenisticum." *New Testament Studies* 3 (1957) 254–59.

———. "'Tiefer Friede' 1. Klemens 2,2." *Vigiliae Christianae* 24 (1970) 261–79.

———. "Words Come to Life: The Work for the 'Corpus Hellenisticum Novi Testamenti.'" *Novum Testamentum* 13 (1971) 199–216.

Valantasis, Richard. "Demons, Adversaries, Devils, Fishermen: The Asceticism of 'Authoritative Teaching' (NHL, VI, 3) in the Context of Roman Asceticism." *Journal of Religion* 81 (2001) 549–65.

Van der Horst, Pieter W. "Chariton and the New Testament: A Contribution to the Corpus Hellenisticum." *Novum Testamentum* 25 (1983) 348–55.

———. "Cornutus and the New Testament: A Contribution to the Corpus Hellenisticum." *Novum Testamentum* 23 (1981) 165–72.

———. "Corpus Hellenisticum Novi Testamenti." *Journal of Biblical Literature* 30 (1964) 17–33.

———. "Hierocles the Stoic and the New Testament: A Contribution to the Corpus Hellenisticum." *Novum Testamentum* 17 (1975) 156–60.

———. "Macrobius and the New Testament: A Contribution to the Corpus Hellenisticum." *Novum Testamentum* 15 (1973) 220–32.

———. "Musonius Rufus and the New Testament: A Contribution to the Corpus Hellenisticum." *Novum Testamentum* 16 (1974) 306–15.

———. "Pseudo-Phocylides Revisited." *Journal for the Study of the Pseudepigrapha* 3 (1988) 3–30.

Van der Stockt, Luc. "'Never the Twain Shall Meet?': Plutarch and Philostratus' Life of Apollonius: Some Themes and Techniques." In *Theios Sophistes Electronic: Essays on Flavius Philostratus' Vita Apollonii*, edited by Kristoffel Demoen and Danny Praet, 187–210. Leiden: Brill, 2009.

Vander Waerdt, Paul A. "The Justice of the Epicurean Wise Man." *Classical Quarterly*, n.s., 37 (1987) 402–22.

Vardi, Amiel. "Gellius against the Professors." *Zeitschrift für Papyrologie und Epigraphik* 137 (2001) 41–54.

Venit, Marjorie Susan. "Women in Their Cups." *Classical World* 92 (1998) 117–30.

Vidén, Gunhild. *Women in Roman Literature: Attitudes of Authors under the Early Empire*. Studia Graeca et Latina Gothoburgensia 57. Gothenburg, Sweden: Acta Universitatis Gothoburgensis, 1993.

Visscher, Gerhard H. *Romans 4 and the New Perspective on Paul: Faith Embraces the Promise*. New York: Lang, 2009.

Vlachos, Chris. *The Law and the Knowledge of Good and Evil: The Edenic Background of the Catalytic Operation of the Law in Paul*. Eugene, OR: Wipf & Stock, 2009.

Vlastos, Gregory. "Socrates' Disavowal of Knowledge." *Philosophy Quarterly* 35 (1985) 1–31.

Works Cited

Vos, Johan. "Rhetoric and Theology in the Letters of Paul." In *Paul and Rhetoric*, edited by J. Paul Sampley and Peter Lampe, 161–79. London: T. & T. Clark, 2010.

Waithe, Mary Ellen. *Ancient Women Philosophers, 600 B.C.–500 A.D.* Boston: Kluwer Academic, 1987.

———. "On Not Teaching the History of Philosophy." *Hypatia* 4 (1989) 132–38.

Walbank, Mary E. Hoskins. "Aspects of Corinthian Coinage in the Late 1st and Early 2nd Centuries A.C." *Corinth* 20 (2003) 337–49.

———. "What's in a Name? Corinth under the Flavians." *Zeitschrift für Papyrologie Epigrapik* 139 (2002) 251–64.

Walker, William O., Jr. "1 Corinthians 11:2–16 and Paul's Views regarding Women." *Journal Biblical Literature* 94 (1975) 94–110.

———. "The Portrayal of Aquila and Priscilla in Acts: The Question of Sources." *New Testament Studies* 54 (2008) 479–95.

———. "The Vocabulary of 1 Corinthians 11:3–16: Pauline or Non-Pauline?" *Journal for the Study of the New Testament* 35 (1989) 75–88.

Wallace-Hadrill, Andrew. "Domus and Insulae in Rome: Families and Housefuls." In *Early Christian Families in Context: An Interdisciplinary Dialogue*, edited by David L. Balch and Carolyn Osiek, 3–18. Grand Rapids: Eerdmans, 2003.

———. *Houses and Society in Pompeii and Herculaneum*. Princeton: Princeton University Press, 1994.

———, editor. *Patronage in Ancient Society*. London: Routledge, 1989.

Wanamaker, Charles A. "Connubial Sex and the Avoidance of Porneia: Paul's Rhetorical Argument in 1 Corinthians 7:1–5." *Scriptura* 90 (2005) 839–49.

———. *The Epistle to the Thessalonians: A Commentary on the Greek Text*. New International Greek Testament Commentary. Grand Rapids: Eerdmans, 1990.

Ward, Julie K., editor. *Feminism and Ancient Philosophy*. New York: Routledge, 1996.

Ward, Roy Bowen. "Why Unnatural? The Tradition behind Romans 1:26–27." *Harvard Theological Review* 90 (1997) 263–84.

Warren, James. *Epicurus and Democritean Ethics: An Archaeology of Ataraxia*. Cambridge: Cambridge University Press, 2002.

Warren, Karen. *An Unconventional History of Western Philosophy: Conversations between Men and Women Philosophers*. Plymouth, UK: Rowan & Littlefeld, 2009.

Warren, Mary Anne. "Feminist Archeology: Uncovering Women's Philosophical History." *Hypatia* 4 (1989) 155–59.

Wassermann, Emma. "Paul among the Philosophers: The Case of Sin in Romans 6–8." *Journal for the Study of the New Testament* 30 (2008) 387–415.

Waters, Guy Prentiss. *Justification and the New Perspectives on Paul: A Review and Response*. Phillipsburg, NJ: Presbyterian & Reformed, 2004.

Waters, Larry J. "Paradoxes in the Pauline Epistles." *Bibliotheca sacra* 167 (2010) 423–41.

Watson, Alan. "Roman Private Law and the Leges Regiae." *Journal of Roman Studies* 62, (1972) 100–105.

Watson, Duane. "The Contributions and Limitations of Greco-Roman Rhetorical Theory for Constructing the Rhetorical and Historical Situations of a Pauline Epistle." In *The Rhetorical Interpretation of Scripture: Essays from the 1996 Malibu Conference*, edited by Stanley E. Porter, 123–51. Novum Testamentum Supplement 180. Sheffield, UK: Sheffield Academic, 1999.

Works Cited

Watson, Francis. *Paul, Judaism, and the Gentiles: Beyond the New Perspective*. Grand Rapids: Eerdmans, 2007.

Watson, Patricia. *Ancient Stepmothers: Myth, Misogyny and Reality*. Leiden: Brill, 1995.

Weaver, P. R. C. "Social Mobility in the Early Roman Empire: The Evidence of the Imperial Freedmen and Slaves." *Past & Present* 37 (1967) 3–20.

Webb, Clement C. J. *A History of Philosophy*. London: Williams & Norgate, 1915.

Weber, Alfred. *History of Philosophy*. Translated by Frank Thilly. New York: Schribner, 1896.

Weigel, Richard D. "Roman Colonial Commissioners and Prior Service." *Hermes* 113 (1985) 224–31.

Weir, Robert G. A. *Roman Delphi and Its Pythian Games*. British Archaeological Reports International Series 1306. Oxford: Hadrian, 2004.

Welborn, L. L. "Mōros Genesthō: Paul's Appropriation of the Role of the Fool in 1 Corinthians 1–4." *Biblical Interpretation* 10 (2002) 420–35.

———. "On the Discord in Corinth: 1 Corinthians 1–4 and Ancient Politics." *JBL* 106 (1987) 101–3.

———. *Politics and Rhetoric in the Corinthian Epistles*. Macon, GA: Mercer University Press, 1997.

Wender, Dorothy. "Plato: Misogynist, Paedophile, and Feminist." In *Women in the Ancient World*, edited by John Peradotto and J. P. Sullivan, 213–28. Albany: State University of New York Press, 1984.

Wells, Benjamin W. "Trade and Travel in the Roman Empire." *Classical Journal* 19 (1923) 67–78.

Wells, Collin. *The Roman Empire*. 2nd ed. Cambridge: Harvard University Press, 1992.

Wenham, David. "Paul's Use of the Jesus Tradition: Three Samples." In *Source: Jesus Tradition Outside the Gospels*, edited by David Wenham, 7–37. Sheffield, UK: JSOT, 1984.

Wenckebach, E. "Der hippokratische Arzt als das Ideal Galens." *Quellen und Studien zur Geschichte der Naturwissenschaften und Medizin* 3 (1933) 170–75.

West, Allen B., editor. *Latin Inscriptions, 1896–1926*. Corinth series 8.2. Cambridge: Harvard University Press, 1931.

———. "Notes on Achaean Prosopography and Chronology." *Classical Philology* 23 (1928) 258–69.

West, M. L. "Corinna." *Classical Quarterly*, n.s., 20 (1970) 277–87.

———. "Dating Corinna." *Classical Quarterly*, n.s., 40 (1990) 553–57.

———. "Erinna." *Zeitschrift für Papyrologie und Epigraphik* 25 (1977) 95–119.

Westerholm, Stephen. *Israel's Law and the Church's Faith: Paul and His Recent Interpreters*. Eugene, OR: Wipf & Stock.

———. *Perspectives Old and New on Paul: The "Lutheran" Paul and His Critics*. Grand Rapids: Eerdmans, 2000.

Wettstein, Johann J. *Novum Testamentum Graecum editionis receptae cum lectionibus variantibus codicum mss., edition aliarum, versionum, et patrum nec non commentario pleniore ex scriptoribus veteribus Hebraeis, Graecis et Latinis historiam et vim verborum illustrante*. Amsterdam: Ex Officina Dommeriana, 1751–52.

Wheatley, Alan B. *Patronage in Early Christianity: Its Use and Transformation from Jesus to Paul of Samosata*. Eugene, OR: Pickwick, 2011.

Whelan, Caroline F. "Amica Pauli: The Role of Phoebe in the Early Church." *Journal for the Study of the New Testament* 49 (1993) 67–85.

Works Cited

White, F. C. "Love and Beauty in Plato's Symposium." *Journal of Hellenistic Studies* 109 (1989) 149–57.

White, John. *Light from Ancient Letters*. Philadelphia: Fortress, 1986.

White, L. Michael. "Social Authority in the House Church Setting and Ephesians 4.1–16." *Restoration Quarterly* 29 (1987) 209–28.

———. "Synagogue and Society in Imperial Ostia: Archaeological and Epigraphical Evidence." *Harvard Theological Review* 90 (1997) 23–58.

White, Peter. "Amicitia and the Profession of Poetry in Early Imperial Rome." *The Journal of Roman Studies* 68 (1978) 74–92.

———. "The Friends of Martial, Statius, and Pliny, and the Dispersal of Patronage." *Harvard Studies in Classical Philology* 79 (1975) 265–300.

Whitmarsh, Tim. "Greek and Roman in Dialogue: The Pseudo-Lucianic Nero." *Journal of Hellenistic Studies* 119 (1999) 142–60.

Wicker, Kathleen O'Brien. "Mulierum virtutes." In *Plutarch's Ethical Writings and the New Testament*, edited by Hans Dieter Betz, 106–35. Leiden: Brill, 1978.

Wiedemann, Thomas. "Children and Benefactors in the Eastern Part of the Roman Empire." *POLIS. Revista de ideas y formas políticas de la Antigüedad Clásica* 18 (2006) 163–86.

Wilder, Kathleen. "Women Philosophers in the Ancient World: Donning the Mantle." *Hypatia* 1 (1986) 21–62.

Wilken, Robert Louis. *The Christians as the Romans Saw Them*. New Haven: Yale, 2003.

———. "Collegia, Philosophical Schools, and Theology." In *The Catacombs and the Colosseum: The Roman Empire as the Setting of Primitive Christianity*, edited by Stephen Benko and John J. O'Rourke, 268–91. Valley Forge, PA: Judson, 1971.

———. *Remembering the Christian Past*. Grand Rapids: Eerdmans, 1995.

Williams, Charles Kaufman, II. "The City of Corinth and Its Domestic Religion." *Hesperia* 50 (1981) 408–21.

Williams, Craig A. *Roman Homosexuality: Ideologies of Masculinity in Classical Antiquity*. New York: Oxford University Press, 1999.

Williams, M. H. "The Structure of Roman Jewry Re-considered – Were the Synagogues of Ancient Rome Homogeneous?" *Zeitschrift für Papyrologie und Epigraphik* 104 (1994) 129–41.

Wilson, Kenneth T. "Should Women Wear Headcoverings." *Bibliotheca sacra* 148 (1991) 442–62.

Wilson, Nigel Guy. *Encyclopedia of Ancient Greece*. New York: Routledge, 2006.

Wimbush, Vincent L. *Paul, the Worldly Ascetic: Response to the World and Self-Understanding According to 1 Corinthians 7*. Macon, GA: Mercer University Press, 1987.

Windisch, Hans. *Der zweite Korintherbrief*. 9th ed. Kritisch-exegetischer Kommentar über das Neue Testament. Göttingen: Vandenhoek & Ruprecht, 1970.

———. *Paulus und Christus: Ein biblisch-religionsgeschichtlicher Verglich*. Untersuchungen zum Neuen Testament 24. Leipzig: Hinrichs, 1934.

Winkler, John J. *The Constraints of Desire: Essays in the Anthropology of Sex and Gender in Ancient Greece*. New York: Routledge, 1989.

Winter, Bruce. *After Paul Left Corinth: The Influence of Secular Ethics and Social Change*. Grand Rapids: Eerdmans, 2001.

———. "Favorinus." In *The Book of Acts in Its First-Century Setting*, edited by B. W. Winter and A. D. Clarke, 196–205. Grand Rapids: Eerdmans, 1993.

Works Cited

———. "1 Corinthians 7:6-7: A Caveat and a Framework for 'The Sayings' in 7:8-24." *Tyndale Bulletin* 48 (1997) 57-65.

———. *Philo and Paul among the Sophists*. Society for New Testament Studies Monograph Series 96. Cambridge: Cambridge University Press, 1997.

———. "Philodemus and Paul on Rhetorical Delivery (ὑπόκρισις)." In *Philodemus and the New Testament World*, edited by John T. Fitzgerald et al., 323-42. Leiden: Brill, 2004.

———. "The Public Honoring of Christian Benefactors: Romans 13.3-4 and 1 Peter 2.14-15." *Journal for the Study of the New Testament* 34 (1988) 87-103.

———. *Roman Wives, Roman Widows: The Appearance of New Women and the Pauline Communities*. Grand Rapids: Eerdmans, 2003.

———. *Seek the Welfare of the City: Christians as Benefactors and Citizens*. Grand Rapids: Eerdmans, 1994.

———. "The Toppling of Favorinus and Paul." In *Early Christianity and Classical Culture: Comparative Studies in Honor of Abraham J. Malherbe*, edited by John T. Fitzgerald et al., 291-306. Leiden: Brill, 2003.

Wire, Antionette. *The Corinthian Women Prophets: A Reconstruction through Paul's Rhetoric*. Minneapolis: Fortress, 1990.

———. "Prophecy and Women Prophets in Corinth." In *Gospel Origins and Christian Beginnings: Essays in Honor of J. M. Robinson*, edited by James E. Goehring et al., 134-50. Forum Fascicles 1. Sonoma, CA: Polebridge, 1990.

Wirszubski, C. *Libertas as a Political Idea at Rome*. Cambridge: Cambridge University Press, 1950.

Wiseman, James. "Corinth and Rome 1: 228 BC-AD 267." In *Aufstieg und Niedergang der römischen Welt: Geschichte und Kultur Roms im Spiegel der neueren Forschung*, vol. 2.7.1, edited by Hildegard Temporini and Wolfgang Haase, 438-548. New York: de Gruyter, 1979.

———. "Excavations in Corinth, the Gymnasium Area, 1967-1968." *Hesperia* 38 (1969) 64-106.

Wissowa, G. "Zur Geschichte des kapitolinischen Agons." In *Darstellungen aus der Sittengeschichte Roms 4*, edited by L. Friedländer, 276-80. Leipzig: Hirzel, 1921.

Witherington, Bruce, III. *Conflict and Community in Corinth: A Socio-Rhetorical Commentary on 1 and 2 Corinthians*. Grand Rapids: Eerdmans, 1995.

Witt, R. E. "The Hellenism of Clement of Alexandria." *Classical Quarterly* 25 (1931) 195-204.

Wong, Eric K. C. "The Deradicalization of Jesus' Ethical Sayings in 1 Corinthians." *New Testament Studies* 48 (2002) 181-94.

Woodhull, Magaret L. "Matronly Patrons in the Early Roman Empire." In *Women's Influence on Classical Civilization*, edited by Fiona McHardy and Eireann Marshall, 75-91. New York: Routledge, 2004.

Wooten, Cecil W., editor. *The Orator in Action and Theory in Greece and Rome: Essays in Honor of G. A. Kennedy*. Leiden: Brill, 2001.

Wright, N. T. *The Climax of the Covenant: Christ and the Law in Pauline Theology*. Minneapolis: Fortress, 1992.

———. "Gospel and Theology in Galatians." In *Gospel in Paul: Studies on Corinthians, Galatians and Romans for Richard N. Longenecker*, edited by L. Ann Jervis and Peter Richardson, 222-39. Journal for the Study of the New Testament Supplement 108. Sheffield, UK: Sheffield Academic, 1994.

———. *Justification: God's Plan and Paul's Vision*. Downers Grove, IL: InterVarsity, 2009.

———. "The Letter to the Galatians: Exegesis and Theology." In *Between Two Horizons: Spanning New Testament Studies and Systematic Theology*, edited by Joel B. Green and Max Turner, 205-36. Grand Rapids: Eerdmans, 2000.

———. "New Exodus, New Inheritance: The Narrative Substructure of Romans 3-8." In *Romans and the People of God: Essays in Honor of Gordon D. Fee on the Occasion of His 65th Birthday*, edited by S. K. Soderlund and N. T. Wright, 26-35. Grand Rapids: Eerdmans, 1999.

———. *Paul: In Fresh Perspective*. Minneapolis: Fortress, 2005.

———. "The Paul of History and the Apostle of Faith." *Tyndale Bulletin* 29 (1978) 61-68.

———. "Redemption from the New Perspective." In *Redemption*, edited by S. T. Davis et al., 69-100. Oxford: Oxford University Press, 2004.

———. "Romans and the Theology of Paul." In *Pauline Theology*, edited by Jouette Bassler et al., 3:30-67. Minneapolis: Fortress, 1995.

Yarbrough, O. Larry. *Not Like the Gentiles: Marriage Rules in the Letters of Paul*. Atlanta: Scholars, 1985.

Yeo, Cedric A. "The Founding and Function of Roman Colonies." *Classical World* 52 (1959) 104-7, 129-30.

Yeo, Khiok-Khng. "Differentiation and Mutuality of Male-Female Relations in 1 Corinthians 11:2-16." *Biblical Research* 43 (1998) 7-21.

———. *Rhetorical Interaction in 1 Corinthians 8 and 10: A Formal Analysis with Preliminary Suggestions for a Chinese, Cross-Cultural Hermeneutic*. Leiden: Brill, 1995.

Young, David C. *A Brief History of the Olympic Games*. Oxford: Blackwell, 2004.

Zakopoulos, Athēnagoras Ch. *Plato and Saint Paul on Man: A Psychological, Philosophical, and Theological Study*. Thessalonica: Melissa, 2002.

Zanker, Paul. *The Power of Images in the Age of Augustus*. Ann Arbor: University of Michigan Press, 1988.

Zedler, Beatrice. Introduction to *The History of Women in Philosophy*, by Gilles Ménage. Translated by Beatrice Zedler. New York: University Press of America, 1984.

www.ingramcontent.com/pod-product-compliance
Lightning Source LLC
Chambersburg PA
CBHW061424300426
44114CB00014B/1535